# THE ILLUSTRATED WHO'S WHO OF HOLLYWOOD DIRECTORS

ALSO BY MICHAEL BARSON

*Flywheel, Shyster and Flywheel: The Marx Brothers' Lost Radio Show*

*Lost, Lonely & Vicious*

*Born to Be Bad*

*Rip It Up!*

*Career Girls*

*Boy Loves Girl, Girl Loves Boy*

*"Better Dead Than Red!"*

*I Married a Monster from Outer Space*

# THE ILLUSTRATED WHO'S WHO *of* HOLLYWOOD DIRECTORS

## VOLUME I: THE SOUND ERA

MICHAEL BARSON

AN ARCHIVE PHOTOBOOK
FARRAR, STRAUS AND GIROUX • NEW YORK

Published simultaneously in Canada by HarperCollins*CanadaLtd*
Printed in the United States of America
Designed by Debbie Glasserman
First edition, 1995

Library of Congress Cataloging-in-Publication Data
Barson, Michael.
The illustrated who's who of Hollywood directors / Michael Barson.
—1st ed.
p. cm.
Includes index.
Contents: v. 1. The studio system in the sound era
1. Motion picture producers and directors—United States.
2. Motion picture producers and directors—United States—Pictorial works. I. Title.
PN1998.2.B368 1995 791.43'0233'092273—dc20 94-40212 CIP

All photographs are from the Archive Photos Collection;
all poster and advertising art are from the
collection of the author.

*To my wife, Jean, who had to live with this (and me) for longer than the Geneva Convention requires. P.S.—You can have the computer back now.*


# ACKNOWLEDGMENTS

Heartfelt thanks to the five other people who helped with this project so much, so often, and for so long:

My editor, Elisabeth Kallick Dyssegaard, patient beyond reproach

My agent, Nancy Stauffer, loyal beyond expectation

My designer, Debbie Glasserman, inventive beyond hope

My friends Brian Rose and Eric Rachlis, supportive beyond reason

# CONTENTS

# INTRODUCTION

## *"The Director's the Guy That Makes the Picture, You Bet Your Life He Is"*

*A director doesn't draw anybody in to [see] a picture. I'm sorry. Maybe in Hollywood or New York, but nowhere else. Don't tell me that a guy's going to go and see a picture and say, "Look, Jesus, that was beautifully directed." They don't know what a director is . . . The director's the guy that makes the picture, you bet your life he is, but he isn't the guy that sells tickets. I don't care who he is. Hitchcock maybe, maybe Orson Welles . . . But that's as far as I go.*

So William Wellman opined in an interview with Richard Schickel for Schickel's book *The Men Who Made the Movies*. It's a valid question: Do ticket buyers know and appreciate a film's director the way they do its stars? Or are they oblivious to his contribution? Certainly it's difficult to conceive of any 1994 moviegoer attending *Pulp Fiction* and not realizing that it was made by instant media darling Quentin Tarantino, winner of the New York and Los Angeles Film Critics Awards for best direction and the most feted young writer-director since . . . well, since Orson Welles in 1941. But then, that's precisely Wellman's point: Hollywood directors who can claim to have a household name are as rare as hen's teeth.

Whenever a director's importance to filmmaking is debated, at least one conundrum can be counted on to introduce itself sooner or later; namely, if it is the director who is chiefly responsible for the quality of a film—who exerts the most control over the shape it finally assumes—then why do so many movies made by front-line directors turn out to be of mediocre quality, or worse? On the other hand, if it is *not* the director who exerts the most influence over a movie's quality—if, instead, filmmaking is a collaborative venture in which directing is merely one component among many—then why are the works of a top director, viewed collectively, markedly better than the collected works of a director of lesser stature?

The problem is further complicated by the fact that those unanimously deemed "great" Hollywood directors and "great" Hollywood films represent about 5 percent of the candidates. Voting in John Ford and *The Searchers* makes perfect sense, and certainly Howard Hawks and *Rio Bravo*, Orson Welles and *Citizen Kane*, and Alfred Hitchcock and *North by Northwest* must be admitted to the club. But even Ford, Hawks, Welles, and Hitchcock made pictures that fell far short of the above masterpieces—despite having approximately the same level of resources (casts, scripts, cameramen, budgets, etc.) available to them. The simplest explanation for their occasional misfires is that no one—not even these four titans—bats .1000. Such folk wisdom may not sound very scientific, but does serve to illustrate why directing films can be viewed as an art, a craft, and a business—anything *but* a science.

Consider this scenario based on the making of a big-budget picture under the aegis of the studio system. A famous Oscar-nominated director has been assigned by the studio to which he is under contract to adapt a popular Broadway play (acquired at great cost) for the screen. His charismatic, highly paid star (who collaborated successfully with the director on other films) is joined by a revered screenwriter, a team of prize-winning art directors, and one of the industry's top costume designers. Several of these people have won Oscars after working with the director on other projects. The film is being produced by the same studio executive who oversaw many of the director's earlier successes, one of which earned him the best picture Academy Award as the producer of record.

The signs all seem promising—but things begin to go wrong almost immediately. The plan to shoot on location has to be scrapped because of inclement weather; work must continue on hastily erected, highly stylized soundstages. The star has his own agenda for the film and tugs in directions in which the director does not want to go. The leading lady walks through her part like an automaton, and no one in the cast can settle on a consistent accent. Finally, the picture is completed and released; it enjoys a brief moment of popularity with moviegoers and some respectful reviews but never manages to earn back its cost. Not exactly a disaster, but ultimately it must be judged an artistic and commercial failure.

Such was the making of the 1954 MGM musical *Brigadoon*. The director at the helm was Vincente Minnelli, who over the previous ten years had been one of the studio's premier directors. In retrospect, the disappointment of *Brigadoon* should have been shared by all hands—producer Arthur Freed, stars Gene Kelly and Cyd Charisse, screenwriter and librettist Alan Jay Lerner (who also co-authored the original Broadway show)—even MGM itself, which in a cost-cutting measure scotched Minnelli's plan to shoot the picture on location in the highlands of Scotland. But when *Brigadoon* is discussed today, it is inevitably referred to as a Vincente Minnelli movie, by virtue of his having directed it; never mind all those other collaborators. This is the way we watch Hollywood movies, and such is the importance we ascribe—rightly or wrongly—to those who direct them.



Somehow, over time, we have come to accept film directors as "the men [and women] who made the movies," to quote a phrase coined by Richard Schickel. It still seems perfectly logical to approach Hollywood movies through the organizing principle of the directors who "made" them, despite knowing that even the greatest of them often had only partial control over the production—let alone what went on in the editing room after filming was completed (e.g., *Brigadoon*). And if elite members of Hollywood's directorial community like Vincente Minnelli, John Huston, and King Vidor sometimes watched helplessly as their pictures spun out of control, imagine the frustration if you were a relatively unempowered director like Stuart Heisler, Richard Fleischer, or Sidney Lanfield.

It was a simpler question in the early years of the century, the prehistoric era when a moving picture was just a novelty—a smart but uncouth notion, like the Sunday funnies. It wasn't until 1913 that the radical concept of producing "feature-length" entertainments was implemented, but that step only augmented the power already being enjoyed by the screen director—the one man who could deliver a product that millions of consumers suddenly had decided to consume. In this prehistoric era, it was the name of David Wark Griffith that came before all others—he who made 44 one- and two-reelers for Biograph in 1908, an eye-popping 145 in 1909, and another 83 in 1911. No wonder industry reporter W. Stephen Busch was prompted to issue this effusive paean to him in a 1915 issue of the weekly *Motion Picture World*:

> In point of brilliancy, in psychological depth and in the power of condensation, David W. Griffith stands in a class by himself. The sun of his genius poured its rays upon the motion picture in the early formative period and has left its impress upon the art to this day . . . He was the first to speak the language of the screen. The rise of Griffith came at a time when the identity of player and director was unknown to the general public . . . If some disaster like Pompeii were to overtake us, leaving only dead relics for the judgment of posterity, I would not hesitate in choosing as the choicest specimens of our art the pictures that Griffith directed in 1908, 1909 and 1910.

The potency of motion pictures has not flagged in the eight decades that have passed, but over time the stature of the director has ebbed and risen with the tides of theoretical discourse. Some argue that he is, after all, simply a well-paid sorcerer's apprentice—a tool of the producers who assembled the package of which he is but one part of many. By these lights, the director at best possesses a tenuous authority which can be, and usually is, exhausted as he tries (in vain) to control the myriad forces that beset each and every movie ever filmed.

As Thomas Schatz argues so eloquently in his bold reassessment of the "golden age" of moviemaking, *The Genius of the System* (1988), for many years it was the Hollywood studio itself—and not the brilliance of individual auteurs—that so often shaped the finished film, regardless of how talented (or talentless) the director working on it was. Only those directors who had the negotiating power to also *produce* (and perhaps in addition to write, with

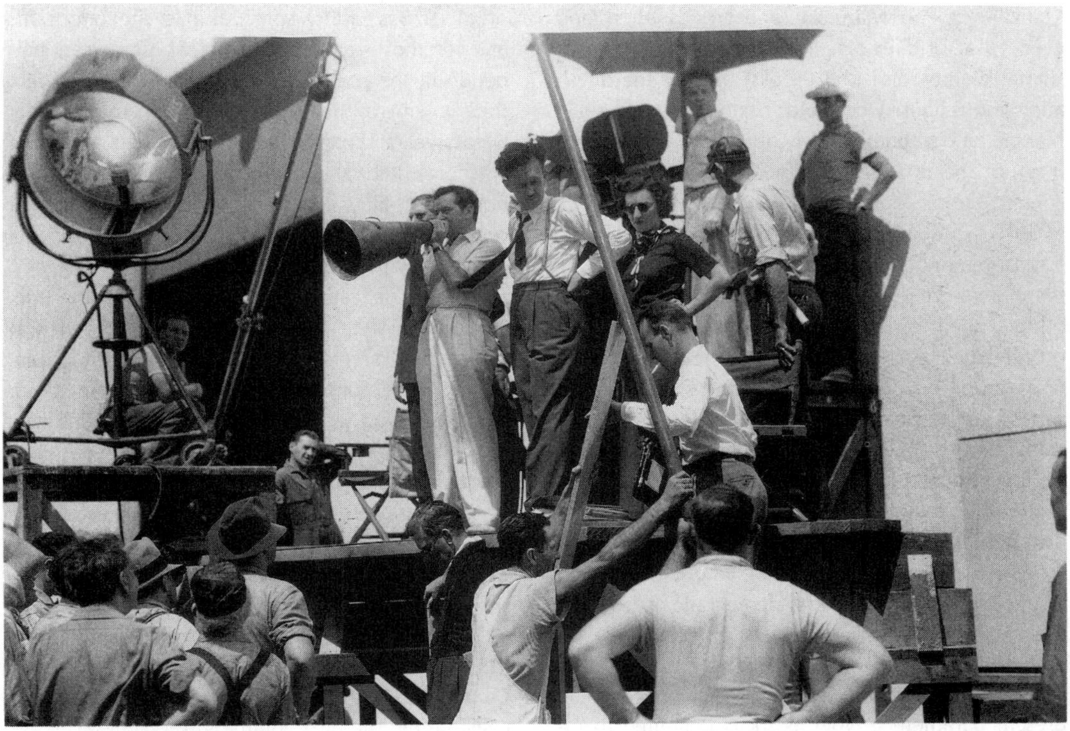

or without credit) their pictures would have had that degree of control over their projects—industry powerhouses like DeMille and King Vidor in the Twenties, and Frank Capra, John Ford, Alfred Hitchcock, and Howard Hawks in the Thirties, Forties, and Fifties. For the rest, even aspiring to mold a movie to some sort of "auteurist" specifications would have been little more than a pipe dream (although such pipe dreams did occasionally make it to America's screens).

Of course, even having that control didn't *guarantee* a great movie as the end product—which is why a certain number of films made by Capra, Ford, Hitchcock, and Hawks aren't as good as the better work of less talented (and less autonomous) directors.

The reverse of this corollary is that a director of much lesser stature can be, and often is, entirely capable of making a terrific movie. Even if no one seems particularly inclined to give that director credit for such a success, viewing it as some sort of anomaly, the truth is that this happens far more frequently than one might think. It happened in the heyday of the old studio system, and it is still happening today.

Still, it is a given that some directors—like some actors, screenwriters, set designers, composers, and cinematographers—are more talented than others; they are more skillful, more resourceful, better able to tap the talent that surrounds them and elicit the best from it on a regular basis. There is no use pretending that the only reason Alfred Hitchcock is more famous than, say, Archie Mayo is that Hitchcock had bigger budgets to work with, or a better story scout. If one *had* to choose between the bodies of work those two men directed, it would be madness not to select the oeuvre of Hitchcock. But since no one is forcing us to make that choice, why not welcome them both to the club? The legacy of Archie Mayo's films is surely less rich than Hitchcock's, but there are pleasures to be found in the likes of *Bordertown*, *Black Legion*, and *Moontide*. (And it's worth noting that under Mayo's handling the stars of those pictures—Bette Davis, Paul Muni, Humphrey Bogart, Jean Gabin, and Ida Lupino—come off as well as, or better than, they did in any of their other contemporaneous work.)

The elitist approach to Hollywood directors, which all too often pervades even the best works about filmmaking in America, relegates all too many able craftsmen to the level of maître d's. Granted, it may seem easier to assign credit to high-profile writer-directors like Welles, Preston Sturges, Joseph

Mankiewicz, Paul Mazursky, and Woody Allen (and even to actor-directors like Allen, Clint Eastwood, Warren Beatty, and Mel Brooks) than to the quasi-anonymous figure who stands next to a camera while his cinematographer actually operates it—but, then, it is not the province of this volume to assign (or contest) authorship of individual films.

While studying *only* the elite members of this profession may not seem that grievous an oversight—there are a great many directors who rate, and have gotten, their own book-length studies—that approach does tend to imply that nine-tenths of the work produced during the sound era may not be worthy of viewing, let alone discussion. From the standpoint of Art, with a capital *A*, this may indeed be true. But the hundreds and hundreds of movies that would thus be overlooked can stand as their own defense.

As it is, *The Illustrated Who's Who of Hollywood Directors* is not able to be as democratic as it would like to be. If space were not a consideration—and with illustrations accompanying each entry, it surely is—this book would have expanded far beyond the present parameters. Now its focus is limited to directors who worked primarily in Hollywood, whose films were for the most part sound features (and even then, not exclusively programmers or drive-in fare), and whose careers were under way by 1975. As it is, several dozen directors whose careers met those definitions but whose output seemed on the whole to be relatively minor—including Ralph Nelson, Lewis Allen, Byron Haskin, Carl Reiner, James Bridges, Frank Perry, Mark Rydell, and George Seaton—were relegated to the "Short Subjects" appendix because of space constraints.

Why only Hollywood? Because it already contains multitudes; its influence is so pervasive that the world beyond it—the film industries of other countries, and even the independent releases made in the United States—could not also be represented in a meaningful way without making the book the size of a Cadillac. The sound era was chosen as a boundary at least in part because so many silent features have been lost, apparently forever, which makes any present-day examination of a director's work from that era fragmentary at best; of course, another reason is that there are so many directors of silent films that they demand their own book. The arbitrary cut-off of 1975 is easily justifiable: space limitations, first and foremost—so the directors whose careers have begun in the past twenty years can (and will) fill a thick volume of their own. (It also pays to recall that, twenty years into their careers, John Ford and Alfred Hitchcock had already made a number of Oscar-nominated films—but each had another quarter-century of work lying before him, work that outshone what came before it.)

A more delicate question is, wherefore the Brits? Quite simply, the ones who spent a significant fraction of their careers in Hollywood (like Hitchcock and Robert Stevenson) are present and accounted for, and those who worked primarily in the British film industry—even Oscar winners like Carol Reed, David Lean, and Tony Richardson, as well as Ken Russell, Anthony Asquith, and Terence Fisher—must wait for their own volume.

Those Hollywood veterans who did not assume the mantle of directing feature films until after 1975—like Oliver Stone, Ridley Scott, Alan Rudolph, Martha Coolidge, Ivan Reitman, Alan Parker, Joe Dante, Rob Reiner, and Robert Zemeckis—will be evaluated in the next volume in this series.

In the meantime, here are profiles of more than one hundred and fifty Hollywood directors, each illustrated with contemporary photographs of the director—at work or at play—accompanied by graphics representing one of his or her most important films. Within these pages, the great and near-great coexist happily with the merely good and the only competent—and why not? Even the "pantheon" directors made their share of lemons, and they (usually) have been forgiven for them; it ought to follow that even the humblest Hollywood contract director was capable of making at least a handful of enduring motion pictures over the course of a forty-year, fifty-film career. "Enduring" is the key here: whether a film constitutes Art is one thing; whether it is still watched and enjoyed another. The profiles in *The Illustrated Who's Who of Hollywood Directors* are not conceived to answer the question of whose movies get a bigger capital "A" for artistic achievement but rather to celebrate the craft that has delivered to us movie lovers these terrific entertainments that (with certain exceptions) can still be savored decades after their creation. If that isn't achievement enough, then there never was a Hollywood.

# THE ILLUSTRATED WHO'S WHO OF HOLLYWOOD DIRECTORS

## ● ROBERT ALDRICH (1918–1983)

One of the most provocative directors of the 1950s, Robert Aldrich went through a number of peaks and valleys, each phase lasting several years. But to his credit, he made as many good films late in his career as he did when he was a young turk, and somehow the pleasures of the ones that worked seem to outweigh the problems of the many that didn't.

Born in Cranston, Rhode Island, Aldrich took a job at RKO as a production clerk in 1941, after studying law at the University of Virginia. Soon he was assisting Edward Dmytryk, among others, on "B" features at RKO. In 1945 he went freelance, working as an assistant director for Lewis Milestone on a number of pictures, as well as for William Wellman, Fred Zinnemann, Robert Rossen, and Joseph Losey. He then gravitated toward television, directing dramas on *Four Star Playhouse* and pilots for *Adventures in Paradise* and other series. His first feature film, *The Big Leaguer* (1953), was a rather clumsy baseball yarn with Edward G. Robinson and Vera-Ellen. *World for Ransom* (1954) was better, a suspenseful espionage tale starring Dan Duryea.

Aldrich now signed a contract with United Artists, where he made the exciting *Apache* (1954) with Burt Lancaster, based on the novel *Bronco Apache* about a Geronimo-like protagonist. Lancaster and Gary Cooper were soldiers of fortune trying to overthrow Maximilian in 1860s Mexico in *Vera Cruz* (1954). But none of these could have prepared moviegoers for *Kiss Me Deadly* (1955), one of the last of the great noirs and perhaps the nastiest of them all. Aldrich's genius was to take something that has already gone too far—Mickey Spillane's hyperventilating, multimillion selling paperback mystery—and move it five steps further; Ralph Meeker was well cast as ruthless (some would say psychotic) private eye Mike Hammer. Frightening but stylish, this film is a hopped-up ode to violence that lets the candle burn at both ends and then rubs your face in the hot puddle of wax.

This box-office success enabled Aldrich to form his own production company, whose first release was *The Big Knife* (1955). This slash-and-burn look at the moviemaking game, via Clifford Odets's play, offered a memorable group of loathsome producers, egomaniacal actors, spineless agents, betrayed wives, and amoral starlets as embodied by Rod Steiger, Jack Palance, Ida Lupino, Wendell Corey, and Shelley Winters. *Autumn Leaves* (1956) was a potboiler, with Joan Crawford as a spinster typist

who marries much-younger Cliff Robertson, only to learn he's murderously schizophrenic. Many shock treatments later, Cliff is cured (no thanks to the film's omnipresent theme song).

*Attack!* (1956) returned to the high ground of action in a taut tale about a platoon of American soldiers at the Battle of the Bulge. The great cast included Jack Palance, Lee Marvin, and—in a clever bit of casting against type—Eddie Albert as the cowardly captain. Aldrich had almost completed *The Garment Jungle* (1957) when Columbia fired him from the production for refusing to tone down the script's frank exposé of New York's crime-infested garment industry; Vincent Sherman finished it. Aldrich exiled himself from Hollywood for the next five years, making the World War II pictures *The Angry Hills* (1959), with Robert Mitchum in fine form as a war correspondent, and *Ten Seconds to Hell* (1959), which offered the odd casting of Jack Palance and Jeff Chandler as German demolitions experts. *The Last Sunset* (1961) was a long, chatty Western in which Kirk Douglas, Rock Hudson, and Dorothy Malone exchanged their views on the universe during a cattle drive, while *Sodom and Gomorrah* (1963) was a two and a half-hour Italian-French production about the Bible's most spectacular sinners, with Stewart Granger and Pier Angeli heading the proverbial international cast.

Warner Bros. provided Aldrich with his entry back to the Hollywood film community, hiring him to produce and direct the neo-gothic *What Ever Happened to Baby Jane?* (1962). A vicious black comedy played for all it was worth by stars Bette Davis and Joan Crawford, the picture was either reviled as grotesque overindulgence or hailed as an avatar of high camp; it seems fair to say, with the benefit of thirty years of hindsight, that it was both (and then some). Davis was Oscar-nominated for her florid performance (oh, how that galled Crawford!), as was Victor Buono in the supporting actor category. The more mundane *Four for Texas* (1963) was a quasi–Rat Pack adventure, starring Frank Sinatra and Dean Martin, although the supporting cast of Victor Buono, Ursula Andress, and Anita Ekberg stole the show.

The phenomenonal box-office success of *Baby Jane* led to *Hush . . . Hush, Sweet Charlotte* (1964), with alumni Bette Davis (here the victim) and Victor Buono joined by Olivia de Havilland, Agnes Moorehead (who was Oscar-nominated), and Joseph Cotten in this surprisingly effective thriller. *The Flight of the*

▲ *Aldrich and Kim Novak on the set of* The Legend of Lylah Clare

*Phoenix* (1965) was exciting in its own right, a survival yarn set in the Arabian desert that hinges on whether ten men can rebuild their cracked-up airplane from scratch before their meager supply of water runs out. Although the film is a half hour longer than necessary, its tension rarely lags; the superlative cast includes James Stewart, Richard Attenborough, Peter Finch, Hardy Kruger, and Dan Duryea.

Aldrich's most successful film of the Sixties was *The Dirty Dozen* (1967), a peerless (though much imitated) World War II adventure based on a best-selling novel about a group of military convicts who are coerced into attempting a suicide mission (blowing up a château used as a retreat by Nazi officers) in exchange for commutation of their sentences. The training sequences are actually the movie's better half, but the fabled tough-guy cast—Lee Marvin, Jim Brown, John Cassavetes (Oscar-nominated), Charles Bronson, Donald Sutherland, Telly Savalas, Ralph Meeker, Robert Ryan, et al.—makes even the more formulaic elements a delight for fans of two-fisted, stubble-faced, foul-mouthed action. One of the biggest hits of the decade, *Dozen* may not be Aldrich's best movie, but it's far and away the one most people have seen (and that's no thanks to the three vastly inferior made-for-TV movies that emerged twenty years later).

This enormous success enabled Aldrich to set up his own mini-studio, Cinerama Releasing Corp., which went bust after a few years of hitless productions. But first he made *The Legend of Lylah Clare* (1968) for MGM, a made-for-cult-status exercise that was too long, too inside-Hollywood, and too complicated to appeal to a mass audience—and it didn't. Aldrich's first Cinerama release was *The Killing of Sister George* (1968), an adaptation of the Frank Marcus play (set and filmed in England) about an aging soap opera actress (Beryl Reid) who fears she's losing both her television role and her young lesbian lover (Susannah York). It was well made, but its initial "X" rating (for a rather explicit sexual encounter) doomed its commercial prospects. *Too Late the Hero* (1969) marked Aldrich's return to the more comfortable terrain of World War II in this exciting (if long) account of two soldiers (Michael Caine and Cliff Robertson) trying to outwit a Japanese officer while stuck on a Pacific atoll.

Aldrich's final Cinerama production was *The Grissom Gang* (1971), a wild-and-woolly adaptation of James Hadley Chase's ultra-violent novel *No Orchids for Miss Blandish*. His most blackly humorous work since *Baby Jane*, it, too, failed to attract a large enough audience and Aldrich was forced to fold the company. But *Ulzana's Raid* (1972), made under the aegis of Universal, turned out to be Aldrich's best picture in several years, a superb Western starring Burt Lancaster as a veteran Indian fighter who has to rely on the help of cavalry officer Bruce Davidson to capture the wily Apache Ulzana. *Emperor of the North Pole* (1973) was nearly as fine, a violent hymn to the railroads and the men who ride them, legally and otherwise. Set during the Depression in the Northwest, *Emperor* pits hobo supreme Lee Marvin and raw rookie Keith Carradine against sadistic Ernest Borgnine, with a payoff that is Aldrich at his bloody best.

*The Longest Yard* (1974) was a box-office smash, with Burt Reynolds at his most charismatic. He plays a former pro quarterback who blew his career by throwing a game, and who then earns a prison sentence for impulsively drowning his girlfriend's car. Reynolds gets a chance for redemption when he leads the prisoners' football team against the guards'—a pair of goon squads only the man who made *The Dirty Dozen* could have dreamed up. In the gratuitously nasty *Hustle* (1975), Reynolds plays a cynical cop who falls for call girl Catherine Deneuve against his better instincts. Aldrich lost control of the overlong antiwar polemic *Twilight's Last Gleaming* (1977) somewhere along the line, although Burt Lancaster is impressive as usual. But *The Choirboys* (1979), from the Joseph Wambaugh bestseller about a precinct of rogue cops, was an unmitigated disaster, and *The Frisco Kid* (1979)—Gene Wilder as a rabbi in the West of 1850—was amiable but forgettable. More amusing was . . . *All the Marbles* (1981), with Peter Falk as the unprincipled manager of a pair of women wrestlers; exploitative and crude, to be sure, but good (if not clean), rowdy fun. Declining health made this Aldrich's swan song, but he left behind a passel of tough, tangy pictures that promise to hold up better than the work of many of his more heralded contemporaries.

## ● WOODY ALLEN (1935– )

He was the touchstone for a generation that fell in love with his comic persona of a nebbishy New York Jew who might be consumed at any moment by his galaxy of anxieties were he not equally obsessed with bedding down sundry attractive females apparently not of the Hebrew faith. As a film director, though, the prolific (twenty-three films in twenty-five years) Woody Allen bears little resemblance to his gallery of whining characters like Alvy Singer and Miles Monroe. Indeed, he carries a reputation as a fierce perfectionist who does not hesitate to recast a part in mid-production and who parcels out the pages of his scripts to his actors like a miser parting with the gold in his teeth.

But an uneven track record with his films over the past fifteen years and disastrous recent turns in his personal life have combined to dull the glow that made Woody Allen the premier actor/writer/director of the Seventies. And yet who has stepped forward to replace him as the triple threat of the Eighties and Nineties? For all his flaws as an artist and as a human being, Woody Allen is still unique, and uniquely productive, as a filmmaker.

Born Allen Stewart Konigsberg in Brooklyn, New York, he was a child prodigy when it came to comedy, selling jokes to professional comedians while still in high school—Brooklyn's Midwood High, to be precise. After graduating in 1952, he joined the staff of Sid Caesar's esteemed television revue *Your Show of Shows*, a coveted spot for any writer, let alone an eighteen-year-old. He tried attending college while continuing to write for stand-up comics, as well as newspaper columnists like the nationally syndicated Earl Wilson. He also dabbled with performing, Greenwich Village among his venues. But ultimately he found himself expelled from both N.Y.U. and C.U.N.Y.

Having cast his lot, Woody found the demand for his comic services growing and worked as a writer for Garry Moore's television show as well as for other high-profile personalities. In 1961 he decided to strike out on his own as a performer. He developed a nightclub act, recorded it on a few albums, and made occasional appearances on television. His first Broadway play, *Don't Drink the Water*, opened to wide acclaim in 1966, the same year he made his first film, *What's Up, Tiger Lily?*, in which he redubbed the 1964 Japanese spy flick *Kagi No Kag* into a burlesque of *Goldfinger*.

*Take the Money and Run* (1969) was Allen's actual debut behind the camera, and it was an accomplished one. An uneven but often riotously funny pseudo-documentary, the film starred Allen as Virgil Starkwell, a hopelessly inept thief who apparently learned his trade from watching old Warner Bros. prison pictures. Janet Margolin is the woman who loves, marries, and stoically waits for Virgil as he serves his time in the big house after each misbegotten caper, including one sentence scheduled to run for 800 years. Made for under $2 million, the film did well enough to earn Allen a three-picture deal with United Artists, the studio where he would toil through 1980.

Before undertaking his second feature, Allen starred on Broadway from 1969 to 1970 in his well-received romantic comedy *Play It Again, Sam*, which would reach the screen successfully in 1972, with Allen, Diane Keaton, and Tony Roberts, directed by Herbert Ross. *Bananas* (1971), the first of Allen's UA movies, was co-written with *Money* collaborator Mickey Rose and starred Woody as the hapless Fielding Melish, a horny and neurotic Manhattanite who's drawn into a revolution in the fictional Central American country of San Marcos by the woman he has a crush on (Louise Lasser, Allen's real-life wife at

WOODY ALLEN
DIANE KEATON
TONY ROBERTS
CAROL KANE
PAUL SIMON
SHELLEY DUVALL
JANET MARGOLIN
CHRISTOPHER WALKEN
COLLEEN DEWHURST

# "ANNIE HALL"

A nervous romance.

A JACK ROLLINS-CHARLES H. JOFFE PRODUCTION
Written by WOODY ALLEN and MARSHALL BRICKMAN · Directed by WOODY ALLEN
Produced by CHARLES H. JOFFE

PG PARENTAL GUIDANCE SUGGESTED
SOME MATERIAL MAY NOT BE SUITABLE FOR PRE-TEENAGERS

United Artists
A Transamerica Company

THEATRE

the time). Undisciplined and sometimes unreliable—the Howard Cosell routine at the end falls flat on its face—*Bananas* does offer high points of absurdist humor that rank among Allen's peaks.

*Everything You Always Wanted to Know about Sex (but Were Afraid to Ask)* (1972) was a clever if erratic adaptation—to use the term loosely—of Dr. David Reuben's insufferably cheerful but phenomenally popular bestseller about sex, which Allen mercilessly turns on its head. Of *Sex*'s seven segments, the best is probably "What Happens during Ejaculation?," in which Burt Reynolds leads a team of sperm into battle as orgasm approaches during a hot date, while Gene Wilder in "What Is Sodomy?" and Lou Jacobi in "Are Transvestites Homosexual?" fare less well. (Allen's parody of the Michelangelo Antonioni technique in "Why Do Some Women Have Trouble Reaching Orgasm?" was the first indication that he aspired to, and could deliver, more than anarchic Borscht Belt upgrades.)

*Sleeper* (1973) was a far more cohesive work, with Allen as Miles Monroe, a typically neurotic protagonist. A Greenwich Village health-food mogul who goes into the hospital for a simple operation that is botched, Monroe learns that his doctors flash-froze him when he awakes two hundred years later, a strange visitor in an even stranger land. Sex is forbidden—a notion inimical to any Woody Allen protagonist—and so Miles helps the rebel underground, led by dishy dilettante Diane Keaton, overthrow the repressive government, whose leader is a cloned nose. It's utter foolishness, but this goof on *1984* established Allen as a satirist of the first order. *Love and Death* (1975), a parody of Tolstoy, Sergei Eisenstein, and a half dozen other watermarks of Russian culture, was less universally applauded. Still, it had moments as hilarious as any in a Woody Allen picture, and the running philosophical debates between Woody's Boris Grushenko and Diane Keaton's Sonja are film's nearest equivalent of Allen's brilliant literary pastiches in *The New Yorker*.

After submitting an excellent "straight" performance as the protagonist in Martin Ritt's fine drama about blacklisting, *The Front* (1976), Allen made the semiautobiographical *Annie Hall* (1977). It was his breakthrough work, an elliptical account of the rise and fall of a romance that for the first time blended genuine sentiment with Allen's patented theater-of-the-ridiculous. Though really no more unified than his last few films, the poignancy of *Annie*'s love story (he and co-star Diane Keaton had been lovers but had called it quits by the time the film was shot) more than compensated for the clever but predictable excursions into Borscht Belt comedy and existential wisecracks—though the one featuring Toronto philosopher Marshall McLuhan was a beaut. As comedian Alvy Singer, Allen was supported by an unusually strong cast, including worldly pal Tony Roberts, Carol Kane (an analogue for the Louise Lasser phase of Allen's neurotic love life), and Christopher Walken and Colleen Dewhurst as Keaton's terrifying brother and mother.

At Oscar time, *Annie Hall* startled Hollywood by winning for best picture, best actress (Keaton), best direction, and (perhaps less surprisingly) best screenplay for Allen and collaborator Marshall Brickman. It was a stunning triumph for Allen, who further astounded Hollywood by playing his clarinet at Manhattan's Michael's Pub, per usual, on the Monday night of the Academy Awards. Allen was also nominated for best actor for the first and only time; his loss to Richard Dreyfuss (for *The Goodbye Girl*) made more sense then than it does now. *Annie Hall* grossed about $20 million, one of his few movies to attain that level.

Filmgoers of the Western world were waiting to see how Allen could possibly top himself, so when *Interiors* was released, the bewilderment and disappointment were almost palpable. An expert homage to the weighty psychodramas of Ingmar Bergman, its tale of a dysfunctional family (Geraldine Page, Maureen Stapleton, E. G. Marshall, Mary Beth Hurt, Diane Keaton) was extremely well done for what it was—although some critics gave it a mixed reception, reacting to what they perceived as unmitigated pretentiousness. *Interiors* was greeted at the box office with either total hostility or utter indifference. (Considering how it forsook all the elements that had attracted Allen's following over the years, this should not have been a surprise.) But in the end the picture earned Allen Academy Award nominations for his direction and original screenplay, with Page and Stapleton also nominated as, respectively, best actress and best supporting actress.

*Manhattan* (1979) restored Allen's covenant with his fans. It is a lyrically photographed (in black-and-white, by Gordon Willis), deftly written (by Allen and Brickman, whose screenplay was nominated for an Academy Award), wonderfully scored (music by George Gershwin) ode to the city from which Woody

Allen derived his identity and, ultimately, his fame. The plot, such as it is, involves the attempts of television writer Isaac Davis (Woody) to find a more meaningful career and a less confused love life—he's involved with a seventeen-year-old acting student (Mariel Hemingway, who received an Oscar nomination) as well as Diane Keaton, the woman his philandering best friend (Michael Murphy) is having an affair with. (In a small role, Meryl Streep is hilarious as Allen's former spouse, who left him and moved in with a lesbian.) More polished and less sentimental than *Annie Hall*, *Manhattan* has some claim to being Allen's best film, although it did not enjoy the broad success of its predecessor.

The sour *Stardust Memories* (1980), in which Allen plays a filmmaker who's becoming increasingly contemptuous of his fans and his work, was apparently his attempt to wed the storytelling style of Fellini (another of his idols) to his own particular vision. But here the graft doesn't take as it did in *Interiors*; the visual surrealism is an uneasy companion to Allen's familiar (and now often tiresome) obsessions. The period piece *A Midsummer Night's Sex Comedy* (1982), his first release under a new deal with Orion, was more pleasing, although its sexual roundelay among six turn-of-the-century vacationers (an homage to the plot of Bergman's superior *Smiles of a Summer Night*) was less than compelling. Still, the film will be remembered for pairing Allen on screen with Mia Farrow for the first time (Mary Steenburgen, José Ferrer, Tony Roberts, and Julie Hagerty play the other couples).

*Zelig* (1983) created considerably more excitement, in large part due to its groundbreaking use of period film footage as the backdrop for what is basically an amusing *faux*-documentary. Woody plays "human chameleon" Leonard Zelig, who has an uncanny ability to appear at the most critical junctures of history in the 1920s—listening to Hitler stir a crowd to frenzy, watching Babe Ruth swat a homer—although he himself desires only anonymity. Mia Farrow, as Zelig's analyst, is the only other character in the picture, which feels slight despite its technical brilliance. Gordon Willis's cinematography was nominated for an Oscar. (Its technique, much advanced, was employed several years later for a much wider audience in Robert Zemeckis's *Forrest Gump*.)

*Broadway Danny Rose* (1984) was another mixed

bag, with Woody now as a marginal booker of oddball burlesque acts; he runs afoul of the mob when he falls for the hard-boiled girlfriend of gangster Lou Canova (Nick Apollo Forte)—Mia Farrow, cast wildly against type and reveling in the opportunity. The Catskill-comic ambiance, which Allen had discarded a decade earlier, returns to good effect, although the use of black-and-white cinematography (expertly overseen, as usual, by Gordon Willis) actually inhibits the zany mood Allen is aiming for. Even so, Allen's screenplay was nominated for an Academy Award. *The Purple Rose of Cairo* (1985) was also marred by an unevenness of tone, although there was more working in this poignant story of a Depression-era New Jersey shopgirl (Mia Farrow) whose lackluster life is enlivened only through her daydreams about the cinema. Those fantasies molt into a startling new reality when the object of her adoration, swashbuckling actor Jeff Daniels, literally walks off the screen and into her world. A charming but ultimately downbeat tale, *Purple Rose* offered memorable performances by Danny Aiello and Dianne Wiest, and earned Allen yet another Oscar nomination for his original screenplay.

After this lengthy string of quasi-successes, the triumph of *Hannah and Her Sisters* (1986) must have felt sweet indeed. A complex modern romance that balanced the travails of three sets of couples, it boasted a superb ensemble cast that included Michael Caine—husband to Hannah (Mia Farrow) but pathetically smitten by Hannah's sister Lee (Barbara Hershey at her most appealing)—as well as Dianne Wiest as Holly, the third sister, and Woody himself in an atypically self-effacing (and sweet) role as Hannah's ex-. The film performed only respectably at the box office ($20 million, a level he has not reached since), but was heavily represented among the year's Academy Award nominees, with the film nominated as best picture and Woody as best director (losing to Oliver Stone and *Platoon* on both counts); Caine and Wiest won Oscars as the year's best supporting actors, and Allen was given the Academy Award for his original screenplay, which indeed was his most satisfying to date.

*Radio Days* (1987) was an amber-hued but rambling valentine to the New York of the early 1940s, with Allen narrating the colorful but overly familiar tale of his loony Rockaway Beach family. Michael Tucker and Julie Kavner are his perpetually squabbling parents, Josh Mostel his peculiar uncle, and Dianne Wiest his doomed-to-remain-maiden aunt, while Seth Green stands in as the eleven-year-old

Woody. Allen's vignettes of broad Jewish comedy we've seen before, but here they're intercut with the glory days of radio, with Mia Farrow and a seriously miscast Wallace Shawn among the larger-than-life stars from what apparently is Allen's notion of Paradise Lost. The details are rendered with loving care, including a marvelous soundtrack of the day's pop hits, but it felt thin after the emotional richness of *Hannah*. Even so, Allen received another Oscar nomination for his screenplay.

The grim *September* was a return to the territory of *Interiors*, but despite a capable cast (Dianne Wiest, Elaine Stritch, Denholm Elliott, Sam Waterston, and, inevitably, Mia Farrow), the picture's weighty psychodrama lay like a ten-ton lox across the screen. *Another Woman* (1988) didn't promise to be any more convincing, but this time Woody's Bergmanesque approach to his story—a professionally successful woman's growing awareness of the waste she's made of her life—pays off. Gena Rowlands is nothing less than superb as the philosophy professor who undergoes an epiphany that turns her life inside out, and such unfamiliar Allen performers as Gene Hackman, Sandy Dennis, Blythe Danner, Martha Plimpton, and John Houseman help maintain the element of surprise. (Sven Nykvist, the Oscar-winning cinematographer for many of Bergman's greatest films, is also due much of the credit for the film's impact.)

The segment Woody contributed to the triptych *New York Stories* (1989), "Oedipus Wrecks," was widely acknowledged to be the film's strongest; it is an often hilarious fable about a Manhattan-based Jewish attorney (Allen, of course) whose guilt over his impending marriage to shiksa Mia Farrow transmogrifies his nagging mother (the delightful Mae Questel) into an omniscient specter. (In retrospect, it seems unfortunate that one with the proven short-story talents of Woody Allen doesn't work more often in the short-film form.) *Crimes and Misdemeanors* (1989) was far more ambitious, a Dostoevskian meditation on the nature of evil and culpability, with Martin Landau as a respected ophthalmologist who slays mistress Anjelica Huston when she threatens to reveal their affair to his wife (Claire Bloom); he then wrestles with the burden of his guilt. As a counterpoint is the less serious story of a married maker of documentary films (Woody) who detests the subject of his latest opus (cocky TV producer Alan Alda) while lusting after one of the mogul's underlings (Mia Farrow). This was Allen in top form, and he received a well-deserved Oscar nomination for his direction.

*Alice* (1990) was a much quieter film. And yet it contains Mia Farrow's best performance in any of his films. She is set center stage as a wealthy Park Avenue wife who wiles away her days in idleness enforced by her philandering husband (William Hurt, whose essential coldness is used to great effect here). When an encounter with the handsome father of one of her children's schoolmates (the magnetic Joe Mantegna) awakens her to the barrenness of her emotional and spiritual lives, she seeks out an ancient Chinese sage (the wonderful Key Luke), who dispenses wisdom—along with a number of mysterious potions that embolden her to undertake an affair. Like so many of Allen's films in which he does not act, *Alice* received indifferent reviews, but it actually achieves its modest goals and boasts a terrific cast that includes Judy Davis, Blythe Danner, and Bernadette Peters (none of whom are onscreen enough).

After performing opposite Bette Midler in Paul Mazursky's 1991 disaster *Scenes from a Mall*, Woody made his own stinker, the universally reviled *Shadows and Fog* (1992). As happened with some of Allen's previous homages to the likes of Federico Fellini and Bergman, this incoherent "tribute" to Kafka may have sounded like a great idea on paper, but its execution proved fatal for the few moviegoers who saw it. Woody performs alongside Kathy Bates, Mia, John Cusack, and Jodie Foster (among many other stars who pop up for purposeless cameos), but even with a murder mystery to propel the plot, it all comes to naught.

In the midst of the 1992 media blitzkrieg that descended when Allen's affair with Farrow's twenty-one-year-old adopted daughter, Soon-Yi Previn, became public knowledge, Allen made *Husbands and Wives*, a darkly comic tale that revolved around a couple (the Oscar-nominated Judy Davis and Sydney Pollack) whose impending split (which ultimately never takes place) inspires their best friends (Woody and Mia) to break up and seek out new lovers—Liam Neeson for Mia and young Juliette Lewis for Woody. Although widely admired, *Husbands* also endured numerous complaints about Woody's faux-documentary, hand-held camera technique. But further debacles in Allen's personal life, in particular charges of child abuse leveled against him by Mia, distracted from the many merits of *Husbands* and made its ironies play more like burlesque.

After a year of tabloid headlines, the lighthearted *Manhattan Murder Mystery* (1993) seemed like a breath of fresh air. It featured the welcome return of Diane Keaton as Allen's leading lady (absent since *Manhattan* in 1979), playing an amateur sleuth who stumbles into a *Rear Window* scenario in which she suspects a neighbor has committed a murder. Encouraged by friend (and would-be lover) Alan Alda, she drags her unwilling husband (Woody at his most kvetchy) along to investigate. *Mystery* has an insistent effervescence that seems forced at times; still, it's a pleasant-enough concoction.

*Bullets over Broadway* (1994) starred John Cusack as a Prohibition-era playwright who finds his first Broadway effort transformed through the contributions of *grande dame* Dianne Wiest (a terrific evocation of all the Tallulah Bankheads who ever trod the boards), bubble-headed Jennifer Tilly (whose mobster boyfriend will help underwrite the production only if she gets a part in it), and brooding Chazz Palminteri, an enforcer who, it turns out, has more of a knack for playwrighting than does the pretentious Cusack. Both Tilly and Palminteri were nominated for Oscars, and Wiest copped the Award for best supporting actress.

Allen got enthusiastic notices and was nominated for an Academy Award for best direction. But he must have winced when he read the reviews a few months later of his made-for-television movie *Don't Drink the Water* (also 1994), which he both directed and starred in for ABC-TV. It was nice of Allen to bring himself to the masses, but his 1966 play did not date well, and his own performance was an embarrassment. A book of conversations with Allen, *Woody Allen on Woody Allen*, was published in 1995.

MANHATTAN

## ● ROBERT ALTMAN (1925- )

If, as Scott Fitzgerald claimed, there truly are no second acts in American life, Robert Altman could not exist. The toast of Hollywood for the first half of the Seventies, during which time he was twice nominated for Academy Awards while revolutionizing what form and content could be in a Hollywood movie, he went into eclipse after a string of flops and spent much of the Eighties filming plays for limited theatrical release and television. But the Nineties have seen him return with a vengeance, and if *The Player* and *Short Cuts* are any indication, his time spent in the wilderness outside the gates of tinseltown only provided him with raw meat to tear into.

Born in Kansas City, Missouri, Altman completed wartime service as a pilot and then entered the industrial film business, taking a job with the Calvin Company in Kansas City, where he directed untold scores of industrials. He shot *The Delinquents* (1957) in Kansas City as well, an entry in the then-burgeoning Juvenile Delinquent genre; it was no better or worse than most of its ilk, with Tom Laughlin as a "good kid" who gets mixed up with Richard Bakalyan's gang out of spite. That same year he made *The James Dean Story*, a middling documentary co-directed with George W. George. But Hollywood did not swoon when presented with this accomplishment, and Altman moved on to television, where he carved out a respected niche by directing episodes of *Combat*, *Bonanza*, and *Alfred Hitchcock Presents*.

In 1964 Altman made the television film *Nightmare in Chicago* as well as a handful of 16mm shorts, but it wasn't until 1967 that he directed another feature, the meticulously realized, documentary-flavored *Countdown* (1968), with Robert Duvall and James Caan heading a team of astronauts en route to the moon. Altman went to Canada to shoot *That Cold Day in the Park* (1969), a portentous modern gothic starring Sandy Dennis at her most overwrought as a tightly wound spinster who impulsively brings home young Michael Burns, with predictably dire results.

But this disaster was quickly erased by the phenomenal success of *M*A*S*H* (1970), a bold and brilliant black comedy that stood for many years as the best Vietnam movie (ostensibly *not* about Vietnam) ever made. Elliott Gould and Donald Sutherland, as the madcap surgeons Hawkeye and Trapper John, struck a chord with the counterculture for their refusal to kowtow to (or even politely acknowledge) authority, and Sally Kellerman and Robert Duvall gave superb support. But it was Altman's movie all the way, from his use of overlapping dialogue—a breathtaking innovation at the time—to his cutting suddenly from bawdy slapstick to the shocking horrors of war, slapping the complacency out of viewers in a way no Hollywood movie had ever done. Ring Lardner, Jr., won a well-deserved Oscar for his blistering screenplay, and the film (which actually made a pile of money), Kellerman, and Altman were also nominated for Academy Awards. Even though *M*A*S*H* didn't win—ironically, *Patton* was named best picture of 1970—its impact was such that Altman was permitted to write his own ticket for some time thereafter.

He used his *carte blanche* to make the peculiar fable *Brewster McCloud* (1970), with Bud Cort as a nerd who wants to fly inside the Houston Astrodome; Sally Kellerman and Michael Murphy try to help him realize his dream. Its relentless quirkiness created a thud at the box office at the time, but today the film seems a pleasant bit of whimsy. Even more interesting was *McCabe and Mrs. Miller* (1971), an iconoclastic frontier tale of rare beauty. Warren Beatty is at his most appealing as a rather dense small-time gambler whose ambitions prove too big to swallow. Co-scripted by Altman, with a wonderfully dreamy score by Leonard Cohen, the film (which did not do well at the box office) also offers Julie Christie's Oscar-nominated performance as a canny brothel madam who loves but cannot save McCabe, and poetic cinematography by Vilmos Zsigmond. *Images* (1972), starring Susannah York as a disturbed woman who has trouble separating fantasy from reality, was Altman's ambitious venture into Bergman territory; while not a disaster, it was not wholly successful.

Altman created a stir with *The Long Goodbye* (1973), a revisionist take on the icon of the hard-boiled private eye; it used (some cried, *abused*) Raymond Chandler's 1953 novel featuring his noble, world-weary hero Philip Marlowe, portrayed here by aggressively antiheroic, ignoble *schlub* Elliott Gould. Although Altman actually hews close to Chandler's plot, simply transposing the time frame to contemporary L.A., his deliberately provocative tone was too rude for moviegoers who still bought into the mythos—and there were plenty of them, as the success of Polanski's *Chinatown*, set in 1937 L.A., a year later, showed. Leaving aside the question of Gould's mumbling, cat-loving, rather sweet Marlowe, *Goodbye* was enhanced by the work of Sterling Hayden, Nina Van Pallandt, and especially once-and-future director Mark Rydell, most convincing as a civilized but vicious gangster.

*Thieves Like Us* (1974) was a faithful adaptation (by Altman, Calder Willingham, and Joan Tewksbury) of Edward Anderson's 1930s novel about a gang of bank robbers, perhaps inspired by the recent achievements of Bonnie and Clyde. Keith Carradine and Shelley Duvall are fine as the doomed young lovers, and Altman wisely eschews his usual stylistic flourishes to create a nice period look (and sound) for the production, but in the end he doesn't accomplish much more than Nicholas Ray did in his 1949 noir *They Live by Night* (based on the same source). *California Split* (1974) was a loosely structured, almost existential meditation on the joy and despair of gambling, with Elliott Gould and George Segal as a pair of cardsharps trying to score big by setting up a high-stakes poker game in Reno. Altman seems to let his actors improvise almost at will here, and with his multichannel soundtrack further obfuscating the narrative, he creates a challenge that not every viewer may be interested in meeting.

The tepid reaction to *Split* might have convinced another director to back off from experimenting with free-form narrative. But even though Altman hadn't had a hit since *M*A*S*H*, he pushed the envelope even further with *Nashville* (1975), a wildly inventive profile of some two dozen characters who congregate in Nashville over the course of a weekend, some to attend a political rally, some to break into the music business, and some because it's there and so are they. Using his stock company (Keith Carradine, Shelley Duvall, Michael Murphy, Gwen Welles, Bert Remsen) alongside newcomers Lily Tomlin, Ronee Blakely, Karen Black, and Barbara Harris, Altman weaves an impressionistic tapestry out of his motley threads that somehow conveys the essence of the American dream. How he did it no one was certain —perhaps not even Altman himself—but the film received near-unanimous accolades from the critics, performed respectably at the box office, and received Academy Award nominations for best picture, direction, supporting actress (both Tomlin and Blakely), and song (Carradine's "I'm Easy," the only Oscar winner in the group).

Following a masterpiece is never easy, but *Buffalo Bill and the Indians, or Sitting Bull's History Lesson* (1976) was a major letdown, a pretentious, long-winded, self-conscious treatise, adapted (not very faithfully) from Arthur Kopit's play *Indians* by Altman and Alan Rudolph. Paul Newman lugs the heavy water as the fraudulent showman, while the fine cast (Joel Grey, Will Sampson, Burt Lancaster, Harvey Keitel, Geraldine Chaplin) mills about impersonating various historical figures. Before you know it, the two hours have passed and you can awaken. (The penalty for laying this egg was Altman's falling out of consideration for *Ragtime*, and probably other projects as well.) Undaunted, he next donned the hats of producer, director, *and* writer for *Three Women* (1977), a mystical investigation into the nature of identity (based on a dream Altman had), with Shelley Duvall, Sissy Spacek, and Janice Rule. It polarized the critics, some of whom found it pretentious and tedious, while others argued for its profundity.

*A Wedding* (1978) recalled the ambitions of *Nashville* in its promiscuous use of characters—here there are more than fifty—but there the resemblance ends, as the story becomes so diffuse that it floats off into the ozone. (It did, however, provide the only known teaming of Lillian Gish and Desi Arnaz, Jr.) Paul Newman worked with Altman again on the allegorical science-fiction yarn *Quintet* (1979), but the effect was like watching ice freeze. The little-seen *A Perfect Couple* (1979) was a genuine anomaly for Altman, a rather sweet romantic comedy starring Paul Dooley and Marta Heflin as a couple that meets through a computer dating service. *H.E.A.L.T.H.* (1979) was the old acerbic Altman: a health-food convention serves as the backdrop for political commentary. The impressive cast included James Garner, Carol Burnett, Lauren Bacall, Glenda Jackson, and Alfre Woodard, but the film sat on the shelf for two years and failed to find an audience when finally released.

How Paramount decided that Altman was the man to direct their big-budget musical version of *Popeye* (1980) is anyone's guess—but to put it simply, he wasn't. Scripted without wit by Jules Feiffer, scored with a tin ear by Harry Nilsson, and acted strenuously by Robin Williams, Shelley Duvall, and Ray Walston, this was a disaster in every area except set design, and even that felt cloying after a while. Altman then bade farewell to $20 million budgets and took nineteen days to film *Come Back to the 5 & Dime, Jimmy Dean, Jimmy Dean* (1982), a play he had directed on Broadway, using Super 16mm cameras. Karen Black, Sandy Dennis, and Cher (who resuscitated her film career with this) were among the original cast members who appeared in this stagebound but still effective production. *Streamers* (1983), adapted by David Rabe from his Broadway play, featured Matthew Modine, David Alan Grier, and Michael Wright as inductees circa 1965 waiting in their barracks for the call to Vietnam, while *Secret Honor* (1984) was Philip Baker Hall's one-man show, in which the rantings and ravings of Richard Nixon are neatly served up for posterity.

Altman made *The Laundromat* (1985) for Canadian television, then filmed Sam Shepard's claustrophobic *Fool for Love* (1985) with Shepard and Kim Basinger as the warring ex-lovers. He went to Paris to film *Beyond Therapy* (1987), an adaptation of a play by Christopher Durang, but even such high-wattage actors as Glenda Jackson, Jeff Goldblum, and Tom Conti couldn't transform this comedy about New Yorkers and their shrinks into something worth

▲ *Warren Beatty and Julie Christie are guided by Altman during the filming of* McCabe and Mrs. Miller

sacrificing a session to see. *O.C. & Stiggs* was released in 1987 after four years on the shelf, and despite its prevailing incoherence, this teen comedy did have its charms, not the least of which were turns by Dennis Hopper, Martin Mull, Tina Louise, and Jane Curtin. Altman shot *The Dumbwaiter* (1987), starring John Travolta, and *The Room* for television, then contributed a segment to the unfortunate British anthology *Aria* (1988).

He broke out of this prolonged slump with a project for network television. *The Caine Mutiny Court-Martial* (1988) was made for CBS-TV, with Eric Bogosian, Jeff Daniels, and Brad Davis reinvigorating Herman Wouk's play (also the basis of Dmytryk's 1954 film). *Vincent & Theo* (1990) originated as a miniseries for European television, but its roots are not evident in either the stunning photography by Jean Lepine or the work of Tim Roth as the tortured Vincent Van Gogh (Kirk *who?*) and Paul Rhys as his supportive brother, Theo.

Altman's return to form was apparently noticed by Hollywood, where he made a triumphal return with *The Player* (1992). A corrosive portrait of the film industry, it fairly drips with venom. Tim Robbins's portrayal of a rising studio executive who kills to maintain his place in the pecking order is potent, but Altman's doodling at the edges of the story—the showy camerawork, the quick-as-a-flash star cameos—is almost more fun than the gripping plot. And the staging of the mini-movie gas-chamber scene provided the year's biggest laugh. Both Altman and the film were nominated for Academy Awards, his first in seventeen years. *Short Cuts* (1993) also created quite a stir; it was an ambitious, 189-minute-long attempt to adapt nine of the stories in Raymond Carver's collection by the same name. Altman makes a token effort to unify the stories, but what we end up with is a kaleidoscopic grab bag of corrosive character profiles; this worked well as a structure in *Nashville*, and Altman makes it work again here. Tim Robbins, Jennifer Jason Leigh, Lyle Lovett, Madeleine Stowe, Chris Penn, Anne Archer, and Peter Gallagher are among the actors representing an array of dysfunctional Los Angeles types. Some of their stories are tragic, some hilarious, and some just bizarre, but Altman somehow holds this nine-ring circus together. His Academy Award nomination for best direction came as a surprise to many, especially Martin Scorsese, whose slot he "took"—but *Short Cuts* is a convincing argument for how a director can make a difference on a project.

Altman must have also made a difference on *Ready to Wear* (1994; aka *Prêt-à-Porter*), but this impressionistic look at the Paris high-fashion biz quickly falls apart at the seams. It's wonderful to see Sophia Loren and Marcello Mastroianni paired again after so many years, and as usual Altman has enticed many of the day's buzz-name actors (Stephen Rea, Tim Robbins, Julia Roberts) to join in, along with such screen legends as Anouk Aimee and Lauren Bacall. But while its narrative resembles those of *Nashville* and *Short Cuts*, *Ready to Wear* isn't a patch on those tours de force. Despite a blizzard of publicity both during the film's location shooting and in its first weeks of release—most of it concerned with the outrage expressed by members of the fashion community at the liberties this broad satire had taken—American audiences stayed away in droves, and the critics were less than kind. But Altman had survived that experience a dozen times already.

## ● JACK ARNOLD (1916–1992)

Best remembered for overseeing several of the very best science-fiction films of the Fifties, this New Haven, Connecticut, native began his career directing and producing dozens of industrial films and documentaries for the government and the private sector. In 1953 he joined Universal, where he directed one of the first Juvenile Delinquent pictures, *Girls in the Night* (1953). Telling the "Tense, Terrifying Truth About the BIG CITY's Delinquent Daughters!," it never rose above its "B" budget and cast, but did help pave the way for *The Wild One* and *The Blackboard Jungle*. Arnold's next film was the groundbreaking *It Came from Outer Space* (1953). Based on a Ray Bradbury story, this quietly creepy yarn about aliens taking over the identities of small-town Arizonans as they repair their spaceship is high on anyone's list of seminal SF cinema, and it also boasted one of the more effective uses of the 3-D process (during that short-lived craze). *The Glass Web* (1953), also shot in 3-D, was a murder mystery with a TV background, starring Edward G. Robinson and John Forsythe.

But it was *The Creature from the Black Lagoon* (1954) that cemented Arnold's position as the new master of *cinema fantastique*. More an old-fashioned monster movie than an exercise in science fiction, *Creature* was shot in 3-D but achieved its fame largely through release in a standard format. Not to make more of it than it deserved, this was the blueprint for scores of SF flicks to come, most of them offering inferior versions of its effective rhythms, gripping score, and constant suspense. It also made a ton of money for Universal. Arnold's reward was to be assigned the sequel; though not up to the original, *Revenge of the Creature* (1955) has merit (but not, alas, Julia Adams).

*The Man from Bitter Ridge* (1955) was an unremarkable Lex Barker Western, but the more memorable *Tarantula* (1955) was a Big Bug entry second only to the previous year's *Them!* in effectiveness. Again Universal insisted on saddling Arnold with fodder from other genres, resulting in the formulaic *Outside the Law* and *Red Sundown* (both 1956). Blessedly, Arnold's next project was the classic *The Incredible Shrinking Man* (1957), a strong adaptation of the fine novel by author Richard Matheson. Although its special effects are crude compared to the marvels wrought in today's cinema, the film imparts a sense of wonder more vital than that of many big-budget epics.

*The Tattered Dress* (1957) was a contemporary melodrama featuring Jeanne Crain and Gail Russell. Then it was back to the Old West for *Man in the Shadow* (1957), a relatively painless drama starring Orson Welles (in his only Western, thank goodness) and Jeff Chandler. *The Lady Takes a Flyer* (1958) used Chandler again, pairing him with Lana Turner as a pilot who doesn't fancy being domesticated; Turner had just been Oscar-nominated for *Peyton Place*, and Arnold probably had to pinch himself to be working with bankable stars on a mainstream romance. *High School Confidential!* (1958) was a wonderfully trashy, profoundly awful Juvenile Delinquent pic with Mamie Van Doren and Russ Tamblyn, returning Arnold to the land of the "B"s in no uncertain fashion. *The Space Children* (1958) was a solemn story of mysteriously brainwashed children sabotaging a nuclear test site, while (completing a very busy 1958) *Monster on the Campus* had a less weighty message: one shouldn't ingest the blood of a prehistoric fish, unless he wants to devolve into a caveman. (Or did you already know that?)

So far Arnold's only extraordinary work had been within the SF genre. But in 1959 he helmed the British production of the hilarious Leonard Wibberley novel *The Mouse That Roared* and turned in a comic masterpiece, in no small part thanks to the talents of

Peter Sellers. This must have signaled to Arnold that he was ready to break away from the genre ghetto, because he never made another science-fiction film. Unfortunately, most of his subsequent work wasn't up to the level of *The Mouse.* After the decent Audie Murphy Western *No Name on the Bullet* (1959), he made the lame Bob Hope–Lana Turner comedy, *Bachelor in Paradise* (1961); *The Lively Set* (1964), with James Darren romancing Pamela Tiffin in between drag races; another Bob Hope misfire, *A Global Affair* (1964); and the hopelessly unfunny comedy *Hello Down There* (1969), with Tony Randall, Janet Leigh, and Merv Griffin.

Working less and less frequently, Arnold turned out a pair of blacksploitation pictures, *Black Eye* (1974) and *Boss Nigger* (1975), along with the sexploitation entry *The Games Girls Play* (1974). For television he made *Sex and the Married Woman* (1977) and *Marilyn: The Untold Story* (1980), after which he retired—a rather unsatisfying final act for one of the 1950s' most enjoyable fantasists. With hindsight, one can argue that Arnold should have remained within the science-fiction genre, where he had consistently excelled. But given the opportunity to break out of the low-rent "B"-picture neighborhood, any director of that time would have acted as Arnold did. Would that he fared better in his grab for the brass ring.

## ● DOROTHY ARZNER (1900-1979)

The most amazing thing about Dorothy Arzner's colorful life is that it hasn't yet been made into a movie—although that may change shortly. Born in San Francisco two days after the century turned, she worked in her father's restaurant before volunteering to drive an ambulance in World War I at the age of seventeen. Arzner studied medicine at the University of Southern California but dropped out in 1919 to take a job as a steno in the Famous Players–Lasky script department; soon she rose to supervisor, then film cutter. By now the company was doing business as Paramount, and she worked in its subdivision Realart as an editor on low-budget fodder before getting a chance to edit such major productions as James Cruze's 1923 epic *The Covered Wagon* and Fred Niblo's Valentino showcase *Blood and Sand*. Soon she began to write screenplays as well: *Inez from Hollywood*, *Red Kimono*, and *When Husbands Flirt*, among others. Impressed with her acumen, Cruze hired her to both write and edit his 1926 opus about the early days of the Merchant Marine, *Old Ironsides*.

Arzner was rewarded with her first directorial assignment, the 1927 comedy *Fashions for Women*, which was followed in short order by *Ten Modern Commandments* and *Get Your Man*, the latter with Clara Bow. *Manhattan Cocktail* (1928) was wonderfully trashy: Nancy Carroll's Broadway aspirations lead to rape, the death of her brother, and assorted infidelities; while *The Wild Party* (1929)—Paramount's first sound release—featured Clara Bow as a college temptress who earns expulsion after a torrid dalliance with professor Fredric March, who gets shot for his trouble. Uncredited, Arzner co-directed *Charming Sinners* (1929) with Broadway director Robert Milton, then made *Sarah and Son* (1930), a prime weeper that featured Ruth Chatterton as an opera star searching for her long-lost lad with the help of attorney Fredric March. She contributed "The Gallows Song" sequence to the all-star revue *Paramount on Parade* (1930), then made *Anybody's Woman* (1930), another Ruth Chatterton soap opera.

*Honor Among Lovers* (1931) featured rising star Claudette Colbert as a secretary who is in love with boss Fredric March but marries a stock-market plunger in a weak moment and nearly pays for the mistake with her life. *Working Girls* (1931) let small-town Frances Dee loose on New York City, while Buddy Rogers and Paul Lukas competed for her favors. Arzner's final picture at Paramount was *Merrily We Go to Hell* (1932) with Fredric March and Sylvia Sidney, a turgid weeper about an heiress who unwittingly marries an alcoholic playwright; they separate, but pregnancy reunites them in time to save their marriage. Now a freelancer, Arzner made *Christopher Strong* (1933) at RKO with Katharine Hepburn, a wild drama about a liberated aviatrix (in skin-tight, silver lamé flying togs, no less) who has an affair with married Colin Clive (why?) and then commits suicide when she learns she's carrying his child. *Little Women* it wasn't, and few paid to see it, but its theme and imagery allowed Arzner to express herself more fully than any of her other films to date.

Arzner next made *Nana* (1934) for Samuel Goldwyn, whose five-year plan to turn his discovery, Russian actress Anna Sten, into the next Garbo never succeeded. This well-mounted adaptation of the Zola story had a tragic ending—another suicide for Arzner to stage—but the film grinds to a halt long before Sten's demise. A more interesting effort was *Craig's Wife* (1936), adapted from George Kelly's Pulitzer Prize–winning play about a materialistic woman (Rosalind Russell) who is less interested in her husband (John Boles) than maintaining the gleam of her showcase domicile. The story had been filmed as a silent in 1928 and would surface again in 1950 as *Harriet Craig* with Joan Crawford, but this version remains potent.

It was, in fact, Crawford whom Arzner next directed in *The Bride Wore Red* (1937), a disappointingly conventional production that starred Joan as a singer in a waterfront dive who gets the chance to pass herself off as a society dame and runs with it. It was adapted from Molnar's play *The Girl from Trieste*, but he couldn't have anticipated the MGM gloss it would receive here (in spite of which it died at the box office). Arzner's next screen credit was at RKO, where she replaced Roy Del Ruth on *Dance, Girl, Dance* (1940); Lucille Ball has one of her best early roles as Bubbles, a burlesque dancer who convinces aspiring ballerina Maureen O'Hara to give up her dream and learn to bump 'n' grind. One good cat fight and several speeches later, O'Hara has taught the cynical Ball a lesson. Today *Dance* is celebrated as a proto-feminist work, but in 1940 RKO took a bath on the film.

It was another three years before Arzner made her final film, *First Comes Courage*. Here exotic-looking Merle Oberon is a Norwegian who uses her wiles to leach secrets from Nazi major Carl Esmond; in the end she nobly rejects Brian Aherne's offer to flee with him to the safety of England so that she can continue her undercover efforts. It was patriotic as all get-out, but no more credible than the sight of the Eurasian Oberon as a Scandinavian.

Arzner never directed another studio picture, although she spent the rest of the war years making WAC training films. Later she taught at U.C.L.A. and made the occasional Pepsi commercial. A number of tributes in the Seventies brought home to her the fact that, although much of her early work may have been forgotten or lost, her role as a female pioneer in the film industry was very much remembered. Her unabashed lesbianism has today made her a symbol to many, regardless of the obscurity of many of her films.

## ● HAL ASHBY (1936-1988)

Although Hal Ashby was one of the premier directors of the Seventies, his career suddenly, strangely, derailed in the decade that followed, and his early death prevented him from demonstrating whether he might have set it aright. But he made as many good movies in his first ten years of directing as anyone in Hollywood, and some were among the best films of the day.

Born in Ogden, Utah, Ashby hitchhiked to Hollywood after graduating from Utah State and got a job at Universal in the script department. He worked at Republic in the early Fifties in their poster-printing operation, then became an assistant editor to directors like William Wyler (on *Friendly Persuasion* and *The Big Country*) and George Stevens (on *The Diary of Anne Frank* and *The Greatest Story Ever Told*). As head editor, he worked with Tony Richardson on *The Loved One* and Norman Jewison on *The Cincinnati Kid* and *In the Heat of the Night*; Ashby won an Oscar for his work on the last.

Jewison helped Ashby land his first directing assignment, the socially conscious comedy *The Landlord* (1970), with Beau Bridges as a quirky Yuppie (before the term existed) who bonds with the tenants living in the Brooklyn tenement he has purchased on a whim. The film's potent cast included Lou Gossett, Pearl Bailey, Lee Grant, and Susan Anspach. *Harold and Maude* (1972) was received rather coolly at first, but this black comedy about a twenty-year-old boy (Bud Cort) who has a passionate affair with a lusty octogenarian (Ruth Gordon) slowly found its audience and is now a genuine cult classic. But it was *The Last Detail* (1973) that advanced Ashby to the front rank of mainstream directors. Offering a hilarious (and profane) turn by Jack Nicholson as a Navy lifer who (along with partner Otis Young) draws the unpleasant task of escorting petty thief Randy Quaid from West Virginia to the Portsmouth, New Hampshire, naval prison where he will spend the next eight years. Robert Towne's superb, Oscar-nominated screenplay helped make this one of the year's best films, and Nicholson and Quaid were also nominated by the Academy for their performances.

One of 1975's biggest—and most controversial—hits, *Shampoo* was a splendid satire of 1968 Los Angeles society, with charismatic starring performances by Warren Beatty, Julie Christie, and Goldie Hawn, great supporting work by Lee Grant and Jack Warden, and a clever, bold screenplay by Towne and Beatty, who were nominated for an Academy Award; Warden and Grant were also nominated, with Grant winning an Oscar. Based on his autobiography, *Bound for Glory* (1976) was a biopic about the life of activist folk singer Woody Guthrie (David Carradine), gorgeously photographed by Haskell Wexler, who won an Oscar. Although the hagiography is laid on thick, it was well received by the critics (despite an indifferent box office); among its slew of Academy Award nominations was one for best picture.

Ashby's most lauded film is also one that many critics are on record as loathing, an appropriately polarized reaction to a film about the effects of the Vietnam War on the homefront. But if *Coming Home* (1978) is too sanctimonious by half (it was, after all, made by Jane Fonda's production company), at least it had the courage of its (safely liberal) convictions and some powerhouse performances. In fact, all its principal actors were nominated for Oscars—Jon Voight, Jane Fonda (both winners), Penelope Milford, and Bruce Dern (this last a tad dubious). Ashby also received his only nomination for best direction, and the screenplay won an Oscar as well. Quite an act to follow, but Ashby did nearly as well (some would say better) with *Being There* (1979), a sometimes brilliant adaptation by Jerzy Kosinski of his novel, with an inspired performance by Peter Sellers as the idiot gardener who becomes a savant to all who behold him. Sellers was Oscar-nominated, but it was Melvyn Douglas who took home a best supporting actor award.

After that impressive string of seven good-to-great films, *Second-Hand Hearts* (1981) came as something of a shock. But there's no way around it—this is one awful picture. Suffice it to say that leading man Robert Blake has never been worse—a frightening statement—and that his performance is matched in every other creative category. Nor was this disaster an anomaly. *Lookin' to Get Out* (1982), which actually was filmed before *Hearts* but (understandably) left on the shelf for two years, was just as excruciating. Jon Voight and Burt Young go down in flames as one of the least funny comedy teams ever recorded on celluloid, and for co-scripting and co-producing, Voight had only himself to blame.

Understandably searching for a change of pace, Ashby next directed *Let's Spend the Night Together* (1982), a Rolling Stones concert film that he assembled in workmanlike fashion—no more—from their 1981 tour. *The Slugger's Wife* (1985) held out the promise of something better, with an original Neil Simon story about a baseball player (Michael O'Keefe) infatuated with a singer (Rebecca DeMornay), much to the dismay of his manager (Martin Ritt, of all people!). But it, too, bombed. Ashby's final film, *8 Million Ways to Die* (1986), was marginally better, a freewheeling, often flabby adaptation of a Lawrence Block novel, with Jeff Bridges somewhat miscast as alcoholic private eye Matt Scudder. But Rosanna Arquette was fine as a good call girl–in–trouble, and Andy Garcia is most amusing (if sometimes incoherent) as her smug pimp—much of his performance was reported to have been improvised, and it looks it.

What went wrong with Hal Ashby's career? We may never know. But when one compares his initial seven films with his final five, it seems as if two different beings took turns inhabiting his body—the first with talent to burn, the second merely burned out.

▲ *Ashby and Jane Fonda confer on the set of* Coming Home

▲ *Lloyd Bacon and superstar Al Jolson on the set of* The Singing Fool, *one of the first "talkies," in 1928*

## ● LLOYD BACON (1890–1955)

For nearly eighteen years, Lloyd Bacon was one of Warners' top directors, making more than half his one hundred films under its aegis (including ten silents); for a while he averaged five pictures a year. After Warners, he made another twenty-three films, mostly period musicals for Fox. Looking at those ninety sound pictures, one finds a classic company man turning out work that rarely fell below a certain standard of competency and just as rarely exceeded it, regardless of the genre. When compared to Warners' other front-line directors, Bacon falls somewhere among Roy Del Ruth, William Keighley, and Archie Mayo, but well below Michael Curtiz. In short, his work was professional but (with certain exceptions) uninspired.

Born in San José, California, he became a member of David Belasco's Los Angeles stock company in 1911, and two years later had broken into films as a heavy in comedy shorts. He worked with Charlie Chaplin in 1915 and 1916, before entering the war as a photographer for the Navy, after which he rejoined Chaplin. He was given the chance to direct by Mack Sennett in 1921, and joined Warner Bros. in 1926, where his first feature was the cautionary melodrama *Broken Hearts of Hollywood. Women They Talk About* and *The Lion and the Mouse* (both 1928) were part-talkies that paved the way for *The Singing Fool* (also 1928), Bacon's enormously successful follow-up to *The Jazz Singer*, with Al Jolson again regaling audiences with his singing in an otherwise creaky tearjerker.

Bacon's five 1929 releases included *Honky Tonk* with Sophie Tucker and *So Long Letty*, a musical comedy via Broadway that included the standard "Am I Blue?" *Moby Dick* was the most interesting of Bacon's five 1930 efforts, with John Barrymore repeating the role of Ahab he first portrayed in the 1926 silent *The Sea Beast*. Bacon was called on five times again in 1931 for such forgettable productions as *Fifty Million Frenchmen* and *Gold Dust Gertie*, a pair of Olsen and Johnson comedies, and *Sit Tight*, with Joe E. Brown as a hapless wrestler. Bacon's name appeared on an incredible seven releases in 1932, including the obscure newspaper exposé *The Famous Ferguson Case*, the Joe E. Brown comedy *Fireman Save My Child*, and *Crooner*, an interesting dissection of the rise and fall of a radio star (David Manners) whose hubris is the instrument of his destruction.

*42nd Street* (1933) was Bacon's most successful film to date (he replaced the ailing Mervyn LeRoy); the archetypal backstage musical, it featured Ruby Keeler, Dick Powell, Ginger Rogers, and Warner Bax-

▲ *Bacon (center) coaches George Brent and Ann Sheridan on the set of* Honeymoon for Three

ter on the acting front. Even more critical to its success was the wealth of talent behind the camera, notably composers Al Dubin and Harry Warren and dance director Busby Berkeley. *Picture Snatcher* (1933) wasn't as big a hit, but it remains one of James Cagney's pre-Code delights; he plays an unscrupulous news photographer who snaps a photo no one else can get. *Mary Stevens, M.D.* (1933) was a ridiculously melodramatic story of a woman doctor's frequent trials and tribulations, with Kay Francis suffering nobly, as only she could do. But *Footlight Parade* (also 1933) was another backstage classic, with Cagney showing what he could do under Busby Berkeley's dance direction for the first and last time; he was pretty swell in the rest of the movie as well, as a hyperkinetic director exhorting Joan Blondell, Keeler, and Powell onward, with barely a pause to breathe.

*Son of a Sailor* (1933) was one of Joe E. Brown's better vehicles, and Thelma Todd was a welcome comic presence. *Wonder Bar* (1934) transported the Warners musical formula and players to a Parisian nightclub with uneven results, the nadir being Al Jolson's infamous number "Goin' to Heaven on a Mule," sung in blackface to two hundred darling pickaninnies—er, black children—dressed as angels. Bacon couldn't elevate either *Here Comes the Navy* or *He Was Her Man* (both 1934) despite the presence of Cagney—in fact, both were among his dullest pictures for Warners—while *A Very Honorable Guy* and *Six Day Bike Rider* (both 1934) featured Joe E. Brown, again and yet again. *Devil Dogs of the Air* (1935) provided Cagney with the promising setting of the Marine Air Corps for the inevitable rivalry with Pat O'Brien, but again the result was unimpressive.

Having proved merely competent in handling adventure, Bacon returned to the confines of the musical comedy with *In Caliente* (1935), but Dolores Del Rio and Pat O'Brien were no Rogers and Astaire. *Broadway Gondolier* (1935) was better, if only for the chemistry between Dick Powell and Joan Blondell and the presence of the Mills Brothers. Bacon finished 1935 with two more subpar Cagney vehicles, the sentimental boxing pic *The Irish in Us* and the Barbary Coast drama *Frisco Kid* (which came out the same year as Hawks's far superior *Barbary Coast*). Someone at Warners took pity on Bacon and assigned him just three productions for 1936: *Sons O'Guns*, with Joe E. Brown fighting World War I for the French; *Cain and Mabel*, a terrible musical comedy/romance with Clark Gable and Marion Davies floundering throughout; and *Gold Diggers of 1937*, a blessed return to the backstage formula with Powell, Blondell, and Busby Berkeley's saving dance direction.

*Marked Woman* (1937) was Bacon's best picture

in years. Bette Davis starred as the Code-correct "nightclub hostess" who agrees to testify for D.A. Humphrey Bogart against mob czar Eduardo Cianelli after he kills her sister. Based on the recent trial of Lucky Luciano, which sent him to prison for trafficking in prostitution after several of his "girls" testified against him for D.A. Thomas Dewey, the film had a particular veracity. But *Ever Since Eve*, a Marion Davies comedy, and *Submarine D-1* (both 1937), with Pat O'Brien as the commander of a peacetime sub, just barely made par. Bogart was in *San Quentin* (1937), but it was such a mundane prison yarn that his presence hardly registered. *A Slight Case of Murder* (1938) was thus a pleasant surprise: an amiable crime comedy based on a play by Damon Runyon and Howard Lindsay that permitted Edward G. Robinson to playfully send up his Capone-like persona as a bootlegger gone straight.

*The Cowboy from Brooklyn* (1938), with Dick Powell as a cowhand who becomes a radio star thanks to promoter Pat O'Brien, sounded like more fun than it proved to be, while *Racket Busters* (1938) was another in the seemingly endless skein of formulaic gangster pictures Bogart was mired in at that point in his career. *Boy Meets Girl* (also 1938), from the Broadway play, featured Cagney and Pat O'Brien as a pair of wise-guy Hollywood screenwriters—better roles than they were used to of late—but *Wings of the Navy* (1939) was unadorned hokum about pilots George Brent and John Payne, both politely lusting after Olivia de Havilland. *The Oklahoma Kid* (1939) again paired Cagney and Bogart, who had recently proved to be dynamic screen foes, but here the sight of Bogart in a Cisco Kid mustache and the sound of Cagney's Lower East Side patois made it impossible to take the plot (Cagney's revenging his dad's murder) seriously.

Bacon's spot in the Warners pecking order had been slipping for some time now, as top stars like Errol Flynn and Paul Muni went with Michael Curtiz or William Dieterle, and now Cagney would be beyond his reach as well. But he did what he could with such second-tier properties as *Indianapolis Speedway* with Pat O'Brien and John Payne, *Espionage Agent* (both 1939) with Joel McCrea and Brenda Marshall, and *A Child Is Born* (1940), a remake of the 1932 *Life Begins*, with Geraldine Fitzgerald as a convict sent to a "civilian" maternity ward to have her baby. *Invisible Stripes* (1939) was better: ex-con George Raft tries to keep kid brother William Holden

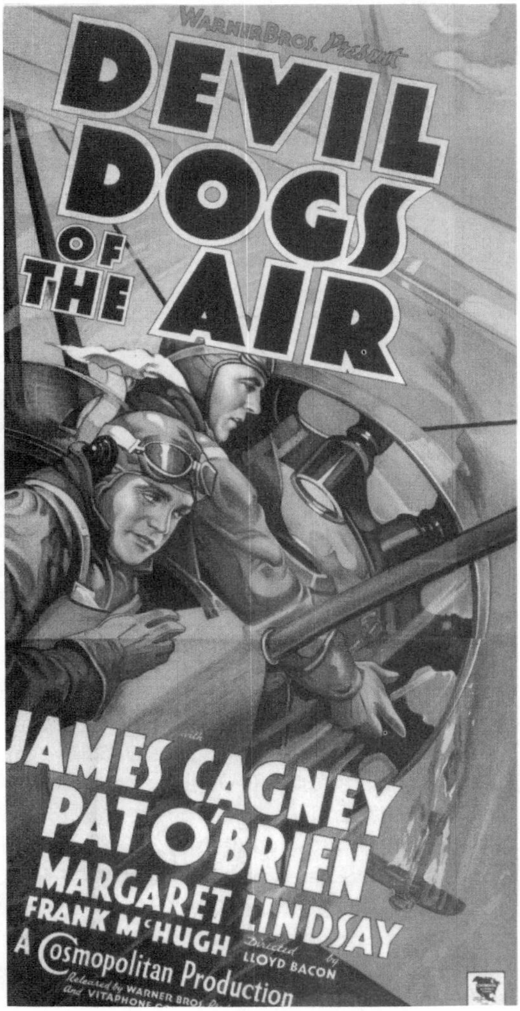


from hooking up with erstwhile partner Humphrey Bogart; but then it was back to blarney hell with Thomas Mitchell as an over-the-hill beat cop in *Three Cheers for the Irish* (1940).

*Brother Orchid* (1940) was a clever post-gangster comedy, with Edward G. Robinson as a reformed racketeer who hides out in a monastery only to discover he likes the life. *Knute Rockne, All American* (1940), with Pat O'Brien in rare form, was one of the era's best sports biopics, while *Honeymoon for Three* (1941) was a painless comedy, with George Brent as an irresistible novelist (hah!) who's blind to the charms of gorgeous secretary Ann Sheridan. Bacon got his one chance to direct Errol Flynn in *Footsteps in the Dark* (1941)—but just his luck, it used Flynn not as a swashbuckler or war hero but rather as a gentleman sleuth for lackluster comedy. *Affectionately Yours* (1941) was a casting mess, with Rita Hayworth, Merle Oberon, and Dennis Morgan hardly forming an equilateral triangle, but *Navy Blues* (also 1941) fared better with Ann Sheridan, Martha Raye, and four Mercer-Schwartz tunes.

Bacon made good use of Edward G. Robinson's comic gifts for a third time in *Larceny, Inc.* (1942), with Broderick Crawford and Edward Brophy joining him as ex-cons using a luggage shop as a front for drilling into the bank next door. *Wings for the Eagle* (1942) was Warners patriotism in full swing, with Ann Sheridan working in an airplane factory alongside Dennis Morgan, but *Silver Queen* (also 1942) was a lame Civil War yarn featuring George Brent and Priscilla Lane. *Action in the North Atlantic* (1943) was more patriotism, a salute to the Merchant Marine (screenplay by John Howard Lawson) with Humphrey Bogart and Raymond Massey defending their ship from a German sub attack. It was probably Bacon's best action picture at Warners—so naturally it proved to be his last at the studio.

Moving to 20th Century-Fox and old boss Darryl Zanuck, Bacon was put to work on *The Sullivans* (1944), a moving account of five real-life brothers who lost their lives when their Navy ship was sunk at Guadalcanal. *Captain Eddie* (1945) was another biopic, this time about the life of World War I ace Eddie Rickenbacker, played rather dully by a miscast Fred MacMurray. With the war over, Bacon handled more frivolous fare: *Home Sweet Homicide* (1946), your basic murder mystery/comedy/romance, and *Wake Up and Dream* (1946), a bizarre fantasy of a girl's search for her MIA brother, with June Haver and John Payne the romantic leads. Bacon hadn't directed many musicals since the mid-Thirties, but he now was assigned a string of Technicolor productions, commencing with *I Wonder Who's Kissing Her Now* (1947), a pleasant biography of Gay Nineties vaudeville star Joe Howard, starring Mark Stevens and June Haver. *You Were Meant for Me* (1948) featured Dan Dailey and Jeanne Crain as a bandleader and his wife struggling through the Depression, while *Give My Regards to Broadway* (1948) had Dailey again in another nostalgic peek at old-time show biz.

*Don't Trust Your Husband* (aka *An Innocent Affair*, 1948) was a feeble farce with Madeleine Carroll suspicious of hubby Fred MacMurray's affairs (there weren't any), while *Mother Is a Freshman* (1949) was a sweet comedy with mom Loretta Young competing with daughter Betty Lynn for college prof Van Johnson. *It Happens Every Spring* (1949) was a hilarious baseball comedy, one of the best ever made: Ray Milland is a chemistry professor who discovers a formula that makes bats repel baseballs, inspiring him to embark on a new career as a star pitcher.

Bacon spent a year at Columbia making *Miss Grant Takes Richmond* (1949), a showcase for Lucille Ball's screwball talents as she outwits William Holden's gang of bookies, and *Kill the Umpire* (1950), which used William Bendix to good effect as a baseball fanatic who has to take a job as an umpire to make ends meet. Frank Tashlin worked on the screenplays for both of these, as well as Bacon's slapstick companions *The Good Humor Man*, with Jack Carson foiling a payroll holdup, and *The Fuller Brush Girl* (both 1950), with Lucille Ball mixed up in murder.

Back at Fox, Bacon directed the Betty Grable–Dan Dailey musical *Call Me Mister* (1951), a USO comedy with choreography by Busby Berkeley, and *The Frogmen* (1951), a surprisingly hard-boiled World War II yarn starring Richard Widmark as the leader of a squad charged with sabotaging a Japanese sub base. *Golden Girl* (also 1951) offered Mitzi Gaynor as Civil War–era musical star Lotta Crabtree, while *The I Don't Care Girl* (1953) had Gaynor as vaudeville star Eva Tanguay, with George Jessel and Oscar Levant in support.

At Universal Bacon made *The Great Sioux Uprising* with Jeff Chandler and Faith Domergue, a typical entry in the then-popular Indian Wars genre, and *Walking My Baby Back Home* (both 1953), a rather dumb musical set on an Army base, with Donald O'Connor and Janet Leigh. Bacon's last two movies were for RKO—*The French Line* (1954), with a 3-D Jane Russell in scandalously scant togs, and *She Couldn't Say No* (1954), a stillborn comedy with a miscast Robert Mitchum wooing eccentric benefactress Jean Simmons. That made it an even one hundred pictures for Bacon, who then folded up his tent and retired. He died a year later.

## ● ROBERT BENTON (1932– )

The most famous filmmaker to emerge from Waxahachie, Texas, Robert Benton has disappeared for years at a time from the awareness of American moviegoers—eight films spread out over twenty-three years has a way of doing that to a director's reputation. But just when you've forgotten him, Benton comes back, bearing some totally unexpected gift with him. He began his career in movies as a screenwriter in 1967, debuting on no less a production than Warren Beatty's *Bonnie and Clyde*; he would continue to script or co-script most of his own pictures. If Benton worked more frequently, we might think of him now as our greatest writer/director.

Before he ever thought of a himself as a Hollywood director, Benton had already sampled several interesting careers. While in the Army in the 1950s he painted dioramas; in 1958 he began a six-year stint as the art director of *Esquire* magazine, switching in 1964 to the post of contributing editor. Along the way he wrote a few books, and (with fellow *Esquire* editor David Newman) came up with the "book" for the 1966 Broadway show, *It's a Bird . . . It's a Plane . . . It's Superman*. He wrote *Bonnie and Clyde* with Newman—their script was nominated for an Academy Award—and subsequently earned writing credits on *There Was a Crooked Man*, *What's Up, Doc?* and *Oh, Calcutta!*

That took Benton up to 1972, when he directed *Bad Company*, an iconoclastic little Western that starred Jeff Bridges and Barry Brown as a pair of Civil War draft dodgers who avoid the war by heading West with a few friends, robbing and stealing to support themselves. The film (which Benton wrote with Newman) exhibits some nice touches of black humor, and cinematographer Gordon Willis gives it a lovely palette (he also shot *The Godfather* that year). With that modest success, Benton was able to leave *Esquire* (which always will be grateful for his having invented, with Newman, the annual Dubious Achievement Awards) and devote himself to films full time.

He next directed *The Late Show* (1977) from his own screenplay about an aging private eye who gets dragged into a case (isn't it always that way?) trying to help a kooky dame who's lost her cat. Art Carney was splendid as Ira Wells, the gumshoe who's falling apart at the seams, and Lily Tomlin gives what just may be her finest performance as his client who, much to her surprise, finds herself falling for the overweight, cranky lug. Howard Duff has a nice cameo as Ira's doomed partner, and Bill Macy, Joanna Cassidy, and John Considine all score as the criminally inclined.

Benton paid some bills by co-scripting the first *Superman* movie for Richard Donner in 1978, then hit paydirt with *Kramer vs. Kramer* (1979), a lovely adaptation (scripted by Benton) of Avery Corman's moving novel about a father who must raise his young son after his wife deserts them. Dustin Hoffman was never more sympathetic than here as the dad who sacrifices his job and love life to care properly for his son (the irresistible Justin Henry), and Meryl Streep gives an amazing performance as the selfish wife whose need to "find herself" proves disastrous for those she leaves behind. Manipulative, to be sure—but it was an enormous box-office hit, and won the Academy Award for best picture, with Streep and Hoffman also winning; Benton took home two Oscars, one for best direction and one for best screenplay adaptation. It was a virtual sweep of the major awards and a stunning triumph for Benton.

Who would have thought that a writer/director that hot would take three years to launch his next project? And *Still of the Night* (1982) hardly seemed worth the wait—a derivative thriller (written by Benton and Newman) that miscast Meryl Streep as a woman suspected of murder, with Roy Scheider less than compelling as the Manhattan psychologist who tries to fathom whether she's the actual killer or just disturbed.

*Places in the Heart* (1984) was more comfortable territory for Benton, and it showed. Set in his hometown of Waxahachie circa 1935, the film features Sally Field as a god-fearing woman who is suddenly widowed and must provide for her children by working her forty-acre cotton field with just her own two hands and the aid of quirky black laborer Danny Glover—the townspeople are entirely unsympathetic to her plight. John Malkovich is almost too saintly as her blind boarder, and Lindsay Crouse, Amy Madigan, and Ed Harris also register in support, but this is really Field's show. She won the best actress Oscar for the second time ("You like me! You really like me!"), and Benton took home another Academy Award for his original screenplay; the film was also nominated for best picture, as were Malkovich and Crouse for their acting.

*Nadine* (1987) allowed Benton to let down his hair; it was another Texas yarn, this time set in 1954 Austin. Kim Basinger gives what's probably her best performance (faint praise, it's true) as a madcap manicurist who's pregnant by hubby Jeff Bridges and so is stalling on their divorce; when she tries to recover some nude photos of herself from a photographer's studio, she stumbles across plans for a superhighway that developer Rip Torn would kill to recover. *Nadine* was supposed to be all-out fun, and does have its moments, but in the end it leaves us feeling that it could have been even better.

The same was said of *Billy Bathgate* (1991), Benton's elegant but muted version of E. L. Doctorow's novel about a kid from the Bronx (Loren Dean) who becomes involved with notorious gangster Dutch Schultz (a miscast Dustin Hoffman) and the widowed moll (Nicole Kidman) of a rival Dutch disposed of (Bruce Willis, who dies well). Tom Stoppard did the adaptation, but this was not a book that cried out for a screen treatment, as the lack of box-office interest in it demonstrated. Benton cast *Nobody's Fool* (1994) more cannily; Paul Newman, looking great, plays Sully, a bone-weary, cynical, misanthropic handyman in a small, economically depressed town in upstate New York. In Richard Russo's excellent novel, Sully is self-deluding; here he's just adorably cranky as he interacts with Carl, the wise-aleck construction kingpin who intermittently employs Sully (an expert turn by an unbilled Bruce Willis), Carl's sexy but neglected wife (Melanie Griffith, ditto), his estranged son (Dylan Walsh), and—best of all—his landlady and former eighth-grade teacher, Miss Beryl (Jessica Tandy, who died shortly after filming was completed). Benton, a notorious perfectionist, admitted in an interview that he had rewritten his script at least twenty times, and at least one actor was glad he did: Newman won the New York Film Critics Circle award for best actor and also received an Oscar nomination, while Benton was nominated for his screenplay adaptation.

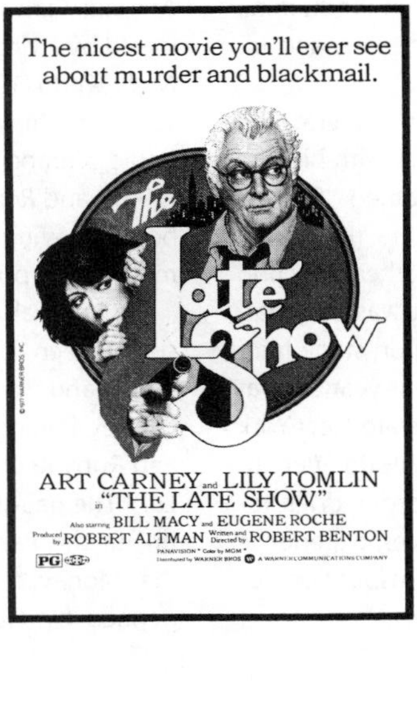

▲ *Busby Berkeley and Mickey Rooney yuk it up during* Strike Up the Band

## ● BUSBY BERKELEY (1895–1976)

In his palmy days, Busby Berkeley was the cinema's most innovative stager of dance sequences—showy geometric spectacles laden with sexual imagery that remain visual delights even sixty years after their technique has been decoded and duplicated by others. But that phase of his career, which covered the Thirties, was followed by several years at the more sedate MGM, and Berkeley never regained his early, feverish momentum. Plagued by a debilitating series of problems in his personal life—including a mother he couldn't break away from—he lacked the stamina needed to fuel his particular sort of genius, and ultimately he broke down.

A child of Los Angeles in its pre-cinema era, William Berkeley Enos moved to New York with his parents at the age of three; he was nicknamed "Busby" by his stage-actress mother during the heyday of Broadway star Alice Busby. With a father directing plays and a mother acting in them, it was only natural that young Busby was appearing on stage himself as the century turned. But an eight-year stint at the Mohegan Military Academy in upstate New York was followed by service in the First World War; as one of his duties he oversaw close-order drills for both the American and the French forces, experience that later would serve him well as inspiration for many of his cinematic flights of fancy.

He returned to the stage after the war, acting a bit and directing stock, before conquering Broadway as one of its most coveted dance directors. In 1927 he choreographed *A Connecticut Yankee*, which led to an offer to direct his first Broadway show, *A Night in Venice*, in 1928. Thus he became the first Broadway director to also choreograph the dance numbers (how many have followed in his footsteps?). Those successes brought Berkeley to the attention of Hollywood, and Sam Goldwyn imported him in 1930 to work on the choreography for Eddie Cantor's film *Whoopee!* which had been a successful Ziegfeld show. Another Cantor vehicle, *Palmy Days* (1931), was followed by *Flying High* (1931), a Bert Lahr musical, and *Night World* (1932), a gangster tale with Boris Karloff, set in a nightclub. Berkeley choreographed two more Eddie Cantor extravaganzas—*The Kid from Spain* (1932) and *Roman Scandals* (1933), both huge hits—before leaving Goldwyn for Warner Bros., where his most eye-popping work would be created.

In 1933 alone he staged the dances for three musical screen classics: *42nd Street*, *Gold Diggers of 1933*, and *Footlight Parade*, the latter with Jimmy Cagney joining regulars Joan Blondell, Dick Powell, and Ruby Keeler in the spectacular finale, "Shanghai Lil." The naughty ditties in this triad (including "Pettin' in the Park," "Honeymoon Hotel," "We're in the Money," and "Shuffle Off to Buffalo") were penned by Harry Warren and Al Dubin, but it is

Berkeley's unfettered staging of them—the Code was not yet in effect—that makes them so brazenly erotic. He co-directed (with George Amy) *She Had to Say Yes* with Loretta Young that same fruitful year, then handled the production numbers for three more musicals in 1934: *Dames*, *Wonder Bar*, and *Fashions of 1934*, the last with the climactic "Spin a Little Web of Dreams," ostrich-plumed ship and all.

*Go Into Your Dance* (1935), an Al Jolson–Ruby Keeler showcase with "A Latin from Manhattan," was just passable, while *In Caliente* ("Muchacha") and *Stars over Broadway* (both 1935; the latter's elaborate "September in the Rain" number scratched for budget reasons) were outright disappointments. But now, at last, Warners made Berkeley a full-fledged director. He responded with some of his best work on *Gold Diggers of 1935*, a somewhat garbled account of the goings-on at a summer resort that commands a place in cinema history just for its extended "Lullaby of Broadway" number, sung by Wini Shaw as pianos undulate and a depressed chorus girl defenestrates herself. The song won an Oscar; Berkeley's dance direction, although nominated, did not. (He would also leave the Awards ceremony a loser in 1936 and 1937.)

*Bright Lights* and *I Live for Love* completed a very busy 1935 for Berkeley—perhaps *too* busy, as those two productions failed to include any dance numbers. But more serious events now commanded Berkeley's attention. He had struck three people while driving, resulting in a manslaughter trial that lasted for years; Berkeley arrived to testify in court on a stretcher at one juncture. He finally was acquitted in 1939, but the damage to his psyche may have been irreparable. Recently divorced for the second time, he saw his third marriage end in an annulment during this same period. But he kept working—compulsively, some said. *Stage Struck* (1936) used the tried-and-true backstage formula with Dick Powell and Joan Blondell (recently mar-

▲ *A spectacular number from* Girl Crazy

ried) and Warren William, although the Yip Harburg–Harold Arlen tunes weren't anything special, and the production numbers were nil.

Berkeley choreographed the mediocre *Gold Diggers of 1937* for Lloyd Bacon, then directed *The Go-Getter* (1937), a pallid melodrama with George Brent that was Berkeley's first nonmusical. (Would that it had been his last!) But *Hollywood Hotel* (also 1937) was a welcome return to his earlier work: Dick Powell simmers in a mad brew with the Lane Sisters, the Benny Goodman Quartet, Louella Parsons, and "Hooray for Hollywood," to fashion an utterly absurd but delicious trifle. Berkeley concluded 1937 by doing the choreography on *The Singing Marine* and *Varsity Show*, two more thin excuses for Dick Powell to warble.

But those were Academy Award material compared to *Men Are Such Fools* (1938), a hopeless tear-jerker about wandering wives and erring husbands that may rate as Humphrey Bogart's worst picture. *Garden of the Moon* (1938) was marginally better—at least it was a musical—but the Warren-Dubin score wasn't up to their usual heights, and Pat O'Brien and John Payne made lead-footed leads (where was Dick Powell when you needed him?). *Comet over Broadway* (1938) had Kay Francis in more soap opera via Faith Baldwin and *Cosmopolitan*; what madman at Warners was assigning material like this to Berkeley? Handling the choreography on the forgettable *Gold Diggers in Paris* (1938) must have seemed a relief. *They Made Me a Criminal* (1939), with John Garfield, Ann Sheridan, and Claude Rains, was a respectable crime melodrama, familiar stuff for Warners, if not for Berkeley. But now MGM beckoned, and—irked at how he'd been misused by Warners—he was quick to accept.

▲ *Esther Williams and Berkeley go over a water-ski routine for* Easy to Love

Berkeley's inaugural project was *Babes in Arms* (1939), the first of the Mickey Rooney–Judy Garland star vehicles, based (not respectfully enough, some felt) on the Rodgers and Hart show. It was a huge hit, but its charms today seem to have withered considerably. *Fast and Furious* (1939) was a pleasant entry in a short-lived series about two rare book dealers (Franchot Tone and Ann Sothern) who get mixed up in murder, this time at a beauty contest, while the lumbering *Broadway Serenade* required Berkeley to handle only Jeanette MacDonald's musical numbers. *Strike Up the Band* (1940) was the Mickey and Judy Show, take 2: Paul Whiteman holds a nationwide radio contest, and (yawn) Mickey's high-school band is determined to win. *Forty Little Mothers* (1940) was clarified treacle—Eddie Cantor played it straight as a teacher at a girls' school—while *Blonde Inspiration* (1941) was a cute "B" about a writer who can't write without a dame nearby.

*Babes on Broadway* (1941) was more prestigious, with Mickey and Judy taking nearly two hours to go through their paces, which included Judy singing the Oscar-nominated "How About You?" and Mickey imitating Carmen Miranda. Berkeley spent the rest of 1941 staging just the production numbers for three films: *Ziegfeld Girl*, *Lady Be Good*, and *Born to Sing*. *For Me and My Gal* (1942) was all his, with Gene Kelly and the mature Judy Garland trying to ignore third wheel George Murphy as they perform in vaudeville circa 1915. It was a hit, but there was friction between him and star Garland, and he was unceremoniously taken off *Girl Crazy* (1943), demoted to choreographer, and replaced by Norman Taurog.

That cinched it for Berkeley, who tired of MGM's yo-yo approach to his assignments and departed for Fox, where he made *The Gang's All Here* (1943), his wildest picture since his pre-Code days at Warners and his first ever in Technicolor. Alice Faye was the nominal star, but the film really belonged to Carmen Miranda, whose stranger-than-fiction persona combined wonderfully with Berkeley's unfettered vision to create a camp masterpiece—proof positive of how his talents had been squandered at MGM. He signed with Warners, but before a single film had been made, the contract was terminated in 1944; so was Berkeley's most recent marriage, begun and annuled that same year. In light of these setbacks, it is not surprising that the tightly wound Berkeley suffered a nervous breakdown, from which he was slow to recover.

He returned to the screen with the feeble *Cinderella Jones* (1946), in which Joan Leslie tries to marry brainiac Robert Alda to qualify for an inheritance. Berkeley seemed finished, but then came MGM's *Take Me Out to the Ball Game* (1949), a proficient period musical starring Frank Sinatra and Gene Kelly as a vaudeville team who begin playing baseball for a team owned and managed by Esther Williams. Ironically, Kelly and Stanley Donen directed the dance sequences, with Berkeley handling the rest. Thereafter he choreographed musicals with Betty Grable and Esther Williams, as well as *Rose Marie* (1954) and *Jumbo* (1962). In 1971 he came out of retirement to supervise the Broadway revival of *No, No, Nanette*, a smash that starred old friend Ruby Keeler. It was a return to happier times, and Berkeley deserved that final glory.

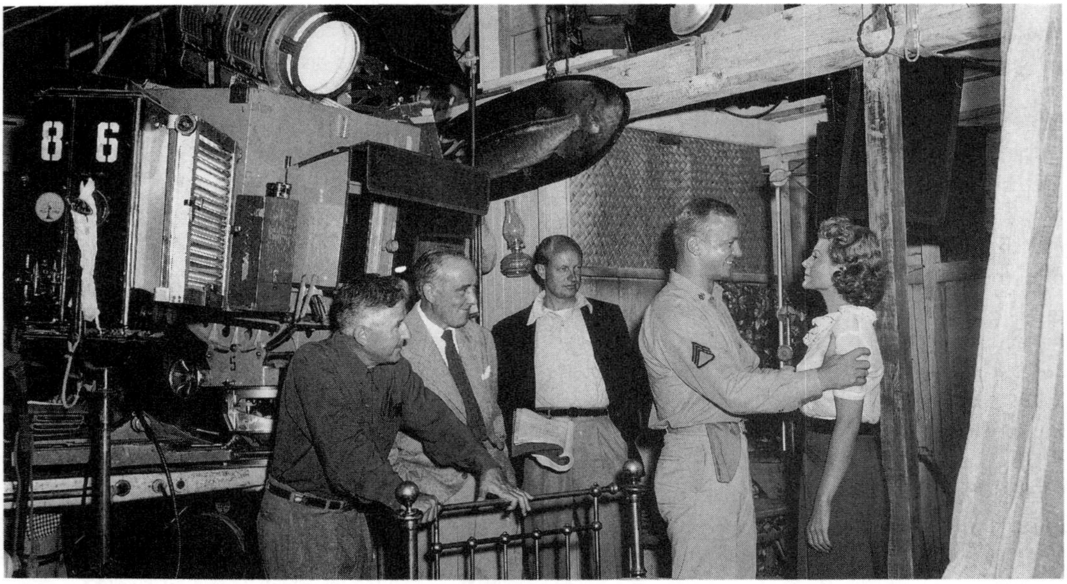


▲ *Bernhardt (left) watches Aldo Ray and Rita Hayworth on the set of* Miss Sadie Thompson

## ● CURTIS BERNHARDT (1899–1981)

Curtis (né Kurt) Bernhardt had already directed a dozen films in his native Germany when an arrest by the Gestapo in 1934 convinced him to move to France. He made one film there, then went to England, where he made *The Beloved Vagabond* (1934) while also producing *The Dictator* (1935). He returned to Paris for a few years before a contract with Warner Bros. brought him to Hollywood in 1940. There he began with two of the studio's strongest female leads. *My Love Came Back* (1940) was a passable Olivia de Havilland vehicle weakened by the presence of leading man Jeffrey Lynn, while *The Lady with Red Hair* (1940) was a biopic with Miriam Hopkins as famed actress Mrs. Leslie Carter, though it was Claude Rains as David Belasco who stole the film.

*Million Dollar Baby* (1941) was an extremely silly romance with Ronald Reagan (as a suffering pianist!) and Priscilla Lane, but *Juke Girl* (1942) was better; Reagan and luscious Ann Sheridan play exploited fruit pickers charged unjustly with murder. *Happy Go Lucky* (1943) was made on loan-out to Paramount; it was a pleasant-enough musical featuring Dick Powell, Mary Martin, and Betty Hutton that was forgotten minutes after it was released. Of more interest was *Conflict* (1945), a Bogart suspenser with an overly contrived plot that nonetheless allowed Bernhardt to use his expressionist background for the moody visuals. *My Reputation* (1946) was his best film to date, an elegant soap opera with Barbara Stanwyck and George Brent.

*Devotion* (1946), a fanciful account of the lives of the Brontë sisters, had been filmed earlier than *Conflict* but was held back for nearly three years before being released; it can't be taken seriously, but Olivia de Havilland and Ida Lupino are fine as Charlotte and Emily. *A Stolen Life* (1946) is much more convincing, with Bette Davis cleverly photographed to be twin sisters who both love Glenn Ford. *Possessed* (1947) was a superior melodrama that offers a memorable crack-up by Joan Crawford, an Oscar-nominated turn. Bernhardt now left Warners and signed with MGM, where his first film was the offbeat noir *The High Wall* (1947), in which Audrey Totter is cast against type as a psychiatrist who tries to help amnesia victim Robert Taylor clear himself of a murder charge.

But next came the insipid *The Doctor and the Girl* (1949) with Glenn Ford and Gloria DeHaven. *Payment on Demand* (1951) was better, a well-mounted drama about Bette Davis's marital problems with Barry Sullivan, with elaborate flashbacks building the suspense. *Sirocco* (1951), a decent period actioner (rare for Bernhardt), had Bogart running guns for and against Zero Mostel and Lee J. Cobb, while *The Blue Veil* (also 1951) was soap opera of a high order, with nurse Jane Wyman repressing her own desires to serve a variety of patients over a lifetime; this nearly forgotten role earned her an Academy Award nomination. But *The Merry Widow* (1952) with Lana Turner was pure MGM hooey, its lavish production values notwithstanding.

Bernhardt got his chance to work with another strong female star with *Miss Sadie Thompson* (1953), a musical remake of *Rain* that featured Rita Hayworth as Somerset Maugham's fallen woman. Hayworth was at less than her best, both physically and emotionally, but held her own in this oft-filmed role. *Beau Brummel* (1954) offered Stewart Granger as Casanova, with Elizabeth Taylor, Robert Morley, and Peter Ustinov on hand to lend color to this typically lavish MGM costumer. *Interrupted Melody* (1955) was a solid biopic about Australian Marjorie Lawrence, with Eleanor Parker as the polio-stricken opera star in another Oscar-nominated performance. But *Gaby* (1956) was a mediocre remake of *Waterloo Bridge*, starring Leslie Caron and John Kerr.

It proved to be Bernhardt's last Hollywood picture for many years. He finally resurfaced in 1960 with the West German production *Stephanie in Rio*, followed two years later by the U.S.–Italian pic *Damon and Pythias*. *Kisses for My President* (1964) was his last film, an overlong but occasionally funny yarn about President of the United States Polly Bergen making life difficult for hubby Fred MacMurray. Not the sort of movie Bernhardt built his reputation on, but a professional job by a onetime master of the "woman's picture."

## ● BUDD BOETTICHER (1916– )

Along with Anthony Mann, Oscar "Budd" Boetticher, Jr., was the most reliable and interesting director of Westerns during the key decade of the 1950s. True, he never made a *Searchers*—but with such modest means as were available to him, Boetticher was able to fashion a plethora of interesting and provocative variations out of the form. It's easy to forget that Westerns comprised only half his output, so much do they dominate his reputation.

Born in Chicago, Boetticher was educated at Ohio State, where he played varsity football and boxed. It was while he was recuperating from a football injury in Mexico that he began to study bullfighting; incredibly, he became proficient enough to become a professional matador. It was that skill that proved his entrée to Hollywood, where he was retained in 1940 as a technical consultant to Rouben Mamoulian's production of *Blood and Sand.* Taking to Hollywood, Boetticher stayed on, working as a messenger boy for the Hal Roach studios until 1943, when he broke in as an assistant director at Columbia on such films as *Destroyer*, *The More the Merrier*, and *Cover Girl*. That earned him a chance to handle "B" features on his own, and he directed five of them for Columbia in 1944 and 1945, including *One Mysterious Night*, a Boston Blackie entry with Chester Morris, and *Escape in the Fog*, a murder mystery with Nina Foch.

Boetticher made one picture for Paramount before being drafted in 1946, and spent his next two years in the service. When he came out, he went to work for Eagle-Lion, making a pair of crime pictures, *Assigned to Danger* and *Behind Locked Doors* (both 1948). At Monogram he made a trio of low-budget action movies, including *Killer Shark* (1950) with Roddy McDowall and Laurette Luez, before being given the chance at Republic to direct a much more personal film. *The Bullfighter and the Lady* (1951), which Boetticher also co-wrote, was produced by John Wayne, who was Republic's biggest star at the time. *Bullfighter* was a minor masterpiece about a young American (Robert Stack) visiting Mexico who is drawn to bullfighting and gets the top matador (Gilbert Roland) to teach him everything he knows—except it isn't enough. (Over two hours long when released, the film was shown for years with a full third lopped off. It was recently restored.)

Boetticher now signed on with Universal, where he would make his next ten pictures. First up was the costumer *The Sword of D'Artagnan* (1951), followed by his maiden Western, *The Cimarron Kid* (1952), an Audie Murphy vehicle that had little to recommend it. But *Red Ball Express* (1952) was a good war picture, with Jeff Chandler in charge of trucking gasoline and arms to supply Patton's troops on their way to liberate Paris. *Bronco Buster* (1952) skated through its formulaic story about rodeo whiz John Lund teaching Scott Brady the tricks of the trade. *Horizons West* (also 1952) wasn't any more original, but at least it had a heck of a cast: Robert Ryan, Rock Hudson, James Arness, Raymond Burr, and Julia Adams.

Boetticher changed his venue for *City Beneath the Sea* (1953), sending Robert Ryan and Anthony Quinn diving off the coast of Kingston, Jamaica, in search of a million dollars in sunken gold. *East of Sumatra* (1953) was more high adventure; Jeff Chandler plays a tin miner who runs into opposition from the island's reigning chief (Anthony Quinn). Such exotica wasn't Boetticher's forte, so he was probably glad to see the script for *Seminole* (1953), an atypically pro-Indian story set in Florida's Everglades, with cavalry officer Rock Hudson doing his best to help his old friend Osceola (Quinn again) resist the Army's efforts to wipe out the native Seminole population.

*The Man from the Alamo* (also 1953) was a tale of redemption: Glenn Ford has to prove himself in battle after leaving the Alamo (at the request of his fellow fighters) before the attack in order to warn Texans about Santa Ana, and is branded a deserter for his efforts. Boetticher's fifth release of 1953 was the 3-D *Wings of the Hawk*, which also dealt with the conflict between the United States and Mexico as Van Heflin tries to regain control of his gold mine after it has been seized by the Federales Colonel Ruiz. Now a freelancer, Boetticher made *The Magnificent Matador* (1955) for Fox, a self-penned tale about his great passion, bullfighting, with Anthony Quinn as an over-the-hill matador who wonders if his nerves are eroding along with his skills, even as he coaches understudy Manuel Rojas. *The Killer Is Loose* (1956) was an atypically contemporary crime yarn, with psychopathic ex-con Wendell Corey swearing revenge on Joseph Cotten, the cop who sent him to prison and accidentally caused the death of his wife.

To this point in his career, Boetticher had demonstrated that he was a capable—though hardly extraordinary—action director with a taste for period material. But he rose to a higher level of accomplishment when he aligned himself in 1956 with writer Burt Kennedy and actor Randolph Scott for a series of taut, psychologically complex Westerns. The first was *Seven Men from Now* (1956), with Scott as an ex-sheriff who methodically tracks down the seven lowlifes who killed his wife, a group headed by a supremely evil Lee Marvin. *The Tall T* (1957) was better still, a suspenseful story (via Elmore Leonard) about an outlaw trio led by Richard Boone that is holding newlyweds Maureen O'Sullivan and her cowardly husband, John Hubbard, for ransom. This time Randolph Scott must use his wits to triumph, and he does so most cleverly.

*Decision at Sundown* (1957) was more pedestrian, possibly because Burt Kennedy was not involved·

▲ *Oscar "Budd" Boetticher visits the set of a low-budget Columbia musical in 1944*

with the script; here Randolph Scott is content merely to drive nemesis John Carroll (who had stolen Scott's wife) out of town. *Buchanan Rides Alone* (1958) had a semi-comical undertone, with a self-mocking Scott defying a corrupt family's stranglehold over a town. *Ride Lonesome* (1959) was all business, though, with Scott as a bounty hunter who gets more than he bargained for in the form of Lee Van Cleef when he brings in Lee's brother, killer James Best. *Westbound* (1959) was one of the lesser entries, again attributable to the absence of Burt Kennedy, with Scott as a cavalry officer who has to oversee a gold shipment bound for the federal bank during the Civil War. The last picture in the cycle was *Comanche Station* (1960), a CinemaScope production that found Scott's lone hero penetrating Indian territory to locate kidnapped Nancy Gates.

Boetticher made one more film in Hollywood, the crime classic *The Rise and Fall of Legs Diamond* (1960) with Ray Danton and Warren Oates, before deciding to pursue a quixotic project close to his heart. He went to Mexico to film a documentary about his friend matador Carlos Arruza—a decision that had disastrous consequences. As he relates in his memoir, *When in Disgrace*, financial and other problems plagued the production, and as time dragged on, Boetticher's personal life collapsed. He was divorced, jailed for a week, went broke, nearly starved, became ill, and finally suffered a nervous breakdown. In the midst of all this, Arruza was killed in a car crash with most of the film crew. It wasn't until 1967 that Boetticher was ready to work again, allying himself with Audie Murphy. They made one film together in Spain in 1969, *A Time for Dying* (1971), before Murphy was killed in a plane crash.

*Arruza* finally was released in 1971, but Boetticher never made another film. His last screen credit was as the writer of Don Siegel's *Two Mules for Sister Sara* (1970), a film that starred an actor with whom Boetticher was never able to work: Clint Eastwood.

## ● PETER BOGDANOVICH (1939– )

The former *Wunderkind* of the early Seventies, Peter Bogdanovich made the transition from being a film critic to directing with more success than any other American (the French patented the process, of course). But now his struggles have persisted for a full twenty years, and it seems he probably will never be restored to his former lofty position as a peer of Coppola, Scorsese, and the other young turks of the time.

Born in Kingston, New York, Bogdanovich studied acting under Stella Adler and performed on stage in the 1950s with the American and New York Shakespeare Festivals. He directed Odets's *The Big Knife* Off-Broadway in 1959, then began writing about moviemakers for *Esquire* and *Cahiers du Cinema*. His monographs on Orson Welles (1961), Howard Hawks (1962), and Alfred Hitchcock (1963) for MoMA were published to much acclaim, and volumes on Lang (1967), Ford (1968), and Allan Dwan (1971) would follow. As befit an unreconstructed auteurist, he began his film career assisting Roger Corman on *The Wild Angels* (1966), then directed new sequences for the Russian import *Voyage to the Planet of Prehistoric Women* (1968) and a documentary on Hawks for BBC-TV. Corman then gave him backing for his first feature, *Targets* (1968), a showy but suspenseful study of a sniper, psychopathic Vietnam vet Tim O'Kelly, which Bogdanovich scripted with his then-wife Polly Platt. Boris Karloff, as a horror-movie star who wants to retire, was provided with a marvelous vehicle in one of his last screen appearances.

The American Film Institute financed Bogdanovich's 1971 documentary *Directed by John Ford*, but it was *The Last Picture Show* (also 1971) that finally established him as a director of immense gifts. With its elegaic tone, elegant black-and-white cinematography (by Robert Surtees), and small-town Texas location, *Picture Show* resembled certain works by Welles and Ford, as Bogdanovich no doubt intended. Yet in some ways this story of two high-school friends (Timothy Bottoms and Jeff Bridges) who aspire to manhood but lose much of their hope along the way is even more moving than the classic films that inspired it. Bogdanovich was Oscar-nominated for best direction, and nominations also went to the film, the screenplay by Bogdanovich and Larry McMurtry (on whose novel it was based), Surtees's cinematography, and half the cast—Bridges, Ellen Burstyn, Cloris Leachman, and Ben Johnson, with the last two winning Oscars. But the film's success was nearly overshadowed by Bogdanovich's affair with actress Cybill Shepherd, ending his marriage to Platt, who had handled the film's evocative production design.

*What's Up, Doc?* (1972) was less impressive, an often strained replica of Hawks's 1938 farce *Bringing Up Baby*, based on a story by Bogdanovich. Ryan O'Neal plays a musicology professor who lugs around a suitcase full of prehistoric rocks, and Barbra Streisand is the loony live wire who helps misplace the priceless antiquities, complicating his life but freeing him up for romance. It probably was as close to a re-creation of the classic screwball comedies as anyone will ever come, but (to state the obvious) O'Neal and Streisand were not Cary Grant and Katharine Hepburn. Bogdanovich tried to replicate another kind of Thirties picture with *Paper Moon* (1973), filmed in the black-and-white appropriate to the 1936 setting. Ryan O'Neal is a con man "temporarily" saddled with a nine-year-old (his real-life daughter, Tatum O'Neal) who may or may not be his actual daughter but who refuses to leave his side. As they travel about the Depression Midwest (wonderfully re-created by Polly Platt) inventively bilking widows, clerks, and even bootleggers with a variety of schemes, they bond. Tatum O'Neal won an Oscar for her precocious film debut, but one of the supporting actresses she was selected over—her co-star, Madeleine Kahn—actually stole *Moon* as the blowsy tart Trixie Delight.

*Daisy Miller* (1974) was the first of Bogdanovich's films to star paramour Cybill Shepherd, and critics gleefully pronounced her totally inadequate for the demands of her role as Henry James's Europhiliac American. (In any case, it fared even less well at the box office than *The Great Gatsby*, another high-profile, disappointing literary adaptation made by Paramount that year.) Bogdanovich refused to kowtow to popular opinion and fashioned another elaborate production around the talents of Shepherd, the gruesome *At Long Last Love* (1975). A lovingly re-created homage to the gloriously inane musical romances of the Thirties, complete with sixteen songs by Cole Porter, it was doomed as soon as Shepherd and Burt Reynolds were cast as the leads; Astaire and Rogers would have been spinning in their graves had they not still been alive.

*Nickelodeon* (1976), co-written by Bogdanovich, was a more modestly conceived project, a tribute to the pioneers of the film industry. Ryan O'Neal plays a lawyer transformed by accident into a director of one-reelers and Burt Reynolds a rodeo star who becomes a screen idol; Tatum O'Neal and Stella Stevens are among the effective supporting players. Although it did nothing at the box office, its verisimilitude (Bogdanovich incorporated anecdotes he'd been given by Raoul Walsh, John Ford, and Allan Dwan, among others) and sincerity make it a worthy failure. Having worn out his welcome at the major studios, Bogdanovich now was helped by Roger Corman to make the low-budget but atmospheric *Saint Jack* (1979), a welcome respite from his nostalgic pastiches. An existential drama based on a novel by Paul Theroux, it starred Ben Gazzara as a good-natured pimp stuck in Singapore, with Denholm Elliott as a lowlife he feels compelled to aid.

*They All Laughed* (1982) was a sweet, quirky romantic comedy with an appealing cast that included Audrey Hepburn, Ben Gazzara, Colleen Camp, and

▲ *Bogdanovich and Barbra Streisand share a thought while filming* What's Up, Doc?

◀ *On the set of* Paper Moon *with Tatum O'Neal*

John Ritter. Bogdanovich's meandering screenplay leaves something to be desired, but the film has a pleasant aura made bittersweet through the presence of the luminous Dorothy Stratten, who was murdered by her husband before the film was released because of her affair with Bogdanovich. *Mask* (1985) reached a wider audience, with Cher memorable as the hard-boiled but loving mother of a teenage boy (Eric Stoltz, whose Oscar-winning makeup almost obscured his affecting performance) afflicted with "Elephant Man's" disease. But *Illegally Yours* (1988) squandered the goodwill earned by *Mask* with a pathetic attempt to make yet another modern *Bringing Up Baby*; Rob Lowe was way out of his league in the Cary Grant role.

*Texasville* (1990), from Larry McMurtry's novel, seemed Bogdanovich's best opportunity to win back some of the territory he had lost—but he succeeded only in making an aimless, flat sequel to *The Last Picture Show*, despite the presence of original cast members Bottoms, Shepherd, Leachman, and Bridges. More encouraging was his proficient adaptation of *Noises Off* (1992), Michael Frayn's acclaimed Broadway play, with Carol Burnett, Michael Caine, Christopher Reeve, John Ritter, and Marilu Henner as members of a cast engaged in a sex farce both on and off the stage. That same year saw the release of the fascinating documentary *Picture This: The Times of Peter Bogdanovich in Archer City, Texas*, made by George Hickenlooper while Bogdanovich was shooting *Texasville*; both the actors (Shepherd, Bridges, Bottoms, etc.) and the townspeople of Archer City are interviewed about their perceptions of what Bogdanovich had wrought with *Last Picture Show* and its sequel.

*The Thing Called Love* (1993) was another meditation on the elusiveness of dreams, starring River Phoenix as an aspiring songwriter trying to penetrate the barriers of Nashville; he and *Speed* star Sandra Bullock are but two of a group of would-be country-and-Western stars who we know will probably never make it, but whom we can't help rooting for. It's *Nashville* writ small, and unfortunately received only a limited theatrical release before moving to video.

## ● JOHN BOORMAN (1933– )

One of the most distinctive stylists of the last twenty-five years, John Boorman also created some of the day's most wildly fluctuating work. Born outside London, Boorman was already writing film reviews while still a teenager. After a stint in the British military, he began working in television in 1955, editing and filming documentaries. He joined the BBC a few years later, rising to the head of their documentary division by 1962.

His first feature was *Having a Wild Weekend* (aka *Catch Us If You Can*; 1965), a stab at doing for the Dave Clark Five what Richard Lester's *A Hard Day's Night* had done for the Beatles a year earlier. While not up to the inspired madness of Lester's film, Boorman did an adequate job with his less talented stars. After making a BBC documentary on D. W. Griffith, Boorman made his first American film, *Point Blank* (1967), a scalding adaptation of Richard Stark's crime novel *The Hunter*, with Lee Marvin superbly cast as small-time hood Parker, out for revenge against his wife (Angie Dickinson) and the syndicate that left him for dead. Considered a minor genre release at the time, it now has earned a reputation as one of the best films of the Sixties, a paradigm of nihilistic violence that looks better with each passing year.

*Hell in the Pacific* (1968) pitted Marvin against the great Toshiro Mifune as the two lone survivors on an island during World War II. *Leo the Last* (1970) was a quirky, philosophical tale about a royal hermit (Marcello Mastroianni) who re-enters the world to find that he now lives in a black ghetto. It won Boorman the best director prize at Cannes, though it was not a commercial success. But *Deliverance* (1972) was a huge critical and box-office hit. Adapted by James Dickey from his novel (he also appears in a small role) about four businessmen whose weekend canoe trip down a Georgia river turns into a nightmare, it starred Burt Reynolds, John Voight, Ronny Cox, and Ned Beatty—all were excellent. The film was Oscar-nominated for best picture and Boorman for best direction.

On the heels of that undisputed triumph, Boorman chose to make one of the oddest films of the Seventies (and that's saying something!), the dystopian sci-fi allegory *Zardoz* (1974). Featuring a pony-tailed Sean Connery and an ice-eyed Charlotte Rampling, this futuristic parable about the dangers of technology was long on gorgeous visuals and short on logic—but it was never boring. Boorman's bent toward mysticism was fully indulged in *The Exorcist II: The Heretic* (1977); unfortunately, this was the wrong property to turn into a metaphysical exploration of evil. A disaster of mega-proportions that instantly became one of the most reviled films of the decade, it now boasts its own cult audience. (The cult of Pazuzu?)

Boorman's dream long had been to make a film about the Arthurian legends, but after *Exorcist II* he found few backers. Agreeing to waive his salary for a percentage of the profits, he filmed *Excalibur* (1981) in Ireland and created a spellbinding blend of sensuality, violence, and magic. Although a bit long and occasionally overplayed by its top-notch English-Irish cast (Nicol Williamson, Patrick Stewart, Helen Mirren, Liam Neeson), *Excalibur* has a visual intensity (thanks in part to Alex Thomson's Oscar-nominated cinematography) that is almost hypnotizing. Just as visually distinctive—and as loonily mystical—was *The Emerald Forest* (1985), a fanciful, sometimes thrilling story of a boy (Charles Boorman, John's son, in a terrific acting debut) kidnapped and raised by an Amazonian tribe, whose father (Powers Boothe) finds him after a ten-year search. On some levels absurd, the film maintains the courage of its convictions and somehow works—though not everyone would agree.

Boorman left behind his beloved Nature Primeval for *Hope and Glory* (1987), his first film in fifteen years about ''normal'' people in a setting not tinged with the supernatural. An autobiographical story about a boy growing up in London during the air raids of World War II, it manages to convey the same sense of wonder found in much of Boorman's previous work. He earned his second Academy Award nomination for best direction and another for his screenplay, and the picture was also nominated. But there is little sense of wonder, or even sense, to be found in *Where the Heart Is* (1990), a strained fable about a New York millionaire (Dabney Coleman) who makes his family homeless so they can learn the value of money. Its inconsistent tone and contrived plot made *Heart* a box-office failure, but Boorman has bounced back from worse defeats.

▲ *Boorman on location for* Deliverance

## ● FRANK BORZAGE (1893–1962)

One of a handful of directors who won Oscars for both a silent and a sound movie, Frank Borzage's forty-three-year, ninety-eight-film career has come to seem less impressive over the years. In part this is because so many of his silents have been lost or are simply obscure, but (more significantly) most of his forty-four glossy, often sentimental sound pictures now seem badly dated. But while his batting average was not high (at least not for a double-Oscar winner) Borzage did oversee a number of well-fashioned entertainments, several of which still reward viewing.

Born in Salt Lake City, Utah, he began acting in his teens with a theatrical troupe, doubling as a prop boy before entering films as an actor for Thomas Ince in 1913. After appearing in a number of Westerns and comedies, he must have determined that he knew how to direct as well, because he helmed fifteen movies in 1916, his first year behind the camera. He worked primarily for Triangle from 1917 to 1919, then Paramount and First National. He finally landed at Fox, the scene of his greatest triumphs, in 1925, where he took his place alongside John Ford, Raoul Walsh, Howard Hawks, W. S. Van Dyke, and Jack Conway. Like them he began with a Western—Buck Jones in *Lazybones*—though he soon moved over to domestic comedies like *Early to Wed* and *The Marriage License* (both 1926).

In 1927 he made his breakthrough film, *Seventh Heaven*, a sentimental but beautifully photographed tale of a Parisian sewer worker (Charles Farrell) who saves a homeless beauty (Janet Gaynor) from despair. A bit clumsy, perhaps, but in its time it dominated the first Academy Awards with nominations for best picture, actress, screenplay adaptation, and direction of a dramatic picture, winning Oscars in all but the first category. Gaynor's award was predicated upon her work in *Heaven* as well as F. W. Murnau's *Sunrise* and *Street Angel* (1928), the latter Borzage's equally romantic pairing of her as a circus runaway and Charles Farrell as the painter she inspires. They were teamed again under Borzage in *Lucky Star* (1929), and he directed Will Rogers in his first sound picture, *They Had to See Paris*, which became one of Fox's biggest hits in 1929.

The misleadingly titled *Bad Girl* (1931) was his next important success, a sentimental account of a New York tenement couple (Sally Eilers and James Dunn) who meet, marry, and have a child in the space of a year. Nominated for a best picture Academy Award, it earned Borzage his second best direction Oscar (over King Vidor and Joseph von Sternberg). He made another comedy with Will Rogers, *Young as You Feel* (1931), followed by the Charles Farrell drama *After Tomorrow* (1932) and one of Spencer Tracy's first efforts, *Young America* (1932). That brought his tenure at Fox to an end.

Borzage began freelancing, going to Paramount for the 1932 Oscar nominee *A Farewell to Arms*, the picture with which Borzage is today most closely identified. Gary Cooper starred as an American volunteer who is wounded while serving as an ambulance driver for the Italian Army in World War I; English nurse Helen Hayes restores him to health, and they fall wildly in love. Shamelessly romantic, the film predictably altered the tragic ending of the Hemingway novel, disgusting Ernest but probably adding millions to its box-office take. *Secrets* (1933) was Mary Pickford's last movie, an awful frontier soap opera with Leslie Howard as her unfaithful husband. But *Man's Castle* (1933) was a colorful if overwrought romance, starring Spencer Tracy as a hard-boiled resident of New York's "Hoover Flats" shantytown who takes in homeless waif Loretta Young; when she becomes pregnant, he decides to rob for her and their unborn child.

*No Greater Glory* (1934) was a sentiment-drenched tale of a boy (George Breakston) who overcomes his ill health to join a gang headed by Frankie Darro. Of more import was the 1934 *Little Man, What Now?*, an affecting drama set in the Weimar Republic, with Margaret Sullavan as a newlywed who becomes pregnant, alarming penniless husband Douglass Montgomery. Its sympathetic dramatization of the terrible conditions in Germany that made the Nazi movement so appealing was a first for a Hollywood production. Borzage now signed with Warner Bros. He began his three-year tenure there with *Flirtation Walk* (1934), a harmless Dick Powell–Ruby Keeler musical set at West Point, while *Living on Velvet* (1935) was a turgid soaper in which George Brent plays a guilt-racked pilot responsible for the deaths of his family in a plane crash and Kay Francis is the socialite who helps him face up to his trauma.

*Stranded* (1935) set Brent and Francis down in San Francisco and covered the underwhelming details of their nine-year romance, while *Shipmates Forever* (also 1935) was another sappy Powell-Keeler vehicle, redeemed (partially) by five tunes by Dubin and Warren. *Hearts Divided* (1936) tried pairing Powell with Marion Davies (then in the last stages of her film career) in a costume musical set in the time of Napoleon—so what was the spiritual "Nobody

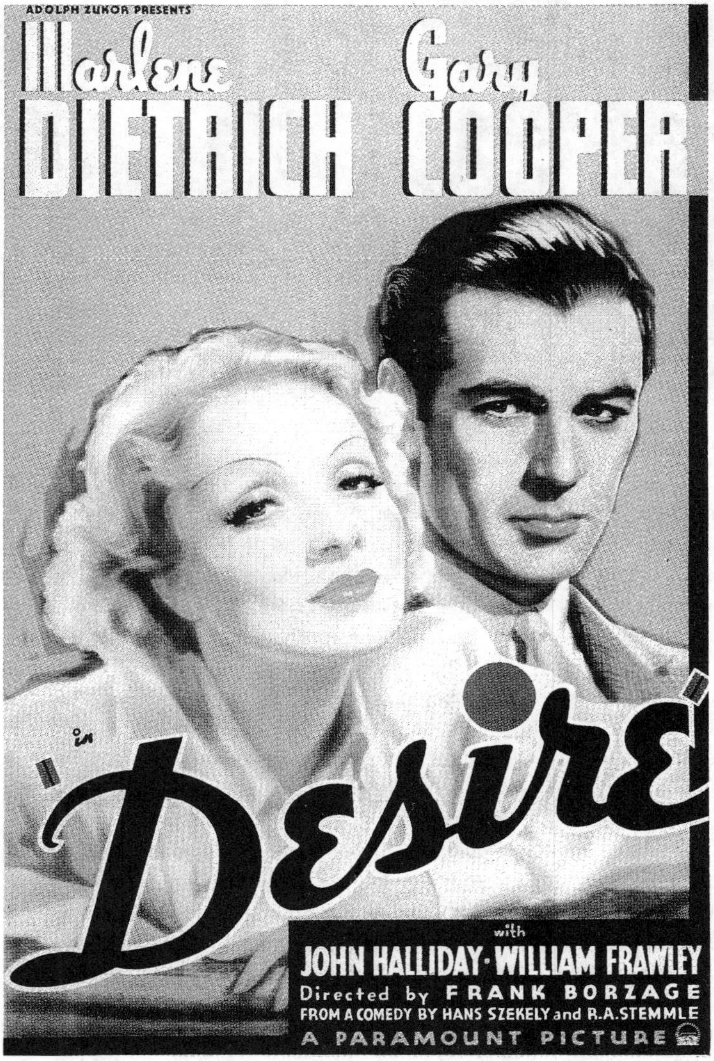

▲ *Ann Sothern and Red Skelton relax with Borzage on an MGM set*



Knows the Trouble I Seen'' doing amid the Dubin-Warren ditties? Far better was *Desire* (1936), made on loan-out to Paramount under the supervision of Lubitsch, with Gary Cooper as an American engineer on vacation in France who becomes a patsy for glamorous jewel thief Marlene Dietrich. As they chase each other around Spain, they fall in love—but who gets to keep the priceless pearl necklace? Borzage was, for the first time in a good while, in his element with these sophisticated dallyings; the Warners' concern for the common man was not close to his heart.

And so he left the studio after a final picture, the quasi-religious medical drama *The Green Light* (1937); Errol Flynn atypically was cast as a noble surgeon who sacrifices his own career to cover another doctor's fatal mistake. *History Is Made at Night* (1937) was a farfetched but ultra-romantic melodrama; Charles Boyer plays the world's suavest fugitive from justice, posing as a waiter aboard an ocean liner, Jean Arthur is the runaway socialite who falls in love with him, and Colin Clive plays her jealous, murderous husband. It didn't make much sense, but Gregg Toland's elegant photography ensured that the stars looked great.

Borzage now touched down at MGM, a studio that specialized in the gloss he favored—although that was not immediately apparent from *Big City* (1937), a Warners-style yarn about a cabdriver (Spencer Tracy) who takes on the mob with the support of pregnant wife Luise Rainer. (She would win the Academy Award in 1937—but not for this!) *Mannequin* (1938) was more like it: Joan Crawford rises from poverty to the upper reaches of society, thanks to shipping tycoon Spencer Tracy (and despite her loser husband, Alan Curtis). A true oddity, and not very good when you get right down to it, but Joan gets to wear some amazing outfits and declaim poetically. *Three Comrades* (1938), co-scripted by F. Scott Fitzgerald from a novel by Erich Maria Remarque, offered Margaret Sullavan dying spectacularly of TB while ex-soldiers Robert Taylor, Robert Young, and Franchot Tone suffer abject poverty in Germany after World War I. Sullavan, who forced producer Joe Mankiewicz to jettison much of Fitzgerald's dialogue, was rewarded with a best actress Oscar nomination—proof once again of the virtues of dying nobly onscreen.

*The Shining Hour* (also 1938) tossed together Crawford and Sullavan—who combined like oil and water—in a salad with Robert Young and Melvyn Douglas, but the resulting adaptation of Keith Winters's stage play was largely unpalatable. While MGM was gearing up for its sensational slate of 1939 releases, Borzage was loaned to Paramount to make *Disputed Passage* (1939), an adaptation of a Lloyd C. Douglas novel about an older scientist (Akim Tamiroff) who advises his understudy (John Howard) that there's no room for a wife (Dorothy Lamour) in the life of a true scientist. Back at MGM Borzage was assigned to the strange *Strange Cargo* (1940), a weighty but in the end risible parable that had Clark Gable and Joan Crawford (in their eighth film together) smooching amid the island palms while convicts Peter Lorre and Paul Lukas escape from Devil's Island with the help of—could it be Jesus? (Ian Hunter). Without divine intervention, the film bombed.

*The Mortal Storm* (1940), with James Stewart, Robert Young, Margaret Sullavan, and Frank Morgan as a German family torn apart by the Nazis' rise to power, was a compelling drama—partial redemption for MGM rajah Louis B. Mayer, who had ordered Borzage to expurgate the anti-Nazi material from *Three Comrades* two years earlier. But *Flight Command* was cornball fly-boy stuff with Robert Taylor trying like blazes to qualify as a Navy pilot; 116 minutes later he succeeds, an outcome that delighted dozing filmgoers in 1940. Borzage was permitted to forgo the patriotic crowd-pleaser to direct *Smilin' Through* (1941) with Jeanette MacDonald, a remake of Sidney Franklin's 1932 drama with Norma Shearer and Fredric March, now gilded with songs, Technicolor, and MacDonald's real-life husband, Gene Raymond.

Borzage's record at MGM had been spotty, to be sure, and his stock must have been plummeting, because his next assignment was *The Vanishing Virginian* (1942), a perfectly decent bit of Americana that starred character actor Frank Morgan and newcomer Kathryn Grayson—but where were Gable, Turner, Tracy, and Taylor? *Seven Sweethearts* (1942) was similarly unprepossessing, a glorified "B" showcasing Grayson's spectacular soprano, with Van Heflin thrown in for romantic interest. That wrote *finis* to Borzage's time at MGM. His star would continue to dim from that point on.

He oversaw the all-star revue *Stage Door Canteen* (1943) at UA, a charity-driven project that offered every celebrity from Peggy Lee to Gypsy Rose Lee. Then came the formulaic Deanna Durbin vehicle *His Butler's Sister* (1943), with Franchot Tone as a big-time Broadway composer who reluctantly agrees to take Durbin under his wing. *Till We Meet Again* (1944) was wartime adventure, with nun Barbara Britton helping Allied pilot Ray Milland escape from behind enemy lines by posing as his wife, while *The Spanish Main* (1945) was piracy most foul, with the miscast Paul Henreid taking on the Errol Flynn role to save Maureen O'Hara from oily Walter Slezak. *I've Always Loved You* (1946) brought Borzage to lowly Republic Studios as a producer-director—but surprisingly, this tale of romance between classical musician Philip Dorn and Catherine McLeod had class to spare.

*The Magnificent Doll* (1946) was less fortunate; Burgess Meredith was an unlikely President Madison, David Niven a dubious Aaron Burr, and Ginger Rogers a preposterous Dolley Madison. *That's My Man* (1947) was a typical racetrack drama, with Don Ameche, but *Moonrise* (1948) showed a flash of Borzage's old form, with Dane Clark as a hothead who accidentally murders an old enemy and Gail Russell the girl who tries to keep him from going off the deep end. It was an encouraging piece of work that might have boosted Borzage beyond Republic, but he found himself blacklisted (although his work, except for the anti-Nazi pictures, hardly leaned far left of center), and he was forced into retirement.

Ten years later he found it safe to return to Hollywood, making *China Doll* (1958), an embarrassing soap opera, with Victor Mature buying the eponymous Li Li Hua in China, then falling in love with her. *The Big Fisherman* (1959), made for Disney, adapted the Lloyd C. Douglas novel about the life of St. Peter, with Howard Keel as the saver of souls. At three hours running time, it was half again what was needed, but it gave Borzage the chance to exit with his head held high; Hollywood owed him that much.

## ● MEL BROOKS (1926– )

Arguably the funniest man ever to work in Hollywood, the former Melvin Kaminsky was born in Brooklyn, New York; his father, a process server, died when he was two. Brooks toiled as an amateur comedian in the Catskills before serving in the war as a combat engineer, after which he returned to work as a drummer at various Catskills resorts. Graduating to the post of social director at Grossinger's, he also moonlighted as a stand-up comic. In 1949 he was spotted by Sid Caesar, who asked him to write for his TV show *Broadway Revue*, which led to a spot in 1950 as both a writer and a performer on *Your Show of Shows* and other Caesar enterprises. In 1960 Brooks recorded his classic comedy routine "The 2,000-Year-Old Man" with Carl Reiner as straight man. Brooks's first filmwork was in the Oscar-winning animated short *The Critic* (1963), which Brooks wrote and narrated.

In 1965 Brooks teamed with Buck Henry to create the popular spy spoof *Get Smart* for television. When its three-year run was over, Brooks wrote and directed *The Producers* (1968), a way-over-the-top, extremely rude comedy that has developed a passionate cult following over the years. The great Zero Mostel stars as a desperately overextended producer who sets about selling 25,000 percent of his show *Springtime for Hitler* to investors with the help of malleable accountant Gene Wilder, then finds to his horror that the stiff has become a hit despite its deliberate awfulness. Brooks won an Oscar for his original screenplay, and Wilder was also nominated. *The Twelve Chairs* (1970), filmed in Yugoslavia, starred Ron Moody as a debt-ridden Russian nobleman who teams with beggar Frank Langella to hunt down a widely scattered set of chairs, one of which houses a fortune in jewels within its upholstery. Their quest fails, and so did the box-office for this little comic gem.

There was nothing little or restrained about *Blazing Saddles* (1973), the film that put Brooks on the map as a bankable filmmaker and put moviegoers into convulsions. An uneven parody of Western movie (and TV show) conventions so vulgar that it managed to insult every one of America's ethnic and racial constituencies, it starred Cleavon Little, Gene Wilder, Harvey Korman, Slim Pickens, and—in a superb, Oscar-nominated takeoff of Marlene Dietrich in *Destry Rides Again*—Madeline Kahn. Written by Brooks, Andrew Bergman, and Richard Pryor, among others, the picture's success can be credited to their anarchronistic, Borscht Belt humor: Korman's villain is named "Hedly Lamarr," while references to the size of Little's equipment pop up like prairie dogs. All this, and a terrific theme song, sung by Frankie Laine (composed by Brooks and John Morris), too! Of course some loathe the film for its sophomoric, tasteless humor, but it did gross $48 million, making it the most popular (anti-) Western to that time.

Grasping that genre spoofs were his métier, Brooks next made a big-budget parody of the old Universal horror movies. *Young Frankenstein* (1974), with Wilder, Kahn, Teri Garr, Cloris Leachman, and Peter Boyle (as the monster), was more carefully structured than *Saddles*, and its elegant black-and-white cinematography actually manages to replicate the look of the 1935 *Bride of Frankenstein* (some of the lab equipment used is original to that film). Brooks, who co-wrote the film with star Gene Wilder (for which they received an Academy Award nomination), actually reins in his more anarchic impulses, tossing in just enough lewd jokes so you don't forget whose movie you're watching. The result is more sophisticated and technically better than the kamikaze *Saddles*; whether it's funnier is a matter of taste, but it also was a box-office smash. Less successful was *Silent Movie* (1976), in which Brooks himself starred as a washed-up movie director who convinces studio head Sid Caesar to make a silent picture. Without dialogue and loaded with sight gags, it was less of a spoof than an affectionate reference to the Mack Sennett comedies—but that gentleness didn't appeal to Brooks fans, who loved him for his undiluted bawdiness.

*High Anxiety* (1977) was a more centered parody, with the films of Alfred Hitchcock as the target. Brooks again stars (as well as producing, co-writing, and even singing the theme song) as a psychiatrist whose life is put in jeopardy when he goes to work at the Institute for the Very, Very Nervous, which is staffed with sinister Cloris Leachman and Harvey Korman. Before he manages to save (and be saved by) Madeline Kahn, Brooks cleverly alludes to *Vertigo*, *Spellbound*, and *Psycho*, among other Hitchcock suspense classics. The in-jokes pleased savvy moviegoers, and the film was a modest hit. *History of the World—Part I* (1981) had a less happy fate, despite a cast that included Sid Caesar, Kahn, Korman,

Brooks, and Leachman. Maybe it was Orson Welles's narration that sank it, or the casual sketch format; in any case, it bombed.

*Spaceballs* (1987) was a flaccid takeoff on *Star Wars* and its ilk—although it really had been needed a decade earlier. Brooks starred in a dual role (Yogurt being the funnier of the two) along with John Candy (as Barf the Mawg), Rick Moranis (Lord Dark Helmet), and Daphne Zuniga (Princess Vespa). Not exactly an embarrassment, the film did suggest that Brooks's once limitless powers of invention were waning. That was more than confirmed by the shockingly limp *Life Stinks* (1991), a formless, almost gagless statement about homelessness that starts out slowly and plummets steeply downhill from there, with a "sincere" conclusion that Brooks himself would have had a field day mocking twenty years earlier. Most recently Brooks directed *Robin Hood: Men in Tights* (1993), a send-up of Kevin Costner's 1991 version of the Robin Hood legend. But Brooks had had better results with his 1970s television series *When Things Were Rotten*, evidence that he requires a target worthy of his parodic genius.

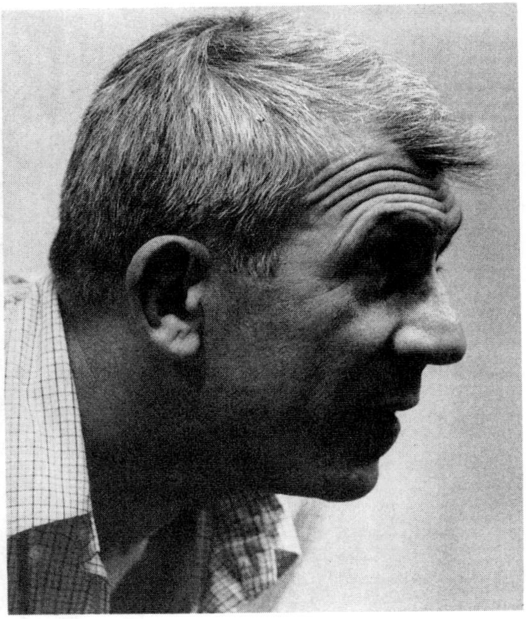

## RICHARD BROOKS (1912-1992)

Long before he directed his first film at the age of thirty-eight, the Philadelphia-born Brooks had contributed mightily to the medium with his screenplays and stories. A former newspaper sports reporter and radio commentator for NBC, Brooks began his Hollywood career in the early Forties at Universal, working on the screenplays for delirious Maria Montez vehicles like *White Savage* and *Cobra Woman*. He then joined the Marines, an experience that provided background for his novel *The Brick Foxhole*, which was the basis for Edward Dmytryk's noir classic *Crossfire* in 1947. Brooks then scripted the fine Jules Dassin noir *Brute Force* and John Huston's *Key Largo*, along with less important pictures like *Swell Guy* and *To the Victor*.

In 1950 he was given the chance to direct his own script for *Crisis*, thanks to its star, Cary Grant, who interceded with MGM on Brooks's behalf. The film involved South American politics and was rather turgid, but for a maiden effort it wasn't half bad. *The Light Touch* (1951), shot on location in Europe, was a standard caper, starring Stewart Granger as an art thief. *Deadline U.S.A.* (1952) was a significant step forward, however, using Brooks's background in the newspaper biz to provide Humphrey Bogart with one of his better late films. (It also has one nice in-joke—Paul Stewart's sports reporter captures a criminal.) *Battle Circus* (1953) had Bogart and June Allyson as MASH unit officers who fall in love: not enough battle, and certainly no circus.

*Take the High Ground* (1953), an account of Army basic training with Richard Widmark and Karl Malden, was better, but *The Flame and the Flesh* (1954) was a Lana Turner howler, and *The Last Time I Saw Paris* (1954) attempted to graft Liz Taylor onto F. Scott Fitzgerald, without much success. Brooks rebounded from this rather indifferent batch of work with *The Blackboard Jungle* (1955). Based on a popular novel by Evan Hunter, the film was an anomaly for MGM, with its nasty vignettes of teenage hoodlums Vic Morrow, Sidney Poitier, Paul Mazursky, and Jamie Farr terrorizing their school until teacher Glenn Ford stands up to them. Extremely influential, it helped speed the rock 'n' roll phenomenon by using "Rock Around the Clock" by Bill Haley and the Comets as its theme. Brooks's screenplay received an Oscar nomination.

One of Brooks's few Westerns, the fine *The Last Hunt* (1956), with Robert Taylor and Stewart Granger on the trail of buffalo, was followed by *The Catered Affair* (also 1956), with Bette Davis and Ernest Borgnine—one of those earnest Paddy Chayevsky TV plays about the "little people" that today sets one's teeth on edge. But Brooks's adaptation of Robert Ruark's bestseller *Something of Value* (1957), an account of the Mau Mau uprising in Kenya, offered Rock Hudson, Sidney Poitier, and Wendy Hiller at their best. Now Brooks always would work from his own screenplays, a situation which gave him an unusual degree of control over his finished work.

*Cat on a Hot Tin Roof* (1958) was Brooks's adaptation of the Tennessee Williams play. Cleaned up considerably for the screen—Paul Newman's "affliction" is treated quite coyly—it still comes across with considerable force. The picture, Newman, Elizabeth Taylor, Brooks's direction, and the screenplay by Brooks and James Poe were all Oscar-nominated. *The Brothers Karamazov* (1958), starring Yul Brynner, William Shatner, Lee J. Cobb, and Claire Bloom, was no masterpiece but far from an embarrassment. It was to be Brooks's last film as an MGM contract director.

Brooks produced and directed *Elmer Gantry* (1960), an adaptation of Sinclair Lewis's novel that won Academy Awards for Burt Lancaster, Shirley Jones, and Brooks himself—for best screenplay, rather than direction. A cynical masterpiece, the film has dated a bit—Lancaster's signature mannerisms are now overly familiar—but retains much of its power. (Brooks married leading lady Jean Simmons after filming was completed.) His second brush with Tennessee Williams was *Sweet Bird of Youth* (1962), with Paul Newman, Geraldine Page, and Ed Begley in an Oscar-winning supporting role. Not as potent as the undiluted play, it still holds its own with most screen versions of Williams.

The ambitious *Lord Jim* (1965), with Peter O'Toole as Conrad's guilt-racked protagonist, is far too long (154 minutes) and self-indulgent, although good moments reside within its amphorous mass. Brooks also functioned as producer/director/screenwriter on *The Professionals* (1966), but he kept it under two hours and ended up with one of the decade's best Westerns. A precursor to *The Wild Bunch*, the picture boasted a dream cast—Lee Marvin, Robert Ryan, Burt Lancaster, Jack Palance, Woody Strode, and Claudia Cardinale—and earned Brooks Oscar nominations for both direction and screenplay.

His next film remains the one with which he is most closely identified. *In Cold Blood* (1967) was based on the Truman Capote bestseller, a book that was shocking in its willingness to enter the minds of two psychopathic killers who murdered an entire Kansas family in 1959. Robert Blake and Scott Wilson are well cast as Perry Smith and Dick Hickock, and Brooks's docudrama approach approximates Capote's own technique. *In Cold Blood* was a favorite with critics, but its implicit argument against capital punishment may have kept its box office modest. Brooks earned Academy Award nominations once again for both his screenplay and his direction.

*The Happy Ending* (1969) was a turgid soaper about a wife (Jean Simmons) walking out on her family to find herself, while *$ (Dollars)* (1971) was a complicated but exciting caper yarn in which security expert Warren Beatty and hooker Goldie Hawn steal millions of bucks from a West German bank. *Bite the Bullet* (1975), which suicidally opened the same week as *Jaws*, was a well-made throwback to an era when audiences actually cared about Westerns; despite fine performances by Gene Hackman, James Coburn, and Ben Johnson, it sank without a trace. The much-anticipated *Looking for Mr. Goodbar* (1977) proved to be an ugly adaptation (by Brooks) of Judith Rossner's bestseller, with Diane Keaton as the teacher in search of unsafe sex and Richard Gere, William Atherton, and Tom Berenger as the men she finds it with. A controversial moneymaker upon its release, the scathing reviews it received were a blow from which Brooks never truly recovered.

*Wrong Is Right* (1982) didn't offend anyone, but Brooks's screenplay missed its satirical target—the power of the media—by a country mile, wasting Sean Connery and a cast of familiar faces from the Sixties. His last movie was *Fever Pitch* (1985), an unmitigated disaster (written by Brooks), starring Ryan O'Neal as a gambling addict; its utter failure sent Brooks into retirement. It was an unfortunate ending to a quietly distinguished career.

◀ *Brooks rehearses Scott Wilson and Robert Blake during the filming of* In Cold Blood

# ● CLARENCE BROWN (1890–1987)

Every one of Clarence Brown's thirty-six sound movies was made for MGM, and in many ways his tasteful romances, well-mounted historical adventures, and elaborate costume dramas embody all the virtues (and some of the defects) with which the studio is most closely identified. Few of these pictures seem wildly exciting to a modern sensibility, but a great many of them are considered classics of their kind, and it was not for nothing that Brown received Academy Award nominations for best direction six times.

Born in Clinton, Massachusetts, Brown took engineering courses at college and by 1913 had become an entrepreneur, founding the Brown Motor Car Company. But soon after, he observed Maurice Tourneur making a film in Fort Lee, New Jersey, and fell in love with motion pictures. He sold his car company and spent the next six years as Tourneur's assistant, rising to the post of editor. After serving as a pilot in World War I, he co-directed *Last of the Mohicans* (1920) with Tourneur. His first solo credit was *The Light in the Dark* (1922), after which he signed with Universal. His most important silent during this period was *The Eagle* (1925), with Rudolph Valentino and Vilma Banky.

That brought him to the attention of MGM, with whom he signed in 1926. Brown's second picture there, *Flesh and the Devil* (1927), starred a recent Swedish import named Greta Garbo (in her third American movie) alongside matinee idol John Gilbert. The film helped establish her as a top-ranking star and was the first of the seven pictures she made with Brown, one of her favorite directors. The following year he made *A Woman of Affairs* with Garbo and Gilbert, who by now were involved in a torrid affair. *The Wonder of Women* (1929) was one of the transitional part-talkies, so Brown's first real sound movie was the 1929 William Haines comedy *Navy Blues*—one of the few comedies Brown would attempt during his long career.

More famous was *Anna Christie* (1930), the adaptation of Eugene O'Neill's play about a prostitute who finds true love that dragged Garbo, rather reluctantly, into the sound era. (A more explicit German-language version was shot almost simultaneously under the direction of Jacques Feyder, which many find superior to Brown's.) *Romance* (1930), with Garbo as an Italian opera star, was less successful, thanks in part to inept leading man Gavin Gordon—but Garbo and Brown both received Academy Award nominations for it, in conjunction with their work on *Anna*.

*Inspiration* (1931) paired Brown and Garbo yet again in a creaking tale about a Parisian model who gives up love-of-her-life Robert Montgomery to avoid staining him with her tawdry past, while *A Free Soul* (1931) starred Lionel Barrymore as a boozing attorney whose glibness gets a gangster (Clark Gable) off the hook for homicide; he then finds his daughter (Norma Shearer) has fallen for the lug. Barrymore won a best actor Oscar, largely on the strength of his fourteen-minute closing soliloquy, and Shearer and Brown were also nominated. *Possessed* (also 1931) had rich lawyer Clark Gable putting mistress Joan Crawford through her paces; it was their first pairing, and remains one of their best.

*Emma* (1932) was a tearjerker of the first order, with Marie Dressler as the lower-class housekeeper who falls in love with, and eventually marries, head-of-the-house Jean Hersholt, despite opposition from his spoiled children. *Letty Lynton* (1932) starred Crawford as a woman unjustly accused of murder, cleared by dashing Robert Montgomery, while the 1932 *The Son-Daughter* (now there's a title!) depicted romance in Chinatown, with Helen Hayes, Ramon Navarro, and Warner Oland in Oriental garb—but the laughs were wholly unintentional. *Looking Forward* (1933) was a drama about the Depression, with

Londoner Lewis Stone trying to keep his department store from going under as employees Lionel Barrymore and Colin Clive keep a stiff upper lip. *Night Flight* (1933) employed most of MGM's top stars—the Barrymore brothers, Clark Gable, Helen Hayes, Myrna Loy, and Robert Montgomery chief among them—but this attempt to create another *Grand Hotel* out of a South American airline setting didn't fly.

Brown came out of his two-year slump with *Sadie McKee* (1934), a nifty vehicle for Joan Crawford: hard-drinking millionaire Edward Arnold vies with Gene Arnold for working-girl Joan while Franchot Tone gives her moral support. Crawford was also fine in the 1934 *Chained*, with her romantic options now upgraded to Clark Gable and Otto Kruger (that's a contest?). But it was *Anna Karenina* (1935) that again brought critical accolades to Brown. A handsomely staged Selznick production of the Tolstoy novel, it featured Garbo and Fredric March as the tragic lovers in nineteenth-century Russia who can be happy neither together nor apart. Filmed in 1927 as the silent *Love* with Garbo and Gilbert, this is by far the better version. *Ah, Wilderness* (1935) was also impressive, a well-cast staging of Eugene O'Neill's slice-of-life play set in a turn-of-the-century small town, with Eric Linden, Frank Albertson, Mickey Rooney, Wallace Beery, and Lionel Barrymore as the Miller family.

*Wife vs. Secretary* (1936) was one of Brown's few comedies, with the terrific cast of Jean Harlow, Clark Gable, and Myrna Loy; while the film's not a botch, the romantic complications don't crackle the way they might have in the hands of Jack Conway or W. S. Van Dyke. *The Gorgeous Hussy* (1936) offered Lionel Barrymore as Andrew Jackson and Beulah Bondi as his wife, but as the Southern belle who disgraces her family, Joan Crawford was less than perfectly cast. (Ditto Robert Taylor and Jimmy Stewart.) Brown was clearly more comfortable with the material provided in *Conquest* (1937), a long, slow, but lavish historical romance, with Charles Boyer as Napoleon and Garbo as Marie Walewska, the Polish countess he loved. (This was Brown's seventh and

▲ *Brown shows his old high-school photo to actress Cecilia Parker*

final picture with Garbo, and his work with her is just a notch below that of Edmund Goulding, George Cukor, and Reuben Mamoulian.)

*Of Human Hearts* (1938) starred Walter Huston as a rural preacher who can reach his flock but not his rebellious son James Stewart. Beulah Bondi was Stewart's long-suffering mom and John Carradine appeared in a cameo as Abraham Lincoln. *Idiot's Delight* (1939) was the much-anticipated—but much-censored—adaptation of Robert Sherwood's Pulitzer Prize–winning antiwar play. Clark Gable and Norma Shearer weren't exactly Lunt and Fontanne (who had starred in the original Broadway production), though Gable's smirking vaudevillian was fun for a change (although his tap dancing to "Puttin' on the Ritz" isn't much better than Peter Boyle's in *Young Frankenstein*). *The Rains Came* (1939), with Tyrone Power as a rajah whose love for Myrna Loy is doomed, wasn't particularly compelling, but Brown did furnish his adaptation of the Louis Bromfield novel with Oscar-winning special effects (notably, a climactic earthquake).

The more modestly scaled *Edison the Man* (1940) was better; Spencer Tracy was well cast as the great inventor. In *Come Live with Me* (1941) James Stewart agrees to marry Hedy Lamarr so that she won't be deported, then finds himself attracted to her (some surprise). *They Met in Bombay* (1941) matched Gable with Rosalind Russell for the first and only time as rival jewel thieves who "meet cute" in the Far East, with predictable results. Brown both produced and directed *The Human Comedy* (1943), William Saroyan's smart, sensitive drama about how the war affects the inhabitants of a small town. Mickey Rooney, Frank Morgan, and Donna Reed starred, and William Saroyan won an Oscar for his original story; the film was also nominated for an Academy Award as best picture, and Brown received a best-direction nomination.

*The White Cliffs of Dover* (1944) was another sen-

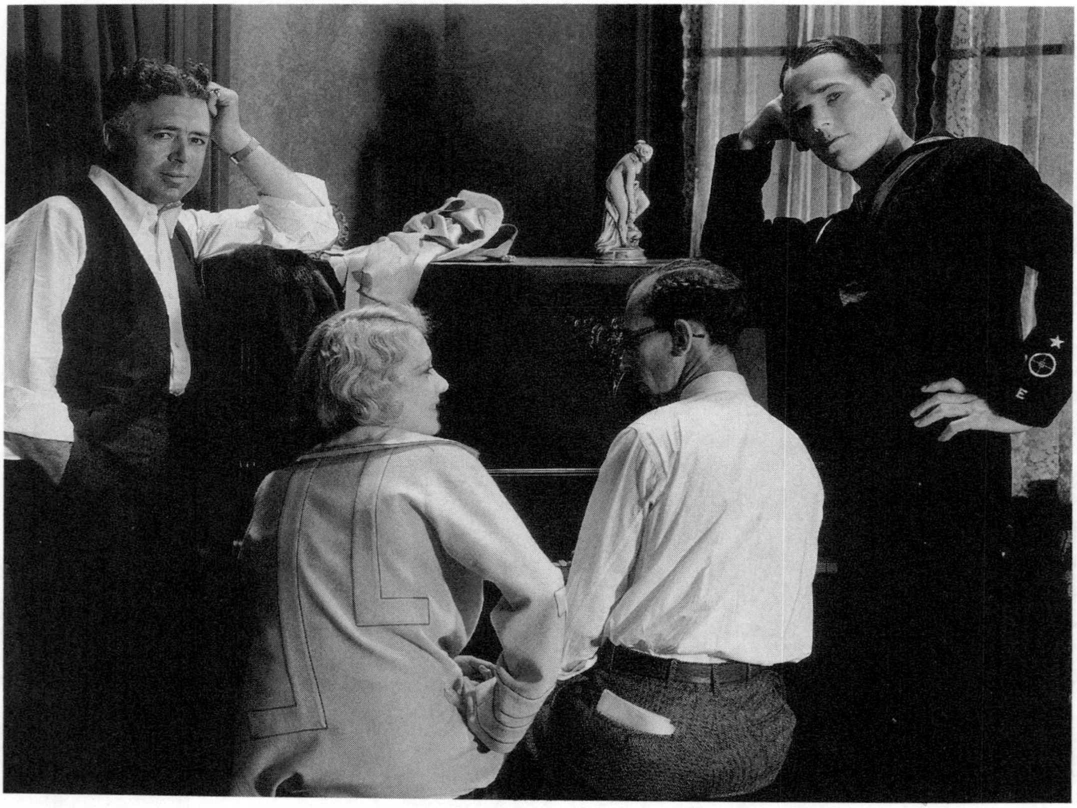

▲ *Brown and William Haines (right) on the set of* Navy Blues *in 1929*

timental but nicely observed tale. Irene Dunne plays an American who marries British aristocrat Alan Marshal, who is then killed in World War I; Van Johnson, Roddy McDowall, and Peter Lawford were also on hand for the sprawling story, as was an unbilled Elizabeth Taylor. Taylor got her billing a few months later in Brown's *National Velvet*, the beloved classic about a young English girl's quest to have her horse race in the Grand National Steeplechase. Mickey Rooney was in rare form as Velvet's trainer, and Anne Revere won an Oscar for her supporting role as Taylor's sacrificing mother; Brown, too, was nominated for his direction. (Taylor was undoubtedly grateful that RKO hadn't made the picture in 1935 with Katharine Hepburn, as they'd hoped to.)

Just as moving—and successful—was *The Yearling* (1946), based on Marjorie Kinnan Rawlings's novel about a boy growing up in the Florida Everglades who raises a fawn as a pet, then has to kill it when the full-grown deer begins to eat his poverty-stricken family's crops. Claude Jarman, Jr., laid on the "Shucks, Paw!" a bit heavily by today's standards but was given a special Oscar at the 1947 Awards; Gregory Peck as his sympathetic father and Jane Wyman as his unsympathetic mother were also Oscar-nominated, as were the film, the cinematography, and Brown—who shot the film on location under the difficult conditions that had foiled it back in 1941, when first Victor Fleming and then King Vidor tried making it with an entirely different cast. *Song of Love* (1947) was less satisfying, a sumptuous but synthetic account of the friendship among Robert Schumann, his wife, Clara, Brahms, and Liszt (Paul Henreid, Katharine Hepburn, Robert Walker, and Henry Daniell). Still, the music was rendered splendidly.

Brown next produced and directed an ambitious adaptation of Faulkner's *Intruder in the Dust* (1949). The great Juano Hernandez starred as a black man unjustly accused of murder in the Deep South, now facing a bloodthirsty lynch mob, and only Claude Jarman to believe in his innocence. Shot on location near Oxford, Mississippi, with hundreds of locals among its milling cast, this antiracist gem failed at the box office. *To Please a Lady* (1950) was plain foolishness, with Clark Gable as a race-car driver and Barbara Stanwyck the tough reporter who loves the big lug. But *Angels in the Outfield* (1951) was a good baseball fantasy, with Paul Douglas guiding the heavenly blessed Pittsburgh Pirates through a pennant race.

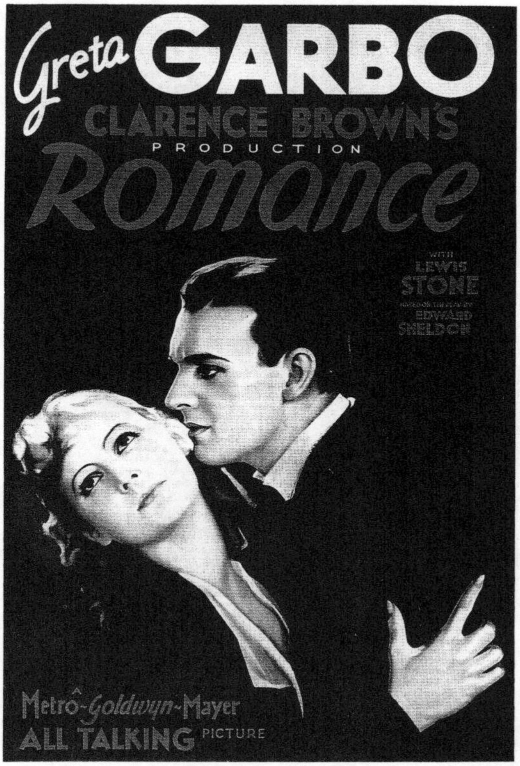


Brown directed a segment of *It's a Big Country* (1951), then made *When in Rome* (1952), a religious comedy/drama in which San Quentin escapee Paul Douglas finds his faith while disguising himself as a pilgrim on the way to the Vatican. Last came *Plymouth Adventure* (1952), a colorful but overwrought tale of the *Mayflower*'s historic voyage; Spencer Tracy is his most unlikable as the surly captain. The film won an Oscar for its special effects, which consisted primarily of storms, including one that tossed Gene Tierney into the drink. Brown produced one last picture, Delmer Daves's *Never Let Me Go* (1953), then retired, to live to age ninety-seven.

## ● TOD BROWNING (1882-1962)

Now a cult director because of his association with fabled silent star Lon Chaney and his proclivity for outré fantasy and horror pictures, Tod Browning made only a handful of sound pictures versus almost forty silents. But the impact of those films still lingers, making his early retirement seem more significant today than it probably did in 1939.

Born in Louisville, Kentucky, with the given name Charles Albert, Browning ran away from home at age sixteen to join a carnival, and later performed as a comedian on the vaudeville and burlesque circuits—experiences which would loom large in his subsequent film work. He began acting at Biograph around 1914, and directed his first movie, *The Lucky Transfer*, in 1915. He had a role in D. W. Griffith's *Intolerance* (1916) while also functioning as an assistant director on it, then moved to Fine Arts–Triangle in 1917, where he co-directed three pictures with Wilfred Lucas. He spent a year at MGM before signing with Universal in 1918; he wrote or helped adapt most of the films he made there, including *Outside the Law* (1921), his first with Lon Chaney, and *Under Two Flags* (1922).

In 1925, Browning went to MGM, where his first project became the shocking (for the time) circus tale *The Unholy Three*, with Lon Chaney as a transvestite ventriloquist who teams with midget Harry Earles, strongman Victor McLaglen, and pickpocket Mae Busch to go on a crime spree that culminates in murder. Browning and Chaney worked together on *The Black Bird, The Road to Mandalay, The Unknown, London after Midnight, The Big City, West of Zanzibar*, and the macabre *Where East Is East*, in which Chaney is an animal trapper in Indochina who kills his wife and then himself by letting loose a wild gorilla.

Browning's first talkie was *The Thirteenth Chair* (1929); because Chaney wasn't yet open to the notion of making a sound picture, Bela Lugosi was recruited to play the creepy séancegoer suspected of murder. Chaney finally made one sound film, a remake of *The Unholy Three*, before his sudden death from bronchial cancer in 1930—but Jack Conway directed it instead of Browning, who had jumped to Universal and couldn't take the property with him. Instead, he remade another of his Chaney silents, *Outside the Law* (1930), with Edward G. Robinson taking the part left vacant by Chaney's death.

*Dracula* (1931) was supposed to star Chaney as well, although it's now hard to imagine how even that master of disguise could have delivered the unctuous line readings that Bela Lugosi made inseparable from the character of the elegant vampire. Lugosi had played the part of the Count on stage for three years anyway, and that version was the primary basis for the film. But *Dracula*'s reputation as a horror classic was never truly deserved, as was that of James Whale's contemporary *Frankenstein*; Browning's early atmospherics soon dissipate, leaving us with a stiff, talky production. (The 1958 Hammer version with Christopher Lee, *Horror of Dracula*, and Francis Ford Coppola's 1992 *Bram Stoker's Dracula* are both far superior.)

*Iron Man* (1931), from the W. R. Burnett novel, starring Lew Ayres as the prizefighter and Jean Harlow as his disloyal girlfriend, also creaked. But back at MGM, Browning delivered the goods with *Freaks* (1932), a truly shocking morality play that boldly cast a number of severely deformed circus performers. Olga Baclanova, as the trapeze artist who marries midget circus owner Harry Earles, only to try killing him for his money, is the film's nominal protagonist, but it is really the "freaks" themselves who make this film so haunting. Browning's obvious affection for the misshapen performers—Randion the "Living Torso," the Siamese twins Daisy and Violet Hilton, et al.—was undoubtedly inspired by his own younger days with the circus. But Irving Thalberg was reportedly appalled when he saw it, and curtailed its distribution. (What did Thalberg expect it to be?)

*Fast Workers* (1933) was a pedestrian drama about the men who erect skyscrapers, with John Gilbert in his last work for the studio he once ruled, but *Mark of the Vampire* (1935) was a lively remake of the now-lost *London after Midnight*—Bela Lugosi is in fine form as a vampire responsible for murder (or is he?), and Lionel Barrymore plays a professor of demonology. Even better was *The Devil Doll* (1936), with Barrymore now scuttling about in drag, Lon Chaney–style, as a madman who shrinks people and bends them to his will, exacting revenge on the judge and jury who sent him to Devil's Island. It's great fun, and is easily one of Browning's best sound efforts.

But after that came only *Miracles for Sale* (1939), a ''B'' mystery with Henry Hull as an ''escapologist'' and Robert Young as a stage magician trying to expose a fake spiritualist. Then the heavy-drinking Browning retired, for reasons that have never been fully explained. Certainly, after Thalberg's death in 1936, he had no one at MGM to champion his peculiar interests. But he left a void in the cinema where once eerieness had spread like graveyard mist.

▲ *Browning and Lon Chaney during one of their many 1920s collaborations*

## ● FRANK CAPRA (1897–1991)

Few major directors have fallen from a state of grace so precipitously as did Frank Capra, if only because few had as far to fall. He was far and away the most honored Hollywood director of the 1930s, winning three Academy Awards while serving as a sort of self-appointed spokesman for the industry. There were successes in the 1940s, too, but they were outweighed by the failures, and by the Fifties Capra was a pale, pale shadow, making just three pictures in the entire decade, none of them very good. He restored interest in himself by writing a lively autobiography, *The Name Above the Title*, in 1971—however, the publication twenty years later of Joseph McBride's masterful but devastating *Frank Capra: The Catastrophe of Success* undid (permanently, it would appear) the relentless PR job Capra had conducted on his own behalf since his retirement from moviemaking in 1961. It is doubtful Capra will ever be thought of again as he was back in 1938, when he became the first director ever to cart off a third Oscar for best direction. In fact, many of today's critics seem on the verge of demanding a recall of Capra's awards.

Born in Bisacquino, Sicily, Capra moved with his family at the age of six to Los Angeles. The Capras had to struggle to support their seven children, and young Frank labored at a number of odd jobs to put himself through Cal Tech—he graduated as a chemical engineer in 1918. After a stint in the Army, Capra worked his way up and down the length of California, trying to earn a living as a door-to-door-salesman and, when that failed, as a card shark. With no experience whatsoever, he convinced a small San Francisco company to hire him in 1922 as the director of a one-reeler; the modest result, *Fultah Fisher's Boarding House*, convinced Capra that this could be his calling. He took a job in a film lab to learn about the medium from the ground up, then caught on as a gagman on Hal Roach's "Our Gang" series.

That experience brought Capra to the attention of Mack Sennett, who hired him to write gags for Harry Langdon, one of the day's top screen comedians. Capra co-wrote and (with Harry Edwards) co-directed *Tramp, Tramp, Tramp* before soloing as director and writer on *The Strong Man* (1926) and *Long Pants* (1927). These were among Langdon's greatest comedies, and Capra was rewarded with a handsome $600 weekly salary; but then Langdon and Capra had a mysterious but bitter falling out that left Capra unemployed. He took an assignment in New York directing *For the Love of Mike* (1927) for First National, but the screen debut of Claudette Colbert failed to click with audiences.

Capra returned to Hollywood to make two-reel comedies for Mack Sennett for a pittance, a dead-end grind from which he was rescued when Harry Cohn, head of Columbia, gave him a contract. During 1928, his first year at Columbia, Capra directed seven silent features, mostly on "B" budgets: *That Certain Thing*, a melodrama that cost less than $20,000 to make; *So This Is Love*, a romantic comedy with a boxing background; *The Matinee Idol*, a romantic comedy with a theatrical backdrop, starring Bessie Love; *The Way of the Strong*, a corny crime melodrama that had a tough bootlegger and a sensitive piano player competing for the affections of a blind violinist (Alice Day); *Say It with Sables*, a tear-jerker with Francis X. Bushman trying to avoid his past, as represented by golddigger Margaret Livingston; *Submarine*, a big-budget (for Columbia, at least) actioner starring Jack Holt as a deep-sea diver trying to save the crew of a stranded submarine from suffocation—the studio's first movie to have a pre-recorded score and sound effects; and *The Power of the Press*, with Douglas Fairbanks, Jr., as an intrepid cub reporter who manages to clear lovely Jobnya Ralston of a trumped-up murder charge.

As the studio moved into the sound era, Capra became ensconced as Harry Cohn's most trusted director. *The Younger Generation* (1929) was a part-talkie about the Goldfish family's upward mobility from the Lower East Side to Park Avenue; Ricardo Cortez was whimsically cast as the son denying his Jewish roots to keep his rich girlfriend, and Jean Hersholt was the embarrassingly down-class Pa Goldfish. (Goldfish was Sam Goldwyn's actual name; was Harry Cohn giving his rival a tweak?) *The Donovan Affair* (1929) was Capra's first all-talkie, starring the stolid Jack Holt as a police inspector who attends a dinner party where a guest is murdered every time the lights go out, while *Flight* (also 1929) featured Holt and Ralph Graves as Marine pilots who alternate heroics over Nicaragua with a good-natured rivalry for Lila Lee's affections. More interesting than the stale flyboy plot was Capra's insistence on staging and filming all the aerial action without tricks or special effects; oddly enough, he never again indulged this appetite for action verisimiltude.

*Ladies of Leisure* (1930), based on an old David Belasco play, was the first of Capra's pictures to star Barbara Stanwyck, with whom he soon would be having an affair. Here Stanwyck plays a golddigger reformed by her love for a sensitive painter (the inert Ralph Graves). The musical comedy *Rain or Shine* (1930) had been a hit on Broadway in 1928, and now Capra set it onto celluloid nearly intact, with comedian Joe Cook repeating his stage role as the savior of a circus in dire need of funds. More ambitious was *Dirigible* (1931), an expensive aerial adventure set at the South Pole, starring the inexplicably popular screen team of Jack Holt and Ralph Graves—as wooden a pair of hearth logs as ever lay across the silver screen—with Fay Wray wasted in a supporting role. Capra was probably grateful to have Stanwyck back for *The Miracle Woman* (1931), a thinly disguised take on the Aimee Semple McPherson story (via a recent Broadway dramatization by Robert Riskin and John Meehan titled *Bless You, Sister*); Stanwyck is an evangelist transformed into a cynical fraud by unscrupulous promoter Sam Hardy, who hears the jingle of cash registers every time she preaches.

Playwright Riskin was hired as one of the writers of *Platinum Blonde* (1931), a comedy of manners starring Jean Harlow as a society dame who marries fast-talking reporter Robert Williams and Loretta Young as a peppy journalist who earns his love and brings him back to the newsroom; the film owed a lot to *The Front Page* (and foreshadowed the romances between journalist and commoner that fortify such later Capra-Riskin efforts as *Mr. Deeds Goes to Town* and *Meet John Doe*). *Forbidden* (1932) found librarian Barbara Stanwyck again a victim of the cruel fates: wealthy attorney Adolphe Menjou, the father of her child, maintains Stanwyck as his mistress, but she agrees to marry his political foe Ralph Bellamy in order to protect Menjou from disgrace; after all that, she has to kill Bellamy anyway, and goes to prison for her crime.

*American Madness* (1932) had more serious concerns at its center. Walter Huston plays a compassionate bank president trying to stem the tide of Depression-panicked customers making a run on his beleaguered institution; the story (which Capra would recycle as part of *It's a Wonderful Life*) was written by Robert Riskin. The film qualifies as the first New Deal drama (though released months before F.D.R. was even elected), and is also the first of Capra's pictures with what we now think of as a "Capraesque" theme: the little people against heartless Big Business. *The Bitter Tea of General Yen* (1933) is easily Capra's most erotic work; Barbara Stanwyck stars as a missionary visiting war-racked Shanghai who becomes the unwilling guest of Chinese warlord Nils Asther (a Swede, but nevertheless convincing), who falls hopelessly in love with her. An anomaly in Capra's oeuvre, *Bitter Tea* has lush, intoxicating cinematography by Joseph Walker that makes the picture look more like a Josef von Sternberg production—and its hint of miscegenation was possibly only because the Production Code was still a year away from taking effect. This was the film selected for the opening of Radio City Music Hall, although that prestigious launch did not make it a box-office success.

But the sentimental *Lady for a Day* (also 1933) was. Capra, who both produced and directed, had Riskin adapt Damon Runyon's short story "Madame La Gimp" about decrepit peddler Apple Annie (May Robson), who enlists sympathetic gangster Dave the Dude (Warren William) to transform her into a society lady so that her estranged daughter (Jean Parker) won't be embarrassed by her lowly station when she visits from Europe with her fiancé and prospective in-laws. It's a charming comedy with a touching payoff, and was nominated for an Academy Award as best picture; Capra, Robson, and Riskin were also Oscar-nominated. (Capra would remake this in 1961 as *Pocketful of Miracles*, his last film.)

Nineteen thirty-four was the year Capra was elevated to the peak of his profession, winning the Academy Award for best direction for his work on *It Happened One Night*, which also became the first movie to win all the other major Oscars as well—best picture, actor (Clark Gable), actress (Claudette Colbert), and writing (Robert Riskin). The making of this enduring romantic comedy about a runaway heiress and the brash newspaper reporter who tracks her down and falls for her is now familiar Hollywood lore: MGM king Gable and Paramount diva Colbert were shunted over to Harry Cohn's bargain-basement operation as punishment for misdeeds long since forgotten, but they, Columbia, and Capra had the last laugh. This remains one of the best-loved movies of the Thirties and is an object lesson in why a movie doesn't need a big budget to hit on all cylinders.

Capra's second 1934 effort may have been less memorable, but *Broadway Bill*, a racetrack soap opera adapted by Riskin from a Mark Hellinger story, had its moments. Warner Baxter stars as a disillusioned businessman who drops his job and unpleasant wife (Helen Vinson) to race his horse, the eponymous Bill, with only sister-in-law Myrna Loy to spur him on against staggering odds. The tear-jerking denouement is a bit much, but the film would have more of a reputation today had Capra not withheld it from rerelease for many years so as not to compete with his inferior 1950 musical remake, *Riding High*. Capra was absent from the screen in 1935, the result of peritonitis and other complications following a burst appendix that had him on the brink of death, but he returned in 1936 with a new, extremely lucrative contract and the smash hit *Mr. Deeds Goes to Town*.

One of the three or four pictures with which Capra remains most closely identified, *Mr. Deeds* was adapted by the indispensable Robert Riskin from a story by Clarence Budington Kelland—a David-vs.-Goliath populist fable that may be corny and naïve by today's wised-up standards but was certainly inspirational in the midst of the Depression. Gary Cooper stars as Longfellow Deeds, a tuba-playing writer of greeting-card sentiments from a small town in Vermont who inherits his uncle's $20 million estate and moves to New York to administer it; when Deeds decides to give it away to benefit the less fortunate, he's put on trial by the nabobs to determine his sanity. Jean Arthur is luminous in her first major romantic role as a hard-boiled reporter who is suspicious at first of Deeds's motives but who falls for him once she realizes that he's sincere; such fine character actors as Lionel Stander, Douglas Dumbrille, and H. B. Warner lend able support. The film was nominated for an Academy Award as best picture, and Cooper and Riskin also received nominations, while Capra—then the president of the Academy of Motion Picture Arts and Sciences—was given his second Oscar for best direction.

James Hilton's immensely popular 1933 novel, *Lost Horizon*, should have become an equally great success for Capra, but after he spent a full year and over $2 million filming it, 1937 audiences yawned at the verbose, grandiose production—Columbia's most expensive ever to that point. Adapted, as usual, by Robert Riskin, it starred Ronald Colman as the intrepid British diplomat Robert Conway, whose accidental plane crash brings him to the hidden utopia known as Shangri-La; he and fellow travelers Thomas Mitchell, John Howard, and Edward Everett Horton are entertained by the mysterious Chang (H. B. Warner), the lovely Sondra (Jane Wyatt), the bitter Maria (Margo), and the dying High Lama (Sam Jaffe), who wants Conway to take his place.

As allegory, the picture worked, but as entertainment, its pace and general lack of action proved problematic. (Capra actually screened a three-and-a-half-hour version for a preview audience in 1936; Harry Cohn finally stepped in to cut it to a manageable two-hour running time.) Capra exposed over a million feet of film—enough for a dozen "A" productions—trying to get it right before wrapping. While less than an utter disaster—it did finally make a profit after several years and many reissues—*Lost Horizon* was hardly "Mightiest of All Motion Pictures . . . Frank Capra's Greatest Production," as its advertising proclaimed. And while nominated for an Academy Award as best picture, it won only in the relatively minor categories of art direction—the sets *are* spectacular—and editing; Capra was not so much as nominated.

Capra's refusal to share credit with Riskin instigated a temporary split between the two. But after his first and only effort at directing failed, Riskin returned to script *You Can't Take It with You* (1938) for Capra, an adaptation of the George S. Kaufman–

◀ *Capra and James Stewart confer on the set of* It's a Wonderful Life

Moss Hart Broadway smash which had recently been awarded the Pulitzer Prize. Made in under two months and boasting a lickety-split pace, this frenetic comedy was a dramatic about-face from the self-important weight of *Lost Horizon*, with James Stewart, Lionel Barrymore, Jean Arthur, and Edward Arnold top-billed. This is a professional piece of work, if not exactly the inspired lunacy Capra and the play were aiming for, but the fact that *You Can't Take It with You* won an Academy Award as the best picture of 1938 is still a jaw dropper. And Capra's third Oscar for best direction (over Michael Curtiz, King Vidor, and Norman Taurog) is almost as great a stretch. Small wonder that *Time* magazine, which had put Capra on the cover of its August 8, 1938, issue, hailed him as "the top director of his industry," a claim that was strengthened when Capra was voted president of the recently established Screen Directors' Guild while simultaneously holding down the presidency of the Academy. (Capra was instrumental in negotiating a critical settlement between the two warring factions early in 1939.)

*Mr. Smith Goes to Washington* (1939) had been claimed as a project by Rouben Mamoulian, but according to Joseph McBride's splendid biography, Capra traded Mamoulian his dibs on Clifford Odets's *Golden Boy* for the right to make it. And no wonder: its story about a freshman senator from Montana who uproots pork-barrel corruption in the Senate at the risk of his own career and well-being was quintessential Capra. The picture stars Jimmy Stewart as the idealistic Jefferson Smith and Jean Arthur as the cynical Washington secretary who is won over by his crusade, and was the first Capra production since 1933 not written by Robert Riskin—he had departed Columbia to work for Sam Goldwyn for an enormous salary increase. Sidney Buchman, who had done some rewrites on *Lost Horizon*, inherited the scripting chores.

Even more than *Mr. Deeds*, *Mr. Smith* embodies the favorite Capra theme of an Everyman who refuses to sell out his all-American ethics in the face of enormous pressure from greedy, amoral power brokers—here embodied by Claude Rains's venal Senator Paine, who has sold out to the political machine run by Edward Arnold. An enormous popular and critical success (thanks in no small part to the highly politicized Buchman, who later was revealed to have joined the Communist Party just before filming commenced), *Mr. Smith* earned eleven Academy Award nominations, including ones for best picture, actor, direction, screenplay, and supporting actor (Harry Carey); the only winner turned out to be Lewis R. Foster for his original story, but then, 1939 was the Oscars' most competitive year ever.

Capra now departed Columbia and Harry Cohn to follow the lure of independent production. Surprisingly, Robert Riskin agreed to leave the green pastures of Sam Goldwyn's operation to join him and Frank Capra Productions. Their first project was *Meet John Doe* (1941), which was made at Warner Bros. after Capra signed a complicated deal to have the studio underwrite and distribute the picture. Gary Cooper, who had been Capra's first choice for *Mr. Smith*, was acquired at great cost on loan-out to star as Long John Willoughby, an unemployed former baseball player hired by cynical newspaper reporter (a fixture in a Capra picture) Barbara Stanwyck to appear in public as the fictitious "John Doe" she has been writing about in her columns, who has vowed to jump off the roof of City Hall to protest how "the whole world's gone to pot."

Naturally Stanwyck falls for the big lug—and naturally the big lug decides to actually carry out the suicide pledge when he realizes how he's been made a party to manipulating the masses who have come to idolize him. Evil media baron Edward Arnold, representing the forces of Fascism, is the most interesting character in the film, which was tested with several different endings—Capra and Riskin never could decide which one worked best. The "true" ending, in which John Doe actually jumps, didn't test well, and neither did any of the other variations, including the one the film had when it went into release. Capra and Riskin had a different ending appended to the prints after the film had premiered, and took the even more unusual step of shooting yet another ending a few weeks later for the picture's national release. Given the creators' confusion, it's no wonder that *Meet John Doe* ends with a whimper rather than a bang. And while the film turned a profit, it wasn't enough to keep Frank Capra Productions from dissolving by the end of 1941.

Riskin now moved to London to work for the Ministry of Information; Capra was again without a partner. He dickered for several months with United Artists over a prospective partnership before giving it up, instead signing a deal to direct *Arsenic and Old Lace* for Warners. At the time the Howard Lindsay–Russel Crouse gothic comedy was a huge hit on Broadway, and the creators sold the rights on condition that the film version not be released until the Broadway run was completed. Capra completed filming in December of 1941, but as the play ran for almost fifteen hundred performances, Warners had to let the picture sit on the shelf until September 1944. Cary Grant renders what he considered the worst performance of his career as the "normal" nephew of loony aunts Josephine Hull and Jean Adair (given a two-month leave from Broadway to make this film); Raymond Massey replaced stage star Boris Karloff as the lumbering killer Jonathan, and the screenplay was written by Philip and Julius Epstein. But the haste with which Capra worked is evident, and *Arsenic* is an extremely minor footnote to his résumé.

Less than a week after Pearl Harbor, Capra reenlisted, joining the Army Signal Corps as a major, with the understanding that he would oversee a series of orientation films under the rubric of "Why We Fight." Working out of Washington and then Hollywood, Capra helped produce *Prelude to War* (1942), *The Nazis Strike* (1942; co-directed with Anatole Litvak), *Divide and Conquer* (1943; with Litvak), *Battle of Britain* (1943), *Battle of Russia* (1943; with Litvak), *Battle of China* (1943; with Litvak), and *War Comes to America* (1944); of these, only *Prelude* (which shared an Oscar for best documentary of 1942) and *Russia* were released theatrically during the war. The seven films, which consisted in large part of edited newsreel footage and scenes from Hollywood and foreign war movies, were made for a mere $400,000. (While Capra was thus engaged, Robert Riskin was working as the head of the Overseas Motion Picture Bureau of the Office of War Information out of New York.)

Capra left the Army with the rank of full colonel and the Distinguished Service Medal, pinned on him personally by General George Marshall. But back in Hollywood, he had the same difficulty readjusting that so many returning servicemen did—his former workplace didn't want him. In Capra's case, this meant that the studios weren't rolling out the red carpet in the form of lucrative independent production deals. And so, in 1945, Colonel Capra banded together with Colonel George Stevens, Colonel William Wyler, and Colonel Sam Briskin to form Liberty Films, with nine pictures (three from each director) to be distributed by RKO. (Robert Riskin cut his own deal with RKO.)

Liberty's first release was *It's a Wonderful Life* (1946), the now-classic Christmas tale about a banker driven to despair who wishes aloud that he'd never been born, then gets to see how much poorer the world would have been without him. Based on "The Greatest Gift," a Christmas pamphlet sent out to his friends by Philip Van Doren Stern and later published in *Good Housekeeping*, it had been purchased by RKO in 1943. Capra bought the story from the studio and developed it with writers Frances Goodrich and Albert Hackett (Jo Swerling also worked on it, as did the uncredited Dalton Trumbo and Dorothy Parker). Released in the Christmas season of 1946, *Wonderful Life* starred Jimmy Stewart as Bedford Falls banker George Bailey, Donna Reed as his wife, Lionel Barrymore as the conniving Mr. Potter, and Henry Travers as Clarence Oddbody, the angel sent to guide George.

Given the classic status of the film today, it's hard to appreciate that it was not especially popular with contemporary audiences. Its heart-tugging, warm conclusion could not erase the film's dark, dark vision of the cruelty of life, and perhaps the day's audiences were not ready to embrace a nihilistic Christmas yarn. That was unfortunate, because according to Joseph McBride, this was the most expensive film of Capra's career, leaving Liberty almost a half-million dollars in the red after receipts were tallied. (Ironically, the movie that Liberty partner William Wyler made outside the company at the same time, *The Best Years of Our Lives*, became the year's biggest hit.) Even so, *Wonderful Life* was nominated for an Academy Award as best picture, and Stewart and Capra were also nominated, Capra for the sixth and final time. But Wyler's *Best Years* took all the major awards.

Disillusioned, Capra and his partners sold Liberty Films to Paramount and went back to working for someone else. Capra now eyed *State of the Union* (1948), a Broadway success for Lindsay and Crouse that had recently won the Pulitzer Prize; he made a one-picture deal with MGM to acquire the rights. After failing to secure Gary Cooper as the lead, Capra settled for Spencer Tracy as Grant Matthews, a wealthy industrialist whom the Republicans want to run for President. Only one problem: he's estranged from his wife, and their dysfunctional marriage needs to be patched up for public-relations purposes when Matthews begins his campaign.

Katharine Hepburn doesn't have a great deal to do as Mary Matthews except show disapproval of her husband's growing propensity for selling out to special-interest groups. But Angela Lansbury is deliciously evil as the newspaper publisher supporting Grant's candidacy while having an affair with him, Adolphe Menjou is morally repulsive as Grant's cynical campaign manager, and Van Johnson is appealing as his publicist. The film wants very much to be as stirring as *Mr. Smith Goes to Washington*, but Capra seems to have lost his knack for rabble-rousing—not to mention his sense of drama; Grant's final repudiation of his manipulative pals and embrace of the "honest" masses makes Tracy sound as though he's reading his lines from the back of a cereal box.



For all its shortcomings—let's cite ideology, pace, and timing for starters—*Union* would prove to be Capra's last solid piece of moviemaking. *Riding High* (1950), an uninspired remake of *Broadway Bill*, had Bing Crosby taking over the Warner Baxter part (warbling five tunes), Coleen Gray the Myrna Loy role; racing footage from the 1934 movie was reused (rather clumsily) as a cost-cutting measure. (The horse still died at the end, but this picture expired long before that final race.) *Here Comes the Groom* (1951), from a story by Robert Riskin and Liam O'Brien, starred Bing Crosby again, with similarly underwhelming results. Here Crosby is reporter Pete Garvey, who returns to the States from France with two orphans in tow; he can keep them only if he gets married in the next five days. Can Bing's crooning of the Oscar-winning ditty "In the Cool, Cool, Cool of the Evening" steal Jane Wyman away from Franchot Tone and his millions? Thus it is preordained—but who believed it? or cared?

After failing to get *Roman Holiday*, the classic romantic comedy that William Wyler finally made in

1953, off the ground, the burned-out Capra (who also felt he was the victim of subtle blacklist pressures for his political progressivism during the Thirties) did not get another picture into movie theaters for eight years. He did direct four hour-long programs for Bell Telephone's television science series for children: *Our Mr. Sun* (1956), *Hemo the Magnificent* (1957), *The Strange Case of the Cosmic Rays* (1957), and *The Unchained Goddess* (1958; actually directed under Capra's supervision by actor Richard Carlson).

He finally returned to feature filmmaking with *A*

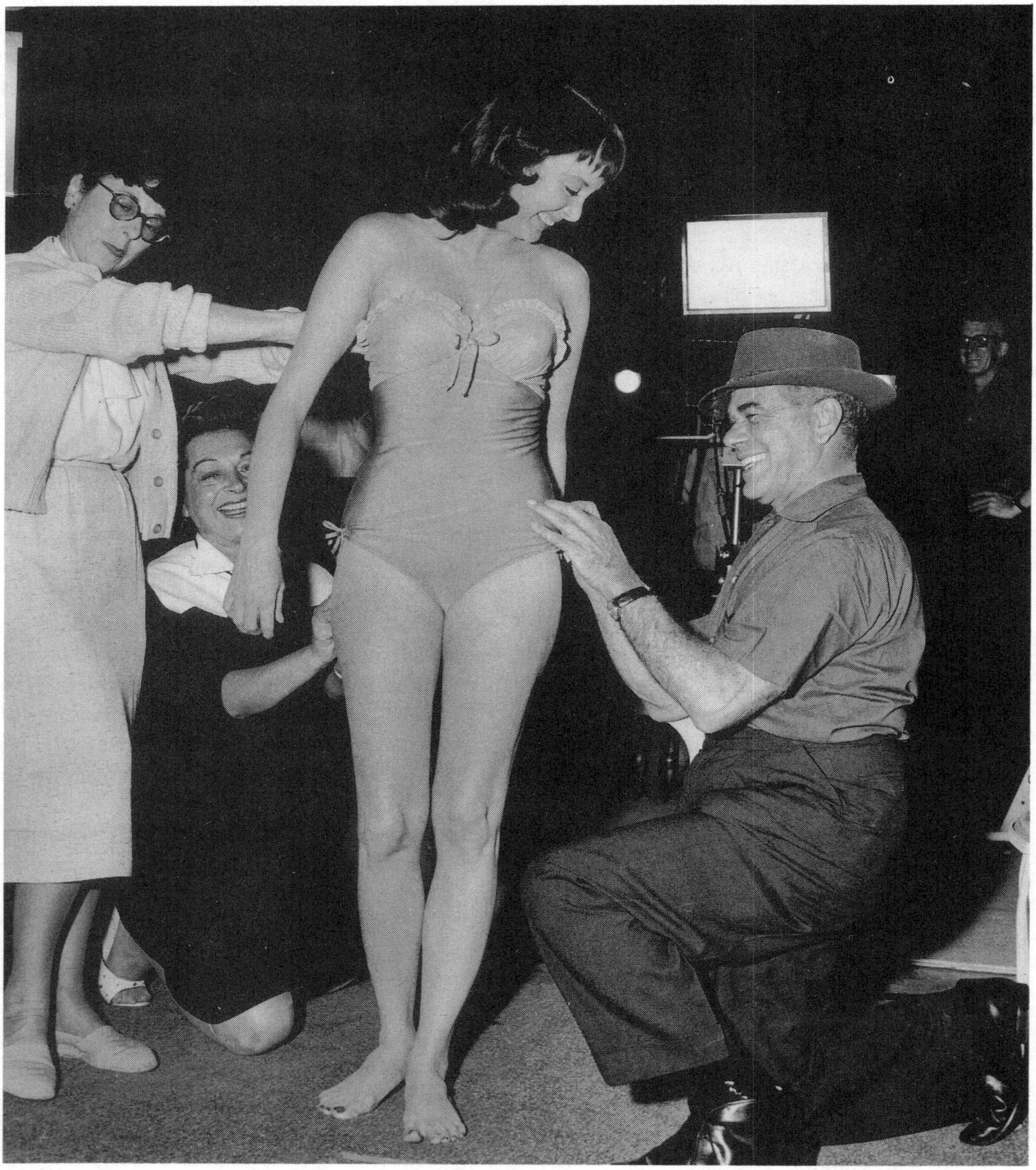

▲ *Carolyn Jones and Capra share a laugh while filming* A Hole in the Head

Hole in the Head (1959), a rather sour (and decidedly unromantic) romantic comedy. Frank Sinatra starred in (and co-produced) this adaptation of Arnold Shulman's Broadway play about a no-goodnik hotelier in Miami Beach whose irresponsibility nearly costs him custody of his son (Eddie Hodges); Eleanor Parker is the wealthy widow he romances, hoping she'll give him enough money to keep his hotel from being repossessed, Carolyn Jones is his masochistic beatnik girlfriend and Edward G. Robinson his unsympathetic older brother. The most that can be said for this rather nasty comedy-of-no-manners, which inexplicably made a killing at the box office, is that, like Capra's previous film, it spawned an Oscar-winning song: the infectious "High Hopes" by James Van Heusen and Sammy Cahn.

*A Hole in the Head*'s financial success enabled Capra to remake one of his earliest triumphs, *Lady for a Day*. There would be no such honors accorded *A Pocketful of Miracles* (1961), however; it was an object lesson in why remakes of classic movies—even by their original directors—should be against the law. Bette Davis now stars as Apple Annie alongside Glenn Ford's Dave the Dude, with Peter Falk, Hope Lange, veterans Edward Everett Horton and Thomas Mitchell, and (in her screen debut) Ann-Margret in support. With the film at a swollen 136 minutes (vs. *Lady*'s 96), one is justified in asking exactly what Capra and his writers did to "improve" on Riskin's original screenplay. The answer is: not enough and too much. As the picture limps along, dragging the plot three paces behind, one almost feels embarrassed for the former master of the sentimental comedy. The picture failed to earn back its cost, and the critics called it "listless."

Capra must have realized that he had stayed too long at the fair, because he never directed another feature film—although he was briefly considered for Gore Vidal's political drama *The Best Man* (which Franklin Schaffner ultimately directed in 1964). In 1964 Capra made a short for NASA called *Rendezvous in Space* for exhibition at the New York World's Fair. His autobiography—or, as one wag called it, "autohagiography," *The Name Above the Title*, was published in 1971 to a warm reception. But Capra's selective memory and often fanciful representations of who did (and, more significantly, didn't) help him make his films was revealed in all its pathetic self-delusion in Joseph McBride's 1992 book. Capra died in 1991 at the age of ninety-four.

## ● JOHN CASSAVETES (1929–1989)

He was a maverick every time he stepped behind the camera, and most of his films were independently (and painstakingly) made over many months and even years, financed by the acting offers that kept rolling in from the same studios that (perhaps sensibly) were afraid to back his pictures. So John Cassavetes carved out his own one-man domain, which, while not truly part of Hollywood, eventually earned the respect and admiration of those within the gates of the kingdom.

Born in New York City at the dawn of the Great Depression, Cassavetes started acting while an undergraduate at Colgate, subsequently enrolling in the American Academy of Dramatic Arts. After working in stock for a few years, he began to get small roles in films (*The Night Holds Terror* in 1954 was one of his first credits) and larger roles on television shows; by his own count, he acted in thirty-seven live television shows in 1955, including several installments of *Omnibus*. In 1956 Cassavetes appeared in Don Siegel's Juvenile Delinquent opus *Crime in the Streets*, the same year he established an improvisational acting class. In Martin Ritt's *Edge of the City* (1957), Cassavetes starred alongside Sidney Poitier, a high-profile role that helped him land the lead as the eponymous private eye in the 1959 television series *Johnny Staccato*. It ran for only one season, but Cassavetes's salary—augmented by $20,000 in donations—helped him complete the film he had begun working on in 1957.

Shot with a 16mm camera, and almost entirely improvised by his cast (who were enrolled in Cassavetes's own Variety Arts Studio in New York), *Shadows* (1960) was a downbeat slice of *cinema verité* about a frustrated black jazz musician (Hugh Hurd) who spends his nights blowing the trumpet at crummy strip joints and his days trying to help his younger, lighter-skinned siblings (Lelia Goldoni, Ben Carruthers) find their way in the world, even while battling his jealousy over their ability to pass for white. Not exactly *Please Don't Eat the Daisies*, so when Cassavetes couldn't find an American distributor, he entered it in the Venice Film Festival, where it won the Critics Award. *Shadows* was then picked up for exhibition in England, and finally made its way to the States, where critics were unanimous in their praise. It is generally acknowledged as inaugurating the New American Cinema of independent filmmaking.

The studios were intrigued by this promising new talent, and Cassavetes was inundated with offers. He signed with Paramount to produce and direct *Too Late Blues* (1961), another downbeat film about a jazz musician. Erstwhile teen idol Bobby Darin plays the leader of a jazz combo waiting for its big break; one night he picks up lovely, unpretentious Stella Stevens, in tears after being verbally abused by her big-shot boyfriend. But Darin's foolish pride causes him to blow his chance with her. He also alienates his pals (Seymour Cassel, Cliff Carnell), whom he ditched to become the gigolo of a rich dame "sponsoring" him to play at upscale cocktail lounges. *Blues* has a nice, improvised feel, with plenty of funky club atmosphere, and Stevens is positively luminous. But Darin's petulant hipster alternates between pathetic and obnoxious—it's a pleasure to watch bully Vince Edwards beat the crap out of him—sinking the picture into a quagmire from which Cassavetes cannot extricate it.

Cassavetes signed a multipicture deal with Paramount, but left the studio a year later without having made another movie, citing interference. Independent producer Stanley Kramer then signed him to direct *A Child Is Waiting* (1963), an earnest drama written by Abby Mann about dedicated teachers Burt Lancaster and Judy Garland helping devise treatments for retarded children; Cassavetes's future wife, Gena Rowlands, was also in the cast. But displeased

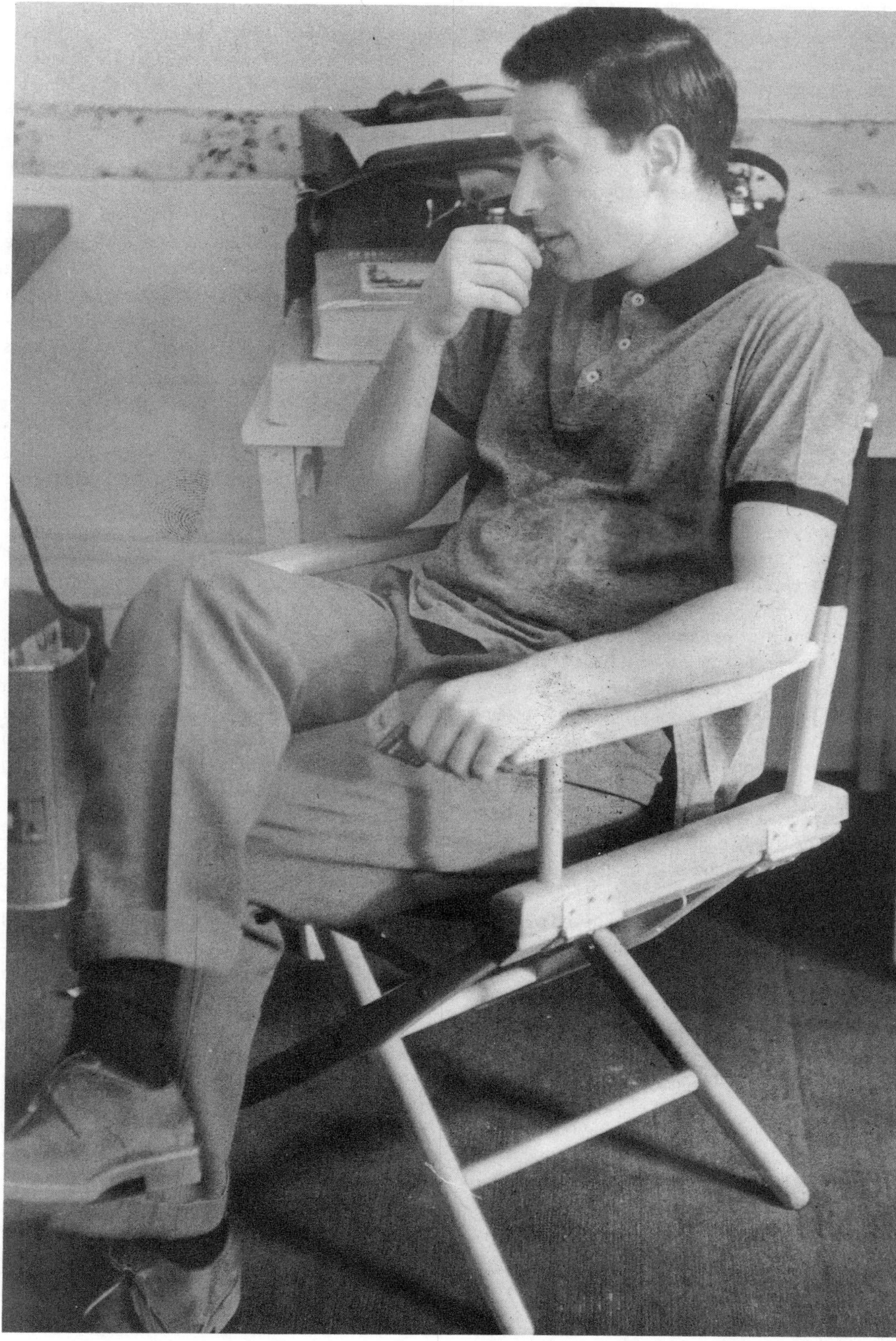

with Kramer's "input"—Kramer took the picture out of Cassavetes's hands and recut it, changing the film's message about the dependency of the retarded—Cassavetes made his break with Hollywood. He spent a year in unenforced idleness, working on screenplays, before trying to develop a TV series in partnership with Screen Gems. When that didn't work out, Cassavetes decided to begin filming his next 16mm opus.

*Faces*, which Cassavetes wrote in 1965 and shot in '66, "stars" John Marley and Lynn Carlin as a husband and wife facing a split after fourteen years of marriage; Gena Rowlands is the prostitute who sleeps with Marley one night, and Seymour Cassel is a hippie who picks up and beds down Carlin that same evening. Originally six hours, the film was painstakingly edited down over the next two years to slightly over two hours and released on the independent circuit in 1968 to rave reviews. Somewhat surprisingly, Cassavetes received an Academy Award nomination for his screenplay, and Carlin and Cassel were nominated as best supporting actors. (The picture even made a little money.)

Cassavetes had helped finance *Faces* by taking acting jobs on films like Aldrich's *The Dirty Dozen*, for which he was Oscar-nominated as best supporting actor, and Polanski's *Rosemary's Baby*. For *Husbands* (1970), his first color 35mm effort, Cassavetes assembled his first "name" cast: Peter Falk, Ben Gazzara, and himself. They portray a triumvirate of suburban hubbies who, shocked by the sudden death of a pal, treat themselves to a forty-eight-hour spree of boozing, basketball, and balling. "Agonizingly banal," Pauline Kael opined, and it's true that the friends' seemingly endless confessions and ruminations—mostly improvised, of course—become tedious halfway through the film's two and a half hours. Still, there are moments of uncommon power, and with a more judicious editing job, *Husbands* might have earned Cassavetes the sobriquet of the American Bergman.

Released by Columbia, *Husbands* became his most widely seen film to date (though hardly a hit by Hollywood standards), which helped *Minnie and Moskowitz* (1971) get made (for Universal) without the usual lengthy delay. More hopeful and romantic than any of his other pictures, this is Cassavetes's version of a screwball comedy. Seymour Cassel plays a slightly demented parking lot attendant with a crush on museum curator Gena Rowlands, who's trying to pull herself together after being dumped by her married lover (John Cassavetes). It's an impossible match, one that makes no sense even in movie terms—but by the end Cassavetes has us rooting for Cassel and Rowlands to get together (and of course they do).

But it was back to psychodrama in *A Woman under the Influence* (1974), a harrowing, unrelievedly raw portrait of a Los Angeles housewife's nervous breakdown. Originally intended as a stage vehicle for Gena Rowlands (who understandably didn't want to crumble into pieces seven times a week), it was made for Cassavetes's newly formed Faces International production company. Peter Falk is appropriately detestable as Rowland's brutish construction-worker husband, and no one can gainsay the majesty of Rowland's performance, which earned her a best actress Oscar nomination. But as with *Husbands*, Cassavetes is too indulgent of his whims, letting the big scenes run on far too long and dissipating much of their hard-won power. Nevertheless, *Woman* was his biggest hit yet, and Cassavetes received his only Academy Award nomination for best direction.

It seemed as if Cassavetes had beaten the system, making deeply personal, deliberately uncommercial movies entirely on his own terms and still winning the admiration of the industry on which he'd turned his back. But *The Killing of a Chinese Bookie* (1976) seems a miscalculation. Ben Gazzara is convincing enough as Cosmo Vitelli, the debt-ridden owner of a strip joint forced by the mob to commit a murder, and Timothy Carey and Seymour Cassel provide their usual fine support. But this may have been the wrong genre for Cassavetes—perhaps *every* genre but his own unique one was wrong for him—and the sleazy atmosphere and muddled, drawn-out dramatics alienated both his new fans and his longtime admirers.

The ambitious *Opening Night* (1977) also had its problems, including the usual one of excessive length, but Gena Rowlands again excelled as a stage actress suffering an existential crisis after a fan dies on the opening night of her new play, *The Second Woman*. As her co-star, Cassavetes is also terrific (he was surely as good an actor as he was a director), and veteran character actress Joan Blondell adds a welcome dimension as the playwright. It may have been nothing more than coincidence, but *Gloria* (1980), which was made for Columbia rather than

Faces International, was far more enjoyable. Rowlands is superb as a former moll/hooker who goes on the lam with an eight-year-old boy (John Adames) after his family is eradicated by the mobsters who employed his dad as an accountant. It's great to see Gena (who again was nominated for an Academy Award as best actress) shooting it out with hoodlums for a change instead of paralyzed by neuroses, and in between killings the film offers plenty of Cassavetes's distinctive humor. Though he fails to attend to the narrative as the genre demands, *Gloria* remains one of Cassavetes's most accessible pictures.

Cassavetes had been acting less frequently at that time—roles in Elaine May's *Mikey and Nicky* (1976) and Brian De Palma's *The Fury* (1978) were his most significant credits—but he and Gena Rowlands played the leads in Paul Mazursky's 1982 *The Tempest*, the first time they had acted together in a non-Cassavetes picture. He and Rowlands then starred in his own *Love Streams* (1984) as a brother and sister who lead wildly differing lifestyles—he's doing field research for a book about prostitution, she's struggling with ex-husband Seymour Cassel for custody of their children—but who care deeply about each other. The typical narrative longueurs aside, this is a moving and unusual love story.

Cassavetes's final project was the goofy *Big Trouble* (1985)—*Double Indemnity* done for laughs. Alan Arkin stars as an insurance salesman who agrees to knock off sex bomb Beverly D'Angelo's husband (Peter Falk) in order to finance his kids' Ivy League education; the terrific cast also featured Charles Durning, Paul Dooley, and Robert Stack. But this belated bid for mainstream acceptance—if that's what it was—ironically was seen by fewer people than almost any other Cassavetes picture, proving an unfortunate (and unfortunately premature) ending to an adventurous and scintillating filmmaking career.

▲ *Cassavetes and wife, Gena Rowlands, relax at home in 1958*

## ● WILLIAM CASTLE (1914–1977)

Ever so important as a promotion and marketing innovator, New York City–born William Castle eventually would be credited with directing fifty-five feature films, only a few of which are memorable for more than the genius with which they were exploited. As he cheerfully admits in his 1976 autobiography, *Step Right Up! I'm Gonna Scare the Pants Off America*, Castle considered himself the P. T. Barnum of the cinema. But while his Hollywood career for a long while resembled those of any number of career "B" directors, after 1958 Castle succeeded in making a unique (if modest) contribution to the American cinema.

After several fruitless years in the Off-Broadway theater, Castle apprenticed as a dialogue coach at Columbia. He was given the chance to direct his first features in 1943, and in 1944 he made three excellent low-budget noirs, *The Whistler*, featuring Richard Dix as the death-obsessed protagonist; *Mark of the Whistler*, again with Dix; and *When Strangers Marry*, a taut thriller that felicitously cast Robert Mitchum as the murderous spouse of Kim Hunter. After making *The Voice of the Whistler* in 1945, he took over the "Crime Doctor" series, which starred Warner Baxter, and contributed four good entries.

In 1949 Castle moved to Universal, where he made more good crime pictures, including *Johnny Stool Pigeon* with Shelley Winters and Dan Duryea, and *Undertow* (both 1949) with Scott Brady. After directing the indescribable midget melodrama *It's a Small World* (1950), Castle would work in every conceivable genre: Westerns like *Fort Ti* and *Conquest of Cochise*; spectacles like *Serpent of the Nile* (all 1953), featuring Rhonda Fleming as Cleopatra, and the cheesy biblical tale *Slaves of Babylon* (also 1953); crime pics like *New Orleans Uncensored* (1954), and period adventure yarns like *Charge of the Lancers* and *The Iron Glove* (both 1954).

Castle might have continued grinding out such hackwork forever, but in 1958 he had a revelation: he decided to produce and direct a series of shockers, overcoming the limitations of casts and budgets by creating a gimmick with which each one could be exploited. Thus, the intense horror yarn *Macabre* (1958) was advertised with the prominent guarantee "We insure you for $1,000 against fright!" (Needless to say, no one ever had to have a claim filed on their behalf.) *House on Haunted Hill* (1959), which had Vincent Price at his most malevolent and was probably the best of Castle's tongue-in-cheek shockers, featured "Emergo," which theoretically sent a luminescent skeleton floating over the heads of theatergoers (assuming the exhibitor was cooperating, which rarely happened).

*The Tingler* (1959), a clever tale about the nature of fear, had "Percepto," which required that electric buzzers be wired under selected patrons' seats; star Vincent Price instructed the audience from the screen that they must scream aloud if the parasitic Tingler was to be destroyed. For *13 Ghosts* (1960), Castle

▲ *Castle encourages Rhonda Fleming during* Serpent of the Nile

offered "Illusion-O," basically a pair of glasses with tinted plastic lenses that made the ghosts visible on-screen when worn. *Homicidal* was a knockoff of *Psycho*, with the added fillip of a "Fright Break" that offered audiences a refund if they left during the film's last five minutes. *Mr. Sardonicus* (1961) was a rare period outing for Castle, in which disfigured Guy Rolphe has his fate decided at film's end by the audience's vote during a "Punishment Poll."

*Zotz!* (1962) was one of Castle's few disappointments during this creative burst; a middling Cold War comedy starring Tom Poston, it offered only a plastic coin to patrons as its promotional tie-in. *13 Frightened Girls* (1963) also relied on the Cold War for its plot, while *The Old Dark House* (also 1963), shot in England, was a tongue-in-cheek remake of the 1932 Universal chiller; now Tom Poston is installed in a creepy mansion amid the wacky Femm family. Noting that his box-office grosses had dipped while fiddling with macabre comedy, Castle returned to the business of shocking audiences with *Strait-Jacket* (1964), which featured Joan Crawford as an erstwhile ax murderer who fears she's reverting to her old ways; written by Robert Bloch, the picture featured the now-classic tag line, "Just keep saying to yourself: It's only a movie, it's only a movie . . ."

Bloch also wrote *The Night Walker* (1965), a middling suspenser whose chief attraction was its use of old-timers Barbara Stanwyck, Robert Taylor, and Rochelle Hudson as headliners. Crawford was back in *I Saw What You Did* (also 1965), but it was really John Ireland as a murderous psycho on the hunt for two teenage girls that held things together. Castle's subsequent films never again reached that level: *Let's Kill Uncle* (1966) set a couple of kids against a homicidal British soldier, while *Project X* (1968) was a dubious science-fiction adventure starring Christopher George.

But Castle was able to enjoy one more moment of glory. Having acquired the rights to *Rosemary's Baby*, Ira Levin's bestseller about witchcraft in modern-day New York City, Castle was able to help guide it to becoming one of the year's best films, a box-office smash that remains an all-time suspense classic. He even got over the disappointment of Paramount studio head Robert Evans not allowing him to direct it, instead handing the reins to Roman Polanski. Castle's larger-than-life persona as a cigar-chomping, half-huckster, half-savant was captured to a T by John Goodman in Joe Dante's enjoyable *Matinee* (1993), set in Florida during the Cuban missile crisis—Castle's heyday. It was a loving tribute, the likes of which few directors ever have had the good fortune to receive.

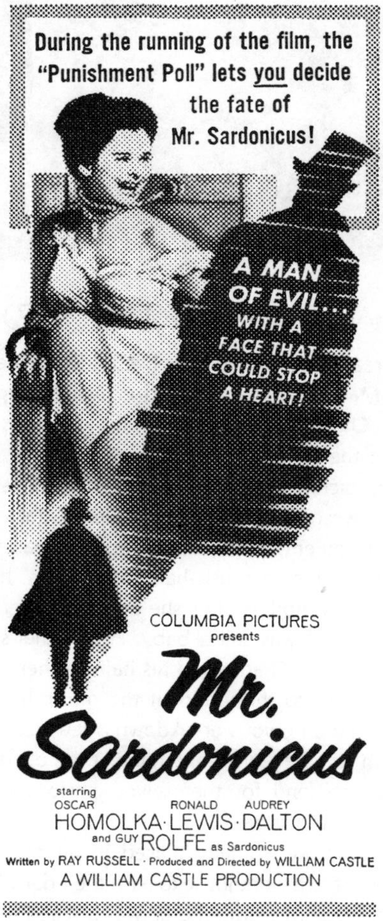
During the running of the film, the "Punishment Poll" lets you decide the fate of Mr. Sardonicus!
A MAN OF EVIL... WITH A FACE THAT COULD STOP A HEART!
COLUMBIA PICTURES presents
Mr. Sardonicus
starring OSCAR HOMOLKA · RONALD LEWIS · AUDREY DALTON
and GUY ROLFE as Sardonicus
Written by RAY RUSSELL · Produced and Directed by WILLIAM CASTLE
A WILLIAM CASTLE PRODUCTION

## ● CHARLIE CHAPLIN (1889-1977)

"The greatest artist who ever lived." So former employer Mack Sennett described erstwhile employee Charles Chaplin. While few of his triumphs were made in the sound era, and fewer still were actual "talking pictures," Chaplin's screen achievements were as awesome as his personal life was (at various points) turbulent, petty, and simply embarrassing. Born in London to music-hall entertainers, he was raised by his mother after she and his father separated when he was still a baby. His mother's stage career provided Charlie and his half brother Sydney with an entry to the world of the music halls, but she suffered a nervous breakdown a few years later, and with Charlie's alcoholic father now dead, they were left to fend for themselves, performing and sleeping on the streets.

The boys were finally placed in an orphanage and sent off to a workhouse to earn their daily bread. But at the age of eight, Charlie was rescued from his *Oliver Twist*-like existence by joining a troupe of child dancers. By the time he was eleven, he was appearing at London's newly opened Hippodrome and acting in stage productions around town. In 1906 Charlie joined the older Sydney at Fred Karno's Pantomime Troupe, with which he spent the next several years performing all over England.

Charlie visited the United States with one of Karno's troupes in 1910, and paid another visit in 1912. It was then that he came to the attention of Mack Sennett, the head of Keystone, which specialized in short comic films. Late in 1913, Sennett hired Charlie, and his screen career was under way. Chaplin began to refine the sensitive vagabond character who would soon make him the world's most recognized movie actor—relying on just a fake mustache, a bowler hat, impossibly baggy pants, and a twirling cane—making his presence felt in support of star comics like Fatty Arbuckle, Chester Conklin, and Mabel Normand. It was not long before Charlie was directing, writing, and starring in his own shorts, and by 1914 he was one of Keystone's stars, in that single year making thirty-five shorts, as well as the six-reel "epic" *Tillie's Punctured Romance*. In 1915 he jumped to the Essanay studio, which offered him the impressive sum of $1,250 a week to make two-reelers like *The Tramp*, which established the Little Tramp screen persona in its final, noble form.

So successful were Chaplin's shorts that Essanay quadrupled his salary in 1916, but that still wasn't enough to keep him from jumping to the rival Mutual studio a few months later for the staggering sum of $10,000 a week, the promise of complete creative control, a $150,000 bonus, and an obligation of just twelve films per year. *Easy Street*, *The Rink*, and *The Immigrant* were just a few of his Mutual triumphs during this period, but in 1917 Chaplin found himself attacked for the first (though hardly the last) time by the press for not enlisting to fight in the First World War. (He actually had been rejected as being unfit for medical reasons, but did devote himself to raising funds for the troops in bond drives.) In 1918 he jumped studios yet again, accepting a million-dollar offer from First National to make just eight two-reelers; one of the first was *Shoulder Arms*, a comic look at the world war Charlie had just missed.

After marrying sixteen-year-old extra Mildred Harris in 1918—the first in a procession of child brides—Chaplin made the most momentous business decision of his career, joining forces in 1919 with D. W. Griffith, Douglas Fairbanks, Jr., and Mary Pickford to form United Artists, the company through which all his subsequent films would be released. *The Kid* (1921) was Chaplin's first feature-length film, a tearjerking tale that featured the (then) irresistible Jackie Coogan as a young boy befriended and aided by the Little Tramp. After making a few more shorts, Chaplin paid a visit to Europe that codified his international stardom. Then came *A Woman of Affairs* (1923), a seriocomic drama that featured Adolphe Menjou and Edna Purviance but, more significantly, did *not* co-star Chaplin; reviews were respectful, but the box-office take was weak.

Having divorced Mildred after two years, Chaplin now married sixteen-year-old Lolita MacMurray, who shortly would become known to the world as film star Lita Gray (they would be noisily divorced in 1927). He then set to work making what would come to be regarded as his greatest silent picture, *The Gold Rush* (1925). The protagonist, as usual, was the Little Tramp, but Chaplin here placed him in the epic setting of the Yukon, amid bears, snowstorms, and fearsome prospector Mack Swain; his love interest was a beautiful dance-hall queen (the lovely Georgia Hale). All this provides a wider scope for the great comic set pieces, and the film's well-earned (if inevitable) pathos seems emotionally richer than in previous works; the scene where the Tramp must eat his shoes to stay alive can induce chuckles and tears simultaneously. Cut by ten minutes, *The Gold Rush* was reissued in 1942 with narration and a prerecorded score; in either format, it remains one of the silent cinema's timeless, endlessly rewarding masterpieces.

*The Circus* (1928) was Chaplin's much-anticipated follow-up, and it did not disappoint. Released at a time when sound was still considered an experiment that might or might not catch on, this polished effort was easily one of the year's best pictures. Chaplin plays a simple soul who accidentally joins up with a traveling circus and quickly finds himself falling in love with pretty bareback rider Merna Kennedy, in between lion-taming and other big-top pursuits. The film earned Chaplin his only Oscar nomination for best direction, in the inaugural year of the Academy Awards; more unusual was the special Oscar he was awarded for making *The Circus*, "for versatility and genius in writing, acting, directing and producing" —as if it would have been unfair to Hollywood's other filmmakers to have to compete with him on the same playing field!

By the time Chaplin made *City Lights* (1931), however, the "problem" of sound could no longer be

ignored, and the silent film was suddenly a museum artifact. Except, of course, to Chaplin. He simply proceeded as if nothing had happened, and produced a sweet, unabashedly sentimental story in which the Little Tramp falls in love with blind flower girl Virginia Cherrill; he vows to restore her sight, then loses her to his rival upon succeeding. In other hands the story might have become maudlin, but Chaplin keeps the pathos affecting without crossing the line. The musical score, the lone "sound" element the film offered, was composed by Chaplin, and he also conducted its recording; no matter the lack of dialogue, it was a huge success.

In 1933 Chaplin secretly married nineteen-year-old starlet Paulette Goddard at sea; they managed to keep their marriage secret for three years. Also in 1933, United Artists announced Chaplin's next project in the trade journals, but *Modern Times* did not appear in theaters until 1936. Incredibly, it, too, was a silent film, with just sound effects (many created by Chaplin), a nonsense song, and a score (again, composed and conducted by Chaplin) differentiating it from Chaplin's 1920s features. Chaplin stars as a nameless factory worker who has been totally dehumanized by the mindless task he has to perform—tightening bolts on parts that fly by on an assembly line (a task perhaps reminiscent to Chaplin of his childhood days working at a printing press in London); Goddard is Gamine, the waif who comes under his wing. It was essentially the only silent feature to come out of Hollywood during that decade, but audiences still turned out to see it.

*The Great Dictator* (1940) was Chaplin's most overt political satire, and it was his first sound picture. Made on the eve of the Second World War, it starred Charlie in a dual role as a nameless Jewish barber and as Adenoid Hynkel, Dictator of Tomania—a dead-on parody of Hitler, to whom Chaplin bore a remarkable physical resemblance. Paulette Goddard is Hannah, the barber's Jewish friend, who flees Germany after the barber is arrested and sent to a concentration camp, and Jack Oakie gives a hilarious impersonation of Mussolini as Napaloni, Dictator of Bacteria. The *Mad*-magazine tone of the picture's lampoons is a welcome movement away from Chaplin's usual poetic approach—*The Great Dictator* is simply too bitter and too outraged to permit much in the way of gentle comedy. The film, which Chaplin promoted and publicized heavily, did well at the box office, and he received his only Academy Award nomination as best actor. (The New York Film Critics gave him their best actor award, but he refused to accept it.)

After making just three movies over a ten-year period, Chaplin would take seven more years before shepherding his next project to the screen. Problems in his personal life were again partly to blame. In 1942 a paternity suit was brought against him by young would-be actress Joan Barry; the courts ruled against Chaplin, and he was named the father of her child, although cleared of the more serious charges of violating the Mann Act. Weeks later, he and Goddard finalized their divorce. In 1943 he married eighteen-year-old Oona O'Neill, the daughter of playwright Eugene; again he was accused of cradle-robbing.

It wasn't until 1947 that his darkest comedy, *Monsieur Verdoux*, was released, and by then Chaplin was in the headlines again, defending himself against charges by the House Un-American Activities Committee of having Communist affiliations; so vociferous were the accusations that the picture's play dates were compromised. Chaplin starred in this "Comedy of Murders" (as the film was promoted) as the eponymous protagonist, Henri Verdoux, a happily married former bank clerk and father who becomes the scourge of 1930s Paris by romancing and then killing a series of rich widows and spinsters for their fortunes. (Chaplin based his character on a mass murderer named Landru, who was known as the Bluebeard of France when he went on his killing spree during the early 1900s.) Mady Correll played Verdoux's unknowing wife; his targets included Martha Raye, Audrey Betz, Isobel Elsom, and Margaret Hoffman. *Verdoux* was an utter failure commercially upon its release—his first in over twenty years—and critical opinion was divided, although Chaplin's screenplay was nominated for an Oscar. It is still difficult to determine whether this rather uneven satire (or parable about pacifism, as Chaplin described it) would have been received more warmly had he not been suffering from the attentions of HUAC; they invited (rather than supoenaed) Chaplin to testify, but he refused, advising them, "I am what you call a peacemonger"—as if that explanation would have called off the wolves.

Keeping a low profile during this heyday of Red-baiting, Chaplin took another five years to launch his next film, the melancholy *Limelight* (1952). Chaplin plays Calvero, an erstwhile music-hall idol whose day has passed, and British actress Claire Bloom (then nineteen) co-stars as Terry, a ballet dancer whom Chaplin saves from a suicide attempt; he shelters, encourages, and finally helps elevate her to the top of her profession, even as his own star dims and then blinks out. Sydney Chaplin and Charlie Jr. both have small parts, and Buster Keaton has a key role as a theater pianist who watches Calvero expire. (*Limelight* would be given an Oscar for its score, to which Chaplin contributed, in 1972, the year the picture received the requisite release in Los Angeles.) The film is vitiated somewhat by a surfeit of self-pity and an excessive running time (almost two-and-a-half hours); nor is its poignancy necessarily preferable to the blackhearted cruelty of *Verdoux*. *Limelight* was not a popular success, and for Chaplin its release was further tainted by the U.S. Immigration Service advising him (as he sailed on an ocean liner with Oona) that he would be denied re-entry to the United States unless willing to face charges "of a political nature and of moral turpitude." The Chaplins continued on their way to England; she returned to the States to close out their business affairs, while he kept going, finally settling in Vevey, Switzerland, where he and Oona would live for the rest of their lives. Chaplin also liquidated his interest in United Artists.

It was to be expected that Chaplin would make use of his own experiences as a victim of McCarthyism in his next film, and in the British-made *A King in New York* (1957), he did. Satirizing the very witch-hunts that sent him into self-imposed exile, Chaplin fashioned a diatribe against the foibles of 1950s America that only occasionally managed to nail its target. Ironically, the film (which featured son Michael Chaplin) wasn't even shown in the United States until 1973, so whatever revenge Chaplin might have been intending to exact was delayed until its blade had been dulled to a safely nostalgic edge. While a Chaplin anthology entitled *The Chaplin Revue* (comprised of the shorts *A Dog's Life*, *Shoulder Arms*, and *The Pilgrim*) was being given a theatrical release in the United States in 1959, Chaplin again retired to Switzerland to lick his wounds and begin work on his memoirs. Published in 1964, *My Autobiography* was a substantial work that provided a great deal of information about Chaplin's childhood and rise to stardom, but which failed (as so many autobiographies do) to examine his work and adult life in a wholly forthcoming manner. Still, the warm reception it was accorded helped rehabilitate Chaplin's unjustly sullied image, and made another film project viable.

The passing of a full decade since *King* and the radical change in the political climate of the United States ensured that there would be much anticipation surrounding *A Countess from Hong Kong* (1967), Chaplin's British-made romantic comedy starring Marlon Brando and Sophia Loren. The media had a sense of how Chaplin had been ignored and abused over the past twenty years, and a torrent of publicity accompanied the film's release, with scenes of Chaplin blocking out scenes with his handsome leads—the biggest names he had had to work with since the days when he himself was a premier box-office draw—played up in newspapers and magazines. But despite that goodwill (and cameo appearances by the Chaplin *frères*), *Countess* proved to be disappointingly flaccid, with the miscast (and mismated) Brando and Loren hitting their marks without ever striking a spark. Still, it was an honorable failure and enabled Chaplin to retire from filmmaking in a dignified fashion.

In his last years Chaplin was accorded many of the honors that had been withheld from him for so long. In 1972 he returned to the United States for the first time in twenty years to accept a special Academy Award for "the incalculable effect he has had on making motion pictures the art form of this century." Three years later, he was knighted by Queen Elizabeth, and was addressed thereafter as Sir Charles Spencer Chaplin for the two last years of his life. However, he will always be remembered not as Sir Charles but as the eternally beloved Little Tramp.

## ● JACK CONWAY (1887-1952)

A classic example of a talent whose efforts were subsumed by the studio system, Jack Conway is best remembered as a house director for MGM, where he toiled from 1925 until his retirement in 1948. While many of the thirty-four sound pictures he made for MGM may have been of less than Oscar caliber, they did feature the pride of the studio—Harlow, Powell, Loy, Robert Taylor, the Barrymores, Turner, Colman, Tracy, Garson, Gable—few of whom had grounds for complaint when Conway's work was finished. And so his reputation as a studio hack seems unwarranted.

Born in Graceville, Minnesota, in 1887, Jack Conway entered the film industry as an actor in 1909, performing in *Her Indian Hero* and *Indian Bill* for the Nestor Studio. After assisting D. W. Griffith on a number of shorts, Conway directed his first film, *The Old Armchair*, in 1913. By 1917 he was directing as many as eight features a year for studios like Triangle, Red Films, Bluebird, and Pathé. In 1921 he landed at Universal, where he stayed for three years, followed by a short stint at Fox. He commenced his long stay at MGM with eight silent features, including *Brown of Harvard* (1926), *Bringing Up Father* (1928), and the Lon Chaney gangster picture *While the City Sleeps* (1928). He made MGM's first sound picture, *Alias Jimmy Valentine*, with William Haines and Lionel Barrymore, in 1928. That experiment was followed by *Our Modern Maidens* (1929), Joan Crawford's last silent, and *Untamed* (1929), her first talkie, in which Joan plays an oil heiress who gets to sing "Chant of the Jungle" to Robert Montgomery.

In 1930, Conway had the distinction of directing Lon Chaney in his only talkie, the remake of Tod Browning's *The Unholy Three*, which proved to be Chaney's last picture. *New Moon* (1930) was a rare musical for Conway, a teaming of opera stars Grace Moore and Lawrence Tibbett, while *The Easiest Way* (1931) was a romantic melodrama starring Constance Bennett and Robert Montgomery. *Just a Gigolo* (1931) was a romantic comedy with William Haines, who also handled the film's art direction. Conway began to hit his stride in 1932, making *Arsene Lupin* with the Barrymore brothers and *But the Flesh Is Weak* with Robert Montgomery. The smash hit *Red-Headed Woman* (1932), became the comeback vehicle that elevated naughty Jean Harlow to unequivocal stardom, with Anita Loos's unblushing script, which was one of the sexiest pre-Code comedies.

Conway's three 1933 releases were unremarkable, but in 1934 he made the fine Harlow showcase *The Girl from Missouri*, with sidekick Patsy Kelly delivering many of Anita Loos's best wisecracks, as well as the exciting *Viva Villa!*, with Wallace Beery as the legendary revolutionary. Conway actually inherited the latter after it had been begun by Howard Hawks, and both the film and Ben Hecht's screenplay were Oscar-nominated. *The Gay Bride* (1934) was a disappointment, considering it starred Carole Lombard as a gold-digging showgirl, while *One New York Night* (1935) was a minor comic mystery that should have been beyond Conway by this point. But *A Tale of Two Cities* (1935) was certainly prestigious enough, a lavish Selznick production with Ronald Colman as Dickens's heroic Sydney Carton and Basil Rathbone and Blanche Yurka as his Reign of Terror nemeses. *Libeled Lady* (1936) was one of the best comedies of the decade, a cleverly plotted romp with Jean Harlow, Spencer Tracy, William Powell, and Myrna Loy all in peak form. (Who needs a supporting cast with those four?) It received a best picture Academy Award nomination, one of ten nominees that year.

Conway directed Harlow again in *Saratoga* (1937) with less happy results; she was dying, though no one knew it, and actually expired before the production was completed, requiring stand-in Mary

Dees to finish several scenes for her. With that bit of history it's hard to watch, despite a fine cast that includes Clark Gable, Walter Pidgeon, and Lionel Barrymore. *A Yank at Oxford* (1938) was a pleasant enough vehicle for Robert Taylor, with Maureen O'Sullivan and Vivien Leigh among his extracurricular studies, while *Too Hot to Handle* (1938) was a first-rate romantic adventure, with Clark Gable and Walter Pidgeon as rival newsreel photographers competing ferociously for both stories and Myrna Loy. *Let Freedom Ring* (1939) set dreaded tough guy Nelson Eddy loose on his town's corrupt bosses, while *Lady of the Tropics* (1939) was a patently ridiculous romance between rich Robert Taylor and half-breed Hedy Lamarr—not much to show for that grandest of cinema years, it's true.

▲ *Conway on the set of* A Yank at Oxford

But Conway rebounded with the lively *Boom Town* (1940), starring Clark Gable, Claudette Colbert, Hedy Lamarr, and Spencer Tracy, who change partners amid the oilfields of the Old West until the right couplings are aligned. *Love Crazy* (1941) was a deft comedy—William Powell is about to be divorced by Myrna Loy until he hits on the notion of making himself appear insane to forestall the proceedings. *Honky-Tonk* had Gable out West again, this time as a gambler romancing proper Lana Turner, while blackmail victim William Powell was married to Hedy Lamarr (for a change) in the suspenseful *Crossroads* (1942). The patriotic *Assignment in Brittany* (1943) suffered from low-wattage stars—Susan Peters, Jean-Pierre Aumont, and Signe Hasso, and casting was also a problem on *Dragon Seed* (1944), with Katharine Hepburn as Pearl Buck's Chinese heroine repelling the Japanese invaders; Conway co-directed it with Harold Bucquet, and one of them made it a half hour too long.

*High Barbaree* (1947) was a mediocre wartime yarn with Van Johnson and June Allyson, but *The Hucksters* (also 1947) was more interesting, a snappy satirical drama (from the bestselling novel) about life on Madison Avenue, with Clark Gable as a no-nonsense ad exec, Deborah Kerr as his object of desire, and Sydney Greenstreet as a loathsome client. Finally there was *Julia Misbehaves* (1948), a playful comedy with Walter Pidgeon and Greer Garson teaming one last time as the bickering parents of about-to-marry Elizabeth Taylor. Not a classic, perhaps, but a good piece of work, such as Conway submitted so many times.

## ● FRANCIS FORD COPPOLA (1939– )

A former Corman alumnus who went on to make one of the biggest-grossing pictures in history, Francis Ford Coppola has fallen on hard critical times since his mid-Seventies heyday. But the commercial success of *Bram Stoker's Dracula* has earned him back at least some of the respect he squandered—and as any viewer of a Coppola film knows, respect is all.

Born in Detroit to a father who played the flute in Toscanini's NBC Symphony Orchestra, Coppola was raised in Westchester in New York State and attended Hofstra before enrolling in U.C.L.A.'s film studies program. One of his projects there was the soft-core sexer *Tonight for Sure* (1961); it was accomplished enough to convince Roger Corman to put the lad to work handling sound, second-unit photography (never with credit), re-editing, and dubbing foreign pickups like *The Magic Voyage of Sinbad* and *Battle Beyond the Sun*, both from Russia. Within a year's time he had impressed Corman sufficiently for AIP to bankroll the $22,000 production *Dementia 13* (1963), a gory horror yarn which Coppola shot in Ireland after helping Corman on another picture in Europe.

After contributing to the scripts of *This Property Is Condemned* and *Is Paris Burning?*, Coppola filmed the coming-of-age gem *You're a Big Boy Now* (1966). It was his master's thesis at U.C.L.A., and presumably earned him an A, if only for his handling of its remarkable cast: Elizabeth Hartman, Karen Black, Rip Torn, Dolph Sweet, Julie Harris, and Geraldine Page. The story is elementary: post-teen Peter Kastner moves to New York City, falls for a coldhearted beauty (Hartman), then finds true love with the loyal Black. Short on plot but rich with incident, the film even had a score by the Lovin' Spoonful—Coppola could pick 'em. Warner Bros. rewarded him for his proficiency by signing him to direct the big-budget musical *Finian's Rainbow* (1968), a Burton Lane–Yip Harburg Broadway hit twenty years earlier, famous for its subversive satire on racism. Now it became an overlong, anachronistic, and underchoreographed bomb, with poor Fred Astaire as an Irishman living in the Deep South whose leprechaun (the execrable Tommy Steele) tracks him down to reclaim his stolen pot o' gold. Long before Senator Keenan Wynn is magically turned black for espousing racism, veteran movie watchers will sense they are witnessing a "disaster," to quote Coppola's assessment of it some years later.

*The Rain People* (1969) was a small "personal" drama, scripted rather portentously by Coppola. Pregnant Long Island housewife Shirley Knight goes AWOL and leaves her husband to take to the road; Along the way she picks up brain-damaged ex-jock James Caan, and they crisscross the United States. Knight has an affair with Nebraska cop Robert Duvall, but Caan goes haywire and is shot to death. A bit pretentious and laden with confusing flashbacks, *People* nonetheless works on an emotional level. Coppola next co-scripted the mega-hit *Patton* (1970) for Franklin Schaffner, earning an Oscar in the process, then helped George Lucas by executive producing on *THX-1138*.

But his breakthrough came with *The Godfather* (1972), Coppola's brilliant, enormously successful, muscular adaptation of Mario Puzo's blockbuster novel. Such is the familiarity of this epic tale of the Mafia's rise in America that today, more than twenty years on, the plot requires no recapitulation. Still one of the top-twenty-five grossing pictures in history, and for a brief time the biggest ever, *The Godfather* was the fifth-biggest movie of the decade, and just may have been the best. It won Academy Awards for best picture, actor (Marlon Brando), and screenplay (Coppola and Puzo), and also earned nominations for Coppola's direction and cast members James Caan, Robert Duvall, and Al Pacino. (Incredibly, neither Nino Rota's evocative score nor Gordon Willis's brooding cinematography were nominated.)

Coppola now was empowered to make a less commercial, more personal film, and that he did with *The Conversation* (1974), a stunning meditation on technology's dehumanizing power. Gene Hackman starred as a surveillance expert who invades others' privacy to earn a living; when he suspects that a couple he has recorded are about to be murdered for conducting an illicit affair, he tries desperately—but futilely—to save them. Too bleak for some tastes, the film is brilliant on every level, from its nihilistic screenplay (written some years back by Coppola) to the acting of John Cazale, Allen Garfield, and, especially, Hackman. Its Oscar nominations included best picture, screenplay, and, fittingly, sound—although the exclusion of Hackman and Coppola by the Academy seems less than astute.

But, then, Coppola only would have been competing with himself for *Godfather II* (also 1974), the sequel he and Puzo concocted with the aim of surpassing their first triumph. And they just may have succeeded, if not in dollars—it grossed less than half as much—then in artistic achievement. Moving both forward in time through the 1950s and back to the early years of the century, *II* bookends *The Godfather* with contrapuntal stories that enrich each other (and, in the process, the original film as well). Robert De Niro plays the young Vito Corleone, taking over Little Italy bit by bit as he ruthlessly ascends to the rank

► *With Robert De Niro during the filming of* The Godfather II

of "family" head, while in the 1950s Al Pacino endeavors (just as ruthlessly) to make the Corleones legit. De Niro, Michael Gazzo, Lee Strasberg—all of whom were nominated for Oscars—collectively compensate for the absence of Brando, and Coppola even found a bit part for old mentor Roger Corman. The film won the best picture Academy Award, which Coppola accepted as producer, and he won two more statues for best direction and (co-) screenplay. De Niro was given his first Academy Award, and the score by Nino Rota and Carmine Coppola, Francis's dad, also won.

Now at the peak of his influence—what other director had had two best picture nominations and two best screenplay nominations in the same year?—Coppola set about the arduous task of filming *Apocalypse Now* (1979), which transposed Joseph Conrad's *Heart of Darkness* to Vietnam. Written by Coppola with John Milius and Michael Herr, this was a troubled production plagued by location miseries (shot on location in the Philippines, it was struck by a typhoon and an earthquake), acts of God (co-star Martin Sheen suffered a heart attack and nearly died), and simple Hollywood hubris: Coppola's original $12 million budget finally exceeded $30 million, much of it due to profligacy (a goodly portion of which he had to restore out of his pocket). The details are reported by Coppola's wife, Eleanor, in her journal *Notes* and in *Hearts of Darkness* (1991), the superb documentary about the film's turbulent making, which incorporates footage shot by Eleanor.

Leaving aside the feeding frenzy the press indulged in when it became clear how royally Coppola had screwed up, the film he delivered is not unimpressive, particularly when Robert Duvall and Frederic Forrest are front and center. As for the section with Brando—well, Coppola had given him his head in *Godfather* and looked like a genius, so he can't be blamed too much for letting the Great One improvise again. Nor was the film a total flop—at $40 million, it was the thirty-second-biggest grossing movie of the 1970s. With Oscar nominations that included best picture, direction, supporting actor (Duvall), and screenplay, neither could it be labeled a critical disaster. But Coppola's reputation as the crown prince of Hollywood directors had been besmirched, possibly forever.

Bowed but not broken, Coppola somehow managed to spend $27 million on the ultra-stylized romantic comedy *One from the Heart* (1982), with Teri Garr and Frederic Forrest as Las Vegas lovers who split up and try new partners (Raul Julia and Nastassia Kinski). Written, produced, and directed by Coppola, it was a total misfire, a failure with both critics and (more seriously) moviegoers that cost him control of his Zoetrope Studio (and nearly his home). Coppola retrenched by adapting a pair of S. E. Hinton novels about troubled adolescents, *The Outsiders* and *Rumble Fish*, both of which were released in 1983. Of the two, the expressionistic, black-and-white *Rumble Fish* is the better, with Matt Dillon and Dennis Hopper as a son and father who can't connect except through blows, and Mickey Rourke as the zenlike older brother who would help Dillon if he could. Adapted by Hinton with Coppola and featuring an experimental-music score by Stewart Copeland of The Police, this is a moving if rather muddled work, with striking performances by a terrific cast (which also includes Diane Lane, Vincent Spano, and Nicolas Cage). But many found it laughable, and few paid to see it.

*The Outsiders*, made first, is less believable and just as pretentious, but it was more popular. A *Rebel Without a Cause* yarn with delusions of being *Gone with the Wind*, it, too, featured Matt Dillon, along with an impressive array of post-teen hunks: Patrick Swayze, Tom Cruise, Ralph Macchio, Rob Lowe, Emilio Estevez, and C. Thomas Howell among them. Diane Lane is also on hand as this Oklahoma town's primary object of desire. But the posturing and melodrama, no doubt intended by Coppola to be operatic in their exaggeration, simply get out of hand. *The Cotton Club* (1984) was his much-anticipated return to big-budget gangsterdom, but this time Coppola's reach exceeded his grasp. Stylish, well cast, and opulent, this is a classic case of a film undone by careless scripting (credit Coppola, William Kennedy, and Mario Puzo for the incoherent storytelling) and production distractions (well documented by the press in uncountable stories). Despite the inadequacies of leads Richard Gere and Diane Lane, *Club* has a strong supporting cast and splendidly re-creates 1930s Harlem, enhanced by the evocative music of Duke Ellington.

*Peggy Sue Got Married* (1985) was an oddball, atypical effort for Coppola. Unhappily married Kathleen Turner is transported back to her senior year in high school, where she gets a second chance to evaluate her awful husband (Nicolas Cage at his most grating). Less plot-driven than that year's similar *Back to the Future*, this quirky film wants to be better than it is. Still, it possesses moments of brilliance, thanks in no small part to Turner's astonishing impersonation of a seventeen-year-old. The more somber *Gardens of Stone* (1987) was a well-conceived portrait of the soldiers assigned to Arlington National Cemetery during the Vietnam War, with James Caan as the sergeant in charge of the Guard, Anjelica Huston as his girlfriend, and D. B. Sweeney as the gung-ho kid whose wish to fight overseas is tragically granted. Coppola suffered through both poor reviews and box office on this; worse, his son Giancarlo perished in a boating accident during its making.

*Tucker: The Man and His Dream* (1988) fared no better commercially, but this handsome biopic was Coppola's best film in years. Jeff Bridges plays the visionary car designer whose superior product (the "Tucker Tornado") is squelched through the collusion of Detroit's giant manufacturers and their Washington lobbyists; Martin Landau is terrific as Tucker's partner. (Some noted that Coppola could identify with the brilliant artist/craftsman whose work was undermined by crass philistines.) Coppola contributed the "Life without Zoe" segment to *New York Stories* (1989), but it was far weaker than Martin Scorsese's and Woody Allen's.

Coppola and Mario Puzo were invited by Paramount to submit another installment of the *Godfather* saga, and the result was *The Godfather, Part III* (1990). While surely not in the league of the first two pictures—particularly in regard to its diffuse, overlong story—it does possess some merit. Also, there is a splendid cast that includes Al Pacino, Andy Garcia, Diane Keaton, Talia Shire, Joe Mantegna, and Eli Wallach. But there is also Sophia Coppola, his daughter, in a key role; a last-minute replacement for Winona Ryder, she simply is lost at sea. The decent box office of *III* helped Coppola get the big-budget *Bram Stoker's Dracula* (1992) made. A florid, bloody, occasionally silly, violently erotic version of the oft-filmed tale with eccentric Brit Gary Oldham as the Count and Ryder as his (possibly) reincarnated love, it's easily the most faithful and horrific version of the Stoker novel. But what audiences remember are the film's peerless sets, makeup, and costumes, all of which won Oscars. It also returned Coppola, at long last, to bankability—Hollywood's enduring mark of respect.

## ● ROGER CORMAN (1926- )

It's not every director who can look at the movies he made and recollect how many *days* it took to shoot each one, rather than weeks or months; but on just such expediency is the reputation of Roger Corman based. The drive-in staples he directed in the Fifties and Sixties have earned him the reputation among cultists as the D. W. Griffith of the exploitation picture—but his contributions as a producer and mentor to young, unproven talent may be his more significant legacy, giving starts as he did to the likes of Francis Ford Coppola, Jack Nicholson, Martin Scorsese, Peter Bogdanovich, and Jonathan Demme.

Born in Detroit, Corman earned an engineering degree at Stanford before serving in the Navy for three years, then worked briefly for Twentieth Century-Fox as a reader before moving to England for postgraduate work in literature at Oxford. He then returned to Hollywood to work as a screenwriter, and by 1955 was ready to both produce and direct his own pictures. Corman's first efforts at "B"-picture factories American International Pictures (AIP) and Allied Artists were ultra-low-budget Westerns like *Apache Woman*, *Five Guns West* (both 1955), and *The Oklahoma Woman* (1956); science-fiction/monster pictures like *The Day the World Ended* and *It Conquered the World*; and "bad girl" melodramas like *Swamp Women* (all 1956), *Teenage Doll*, and *Sorority Girl* (both 1957).

Since most of Corman's early work was shot in less than a week, the films tended to have better poster art than content—in fact, several of the stories were developed *from* the poster art. But there is some merit in the 1957 SF thrillers *Attack of the Crab Monsters* and *Not of This Earth*, which Allied Artists released on a double bill. On the other hand, *Rock All Night*, *The Viking Women and the Sea Serpent* (also 1957), *The She-Gods of Shark Reef* and *Teenage Caveman* (both 1958) are absolutely the pits. *War of the Satellites* was a passable SF quickie starring Corman regular Dick Miller, and *Machine Gun Kelly* (also 1958) gave Charles Bronson a good role as the notorious 1930s bank robber. *I, Mobster* (also 1958) was a less successful crime yarn.

But Corman at the same time made two of his best pictures, the beatnik chiller *A Bucket of Blood* (also 1959) and *The Little Shop of Horrors* (1960). Both were written by Charles Griffith, and *Shop* was shot in less than three days on a leftover set; both are genuinely original masterpieces of horrific humor, and the latter features a memorable cameo by Jack Nicholson. *The Wasp Woman* (1960), in which star Susan Cabot gets some of the worst makeup of the decade, was basically awful. The post-apocalypse yarn *The Last Woman on Earth* (also 1960) was written by Robert Towne, whom Corman also drafted as an actor, but Towne disguised both contributions under the pseudonym "Edward Wain."

Corman cast himself as a skier in his cheapo World War II opus *Ski Troop Attack*, but *The House of Usher* (both 1960) was a fine, stylish mounting of the Edgar Allan Poe story, with excellent production values. Vincent Price is at the top of his game as the hypersensitive Roderick Usher. "Edward Wain" (aka Robert Towne) appeared again as both actor and screenwriter in the pitiable *Creature from the Haunted Sea*, and the cheesy *Atlas* (both 1961), filmed in Greece, demonstrated that Corman's strength wasn't mythological spectacles. *The Intruder* (1961) was a serious parable about race relations, with William Shatner as a rabble-rousing racist in the South, while *The Pit and the Pendulum* (also 1961) was a splendid rendering of Poe's classic chiller, scripted by Richard Matheson and starring Vincent Price and the formidable Barbara Steele. *The Premature Burial* (1962), starring Ray Milland as the claustrophobic protagonist, was the only one of Corman's Poe adaptations not to star Vincent Price.

*Tales of Terror* (also 1962), Richard Matheson's

adaptation of three of Poe's best stories (including "The Black Cat"), featured Price alongside veteran character actors Basil Rathbone and Peter Lorre; Price also starred in *Tower of London* (1962), an inferior remake of the 1939 period chiller. The delightful spoof *The Raven* (scripted by Matheson) offered Price, Boris Karloff, and Peter Lorre as fifteenth-century sorcerers (Jack Nicholson also had a bit role), while *The Terror* (both 1963) used *The Raven*'s leftover sets and leftover actors Nicholson and Karloff for a hastily invented ghost story that was filmed in three days; Francis Ford Coppola and Nicholson also directed parts of the picture.

Corman's productive 1963 continued with three more features: *X—The Man with the X-Ray Eyes*, in which scientist Ray Milland goes a little too far in probing life's little mysteries; *The Haunted Palace*, based on an H. P. Lovecraft novel and starring Vincent Price as the possessed ancestor of a warlock who'd been burned at the stake; and the Grand Prix racing yarn *The Young Racers*, filmed on location while Corman was vacationing in Europe. After making the World War II adventure *The Secret Invasion* in Yugoslavia, Corman directed *The Masque of the Red Death* (both 1964); adapted by Charles Beaumont, it was another eerie Poe tale starring Vincent Price, who this time finds himself cast as an evil, devil-worshipping prince in twelfth-century Italy (the film was actually shot in England and took an atypically long five weeks to complete). *The Tomb of Ligea* (1965) was the last of Corman's Poe cycle; written by Robert Towne, it predictably starred Vincent Price as a nineteenth-century nobleman whose late wife's spirit seems to be taking over the personality of his new bride.

Few of Corman's subsequent efforts would attain the same level of quality as those period pictures. *The Wild Angels* (1966) was a sordid biker pic based on the exploits of the Hell's Angels, who supplied screenwriter Charles Griffith with anecdotes. Peter Fonda, Bruce Dern, and Nancy Sinatra starred, all of whom probably get a good laugh out of it now, but the film did have a good sound track. *The St. Valentine's Day Massacre* (1967) was a relatively faithful

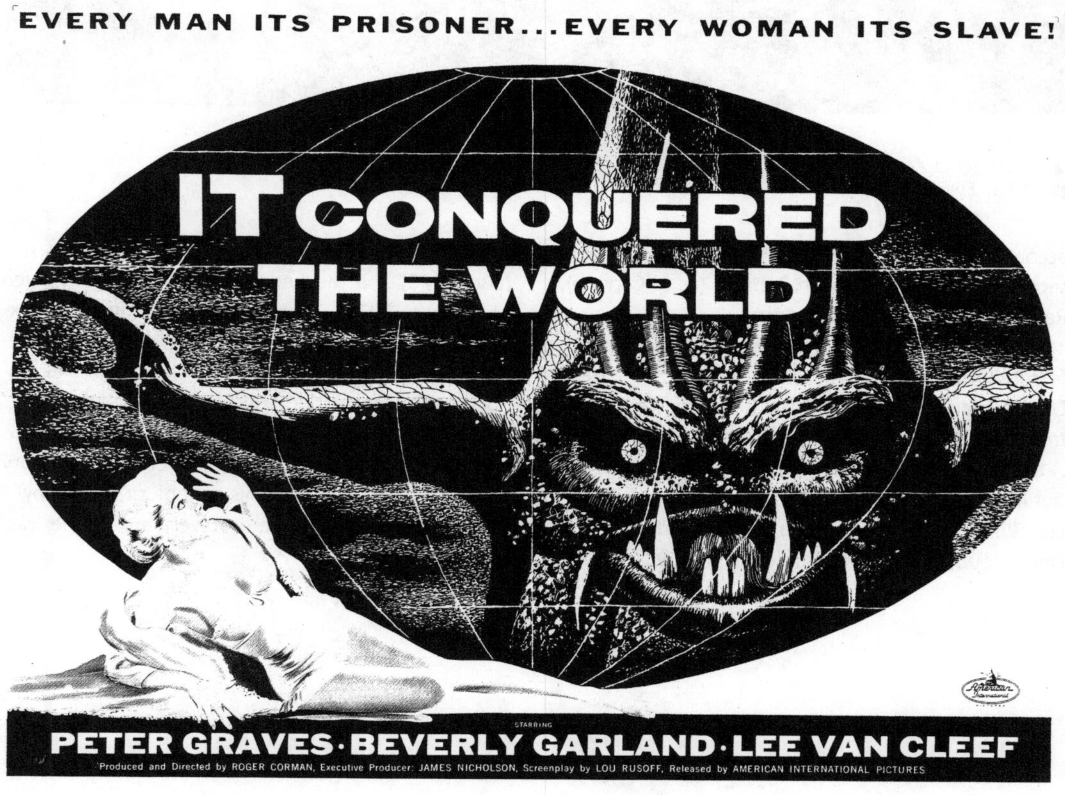

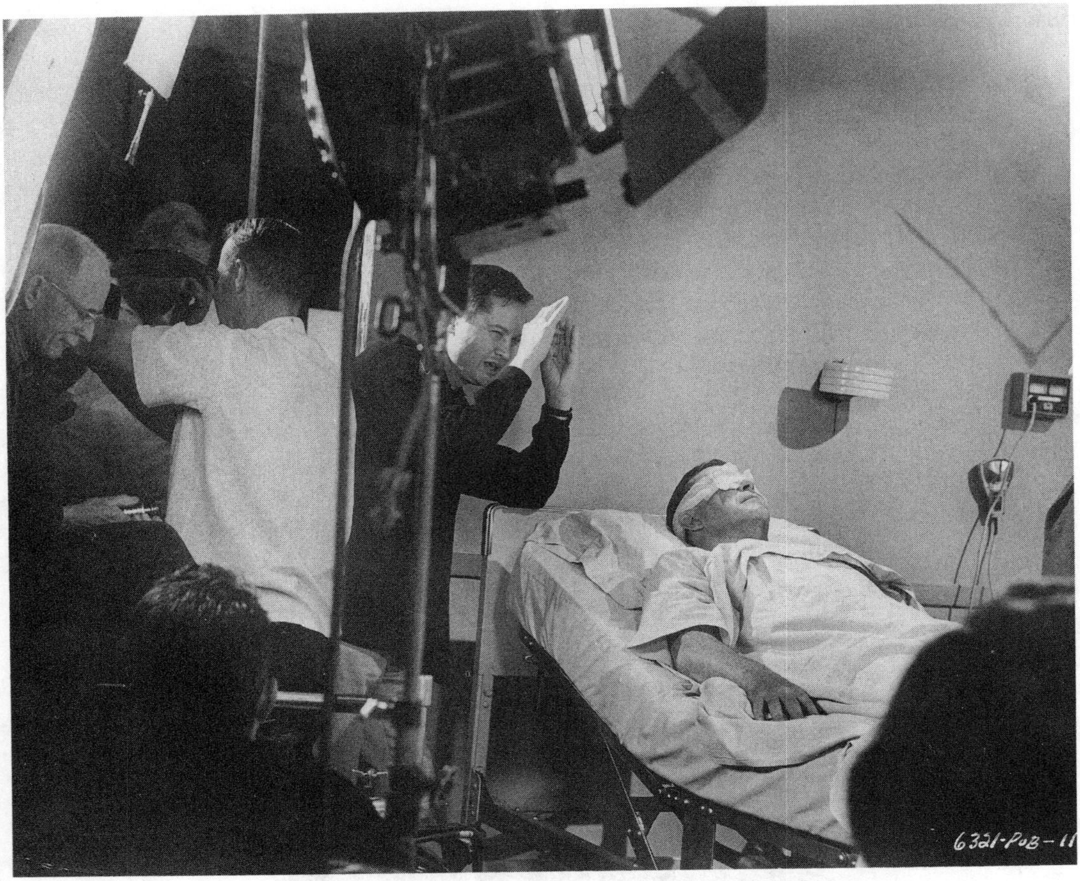


▲ *On the Set of* X—The Man with the X-Ray Eyes *with Ray Milland*

account of the notorious 1929 slaughter, starring such upscale actors as Jason Robards (as Al Capone), Ralph Meeker, and George Segal.

*The Trip* (also 1967), written by Jack Nicholson, featured Peter Fonda, Susan Strasberg, and Bruce Dern as acid heads who share in Fonda's very bad trip: "Touch the Scream That Crawls up the Wall!" is the way the ads put it. *Bloody Mama* was a violent but lousy portrayal of the Ma Barker story, with Shelley Winters a believable Ma and Robert De Niro, Don Stroud, and Robert Walden as her twisted sons. After directing the counterculture SF opus *Gas-s-s-s* (also 1970) and the Red Baron yarn *Von Richthofen and Brown* (1971), Corman restricted himself to executive producing and distributing. In 1990 he returned to direct *(Roger Corman's) Frankenstein Unbound*, a disappointing version of the horror classic, starring Raul Julia as the mad doctor, John Hurt as a time-traveling scientist, and Bridget Fonda as Mary Shelley. That same year his autobiography, *How I Made a Hundred Movies and Never Lost a Dime*, was published.

## ● JOHN CROMWELL (1888–1979)

He was forty before he ever worked in Hollywood, but that still left John Cromwell sufficient time to direct some forty-five films, a total that is all the more remarkable for his having spent most of his post-1951 career blacklisted. His filmography is impressive enough to raise the question of why Cromwell was never nominated for an Academy Award.

Born in Toledo, Ohio, as Elwood Dager, Cromwell began acting on the stage while still in his teens, and was appearing on Broadway by 1910. He assumed the Cromwell moniker in 1912, around the time he began acting and directing for the New York Repertory Company. His entire career might have been played out on the stage but for a touring production of the crime drama *The Racket* that showcased him along with Edward G. Robinson in Los Angeles. The exposure got him an offer from Paramount to become a dialogue director, but only a year later Cromwell was co-directing his first feature, *Close Harmony* (1929), with Eddie Sutherland. They also collaborated on *The Dance of Life* (1929), and then Cromwell was on his own. His first solo projects were *The Mighty* (1929) with George Bancroft and *Street of Chance* (1930), one of Jean Arthur's first talkies. (Cromwell had bit parts in both.)

He directed four pictures for Paramount in 1930, including the Jackie Coogan version of *Tom Sawyer* and *The Texan* with Gary Cooper. There were four more in 1931, notably *Scandal Sheet* and *Vice Squad*, both with Kay Francis. *The World and the Flesh* (1932) had George Bancroft coming to the aid of Miriam Hopkins during the Russian Revolution; it was utter nonsense. That was Cromwell's last work for the studio, as a rift developed over his next picture that culminated with him walking off the lot for good. He quickly was signed by RKO, which was reeling from the sudden exit of George Cukor, and he was put to work on the Edna Ferber story *Sweepings* with Lionel Barrymore, Gloria Stuart, and Gregory Ratoff, and *The Silver Cord* (both 1933), a romantic drama with Irene Dunne and Joel McCrea. *Ann Vickers* (1933) was an adaptation of the Sinclair Lewis novel, with judge Walter Huston vying with Bruce Cabot for prison reformer Irene Dunne's affections; *Double Harness* (also 1933) was a snappy comedy starring William Powell and an atypically unrefined Ann Harding.

*Spitfire* (1934) was an utter disaster, with Bryn Mawr's Katharine Hepburn absurdly miscast as Ozarks tomboy Trigger Hicks, who falls for suave (and married) city slicker Robert Young. *This Man Is Mine* (1934) wasn't much better—pure soap, with Irene Dunne struggling to win the love of Ralph Bellamy. But *Of Human Bondage* (also 1934) was a revelation, a gritty adaptation of the Somerset Maugham novel; incredibly, neither the picture, Cromwell, nor star Bette Davis was nominated for an Academy Award. (At least Davis had it made up to her in the 1935 awards.) *The Fountain* (1934) was another Ann Harding "women's picture," which is to say an antiquated tearjerker now barely endurable as a viewing experience, while *Village Tale* (1935) had Randolph Scott trying to take Kay Johnson away from loutish husband Arthur Hohl.

*Jalna* was a busy family drama set on a Canadian farm with Kay Johnson, Ian Hunter, and Nigel Bruce, while *I Dream Too Much* (both 1935) had real-life opera star Lily Pons playing a French peasant who falls in love with opera conductor (!) Henry Fonda. David O. Selznick, who now had formed his own production company, hired Cromwell to direct *Little Lord Fauntleroy* (1936), a tasteful if slightly cloying treatment of the popular novel, with Freddie Bartholomew and Mickey Rooney. Cromwell went to Fox to make *To Mary—With Love*, a marital drama starring Myrna Loy and Warner Baxter, and *Banjo on My Knee* (both 1936), an enjoyable riverboat musical with

THE GREATEST NOVEL OF THE TWENTIETH CENTURY NOW BRINGS TO THE SCREEN HUMANITY'S TORTURED HEART-CRY!
LESLIE HOWARD
IN
"Of Human Bondage"
By W. Somerset MAUGHAM
The story of a man who burnt up his soul for an idol cold as ice! . . . with
BETTE DAVIS
FRANCES DEE · KAY JOHNSON
REGINALD DENNY
AN RKO-RADIO PICTURE
Directed by John Cromwell
A Pandro S. Berman Production

Barbara Stanwyck and Joel McCrea. This was the beginning of Cromwell's own personal golden age, signaled by his classic adaptation of *The Prisoner of Zenda* (1937) for Selznick, in which Ronald Colman and Douglas Fairbanks, Jr., are at their most dashing. The best of the five versions of the story set to celluloid, it compares well to the top Errol Flynn swashbucklers.

*Algiers* (1938) was a good Hollywoodization of the Duvivier classic *Pepe Le Moko*; if not quite at the level of the original, it was still a fine entertainment, starring Hedy Lamarr (in her American screen debut). Charles Boyer, as the small-time crook hiding out from the law, earned an Oscar nomination. *Made for Each Other* (1939) was a classy tearjerker, with James Stewart and Carole Lombard, while *In Name Only* (1939) was virtually a companion piece, with Lombard this time trying to extract true love Cary Grant from the clutches of his evil wife, Kay Francis. (Coincidentally, Charles Coburn plays the dad in both pictures, which were made for different studios.) *Abe Lincoln in Illinois* (1940) was based on the Pulitzer Prize–winning play, with an Oscar-nominated performance by Raymond Massey as the great man; Ruth Gordon was Mary Todd Lincoln and Cromwell played John Brown. *Victory* (1940), from Conrad's novel, was somewhat less successful, although Fredric March was excellent as the island loner who is forced to fight for his life.

*So Ends Our Night* (1941) starred March again, this time in a fine thriller about a German trying to escape his homeland as Nazi agents pursue him, while *Son of Fury* (1942) was one of Tyrone Power's best costume pictures; beauteous Gene Tierney supplies the love interest and George Sanders the villainy. Cromwell then was reunited with Selznick for his prestigious *Since You Went Away* (1944), a lengthy but exquisite rendering of a family's trials and tribulations during the war years (Selznick scripted it himself). It was nominated for a best picture Academy Award, and Claudette Colbert was also cited; of course, Cromwell's name never came up. The haunting *The Enchanted Cottage* (1945) was much more modest, a love story with fantasy elements that starred Dorothy McGuire and Robert Young.

*Anna and the King of Siam* was one of the big releases of 1946, an elaborate production of the real-life story of a British governess (Irene Dunne) who dares to challenge the ruler of Siam (Rex Harrison). Unfortunately, this film has been almost completely overshadowed by Walter Lang's 1956 musical remake, *The King and I*. *Dead Reckoning* (1947) was quite a change of pace for Cromwell, a solid film noir in which Humphrey Bogart is betrayed in high style by femme fatale Lizabeth Scott, Columbia's answer to Lauren Bacall. He had gone more than ten years without a misfire, an incredible streak that even the greatest directors would be hard-pressed to match, but *Night Song* (1947), a ridiculous yarn that dared to present hard-boiled Dana Andrews as a blind concert pianist, ended Cromwell's run. He rebounded in 1950 with *Caged*, one of the best (and most harrowing) of the women's prison pictures; Eleanor Parker is cast against type as the new inmate who must learn the ropes, a performance that earned her a best actress Academy Award nomination.

Returning to RKO, Cromwell made *The Company She Keeps* (1951), with Lizabeth Scott as a parole officer and Jane Greer as an ex-con who have both set their sights on Dennis O'Keefe. *The Racket* (1951), with Scott, Robert Mitchum, and Robert Ryan, was a passable remake of Milestone's early talkie with Louis Wolheim; it must have been a special treat for

Cromwell to direct this, an updating of the play that he and Edward G. Robinson had acted in back in 1928. (Reportedly, Nicholas Ray directed some of the scenes in the film.)

But in the heat of the House Un-American Activities Committee's (HUAC's) Hollywood witchhunts, Cromwell's career soured. Howard Hughes accused him of being a Communist, and although the charge was patently false, Cromwell was blacklisted. Unable to work in motion pictures, he returned to the stage, where he performed on Broadway as Henry Fonda's father in *Point of No Return*. He would not direct a film again until 1958, when he made the interesting *The Goddess*, Paddy Chayevsky's dissection of the Marilyn Monroe phenomenon, with Kim Stanley as a troubled actress. *The Scavengers* (1959) was his last Hollywood film; a movie made in Sweden in 1961 followed, after which Cromwell moved to Minneapolis and performed at the Guthrie Theater. Late in life he returned to the screen as an actor in Robert Altman's *Three Women* (1977) and *A Wedding* (1978).

## GEORGE CUKOR (1899-1983)

It's hard to believe that a director with as many acknowledged masterpieces under his belt as George Cukor could have won only a single Academy Award (and that for one of his least interesting films) while making more than fifty movies over the course of a half century. But as an "actor's director," he was sometimes given less than full credit for the visual elegance of his films. Today it is clear that his body of work places him among the top ten Hollywood directors, and that in the handling of actors—many of whom gave their greatest performances for him—he was second to none.

Born in New York City, Cukor began his career in show business as the assistant stage manager of a theater troupe in Chicago before he was twenty. He worked for the Shuberts on Broadway, and spent summers in Rochester, New York, as the resident director of a stock company. Working under Gilbert Miller, he directed Broadway productions of *The Great Gatsby* and *The Constant Wife* with such stars as Jeanne Eagels and Ethel Barrymore. He was invited to Hollywood in 1929 along with many other Broadway directors (probably at the suggestion of Rouben Mamoulian) to handle dialogue for Lewis Milestone's *All Quiet on the Western Front*. Paramount then signed him to co-direct three features out of their Astoria studio in Queens—*Grumpy*, *The Virtuous Sin*, and, best of all, *The Royal Family of Broadway* (all 1930), from the Ferber-Kaufman stage hit; Cukor was put in charge of the actors and Cyril Gardner handled the technical camerawork. *Tarnished Lady* (1931), a glossy soap opera with stage star Tallulah Bankhead and Clive Brook, was his first solo effort, while *Girls about Town* (1931), starring Kay Francis and Joel McCrea, was the kind of naughty comedy that the Code would soon render extinct.

Cukor's next film was the Jeanette MacDonald–Maurice Chevalier musical romance *One Hour with You* (1932), but in the midst of filming, producer Ernst Lubitsch decided to take an active role. To Cukor's fury Lubitsch ended up with the "Directed by" credit after an acrimonious arbitration battle that ultimately left Cukor free to follow his friend David O. Selznick to RKO. There he made *What Price Hollywood?* (1932), the fine precursor to *A Star Is Born*, with Constance Bennett as the Brown Derby waitress who rises to acting stardom while her alcoholic mentor (Lowell Sherman) plummets into disgrace. The Broadway drama *A Bill of Divorcement* (1932) came next, with Katharine Hepburn (in her movie debut) as the daughter of an escaped mental patient, played with great sensitivity by John Barrymore. (Hepburn and Cukor would collaborate again nine times.) *Rockabye* (1932) was just a corny melodrama with Constance Bennett and Joel McCrea, while *Our Betters* (1933) used Bennett again as a rich American who marries a British lord (Gilbert Roland, who later *did* marry Bennett). It was adapted from a Somerset Maugham play, indicating early on Cukor's preference for filming theatrical properties.

He made *Dinner at Eight* (1933) at MGM, adapting the brilliant Kaufman-Ferber play with great aplomb. The star-studded cast included Jean Harlow, Wallace Beery, Marie Dressler, and the Barrymore brothers, making it a *Grand Hotel* with laughs. That triumph was followed by the splendid *Little Women* (also 1933), with Katharine Hepburn, Joan Bennett, Jean Parker, and Francis Dee as Alcott's sisters Jo, Amy, Beth, and Meg. It was a major box-office success and earned Cukor his first Academy Award nomination for best direction. Following Selznick to MGM, Cukor directed *David Copperfield* (1935), one of the best adaptations of Dickens ever brought to the screen, with a delightful cast that included W. C. Fields, Basil Rathbone, Edna May Oliver, and Elsa

Lanchester. It, too, was Oscar-nominated as best picture, further establishing Cukor's credentials as one of Hollywood's premier young talents.

*Sylvia Scarlett* reunited Cukor with Hepburn, but this gender-bender was perhaps a bit *too* offbeat for moviegoers in 1935, with Cary Grant as a Cockney con artist in Victorian times who takes a disguised Hepburn under his wing, believing her to be a boy. Although expertly played, the film's sexual ambiguity apparently made audiences uncomfortable, and it was RKO's biggest flop that year. (This helped Hepburn earn the sobriquet of "box-office poison.") *Romeo and Juliet* (1936) was one of Irving Thalberg's last productions, a handsome version of the classic that managed to overcome the casting of thirty-something Norma Shearer and forty-something Leslie Howard as the star-crossed youths; both the film and Shearer were nominated for Oscars. *Camille* (1937) was a gorgeously mounted production of the Dumas tale, with Garbo (in an Oscar-nominated performance) at her most incandescent as the noble, tuberculosis-racked courtesan—

although Robert Taylor as Armand was just barely able to keep up.

*Holiday* (1938) was lighter fare, a bright adaptation of Philip Barry's Broadway success, with Hepburn and Grant delightfully paired as the would-be lovers who must defy convention—and New York City society—in order to be together. (Hepburn had understudied the role on Broadway a decade earlier.) But *Zaza* (1939) was a rare misfire for Cukor, a version of the old chestnut (last filmed in 1923 with Gloria Swanson), with Claudette Colbert as a French music-hall performer. Colbert was coached by Fanny Brice for her singing and by silent star Nazimova as well, but the results were uneven. Far superior was *The Women* (1939), a wholly enjoyable adaptation of Clare Boothe's bitch-fest with a once-in-a-lifetime, all-female cast that included Joan Crawford, Rosalind Russell, Norma Shearer, Joan Fontaine, Paulette Goddard, and Hedda Hopper.

Cukor would have been credited with a third 1939 release had he not been unceremoniously relieved of his command on *Gone with the Wind* at Clark Gable's insistence earlier in the year, despite having worked on preproduction for the film since 1937. (Their differing sexual preferences were reported to be at the root of Gable's pressure on Selznick; Gable's hunting pal Victor Fleming was installed in Cukor's stead.) But *The Philadelphia Story* (1940) helped relieve that ignominy, with Hepburn repeating her stage role opposite Cary Grant and James Stewart, creating one of the cinema's most delightful love triangles. Hepburn herself had shepherded the Philip Barry play—which had been written for her, and in which she had performed more than four hundred times—into MGM's and Cukor's hands, and the result was serendipity. Cukor, Hepburn, Ruth Hussey, and the picture were all Oscar-nominated, with James Stewart and Donald Ogden Stewart's screenplay the film's two winners; Hepburn lost to Ginger Rogers in *Kitty Foyle* (an outrageous choice), while the best direction award went to John Ford.

*Susan and God* (1940), from the Rachel Crothers play, had been a success on Broadway with Gertrude Lawrence, but Joan Crawford was out of her depth as the upper-cruster comically possessed by a religious conversion. Crawford fared better in *A Woman's Face* (1941), a rare foray by Cukor into the crime genre; the story had been filmed with Ingrid Bergman in Sweden in 1937. Here Joan was a terribly scarred woman who had undergone plastic surgery but whose criminal past (in the form of Conrad Veidt) continued to haunt her. *Two-Faced Woman* (1941) reunited Cukor and his beloved Garbo, but at what cost? Passing through many hands and out of Cukor's long before the final cut, this supposedly sprightly comedy about a woman who pretends to be her own sister in order to spy on husband Melvyn Douglas, thudded along, marching Garbo straight into what proved to be a permanent retirement. To add insult to injury, it was condemned by the Legion of Decency and had to be reshot.

*Her Cardboard Lover* (1942) was even worse, a creaking adaptation of a play directed by Cukor fifteen years earlier; it, too, ended a career—that of star Norma Shearer. (Not an enviable record for someone tagged, albeit against his will, as a "woman's director.") Cukor's final film before enlisting in the armed services was *Keeper of the Flame* (1942), a strained, atypically grim vehicle for Spencer Tracy and Katharine Hepburn, with Tracy as a reporter who uncovers the secret Fascist activities of a beloved figure who has just died. After this string of disappointments, Cukor might have welcomed his stint in the Army, but he entered the Signal Corps as a lowly private, where he made unadorned instructional films (including one about latrines and another about electricity). He was never promoted to the officer status he desired, and finally applied for a discharge.

Happy to be back in Hollywood, Cukor filmed *Gaslight* (1944), his acclaimed adaptation of the Broadway success *Angel Street*, which had been filmed in England only four years earlier by Thorold Dickinson. But American audiences were unfamiliar with that version, and Cukor was able to fashion this gothic thriller into an Oscar-winning showcase for Ingrid Bergman; Angela Lansbury (in her film debut), the screenplay, the art direction, and the film itself were also nominated. *Winged Victory* (1944) was a collaboration with Moss Hart, whose purply patriotic play about the training of young pilots Cukor inherited when William Wyler had to withdraw. The ill-fated *Desire Me*, with Robert Mitchum and Greer Garson, was ultimately released in 1947 without any director's credit after Cukor abandoned it and asked to have his name removed; Mervyn LeRoy and Jack Conway completed it but didn't want their names attached, either.

*A Double Life* (1947) brought happier results; Ronald Colman won his only Academy Award for his

◀ *Cukor offers Lana Turner a snack on the set of* A Life of Her Own

portrayal of a high-strung actor whose role as Othello begins to take over his real life as well. Ruth Gordon and Garson Kanin wrote the Oscar-nominated screenplay, inaugurating a series of collaborations between them and Cukor. *Edward, My Son* (1949), filmed in England, was an artificial drama, with Spencer Tracy and Deborah Kerr (Oscar-nominated) as an unhappy couple whose son commits suicide. But the Gordon Kanin yarn *Adam's Rib* provided Cukor with one of his strongest properties, and he turned this riotously funny battle of the sexes into what may be the best Tracy-Hepburn teaming. A high-water mark for Cukor as well, neither the film nor the principals were nominated for Academy Awards in any category, the sort of oversight that seemed to plague Cukor throughout his career.

The regrettable *A Life of Her Own* (1950) was a second-rate Lana Turner sudser that exhibited little involvement on Cukor's part, but *Born Yesterday* (also 1950) was a sparkling adaptation of the hit Garson Kanin play that allowed Judy Holliday to reprise her stage role of dumb-like-a-fox Billie Dawn (she had performed it on Broadway over 1,600 times). It won Holliday an Oscar, and earned nominations for the picture, the screenplay, and Cukor. *The Model and the Marriage-Broker* (1951) is less well remembered, but it, too, has its charms; Thelma Ritter is most appealing as the marriage broker who puts model Jeanne Crain together with hospital worker Scott Brady. The Garson Kanin script for *The Marrying Kind* (1952) was far darker, as Judy Holliday and Aldo Ray recollect their happier times while poised on the brink of divorce.

This was followed by the sunny *Pat and Mike* (1952), with Tracy and Hepburn again splendid as, respectively, low-class sports promoter Mike and high-class, multitalented athlete Pat; the hilarious Gordon Kanin screenplay earned them another Academy Award nomination. *The Actress* (1953) was based on Ruth Gordon's autobiographical play about growing up in Massachusetts, but the casting of Spencer Tracy as her insensitive father and Brit Jean Simmons as the teenaged Gordon didn't really click, and the film was a box-office failure. From solo Ruth Gordon, Cukor proceeded to solo Garson Kanin with *It Should Happen to You* (1954), a pleasing fairy tale featuring Judy Holliday as the ambitious Gladys Glover, who comes to New York City to make a name for herself and rents a billboard space to get things started. Although Kanin was unhappy with the final film, it's really quite good, with equal portions of comedy, romance, and satire (target: the advertising industry).

*A Star Is Born* (1954) has taken on the patina of legend, despite (or because of) its problems during filming (and they were legion) and its flaws as released—Warners cut 27 minutes after the premiere. Now partially restored, this watershed musical drama owns a high spot in the filmographies of both Judy Garland and George Cukor. His first Tech-

▲ *Rehearsing Audrey Hepburn during* My Fair Lady



nicolor (and CinemaScope) production, Cukor worked with screenwriter Moss Hart to transform the 1937 version of *Star* into a harrowing Hollywood odyssey. It's punctuated by wonderful Harold Arlen–Ira Gershwin songs, the best of which is "The Man That Got Away," one of the all-time great torch songs. Jack Carson is terrific as a hard-boiled press agent, and James Mason and Judy Garland were both Oscar-nominated. Garland's loss to Grace Kelly (for *The Country Girl*) the night of the Academy Awards remains a key part of Judy's mystique as a hard-luck loser.

*Bhowani Junction* (1956) was beautifully photographed on location in India, with Ava Gardner as a half-caste whose affair with British officer Stewart Granger is fated for tragedy; in the end the spectacle and anti-Communist politics overwhelmed the love story. Cukor returned to the stage for the only time to direct *The Chalk Garden* in 1955, although he was abruptly fired from the production by producer Irene Selznick while it was still in out-of-town tryouts after it became clear that he had lost his knack for staging a play. The highly stylized *Les Girls* (1957) had Cukor returning to the musical, with Mitzi Gaynor, Taina Elg, and Kay Kendall testifying to French magistrate Henry Daniell about the cad who romanced them all: Gene Kelly.

*Wild Is the Wind* (1957) was an overheated, underscripted soap opera starring Anthony Quinn, Anna Magnani, and Tony Franciosa, and *Heller in Pink Tights* (1960) a rather formless (if colorful) Western—the only one ever attempted by Cukor—that sent Sophia Loren and her theatrical troupe off to the Pecos. *Let's Make Love* (1960) offered Marilyn Monroe the opportunity to sing, dance, and romance co-star Yves Montand, and Cukor extracts one of her best performances (too bad he didn't work with her at least a few more times). He gallantly completed the Liszt biopic *Song without End* (also 1960) for the suddenly deceased Charles Vidor without taking screen credit, although he reshot the entire film; then he made *The Chapman Report* (1962), adapting Irving Wallace's slick, trashy bestseller about a team of sex-institute researchers who find every case history they could dream of in the suburbs. Its female stars were excellent—Claire Bloom (as the nympho), Jane Fonda, Glynis Johns, Shelley Winters—but what was Cukor to do with Efrem Zimbalist, Jr.? As had happened with so many of Cukor's projects, it was edited and completed without his presence or approval, and he finally disowned it.

*Something's Got to Give*, a remake of Garson Kanin's great 1940 comedy *My Favorite Wife*, would have been Cukor's next film, but insoluble problems with Marilyn Monroe culminated with Fox firing her, and the production soon shut down entirely. (She died two months later.) But *My Fair Lady* enjoyed a far more pleasant fate, winning the Academy Award as the best picture of 1964, as well as the New York Film Critics Award. Oscars also went to Rex Harrison, André Previn's scoring, the art direction (color), Cecil Beaton's costume design, and—at long last—Cukor. (Ironically, top-billed Audrey Hepburn wasn't even nominated, while the actress who played the part of Eliza five thousand times on stage, Julie Andrews, won the Oscar for *Mary Poppins*.) Far from Cukor's best film or even his best musical, *Lady* was a by-the-numbers presentation of the Lerner-Loewe blockbuster that offers little in the way of invention or personality but oceans of artificiality. When all's said and done, it's something of a dinosaur, with a bland star turn by Audrey Hepburn. Still, it was the first box-office triumph for Cukor in many, many years.

Over the next seventeen years, Cukor made just six more films, two of them for television. He was called in to rescue *Justine* (1969) for Fox, after a five-year period of unrealized projects; this ambitious attempt to capture Lawrence Durrell's *Alexandria Quartet* on film was shot in Tunis with a motley cast but came off surprisingly well. *Travels with My Aunt* (1972), a quirky version of the Graham Greene book, was made in Spain with Maggie Smith (who ended up nominated for an Oscar) after the vacillating Katharine Hepburn was removed from the film by MGM just days before filming was scheduled to begin. Oddly, the script was mostly written by Hepburn, who was denied screen credit. But Cukor was soon able to work again with his old friend on the television production of *Love Among the Ruins* (1975), a romantic comedy shot in England in six weeks with Hepburn and Laurence Olivier. It was a triumph for all involved, winning Emmy Awards for Cukor, Hepburn, Olivier, and writer James Costigan.

But Cukor was only briefly able to bask in his great notices. His next film, *The Blue Bird* (1976), was an unmitigated disaster. This joint venture between Russia and the United States, based on the classic fairy tale, surely was one of the worst films of the year (considering the talent surrounding it), and certainly one of the most boring. Retreating to television, Cukor made a lovely version of *The Corn Is Green* (1979). Hepburn again was marvelous in the role of the spinster schoolteacher in Wales. This was their tenth and final collaboration, and a splendid way to conclude one of the cinema's most fruitful relationships.

His last film was *Rich and Famous* (1981), an enjoyable remake of the 1943 *Old Acquaintance*, with Jacqueline Bisset and Candice Bergen as the writers who struggle to remain friends through twenty years of turmoil. The film is not without its flaws, but it was quite an accomplishment for an eighty-one-year-old director. Unfortunately, generally unkind reviews convinced Cukor that the strain wasn't worth it, and he retired. He died the night before he was to see the restored version of *A Star Is Born*, making its debut at Radio City Music Hall.

## ● IRVING CUMMINGS (1888–1959)

A former actor both on stage (once touring with Lillian Russell) and in silent films, Cummings was a proficient director whose films could have been (and in memory often *seem* to have been) directed by other of his contemporaries. Most of his forty-two sound pictures were done for Fox, action tales that eventually gave way to lavish musicals of the sort the studio was famed for—more so then than now. And yet his filmography is not unimpressive, as impersonal as each individual work may be.

Born in New York City, Cummings made the switch from actor to director in 1922 with *The Man from Hell's River*. Over the next seven years he handled a wide assortment of silent dramas of every description, from *The Johnstown Flood* and *Bertha the Sewing Machine Girl* to *The Brute* and *Dressed to Kill*. In 1929 he was rushed into service as a replacement for Raoul Walsh, who had been seriously injured while filming *In Old Arizona* on location. Cummings took over the film, a Cisco Kid adventure with Warner Baxter, and earned an Academy Award nomination for his efforts (Walsh did not, although officially he is listed as co-director). Few of his early Fox sound pictures are shown today—some may not have even survived—but they include *The Cisco Kid* (1931), with Warner Baxter again as the Robin Hood of the Southwest, the Jack Holt gangster yarn *Man Against Woman* (1932), and *Night Club Lady* (1932), with hard-boiled Mayo Methot as a murder victim.

But he didn't enjoy another mainstream hit until *Curly Top* (1935), a remake of Mary Pickford's 1919 *Daddy Long Legs*, with new phenomenon Shirley Temple playing matchmaker between sister Rochelle Hudson and millionaire John Boles. (Her secret? "Animal Crackers in My Soup.") Lightning struck again with *Poor Little Rich Girl* (1936), one of Shirley's strongest vehicles, thanks in no small part to the superior support of Alice Faye, Jack Haley, and Gloria Stuart. *Girls' Dormitory* (1936) was unremarkable save for marking the film debuts of Simone Simon (in America) and Tyrone Power, while *White Hunter* (also 1936) sent Warner Baxter on an African trek across dangerous studio lots rife with treacherous location footage.

*Vogues of 1938* (1937) had Warner Baxter, Joan Bennett, and Hedda Hopper dallying with New York's fashion industry, but the musical numbers called for Busby Berkeley, who was elsewhere. Cummings fared a bit better with the equally silly *Merry-Go-Round of 1938*, simply because Bert Lahr was on board, while *Little Miss Broadway* (1938) was a typically sentimental outing for Shirley Temple, enlivened by her duets with Jimmy Durante. Obviously pleased with Cummings's commercial touch on the franchise, Fox next gave him *Just Around the Corner* (also 1938), in which Shirley is reteamed with the great Bill Robinson in an otherwise insufferable tale about laughing away the Depression. Time was ticking for the aging moppet, however, and Cummings was able to graduate to features with actual grown-up stars.

First up was *The Story of Alexander Graham Bell* (1939), a good biopic; Don Ameche, in his most famous role as the great inventor, is lent able support by Henry Fonda and Loretta Young. *Hollywood Cavalcade* (1939) used Ameche again, this time as a silent film director who turns Alice Faye into a star even as his own career declines with the coming of sound. The best parts were those that featured erstwhile silent stars Buster Keaton, Mack Sennett, and Rin-Tin-Tin—Cummings must have enjoyed this sentimental journey into his early days in film. *Everything Happens at Night* (1939) was a departure for skating star Sonja Henie, a straight romantic role with just a smidgen of skating interrupting the efforts of rivals Ray Milland and Robert Cummings to win her hand. *Lillian Russell* (1940) provided Cummings with a rare opportunity to fête his old boss; unfortunately, the script didn't give his fine cast of Alice Faye, Henry Fonda, Don Ameche, and Edward Arnold enough to do.

*Down Argentine Way* (1940) was the splashy Technicolor musical that made Betty Grable a star and—not so incidentally—offered the impressive American film debut of Carmen Miranda. *That Night in Rio* (1941) repeated the formula with a tad less success; Ameche and Miranda (who sings "Chica Chica Boom Chic") are joined this time by Alice Faye in a bedroom farce adapted from *Folies Bergère*. The Western biopic *Belle Starr* (1941) was quite a change of pace, with gorgeous Gene Tierney entirely unconvincing as the hard-bitten outlaw who terrorized Missouri alongside her Reb husband (Randolph Scott). Cummings demonstrated a light hand with Bob Hope's comic foolishness in the Irving Berlin creation *Louisiana Purchase* (also 1941), then excelled with the period musical *My Gal Sal* (1942), with Victor Mature as Gay Nineties songwriter Paul Dresser and Rita Hayworth simply luminous as Sally Elliot, the singer he loves. (It was based on the book *My Brother Paul* by Theodore Dreiser, the younger brother).

*Springtime in the Rockies* (1942) was a return to the stylized terrain of *Argentine*; Betty Grable and Carmen Miranda here are paired off with John Payne and Cesar Romero, with Harry James's "I Had the Craziest Dream" one of several musical highlights. Grable and Cummings teamed again on the turn-of-the-century musical *Sweet Rosie O'Grady* (1943), a pleasant-enough bit of work despite Robert Young's lack of appeal as Betty's love interest. Cummings now departed Fox to make two pictures at Columbia. The first was *What a Woman!* (1943), starring Rosalind Russell in top form as a literary agent whose love life is complicated by her sale of a naughty novel to Hollywood. It might have been even better if Roz had been working with romantic leads of more interest than Brian Aherne and Willard Parker.

*The Impatient Years* (1944) also suffered from casting deficiencies: Jean Arthur is saddled with Lee

Bowman as her hubby, a returning soldier who can't adjust to civilian life, married life, or any other kind of life. But the sour story probably wouldn't have worked even with Olivier and Leigh. Cummings made one final Fox musical, *The Dolly Sisters* (1945), with Betty Grable and June Haver well cast as internationally famed vaudeville stars Jenny and Rosie Dolly. Six years later Cummings came out of retirement to make the strained comedy *Double Dynamite* (1951) at RKO with Jane Russell, Frank Sinatra, and Groucho Marx. He should have stood in bed.

## ● MICHAEL CURTIZ (1888–1962)

One of the most prolific and successful directors of the Thirties and Forties, Curtiz was both respected and feared during his long reign as Warner Bros.' cock of the walk. But when the studio system began to unravel in the early Fifties, the source of his power was vitiated. Curtiz kept busy and made more than twenty films from 1951 to 1961, but few of them were as popular—or as good—as his earlier work. Still, though he failed to exit in a blaze of glory, it must be said that the very best of Curtiz's pictures—including (but not limited to) *Casablanca*, *Yankee Doodle Dandy*, *Mildred Pierce*, and all of Errol Flynn's prime costumers—endure to this day as Hollywood classics.

Born Mihaly Kertesz in Budapest, he studied at the Royal Academy of Theater and Art before making his stage debut in 1906. He entered the nascent Hungarian film industry in 1912, and before the year was out had converted himself from an actor to a director. His career was interrupted by the First World War, in which he served Hungary as an infantryman, and for a time he shot newsreels. By 1918 he had made more than two dozen silents, including the first Hungarian feature-length film, but he fled to Germany in 1919, when the newly empowered Communists nationalized the business. Over the next seven years he made several spectaculars (including *Sodom und Gomorrah*), some of which were Danish, French, and/or Austrian co-productions.

In 1927 Jack Warner invited Curtiz to work for him in Hollywood, beginning a twenty-eight-year stint at Warner Bros. That first year he made four forgettable (and forgotten) silent melodramas; just as obscure is *Tenderloin* (1928), a part-talkie with Dolores Costello as a dancer who defies a horde of gangsters. Of his five 1929 feature releases, the most celebrated was the ambitious *Noah's Ark*, which took a page (or several) from Griffith's *Intolerance*, with contrapuntal stories from the Bible and the present day (here a World War I romance between George O'Brien and Dolores Costello). The clunky *Mammy* (1930), with Al Jolson as a minstrel man, used both an Irving Berlin score and Technicolor sequences to become one of the year's big hits, while Frank Fay starred in the comedy *The Matrimonial Bed* and *Bright Lights* (both 1930), a Technicolor musical that also featured Dorothy Mackaill.

*River's End* (1930) was a drama about the Royal Canadian Mounted Police, with Charles Bickford in dual roles, while *A Soldier's Plaything* (1931) was a musical military comedy with Harry Langdon and Ben Lyon. *The Mad Genius* (1931) was a showy vehicle for John Barrymore, playing a crippled puppeteer who longs to be a dancer, while *God's Gift to Women* (also 1931) was a romantic comedy with Frank Fay and Laura La Plante. *The Woman from Monte Carlo* (1932) became an unsuccessful attempt to make a star of German import Lil Dagover, here a married woman having an affair with naval officer Walter Huston. *Alias the Doctor*, a Richard Barthelmess weeper, was co-directed with Lloyd Bacon, and *The Strange Love of Molly Louvan* (both 1932) was a formulaic gangster yarn starring Ann Dvorak and Lee Tracy.

To this point, Curtiz had produced work virtually indistinguishable from that of fellow Warners directors Lloyd Bacon, Roy Del Ruth, William Keighley, and Archie Mayo, and a cut below that of Mervyn LeRoy and William Wellman. But the creepy *Doctor X* (1932), with Lionel Atwill as the mad mastermind and Fay Wray and Lee Tracy as his would-be victims, had a look quite its own, although its scenario now might elicit laughs where screams were intended. Also enjoyable was *Cabin in the Cotton* (1932), with sharecropper Richard Barthelmess waylaid by upper-class trash Bette Davis (whom Curtiz reportedly didn't want in the picture; foolish boy!).

Curtiz was now poised for his breakthrough, and 1933 was the year he made it. *20,000 Years in Sing Sing* was another entry in the already hoary prison genre, but Curtiz made something more of it, with Spencer Tracy (borrowed to replace the salary-striking James Cagney) as the doomed inmate and Bette Davis his loyal moll. Even more impressive was *The Mystery of the Wax Museum* (1933), a quasi-sequel to *Dr. X* that employed the same primitive Technicolor process; deformed sculptor Lionel Atwill and Fay Wray were again in a struggle to the death—and what a horrible death! Two more 1933 films were *The Keyhole*, a turgid romance between Kay Francis and George Brent (two of the decade's dullest stars) and *Private Detective 62* (aka *Man Killer*), which benefited from the presence of William Powell as a shady PI who falls for pigeon Margaret Lindsay.

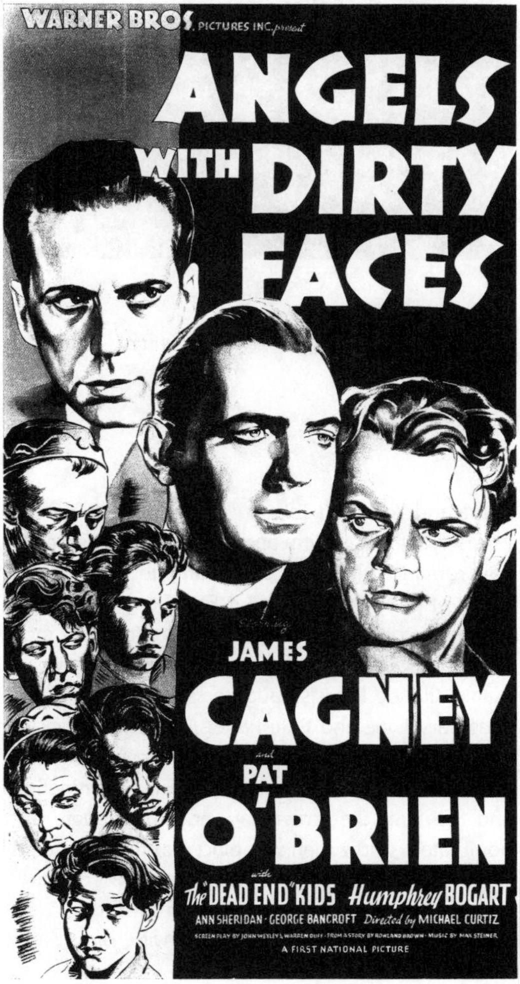
WARNER BROS. PICTURES INC. present
ANGELS WITH DIRTY FACES
JAMES CAGNEY
and
PAT O'BRIEN
with
The DEAD END KIDS Humphrey BOGART
ANN SHERIDAN · GEORGE BANCROFT Directed by MICHAEL CURTIZ
A FIRST NATIONAL PICTURE

Powell displayed his suave side to Mary Astor in *The Kennel Murder Case* (1933), the best of the Philo Vance films and one which laid the groundwork for his Nick Charles the following year. *Goodbye Again* (1933) was a serviceable romantic comedy with Warren William and Joan Blondell, while *Female*—incredibly, Curtiz's seventh release of 1933—cast Ruth Chatterton against type as an automobile tycoon, with George Brent atypically appealing as the engineer who tames her. *Mandalay* (1934), with Kay Francis as the scourge of Rangoon, was simply preposterous, but then Curtiz was overdue for a lemon. He managed to pull out a plum, however, with *Jimmy the Gent* (1934), which offered James Cagney as a charismatic con man who is taught a lesson by Bette Davis; a pity Curtiz and Cagney teamed so infrequently, as each of their pictures was an event.

*The Key* (1934) cast William Powell as a captain in the Black and Tans occupying Ireland during the Twenties; having cuckolded intelligence officer Colin Clive, he has to find a way to redeem his honor. *British Agent* (also 1934) was also a period drama, with the insufferable Kay Francis suffering as a Russian spy in the Revolution of 1917, romancing Brit Leslie Howard in between bouts of angst. Curtiz fared better with the socially conscious *Black Fury* (1935), a dramatization of a real-life case involving a Pennsylvania coal miner who was murdered by company cops. Paul Muni, the Meryl Streep of his day, played the "bohunk" passionately and with a thick (and possibly authentic) Polish accent, but it didn't enjoy the wide success of Warners' earlier exposé *Chain Gang*—being banned in Pennsylvania apparently didn't help.

*The Case of the Curious Bride* (1935) was a rather poor mystery, with Warren William repeating his role as Erle Stanley Gardner's brilliant attorney Perry Mason; what Curtiz was doing on a programmer like this in the first place was the real mystery. He directed Bette Davis for the fourth time in *Front Page Woman* (1935), with Bette and George Brent as rivals competing on their coverage of a fire to see who is the better reporter; its debt to the Hecht-MacArthur *The Front Page* was left unacknowledged. *Little Big Shot* (also 1935) was a deluded attempt to turn South African child star Sybil Jason into another Shirley Temple; the story resembled Shirley's recent *Little Miss Marker* more closely than coincidence could account for.

But *Captain Blood*, Curtiz's fifth picture that year,

was phenomenally successful, a classic swashbuckler that made a star of Errol Flynn and also boosted the careers of Olivia de Havilland (who would star with Flynn eight times in all) and Basil Rathbone. The film earned an Academy Award nomination as best picture, and led to eight more collaborations between Flynn and Curtiz. *The Walking Dead* (1936) was an excellent horror entry—Curtiz's last, alas—featuring Boris Karloff as an unjustly executed man who returns from the grave to exact vengeance. *The Charge of the Light Brigade* (1936) was a big-budget, rather overlong costumer inspired by the Tennyson poem about the 27th Lancers Dragoons, which met its doom—historically in Crimea, here in India—but it was the romance between stars Flynn and de Havilland that carried the picture until the climactic charge.

*Stolen Holiday* (1937) found Parisian model Kay Francis marrying swindler Claude Rains to save him from prison, while *Mountain Justice* (1937) was a minor backwoods drama with a second-rate cast. But *Kid Galahad* (aka *The Battling Bellhop*, 1937) was one of the decade's better boxing pictures. Edward G. Robinson plays a promoter who discovers Wayne Morris, puts him into the ring, then watches mistress Bette Davis switch allegiances to the strapping lad; Humphrey Bogart was also on board as a hood. The nearly (and justly) forgotten comedy *The Perfect Specimen* (also 1937) reunited Flynn and Curtiz—not for derring-do, but rather for the whimsical conceit of upper-crust innocent Flynn learning the facts of life from hard-boiled reporter Joan Blondell. In a word, a waste.

▲ *Curtiz and Ingrid Bergman celebrate Christmas on the set of* Casablanca *in 1942*

That relatively unimpressive year behind him, Curtiz leaped to the forefront of the Warners' roster with a spectacular 1938. It began quietly with *Gold Is Where You Find It*, a conventional gold-rush yarn starring George Brent, de Havilland, and Claude Rains. But then came *The Adventures of Robin Hood*, the studio's biggest box-office performer for 1938. The quintessential Hollywood swashbuckler, *Robin Hood* was a perfect blend of Errol Flynn's swagger, Olivia de Havilland's ethereal beauty, and Claude Rains's and Basil Rathbone's craven villainy, all drenched in Technicolor and served up with a rousing, Oscar-winning score by Erich Wolfgang Korngold. Begun by William Keighley, it was completed by Curtiz when mounting costs and Flynn's discontent forced Jack Warner's hand. (Both the film and Curtiz were nominated for Oscars, but they lost to Capra and *You Can't Take It with You*.) *Four's a Crowd* unwisely let loose Flynn and de Havilland in a screwball romance that had something to do with the world of public relations. But *Four Daughters* was an impressive departure for Curtiz—a gentle and moving drama about the small-town lives and loves of pianist Claude Rains's daughters: Priscilla, Lola, and Rosemary Lane and Gale Page. As one of their suitors, John Garfield gave a naturalistic performance that earned him an Academy Award nomination, and the film, the screenplay, and Curtiz were also nominated. Curtiz then was placed in the unique position of competing with himself for a best direction Oscar when he was also nominated for his next picture, the gangster classic *Angels with Dirty Faces*. James Cagney and Pat O'Brien are archetypally cast as childhood friends who grow up in diametrically opposite directions, one a gangster idolized by the neighborhood ruffians (the Dead End Kids), the other a priest who wants to save their souls. Humphrey Bogart and Ann Sheridan lent able support, and both Cagney and the rather maudlin story by Rowland Brown joined Curtiz as Oscar nominees.

*Dodge City* (1939) sent Flynn and de Havilland back to the Old West with felicitous results, while *Daughters Courageous* was a virtual remake of the previous year's *Daughters*, with a nearly identical cast and plot (courtesy of the Epstein brothers). Moments later came *Four Wives*, the *actual* sequel to *Daughters*, which again recycled the cast sans Garfield, whose character had been killed in the original. *The Private Lives of Elizabeth and Essex* (1939) was a handsomely mounted adaptation of the Maxwell Anderson play, with Bette Davis splendid as the crafty Queen and Errol Flynn game but simply out of his league as the Earl of Essex; Davis had wanted Olivier, and she had a point.

*Virginia City* (1940) was an attempt to repeat the success of *Dodge*, but Miriam Hopkins as Flynn's co-star was less than compelling as a saloon singer, and Bogart's Spanish renegade sported a ridiculous pencil mustache that didn't help matters.

But Flynn and Curtiz had to wait only until their next venture to savor triumph, as *The Sea Hawk* (1940) became one of the year's biggest hits, propelled by Flynn's cocky impersonation of a Sir Francis Drake type, Flora Robson's canny Elizabeth I, the villainy of Claude Rains and Henry Daniell, and Korngold's classic score. In the disappointing 1940 *Santa Fe Trail* Flynn was deprived of his sword and put back on a horse as Jeb Stuart, the cavalry officer in search of abolitionist John Brown (Raymond Massey). Ronald Reagan appeared as Custer and de Havilland returned as Flynn's love interest, but the story was amorphous and the action subpar.

*The Sea Wolf* (1941) was an effective version of the Jack London story; Edward G. Robinson was a convincing Wolf Larsen and John Garfield and Ida Lupino were well cast as the young lovers who match wits with the demented skipper. Flynn and Curtiz worked together for the last time on *Dive Bomber* (1941), a passable drama about the Navy's experiments to help pilots survive high-speed flights; Flynn is a guilt-racked surgeon and Fred MacMurray and Alexis Smith his friend and lover, respectively. Aviation was also the background for *Captains of the Clouds* (1942), with James Cagney doing his patriotic bit for the Royal Canadian Air Force.

But Cagney is much better remembered for his next picture, *Yankee Doodle Dandy* (1942), a musical biography of George M. Cohan that gave Cagney a rare opportunity to demonstrate his considerable hoofing and singing talents onscreen. Corny as Kansas in August, the film nonetheless earned Cagney his only Oscar and also landed one for its scoring; in addition, it earned nominations for best picture, direction, and supporting actor (Walter Huston). It's not often that a director can top a smash success with an even bigger one, but Curtiz did just that with *Casablanca* (1943), the legendary wartime romantic drama that has survived more than a half century to become (arguably) the most popular picture from Hollywood's golden age. Oscar nominations went to Humphrey Bogart (but not Ingrid Bergman!), Claude Rains, and Max Steiner's evocative score, and it won in three categories: best picture, best screenplay (the Epsteins and Howard Koch), and best direction. Curtiz would never ride so high again.

*Mission to Moscow* (1943) fairly dripped prestige, but this elaborate dramatization of former ambassador Joseph E. Davies's memoir about his two years in the Soviet Union turned into one of the studio's biggest embarrassments. Its blatantly pro-Soviet message—politically correct in 1943 but anathema a few years later—eventually landed Jack Warner and screenwriter Howard Koch in front of the House Un-American Activities Committee (HUAC), with Warner explaining that the late F.D.R. himself had confidentially requested a film of the 1941 book to help marshal support for the aid the United States was supplying to the Russians. But that stigma was still in the future, and Curtiz moved on to the ultra-patriotic *This Is the Army* (also 1943), an all-star revue based on Irving Berlin's stage success, with numbers ranging from Kate Smith's "God Bless America" to "I Left My Heart at the Stage Door Canteen."

*Passage to Marseilles* (1944) aspired to be a junior league *Casablanca*—Bogart, Rains, Greenstreet, and Lorre were all on hand—but its impossibly convoluted story prevented it from ever jelling. *Janie* (1944) was a real anomaly for Curtiz, a visit to a small town where a teenage girl (Joyce Reynolds) fantasizes about marrying a soldier, while the biopic *Roughly Speaking* (1945) covered forty-odd years in the life of author Louise Randall Pierson (Rosalind Russell), whose husband (the delightful Jack Carson) was three bricks shy of a load. Then came *Mildred Pierce* (1945), a brilliant, noirish reworking of the James M. Cain novel. Joan Crawford gives her best performance as a driven mother who sacrifices everything for her spoiled daughter (Ann Blyth)—even husband Zachary Scott. It was nominated for Academy Awards as best picture, supporting actress (both Eve Arden and Blyth), and screenplay (Ronald MacDougall), but the big winner was Crawford, who got the part after Bette Davis and Barbara Stanwyck turned it down; she won her only Oscar and resuscitated her then-floundering career.

*Night and Day* (1946) was a synthetic biopic about Cole Porter that optimistically cast Cary Grant as the great tunester (why not John Wayne?); incredibly, it was a hit. But *Life with Father* (1947), adapted from Clarence Day's stories and the long-running (3,224 performances) Broadway show, was at least a high grade of corn with William Powell as the eternally cranky Father and Irene Dunne, Edmund Gwenn, and Elizabeth Taylor as some of his forbearing family. A smash in its day, the film doesn't seem quite as special now, but Powell was nominated for an Oscar and won the New York Film Critics Circle best actor award.

Curtiz made a rare foray into noir territory with *The Unsuspected* (1947), a decent murder mystery starring Claude Rains as a radio dramatist who plots to kill niece Joan Caulfield. *Romance on the High Seas* (1948) was a harmless if attractive musical, with Doris Day impressive in her screen debut (originally intended for Judy Garland) alongside Oscar Levant and Jack Carson, while *My Dream Is Yours* (1949) used Day and Carson again in an updated version of the Dick Powell musical *Twenty Million Sweethearts;* Doris was now cast as the aspiring radio singer. But Curtiz was better suited to overheated melodramas like *Flamingo Road* (1949), with Joan Crawford as a carnival dancer framed for murder by the formidable Sydney Greenstreet, a corrupt Southern politician bent on driving her out of town.

*The Lady Takes a Sailor* (1949) was an awful romantic comedy with the dull duo of Jane Wyman and Dennis Morgan, while *Bright Leaf* (1950), a drama about the building of a tobacco empire, is now memorable chiefly for the struggles of Gary Cooper, Lauren Bacall, and Patricia Neal to keep their nineteenth-century Southern accents operational. But *Young Man with a Horn* (1950) was an above-average biopic based loosely on the life of jazz great Bix Biederbecke; Kirk Douglas's intensity as the tragic Bix was not out of place here, and Lauren Bacall and Doris Day were effective as the yin and yang of his love life (Harry James dubbed Kirk's trumpet playing). Curtiz fashioned the best adaptation of Hemingway to date with *The Breaking Point* (1950), a more faithful version of the novel *To Have and Have Not* than had been made by Hawks in 1944. But despite a terrific performance by John Garfield, the film was not popular.

*Force of Arms* (1951) was a World War II love story between soldier William Holden and nurse Nancy Olson, while *Jim Thorpe—All American* (1951) provided Burt Lancaster with one of his best roles as the American Indian athlete who was the sensation of the 1912 Olympics before being stripped of his medals for having played semi-pro baseball. *I'll See You in My Dreams* (1951) was yet another biopic, this time of songwriter Gus Kahn, whose life afforded Danny Thomas and Doris Day the chance to warble evergreens like "It Had to Be You" and "Pretty Baby." *The Story of Will Rogers* (1952) was able to draw on the not inconsiderable talents of the great man's son, with Eddie Cantor appearing as himself for additional verisimilitude, while *The Jazz Singer* (1953) offered Danny Thomas and Peggy Lee in a contemporary updating of the 1927 antique. (It wasn't much, but it played like *Citizen Kane* next to the 1980 Neil Diamond version.)

Curtiz had seen his stature at Warners decline, slowly but surely, over the past seven or eight years, and his last two films indicated why he jumped ship. The 1953 *Trouble Along the Way* was a gooey yarn, with divorced bookie John Wayne coaching and recruiting a football team for a church that needs to raise $170,000, for which service he will be allowed to keep custody of his daughter, while *The Boy from Oklahoma* (1954) had Will Rogers, Jr., taming a Wild West town with his innate goodness and homespun common sense. It was an anticlimactic ending to Curtiz's twenty-seven-year career at Warner Bros.

He made *The Egyptian* (1954) for Fox, a ponderous costume epic with Edmund Purdom, Jean Simmons, and Gene Tierney, then signed with Paramount, where his very first project proved to be the year's biggest hit. *White Christmas* (1954) was essentially a remake of the 1942 *Holiday Inn*, with Bing Crosby now teamed with Danny Kaye (instead of the original's Fred Astaire) in his endeavor to refurbish a dilapidated country inn. The Irving Berlin tunes

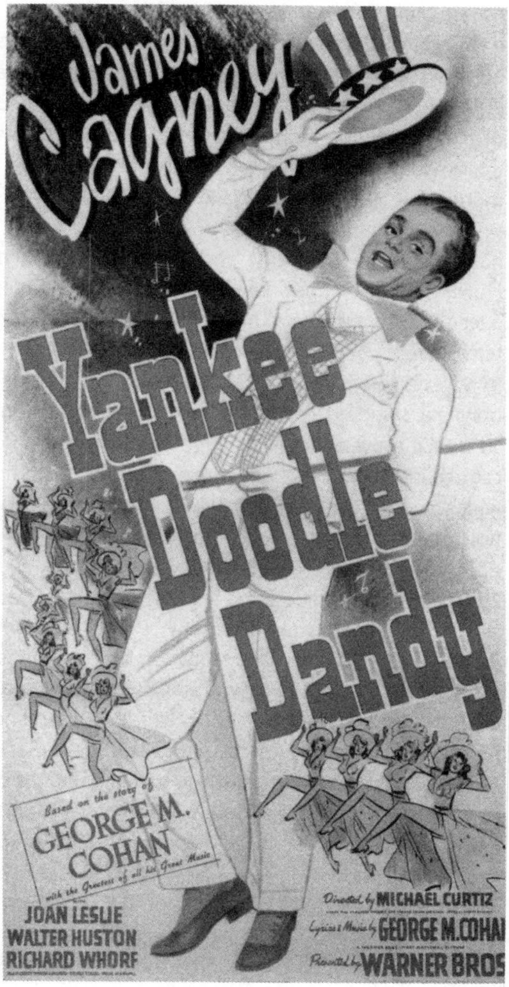


drifted down like so many snowflakes, but the rest of the two hours was like watching ice slowly melt. Having made $12 million for his new bosses, Curtiz now directed the whimsical *We're No Angels* (1955), starring Humphrey Bogart, Peter Ustinov, and Aldo Ray as escaped convicts who move in with a French family; it was too cute by half, but had its moments.

*The Vagabond King* (1956) was the operetta version of the life of François Villon, filmed most recently in 1938 as *If I Were King* with Ronald Colman. As it turned out, the singing of Kathryn Grayson and the acting of Oreste were not enough to power this archaic blunderbuss. *The Scarlet Hour* (1956) was even worse, a lumbering melodrama that deluded itself into relying on Tom Tryon and Carol Ohmart as its stars, while the 1956 *The Best Things in Life Are Free* was a middling biopic of Tin Pan Alley composers DeSylva, Brown, and Henderson. Curtiz returned to Warners to make *The Helen Morgan Story* (1957)—yes, another screen biography, with Ann Blyth laughably miscast as the great torch singer of the 1920s (Gogi Grant did her singing). But Curtiz must be given full credit for the surprisingly effective *King Creole* (1958), a laundered but still tangy version of Harold Robbins's *A Stone for Danny Fisher*, with Elvis Presley as a New Orleans nightclub singer who falls for gangster's moll Carolyn Jones. Even the songs are integrated in a way that few directors attempted with Elvis's vehicles.

*The Proud Rebel* (1958) was made for Disney, with Alan Ladd in an unusually sensitive role as a father trying to get help for his mute son, while *The Hangman* (1959) was conventional Western action with Robert Taylor, Fess Parker, and Jack Lord. The farfetched *The Man in the Net* (1959) tried to fob off Alan Ladd as a Connecticut artist unjustly accused of murdering his slatternly wife (Carolyn Jones). At least *The Adventures of Huckleberry Finn* (1960) had the virtues of former boxing great Archie Moore as Jim and Eddie Hodges as Huck, but *A Breath of Scandal* (1960) needed Lubitsch in his prime and not a seventy-year-old Curtiz to breathe life into the 1928 Molnar story. *Francis of Assisi* (1961) was a longish but well-played biography, with Bradford Dillman as the man who founded a school for monks. (Dolores Hart, Elvis's co-star in *Creole*, left acting soon after this to join a nunnery.)

*The Comancheros* (1961) had John Wayne as a Texas Ranger trying to put Lee Marvin and his gang out of business. It was the best film Curtiz had made in ten years; perhaps he summoned up his fading strength, knowing it would be his last. A year later he was dead, leaving behind dozens of films that remain very much alive.

## ● JULES DASSIN (1911– )

One of many directors whose best work fell in between the war years and the HUAC investigations, Jules Dassin was born in Middletown, Connecticut, and studied drama in Europe. He joined the Yiddish Theater in New York in 1936, then wrote radio scripts for *The Kate Smith Show*. In 1940 he went to Hollywood, where he worked briefly at RKO as an assistant director, moving on to MGM, where he directed shorts. His first features for MGM were the "B"'s *Nazi Agent* with Conrad Veidt, a complicated but ineffective espionage yarn, and the innocuous *The Affairs of Martha* (both 1942) with Marsha Hunt and Richard Carlson. *Reunion in France* (1942) was a dull if patriotic romance that featured one of the screen's all-time odd couples, Joan Crawford and John Wayne, but it was a masterpiece compared to *Young Ideas* (1943), a flaccid comedy with Susan Peters and Richard Carlson. But *The Canterville Ghost* (1944) was a fine piece of work, a charming supernatural comedy with a top Charles Laughton performance.

But it was back to mediocrity with *A Letter for Evie* (1945) as Marsha Hunt tries to choose between Hume Cronyn and John Carroll, while *Two Smart People* (1946) was a comic crime yarn starring Lucille Ball and John Hodiak as art forgers. But if Dassin was not suited to romantic comedy, he found something different awaiting him when he departed MGM for Warners. The classic prison noir *Brute Force* (1947), with Burt Lancaster as a spirited but doomed convict and Hume Cronyn the sadistic warden, holds up well to this day. Almost as good, and even more influential, was *The Naked City* (1948), an on-location, quasi-documentary police procedural, filmed in New York City, with Barry Sullivan and Howard Duff; it would be imitated dozens of times over the next ten years, both in the cinema and on television.

*Thieves' Highway* (1949) was a bit of a comedown, a standard crime pic about California mobsters taking over a trucking firm, with Richard Conte caught in the web. It was made for RKO, a studio which might have been ideal given Dassin's flair for noir material, but he never got the chance to find out. Named before HUAC by Edward Dmytryk as a Communist (he had deserted the Party in 1939), Dassin fled to England (as, ironically, Dmytryk shortly would do). There he made one of his best films, *Night and the City* (1950), with Richard Widmark as an American hustler involved in London's wrestling racket, Gene Tierney as his singer girlfriend, and Mike Mazurki as a wrestler who eventually seals Widmark's doom. One of the darkest of all noirs, *Night*'s 1992 remake only reminded everyone of how great the original was.

Dassin didn't make another film in English until the Sixties, although the French production *Rififi* (1954), a taut caper yarn about a quartet of lowlife jewel thieves, commanded attention in the United States on the art-house circuit and won Dassin a prize at Cannes. *Where the Hot Wind Blows!* (1958) was a disappointing roundelay among Gina Lollobrigida, Melina Mercouri (Dassin's wife), and Yves Montand. But the surprise success of *Never on Sunday* (1960) finally reintroduced Dassin to American audiences. A Greek production, *Sunday* offered Dassin himself in a bit part (as had *Rififi*), but it was Melina Mercouri who stole the show as an incorrigible prostitute, earning an Academy Award nomination for best actress. Dassin was also nominated for his direction and his screenplay, and the film's catchy theme song by Manos Hadjidakis won an Oscar.

Dassin directed Mercouri again in *Phaedra* (1962), in which her character has an affair with stepson Anthony Perkins. She was also in *Topkapi* (1964), a classic caper flick (based on an Eric Ambler novel) about the theft of an emerald-studded dagger from a Turkish museum; it was shot on location in Istanbul, and offered superb suspense and an exceptional cast, including Peter Ustinov (who won an Oscar), Robert Morley, and Maximilian Schell. The little-seen *10:30 p.m. Summer* (1967) was followed by *Survival '67* (1968), a documentary about the Six-Day War. *Up Tight* (1968) was Dassin's first American production in twenty years (and his last). An exciting remake of *The Informer*, with the story transposed to Harlem, it boasted many of the day's top black actors, including Ruby Dee, Raymond St. Jacques, and Roscoe Lee Browne.

*Promise at Dawn* (1970) and *A Dream of Passion* (1978) reteamed Mercouri and Dassin for the seventh and eighth times, but his last film, *Circle of Two* (1981), provided the embarrassing spectacle of Richard Burton wooing jailbait Tatum O'Neal. That's not the way we need to remember this resourceful (if erratic) director, whose impact might have been ever so much greater had the blacklist not stopped him in his tracks.

▲ *Dassin (center) and wife, Melina Mercouri (right), relax with Dr. Martin Luther King, Jr. (left), and Harry Belafonte in 1967*

## ● DELMER DAVES (1904–1977)

A man for all seasons, Delmer Daves at various points during his career was an actor, a screenwriter, a producer, and, of course, a director, often wearing three hats at once. Born in San Francisco, Daves broke into films in 1923 assisting James Cruze, while still in the process of earning his law degree at Stanford. He worked as a consultant on college-theme films, and began acting in 1929 in such pictures as *The Duke Steps Out* and *Good News*. Daves made screenwriting his first serious career, collaborating on such Hollywood gems as *Dames*, *The Petrified Forest*, *Love Affair*, and *You Were Never Lovelier*.

He was given his chance to direct at Warner Bros., where he made the efficient *Destination Tokyo* with Cary Grant and John Garfield in 1943, typically co-writing the screenplay as well. *The Very Thought of You* (1944) was a bland homefront romance with lesser lights Dennis Morgan and Dane Clark, while *Hollywood Canteen* (1944) was an all-star comedy and musical revue with the usual high, middle, and low points, set at an oasis for servicemen founded by Bette Davis and John Garfield. *Pride of the Marines* (1945) was weightier stuff, a hard-hitting account of real-life leatherneck Al Schmid's difficulties in adjusting to civilian life after he was blinded at Guadalcanal. Albert Maltz's screenplay was nominated for an Academy Award, and there were fine performances by Garfield, Dane Clark, and Eleanor Parker.

*The Red House* (1947) was an off-beat, atmospheric thriller starring Edward G. Robinson as a farmer who may or may not be in jeopardy from strange forces, but Daves enjoyed greater success with *Dark Passage* (1947), a vivid adaptation of the David Goodis novel; it starred Humphrey Bogart as an escaped con who gets a new face and Lauren Bacall as his port in the storm. Not quite a classic, but with Agnes Moorehead on hand as a heavy, it delivered plenty of good moments. *To the Victor* (1948) had a powerful premise—collaborators on trial in France—but was hamstrung by the limits of the Warners' stock company. *A Kiss in the Dark* (1949), with David Niven romancing Jane Wyman, hadn't even that much to offer, but the 1949 *Task Force* at least had the virtues of Gary Cooper and a military background, always Daves's strong suit.

Moving to 20th Century-Fox in 1950, Daves made one of his best pictures, *Broken Arrow*, a superlative Western about race relations between the Apaches and the white settlers who are displacing them. Both James Stewart, as the liaison who falls in love with an Indian princess (Debra Paget), and Jeff Chandler as the wise Cochise were terrific, and the movie's strong box office ignited a decade-long cycle of films with American Indian protagonists. Screenwriter "Michael Blankfort" (the blacklisted Albert Maltz) was Oscar-nominated, as was Chandler. Daves was perhaps less comfortable with *Bird of Paradise* (1951), an inferior remake of King Vidor's 1932 South Seas epic, while *Return of the Texan* (1952) was pure formula about a ranching war between Dale Robertson and Richard Boone.

*Treasure of the Golden Condor* (1953) had Cornel Wilde trying on the Tyrone Power role from *Son of Fury* with passable results—but someone forgot to include Gene Tierney and George Sanders to hold up the rest of the picture. Tierney *did* show up in *Never Let Me Go* (also 1953) alongside Clark Gable, but these were the wrong stars for this Cold War tale about a ballerina being smuggled out of Russia by her husband. *Demetrius and the Gladiators* (1954) sounded like sword-and-sandals schlock, but it was actually a decent sequel to the previous year's smash *The Robe*, with Victor Mature and Susan Hayward trying valiantly not to appear too uncomfortable in their togas.

Daves now went freelance, allowing him to avoid

ancient Rome and concentrate on making Westerns. *Drum Beat* (1954) was a welcome return to *Broken Arrow* territory, hampered just a bit by Alan Ladd's congenital impassivity, but Charles Bronson was quite good as the Modoc chief Captain Jack. *Jubal* (1956) was a Freudian Western that used Rod Steiger, Ernest Borgnine, and Glenn Ford to good effect, while *The Last Wagon* (1956) handed the reins to Richard Widmark as a resourceful killer who protects the survivors of a wagon train despite his own agenda. *3:10 to Yuma* (1957) is generally considered one of Daves's gems; a variation on *High Noon*, it pits farmer Van Heflin in a battle of wits with captured killer Glenn Ford, effectively cast against type. *Cowboy* (1958) used Ford well again, this time as the gruff mentor to tenderfoot Jack Lemmon on a cattle drive, while *Kings Go Forth* (1958) depicted a hepster love triangle set in France during the war, with Frank Sinatra, Tony Curtis, and Natalie Wood.

*The Badlanders* (also 1958) cleverly outfitted the urban noir classic *The Asphalt Jungle* with spurs; Alan Ladd and Ernest Borgnine are the robbers who don't dare turn their backs on each other. In 1959 Daves returned to Warner Bros., where he would spend the remainder of his career making films of a very different nature. His first picture there was his last Western, *The Hanging Tree* (1959), with Gary Cooper well cast as a frontier doctor who cares for blind girl Maria Schell. Then came *A Summer Place* (1959), the biggest hit of Daves's career and a high-water mark for cinematic suds. Based on the Sloan Wilson novel, it mined the same rich lode of adultery (enacted stiffly by Richard Egan and Dorothy McGuire) and premarital sex (debated humidly by Sandra Dee and Troy Donahue) as the recent blockbuster *Peyton Place*.

*Parrish* (1961) was cut from the same cloth, but it must have been cut with a pair of hedge clippers; Troy Donahue is again on hand as the youth tortured by his rising sap, but this time the anguish—he's in love with three different girls on a tobacco plantation—plays like watching crops grow. *Susan Slade* (1961) tempts fate by combining the stars of *Summer Place* and *Parrish*—Troy Donahue, Connie Stevens, and Dorothy McGuire—to spin out a tale of illegitimacy and nobility that should be laughable but isn't (at least, not entirely). Warners assigned Daves yet another make-out movie the following year in the form of *Rome Adventure* (1962), which—incredibly—starred Troy Donahue yet again, this time cast as an architect (!?) whose mistress is Angie Dickinson but who really goes for wholesome Suzanne Pleshette.

Daves was released from Donahue hell thereafter, but his last few pictures weren't even as good as those glossy melodramas. *Spencer's Mountain* (1963), a precursor to *The Waltons* TV series, offered Henry Fonda and Maureen O'Hara as a frontier couple overcoming adversity, while *Youngblood Hawke* (1964), from the bestseller by Herman Wouk, forced Daves to use James Franciscus—perhaps the only leading man at the time less capable of carrying a film than Troy Donahue—as the brilliant young Southern novelist who captures the literati of New York City. (In the campy annals of Publishing meets the Cinema, this is at least a match for 1959's sublime *The Best of Everything*.)

Daves's last picture was *The Battle of the Villa Fiorita* (1965), a soap opera in which Rossano Brazzi romances Maureen O'Hara, to the horror of their respective families. As with his previous six Warners pictures, Daves produced and wrote the screenplay as well as directing, and it was competent on its own terms. But in the end, Daves's Sixties filmography is an anticlimax—more what a declining Douglas Sirk might have turned out than what the director of so many superior war pictures and Westerns should have wrought.

▲ *Daves with Troy Donahue and Claudette Colbert on location for* Parrish

▲ *George Raft heeds Del Ruth while shooting* Red Light

## ● ROY DEL RUTH (1895–1961)

"Through his sheer inability to qualify for it, Del Ruth's fecund blankness vindicates the theory of authorship." Harsh words, but David Thomson was not being totally unfair when he wrote them in summary of Roy Del Ruth's thirty-five-year, seventy-film career. A respectable proportion of those films remain watchable today, particularly his early Cagney pictures and the Thirties musicals. But the plain truth is that, if all seventy of his motion pictures (many of them quite successful in their day) suddenly vanished from the face of the earth, only a handful would be missed.

Born in Philadelphia, Del Ruth worked as a newspaperman before entering films in 1915 as a gagwriter for Mack Sennett. He soon was directing comedy shorts, including a number with Harry Langdon. At Warner Bros. he was provided with the opportunity to direct features, and between 1925 and 1929 turned out eighteen of them, including several silent comedies based on stories by Darryl Zanuck and the prehistoric part-talkie *The Terror*. In 1929 he directed the first all-talking, all-singing operetta, *The Desert Song*, as well as *The Gold Diggers of Broadway*, which established the studio's cottage industry of "Gold Diggers" pictures and also unleashed "Tiptoe Through the Tulips" upon an unsuspecting world.

Del Ruth directed six features in 1930, the most memorable of which was the Joe E. Brown boxing comedy *Hold Everything*. But he made a bigger impact a year later with the original version of *The Maltese Falcon*, a competent adaptation of Dashiell Hammett's classic novel (with Ricardo Cortez as Sam Spade) that would be more fondly remembered today had not John Huston's 1941 masterpiece rendered it obsolete. *Blonde Crazy* (1932) was simply terrific, with James Cagney at his snap-crackle-and-pop quickest as a bellhop who teams with chambermaid sidekick Joan Blondell to con Louis Calhern; the film even had a great tune, "When Your Lover Has Gone." Del Ruth also handled Cagney in good vehicles like *Taxi!* (1932), in which he's a pugnacious hack driver trying to keep wife Loretta Young happy in between confrontations with his union, and the 1932 *Winner Take All*, where he's a boxer who loses his way in love; just as he'd had to learn to drive for *Taxi!*, Cagney went into training so he'd be convincing as a boxer.

*Blessed Event* (also 1932) was a crackling comedy,

with Lee Tracy at his best as a gossip columnist willing to do anything to increase circulation, while *Employees' Entrance* (1933) offered Warren William as an unscrupulous department-store manager who wreaks havoc with the lives of those around him. Del Ruth handled five more films that year: *The Little Giant*, with Edward G. Robinson in good comic form as a beer baron who tries to enter society (and win Mary Astor) after the repeal of Prohibition makes him "respectable"; *The Mind Reader*, with Warren William as a con man who pretends he's clairvoyant; *Bureau of Missing Persons*, a silly programmer in which Bette Davis implores Pat O'Brien to search for her kidnapped husband with the help of a carrier pigeon; *Captured!*, with Leslie Howard suffering in a World War I POW camp; and—best of the lot—*Lady Killer*, with Cagney in one of his best comic roles as a gangster on the lam who draws on his experience as a movie theater usher to become a Hollywood star. A productive year, thanks to the studio system and Del Ruth's proficiency—but he would not match it again.

*Upperworld* (1934), his last picture for Warner Bros. (and first under the new Production Code), put Warren William, Mary Astor, and Ginger Rogers through their paces in a murder mystery, while *Bulldog Drummond Strikes Back* (1934) had Ronald Colman repeating his role as London's foremost amateur detective. The delightful *Kid Millions* (1934) found new-made millionaire Eddie Cantor and Ethel Merman in Egypt and in a Brooklyn ice-cream factory, while *Folies Bergère* (1935) had Maurice Chevalier dumping Ann Sothern to woo the more upscale Merle Oberon; the Oscar-winning "Straw Hat" musical finale would be the last glimpse American moviegoers would have of Chevalier for the next twenty-one years. Del Ruth was paired with dance director Dave Gould again for *Broadway Melody of 1936*, a typically lavish MGM hodgepodge that somehow combined Jack Benny, Robert Taylor, Eleanor Powell, and a spiffy group of Freed-Brown tunes into a tasty mixture.

Suddenly a proven expert in the genre, Del Ruth was signed by Fox to handle their stable of musical stars. He started with the snappy *Thanks a Million* (1935), with Dick Powell running for governor assisted by campaign manager Fred Allen, then made the more serious political drama *It Had to Happen* (1936), although George Raft and Rosalind Russell made for an unlikely pairing. *Private Number* (1936) was a sodden soap opera, with wealthy Robert Taylor secretly married to "serving girl" Loretta Young, to the displeasure of nefarious butler Basil Rathbone. But the 1936 *Born to Dance* sent Del Ruth back to MGM for another elaborate musical showcase: Eleanor Powell is paired with an endearingly awkward Jimmy Stewart amid such great Cole Porter songs as "I've Got You Under My Skin" and "Easy to Love." It was a huge hit, as was *On the Avenue* (1937), a Dick Powell–Alice Faye–Madeleine Carroll musical graced with a bevy of Irving Berlin tunes, including "The Girl on the Police Gazette."

MGM borrowed Del Ruth yet again for *Broadway Melody of 1938*, another box-office bonanza with Eleanor Powell: its high point is the interlude with Judy Garland singing "Dear Mr. Gable." Back at Fox, Del Ruth made *Happy Landing* (1938), a subpar Sonja Henie musical with Don Ameche and Ethel Merman, and *My Lucky Star* (also 1938), with Sonja now cast as an unlikely college undergraduate, and Richard Greene her even unlikelier professor. *Tail Spin* (1939) was a pleasantly loony yarn—Alice Faye and Constance Bennett are aviatrixes competing in the Powder Puff High Speed Race. *The Star Maker* (1939), starring Bing Crosby, was a musical biopic about Gus Edwards, vaudeville impresario, but *Here I Am a Stranger* was pure soap, with Richard Greene estranged from dad Richard Dix—yet another unmemorable film from that most memorable of screen years, 1939.

Del Ruth made the lame screwball romance *He Married His Wife* (1940), with Joel McCrea and Nancy Kelly as off-again, on-again marrieds, before directing *Topper Returns*, another sequel to the 1937 classic: Joan Blondell made an amusing substitute for Constance Bennett. Del Ruth then signed with MGM, where he would make five films over the next four years: *The Chocolate Soldier* (1941), with Nelson Eddy and Risë Stevens, grafted the music from the operetta onto the story of *The Guardsman* with fair results, but *Maisie Gets Her Man* (1942) was a decided demotion for Del Ruth, just another entry in the Ann Sothern "B" series. *DuBarry Was a Lady* (1943), with Lucille Ball and Red Skelton, was prestigious enough—it had been a huge success on Broadway—but someone at MGM foolishly canned most of Cole Porter's score, rendering the rest of the production moot. *Broadway Rhythm* (1944) limped along with its pedestrian leads, George Murphy and Ginny Simms, although bandleader Tommy Dorsey provided a few spots of relief. But *Barbary Coast Gent* (1944) was just another tedious Wallace Beery entry, tipping off Del Ruth that his glory days at MGM were behind him.

He finally, ignominiously, landed at Allied Artists, where he made the tedious comedy *It Happened on Fifth Avenue* (1947), with Don Defore and Charlie Ruggles. Then came the nadir of Del Ruth's career, *The Babe Ruth Story* (1948), starring a shamefully miscast William Bendix—arguably the worst sports biopic of all time. *Red Light* (1949), a standard crime yarn with George Raft and Virginia Mayo, had to be an improvement on that. Del Ruth then returned to Warner Bros., rather less grandly than he had left. *Always Leave Them Laughing* (1949) was a fairly interesting story about a comedian's rise and fall, with Milton Berle a canny casting choice, while *The West Point Story* (1950) reunited Del Ruth with Cagney, although the results were less than electrifying. Rather better was *On Moonlight Bay* (1951), with Doris Day and Gordon MacRae starring in a musical version of Booth Tarkington's "Penrod" stories.

*Starlift* (1951) offered cameos of Gary Cooper, Cagney, Day, MacRae, and Mayo entertaining Korea-bound troops, but the romantic subplot was from hunger. *About Face* (1952) was a lame musical remake of *Brother Rat*, and *Stop, You're Killing Me* (1952) remade the fine 1938 comedy *A Slight Case of Murder* with equally unimpressive results. The musical *Three Sailors and a Girl* (1953), with Jane Powell and Gordon MacRae, also left much to be desired. *Phantom of the Rue Morgue* (1954)—shot in 3-D but released "flat"—might have been adequate had it not been for Karl Malden being cast in the Bela Lugosi role from the 1932 original.

Del Ruth was then absent from the screen for several years, resurfacing in 1959 for the well-done, low-budget horror picture *The Alligator People*, with Lon Chaney and Beverly Garland. His final film was *Why Must I Die?* (1960), an interesting alternate treatment of the Barbara Graham murder trial that had recently been filmed by Robert Wise as *I Want to Live!*—although that film's Oscar-winning performance by Susan Hayward is hardly equaled here by lead Terry Moore.

## ● CECIL B. DEMILLE (1881–1959)

Long before he made his first sound picture, Cecil Blount DeMille had earned the status of a cinema legend for his pioneering efforts in the development of silent movies from shorts to feature-length productions, and in helping to establish Hollywood as the new center of the filmmaking industry. Unlike other great directors of the silents like D. W. Griffith, Mack Sennett, and Fred Niblo, DeMille made the transition to sound pictures with nary a hitch, continuing to be productive—and profitable—well into the 1950s. Although his nineteen sound films may not be as significant, or even as good, as his fifty-odd silents, they do stand on their own as an estimable body of work.

Born in the town of Ashfield, Massachusetts, to a minister with playwriting ambitions, DeMille was raised by his mother after his father passed away when he was twelve. He was sent to military school, but went AWOL trying (unsuccessfully) to enlist for the Spanish-American War. He later enrolled in New York's American Academy of Dramatic Art, and after graduating became involved with his mother's DeMille Play Co. as an actor and general manager. With his older brother William he wrote and produced a number of plays, and also collaborated with David Belasco. But he did not become involved in the new world of motion pictures until 1913, when he formed a partnership with Samuel Goldfish (soon to become Goldwyn), Arthur Friend, and Jesse Lasky to found the Jesse L. Lasky Feature Play Company; DeMille was given the grandiose title of Director-General.

Their first Hollywood production was *The Squaw Man* (1914), a six-reel epic that DeMille co-directed with Oscar Apfel and that virtually stood alone as the year's most important release. (Griffith's *Birth of a Nation* would come out the following year.) Seven more features emerged in 1914 under DeMille's direction, including *Brewster's Millions* and *The Virginian*; he had another twelve to his credit in 1915, most famously *The Cheat*, *The Girl of the Golden West*, and *Carmen*. After the company merged with Adolph Zukor's Famous Players in 1916, the Paramount Picture Corp. was formed. There DeMille was in charge of all the films the studio released, including (but not limited to) his own, such as the 1918 remake of *The Squaw Man*, the domestic dramas *Why Change Your Wife?* and *The Affairs of Anatol*, and the biblical epic *The Ten Commandments* (1923). But DeMille's budget overruns were as colossal as the movies themselves, and tensions with Zukor forced him to leave.

He made *The King of Kings* (1927) at Pathé, then joined MGM in 1928 as a producer-director. *Dynamite* (1929), his first talkie, had Conrad Nagel, Charles Bickford, and a young Joel McCrea battling the mines and each other for over two hours. *Madame Satan* (1930), with Kay Johnson, Lillian Roth, and Reginald Denny, boasted a typically extravagant DeMille finale: a costume party held on a zeppelin over New York is struck by a bolt of lightning, necessitating a mass exit via parachutes. Great fun, but the box-office receipts were abysmal. Nor were they much better for *The Squaw Man* (1931), DeMille's third go-round with this hoary tale of love between an English nobleman (Warner Baxter) and the Indian maid (Lupe Velez) who dies for him.

MGM and DeMille let their disappointing association dissolve, but his old friend Jesse Lasky laid down the red carpet for him at Paramount, scene of their early triumphs; DeMille would stay there for the next twenty-five years, but Lasky was forced into retirement before DeMille had finished shooting his first picture. *The Sign of the Cross* (1932), a lavish epic about the dissolution of Rome under Nero, appeared emblematic of DeMille at his most profligate—but he actually had been placed on (and adhered to) a strict budget that the spectacle belied. Claudette Colbert had the sexiest role of her career as the wicked Poppaea, wife of Nero (Charles Laughton at his most delightfully outrageous), bathing in the milk of asses and trying to seduce lipsticked Fredric March right up to the moment the lions gobble her up. (The 1944 reissue trimmed the most erotic material and added a bit of new footage in deference to the Code.) The little-seen *This Day and Age* (1933) was an original turn on the gangster saga, with killer Charles Bickford dealt justice for his crimes by a group of intrepid high-school vigilantes.

*Four Frightened People* (1934) was also atypical for DeMille—a survival yarn in which Claudette Colbert, Herbert Marshall, Mary Boland, and William Gargan try to survive the rigors of the Malayan jungle; much of it was filmed on location on a small, bug-infested Hawaiian island, and the stars look properly miserable. With *Cleopatra* (1934), DeMille returned to the sort of historical spectacular with which he would forever after be associated. Here Colbert exercises her wiles on Henry Wilcoxon (as Marc Antony) and Warren William (Caesar) in less than half the time it took Liz Taylor to seduce Richard Burton, and capped it with one of the best death scenes on film. History it wasn't, but the film was one of twelve Academy Award nominees for best picture of 1934. *The Crusades* (1935) was another lavish spectacle, with Loretta Young a winsome Berangaria of Navarre and Henry Wilcoxon a piece of plywood as Richard the Lionheart—uninspired casting that helped convince the public to stay away in droves.

DeMille learned his lesson and cast *The Plainsman* (1937) with two of the day's most charismatic stars, Gary Cooper and Jean Arthur, who were just coming off the hugely successful *Mr. Deeds Goes to Town*. As the romantically involved Wild Bill Hickok and Calamity Jane, they weren't particularly authentic—but then neither were the soundstage shots that DeMille seemed to prefer over the Montana location footage he'd shot. The thousands of Sioux and Cheyenne Indians he hired as extras were real enough, although the speaking parts were left to impostors like Anthony Quinn (who met DeMille's adopted daughter Katherine during filming and married her in 1937). In any event, it was DeMille's biggest box-office success since returning to Paramount.

*The Buccaneer* (1938) wasn't as big a hit, probably because audiences didn't know (or care) who female lead Franciska Gaal was, but Fredric March made a fine Jean Lafitte and the Battle of New Orleans was staged with flair. This was also the year that DeMille rejected an invitation to run for the U.S. Senate. Instead, he made *Union Pacific* (1939), a sweeping, disaster-packed account of the building of the first transcontinental rail line, with Joel McCrea, Barbara Stanwyck, and Robert Preston as the heroes and gambling-den owner Brian Donlevy the hissable villain. Made with the cooperation of the Union Pacific Railroad, which supplied the antique trains and the crews to run them, the film had more than its share of verisimilitude.

But it was back to pure hokum with *Northwest Mounted Police* (1940), a laughably set-bound extravaganza that was DeMille's first brush with Technicolor. Gary Cooper played a Texas Ranger who roams up to Canada (where DeMille had planned to shoot on location) hunting for his man while half-breed Paulette Goddard (in "redskin" makeup as artificial as the rest of the activity), Robert Preston, and Madeleine Carroll mill around the fake evergreens. Incredibly, it was Paramount's biggest hit of 1940. *Reap the Wild Wind* (1942) was another smash; John Wayne and Ray Milland star as salvagers (circa 1840) competing for Southern hellcats Paulette Goddard and Susan Hayward while battling villain Raymond Massey, storms, shipwrecks, and giant squids. Every cent of the $2 million DeMille spent was up there onscreen, and the film won an Oscar for special effects.

*The Story of Dr. Wassell* (1944), from James Hilton's book, required DeMille to stick close to the facts about the Navy doctor (Gary Cooper) who saved nine wounded men during World War II by sneaking them past the Japanese to the safety of Australia. Patriotic it was, exciting it wasn't; DeMille fared better when his imagination was allowed to run wild. With that in mind, DeMille invited Coop back for *Unconquered* (1947), a $5 million, pitilessly overlong yarn set in colonial times, with Coop as a militia captain who rescues Paulette Goddard from indentured servitude while readying for the attack of the Seneca nation on Fort Pitt—led by that notorious Indian chief Boris Karloff. Even with DeMille's license for artificiality, this was too dumb to swallow, and audiences of the day didn't, incurring a huge loss for Paramount.

He rebounded with *Samson and Delilah* (1949), an equally silly but wildly profitable epic whose $12 million gross ignited Hollywood's mad rush to cash in on the Bible. Victor Mature and Hedy Lamarr

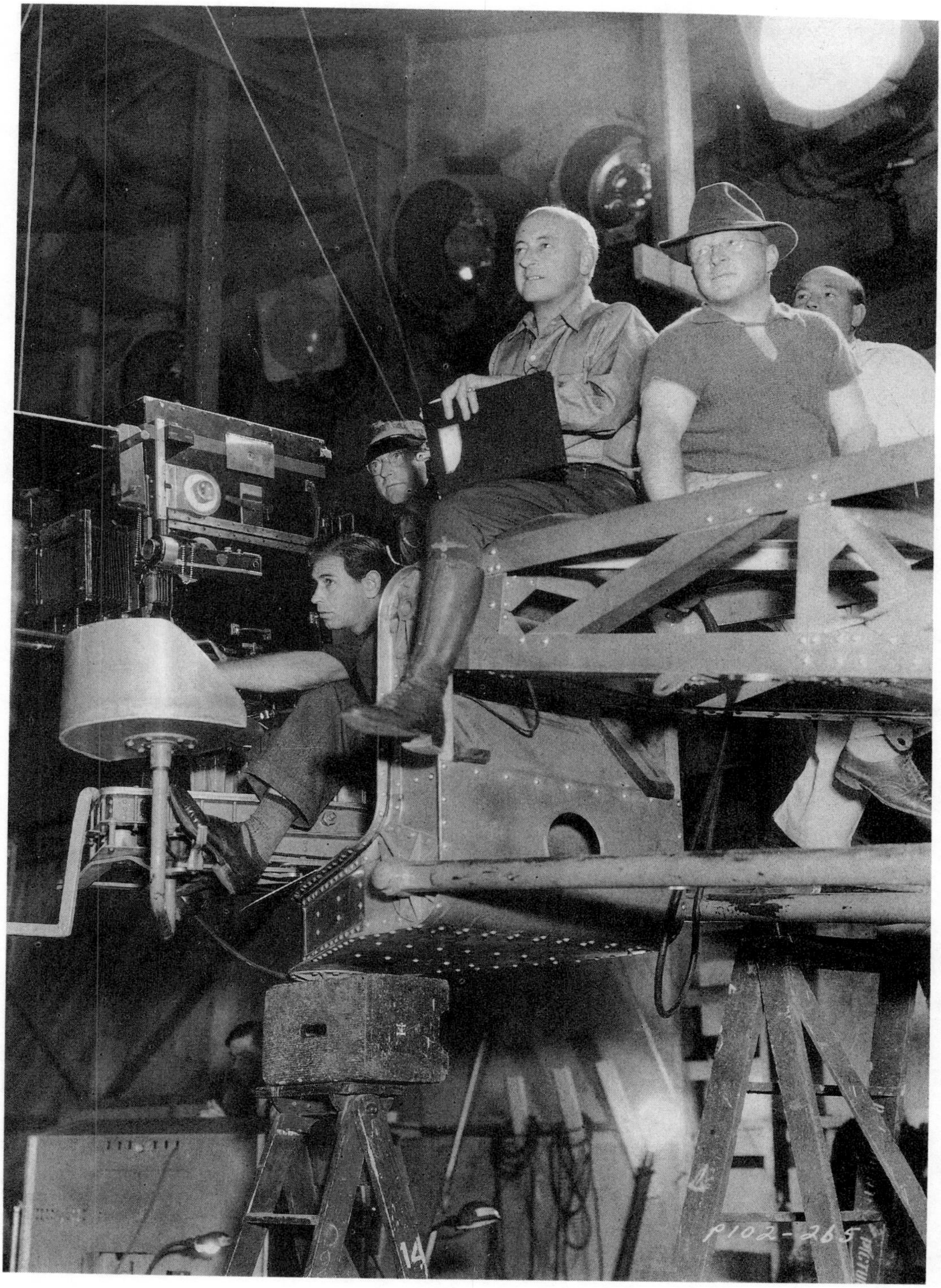


▲ *On the set of the multimillion-dollar epic* Reap the Wild Wind

made terrific leads, and George Sanders was a quietly lethal villain. After taking time to appear as himself in the memorable finale to *Sunset Boulevard*, DeMille made his Oscar-winning *The Greatest Show on Earth* (1952), an all-stops-out salute to the circus that earned him his only nomination for best direction. Charlton Heston was wooden as the big-top boss, but that was compensated for by the fine work of James Stewart, Gloria Grahame, and Cornel Wilde. Heston was much better as Moses in DeMille's final movie, *The Ten Commandments* (1956), with Yul Brynner a worthy foe as Ramses. For once, the excessive approach (this ran almost four hours) and shameless vulgarity worked in the film's favor; it made millions and was Oscar-nominated as best picture—a splendid way for DeMille to complete forty-three years of moviemaking. His *Autobiography* was published in 1959.

▲ *With the circus folk on location during* The Greatest Show on Earth

## ● BRIAN DE PALMA (1940– )

Celebrated in the Seventies as a master of the macabre and derided at the same time as a slavish imitator of Hitchcock, Brian De Palma has managed to broaden his creative horizons without quite settling the question of exactly how important, or even how good, he is as a director. It is more than a bit alarming that, between the critical (if not financial) success of *Blow Out* in 1981 and *Carlito's Way* in 1993, he had exactly one film that both critics and audiences embraced, the 1987 *The Untouchables*, with several near- and outright disasters flanking it.

The son of a surgeon, De Palma was born in Newark, New Jersey, and educated at Columbia and Sarah Lawrence in New York, switching from premed studies to the film courses that propelled him toward his first feature, *The Wedding Party*, co-directed with Wilford Leach and Cynthia Munroe. Shot in 1963 but not released until 1969 (and then just barely), *Party* doesn't have much to offer except the novelty of seeing a very young Robert De Niro and Jill Clayburgh. *Murder à la Mod* (1966) reveals itself through its time-capsule title, but *Greetings* (1968), his first solo feature, was the best of the counterculture pictures. Faint praise, perhaps—but with only $40,000 in financing De Palma managed to capture the raunchy ambience of purple-hazed Greenwich Village with something approaching authenticity; De Niro and Allen Garfield stood out in the cast of semipros. The *Times* hated it, but Pauline Kael was encouraging.

*Dionysus in '69* (1970) was co-directed with Robert Fiore and Bruce Rubin, while *Hi, Mom!* (1970) was the wonderfully loony sequel to *Greetings*, with De Niro back as a would-be porno filmmaker who turns urban guerrilla, smarmy Allen Garfield as his mentor, and Jennifer Salt as his shrewish wife. It didn't make any money, but at least it brought De Palma to the attention of the majors. Warner Bros. signed him in 1970 to make what they considered to be a counterculture comedy. But *Get to Know Your Rabbit*, his first Hollywood movie, was taken out of De Palma's hands after Tommy Smothers fought with him, and De Palma was fired as the picture neared completion. Finished (clumsily) by other hands, it wasn't released until 1972, and offers only intermittent amusing bits by Orson Welles and Allen Garfield.

De Palma was shaken by the experience, but rebounded in 1973 to make the cult chiller *Sisters* for AIP. The first of his many homages to Alfred Hitchcock, right down to the great Bernard Herrmann score, it starred Margot Kidder as Siamese twins separated at birth, one of whom is an insane killer; Jennifer Salt is a reporter who accidentally witnesses one of the gruesome murders. De Palma gets the killings right, but misses badly when he tries to replicate Hitchcock's black humor. *Phantom of the Paradise* (1974) was Faust retold as a rock musical, with clever stylistic references to several classic horror movies, including *Psycho* and of course *Phantom of the Opera*. Paul Williams's score is rather more effective than he is as the evil Swan, but Jessica Harper as the object of desire and Gerrit Graham as the depraved singer Beef are both memorable.

*Obsession* (1976) was a naked recycling of *Vertigo*, and while De Palma expertly mounts the suspense (screenplay by Paul Schrader), the paucity of invention is more than a little disappointing. Genevieve Bujold is quite appealing as the reincarnation of dull Cliff Robertson's dead (or is she?) wife, but Bernard Herrmann's Oscar-nominated score has to carry more than its share of the weight. But *Carrie* (1976) was a genuine shocker, based on a novel by newcomer Stephen King. Sissy Spacek is splendid as the introverted teen whose largely suppressed telekinetic powers come to the fore after she's cruelly humiliated by the high-school in-crowd (Nancy Allen, John Travolta, Amy Irving) and Piper Laurie is chilling as her wacky, fundamentalist mom. Its heart-stopping postscript aside, the film is at its best in its mood-building early scenes, working as an allegory of the confusion and shame wrought by the onset of sexuality, and at its worst during the all-stops-out, blood-soaked conclusion.

*The Fury* (1978), from the John Ferris novel, transposed the telekinetic chills of *Carrie* to the canvas of international intrigue. Kirk Douglas and John Cassavetes battle each other tooth and nail for the souls of "gifted" youngsters Amy Irving and Andrew Stevens; it has some terrific set pieces involving their paranormal powers, but De Palma is barely competent when staging the conventions of spy vs. spy. (If nothing else, Cassavetes gets the most unusual death scene of the decade.) *Home Movies* (1979) was little more than an in-joke, with De Palma's Sarah Lawrence film students making up the crew on this apparently improvised yarn about a self-important director (Kirk Douglas) who helps Keith Gordon win the heart of Nancy Allen.

Gordon and Allen were better served in *Dressed to Kill* (1980), a stylish thriller about a mysterious serial killer that De Palma wrote himself. What distinguishes this nail-biter from something like *Obsession* is De Palma leavening his shocks with well-placed dabs of black humor, giving the film more the flavor of Hitchcock in his prime. But its erotic content—Angie Dickinson as a frustrated Manhattan housewife, Nancy Allen as a spunky hooker—goes far beyond anything Hitch could have gotten away with (although had he worked into the Eighties he might have wanted to try). There's a brilliant sequence that does for elevators what *Psycho* did for showers back in 1960, and Michael Caine's warped psychiatrist is limned as vividly as Anthony Perkins's Norman Bates.

Coming off the best reviews of his career, De Palma made *Blow Out* (1981), a conspiracy-theory thriller again based on his own original screenplay. More or less a cross between Francis Ford Coppola's *The Conversation* and Michelangelo Antonioni's *Blow-Up* (which De Palma's choice of title makes no bones about), it features John Travolta as a sound-effects mixer for trashy movies who accidentally records a sound that suggests that the Chappaquiddick-like drowning of a politician was not the accidental death it was presumed to be. While Travolta gives one of his best performances, and Nancy Allen (now De Palma's wife) is disarming as (again) a helpful prostitute, the nihilistic conclusion tips the film over into *The Parallax View* territory; there is no catharsis, which might explain why it (like *Parallax*) didn't do well at the box office.

Just when the critics were beginning to take De Palma seriously, he made the risible *Scarface* (1983), an over-the-top, past-the-moon updating of Howard Hawks's 1932 version of the life of Al Capone; Al Pacino stars as a Cuban refugee who takes over Miami's cocaine trade before learning that absolute power (and unlimited coke) corrupts absolutely. The lesson is imparted in the film's first hour, but it takes De Palma (and Oliver Stone, who wrote the screenplay) almost two *more* hours of clumsily staged, blood-soaked redundancies to make sure we get it. *Body Double* (1984) was more coherent, but it was weakened by the casting of Craig Wasson as the befuddled protagonist who thinks he has witnessed a murder through his telescope (yes, it's *Rear Window* again, not to mention bits of several other Hitchcock—and even De Palma!—productions). But Melanie Griffith's gum-cracking porno actress is almost enough to carry the day.

The withering reception of *Body Double* steered De Palma away from sex and violence for quite a while. The comic *Wise Guys* (1986) contained none of the excesses or themes that De Palma had been barbecued for so often, but in their place it had precious little to offer beyond the modest premise of Danny DeVito and Joe Piscopo as low-level New Jersey hoods who screw up, earning the ire of bossman Harvey Keitel. That film came and went without making a ripple, but *The Untouchables* (1987) marked a brilliant return to form, with David Mamet's script deepening the 1950s TV series about federal agent Eliot Ness's war against racketeering in general and Al Capone in particular in 1930s Chicago. Although Kevin Costner's deliberately bland portrayal of straight-arrow Ness was—well—bland, the more flamboyant characterizations of Sean Connery's Irish cop (an Oscar winner) and De Niro's Capone provided flavor aplenty, and De Palma's staging of the action was fresh and powerful. The result was the best reviews—and biggest grosses—of De Palma's career.

Stretching in yet another direction, De Palma made the Vietnam drama *Casualties of War* (1989), a David Rabe–scripted tale of American troops that went over the line (based on an actual incident). A miscast Michael J. Fox undercuts the enterprise to a degree, but Sean Penn is superb as the psychopathic sergeant who torments a Vietnamese prisoner (Thuy Thu Le). The lukewarm reception of the film was a bitter disappointment to De Palma, who had gone to great pains to make it a personal statement.

Stung by that indifference, De Palma plunged into a $40 million adaptation of Tom Wolfe's best-selling satire of New York City's warring social strata. But De Palma hadn't demonstrated much flair for comedy in the last twenty years, and he was unable to will *The Bonfire of the Vanities* (1990) into working as social commentary, comedy or drama. The mis-casting of most of the roles in the picture (Tom Hanks, Melanie Griffith, and—most disastrously—Bruce Willis) certainly didn't help, and the changes rung on the original story were without exception ill advised. In the end there is no simple explanation of why *Bonfire* failed to the degree it did, joining the short list of the cinema's all-time, big-budget tur-keys. (A blow-by-blow account of De Palma's and Warners' miscues is provided in reporter Julie Salo-mon's wonderful book *The Devil's Candy*.)

Embarrassed and professionally damaged by the scorn and poor box office that greeted *Bonfire*, De Palma retreated to the safer ground of the thriller, but the over-the-top *Raising Cain* (1992), despite clever homages to Hitchcock and Orson Welles and a wildly entertaining performance by John Lithgow (as twin brothers who are a quart short in the sanity department) failed to please even genre cultists. *Carlito's Way* (1993), however, demonstrated that De Palma hadn't lost his bearings altogether; it's a styl-ish (if somewhat familiar) gambol through the crime-infested streets of New York's Spanish Harlem, with Al Pacino in top form as an ex-con who's dragged back into the rackets against his will by coke-snorting attorney Sean Penn. Redolent of Sidney Lumet's *Prince of the City* and *Serpico*, this handsomely mounted film was a modest success, positioning De Palma for another grab at the brass ring.

BLOW
OUT
Murder
has a sound
all of its own

## ● WILLIAM DIETERLE (1893–1972)

One of Warner Bros.' most reliable directors during the golden Thirties, William Dieterle gave up his filmmaking career in his native Germany to come to the United States, where he made more than fifty films between 1931 and 1957, including some of the best biopics ever to come out of Hollywood. He began acting at the age of nineteen and within a few years had become a member of Max Reinhardt's legendary stage company. Dieterle acted in German films until 1928, but thereafter he committed himself to directing, and by 1930 had overseen a dozen features. That same year he signed a seven-year contract with Warners–First National to come to Hollywood. Dieterle had some peculiar working methods, not the least of which was consulting his astrological chart before deciding if a film could begin shooting. Most of the time, the stars were in alignment.

His first picture for Warners was *The Last Flight* (1931), a Lost Generation drama set in Paris about four World War I airmen whose injuries inhibit them from ever returning to the States; it starred Richard Barthelmess, Elliot Nugent, and Johnny Mack Brown. An impressive seven features bore his name in 1932: *Her Majesty, Love* was an indifferent musical with Marilyn Miller and W. C. Fields, while *Man Wanted* was a romantic comedy, with Kay Francis as a wandering wife; *Jewel Robbery* paired Francis to good effect with the suave William Powell, and *The Crash* sent George Brent to ruination at the hands of high-living wife Ruth Chatterton. *Six Hours to Live!* was the amount of time recently deceased Warner Baxter had to enjoy after a scientist brought him back to life, while *Scarlet Dawn* was a melodrama set during the Russian Revolution, with Douglas Fairbanks, Jr., and Nancy Carroll. Dieterle completed his busiest year with *Lawyer Man*, which featured William Powell as a slick mouthpiece facing blackmail.

*From Headquarters* (1933) was a formulaic police procedural with George Brent, but *Grand Slam* (1933) was more interesting, a deft satire on bridge tournaments, in which Loretta Young competes with her champion ex-husband (Paul Lukas). *Female* (1933), which Dieterle co-directed with Michael Curtiz, was a typical Ruth Chatterton sudser, but *Fashions of 1934* was a tasty morsel; William Powell plays a New York designer who uses secretary Bette Davis to rip off the latest styles from Paris, and the production numbers were brilliantly staged by Busby Berkeley. The 1934 *Fog over Frisco* used Bette Davis again, this time as a larcenous tart whose stepsister (Margaret Lindsay) doesn't believe her capable of crime. *Madame Du Barry* was a highly imaginative account of the life of the infamous French courtesan, with Dolores Del Rio supplying the glamour, while *The Firebird* (both 1934) was a static murder mystery set in Vienna, adapted from a creaky stage vehicle.

Dieterle hadn't been entrusted with Warners' top properties thus far, and the melodrama *The Secret Bride* (1935) was just another programmer, despite the presence of Barbara Stanwyck. But *A Midsummer Night's Dream* was one of the studio's most prestigious releases of 1935, mounted and begun by Dieterle's old mentor Max Reinhardt (who had staged the production in the Hollywood Bowl in 1934). Dieterle was brought in to co-direct when it became clear that Reinhardt was having problems, and the result was a colorful (if imperfect) adaptation of the Bard—some serious miscasting was at the root of many of its problems. Even so, it was nominated for a best picture Oscar (along with eleven other candidates). Now Dieterle found himself handling the studio's better talent. *Dr. Socrates* (also 1935), a crackling crime picture, may not have been one of Paul Muni's most enduring vehicles, but *The Story of Louis Pasteur* (1936) certainly was—Muni won his only Academy Award (in a very tough field) for his performance as the courageous scientist, and the picture was also Oscar-nominated. *The White Angel* (1936) was another elevated biopic about a hero of healing, although Kay Francis was far less convincing as Florence Nightingale than Muni had been as Pasteur.

*Satan Met a Lady* (1936), starring Bette Davis and Warren William, was a pallid remake of Hammett's *The Maltese Falcon* (filmed just five years earlier), with the characters and material foolishly played for laughs, and *The Great O'Malley* (1937) was just as awful, a sentimental crime entry, with Pat O'Brien and Humphrey Bogart done in by a treacly script. *Another Dawn* (1937) was an adequate soaper, with Kay Francis and Errol Flynn trying to restrain their passion for each other in the African desert. Dieterle then landed a prestige property with *The Life of Emile Zola*; Paul Muni plays the outspoken writer who protested in the French courts the unjust charge of treason that had been leveled against Jewish officer Dreyfus by the Army. A box-office success, the film won the Academy Award as the best picture of 1937—Warner Bros.' first-ever win in that category—Dieterle, Muni, and Joseph Schildkraut (who won for his portrayal of Dreyfus) were among the other nominees.

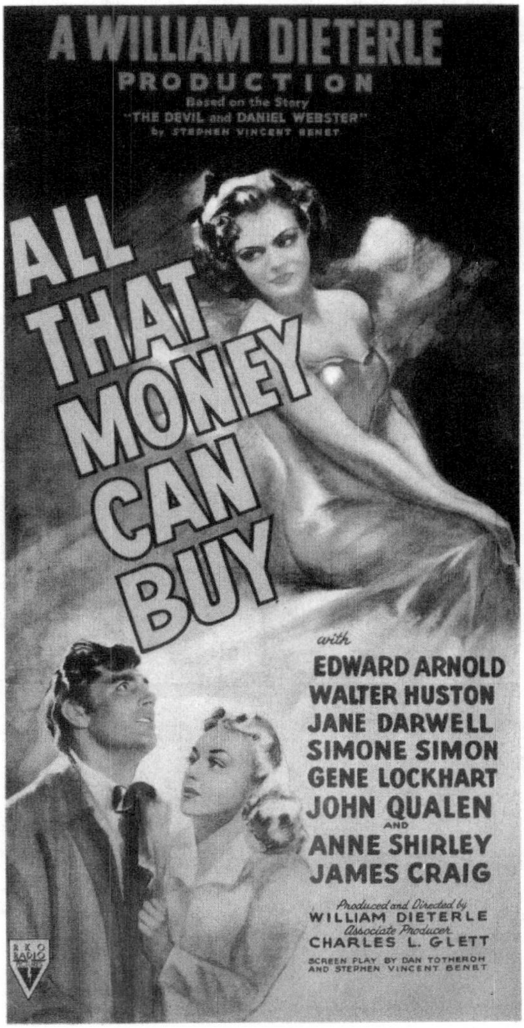


*Blockade* (1938) was a handsomely mounted production, although Henry Fonda and Madeleine Carroll struck few sparks as the lovers torn apart by the Spanish Civil War. *Juárez* (1939), though positioned to be another *Zola*, floundered when Paul Muni's impassive interpretation of the charismatic Mexican leader almost embalmed the picture; only the efforts of Claude Rains, John Garfield, and Bette Davis kept it alive. In 1939 Dieterle remade *The Hunchback of Notre Dame* for RKO, and it was one of his finest (if least typical) works, a lavish production anchored by Charles Laughton's moving performance as Quasimodo, with a fine supporting cast that included Sir Cedric Hardwicke, Thomas Mitchell, and newcomer Maureen O'Hara. *Dr. Ehrlich's Magic Bullet* (1940) was another of Warners' tasteful screen biographies; Edward G. Robinson starred as the German scientist who discovered a cure for venereal disease and Ruth Gordon played his wife.

*A Dispatch from Reuters* (1940) used Robinson as yet another famous nineteenth-century German, the founder of the international news service; however, the picture was not particularly compelling. It proved to be Dieterle's last film for Warner Bros. RKO made him an attractive offer that allowed him to establish his own production company, whose first release was *All That Money Can Buy* (1941), a superb dramatization of Stephen Vincent Benet's classic story "The Devil and Daniel Webster," with Edward Arnold as the tempted Webster and Walter Huston (Oscar-nominated) as the honey-tongued Mr. Scratch. The ambiguous title might have been chosen because RKO already had a film in release called *The Devil in Miss Jones*, but if so, it was a disastrous decision—the film bombed at the box office. By the time *Syncopation*, a clumsy drama about the rise of jazz, was released in 1942, Dieterle and RKO had already parted ways. Moving to MGM, he made the passable biopic *Tennessee Johnson* (1942), with Van

Heflin as our seventeenth President, and *Kismet* (1944), a nonmusical version of the hoary tale, with Marlene Dietrich at her exotic best and Ronald Colman rather bemused by the silly goings-on.

Dieterle now joined forces with David O. Selznick, for whom he directed the inane *I'll Be Seeing You* (1945), starring Ginger Rogers as a paroled jailbird meeting and falling in love with shell-shocked soldier Joseph Cotten during the holidays. The ultra-sudsy *Love Letters* (1945) was another glossy Selznick melodrama, with Jennifer Jones as an amnesiac whose memory is restored after she reads old love letters written by Joseph Cotten; it was scripted by Ayn Rand, of all people, and was inordinately popular. Selznick then prevailed upon Dieterle to take over from King Vidor on *Duel in the Sun* (1946), for which he shot the lively opening saloon scene.

Signing a contract with Hal Wallis at Paramount to produce and direct, Dieterle was force-fed more soap. The 1945 *This Love of Ours*, with Merle Oberon and Charles Korvin, was about an erstwhile wife and husband who rediscover their love for each other twelve years after their breakup. The verbose *The Searching Wind* (1946) was adapted by Lillian Hellman from her Broadway play about war and peace and the love between a diplomat (Robert Young) and a journalist (Sylvia Sidney) over several years; few cared, or paid to see it. But *The Accused* (1948) was an enjoyable noir, with Loretta Young on the run from detective Wendell Corey, and Selznick's *Portrait of Jennie* (1948) was—wonder of wonders—an excellent Jennifer Jones–Joseph Cotten love story with a supernatural twist that has been borrowed several times since.

*Rope of Sand* (1949) pitted *Casablanca* alumni Paul Henreid, Claude Rains, and Peter Lorre against

▲ *Dieterle (wearing gloves) on the set of* Tennessee Johnson *with Van Heflin*

Burt Lancaster searching for a treasure buried in the North African desert. *Paid in Full* (1950) stuck Lizabeth Scott in a truly gruesome soap opera no actress could have survived unscathed; she was treated better in the 1950 *Dark City*, a good if unsurprising noir that also marked the Hollywood debut of Charlton Heston. *September Affair* (1951) should have been awful, but somehow this unabashedly soapy romance between plane-crash absentees Joseph Cotten and Joan Fontaine worked despite the call of common sense. Dieterle probably preferred the scenarios of *Peking Express*, a remake of *Shanghai Express* with Joseph Cotten and Corinne Calvet, and *Red Mountain* (both 1951), a two-fisted account of Quantrill's Raiders, with John Ireland as the bad Reb betrayed by former Raider Alan Ladd.

Dieterle was now having problems with HUAC, which a few years earlier had taken umbrage at his efforts to bring Bertolt Brecht and Kurt Weill to Hollywood. His passport was confiscated, and would be again in 1953. In the meantime, he toiled on, making *The Turning Point* (1952) from a story by Horace McCoy; stars William Holden and Edmund O'Brien purge a city of corruption. Holden worked with Dieterle again that year in *Boots Malone*, a rather pleasant racetrack story, while *Salome* (1953) was Columbia's big entry in the booming biblical adventure genre—but even Rita Hayworth and a cast of British all-stars couldn't disguise the inherent dumbness of this lavish Technicolor production. *Elephant Walk* (1954) was begun with Vivien Leigh, but when her health collapsed, Elizabeth Taylor was recruited to watch the stampeding elephant herd reduce wacko husband Peter Finch's Ceylonese plantation to tinder.

Dieterle made just two more pictures before departing Hollywood. *Magic Fire* (1956) was a turgid biopic of composer Richard Wagner done on the cheap—as one might expect from a studio like Republic, where it was made. At least *Omar Khayyam* (1957) was fun, a foray into ancient Persia with Cornel Wilde, Debra Paget, and John Derek buckling their swashes just like in the old days. The following year Dieterle returned to his homeland, but his experiences with the German film industry weren't any more satisfying than his later years in the States, and after three pictures he gave up moviemaking and returned to the theater.

## ● EDWARD DMYTRYK (1908– )

For a brief, shining moment in the mid-1940s, Edward Dmytryk was making some of the best films to come out of Hollywood. Then disaster struck, and while he managed to survive his misfortune and make dozens of movies over the next three decades, none of them came close to matching the level of his earlier work. In fact, a perilous number of his movies struggled to reach mediocrity.

Born in Canada in 1908 to Ukrainian immigrants, Dmytryk began working in films while still a teenager. At Paramount during the Thirties he edited such films as *Million Dollar Legs*, *Ruggles of Red Gap*, and *Zaza*, while making a lone low-budget feature, *The Hawk* (1935). In 1939 Paramount made him a full-fledged director, and his "B" features for them included *Television Spy* (1939) with Anthony Quinn, *Golden Gloves* (1940) with Richard Denning, and *Mystery Sea Raiders* (1940) with Henry Wilcoxon. He made *Her First Romance* at Monogram in 1940, then moved to Columbia, where he helmed six choice genre entries in 1941: *Under Age*, a white-slavery yarn set in a trailer park, starring the great Tom Neal; *The Devil Commands*, with Boris Karloff inventing a device that allows him to communicate with his dead wife; *Sweetheart of the Campus*, in which Ruby Keeler meets Ozzie and Harriet (an event that probably hastened her retirement); *The Blonde from Singapore* with Leit Erikson; and *Confessions of Boston Blackie* and *Secrets of the Lone Wolf*, two series entries.

After *Counter Espionage* (1942), another well-made "Lone Wolf" mystery with Warren William, Dmytryk moved to RKO, where he would do much of his best work. *Seven Miles from Alcatraz* (1942) was an enjoyable blend of the prison-break and anti-Nazi categories, while *The Falcon Strikes Back* (1943) offered Tom Conway as the urbane detective. *Hitler's Children* (1943) was an exciting propaganda exercise, with Tim Holt and Bonita Granville suffering in Nazi Germany, while cult-favorite *Captive Wild Woman* (also 1943) found John Carradine turning a gorilla into the beautiful Acquanetta—nice work if you can get it. *Behind the Rising Sun* (1943) was more rabid propaganda, with Tom Neal and Robert Ryan battling the Japanese threat in the 1930s Far East.

All that cost-consciousness honed Dmytryk's skills, and in 1943 he was assigned his first "A" production, the sentimental *Tender Comrade*, in which Ginger Rogers lives communally on the homefront while her lout of a husband (Robert Ryan) is away at war; this was one of the pictures that provided HUAC with ammo against Dmytryk and screenwriter Dalton Trumbo a few years later. Then came the sublime *Murder, My Sweet* (1944). A faithful adaptation of Raymond Chandler's 1940 novel, *Farewell, My Lovely* (arguably Chandler's best), it starred erstwhile crooner Dick Powell as the self-deprecating, noble gumshoe Philip Marlowe, up against femme fatale Claire Trevor, dimwitted hood Mike Mazurki, and fraud Otto Kruger. A career saver for Powell, who looked good with stubble and a gat, this remains one of the four or five best films noir, offering style aplenty, with wit, pungent dialogue, and an almost comprehensible plot. Just a notch below that was *Cornered* (1945), another showcase for the new, two-fisted Powell, who plays an ex-serviceman looking for his wife's killer in Buenos Aires; Walter Slezak was a fine villain, but the picture suffered from the inadequacies of the instantly forgettable Micheline Cheirel.

*Back to Bataan* (1945) had John Wayne retaking the South Pacific with the aid of Filipino guerrillas—a rousing bit of World War II hokum—while *Till the End of Time* (1946) was a well-played drama starring Robert Mitchum, Guy Madison, and Bill Williams as returning vets having trouble readjusting to life on the homefront (similar to, but made just before, William Wyler's *The Best Years of Our Lives*). Then came what may be Dmytryk's best work, the noir landmark *Crossfire* (1947). A taut adaptation of Richard Brooks's novel *The Brick Foxhole*, it featured the peerless Robert Ryan as a psychotic whose impulsive off-base murder of a Jewish civilian sets off a manhunt—headed by Robert Young and Robert Mitchum—that ultimately snares him in its web. (The book's black victim here became a Jew.) Nominated for an Academy Award as best picture, *Crossfire* also earned Oscar nominations for Dmytryk, Ryan, Gloria Grahame (in a memorable Bad Girl cameo), and the screenplay.

Where Dmytryk might have gone from here can only be imagined, but a summons from HUAC in 1947 brought his rising star back to earth in a hurry. Charged as one of the Hollywood Ten, he was found guilty of having had Communist affiliations and was sentenced to prison. But he fled to England, where he made three films, including the socialist-themed *So Well Remembered* (1947), narrated by James Hilton, and *Give Us This Day* (1949). But in 1951 he returned from exile, served six months in jail, and publicly recanted, agreeing to cooperate fully with the committee and name names.

He now was free to work again in Hollywood, but his availability elicited only the crummy costumer *Mutiny* (1952). Then Stanley Kramer's production company at Columbia beckoned. Kramer needed someone who could work fast, and Dmytryk took on a mixed slate of low-budget productions.

*The Sniper* (1952) was the best of the group, with Arthur Franz as a compulsive killer whose victims are all women, while *Eight Iron Men* (also 1952) was an efficient World War II tale with Franz, Lee Marvin, and Richard Kiley repelling enemy attacks. *The Juggler* (1953), filmed in Israel, featured Kirk Douglas as a concentration-camp survivor who returns to Israel to start over. Then Dmytryk landed a plum, the adaptation of Herman Wouk's prize-winning bestseller and play, *The Caine Mutiny*. An all-star production with Humphrey Bogart as the deranged Captain Queeg, it received a best picture nomination from the Academy, and Tom Tully, Bogart, and the screenplay were also Oscar-nominated. The 1954 *Broken Lance* was *King Lear* on the range, with Spencer Tracy as the megalomaniacal patriarch who finds his cattle empire and family (Richard Widmark, Robert Wagner) disintegrating before his eyes. Katy Jurado was nominated as best supporting actress, and Philip Yordan's story won an Oscar.

Dmytryk appeared to have triumphed over his scarlet letter. But little of the work that followed over the next twenty years matched what had preceded it. *The End of the Affair* (1955) was a middling version of the Graham Greene novel shot in England; Van Johnson was hardly a match for Deborah Kerr. *Soldier of Fortune* (1936) had Clark Gable rescuing Gene Barry for Susan Hayward in Hong Kong, while *The Left Hand of God* (also 1955) had Humphrey Bogart as a downed flyer impersonating a priest to escape China with Gene Tierney during World War II. But *The Mountain* (1956) was a pretentious bomb, as weighty as Everest itself; Spencer Tracy and Robert Wagner are brothers (!) trying to scale a mountain to reach plane wreckage at the top.

*Raintree County* (1957), starring Elizabeth Taylor and Montgomery Clift (who was seriously injured in a car crash and disfigured during the shoot), was a rambling epic about the antebellum South that should have been pruned by a full hour. The equally inflated *The Young Lions*, from Irwin Shaw's bestselling World War II novel, was one of the biggest hits of 1958. Its strong cast (Brando as a sensitive Nazi officer, Dean Martin as a GI, Montgomery Clift) kept the elaborate story afloat. *Warlock* (1959) was a taut Western, with Henry Fonda, Richard Widmark, and Dorothy Malone, but Dmytryk's 1959 remake of *The Blue Angel*, the von Sternberg classic from 1930, is quite possibly one of the ten worst films of the decade (even allowing that Mai Britt is no Marlene Dietrich).

Almost as bad was *Walk on the Wild Side* (1962), an inept adaptation of Nelson Algren's fine novel, with a laughably miscast Laurence Harvey rescuing old love Capucine from lesbian madam Barbara Stanwyck; Jane Fonda is on hand for decoration. But *Walk* was a masterwork compared to Dmytryk's twin torpedos of 1964, *The Carpetbaggers* and *Where Love Has Gone*, both based on unapologetically trashy bestsellers by Harold Robbins. Between them they featured nearly five hours of bad acting, including (but not limited to) Bette Davis, Susan Hayward, and Joey Heatherton in *Love* (based on the Lana Turner–Johnny Stompanato scandal of 1958), and George Peppard (as Howard Hawks), Alan Ladd, and Carroll Baker (as Jean Harlow) in *Carpetbaggers*. Both pictures have evolved since their release into indisputable camp items, but that surely wasn't Dmytryk's intent.

*Mirage* (1965) was a respectable faux-Hitchcock thriller, with Gregory Peck as an amnesia victim, but *Alvarez Kelly* (1966), starring William Holden and Richard Widmark as foes during the Civil War, was a bit of a bore. *Shalako!* (1968), another Western, managed to waste Sean Connery and Brigitte Bardot, while *Anzio* (also 1968) was a leaden World War II epic, with Robert Ryan and Robert Mitchum teaming for Dmytryk once again. Dmytryk's nadir was *Bluebeard* (1972), a West German–Italian–French production starring a dissipated Richard Burton and, in a memorable teaming, Joey Heatherton and Raquel Welch. Lastly, forgettably, came *The Human Factor* (1975) and *He Is My Brother* (1976), bringing Dmytryk's once-estimable career to a rather ignominious close. He later taught at U.S.C. and wrote a book called *On Directing*.

## ● STANLEY DONEN (1924– )

A former Broadway dancer and choreographer who made the transition to directing films in impressive fashion, Stanley Donen is most closely associated with a number of the Fifties' most adventurous musicals. Born in Columbia, South Carolina, Donen left the University of South Carolina in 1940 to take a job as a chorus boy in the original production of *Pal Joey;* its star was Gene Kelly, with whom Donen would work many times over the next fifteen years. In 1941 he assisted Kelly with the choreography for the stage musical *Best Foot Forward;* when it was put into production as a film, Donen was invited to Hollywood to help choreograph it and repeat his role as a chorus boy. He stayed on at MGM to choreograph such musicals as *Jam Session, Cover Girl, Anchors Aweigh,* and *Living in a Big Way,* most of them alongside Kelly. He even co-wrote the screenplay for Busby Berkeley's *Take Me Out to the Ball Game* (1949), which he also choreographed.

Donen's big chance came when he was asked by Kelly to co-direct and co-choreograph *On the Town* (1949), the classic Comden-Green-Bernstein musical (based on Jerome Robbins's ballet *Fancy Free*) that had been a smash on Broadway in 1944. Shot on location in New York (in one week!) before returning to the Hollywood sound stages, it concerned the exploits of sailors Kelly, Frank Sinatra, and Jules Munshin on a one-day leave in the big city; Vera-Ellen, Ann Miller, and Betty Garrett provide the romance. One of MGM's biggest hits that year, it had an Oscar-winning score (with much of Bernstein now absent) that included "New York, New York" and "Lucky to Be Me." *Royal Wedding* (1951), from the Alan Jay Lerner musical, became Donen's first solo flight, with Fred Astaire and Jane Powell as a brother-sister team who are performing in London when Queen Elizabeth II is getting married. Astaire's dance routines were typically eye-popping and the Lane/Lerner songs ("Too Late Now," etc.) were fine, but the Anglophilia—like casting Winston Churchill's daughter, Sarah—got to be a bit much.

*Love Is Better than Ever* (1952) was a frail structure on which to parade the charms of Elizabeth Taylor, but no such complaint could be made about *Singin' in the Rain* (1952), which Donen co-directed with star Gene Kelly. It was one of the decade's two best musicals, along with Minnelli's *The Band Wagon. Singin'* became Kelly's biggest box-office success, and Jean Hagen was Oscar-nominated for her hilarious performance as a silent-screen star whose grating voice engenders a crisis when sound pictures arrive. The 1952 *Fearless Fagan* was several light-years away from that level of achievement; it was a modest comedy about a circus lion who joins the Army when trainer Carleton Carpenter is inducted. *Give a Girl a Break* (1953) was a so-so musical that offered Debbie Reynolds, Marge Champion, and Helen Wood as actresses trying to grab Broadway's brass ring; the dancing of Bob Fosse and Gower Champion enlivened the proceedings, but not enough.

But *Seven Brides for Seven Brothers* (1954) was another triumph, an inventive extrapolation of Stephen Vincent Benet's story "Sobbin' Women," which itself was based on the old tale of the rape of the Sabine women. The highly theatrical sets, wildly athletic dancing (choreography by Michael Kidd), and appealing cast (Howard Keel, Russ Tamblyn, Jane Powell, Julie Newmar) made this a huge financial and artistic success, earning Oscar nominations for best picture, screenplay, color cinematography, and score (its lone win). *Deep in My Heart* (1954) was a biopic about composer Sigmund Romberg (whose operettas kept Jeanette MacDonald busy for years), an all-star revue with MGM's top musical talent bringing Romberg's most famous works to life. José Ferrer impersonated Romberg, while Gene and brother Fred

Kelly danced, Vic Damone sang, and Cyd Charisse slinked.

Gene Kelly was back to co-direct *It's Always Fair Weather* (1955) with Donen, with a cast that included Cyd Charisse, Dan Dailey, and Michael Kidd. But the Comden-Green story about three Army pals whose ten-year reunion illustrates that they no longer can be friends was perhaps a bit too downbeat. *Funny Face* (1957) was sold to Paramount after the Freed Unit developed it at MGM; why Leo didn't want to handle this superb production remains a mystery, particularly since MGM sent half its talent along to help make it. Set in Paris, it's a magical teaming of Fred Astaire and Audrey Hepburn, and includes one of Gershwin's best scores (''S'Wonderful,'' ''How Long Has This Been Going On''), gorgeous cinematography, art direction, and production design (abetted by consultant Richard Avedon, who helped inspire Astaire's stylish photographer). The finished film—one of Donen's best—bore little resemblance to the stage musical Astaire had starred in with his sister, Adele, back in the late Twenties, but so what?

Now operating freelance, Donen co-directed *The Pajama Game* with George Abbott, who had handled the stage hit. With sparkling choreography by Bob Fosse and most of the Broadway cast on hand, it was about a factory whose workers are about to go on strike unless they get a seven and a half–cent raise. Doris Day played the head of the grievance committee, and the delightful score included ''Hernando's Hideaway'' and ''Steam Heat.'' The 1957 *Kiss Them for Me* was less memorable, a strained Navy comedy that did offer the intriguing cast of Cary Grant, Jayne Mansfield, Ray Walston, and Suzy Parker. *Indiscreet* (1958) used Grant to better effect as a diplomat-playboy who romances famed actress Ingrid Bergman, who's on to him from the get-go; it was adapted by Norman Krasna from his own stage play.

Donen returned to the musical with *Damn Yankees* (1958), again co-directing with George Abbott, who had helmed the Broadway production through a thousand-odd performances and now wrote the screenplay to boot. Combining the Faust legend with baseball was inspired, but the film seems a step off at times, despite having most of the Broadway cast (Gwen Verdon, Ray Walston, Jean Stapleton) and retaining the great score (''Whatever Lola Wants,'' ''[You Gotta Have] Heart''). The problem wasn't Bob Fosse's exciting choreography; perhaps it was Tab Hunter in the lead role. *Once More, with Feeling* (1960) also came from Broadway, but the oft-unpleasant barbs hurled at each other by Yul Brynner and Kay Kendall dragged down what was intended as a frothy romantic comedy. *Surprise Package* (1960) tried Brynner again, this time with Mitzi Gaynor in a caper yarn (from the novel by Art Buchwald). It had its moments, some contributed by Noël

Coward, but positing Brynner as a Damon Runyonesque gangster was not inspired casting.

Donen fared well with the 1960 *The Grass Is Greener*, a pleasant if unremarkable marital comedy with an all-star cast: Cary Grant, Deborah Kerr, Robert Mitchum, and Jean Simmons. *Charade* (1963) was better still, a tongue-in-cheek suspenser that set charismatic stars Cary Grant and Audrey Hepburn (in their only teaming, alas) on the trail of a $350,000 treasure, with Walter Matthau and James Coburn as amusingly nefarious villains. But *Arabesque* (1966) was a confusing espionage yarn set in London, with Gregory Peck as a bewildered American professor; Peck was perhaps a bit *too* stoic, although Sophia Loren made a devastatingly beautiful heroine.

Donen's best nonmusical was *Two for the Road* (1967), a penetrating examination of a marriage's ups and (more plentiful) downs; Audrey Hepburn and Albert Finney are both superb as the couple in trouble. Frederic Raphael's screenplay was Oscar-nominated, but the film was not a commercial success and had to wait a number of years to develop its cult following. *Bedazzled* (1967) is another cult favorite, a great comic vehicle for Dudley Moore and Peter Cooke that explores the seven deadly sins—guess which one is represented by Raquel Welch? But *Staircase* (1968) was a mess, despite the provocative teaming of Rex Harrison and Richard Burton as a gay couple. *The Little Prince* (1974) was armed with a Lerner and Loewe score, a classic children's story, and Bob Fosse as a snake—but Donen failed to assemble these promising parts into a functioning whole.

After making his last five pictures in England, Donen returned to the States for *Lucky Lady* (1975), a big-budget romantic adventure set during Prohibition with Burt Reynolds, Gene Hackman, and Liza Minnelli as rum-runners who can't decide how to make three go into two. An alarming misfire that gets worse as it plods along, it was one of the year's biggest bombs. *Movie Movie* (1978) was a great idea—loving parodies of two of the 1930s most popular genres, the backstage musical and the boxing picture—but audiences were confounded by its oddity. Too bad, because George C. Scott, Eli Wallach, and Art Carney clearly enjoyed themselves making it.

It's hard to believe that Donen ever signed on to make something like *Saturn 3* (1980), with Farah Fawcett and Kirk Douglas menaced in deep space by Harvey Keitel, but presumably it sounded more promising in the development stage. Demi Moore played the Lolita role in *Blame It on Rio* (1984), a leering sex farce for which star Michael Caine probably should not be blamed. Donen made his belated Broadway directing debut with *The Red Shoes*, an expensive musical that closed a week after it opened late in 1993.

◀ *Donen with Albert Finney and Audrey Hepburn on the set of* Two for the Road

## ● RICHARD DONNER (1939– )

Most of today's bankable directors didn't require nearly twenty years to establish themselves, but after a very quiet start Richard Donner has lately emerged as one of Hollywood's most reliable makers of action blockbusters. Born in New York City, he tried his hand acting Off-Broadway, then moved to California, where he scuffled through such unglamorous film jobs as directing industrials and television commercials before graduating to top TV-series work like *Wanted: Dead or Alive.*

Donner directed his first feature film in 1961, a Cold War soaper called *X-15* that starred one of the cinema's least likely couples, Charles Bronson and Mary Tyler Moore. He didn't get his second chance for seven long years, but the lighthearted *Salt and Pepper* (1968), with Sammy Davis, Jr., and Peter Lawford as British club owners in trouble with the mob, was a minor hit. After filming the Charles Bronson sex comedy *Lola* (1969), Donner spent the next five years directing made-for-television films like *Lucas Tanner* (1974), a pilot for the series with David Hartman, *A Shadow in the Streets* with Tony LoBianco, and *Sarah T.—Portrait of a Teenage Alcoholic* (both 1975), another classic bad-girl role for Linda Blair.

On balance, not much to show for fifteen years of moviemaking—but Donner finally hit it big with *The Omen* (1976), a violent, enormously popular supernatural thriller that starred Gregory Peck as an American diplomat whose son, Damien—switched at birth upon the suggestion of a priest—turns out to be the Antichrist. Donner didn't bother making the two sequels, instead accepting the high-profile assignment in 1978, of directing the first *Superman* movie, which starred Christopher Reeve as the Man of Steel, Margot Kidder as Lois Lane, and Gene Hackman as archvillain Lex Luthor. Although the film turned out a bit on the bland side and a half hour too long (the second installment is much better), it went on to gross $134 million.

The honorable failure of *Inside Moves* (1980) and the dishonorable discharge that should have been awarded to the Richard Pryor–Jackie Gleason "comedy" *The Toy* (1982) kept audiences away in droves, and even the enjoyable sword-and-sorcery fantasy *Ladyhawke* (1985), with Rutger Hauer, Matthew Broderick, and Michelle Pfeiffer, barely registered at the box office. *The Goonies* (also 1985), based on a story by Steven Spielberg, was a lively modern-day pirate adventure told from the point of view of its ethnically mixed, gender-balanced juvenile cast, though it sometimes tried *too* hard to re-create the thrills of the old Hardy Boys yarns.

But Donner immediately re-established his commercial savvy with the blockbuster *Lethal Weapon* (1987), written by Shane Black. This spin on the mismatched-partners chestnut—Danny Glover is a by-the-book police detective with a loving family, Mel Gibson a widower with a suicidal bent who breaks every rule for the sheer joy of it—coupled with some truly spectacular action sequences, made this one of the year's biggest hits and started a "Lethal" franchise. But Donner next made the misbegotten *Scrooged* (1988), an updated, presumably comic version of *A Christmas Carol*, starring Bill Murray as a television mogul badly in need of redemption; despite a wonderful array of guest stars, it played as flat as a glass of week-old seltzer.

*Lethal Weapon 2* (1989) still had the star chemistry of Gibson and Glover going for it, along with enough stunts and explosions for a dozen other films—but its thrills feel forced and the film leaves a nasty aftertaste, despite comic relief by Joe Pesci. The well-intentioned but prohibitively expensive *Radio Flyer* (1992) may have been Donner's attempt to keep himself from being typecast as an action director, but its disturbing story about two abused boys who retreat into fantasy never struck the right tone, and neither critics nor audiences gave it a home. Predictably, Donner now returned to the well and made *Lethal Weapon 3* (1992), a bigger if not better variation on the formula: Gibson and Glover wreak havoc on criminals and innocent bystanders alike in between intradomestic spats, and Rene Russo registers as a buffed undercover cop who captures Gibson's fancy, and vice versa.

After Donner co-executive produced the smash children's picture *Free Willy* in 1993, Donner and Gibson (sounds like Santa's reindeer!) teamed again in the amiable but rather bloated *Maverick* (1994), which profited from the presence of James Garner, the original (and still definitive) Bret Maverick, and Jodie Foster—but it needed more substance from William Goldman's anachronistic screenplay. For all that, it raked in $100 million, further confirmation of Donner's newfound golden touch.

▲ *Donner (far right) takes a break from filming*

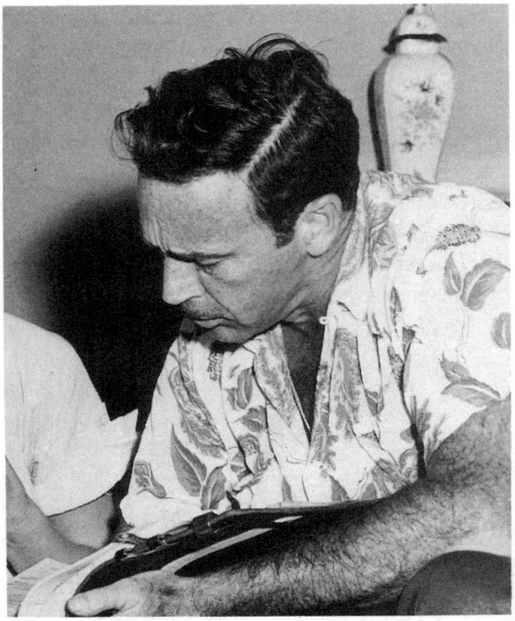

## ● GORDON DOUGLAS (1909–1993)

A generally proficient director whose rather shapeless filmography consists primarily of "B" pictures, genre entries, and other semireputable Hollywood products, Gordon Douglas managed to have his hand in a number of good (if never great) movies—can it be credited to sheer longevity?

Born in New York City, Douglas, who acted on stage as a child, finally made his way to Hollywood just as sound pictures were taking hold. He ended up at the Hal Roach studio. He originally acted in comedy shorts, then became the director of more than thirty "Our Gang" shorts, including the 1936 Oscar-winning short *Bored of Education*; he also co-directed the Our Gang Civil War feature, *General Spanky*, that year. Douglas's first solo features were *Zenobia* (1939) with Oliver Hardy and *Saps at Sea* (1940), one of Laurel and Hardy's best late vehicles. After making a few undistinguished comedies, in 1942 Douglas left Roach for RKO, where he was put to work on the "Gildersleeve" series. He advanced to "B" mysteries like *A Night of Adventure* and *The Falcon in Hollywood* (both 1944), but also was responsible for feeble programmers like *Zombies on Broadway* and *First Yank into Tokyo* (both 1945), the latter a contrived World War II yarn that had Tom Neal infiltrating a Japanese POW camp. *San Quentin* (1946) let Lawrence Tierney do his hard-boiled thing in prison, while *If You Knew Susie* (1948) was a grueling Eddie Cantor musical.

Moving to Columbia, Douglas worked on tough noirs (*Walk a Crooked Mile* [1948] with Dennis O'Keefe), Westerns (*The Nevadan* [1950] with Randolph Scott), and swashbucklers (*The Black Arrow* [1948] starring Louis Hayward, and *The Fortunes of Captain Blood* [1950]—a feeble remake of the Flynn classic). *Rogues of Sherwood Forest* (1950) had John Derek posing as the son of Robin Hood. Douglas's violent 1950 version of Horace McCoy's hard-boiled novel *Kiss Tomorrow Goodbye*, with James Cagney as a psychopathic gangster involved with Barbara Payton, was a cut or two below Raoul Walsh's *White Heat*. *Between Midnight and Dawn* (also 1950) was a mediocre noir—Mark Stevens was pitted against Edmond O'Brien—and *The Great Missouri Raid* (1950) was yet another telling of the James and Younger brothers' exploits.

At Warner Bros., where he would work for the next eleven years, Douglas made the formulaic cavalry-vs.-Indians picture *Only the Valiant* with Gregory Peck and Barbara Payton and *Come Fill the Cup* (both 1951), an interesting James Cagney film about alcoholism, with a memorable performance by Gig Young. The leading entry in the Red-baiting sweepstakes that year was surely the rabid *I Was a Communist for the FBI* (1951), with Frank Lovejoy as self-professed undercover hero Matt Cvetic. Incredibly, the film was nominated for an Academy Award as the best *documentary* of 1951; best unintentional *comedy* would have been more like it. (But it did keep HUAC off Jack Warner's back, which was undoubtedly the point.)

*Maru Maru* (1952) was a treasure-hunt adventure starring the aging Errol Flynn, while *The Iron Mistress* (1952) was a passable biopic with Alan Ladd as Jim Bowie (the title refers to the knife he invented). *She's Back on Broadway*, a musical drama with Virginia Mayo and Steve Cochran, and *The Charge at Feather River*, a 3-D Western with Guy Madison and Vera Miles (both 1953) were presentable examples of their kind, but *Them!* (1954) was considerably more than that. Probably the best of the Giant Creature films of the Fifties, it was also Douglas's best work, making one regret he didn't direct any other films in this much-abused genre.

His musical remake of Curtiz's 1938 success *Four Daughters* was called *Young at Heart* (1954), with Frank Sinatra, Doris Day, and a wealth of great tunes like "Someone to Watch Over Me," "One for My Baby (and One for the Road)," and "Just One of Those Things." *The McConnell Story* (1955) was a workmanlike biopic of the famed test pilot, with Alan Ladd and June Allyson, but *Sincerely Yours* (1955), was one of the decade's biggest hoots, a Liberace musical (Dorothy Malone was cast as his fiancée) so ludicrous that even his fans didn't bother to see it—at least, not enough of them. Douglas wisely stuck with Westerns and war movies for the next two years (*Santiago* and *The Big Land* with Alan Ladd, *Bombers B-52* with Natalie Wood and Efrem Zimbalist, Jr., *Fort Dobbs*), none of them particularly special. Even *The Fiend That Walked the West* (1958), a loose remake of *Kiss of Death*, had little more going for it than future mogul Robert Evans's over-the-top performance as the vicious psychopath played in 1947 by Richard Widmark. *Yellowstone Kelly* (1959) with Clint Walker was a solid Indian Wars tale penned by Burt Kennedy.

Douglas would make movies for another twenty years, but his best work was behind him. Of his last two dozen pictures, only a handful have even small pleasures to offer. *The Sins of Rachel Cade* (1961) had Angie Dickinson as a nurse in the strife-ridden Belgian Congo, while *Follow That Dream* (1962) was an Elvis Presley vehicle with one of his lamest scores ("On Top of Old Smokey"?!?). *Call Me Bwana* (1963) would have been Bob Hope's worst comedy to date had Anita Ekberg and Edie Adams not been along for decoration. *Robin and the 7 Hoods* (1964) was an enjoyable Rat Pack entry—the last—and home of "My Kind of Town," while *Rio Conchos* (1964) was a good Western starring erstwhile football great Jim Brown. Carroll Baker was interesting as a reformed Bad Girl in *Sylvia* (1965), but in the unblushingly trashy biopic *Harlow* (1965) she was left to wallow in a sinkhole.

Douglas's remake of *Stagecoach* (1966), with Ann-Margret and Bing Crosby, was wholly unnecessary, while *Way . . . Way Out!* (1966) was an appalling Jerry Lewis vehicle ("comedy" would be too kind a description) with Connie Stevens. *In Like Flint* (1967) was the loopy sequel to *Our Man Flint*, buoyed by James Coburn's smirking performance. Douglas then made three hard-boiled Sinatra pics, *Tony Rome* (1967), *Lady in Cement* (1968), and (the best of the lot) *The Detective* (1968), with a great cast (Jacqueline Bisset, Robert Duvall, Lee Remick, Ralph Meeker, Jack Klugman) and a nasty, nasty plot, based on the bestseller by Roderick Thorpe. Douglas's Seventies work was spotty: *They Call Me MISTER Tibbs!* (1970), a sequel to *In the Heat of the Night*, with Sidney Poitier as detective Virgil Tibbs, and *Slaughter's Big Rip-Off* (1973), a Blaxploitation entry with Jim Brown and—yikes!—Ed McMahon. His final work, *Viva Knievel!* (1978), is better left on the shelf, unviewed.

◀ *Douglas instructs Liberace in the art of kissing Dorothy Malone during* Sincerely Yours

## ● ALLAN DWAN (1885-1981)

Along with the more celebrated Cecil B. DeMille, Allan Dwan was one of the very few directors who made the transition from the days of the one-reelers through the glory days of the studio system and into the Fifties. He once claimed to have directed more than eighteen hundred films, and even if that estimate more than doubles the likely number (which includes a vast array of now-lost one- and two-reelers), such a prodigious output is mind-boggling. On the debit side, few of those hundreds and hundreds of pictures—nearly seventy of which came in the sound era—are on anyone's list of all-time classics, although their general anonymity doesn't disguise the craft with which they were made.

Born Joseph Aloysius Dwan in Toronto, he moved with his family to Chicago, subsequently earning a degree in electrical engineering from Notre Dame, where he also played football and later coached. In 1908 he got a job with the Peter Cooper Hewitt Company as a lighting engineer, a profession that soon brought him in contact with Chicago's Essanay film company. He began moonlighting for them as a writer, and was soon hired as a story editor. Moving to the American Film Company in 1911, he was given an opportunity to direct when the director of a California production went on a toot, leaving the company stranded. Dwan asked the actors to tell him what he was supposed to do as the director; they did, and he continued doing it for the better part of five decades.

Over the next two years, he turned out as many as 250 one-reelers for American Film—Westerns, comedies, even documentaries, all written, edited, and produced by Dwan. (Few if any of these still exist, but their evocative titles include *The Yiddisher Cowboy*; *Calamity Ann, Detective*; and *The Mormon*.) In 1913 he signed with Universal, but within a year moved to New York's Famous Players Company, and a year after that was working with D. W. Griffith at Triangle. It was Dwan who invented the equipment utilized for the crane shots in *Intolerance* in 1916, and he also is credited with introducing the dolly shot, filming actor William H. Crane's stroll in *David Harum* from a Ford.

Nearly as significant as those innovations were the eleven features he then made with Douglas Fairbanks, Sr., beginning with *The Half-Breed* in 1916 and culminating with *Robin Hood* (1922), one of the great silent pictures. In 1923 Dwan was signed by Paramount, where over the next few years he directed eight pictures starring Gloria Swanson, including *Zaza*, *Manhandled*, and *Stage Struck*. Dwan and Swanson both left Paramount in 1926 at the peak of their popularity, and neither would ever ride so high again. Dwan moved to Fox, but prestige came only with his occasional outside productions, such as the 1929 work *The Iron Mask* with Douglas Fairbanks, Sr., originally shown with some talking sequences, and *Tide of Empire* (also 1929), MGM's big-budget Western with synchronized sound and Renee Adoree.

*The Far Call*, *Frozen Justice*, and *South Sea Rose* (1929) were more modest early talkies done at Fox, but *What a Widow!* (1930) reunited Dwan and Swanson; an elaborate, expensive comedy, its failure precipitated Swanson's split with sponsor Joe Kennedy. *Man to Man* (1930), with Phillips Holmes, and *Chances* (1931), a World War I romance with Douglas Fairbanks, Jr., were made on loan-out to First National, but it was the melodrama *While Paris Sleeps* (1932), with Victor McLaglen and Helen Mack, that became Dwan's biggest hit in some time. Dwan spent the next two years in England, where he made the obscure *Her First Affair* (1933), *Counsel's Opinion* (1933), and *I Spy* (1934), before returning to the States and Fox, where he would labor on "B"s for the most part over the next six years. *Black Sheep* (1935), from Dwan's own story, starred Edmund Lowe as a professional gambler who sees Tom Brown being fleeced by jewel thief Claire Trevor and comes to his aid; it turns out Brown is his long-lost son.

*Navy Wife* (1935) had Trevor again, now as a divorced nurse in a Hawaiian naval hospital who falls in love with officer Ralph Bellamy, while in *The Song and Dance Man* (1936) Trevor is part of a dance team with Paul Kelly; it was adapted from a Broadway show by George M. Cohan, but Dwan didn't have the budget to mount it very grandly. *Human Cargo* (1936), barely an hour long, paired Trevor with Dwan for the fourth consecutive time here; she's a newspaper reporter who vies with rival scribe Brian Donlevy to crack a ring of smugglers specializing in illegal aliens. *High Tension* (1936) was even shorter than *Cargo* and moved nicely, as cable-layer Brian Donlevy tries in vain to avoid wisecracking Glenda Farrell's marital designs, while *15 Maiden Lane* (1936) offered Claire Trevor as an insurance investigator on the trail of jewel thief Cesar Romero.

Dwan remained on Fox's "B" train for most of 1937. The boxing exposé *Woman-Wise* starred Michael Whalen as a crusading sports reporter and Rochelle Hudson as the daughter of a crooked fighter. Hudson appeared again in *That I May Live* as a waitress who helps ex-con Robert Kent extricate himself from a life of crime, and *One Mile from Heaven* featured Claire Trevor as an eager-beaver newspaper reporter who gets in over her head on a story. Dwan finally was given an "A" production with *Heidi* (1937), one of Shirley Temple's better vehicles and still the best of the film versions of Spyri's classic children's story; Jean Hersholt was the loving grandfather from whom the orphaned Heidi is cruelly separated. Its success earned Dwan another go-round with Shirley (no small compliment, as in between the Dwan films she made *Wee Willie Winkie* with John Ford), and *Rebecca of Sunnybrook Farm* (1938) was also popular—although it didn't retain anything from the Wiggins story except the title.

*Josette* (1938) was a charming if minor romantic comedy, with Simone Simon as a nightclub singer courted by both Robert Young and Don Ameche. The spectacular *Suez* (1938) was a fanciful yarn, with Tyrone Power as French engineer Ferdinand de Lesseps (who was actually sixty-four when he finished building the Suez Canal) and Loretta Young as the woman who spurns him to marry Louis Napoleon.

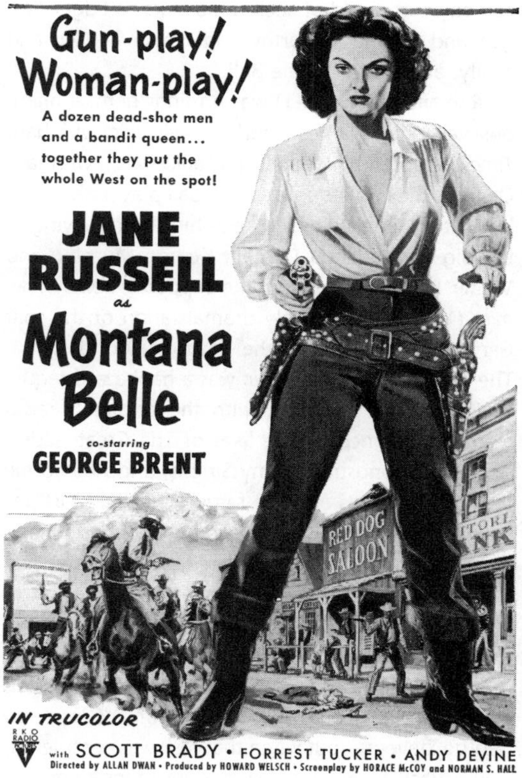


Dwan next directed a slapstick version of *The Three Musketeers* (1939), which had the nerve to pass off the Ritz Brothers as the Musketeers and Don Ameche as a warbling D'Artagnan, although Lionel Atwill was good as de Rochefort. The Ritzes and Atwill tried again in *The Gorilla* (1939), a creaky remake of the 1930 comic mystery; despite the presence of Bela Lugosi, it had been done better as a Three Stooges short.

Dwan's brief flirtation with Fox's "A" list was inexplicably drawing to a close, and so was his term at the studio. *Frontier Marshal* (also 1939) was a perfectly good telling of the Wyatt Earp legend, with Randolph Scott as Earp and Cesar Romero somewhat less inspired as Doc Holliday, but *Sailor's Lady* was romantic pap with Jon Hall and Nancy Kelly, and *Young People* (both 1940) was one of Shirley Temple's least-remembered efforts. Now freelancing, Dwan made *Trail of the Vigilantes* (1940), a comic Western with Franchot Tone as an Easterner who brings Broderick Crawford's gang to justice, and *Look Who's Laughing* (1941), a feeble but popular comedy comprised of such radio stars as Edgar Bergen and Charlie McCarthy and Fibber McGee and Molly, along with Lucille Ball.

*Rise and Shine* (1941) was a minor gem, a hilarious version of James Thurber's *My Life and Hard Times* (adapted by Herman J. Mankiewicz), with Jack Oakie as the hapless college football player abducted by Milton Berle's gang to keep him from playing in the big game; Linda Darnell, George Murphy, and Walter Brennan provided fine support. *Friendly Enemies* (1942) was a timely dramatization of the split Germany underwent at the dawn of World War I. The 1942 *Here We Go Again* was a haphazard sequel to *Look Who's Laughing*, with the original's radio teams now joined by the likes of The Great Gildersleeve and songstress Ginny Simms, and *Around the World* (1943) was another forgettable "all-star" revue, with Kay Kyser and his band performing for soldiers around the world, abetted by comedian Ish Kabibble and starlet Barbara Hale.

In 1943 Dwan was summoned to help train the camera units for Uncle Sam's photographic division —at fifty-eight he was too old to serve alongside Frank Capra, George Cukor, William Wyler, and George Stevens—but when that task was completed, it was back to making low-budget entertainments. *Up in Mabel's Room* (1944), the first of four comedies made for UA, put star Dennis O'Keefe on the hot spot as a husband without a good excuse when old flame Gail Patrick pops up suddenly with a piece of incriminating lingerie, while *Abroad with Two Yanks* (1944) teamed O'Keefe with William Bendix as Marines stationed in Australia who both yearn for Helen Walker.

O'Keefe had one of the best vehicles of his career with *Brewster's Millions* (1945), the oft-filmed George Barr McCutcheon comedy about a man who learns that he stands to inherit $7 million if he's able to first spend $1 million over the next month. (For the record, it's better than the 1914, 1921, 1935, 1961, or 1985 versions, the last with Richard Pryor and appropriately inflated sums.) The 1945 *Getting Gertie's Garter* was a virtual remake of *Mabel's Room*: O'Keefe again must reclaim the eponymous jeweled garter to keep peace on the homefront; Marie McDonald is the flashy Gertie and Sheila Ryan the wife who'd cut his throat if she found out.

These minor successes must not have been enough for Dwan, who signed an exclusive contract with Herbert Yates's Republic Studios in 1946 that tied him up for the next eight years. His first slate of releases was a mixed bag—*Calendar Girl* (1946) with Jane Frazee; *Northwest Outpost* (1947), a dull operetta with Nelson Eddy and Ilona Massey; *Driftwood* (1947), a kind of *Wild Child* with Natalie Wood as the savage youth introduced to civilization; and *The Inside Story* (1948), a fable set in Vermont during the Depression. More interesting was *Angel in Exile* (1948), a religious parable set in the Old West, with John Carroll and Adele Mara, that Dwan co-directed with Philip Ford. *Sands of Iwo Jima* (1949) was a major production, with John Wayne as the hard-boiled Marine sergeant who has to train his green recruits (John Agar, Forrest Tucker) to be tough enough to take Mt. Suribachi; it earned Wayne his first Oscar nomination, and probably was the biggest hit of Dwan's sound pictures.

Dwan's reward was to be entrusted with the career of studio chief Herbert Yates's paramour (and soon-to-be-wife), Vera Ralston. First came *Surrender* (1950), a lavish costumer, followed by *Belle Le Grande* (1951), a forgettable Western. *The Wild Blue Yonder* (1951) was a World War II drama starring Ralston as an Army nurse whose heart is with B-29 flyboys Wendell Corey and Forrest Tucker, while *I Dream of Jeannie* (1952) was a wooden biopic about famed composer Stephen Foster. Dwan had actually shot the risible *Montana Belle* in 1948, but interference from Howard Hughes (he ultimately bought it back from Republic) kept it on the shelf until 1952, when the world was finally treated to the sight of Jane Russell as a blond Belle Starr—in "Trucolor," no less (and no more).

*The Woman They Almost Lynched* (1953) had Audrey Totter running afoul of Brian Donlevy during the Civil War. Dwan's final pictures at Republic were *Sweethearts on Parade* (1953) and *Flight Nurse* (1954), the latter a turgid Korean War romance with Joan Leslie and Forrest Tucker. Moving to RKO—another studio that specialized in genre fare—Dwan made a number of pictures for producer Benedict Bogeaus's Filmcrest Productions. *Silver Lode* (1954) was a noirish Western, with newlywed John Payne framed for murder by Dan Duryea, while *Passion* (1954) set Cornel Wilde down in old California as a man hell-bent on revenge for the killing of wife Yvonne De Carlo. *Cattle Queen of Montana* (also 1954) referred to the formidable Barbara Stanwyck, who as Sierra Nevada Jones outtoughs landgrabbers, Indians, and even helpful Ronald Reagan by a wide margin. *Escape to*

*Burma* (1955) sent Stanwyck from her tea plantation into the jungle trying to help fugitive Robert Ryan.

Now seventy, Dwan kept working at full speed, making *Pearl of the South Pacific* (1955) with Virginia Mayo and Dennis Morgan and *Tennessee's Partner* (also 1955) with John Payne, Rhonda Fleming, and Ronald Reagan. But such fodder was easily eclipsed by *Slightly Scarlet* (1956), Dwan's crackling adaptation of James Cain's novel *Love's Lovely Counterfeit*, with Rhonda Fleming and Arlene Dahl well cast as redheaded sisters in a corrupt town; their odd, quasi-incestuous relationship doesn't put off two-fisted reformer John Payne. The 1956 *Hold Back the Night* was an odd Korean War drama with Payne, Peter Graves, and Chuck Connors, while *The River's Edge* (1957) gave Ray Milland one of his best late roles as a hood trying to make it into Mexico with a suitcase of stolen cash. *The Restless Breed* (1957) was an unremarkable Western with Scott Brady and Anne Bancroft, and *Enchanted Island* (1958) was a clumsy adaptation of Herman Melville's *Typee*. Last came *Most Dangerous Man Alive* (1961; completed 1958), a thriller about a convict transformed by an explosion into something more than human.

Dwan explained his 1958 retirement thusly: "It's just a business that I stood as long as I could and I got out of it when I couldn't stand it any more." His lengthy interview with Peter Bogdanovich was transformed into the book *Allan Dwan: The Last Pioneer* in 1971 (revised edition: 1981).

▲ *Dwan (seated) on the set of* Josette *with Don Ameche and Simone Simon*

## ● CLINT EASTWOOD (1930- )

Jerry Lewis may have been the first actor to assume full control of his career by becoming his own director, but his accomplishments pale alongside Clint Eastwood's during the past twenty-odd years. Rising from laconic TV star to laconic genre star to laconic superstar by almost imperceptible stages, Eastwood is today recognized as a superior director who no longer requires his own charismatic presence to ensure the success of his films—although it never hurts!

Born in San Francisco at the start of the Depression, Eastwood grew up traveling around California with his peripatetic, out-of-work father. After high school—and he attended several—he worked in a variety of rugged jobs before making his way to Los Angeles. A screen test with Universal in 1954 netted him a forty-week contract, but after one renewal and a series of bit parts in movies like *Tarantula!* and *Revenge of the Creature* his option was dropped. He kicked around in "B" Westerns for a few years, then got his break in 1959 by being cast as Rowdy Yates in the newly launched TV series *Rawhide.* Six years of service on the trail made him a minor star in the United States, but it was his decision to appear as the Man with No Name in Sergio Leone's Italian production *A Fistful of Dollars* (shot during *Rawhide*'s 1964 summer hiatus) that jump-started his career. That remake of Kurosawa's *Yojimbo* was followed in 1966 by *For a Few Dollars More*—but neither film was shown in the States, leaving Eastwood an international star everywhere but in America.

Finally, in 1967, Leone's first two films were cleared to play in the States, along with the third film in the cycle, *The Good, the Bad, and the Ugly.* Collectively, the three grossed an enormous sum, and Eastwood was established as a viable box-office star. For his first American Western, *Hang 'Em High* (1968)—Ted Post's expert knockoff of the Leone formula, enlivened by a superior group of character actors—Eastwood formed his own production company, Malpaso, which after 1971 would offer his services exclusively. Also in 1968 he worked with Don Siegel (for the first of five times) on the popular *Coogan's Bluff*; it was Siegel who would teach him most of what he needed to know about directing, a debt Eastwood has often acknowledged.

Eastwood's first directorial effort, the contemporary suspenser *Play Misty for Me* (1971), was a chiller about a disc jockey (Eastwood) who is stalked by an unbalanced listener (Jessica Walter) after he picks her up in a bar for what he thinks will be a one-night affair. (Although it didn't enjoy the commercial success of the similar *Fatal Attraction*, in many ways it is superior to that 1987 blockbuster.) After acting in the mega-hit *Dirty Harry* under Don Siegel, he directed *High Plains Drifter* (1972), a quasi-supernatural Western with Eastwood in his familiar role as a mysterious stranger who helps a panicky town defend itself against a gang of outlaws—for a price. Less successful was *Breezy* (1973), a May-November romance between divorced William Holden and teenaged free spirit Kay Lenz that suffered from an idiotic script and a theme with which Eastwood had had little experience.

*The Eiger Sanction* (1975), based on a popular espionage thriller by Trevanian, turned out to be an overlong, faintly preposterous work that was undermined by a number of problems, not the least of which was Eastwood himself, here an art critic (!) who agrees to use his mountain-climbing skills to assassinate a spy for a CIA-like organization; his reward is an original Pissarro. Eastwood took over *The Outlaw Josey Wales* (1976) from Philip Kaufman, who co-wrote the story of a Missouri farmer driven to violence after his family has been slaughtered by renegade Union soldiers. Stylishly photographed by Bruce Surtees, with a fine performance by Chief Dan George as a Comanche leader who makes his peace with Eastwood, this somewhat overlong work humanized his mythic avenger archetype for the first time.

*The Gauntlet* (1977) was a step backward, a kinetic but formulaic action orgy in which Eastwood plays a cop trying to transport witness (and hooker) Sondra Locke to an Arizona courthouse where she can testify. Although several battalions of crooked cops try their best to waylay the pair, Clint reaches

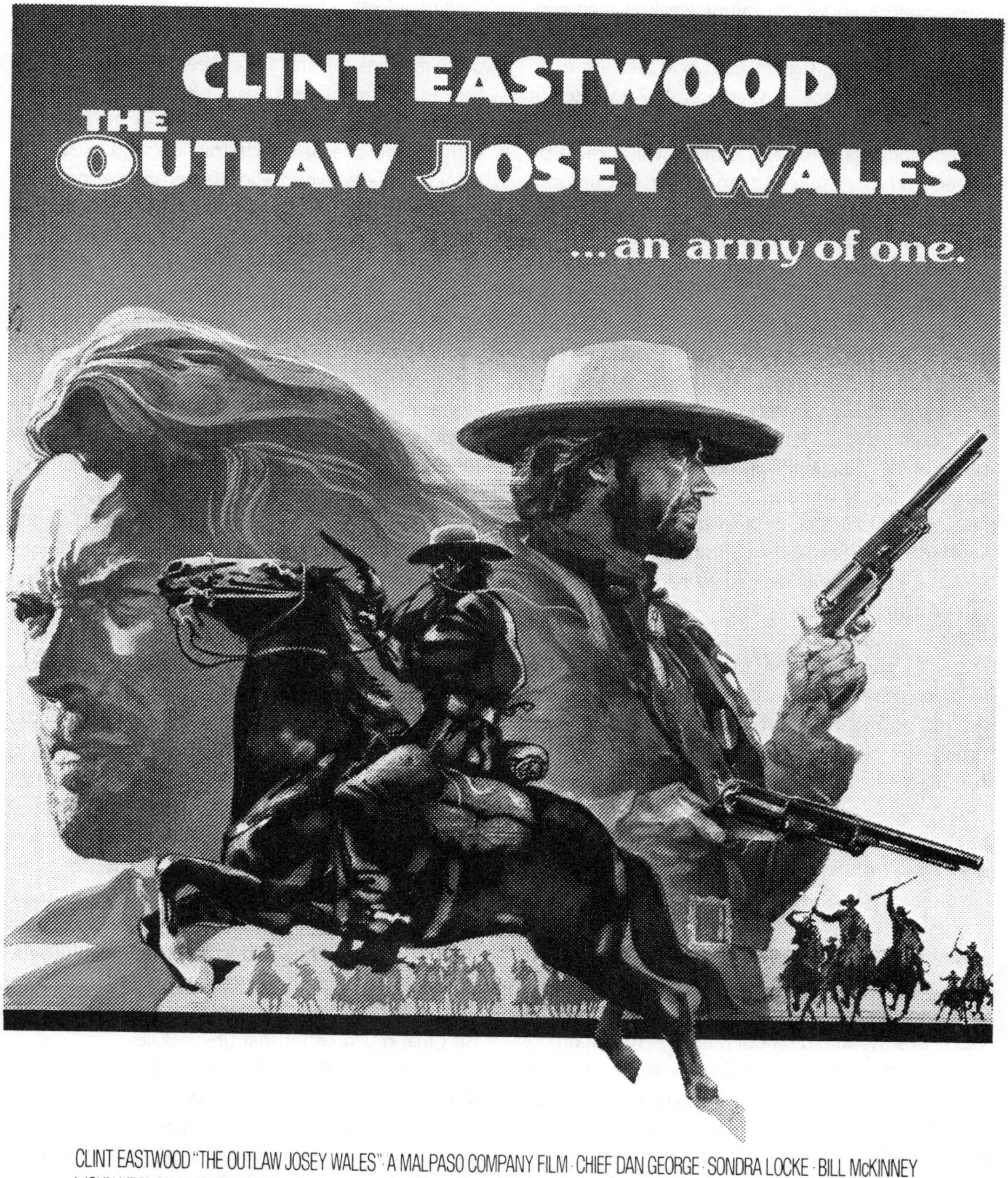
CLINT EASTWOOD
THE OUTLAW JOSEY WALES
...an army of one.
CLINT EASTWOOD "THE OUTLAW JOSEY WALES" A MALPASO COMPANY FILM · CHIEF DAN GEORGE · SONDRA LOCKE · BILL McKINNEY
and JOHN VERNON as Fletcher · Screenplay by PHIL KAUFMAN and SONIA CHERNUS · Produced by ROBERT DALEY · Directed by CLINT EASTWOOD
Music by JERRY FIELDING · Panavision® Color by Deluxe® Distributed by Warner Bros. A Warner Communications Company
PG PARENTAL GUIDANCE SUGGESTED

his destination by commandeering a bus and driving it through enough firepower to obliterate Iraq. The gentle good humor pervading *Bronco Billy* (1980) was far removed from the mayhem of his last few pictures; Eastwood was surprisingly deft as the proprietor and singing star of a two-bit Wild West show who gives shelter to, then falls in love with, runaway heiress Sondra Locke (the film's weakest element). But *Firefox* (1982) was an abysmal high-tech Cold War yarn that had a glum Eastwood stealing a supersonic jet from the Russians; at 137 minutes, it didn't exactly unfold at the speed of sound.

*Honkytonk Man* (1982) was more whimsical, a bit shorter, and more tuneful than *Firefox*, but unfortunately it wasn't much better. Set during the Depression, it features Eastwood as a country singer dying of leukemia whose dream is to make it to the Grand Old Opry before he passes on. Although it offered the novel casting of Eastwood's own son Kyle and the verisimilitude of various country-music stars, the picture is flat-out mawkish. Having wandered rather far afield from his star persona, Eastwood now took over the fourth installment of his Dirty Harry series, *Sudden Impact* (1983); it was the worst entry to date, thanks in part to Sondra Locke's overwrought portrayal of a woman killing off each member of a gang that had raped her and her sister years earlier. In any case, little action seemed to happen suddenly, with or without impact.

Eastwood fared better by returning to his screen roots with the neo-mythic *Pale Rider* (1985), a self-conscious, quasi-religious Western that is almost carried off by Eastwood's iconic presence and Bruce Surtees's gorgeous photography. Had it not recycled *Shane* and a half dozen other Western classics so obviously, its impact might have been greater, and its stately pace almost grinds the picture to a total halt at several junctures. But its popularity was encouraging: *Rider* was one of the few hit Westerns of the Eighties.

Eastwood the director allowed Eastwood the actor to stretch a bit in *Heartbreak Ridge* (1986), a typically overlong but vastly enjoyable drama about Tom Highway, an old-school Marine sergeant on the verge of retirement whose kick-ass approach, long criticized by his wet-behind-the-ears commanding officers, turns out to be just what is needed to whip a bunch of raw recruits into shape in time for the invasion of Grenada. Eastwood wisely spends as much time on his character's efforts to repair his failed marriage to Marsha Mason as his amusing instructional techniques with his wisenheimer squad—although one wishes that something more epic than Grenada had been available as the film's big payoff. (*Ridge* also retires the award for Beefcake on Parade; few of the sweating hardbodies sport more than skivvies for long stretches.)

*Bird* (1988), a biopic about jazz innovator Charlie Parker, was the first film Eastwood had directed without himself as the star since *Breezy* fifteen years earlier, and in many ways it was his most assured work to date. Although an hour too long—a real problem with a grim tale of self-destruction such as we are witnessing—Eastwood elicits a terrific performance from Forest Whitaker as the revered sax genius, and the film's period re-creation and music are beyond reproach. *White Hunter, Black Heart* (1990) was Eastwood's most audacious project, an adaptation of Peter Viertel's wonderful *roman à clef* about his and John Huston's on-location collaboration on *The African Queen* in 1951. Bravely tackling the part of the loquacious Huston, Eastwood is able to suggest the great director's rugged physical presence, but spoils the illusion each time he opens his mouth—that guttural half-whisper hardly evokes the unctuous oratory of Huston! A box-office disaster that earned mixed reviews, the film might have profited from the Merchant-Ivory touch, and someone other than Eastwood in the lead.

A sop to the fans who ignored *Hunter*, the tired *The Rookie* (1990) was the Savvy Old Cop–Obnoxious Young Cop routine, with Charlie Sheen, Sonia Braga, and Raul Julia trying a little too hard to add color to an essentially hopeless enterprise. But *Unforgiven* gave reassurance that Eastwood—who hadn't had a hit in six years—was back. One of 1992's most lauded (some said, overly lauded) releases, it features a towering performance by Eastwood as an erstwhile "regulator" who lays down his plowshare to execute a thug who has disfigured a whore. Both the picture and Eastwood won Oscars, as did Gene Hackman as a thoroughly corrupt sheriff—a rousing embrace for a work that, when all is said and done, isn't *that* much better than *Josey Wales*.

*A Perfect World* (1993) sensibly put superstar Kevin Costner at center stage as a somewhat unbalanced fugitive who kidnaps, then bonds with, a young boy; Eastwood takes a self-effacing, semi-comic role as the laconic Ranger who tracks him down. But despite near-universal accolades and a fine performance by Costner, its box office proved shockingly weak—an exact reversal of Eastwood's earlier track record, for fans of irony. But Eastwood's stature as cinematic royalty remained unscathed—a fact emphasized in September 1993 when His Royal Highness Prince Charles presented Eastwood with the fellowship of the British Film Institute at London's National Film Theatre. He received the Irving G. Thalberg Award for lifetime achievement at the Academy Awards in March of 1995. His ballyhooed adaptation of *The Bridges of Madison County*, the gooey metaphysical romance in which he co-stars with Meryl Streep, was released to glowing reviews in 1995.

▲ *On the set of* Bird

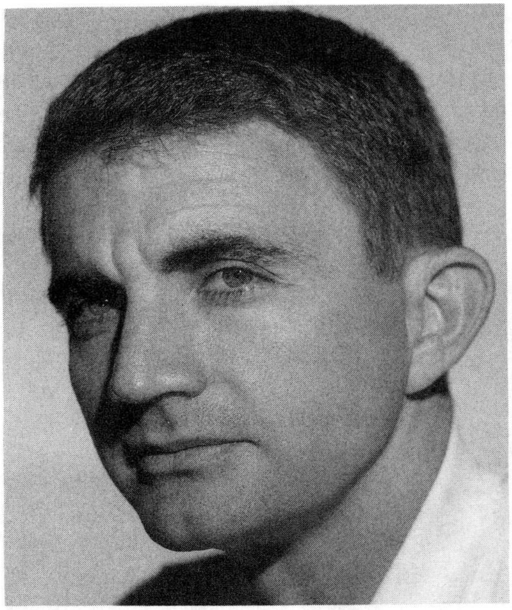

## ● BLAKE EDWARDS (1922– )

A former actor and screenwriter whose reputation as a director now rests on a group of romantic comedies of widely varying merit, Edwards has made films that by his own admission have become increasingly autobiographical since 1983—not always to good effect. Born William Blake McEdwards in Tulsa, Oklahoma, he attended Beverly Hills High School before acting in bit parts in some of the Forties' better war pictures, including *A Guy Named Joe*, *Thirty Seconds over Tokyo*, *They Were Expendable*, and *The Best Years of Our Lives*, with time out for a year in the Coast Guard. He began screenwriting in 1947 with *Panhandle* and followed by scripting a number of Richard Quine's "B" pictures at Columbia, *Leather Gloves* and the Mickey Rooney pictures *All Ashore* and *The Atomic Kid* among them. Along the way he created the hit radio series *Richard Diamond, Private Detective* for Dick Powell.

Edwards began directing at Columbia in 1955 with a pair of Frankie Laine vehicles, *Bring Your Smile Along* and *He Laughed Last* (1956); he also scripted, as he would his next five films. *Mister Cory* (1957) had Tony Curtis as a big-shot gambler returning to his hometown, while *This Happy Feeling* (1958) was a romantic comedy with Debbie Reynolds, John Saxon, and Curt Jurgens. Edwards interrupted his movie career long enough to create two terrific television series, *Peter Gunn* (1958) and *Mr. Lucky* (1959); less successful was his series *Dante's Inferno* (1960). For the big screen he made *The Perfect Furlough* (1959) with real-life husband and wife Tony Curtis and Janet Leigh as Army personnel vacationing in Paris as a psychological experiment. Edwards's first hit was also a military comedy, *Operation Petticoat* (1959), with submarine commander Cary Grant and junior officer Tony Curtis combining their talents as con men to get their leaking vessel repaired. Less acceptable—much less—was *High Time* (1960), a square comedy starring Bing Crosby as a widower who returns to college to get his degree and ends up involved with his instructor; Tuesday Weld and Fabian were on hand for the teens, who must have been bored stiff.

Then came *Breakfast at Tiffany's* (1961), Edwards's breakthrough film and the one on which his reputation rests. A loose adaptation of the Truman Capote novella, it stars Audrey Hepburn in her signature role as Holly Golightly, a free spirit whose zaniness is a mask for insecurity and loneliness. One of the decade's most romantic pictures, it's soft in the center but is carried by Hepburn's incandescence and George Peppard's charm—although they're helped mightily by Henry Mancini's swelling score and Givenchy's outfits (for Audrey, not George). Hepburn and screenwriter George Axelrod were both Oscar-nominated, but it was Mancini who took home the statuettes; fair enough, as "Moon River" (lyrics by Johnny Mercer) is probably the best love theme ever written for a movie.

*Experiment in Terror* (1962) was a suspenseful crime story, with Lee Remick blackmailed by psychopath Ross Martin until FBI agent Glenn Ford steps in. *Days of Wine and Roses* (also 1962) had been a *Playhouse 90* production with Cliff Robertson; Edwards's version used original writer J. P. Miller but changed the cast to Jack Lemmon and Lee Remick for his harrowing look at a woman's descent into alcoholism under the influence of her husband. Both actors were nominated for Academy Awards, and once again the Mancini-Mercer team took an Oscar for the film's theme song. It was quite a distance from that to the inspired foolishness of *The Pink Panther* (1964), but Edwards was clearly in his element with this frenetic parody of the Hercule Poirot school of detection. Propelled by Peter Sellers's eternally bumbling Inspector Clouseau—certainly his most famous characterization—its Continental charm was supplied by

David Niven, Claudia Cardinale, and Capucine. So successful was it that *A Shot in the Dark* (also 1964) was immediately rushed into production; Edwards collaborated on the screenplay with William Peter Blatty. A sequel that for once outstripped the original, it supported the brilliant Sellers with Herbert Lom, Elke Sommer, and George Sanders, and was probably Edwards's most sustained comic vehicle.

*The Great Race* (1965) was another entry in the then-popular, self-indulgent, all-star laughfests that rarely were funny enough to justify their running time (in this case a swollen two and a half hours), although there were moments for Tony Curtis, Natalie Wood, and Peter Falk. *What Did You Do in the War, Daddy?* (1966) was a rowdy World War II comedy starring James Coburn, Aldo Ray, and Carroll O'Connor, while *Gunn* (1967) was Edwards's surprisingly lame feature treatment of his private-eye creation, portrayed (as on TV) by Craig Stevens. *The Party* (1968) was bound to be more interesting, if only for the presence of Peter Sellers as a bewildered Indian actor attending a pretentious Hollywood party; Claudine Longet was most appealing as a guest who becomes interested in him.

But *Darling Lili* (1970) was an expensive musical romantic comedy that featured Edwards's new wife, Julie Andrews, as a German spy in World War I and Rock Hudson as the English soldier she falls for. A total box-office disaster, the film's failure was as much a result of the period it was released in as any intrinsic shortcomings it might have had. Much more modest in scale was *The Wild Rovers* (1971), a fine buddy picture in which William Holden and Robert Ryan play aging cowboys who've just robbed a bank and can't quite figure out how it all happened; dismissed at the time, this film is actually one of Edwards's best. *The Carey Treatment* (1972), a decent mystery set in a Boston hospital, with James Coburn and Jennifer O'Neill, was taken out of Edwards's hands by MGM in postproduction, and his efforts to remove his name from it were fruitless.

The next few years were quiet ones for Edwards. *The Tamarind Seed* (1974), a middling spy story set in a variety of exotic locales, featuring Julie Andrews and Omar Sharif, was all he had to show for 1974. But then United Artists decided to revive the Pink Panther series with Peter Sellers, and in rapid order Edwards made *Return of the Pink Panther* (1975), *The Pink Panther Strikes Again* (1976), and *Revenge of the Pink Panther* (1978), all shot in England and all quite successful at the box office—although only the second entry in this troika, with the lovely Lesley-Anne Down, is up to the level of the earlier pictures. Once more bankable, Edwards returned to the States to make the notorious *10* (1979), an enormous smash thanks to the charms of the wooden but stunning Bo Derek and the deft comic timing of star Dudley Moore; Julie Andrews has less to do as Moore's patient fiancée. The quintessential Seventies sex comedy, *10* hasn't dated well, but it was certainly the must-see sleeper of its time.

*S.O.B.* (1981) might have been a classic satire on Hollywood, but Edwards's savage lampooning of the town that had served him ill not so long ago was both too broad and too bitter to elicit the laughs that were intended. Still, the film occasionally hit its mark, and the talented cast—including William Holden, Julie Andrews, Robert Preston, and Robert Vaughn—was fun to watch. The uneven *Victor/Victoria* (1982), based on a 1933 German film, starred Julie Andrews as a starving performer stuck in 1934 Paris who can find work only by pretending to be a female impersonator; when Chicago nightclub czar

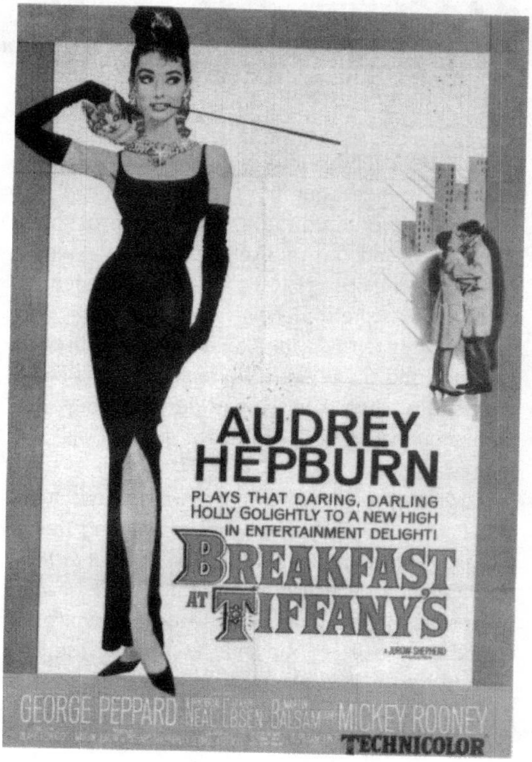

James Garner falls in love with her/him, all sorts of profound gender questions are raised and discussed—a favorite Edwards theme. Little of this is convincing, and the musical numbers by Mancini and Leslie Bricusse are less than what's needed (although their score somehow won a Oscar). But Robert Preston is terrific as the aging queen who tutors Andrews, and Lesley Anne Warren as Garner's floozy girlfriend is better than the part deserves; they were both nominated for Academy Awards, as was Andrews.

Edwards now returned to the well for two more Pink Panther sequels, simultaneously filming *Trail of the Pink Panther* and *Curse of the Pink Panther* (1983), feeble enterprises which relied on the series' earlier guest stars to gloss over the absence of recently deceased Peter Sellers (*Trail* had the nerve to use outtakes of him as Clouseau to draw in theatergoers). A better class of failure was his remake of Truffaut's *The Man Who Loved Women* (1983), with Julie Andrews miscast as the psychiatrist who listens to sculptor Burt Reynolds confess about his affairs with Kim Basinger, Marilu Henner, and the other beauties he has slept with. Edwards's own shrink, Milton Wexler, was the co-author of the screenplay, which lent the therapy sessions verisimilitude without making them interesting.

*Micki & Maude* (1984) was on the mark, though; Dudley Moore plays a philandering husband who manages to get both wife Ann Reinking and girlfriend Amy Irving pregnant. But the aptly titled *A Fine Mess* (1986) was an embarrassing attempt to pass off Ted Danson and Howie Mandel as a latter-day Laurel and Hardy. One of Edwards's most personal films was *That's Life!* (1986), with Jack Lemmon and Julie Andrews and several members of both stars' families in the supporting cast (it was filmed at Andrews and Edwards's home in Malibu). Unlike most films with an exclamation point in their title, this one was really quite good; despite the touchy-feely, transactional-analysis elements, it explores the themes of aging and fear of death without becoming mawkish.

But *Blind Date* (1987) was another gruesome farce that huffed and puffed to no avail, with Bruce Willis as a Yuppie who gets date Kim Basinger drunk even though he's been warned she can't tolerate alcohol. Willis was laughable, but not amusing, as Tom Mix doing some amateur sleuthing in 1920s Hollywood in *Sunset* (1988); a megaton bomb, it did offer James Garner as a predictably smooth Wyatt Earp. Edwards then wrote and directed the television pilot *Justin Case* (1988) with his daughter Jennifer for the Walt Disney Co., with George Carlin as the ghost of a private eye who joins with his daughter to figure out who bumped him off.

*Skin Deep* (1989) was a passable comedy, starring John Ritter as a Hollywood writer inundated with dangerous temptations, while *Peter Gunn* (1990) was another made-for-TV film that mined the TV series' earlier success; daughter Jennifer now plays secretary to sleuth Peter Strauss. *Switch* (1991) had a promising concept—egomaniacal ladykiller Perry King is killed by a jealous girlfriend and reincarnated in the body of Ellen Barkin, attracting the romantic interest of Jimmy Smits—but the execution was clumsy. And *Son of the Pink Panther* (1993) was yet another unsuccessful attempt to install a replacement for Peter Sellers, the ineffectual Robert Benigini. With a Broadway musical version of *Victor/Victoria* in preparation, Edwards was awarded the Preston Sturges Award by the Directors Guild of America and the Writers Guild of America in 1993.

▲ *With the stars of* Micki & Maude

## ● JOHN FARROW (1904-1963)

Equally adept at the noir, the Western, and the historical adventure, John Farrow's versatility was impressive. Born in Sydney, Australia, Farrow began in Hollywood as a writer toward the end of the silent era; among his screenwriting credits are *Ladies of the Mob* (1928), *Wolf Song* (1929), and *Tarzan Escapes* (1936). It was on that last picture that Farrow met Maureen O'Sullivan, whom he would soon wed (their daughter is Mia Farrow). In 1937 Farrow began his directorial career at Warners with such "B"s as *West of Shanghai*, with Boris Karloff as a Chinese warlord, and *Men in Exile*. In 1938 it was *The Invisible Menace* (Karloff again) and three early Ann Sheridan vehicles—*She Loved a Fireman*, *Little Miss Thoroughbred*, and *Broadway Musketeers*—along with a Kay Francis weeper, *My Bill*.

After *Women in the Wind* (1939), in which Kay Francis pilots a plane in a transcontinental race, he moved to RKO, where his busy 1939 continued with a full slate of five "B"s: *Full Confession*, an *Informer* knockoff with Victor McLaglen; *The Saint Strikes Back*, the first in the series to star George Sanders; *Five Came Back*, a good jungle-survival melodrama with Lucille Ball, Chester Morris, and John Carradine; *Reno* with Richard Dix; and *Sorority House*, an Anne Shirley drama written by Dalton Trumbo. *Married and in Love* (1940) was a clever tale about infidelity, but *A Bill of Divorcement* was a so-so remake of the 1932 success, with Maureen O'Hara and Adolphe Menjou taking over for Hepburn and Barrymore.

Farrow had his biggest hit at Paramount with the patriotic *Wake Island* (1942), starring Brian Donlevy, Robert Preston, and William Bendix; it received an Oscar nomination for best picture and brought Farrow his only nomination for best direction. *China* (1943) was a brainless adventure; Alan Ladd and William Bendix blow up half the Japanese invaders while Loretta Young looks on admiringly, and *The Commandos Strike at Dawn* (1942) with Paul Muni and *The Hitler Gang* (1944) were more wartime propaganda. *You Came Along* (1945) sent Robert Cummings on a rather forgettable bond-selling tour, though it did introduce Lizabeth Scott to moviegoers. Farrow then made a pair of period actioners: *Two Years Before the Mast* (1946) depicted flogging on the high seas, another masochistic role for the vastly popular Ladd, and *California* (1946) offered Ray Milland as an unlikely wagonmaster, with Barbara Stanwyck at his side. *Easy Come, Easy Go* (1947) gave recent Oscar winner Barry Fitzgerald the role of a racetrack frequenter who doesn't want daughter Diana Lynn to marry Sonny Tufts, while *Blaze of Noon* (1947) was flyboy corn starring William Holden.

It was Ladd yet again in *Calcutta* (1947), avenging the murder of a pal with the aid of ever-reliable William Bendix. *The Big Clock* (1948), from the fine Kenneth Fearing novel, was a classic noir, with Ray Milland desperately trying to outwit his evil boss, publishing magnate Charles Laughton. (It was remade as *No Way Out* in 1987 with Kevin Costner.) *Beyond Glory* (1948) had Ladd on trial at West Point, with Donna Reed standing by his side; better was Farrow's effectively creepy adaptation of William Irish's novel *Night Has a Thousand Eyes* (1948), with Edward G. Robinson as a clairvoyant who meets a tragic end. *Alias Nick Beal* (1949) was one of Farrow's best works; Ray Milland was cast against type as the Devil, who tries to corrupt honest politician Thomas Mitchell. Farrow was a Roman Catholic convert, and the theme of this picture probably was of special interest to him.

*Red, Hot and Blue* (1949) combined showgirls and gangsters, with Betty Hutton the former and Victor Mature the latter, while *Copper Canyon* (1950) tossed the unlikely duo of Ray Milland and Hedy Lamarr into the Old West. *Where Danger Lives* (1950) had Robert Mitchum as a doctor led down the garden path by Faith Domergue—as if she were the kind of noir temptress who could keep up with him! Mitchum had a field day in *His Kind of Woman* (1951), in which Jane Russell gave as good as she got; Farrow had sense enough to play the overplotted story half for laughs, ending up with an enjoyable parody of Mitchum's hit *Out of the Past. Submarine Command* (1951) had William Holden trying to adjust to peacetime life in the military, while *Ride, Vaquero!* (1953) was an offbeat Western starring Ava Gardner at her most beautiful. *Plunder of the Sun* (1953) sent Glenn Ford to Mexico on a treasure hunt, while *Botany Bay* (also 1953) transported unlucky Alan Ladd to Australia on a convict ship, under the tender offices of Captain James Mason.

The 1953 *Hondo*, shot in 3-D and adapted from a Louis L'Amour novel, featured John Wayne in top form as a cavalry scout trying to save a widow (Geraldine Page) and her son from the Apaches. *A Bullet Is Waiting* (1954) was a moderately interesting Western with Rory Calhoun and Jean Simmons, but *The Sea Chase* (1955) was a peculiar teaming of John Wayne and Lana Turner that asks us to accept the Duke as a German ship captain. (No dice!)

Farrow took time off from directing to co-script *Around the World in 80 Days*, for which he won his only Oscar. He then remade *Five Came Back* as *Back from Eternity* (1956)—now an excuse to have the voluptuous Anita Ekberg crash-landed in the Amazon with only her tattered garments to protect her. *The Unholy Wife* (1957), which Farrow also produced, was unabashed trash: blond bombshell Diana Dors tries to kill nasty husband Rod Steiger to clear time for hunky Tom Tryon. It is a classic of its kind—but its kind was usually left to the likes of Hugo Haas. *John Paul Jones* (1959), with the immobile Robert Stack as its hero, might as well have been phoned in by Farrow, who then retired from filmmaking.

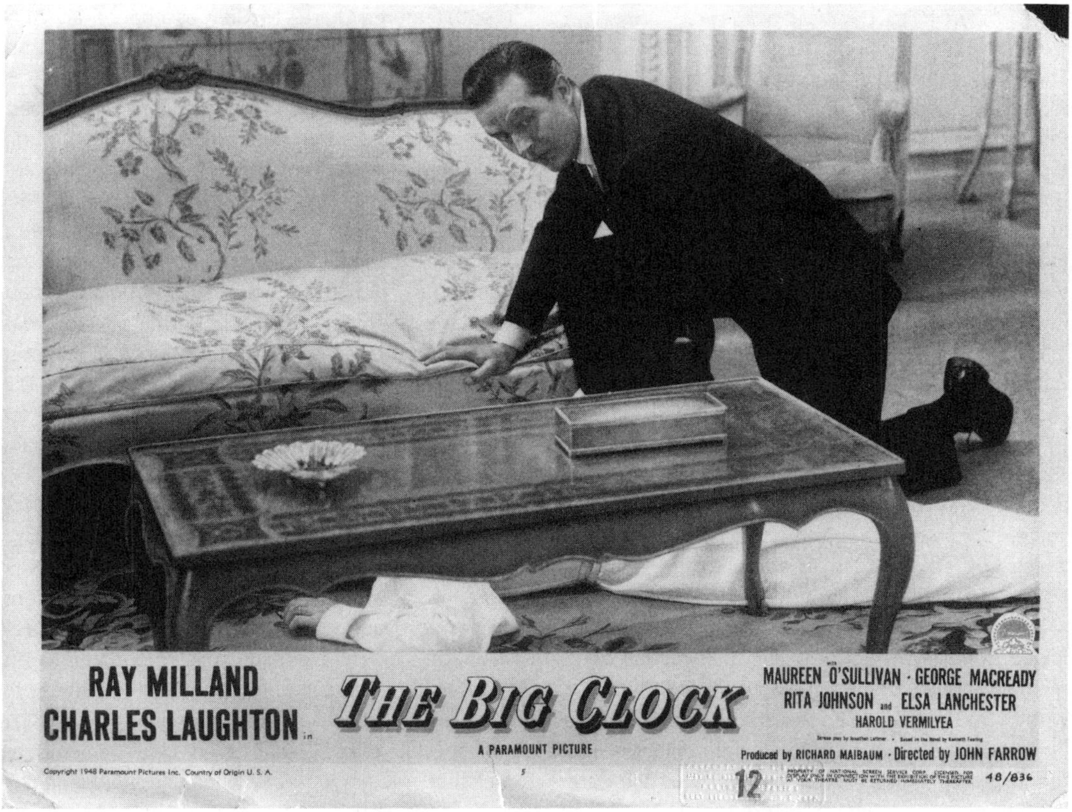

## ● RICHARD FLEISCHER (1916– )

The son of famed animation pioneer Max Fleischer, Richard Fleischer never managed to distinguish himself in the course of making nearly fifty feature films, though several of them were extremely successful. Born in Brooklyn, New York, Fleischer was educated at Brown University but gave up his medical studies to enroll in drama courses at Yale, where in 1937 he founded a theatrical group. In 1942 Fleischer joined RKO as an editor on the Pathé newsreels, and a year later he began directing shorts for RKO's "This Is America" series. After handling a variety of other short subjects, he began directing "B" features at RKO with *Child of Divorce* (1946), a reworking of the 1934 *Wednesday's Child*, starring Sharyn Moffet as a tyke having problems dealing with her parents' divorce. It did well enough to inspire *Banjo* (1947), in which Moffet now tried to adjust to life in a new home up North.

Fleischer was taken off the Moffet watch and allowed to make *Design for Death*, a 48-minute documentary about the psychology of the Japanese, written by Ted and Helen Geisel and co-produced by Fleischer. Assembled from some eight million feet of film captured by the Allied forces, it won the Oscar for the best documentary feature of 1947. On loan to UA he made *So This Is New York* (1948), an amusing adaptation of Ring Lardner's *The Big Town*, with Henry Morgan and Rudy Vallee. *Bodyguard* (1948) was the first of several good, low-budget noirs Fleischer made for RKO; Lawrence Tierney plays a hard-boiled PI who bails Priscilla Lane out of a jam, and vice versa. *Make Mine Laughs* (1949) was simply a compilation of musical numbers and comedy skits from earlier RKO pictures; Ray Bolger and Jack Haley sued RKO and won a judgment for using their performances without recompense.

*The Clay Pigeon* (1949) was another good noir, starring Bill Williams as a seaman who awakens from a coma only to learn that he's about to be court-martialed for treason; writer Carl Foreman used an actual incident as the basis for his screenplay. *Follow Me Quietly* (1949) was a police procedural about a serial killer that failed to maintain the level of suspense offered in the previous year's *He Walked by Night*, but *Trapped* (also 1949) used the faux-documentary style then fashionable to better effect, with Lloyd Bridges and moll Barbara Payton being hunted down by the FBI. *Armored Car Robbery* (1950) featured Charles McGraw as a police detective on the trail of gang leader William Tallman and his burly-q moll Adele Jergens.

*The Narrow Margin* (1952) was one of the best noirs of its day, a taut battle of wits between tough cop Charles McGraw and a group of hoods who want to eliminate their former boss's widow, whom McGraw is delivering via train to testify to the Feds. Made for a song, this modest thriller has held up wonderfully over the years, thanks in no small part to Marie Windsor's cutting performance. This was Fleischer's final film for RKO, closing out his most interesting period. Now freelancing, he made *The Happy Time* (1952), a sentimental period picture set in Canada, with Charles Boyer and Louis Jourdan, and *Arena* (1953), a 3-D Western with a rodeo backdrop that starred Gig Young and Jean Hagen.

*20,000 Leagues under the Sea* (1954) was one of Disney's most successful live-action ventures; Kirk Douglas was at his athletic best as a sailor who signs on for a voyage on the submarine of the megalomaniacal Captain Nemo (James Mason) and gets more than he bargained for—but it's the battle with the giant squid (which helped the film win an Oscar for special effects) that every kid remembers. Fleischer now joined Fox, where he would do the bulk of his work over the next fifteen years. *Violent Saturday* (1955) was a noirish soap opera, with engineer Victor Mature pitted against bank robber Lee

Marvin, while *The Girl in the Red Velvet Swing* (1955) was a well-done version of the Evelyn Nesbit scandal; Joan Collins starred as the seductive showgirl whose affair with famed architect Stanford White (Ray Milland) forces her husband, Harry K. Thaw (Farley Granger), to fatally shoot him.

*Bandido* (1956) was an underrated action picture, with Robert Mitchum as an amoral gunrunner in the revolution-torn Mexico of 1916, while *Between Heaven and Hell* (1956) was a middling World War II yarn about a selfish Southerner (Robert Wagner) learning compassion for others while training for combat. *The Vikings* (1958) was an elaborate adventure starring Kirk Douglas, Janet Leigh, and Tony Curtis; filmed on location in Norway, it included some ponderous narration by Orson Welles. *These Thousand Hills* (1959) was a melodramatic Western, based on an A. B. Guthrie novel, about irresponsible cowboy Don Murray becoming a rancher and a political candidate before having to face up to murderous rival Richard Egan to save dance-hall girl Lee Remick.

The provocative *Compulsion* (1959) was a thinly disguised rendering of the Leopold and Loeb case; Bradford Dillman and Dean Stockwell played the thrill-killers and Orson Welles the Clarence Darrow-esque attorney whose brilliant defense fails to save them. *Crack in the Mirror* (1960), filmed on location in Paris, set Welles and Dillman in a courtroom again, though this time they were given dual roles in contrapuntal plots, vying in each case for the hand of Juliette Greco. *The Big Gamble* (1961), written by Irwin Shaw, paired Greco (the real-life love interest of studio head Darryl Zanuck) with Stephen Boyd as they try to drive a truck deep into the African interior, while *Barabbas* (1962) was a sincere but plodding adaptation of the Par Lagerkvist novel, with Anthony Quinn as the felon whose life changes after Jesus is crucified in his stead.

Fleischer was absent from the screen for four years, but when he returned, it was with his biggest hit in more than a decade, *Fantastic Voyage* (1966). A pop science-fiction landmark, it sent a miniaturized team of scientists, made up of Stephen Boyd, Raquel Welch, and assorted character actors, on a mission impossible through the body of a scientist suffering from a blood clot in his brain. By today's standards the special effects are primitive, but it was the first big-budget SF production in many years, and its success paved the way for *2001* and other, better entries in the genre. More problematic was *Doctor Dolittle* (1967), an excruciating version of the children's classic, with Rex Harrison as the good doctor, Anthony Newley as his insufferable assistant, and fifteen hundred live animals, none worth the price of admission. (A box-office and critical disaster, its legendary production problems are recounted at length in John Gregory Dunne's book *The Studio*.)

But Fleischer rebounded with the gruesome but popular true-crime tale *The Boston Strangler* (1968), a suspenseful (if overly flashy) dramatization of Gerold Frank's bestseller about the Albert De Salvo case; Tony Curtis is quite effective as the schizoid plumber. But *Che!* (1969) was one of the decade's biggest hoots, a dumbed-down account of the revolutionary leader's life; Omar Sharif is inadequate as Che and Jack Palance hopeless as Fidel Castro. The big-budget American-Japanese co-production *Tora! Tora! Tora!* (1970) was a meticulous re-creation of the events leading up to Pearl Harbor, told from both the Japanese and the American vantage points, with a convincing re-creation of the attack on Pearl Harbor that won an Oscar for special effects. (Did Fleischer's *Design for Death* help him land this assignment?)

His contract with Fox now expired, Fleischer made *10 Rillington Place* (1971), a semi-documentary staging of the John Reginald Christie–Timothy Evans murder case that shocked England in the 1940s, with Richard Attenborough as the mass murderer and John Hurt the simpleminded man who is framed for one of the killings and hanged in his place. *See No Evil* (1971) was an atmospheric variation on *Wait Until Dark*, with blind woman Mia Farrow learning to her horror that the other members of her family are being killed one by one by a madman, while *The Last Run* (also 1971) was an offbeat gangster yarn starring George C. Scott and Tony Musante that Fleischer inherited from John Huston. *The New Centurions* (1972), an uneven adaptation of former cop Joseph Wambaugh's gritty bestseller, offered George C. Scott, Stacy Keach, and Jane Alexander as part of its excellent cast.

*Soylent Green* (1973) was a clumsy cautionary science-fiction tale that was impossible to take as seriously as it took itself, although Charlton Heston as a twenty-first-century cop and Edward G. Robinson as an elderly chemist were acceptable. But *The Don Is Dead* (1973) was a crummy knockoff of *The Godfather*, and *The Spikes Gang* (1974) a clichéd Western, in which Lee Marvin teaches runaway Ron Howard

"You rigged it, copper...
Now let her stop a
bullet meant for me!"
Two mystery women on a speeding train...
stalked by the top hoods of the crime
syndicate. One of the women will never
reach the Grand Jury!...
The NARROW MARGIN
with
CHARLES McGRAW
MARIE WINDSOR
JACQUELINE WHITE
RKO RADIO PICTURES
Directed by RICHARD FLEISCHER
Screenplay by EARL FELTON

and his friends how to rob banks. Charles Bronson was well cast in *Mr. Majestyk* (1974) as a watermelon farmer who becomes targeted for a gang hit and fights back with astonishing inventiveness; the unlikely premise somehow made sense in Elmore Leonard's screenplay. But the inexplicably popular *Mandingo* (1975)—a lurid, racist bosom heaver set in the antebellum South—was an embarrassment, despite the presence of James Mason (who should have known better).

At least *The Incredible Sarah* (1976) was tasteful, but this *Reader's Digest*–financed biopic of fabled actress Sarah Bernhardt (Glenda Jackson) had little more to offer. *Crossed Swords* (1978) was a middling version of *The Prince and the Pauper*, starring Mark Lester in the dual role alongside Oliver Reed and Raquel Welch, while *Ashanti* (1979) was an exploitation entry, with Beverly Johnson kidnapped by slave trader Peter Ustinov and pursued over half the continent by missionary husband Michael Caine. But even that was respectable compared to Fleischer's remake of *The Jazz Singer* (1980); Neil Diamond was laughable as the Jewish lad torn between the synagogue and life as a rock musician and Laurence Olivier beyond the pale as his cantor father. The film is now regarded as a camp classic, but that couldn't have been Fleischer's intent.

*Tough Enough* (1983) sat on the shelf for two years, but this tale of country-and-Western singer Dennis Quaid becoming an amateur boxer was at least passable, and *Amityville 3-D*, (1983) was a decent-enough sequel in the series; with Tony Roberts and Tess Harper now the proud owners of Long Island's most active property. *Conan the Destroyer* (1984), however, was an inferior follow-up to John Milius's surprise 1982 hit: Arnold Schwarzenegger is now joined by fellow amateur actors Grace Jones and Wilt Chamberlain. But even that did well enough to inspire the spin-off *Red Sonja* (1985), in which Brigitte Nielsen submits a performance that made Grace Jones in *Conan* look like Meryl Streep. Fleischer's final embarrassment was *Million Dollar Mystery* (1987), a knockoff of *It's a Mad, Mad, Mad, Mad World* that existed primarily as a promotional gimmick for a treasure hunt being conducted by Glad Bags—not exactly the high-water mark of a career that started off so impressively. Fleischer's autobiography, *Just Tell Me When to Cry*, was published in 1993.

## ● VICTOR FLEMING (1883-1949)

He signed his name to some of the most celebrated films of Hollywood's golden age during a career that spanned thirty years, so it comes as something of a surprise that Victor Fleming made only twenty sound pictures and another twenty-odd silents in all that time. But if he was less prolific than some of his peers, he also seemed able to turn out more finely tuned work, whether the matter at hand was an adventure, a romance, or a fantasy. But he won his Oscar for a picture on which, ironically, he contributed far less than he did on any other.

Born in Pasadena, California, Fleming was a chauffeur before breaking into the film industry in 1910 as an assistant cameraman. A year later he began working for Allan Dwan at Flying A studios, and by 1915 he was handling the camera for D. W. Griffith at Triangle. After a year serving as a photographer for the Army Signal Corps, he helped film the Versailles Peace Conference in 1919. Fleming made a couple of Douglas Fairbanks features before signing a contract with Paramount in 1922, where he stayed until the end of the decade. Among the many prestigious silents he helmed were *The Way of All Flesh* with Emil Jannings, *Hula* with Clara Bow, and *Abie's Irish Rose*, an adaptation of the long-running Broadway show. *Wolf Song* (1929) was a part-talkie, with Gary Cooper and Lupe Velez fur-trapping up North, but it was Cooper's other Western that year that made him a star. *The Virginian* had been filmed twice as silents, and would be again in 1946, but Fleming's early talkie remains definitive, thanks to Cooper's laconic charisma and Walter Huston's mustache-twirling villainy.

On the heels of that success Fleming left Paramount, making a pair of features for Fox in 1930 before hooking up with old pal Douglas Fairbanks, Sr., with whom he co-directed the travelogue *Around the World in Eighty Minutes* (1931). Fleming finally touched down at MGM in 1932; he immediately set about becoming one of that top studio's top directors. *The Wet Parade*, from Upton Sinclair's book, was Walter Huston and Myrna Loy playing at Prohibition. *Red Dust* (1932) was an unqualified smash, the first and best of several happy teamings of Clark Gable and Jean Harlow. Fortunately this steamy jungle romance was filmed before the Code came into effect, permitting the sort of teasing sexual byplay that soon would vanish from the screen.

*The White Sister* (1933) was a remake of the 1923 weeper starring Lillian Gish and Ronald Colman, with Helen Hayes now entering a convent when she thinks her lover—Gable again—has been killed in World War I. While Gable was generating tears, Harlow manufactured laughs in *Bombshell* (1933), a wicked, dead-on satire of stardom in which she fearlessly skewered herself along with every conceivable variation of Hollywood parasite, family and otherwise; Lee Tracy was especially funny as her unscrupulous press agent. *Treasure Island* (1934), a crackling good version of the oft-filmed Robert Louis Stevenson novel, starred Wallace Beery as the definitive Long John Silver and Jackie Cooper as Jim.

◀ *Fleming and Harlow on the set of* Bombshell

*Reckless* (1935), though, was one of Fleming's rare misfires at MGM, a grueling musical (Harlow's dancing and singing were performed by stand-ins) that had the bad taste to exploit the 1932 suicide of her husband, Paul Bern, as a thinly—very thinly—disguised plot element, courtesy of David O. Selznick's original story.

Fleming was loaned to Fox for the 1935 *The Farmer Takes a Wife*, a bucolic period piece, with Henry Fonda wooing Janet Gaynor on the shores of the Erie Canal. *Captains Courageous* (1937) was an enormous success, a sentimental but affecting version of the Kipling story about a spoiled rich boy (Freddie Bartholomew) who learns about life when he's rescued by a whaling vessel. Spencer Tracy won his first Academy Award for his performance as the earthy Portuguese fisherman who befriends the boy, and the film was also nominated for a best picture Oscar. The snappy *Test Pilot* (1938) was almost as good; Clark Gable, Myrna Loy, and Spencer Tracy form an atypical but interesting romantic triangle.

Fleming then hit the daily double with two of 1939's biggest hits, both of which remain on everyone's top ten of all-time Hollywood classics—though neither began with Fleming as their director. *The Wizard of Oz* requires little discussion here, so familiar is it to today's audiences thanks to annual television broadcasts that began in the 1950s, but it is worth reflecting on how many of its perfectly realized virtues were the result of provenance. Most important, Shirley Temple would have starred in it had her studio, Fox, permitted her loan-out; its Oscar-winning song, the poignant "Over the Rainbow," was nearly cut from the release print; and the first few weeks of filming under the direction of Richard Thorpe were scrapped by producer Mervyn LeRoy, who then brought Fleming on board. Fleming's accomplishment speaks for itself.

*Wizard* was in the running for a best picture Oscar, but it lost to Fleming's second 1939 production, *Gone with the Wind.* Here again, Fleming was not in the original mix, replacing George Cukor when Clark Gable threatened producer Selznick with a work stoppage unless Cukor was canned; officially the explanation was that Gable was concerned that Vivien Leigh was being favored by Cukor, a "woman's director." (Cukor's knowledge of an early homosexual incident in Gable's career was supposedly what really made the King of Hollywood uncomfortable.) Gable asked for, and got, old hunting pal Fleming. But that was not the end of the production's problems. Fleming suffered a nervous breakdown ten weeks into the shoot and had to be replaced by Sam Wood, who also was borrowed from MGM. Even after Fleming returned to work, Wood stayed on to co-direct. The final cut of *GWTW* includes work by Cukor, Fleming, and Wood, but at Oscar time only Fleming was handed an award for best direction (one of the film's then-record ten Academy Awards). As little as half of what is on screen may be Fleming's handiwork, but it is now impossible to say who did what exactly.

Fully recovered, Fleming next remade *Dr. Jekyll and Mr. Hyde* (1941), which ten years earlier had won an Oscar for Fredric March in Rouben Mamoulian's acclaimed production. Here it was a somewhat miscast Spencer Tracy who starred alongside Ingrid Bergman and Lana Turner, and the result, while not without merit, is surely the lesser of the two sound versions. Fleming then teamed Tracy with Hedy La-

▲ *With Rhett and Scarlett during the making of* Gone with the Wind

marr in a solid adaptation of John Steinbeck's *Tortilla Flat* (1942)—but Tracy's gruff fisherman routine was less effective here than in *Captains Courageous*, although John Garfield and Frank Morgan (who was nominated for an Oscar) fared better. It was Tracy again in *A Guy Named Joe* (1943), co-starring with Irene Dunne in an overlong but often moving love story that recalled *Here Comes Mr. Jordan* at key moments (both shared producer Everett Riskin); in any case, it was better than Spielberg's 1989 remake, *Always*.

Fleming was absent from the screen until 1945, when the ballyhooed *Adventure* was released. "Gable's back, and Garson's got him!" the ads proclaimed, but few ticket buyers were excited by the unlikely pairing, and this strained romantic comedy became a major box-office disappointment. That ended Fleming's long and illustrious tenure at MGM on an unfortunate down note. His next—and final—movie was *Joan of Arc* (1948), which he, Walter Wanger, and Ingrid Bergman formed a production company (Sierra Pictures) to make. It was a hefty—145 minutes in its original road-show cut—rather plodding adaptation of the Maxwell Anderson stage epic. Bergman was a game but fatally dull Joan (although she and co-star José Ferrer both received Oscar nominations). The film's primary sin was that it was too pompous to be entertaining—a flaw not common to his earlier work. Victor Fleming died the following year, his glory days far behind him.

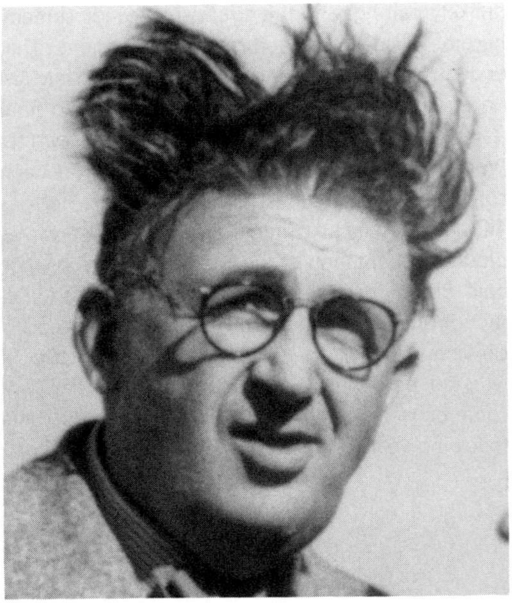

## ● JOHN FORD (1895-1973)

By near consensus, John Ford is the greatest American director, although dissenters do exist. There is a reliably high, nearly classical quality to his sixty-plus sound features (with as many silents preceding them), most of which proffer Ford's uniquely consistent themes and concerns about honor, patriotism, and family. But are those themes redolent of all that is best about the American spirit, or merely (as David Thomson argues so sacrilegiously) "bigoted, grandiloquent and maudlin"? Perhaps it shouldn't matter that so many of Ford's pictures are marinated in sentimentality, or that his formalism sometimes squeezes the juice of innovation out of even his best work. It's the cinematic universe he created and populated over more than four decades that stands as his monument, so much greater than the sum of its (sometimes overly familiar) parts.

Born in Cape Elizabeth, Maine, as Sean Aloysius O'Feeney (aka O'Fearna), he was the youngest of thirteen children, one of whom was Francis, a stage actor who broke into films in 1907 and who branched out into directing (himself, as often as not) by 1913. Francis Ford, as he had christened himself for the stage, took John under his wing around 1914, employing him as an assistant director at Universal on serials and Western two-reelers like *The Broken Coin* and *The Hidden City*. By 1915 John, now working as Jack Ford, was directing his own Universal shorts and features, primarily Westerns along the lines of *Straight Shooting*, *The Phantom Riders*, and *Hell Bent*.

Ford's name appeared on sixteen releases in 1919 (including a version of *The Outcasts of Poker Flats*), several of which starred Harry Carey. In 1920 he began directing pictures outside the auspices of Universal, and by mid-1921 he was working full-time for the William Fox studio, where he would toil for the next ten years alongside the likes of Jack Conway, W. S. Van Dyke, Frank Borzage, Howard Hawks, Raoul Walsh, and Allan Dwan. Many of his silent features apparently are lost works, although one hears about his version of the American folktale *The Face on the Barroom Floor* (1923); *The Iron Horse* (1924), an early epic about the building of the first transcontinental railroad; the sentimental *Four Sons* (1928), a World War I tale laden with as much poignancy (if not poetry) as King Vidor's *The Big Parade*; and the unmitigated blarney of *Riley the Cop* and *Mother Machree* (both 1928).

*Strong Boy* and *The Black Watch* (both 1929) each starred Victor McLaglen, the Irish giant who had once been heavyweight boxing champ of Great Britain; Ford would work (and drink) with him for the next quarter century. But as was the case with most directors' transitional sound pictures, these were unremarkable. *Men without Women* (1930) began Ford's long collaboration with screenwriter Dudley Nichols, while the comic crime yarn *Up the River* (1930) offered nascent screenwork by Broadway actors Spencer Tracy, Humphrey Bogart, and Claire Luce. Lighter fare like *The Brat* (1931) with Sally O'Neil was interspersed with heavy dramas like *The Seas Beneath* (1930), one of many Fox adventures made by Ford starring the stalwart (and dull) George O'Brien.

It wasn't until Ford left Fox to freelance that his films began to stand apart from the pack. He made *Arrowsmith* (1931) for Goldwyn and UA; it was a classy if stolid production with Ronald Colman and Helen Hayes that perversely ignored two-thirds of Sinclair Lewis's source novel about a doctor wrestling with worldly temptations. *Air Mail* (1932) was less restrained, a Hawksian adventure about mail pilots battling the elements and the limits of technology, the conflict between dangerously cocky pilot Pat O'Brien and Desert Airport manager Ralph Bellamy at its hub. (Ford's older brother Francis also appeared in a bit role, the first of many acting jobs John would supply him with.)

*Flesh* (1932) was an atypical product from the MGM gloss factory, a seedy tale about dim-witted wrestler Wallace Beery's infatuation with faithless Karen Morley, while *Pilgrimage* (1933), with Heather Angel and Marian Nixon, was another sentimental story about a family torn asunder by the cruel demands of the First World War. *Doctor Bull* (1933) was pleasant enough Americana, featuring Will Rogers, with whom Ford worked three times. *The Lost Patrol* (1934), still one of Ford's most exciting early works, starred Victor McLaglen as the leader of a band of British soldiers (Boris Karloff and Wallace Ford among them) lost and under attack in the Arabian desert during World War I; Max Steiner's suspenseful score was nominated for an Oscar.

More ambitious, but rather less successful, was *The World Moves On* (1934), starring Franchot Tone and Madeleine Carroll. A sweeping epic about three generations of a family, it starts out in 1800s Louisiana and concludes during World War I with the members scattered all over the globe. Ford seemed more at ease with the gentle whimsy of *Judge Priest* (1934), in which Will Rogers plays the eponymous hero whose eccentricities alternately endear him to, and infuriate, his small-town constituents. The crime comedy *The Whole Town's Talking* (1935) has the trump card of Edward G. Robinson spoofing his snarling gangster persona, playing the dual roles of meek hardware-store clerk Arthur Jones and recently escaped Public Enemy No. 1 "Killer" Mannion, whose fates become intertwined. Co-scripted by longtime Capra collaborator Robert Riskin and co-starring Capra leading lady Jean Arthur, this inventive fable is hard to think of as part of the Ford canon, but Robinson's clever performance is perhaps his best of the Thirties, for which Ford must be given his due.

*The Informer* (1935), the first of a three-picture deal Ford signed with RKO, was adapted by Dudley Nichols from Liam O'Flaherty's novel about a Dublin turncoat who sells out a friend during the Irish civil war of 1922. One of the decade's most admired films, it was atmospheric and intense (if rather heavy-handed), and all the more impressive for being shot in a mere seventeen days on a modest budget. Victor McLaglen—not a subtle actor—got the role of his life as the craven Gypo Nolan, and he was well supported by Preston Foster, Wallace Ford, Heather Angel, and Margot Grahame. Ford, McLaglen, Dudley Nichols, and scorer Max Steiner all won Academy Awards, and the film was nominated as best picture. Ford was also cited by the New York Film Critics Circle for best direction.

But before those awards were meted out, Ford returned to Fox to make *Steamboat 'Round the Bend*, Will Rogers's penultimate film before his untimely death in a plane crash. A lovely piece of nineteenth-century Americana, it featured Rogers as a charismatic hawker of patent medicines floating along the Mississippi in his makeshift barge; Anne Shirley and John McGuire are along for romantic interest and Stepin Fetchit for broad comedy. *The Prisoner of Shark Island* (1936), written by Nunnally Johnson, was set in the same period but concerned itself with a more weighty bit of history. Warner Baxter plays Dr. Samuel Mudd, the doctor who treated John Wilkes Booth's broken ankle after the Lincoln assassination and then was unjustly arrested and sent to an isolated prison camp on the Dry Tortugas for being part of the conspiracy; John Carradine excels as Baxter's tormentor.

*Mary of Scotland* (1936) was Ford's expensive, handsome, but embalmed version of a Maxwell Anderson play (scripted by Dudley Nichols) about Mary Stuart, the queen deposed by Elizabeth I (Florence Eldridge); Katharine Hepburn is at her high-falutin' worst and Fredric March is terribly miscast as her roguish lover, the Earl of Bothwell. Just as close to Ford's heart, but even worse, was *The Plough and the Stars* (also 1936), a plodding adaptation of the Sean O'Casey play about the 1916 Irish Revolution, with Preston Foster, Barbara Stanwyck, and, from Dublin's Abbey Theatre, Barry Fitzgerald. Both pictures lost money for RKO, and *Plough* was reshot and cut by studio execs, infuriating Ford and sending him back to Fox, where he signed an eight-picture contract.

*Wee Willie Winkie* (1937), distantly related to the Kipling story, may have seemed an unlikely project for a recent Oscar winner, but what better way for a director with Ford's sagging fortunes to revitalize his commercial reputation than to work with the day's number-one draw, Shirley Temple? There was only so much he could do with the formula required of Temple pictures—yet this inane variation of *Gunga Din* is mysteriously watchable, and Victor McLaglen, C. Aubrey Smith, and Cesar Romero provide Shirley with unusually expert support. *The Hurricane* (1934),

made for Goldwyn and UA, was even more popular, with Jon Hall and Dorothy Lamour as sarong-clad, google-eyed lovers on the isle of Manikoora, kept apart by cruel governor Raymond Massey. The cast is full of great character actors, including Mary Astor, Thomas Mitchell (who was nominated for an Oscar), and John Carradine, but they're all upstaged when the twenty-minute hurricane sequence—a triumph of the special-effects department—blows Manikoora to kingdom come. The film (on which an uncredited Stuart Heisler assisted) was Ford's biggest hit to date.

*Four Men and a Prayer* (1938) was an intriguing mystery, with sons Richard Greene, George Sanders, David Niven, and William Henry criss-crossing the globe to track down the murderers of their father (C. Aubrey Smith), while *Submarine Patrol* (1938) was a passable World War I adventure in which playboy Richard Greene learns about his shipboard responsibilities from temporarily disgraced seaman Preston Foster.

Far more impressive than that pair was *Stagecoach* (1939), Ford's first Western since the silent era and one of his enduring masterpieces. Filmed in Monument Valley, Arizona, a setting Ford would return to many times over the remainder of his long career, this "*Grand Hotel* on wheels" (as Pauline Kael describes it) was made for Walter Wanger at UA, an arrangement that permitted Ford to assemble a more eclectic cast than would have been possible at a studio like Fox. John Wayne, veteran of some eighty "B" pictures (most recently *Red River Range* and *Santa Fe Stampede*), was lead-billed as the Ringo Kid, and Claire Trevor, Thomas Mitchell, George Bancroft, John Carradine, and Donald Meek are among the principals endeavoring to travel by stage in the 1880s from Tonto, New Mexico, to Lordsburg, directly through the heart of Geronimo's territory. The first "A" Western to make an impact—both commercially and critically—since the early days of talkies, *Stagecoach* was nominated for an Academy Award as best picture. Ford and cinematographer Bert Glennon were also nominated, while the score and Mitchell were both given Oscars. And the New York Film Critics Circle named Ford best director.

On the heels of that unexpected success Ford made *Young Mr. Lincoln* (1939), an excellent biography of Lincoln's early days as a lawyer, with Henry Fonda subtly limning the canny intelligence behind Lincoln's rube façade. Lamar Trotti's original story, which culminates with an exciting murder trial, was nominated for an Academy Award, and in a less awesome year Ford and Fonda probably would have been as well. *Drums Along the Mohawk* was Ford's third film of 1939 and first ever in Technicolor, and while not at the level of the earlier two, it was an exciting treatment of pre–Revolutionary War relations between settlers and Native Americans. Henry Fonda and Claudette Colbert star as newlyweds trying to carve out a home in the untamed Mohawk Valley (for which Ford used the wilds of Utah); resilient neighbor Edna May Oliver was nominated for a best supporting actress Oscar.

*The Grapes of Wrath* (1940) was one of the most eagerly awaited pictures of the year, based as it was on John Steinbeck's enormously popular 1938 novel about the Joad family's epic struggle to survive in Depression-ravaged America. Henry Fonda had the key role of ex-con Tom Joad, while Russell Simpson and Jane Darwell were cast as his parents and John Carradine as the mad ex-preacher Casey. Ford and cameraman Gregg Toland captured the look of Dorothea Lange's famous photographs, and Nunnally Johnson's screenplay is faithful to Steinbeck's prose, pregnant with message as it was. Today the film feels more than a bit stilted and self-conscious of its own importance, but in 1940 it was deemed an unqualified triumph, with Academy Award nominations for best picture, actor (Fonda), and screenplay. Jane Darwell won the best supporting actress Oscar, and Ford took home his second Academy Award for best direction, defeating a stellar field—George Cukor, William Wyler, Alfred Hitchcock, and Sam Wood.

*The Long Voyage Home* (1940), based on four one-act plays by Eugene O'Neill about merchant seamen in the first days of World War II, was adapted by Dudley Nichols into a seamless whole and beautifully photographed by Gregg Toland. John Wayne was cast against type as homesick Swedish sailor Ole Olsen (accent and all), while Thomas Mitchell, Ian Hunter, and Barry Fitzgerald provided fine support. *Voyage* actually competed against *Grapes* for the best picture Oscar, earning nominations for screenplay and cinematography as well. Ford's impressive two-year roll continued in 1941 with *Tobacco Road*, a loose adaptation of Jack Kirkland's long-running Broadway play, itself a tamer version of Erskine Caldwell's then-shocking novel about a dysfunctional, white-trash Georgia clan. Gene Tierney had her patrician beauty smudged to play barefoot temptress Ellie May Lester, but Ford jettisons the story's sweaty sex—with the Code in effect, he had little choice—in favor of the low-down comedy inherent in Charley Grapewin's Jeeter, Marjorie Rambeau's Bessie, and William Tracy's Duke.

That minor accomplishment was soon overshadowed by Ford's second release of the year for Fox, the monumental *How Green Was My Valley*, based on Richard Llewellyn's novel about the struggles of a poor family in a turn-of-the-century coal-mining town in south Wales. Told primarily in flashback from the perspective of Roddy McDowall (whose adult narration is supplied by Jewish actor/director Irving Pichel), *Valley* stars Donald Crisp as the family's stern father, Sara Allgood as the goodhearted mother, and Maureen O'Hara as the sister loved by minister Walter Pidgeon; Barry Fitzgerald was one of the many Irish actors recruited to fill out the cast. (But the singers in the film are Welsh.) Sentimental it may have been, but *Valley* was probably the year's most emotional picture, and it was rewarded with five Academy Awards: best picture, direction (with which the New York Film Critics Circle concurred), supporting actor (Crisp), cinematography (Arthur Miller), and art direction; Allgood and the screenplay by Philip Dunne were also nominated.

Ford thus became the second director to win three Oscars, after Frank Capra. But he was given little time to savor the achievement, as he had been serving since the outbreak of the Second World War as a lieutenant commander in the Navy and chief of the OSS's Field Photographic Branch. (In 1995 the CIA honored Ford for his OSS service.) While overseeing the filming of the encounter that would be released theatrically as *The Battle of Midway* (1942), Ford was wounded, a bit of misfortune that earned him a purple star; later he would also share in the Oscar given to *Midway* as best documentary. *December 7th* (1943), co-directed with Gregg Toland, was awarded an Oscar in the same category a year later. Toward the end of the war Ford began working on a documentary about the Nuremberg trials, but the project was never completed.

Ford's first picture after returning to civilian life was *They Were Expendable* (1945), a gritty but depressing account of the initial failures of the U.S. Navy to hold the Pacific in the early stages of World War II. Robert Montgomery (who helped direct some sequences and had himself just completed a tour of duty in the Navy) and John Wayne star as Navy lieutenants in charge of a torpedo-boat squadron that could hold back the onslaught of the Japanese were they but deployed to do so. But the top brass won't give the green light until it's too late, the Japanese take control of the Philippines, and the lives of many American soldiers are lost. A powerful indictment of U.S. military shortsightedness—and the first with that theme to focus on World War II—this would be the last war movie Ford would make for many years.

*My Darling Clementine* (1946), which concluded Ford's contract with Fox, is widely recognized as one of his masterpieces, despite the scissors taken to it by Darryl Zanuck, who lopped off nearly half an hour. A beautifully observed, almost leisurely telling of the Wyatt Earp–Doc Holliday legend, gorgeously photographed by Joseph MacDonald, it starred Henry Fonda as the impressively iconic Marshal Earp, Victor Mature as a rather robust but still sympathetic Doc, Linda Darnell as the luscious Chihuahua, and Walter Brennan as utterly monstrous Old Man Clanton; Ward Bond, Tim Holt, John Ireland, and Cathy Downs are also part of the remarkable cast. Ford plays fast and loose with the facts of the tale (such as we know them), but forges a poetic reality here that feels more true than any pile of musty clippings could ever be—which is why Monument Valley was a better choice for the location shoot than downstate Tombstone.

Ford now commenced operations on his newly founded Argosy Pictures, at which he would coproduce films with Merian C. Cooper, with RKO releasing the pictures. Argosy's first production was *The Fugitive* (1947), a brooding reshaping of Graham Greene's novel *The Power and the Glory*. Scripted by Dudley Nichols and shot in Mexico, it miscast Henry Fonda as a Central American priest hunted by his unnamed government and haunted by his own shortcomings; Dolores Del Rio is an unwed mother whose child he baptizes, and Ward Bond a distraught American criminal known as "El Gringo" (no one has an actual name in this, a tip-off in itself of the film's pretensions). Ford once inexplicably claimed this to be his best work, but American audiences voted otherwise at the box office.



Fonda was better suited to *Fort Apache* (1948), in which he plays the coldhearted Lieutenant Colonel Owen Thursday, an SOB whose pigheadedness nearly gets his cavalry unit—which includes John Wayne, Ward Bond, and Victor McLaglen—eradicated by Apaches. The film is lovely to look at, but Ford takes more than two hours to embroider his tale with loving vignettes of the fort's social life and horseplay among the soldiers, both of which grow irritating long before the picture ends. *Three Godfathers* (1948) was an enjoyable remake of Peter B. Kyne's oft-filmed story of three fugitives—here John Wayne, Harry Carey, Jr., and Pedro Armendariz—who come across a mother (Mae Marsh) and her baby in the desert; by caring for the infant, they are gradually reformed.

Ford then continued his cavalry trilogy with *She Wore a Yellow Ribbon* (1949), which like *Fort Apache* was also based on stories by James Warner Bellah (adapted by Frank Nugent). Less diffuse than its predecessor, it permitted John Wayne's cantankerous, soon-to-retire Captain Brittles to hold center stage; such frills as the maddeningly cute romance between John Agar and Joanne Dru are kept to an acceptable level. Winton Hoch's stunning color cinematography won an Oscar, capturing the glories of Monument Valley as if Frederic Remington had been behind the camera lens. *When Willie Comes Marching Home* (1950) rarely comes to mind when one ponders this golden period of Ford's career; it is a middling World War II comedy/adventure with Dan Dailey and Corinne Calvet that needed a Preston Sturges at the helm to punch up the satire (although Sy Gomberg's story was nominated for an Oscar).

*Wagon Master* (1950) was developed by Frank Nugent and Patrick Ford (John's son) from Ford's own story. A Mormon wagon train headed by Ward Bond and bound for Utah picks up assorted passengers along the way: cowboys Ben Johnson and Harry Carey, Jr., medicine show performers Alan Mowbray and Joanne Dru, and a tribe of Navajos. Shot modestly in black-and-white, its unpretentious presentation and ensemble acting are rather more likable than the earlier spectacular—but more fussy—Technicolor cavalry sagas. The third installment in that saga, *Rio Grande*, was made in 1950 at Republic Pictures, where Ford and Merian C. Cooper had relocated Argosy. Again based on a James Warner Bellah story, it starred John Wayne as Colonel Cord McNally, whose battles with the Apaches take a back seat to his problems with estranged wife Maureen O'Hara, from whom he's been separated for sixteen years. The Ford stock company fills in the edges of the tale: Ben Johnson, Victor McLaglen, Harry Carey, Jr., Chill Wills, and (warbling the inevitable Irish ditties) the Sons of the Pioneers.

*The Quiet Man* (1952) is one of Ford's most lauded and beloved movies; it also can be one of his most irritating. Set in the 1920s, it features John Wayne as Sean Thornton, an American boxer who (it is later revealed) has killed a man in the ring, forcing his retirement to his homeland of Ireland, where he buys a cottage in the town where he was born. Maureen O'Hara is the fiery maid who captures his heart, Victor McLaglen her mean-spirited giant of a brother, and Barry Fitzgerald the wizened imp who helps bring Wayne and O'Hara together. (Francis Ford also has a small part, as he'd had in twenty-eight of John's previous pictures.) The blarney is so deep it requires a shovel, but Ford's nostalgia is clearly heartfelt, and the film is lovely to look at (shot in part on location in Ireland). It was nominated for an Academy Award as best picture, and McLaglen, Frank Nugent's screenplay, and the art direction were also nominated, with Oscars going to Ford—a record fourth—and cinematographers Winton Hoch and Archie Stout.

Ford's remake of *What Price Glory?* (1952) was not up to Raoul Walsh's 1926 silent classic about World War I, but James Cagney and Dan Dailey as the battling Marines Flagg and Quirt at least kept it respectable. Ford next remade himself with *The Sun Shines Bright* (1953), a revised *Judge Priest* that he later claimed was his favorite among his own works. Charles Winninger has Will Rogers's old role as a small-town politician, and a gallery of such Ford favorites as Milburn Stone, Mae Marsh, Jane Darwell, Slim Pickens, Stepin Fetchit (who also was in the original), and brother Francis fill out the delightful cast.

*Mogambo* (1953) was yet another remake, this time of Victor Fleming's 1932 classic *Red Dust*. Clark Gable repeats his role as an African plantation boss trying to fend off the advances of two beauties, reformed trollope Ava Gardner (in Jean Harlow's role) and refined but married Grace Kelly (in Mary As-

▲ *Relaxing in Africa with the lovely Ava Gardner during* Mogambo

tor's); both actresses received Oscar nominations. Gable is still virile enough to carry off the demands of the part, and with its handsome locations in Kenya and Tanganyika and rich color photography, the film manages to hold its own with the fondly recalled original (although it's hard to believe that it was Ford and not John Huston who made this love letter to Africa). *The Long Gray Line* (1955) brought Ford into *Mr. Chips* territory. Tyrone Power plays a coach of athletics at West Point whose entire life is spent helping his lads realize their dreams and Maureen O'Hara is his supportive wife.

Ford next drew the enviable assignment of bringing Josh Logan's Broadway smash *Mister Roberts* (1955) to the big screen, with Logan and Frank Nugent handling the adaptation. The hand-picked cast was headed by Henry Fonda, repeating his stage role as the Navy cargo officer who must reckon with the whims of Captain James Cagney and the peccadilloes of Jack Lemmon's Ensign Pulver (for which Lemmon won an Oscar); William Powell was also on hand as the ship's wise doctor. Barely a week into filming, Ford and Fonda feuded over their interpretations of the role and Ford left the production, which was completed by Mervyn LeRoy. The result was a rather tame comedy that nonetheless was a huge hit and was nominated for an Academy Award as best picture. What Ford might have wrought with it we'll never know.

*The Searchers* (1956) is probably Ford's greatest achievement, easily the best American film of the year and one of the decade's three or four best—a film that has continued to grow in reputation over time. Based on a competent but unremarkable novel by Alan LeMay (adapted by Frank Nugent), it stars John Wayne as Ethan Edwards, a surly, misanthropic Civil War veteran who shows up at his brother's Texas farm unannounced one sunny day. When much of his brother's family is massacred during an attack by Comanches, Ethan—a fanatic Indian hater—leads a party of men to track them down and recover his kidnapped niece, Deborah (Lana Wood), whom he intends to kill when he finds her, thus purifying her after she was sullied by savages. Seven long years later he and half-breed Jeffrey Hunter, now Ethan's lone partner, locate her (she has grown into the pristine Natalie Wood) and her "buck," Scar, the Comanche leader responsible for the massacre. After killing Scar, Ethan—to his own surprise—brings Deborah back to her family. But the film is really about Ethan's quest; once it's over, he again has no purpose, and the door to civilization literally closes in his face in the film's moving final shot. Wonderfully photographed by Winton C. Hoch (in Monument Valley) and scored by Max Steiner, *The Searchers* was not regarded as a special achievement in its day and didn't receive a single Oscar nomination. Yet its epic canvas and haunted protagonist have a resonance that such contemporary successes as *Around the World in 80 Days* and even *Giant* do not.

*The Rising of the Moon* (1957), based on a trio of stories and plays by Irish writers, was the most purely Irish picture in Ford's canon, shot as it was in Ireland and performed by such Dublin Abbey Players as Cyril Cusack, Maureen Connell, Jimmy O'Dea, and Frank Lawton. *The Wings of Eagles* (1957) was a more commercial venture, an entertaining but self-indulgent biopic about Frank Wead (John Wayne), the heroic World War I aviator who later wrote screenplays for such Ford productions as *Air Mail* and *They Were Expendable*; Ward Bond impersonates Ford during this phase of Mead's life. *Gideon of Scotland Yard* (1958) is one of Ford's least distinguished (and, mercifully, least remembered) efforts, with Jack Hawkins as the eponymous protagonist. *The Last Hurrah* (1958) was an overlong but flavorful adaptation of Edwin O'Connor's bestseller: Spencer Tracy plays a James Hurley-ish Boston mayor preparing for his final campaign; old-timers Donald Crisp, John Carradine, Basil Rathbone, and Pat O'Brien lent a poignancy to the tale.

*The Horse Soldiers* (1959) was an occasionally exciting Civil War yarn in which John Wayne and William Holden are Union officers leading a raiding party into Confederate territory (based on Grierson's Raid of 1863). Far better was *Sergeant Rutledge* (1960), an adaptation of James Warner Bellah's novel *Captain Buffalo* (co-scripted by Bellah), with Ford stock regular Woody Strode now elevated to the starring role of a black cavalry officer who is accused of raping and murdering a white woman. *Two Rode Together* (1961) had the advantage of James Stewart and Richard Widmark heading its cast—incredibly, it was the first time Ford and Stewart had worked together on a picture—but was an otherwise pedestrian story about a ragtag band assembled to rescue captives of the Comanches.

Ford's fourth consecutive Western, *The Man Who Shot Liberty Valance* (1962), was his best since *The*

*Searchers* and, arguably, his last great film. Based on a story by Dorothy Johnson, its setbound activity and black-and-white cinematography make it appear as less than it is, a cosmetic factor that probably contributed to its originally not being embraced by either critics or audiences. John Wayne plays a laconic, cynical ex-gunman who is pressed into service against the vicious Liberty Valance (Lee Marvin at his sadistic best) when tenderfoot James Stewart is maneuvered into a showdown which he can't possibly win. Because it examines, and even tweaks, the nature of mythmaking instead of loudly celebrating it (as so many of his earlier films are wont to do), *Liberty Valance* is one of Ford's more profound works, and the teaming of Wayne and Stewart is a joy to behold.

Ford collaborated with George Marshall and Henry Hathaway on *How the West Was Won* (1962), a lavish, lumbering Cinerama spectacular that traced the history of the West through the experience of the Prescott family over three generations. Icons James Stewart, Gregory Peck, and Henry Fonda share screen time (of which there's nearly three hours) with Lee J. Cobb, Debbie Reynolds, and Carroll Baker; James R. Webb's ambitious screenplay won an Oscar. *Donovan's Reef* (also 1963) was John Wayne's last picture with Ford, and while passable, it wasn't the high-water mark of their time together. A two-fisted comedy with too much testosterone for its own good, *Reef* had something to do with proper Elizabeth Allen's visit to Wayne's Pacific isle agitating him and drinking buddies Lee Marvin and Mike Mazurki; several rounds of fisticuffs finally restore the isle's equilibrium.

By contrast, Ford's well-intentioned *Cheyenne Autumn* (1964) was an epic, dignified account of the shameful 1887 episode in which hundreds of Cheyenne perished while trying to return on foot to their Wyoming homeland from the Oklahoma reservation on which the tribe had been starving—a 1,500-mile trek. Richard Widmark is the cavalry captain charged with recapturing the pitiful band (led by Ricardo Montalban and Gilbert Roland), with Wyatt Earp (James Stewart) reluctantly lending a hand. Considered by some Ford's apology to the Native American peoples for his stereotypical, often cavalier screen portraits of them, the film does demonstrate a heightened consciousness. Still, what does it really say when the Cheyenne leaders Little Wolf and Dull Knife were played by Ricardo Montalban and Gilbert Roland, and the "authentic" Cheyenne actors—even those with speaking parts—were actually Navajos (who happened to live closer to Ford's beloved Monument Valley)?

It seems a pity that the turgid *7 Women* (1965) is Ford's final film. Anne Bancroft, Sue Lyon, Flora Robson, and Betty Field were equal to the task of portraying missionaries in 1935 China, but Ford had been in declining health for years and the difficulties he faced on this production convinced him it was time to retire. This he did, leaving a void that may never be completely filled.

► *Ford and Tyrone Power on the set of* The Long Gray Line

## ● MILOS FORMAN (1932- )

This Czech émigré has already won two Academy Awards for best direction, with just six American releases to his credit, but why does he work so seldom?—only one film, *Valmont*, has appeared since his 1984 multi-Oscar-winner *Amadeus*. Born in Caslav, he was orphaned during the Second World War. Later he was educated at Prague's Academy of Music and Dramatic Art and began working in the Czech film industry in 1955, first as a screenwriter and then as an assistant director. His first feature, *Black Peter* (1964), won an award at the Locarno Film Festival, following his short *Talent Competition*, while the comedies *Loves of a Blonde* (1966) and *The Firemen's Ball* (1968) won him an international reputation, helping to spearhead the Czech New Wave.

He was scouting locations in Paris in 1968 when Russia invaded Czechoslovakia. *Ball* was nominated for an Academy Award as best foreign film, but it was banned by Prague's new government; Forman decided (along with compatriots like director Ivan Passer) to emigrate to the United States, leaving behind his wife and two young sons. After a frustrating three years and a number of stillborn projects, Forman finally got Universal to back him for *Taking Off* (1971), one of the best Generation Gap comedies. Buck Henry and Lynn Carlin are the upscale, uncomprehending parents of runaway hippie Linnea Heacock, whose East Village exploits soon has them going through their own changes; John Guare contributed to the screenplay. Forman next shot the Decathalon segment for the documentary about the 1972 Munich Olympics, *Visions of Eight* (1973).

But it was *One Flew Over the Cuckoo's Nest* (1975) that catapulted Forman to the forefront of Hollywood directors. A potent adaptation of Ken Kesey's acclaimed 1962 novel, it starred Jack Nicholson as Randle P. McMurphy, an irrepressible free spirit who cons his way from a prison work farm into a mental hospital for the soft time it promises. Against his better judgment, he enters into a war of wills with sadistic head nurse Louise Fletcher, who has crushed the spirits of the inmates (Will Sampson, Brad Dourif, Danny DeVito, and Christopher Lloyd). Forman gave the picture a quasi-documentary feel, enhanced by its location filming at the Oregon State Hospital—although in so doing he lost some of the novel's unique, wacky charm. Still, it became the first movie since *It Happened One Night* in 1934 to sweep the Academy Awards' top categories: best picture, actor, actress (Fletcher, in a weak field), direction, and screenplay (Bo Goldman and Lawrence Hauben).

*Hair* (1979) was Forman's much-anticipated version of the Broadway musical, but its time had passed a decade earlier. Forman opens it up impressively, aided by Twyla Tharp's inventive choreography, but leads John Savage, Treat Williams, and Beverly D'Angelo don't have the charisma necessary to carry the picture, which plays as though it's in a time warp. *Ragtime* (1981) was a handsomely mounted, expensive, but ultimately disappointing attempt to capture E. L. Doctorow's brilliant historical fantasy of 1906 America onscreen. Despite a tantalizing cast—James Cagney and Norman Mailer, together for the first time!—Forman simply fails to keep all the balls in the air as the novel did, rendering its American nightmares far too prosaically. Among the film's eight Oscar nominees were Howard Rollins, Jr., as a black radical, Elizabeth McGovern as Evelyn Nesbit, Michael Weller's screenplay, and (most deservedly) Randy Newman's score.

Forman rebounded from those mild disappointments with the acclaimed *Amadeus* (1984), Peter Shaffer's splendid reworking of his stage success. Like *Ragtime*, it's too long for its own good, but F. Murray Abraham's Oscar-winning performance as the jealous Salieri anchors the exquisite production, which features choreography by Twyla Tharp (and Prague as a stand-in for Vienna). As with *One Flew Over the Cuckoo's Nest*, Forman's version may work better if one isn't aware of the original source. And, like *Cuckoo's Nest*, this film won a multitude of Oscars, including best picture, actor, direction, screenplay adaptation, set decoration, costume design, and makeup.

Only a handful of directors have won two Academy Awards within ten years—indeed, within any span of time—and Forman now seemed poised to rise to the very top echelon. But it was five years before *Valmont* (1989) appeared, and it was generally compared unfavorably to the previous year's *Dangerous Liaisons*, whose John Malkovich, Glenn Close, and Michelle Pfeiffer excited more interest than Forman's Colin Firth, Annette Bening, and Meg Tilly. Since then, a number of prospective projects have, for various reasons, evaporated, leaving Forman woefully underutilized.

## ● BOB FOSSE (1927-1987)

A famed Broadway dancer, Bob Fosse made his mark on film primarily as a choreographer. But the five films he directed, three of which earned him Academy Award nominations for best direction, indicate what might have been had he spent more of his regrettably brief career behind the camera.

The son of vaudeville performers, Fosse was born in Chicago and was performing as a dancer in burlesque before he reached his teens. He worked briefly as a nightclub MC, then after graduating high school, enlisted in the Navy, where he was attached to an entertainment unit. After his discharge, he moved to New York to study acting at the American Theatre Wing while dancing as a team with his first wife, Mary Ann Niles, on stage and in shows. He made his Broadway debut in the chorus of *Dance Me a Song* in 1950, and the following year appeared as a dancer on television series like *Your Hit Parade* and *Your Show of Shows*. In 1953, Fosse signed with MGM, which immediately put him to work as a dancer in the films *Kiss Me Kate*, *The Affairs of Dobie Gillis*, and *Give a Girl a Break*. He returned to Broadway in 1954 to choreograph *The Pajama Game*—a maiden effort that won him his first Tony—then returned to Hollywood to choreograph (and dance in) *My Sister Eileen* (1955).

The Broadway-to-Hollywood shuttle continued running for Fosse, who choreographed *Damn Yankees* on stage in 1955 for George Abbott, the film of *The Pajama Game* (1957) for Abbott and Stanley Donen, and the film of *Damn Yankees* (1958) for Abbott and Donen. His debut as a Broadway director was *Redhead* (1959), for which he also did the choreography, as he did for the musicals *How to Succeed in Business without Really Trying* and *Sweet Charity* (written by Neil Simon). When *Charity* was acquired for filming by Universal in 1969, Fosse was finally invited to the party (although his wife, Gwen Verdon, who had starred in the Broadway show, was not). Although the film is hardly a disaster, its extreme length (over two and a half hours) and in-your-face staging mark it as the work of a director not yet wholly aware of how stylized stage business needs to be muted for film. Whether Shirley MacLaine's grating performance as Charity, the hard-luck dime-a-dance hostess, would have been improved with a different director (or a different actress) will never be known.

*Cabaret* (1972) was an ambitious filming of the Fred Ebb–John Kander stage success that itself had been based on the nonmusical play *I Am a Camera*—all of them derived from Christopher Isherwood's *Goodbye to Berlin* stories. This brilliantly detailed tribute to/indictment of the Weimar Republic stars Liza Minnelli, who was a revelation as Sally Bowles—a star turn that is perhaps 10 percent too much but which nevertheless provides high-octane fuel for the production. Joel Grey is unforgettable as the leering, cadaverous nightclub MC, and the new tunes ("Mein Herr," "The Money Song") by Ebb and Kander are terrific. But Fosse was clearly the film's creative center and deservedly won the Oscar (amid stiff competition) for best direction. (Minnelli and Grey also won, but the film itself lost to *The Godfather*.)

*Cabaret* was an impossible act to follow, and *Lenny* (1974) may seem a disappointment next to it. Yet this biography of tragic New Wave comic Lenny Bruce is quite impressive by its own lights. Julian Barry adapted and expanded his own play, and Fosse elected to shoot the film in black-and-white, which in Bruce Surtees's hands works wonderfully. But the core of the movie is Dustin Hoffman's performance, which is almost too powerful for comfort—precisely the effect Fosse was shooting for, of course. Valerie Perrine is also superb as Honey, Bruce's stripper-wife, but the unrelenting misery and uncompromising honesty that permeate this excellent drama make viewing the film more of a task than a pleasure.

*All That Jazz* (1979) is even more problematic, a self-indulgent (though hardly self-serving) autobiography that alternates brilliant passages with scenes that are simply ludicrous. The problem isn't Roy Scheider, who gives the performance of his career as the driven, womanizing, self-destructive Fosse. But Fosse becomes so enamored of his death wish that he makes us wallow in his beautifully mounted hallucinations for unforgivably long stretches; like a madman showing off his family album, Fosse's soul baring, at first fascinating to observe, finally becomes excruciating. (''Bye, Bye'' already!) Yet once again Fosse was nominated for an Academy Award —one of the few directors ever nominated for three consecutive works—as were Scheider, the screenplay, the score (which won), and the film itself.

Fosse's last picture was *Star 80* (1983), an unpleasant treatment of the horrifying tale of Dorothy Stratten, the erstwhile *Playboy* playmate whose nascent acting career was terminated when her unbalanced husband, Paul Snider, brutally murdered her in retaliation for her affair with film director Peter Bogdanovich. This was the stuff of tabloid television, and if that genre had been flourishing then as it is now, perhaps Fosse wouldn't have been as attracted to the material. As it turned out, Mariel Hemingway fell short of capturing the luminous sex appeal Stratten projected, though Eric Roberts was all too convincing as a psychopathic slimeball. Whether a director with a penchant for irony, like Robert Altman, might have made this into more than a sensationalist death march is hard to say, but *Star 80* made clear that true crime wasn't Fosse's forte.

Fosse's ruined health prevented him from working again, and he died four years later at the age of sixty, the recipient of seven Tony awards and one well-earned Oscar.

◀ *Rehearsing a number for* Sweet Charity *with Shirley MacLaine*

## ● JOHN FRANKENHEIMER (1930– )

He peaked early in his career, making his best films in the early Sixties; what followed was a frustrating string of near- and total misses, exacerbated by drinking problems (as he admitted in a 1994 interview). Born in Malba, New York, Frankenheimer was introduced to filmmaking while serving in the Air Force in 1951; he joined the new Film Squadron and eventually learned enough to make several documentary shorts. After his discharge in 1953, Frankenheimer worked briefly as the director of an agricultural show in Los Angeles, then took a job with CBS in New York. He began as an assistant director on *Person to Person* and *The Garry Moore Show*, then was put in charge of the popular *You Are There* series, replacing Sidney Lumet.

In 1955 he began directing teleplays for anthology series like *Playhouse 90* and *Climax*; he adapted a drama from the latter for his first theatrical film, *The Young Stranger* (1957), which featured James MacArthur as a troubled teenager whose wealthy dad (James Daly) doesn't pay attention to him. It was well received by the critics, but Frankenheimer chose to return to television, where he continued to direct dramas for the next four years. In 1961 he made his second film, *The Young Savages*, an overheated but often potent courtroom drama that starred Burt Lancaster as a crusading district attorney who risks his career to exonerate a Spanish Harlem gang member accused of killing a blind boy, to the disgust of socialite wife Dina Merrill.

*All Fall Down* (1962), William Inge's adaptation of a novel by James Leo Herlihy, starred Warren Beatty as the glamorous older brother of adoring Brandon de Wilde, who gradually comes to realize that Beatty's conquests of women young and old (including Eva Marie Saint in the latter category) aren't really the stuff of greatness. Frankenheimer's first popular success was *Bird Man of Alcatraz* (1962), a stately but overly reserved biopic about convicted killer Robert Stroud, who spent his forty years in solitary confinement becoming an authority on birds and their diseases. A tour-de-force for Burt Lancaster, the film (black-and-white like all of Frankenheimer's work to that point) desperately needs a half hour trimmed, but it did garner Oscar nominations for Lancaster, Thelma Ritter (as his suffocating mother), Telly Savalas (as another Alcatraz inmate), and cinematographer Burnett Guffey.

*The Manchurian Candidate* was Frankenheimer's third 1962 release, and it remains his most respected film. A chilling adaptation of the Richard Condon novel, it starred Frank Sinatra and Laurence Harvey as Korean War vets who only gradually learn that they were brainwashed—Sinatra made to believe that Harvey performed heroic deeds and Harvey programmed to kill on command when presented with a code word. Sinatra tumbles to the scheme, but can he stop Harvey before he kills a presidential nominee at the command of Commie double agent Angela Lansbury—his mother!? A political thriller (and satire) that looks better with each passing year, this may have been a bit too dark for its day. Lansbury was nominated as best supporting actress for what is probably the performance (and role) of her career.

*Seven Days in May* (1964), neatly adapted by Rod Serling from the bestseller by Fletcher Knebel and Charles Waldo Bailey III, also mined the vein of Cold War political suspense, but without the black humor of its predecessor. Still, it was an exciting and all-too-plausible rendition of a military coup in Washington, D.C., with Burt Lancaster pitted against Kirk Douglas as heads of warring military factions; Ava Gardner, Fredric March, and Edmond O'Brien fill out the fine cast. Lancaster and Frankenheimer combined forces for the fourth time on *The Train* (1965)—although not by original design, as Arthur

Penn had begun the picture and was fired after two weeks. Lancaster plays a World War II Resistance leader charged with reclaiming a trainload of French art treasures that are bound for Nazi Germany; Paul Scofield is his SS opponent, and Jeanne Moreau and Michel Simon provide the much-appreciated authentic French accents.

*Seconds* (1966) was a New Wavish science-fiction thriller, with John Randolph as a banker bored with his life who pays $32,000 to a mysterious company to have himself surgically altered and to sever all ties to his previous life; now he looks like Rock Hudson, but no matter how much he indulges himself, he still isn't satisfied deep inside. Frankenheimer shows off his technique (in black-and-white, of course) more than is desirable, but it's hard to understand why the film was so ridiculed at Cannes that he didn't dare attend. *Grand Prix* (1966) didn't pretend to be arty or profound, only noisy and long—three hours, nearly, of James Garner and Yves Montand racing at Monte Carlo, Monza, and Brand Hatch, making pit stops only to refuel and romance Eva Marie Saint and Jessica Walter. Frankenheimer's talent for the documentary is evident in the racing sequences, but the rest of the picture (his first in color) is flabby and dull.

*The Fixer* (1968) missed the flavor of Bernard Malamud's acclaimed novel, despite an Oscar-nominated performance by Alan Bates as the Jewish handyman wrongfully imprisoned in czarist Russia; Dirk Bogarde was also memorable as the sympathetic magistrate who tries to make Bates confess for his own good. The script was by Dalton Trumbo, who ladled out Bates's interior monologues like so many matzo balls. *The Extraordinary Seaman* (1969) had been sitting on the shelf for two years, and it's clear why. In all likelihood Frankenheimer's low-water mark, this lame comedy—his first to date,

◀ *With Sinatra during the making of* The Manchurian Candidate

thank heaven—had David Niven, Faye Dunaway, and Alan Alda at sea in World War II. A now forgotten footnote to Frankenheimer's career, it was barely even exhibited.

Far better was *The Gypsy Moths* (1969), an appealing if odd drama about daredevil parachutists in Kansas, with Burt Lancaster romancing Deborah Kerr (no surf crashing about them this time!) with fatal consequences; Gene Hackman and Bonnie Bedelia survived them. *I Walk the Line* (1970) was one of those films spun off from a popular song, in this case a 1963 country hit by Johnny Cash. Gregory Peck is a Tennessee sheriff who goes over the line for lusty Tuesday Weld, the daughter of moonshiner Ralph Meeker and reason enough to entertain a conflict of interest. Four other tunes by Cash were served up to add flavor to this backwoods tragedy, which remains worth viewing for Weld's heavy-breathing coquettry.

Filmed in Afghanistan, *The Horsemen* (1971) had angst-ridden Omar Sharif knocking around a calf's head as per the demands of the polo-like game *buzkashi*, but even his tournament victories cannot please his ultra-competitive father Jack Palance. *The Iceman Cometh* (1973) was a fine, appropriately dark American Film Theatre production of the Eugene O'Neill play; it wisely makes no attempt to disguise its stage origins, and offers remarkable performances by Fredric March, Robert Ryan, Lee Marvin, and Jeff Bridges. The obscure *Impossible Object* (aka *Story of a Love Story*) never received a theatrical release, although this French production with Alan Bates as a fantasizing writer and Dominique Sanda as his married object of desire does sound intriguing.

Frankenheimer understandably now tried for something more commercial, but the appalling gangster "comedy" *99 and 44/100% Dead* (1974)—nice title, guys—wasn't the answer. Nor was *French Connection II* (1975), although it's an honorable failure. Gene Hackman reprises his Oscar-winning role as Popeye Doyle with gusto, now tracking down nemesis Fernando Rey in Marseilles. The film opens strongly, with great location photography (by Claude Renoir) and Hackman's amusing efforts to acclimate himself—but then comes a grueling, gruesome 45-minute sequence devoted to Popeye's epic withdrawal from heroin addiction. It's impressively rendered, but lets all the air out of what, after all, is supposed to be an action picture.

*Black Sunday* (1977) finally gave Frankenheimer his long-awaited hit. An adaptation of Thomas Harris's suspenseful bestseller, it provides Bruce Dern with another of his patented Crazed Vietnam Vet turns, with Israeli officer Robert Shaw and FBI agent Fritz Weaver trying to foil his plan of crashing the Goodyear blimp into the Super Bowl stands. A smash like that should have put Frankenheimer on firm footing, but he squandered it with the absurd horror flick *Prophecy* (1979), while *The Challenge* (1982), shot on location, was a mundane honor-of-the-family saga with Scott Glenn mediating between two Japanese brothers. *The Holcroft Covenant* (1985) had as its source material one of Robert Ludlum's impossibly complicated espionage yarns, from which Michael Caine is never quite able to extricate himself, but *52 Pick-Up* (1986) retained some of the virtues of Elmore Leonard's nasty hard-boiled novel; Roy Scheider plays the victim of sadistic blackmailer John Glover, and Ann-Margret is his resourceful wife.

*Dead-Bang* (1989) was more brutal action, with the hapless Don Johnson as a detective on the trail of white supremacists, while *The Fourth War* (1990) had Scheider again, now as a colonel who has a personal vendetta against Soviet officer Jurgen Prochnow. *Year of the Gun* (1991) was another muddled Cold War thriller devoid of thrills, or even sense. Andrew McCarthy is way over his head as an American novelist in Rome who tries to prevent the Russians from kidnapping their Premier. He has Sharon Stone to help him, but he, she, and especially Frankenheimer need much, much more. But Frankenheimer returned to television in 1994 to direct *Against the Wall* for HBO, a dramatization of the Attica prison riots that starred Kyle MacLachlan. It earned the Emmy for the year's best drama, indicating a potential return to form for Frankenheimer after seventeen years in the wilderness.

▲ *Friedkin confers with Ellen Burstyn on the set of* The Exorcist

## ● WILLIAM FRIEDKIN (1935- )

He will always be remembered as the Oscar-winning director of *The French Connection* and the director who made strong men faint as Linda Blair's head did a 360 in *The Exorcist*, but William Friedkin's work after those two films has been profoundly disappointing.

Born in Chicago, Friedkin began working in local television while still a teenager and by 1956 had worked his way up to nationally broadcast musicals and documentaries. He moved into film directing with the 1967 Sonny and Cher musical *Good Times*, a better-than-average bit of rock 'n' roll whimsy, then took on the more elevated *The Birthday Party* (1968), a respectable if static adaptation of the enigmatic Harold Pinter play, filmed in England with Robert Shaw and Patrick Magee. Equally ambitious was *The Night They Raided Minsky's* (1968), a Norman Lear production that re-created the world of burlesque via the story of an innocent Amish girl (Britt Ekland) visiting New York in the 1920s. Jason Robards, Bert Lahr (who died during filming), Elliott Gould, and Jack Burns were also in the large and colorful cast.

*The Boys in the Band* (1970) was a risk commercially, but Friedkin did a splendid job of adapting the Mart Crowley play about eight (or nine?) gay men at a party without even "opening it up"; doubly unusual was the film's use of the entire original stage company. *The French Connection* (1971) provided Friedkin with his first big-budget property, Robin Moore's bestseller about two real-life narcotics cops who almost make the biggest heroin bust of all time. A kinetic joyride with a great performance by Gene Hackman as "Popeye" Eddie Doyle (based on Eddie Egan, who served as a consultant to the production), the film won five Oscars, including ones for best picture, actor, and direction. Friedkin chose another bestseller for his next project, the William Peter Blatty novel *The Exorcist*. A truly frightening (some would add "nauseating") tale of the supernatural that was the center of much controversy when it was released in 1973—for excessive blasphemy, basically—it became the fourth-biggest hit of the decade, earning Academy Award nominations for Friedkin, Linda Blair, Jason Miller, and Ellen Burstyn, as well as one for best picture.

Friedkin followed those back-to-back smashes by remaking the classic French thriller *The Wages of Fear*, which had been directed in 1952 by H. G. Clouzot and starred Yves Montand. It was a strong property with which to work and one that was not overly familiar to American audiences, but Friedkin's *Sorcerer* (1977), which took years to complete due to the arduous (and expensive) on-location filming in the jungles of Central America, failed both critically and commercially—a classic case of wretched excess (not aided by its no-name cast). To Friedkin's credit, he retrenched and immediately made the modest caper film *The Brinks Job* (1978), an enjoyably goofy version of the famed 1950 Boston armored car heist, starring Peter Falk, Peter Boyle, and Gena Rowlands.

But he apparently couldn't stand prosperity and next chose to film *Cruising* (1980), a universally reviled, fetid tale about a cop, Al Pacino (deep into his own ten-year slump), who goes undercover into the gay S&M subculture of New York City to track down a killer; a bomb of epic proportions, this damaged everyone connected with it. When Friedkin emerged three years later, it was with the lame Chevy Chase comedy *Deal of the Century* (1983), which was intended as a caustic indictment of the international-arms marketplace but managed only to indict itself as a creative mess. Nor did *To Live and Die in L.A.* (1985) salvage Friedkin's reputation, although it actually was an exciting adaptation of Gerald Petievich's ultra-nasty novel about federal agents on the trail of a counterfeiting ring. Violent, gritty, and ugly, it was populated by such irredeemable sleazebags as William Petersen's sociopathic fed, Willem Dafoe's monumentally evil counterfeiter, lowlife John Turturro, and corrupt attorney Dean Stockwell; no wonder it turned off moviegoers. In truth, it was only a Gene Hackman away from being as good as *The French Connection*.

Since then, Friedkin's filmography has been positively embarrassing, with such projects as *Putting It Together: The Making of "The Broadway Album"* (1986), the TV pilots *C.A.T. Squad* and *C.A.T. Squad: Python Wolf*, and the schlocky supernatural entry *The Guardian* (1990). (Surely that's penance enough for *Cruising*!) In 1994 Friedkin's basketball drama *Blue Chips*, with Nick Nolte and Shaquille O'Neal, opened to decent business and respectful reviews—more than Friedkin had had in nigh on twenty years.

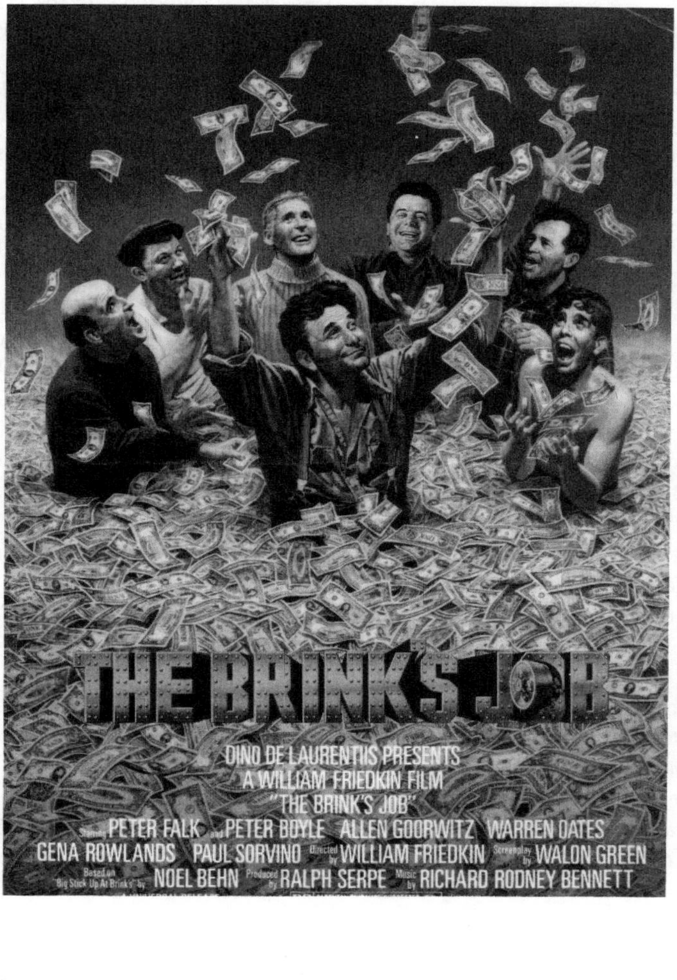

## ● SAMUEL FULLER (1911– )

One of the American cinema's true originals, Samuel Fuller rarely has ventured outside the genre film, with budgets at times below "B" level and casts made up of character actors, has-beens, and never-weres. But in spite of—or perhaps due to—these restrictions, his films have a flavor that is quite heady, and very much his own. Such is the reward for the director who also writes and produces his own pictures as far outside the system as possible. But the drawbacks can be plentiful enough to make even a cigar-chomping rebel weep.

Born in Worcester, Massachusetts, in 1911, Fuller worked as a copy boy on the *New York Journal* at the age of thirteen and by 1928 was covering a crime beat for the *San Diego Sun*. When the Depression struck, Fuller rode the rails for a time and tried his hand at writing fiction. His first novel was published in 1935, and a year later he was working in Hollywood as a screenwriter. He co-scripted James Cruze's *Gangs of New York* (1938), a Republic potboiler starring Charles Bickford, along with several other "B"s; later he would write *Shockproof* (1949), a Douglas Sirk noir with Cornel Wilde. During World War II, Fuller was with the 1st Infantry Division, fighting across North Africa and Italy and being awarded the Silver Star, the Bronze Star, and a Purple Heart—rich material to mine in films to come.

Fuller was given his chance to direct by the humble Screen Guild operation. *I Shot Jesse James* (1949) was a retelling of the now-mythic story from the point of view of killer Bob Ford; it starred Preston Foster and John Ireland. *The Baron of Arizona* (1950) was a fact-based tale about a greedy landowner (Vincent Price chewing up the prairie) who nearly corrals the whole of the Arizona Territory. *The Steel Helmet* (1951) was the first of Fuller's splendid war movies, a blistering account of the Korean War—one of the first out of Hollywood—featuring Gene Evans and Steve Brodie and made for the minor Lippert studio. This film brought Fuller to the attention of the majors, and he was signed by Fox, where he would make seven of his next eight pictures. First came another fine Korean War picture, *Fixed Bayonets!* (1951), with Richard Basehart and Gene Evans as GIs under the gun; James Dean had a bit as a member of the platoon.

He wrote the screenplay for Phil Karlson's *Scandal Sheet*, then directed *Park Row* (1952), a drama based on the 1886 tabloid newspaper wars in the New York City; Gene Evans starred yet again for Fuller as Phineas Mitchell, the founder of the *New York Globe*. Even better was *Pickup on South Street* (1953), a noir with a Cold War theme—scripted, as usual, by Fuller—that seems to grow better with each passing year. Richard Widmark was well cast as a penny-ante pickpocket who unknowingly lifts a roll of microfilm that both the Russians and the FBI want, ultimately landing him on the side of the law, and Thelma Ritter was Oscar-nominated for her colorful role as a hard-luck snitch. *Hell and High Water* (1954) teamed Widmark with Fuller favorite Gene Evans, but this CinemaScope sub adventure was conventional stuff.

More interesting was *House of Bamboo* (1955), a crime story set in Japan, with Robert Ryan as a guilt-ridden Army officer who helps the Japanese police conduct a manhunt for some rogue American ex-soldiers. (Fuller cast himself in a bit part as one of the Japanese cops!) *Run of the Arrow* (1957) also exhibited the distinctive Fuller touch of black humor mixed with a deep streak of cynicism. The somewhat clumsy narrative has a bitter Reb soldier (the florid Rod Steiger) who joins a Sioux tribe as a kind of atonement after the war; Brian Keith, Charles Bronson, and Ralph Meeker were part of the colorful supporting cast. *Forty Guns* (1957) was a more conventional Western, with Barbara Stanwyck as the haughty head of Tombstone, until she is tamed by lawman Barry Sullivan. *China Gate* (also 1957) was an anti-Commie actioner that featured Gene Barry and Nat King Cole as mercenaries working for the French to blow up a munitions stockpile in Vietnam; Angie Dickinson provides the romance.

Fuller now moved to Columbia for three pictures, beginning with *Verboten!* (1959), a drama set in post-war Germany about the romance between American soldier James Best and Berliner Susan Cummings. *The Crimson Kimono* (1959) introduced a provocative element into what otherwise would have been a routine police procedural: Glenn Corbett resents the fact that his L.A. police partner (and Korean War buddy) James Shigeta is having an affair with an artist (Victoria Shaw) to whom Corbett is also attracted. Is his jealousy racially motivated? Fuller teases the question even as the murder mystery unravels. Based on a series of *Saturday Evening Post* articles, the potent *Underworld U.S.A.* (1961) sets Cliff Robertson off on a lifetime of vengeance for the murder of his father. *Merrill's Marauders* (1962) was a hard-boiled World War II adventure about American soldiers (Jeff Chandler, Ty Hardin, Peter Brown) in Burma who help stop the Japanese from invading India.

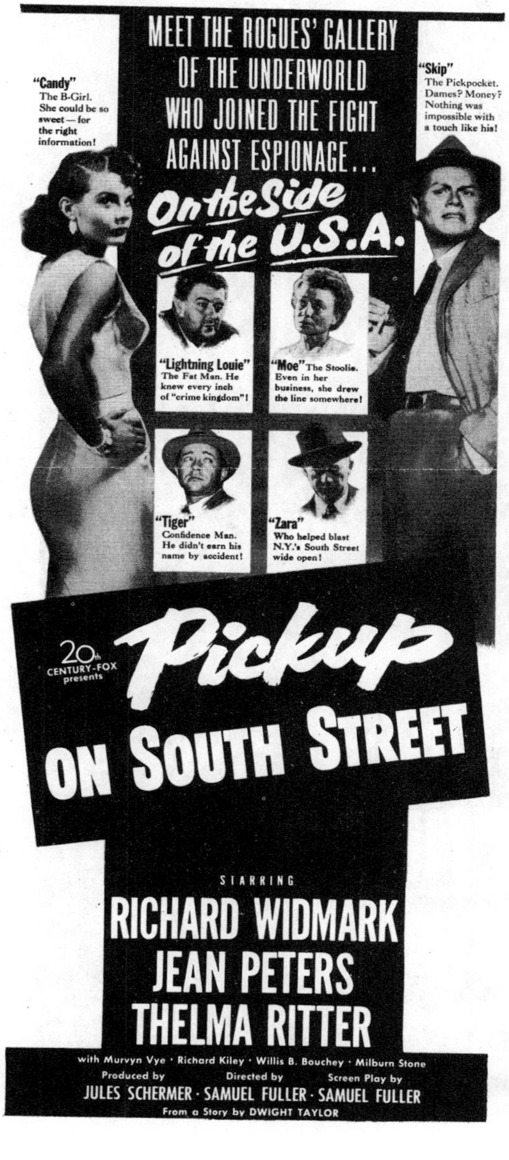


With *Shock Corridor* (1963) and *The Naked Kiss* (1964), both made for Allied Artists, Fuller had almost total freedom, resulting in two of his most accomplished—and disturbing—works. *Shock* starred Peter Breck as a reporter who gets himself committed to an institution in order to track down a murder suspect but loses his sanity in the process, with Gene Evans and Constance Towers providing memorable support. *The Naked Kiss* (1964) was even creepier, as former prostitute Constance Towers tries to attain respectability by moving to a quiet town, only to learn that her new boyfriend (Anthony Eisley) is a child molester. There is no other film quite like *Kiss*, and its unblinking confrontation of utter loathsomeness was strong stuff indeed for the audiences of the day (few of whom paid to see it).

Fuller had gotten his toes wet in television a couple of years earlier when he directed an episode of *The Virginian*, and a paucity of opportunities in film led him back there. He came up with the "bible" for the 1966 series *The Iron Horse*, and directed five episodes. In 1969 he directed Burt Reynolds in *Shark!*, a formulaic treasure-hunt picture that was made as a co-production with a Mexican company. *Dead Pigeon on Beethoven Street* (1972) also was a foreign co-production, this time with West Germany; Glenn Corbett stars as a Chandleresque private eye hired by Christa Lang, Fuller's real-life wife (Fuller himself played a bit as a U.S. senator). As he had done in the past, Fuller wrote a novel-length version of the story, which was published in 1973.

It was eight long years before Fuller's next film (although he did contribute a memorable cameo performance to Wim Wenders's *The American Friend* in 1977)—but it was worth waiting for. *The Big Red One* (1980) was an autobiographical account of Fuller's old unit—the 16th Regiment of Army 1st Division, the insignia for which was, of course, a big

Only
chance
could have
thrown them together.
Now,
nothing can pull them apart.
SAMUEL FULLER'S
THE
BIG RED
ONE

red "1." The film was discursive but powerful, a dose of poetic truth that made this the best war picture in many years. For the first time since the Fifties, Fuller had a first-rate cast to work with; Lee Marvin starred as the indomitable Sarge, and Robert Carradine and Mark Hamill were among the young GIs who grow into manhood while they fight across North Africa, Italy, and Germany.

*White Dog* (1982) was to have followed immediately after, but Paramount deemed the story—a black dog trainer (Paul Winfield) is asked by an actress (Kristy McNichol) to retrain an animal that was reared to attack blacks—too controversial for release. Although the film (based on a Romain Gary novel) is patently antiracist, it sat on the shelf for ten years before finally receiving limited distribution in 1992. (One suspects that Fuller may have relished all the hullabaloo.) *Thieves After Dark* (1983) was a French production that was almost impossible to catch in the United States, while *Street of No Return* (1989) was a laughably purple rendition of David Goodis's 1954 pulp novel about losers trying to hang on to life in the gutter, here transposed to Paris. It was overripe, meandering, foolishly uncommercial—in other words, 100 percent Fuller, God bless 'im.

▲ *Fuller shows young Warren Hsieh how to shoot a film during* China Gate

## ● TAY GARNETT (1894–1977)

A screenwriter for the silents who made the transition to director and never looked back, Tay Garnett was a middling craftsman whose seven or eight superior films are sprinkled among his forty-odd sound pictures like so many chocolate chips in a rather stale cookie. Born in Los Angeles, William Taylor Garnett sold cartoons and stories to the pulp magazines before serving in World War I as a pilot in the Naval Air Service. He taught flying at the San Diego Air Station after the war before breaking into Hollywood in 1920 as a gag writer for Hal Roach and Mack Sennett. He tried his hand at stunting for a spell, but returned to his typewriter to contribute to the screenplays for *Getting Gertie's Garter*, Capra's *Strong Man*, and *Skyscraper*, among a dozen others.



In 1928 Garnett was given his chance to direct at Pathé with *Celebrity*, the first of seven features (many of which he co-scripted) he made there until RKO bought the company. *Bad Company* (1931) was a gangster epic, with Ricardo Cortez as a mob kingpin who entraps solid citizens Helen Twelvetrees and John Garrick in his web, while *Prestige* (1932) was a *Morocco*-flavored romantic adventure, in which rum-soaked Melvyn Douglas and Ann Harding are stuck at a French penal colony in Indochina. *Okay America* (1932) was a perfunctory crime yarn, with corrupt newspaperman Lew Ayres up against politician Edward Arnold. But *One Way Passage* (also 1932) was quite good, with suave William Powell as a con man romancing fatally ill Kay Francis during a cruise. *Destination Unknown* (1933) also went to sea, but its story about a bootlegger (Pat O'Brien) who takes over a rum-running schooner until he is outwitted by Ralph Bellamy was waterlogged.

*S.O.S. Iceberg* (1933) was an oddity, a Rod La Rocque adventure set in the Arctic that incorporated documentary footage of Greenland shot by German geologist Arnold Fanck; Rod's co-star was Leni Riefenstahl (a pairing that regrettably was never encored). *China Seas* (1935) was a more typical star vehicle, boasting the third teaming of top MGM draws Clark Gable and Jean Harlow in a silly but lively tale about modern piracy on the high seas; Wallace Beery supplied the villainy and Robert Benchley the comic relief. That box-office smash was followed by the 1935 *She Couldn't Take It*, a screwball crime comedy with George Raft and Joan Bennett, who proved to be a surprisingly appealing couple. *Professional Soldier* (1936) had young king Freddie Bartholomew stalked by Victor McLaglen, who soon befriends the lad and scotches the plot to kidnap him.

*Love Is News* (1937) was a foray into light romance; heiress Loretta Young outwits obnoxious reporter Tyrone Power—but the comic timing was off. *Slave Ship* (1937) was safer territory for Garnett, a costumer that had Warner Baxter, Wallace Beery, and Mickey Rooney up to their necks in a mutiny on the high seas. (Garnett seemed to find himself at sea with every other picture.) *Stand-In* (also 1937) might have been more than it was, but this passable satire of the Hollywood moviemaking biz still had some pop: Leslie Howard plays a humorless accountant sent to save a floundering movie studio whose chief assets appear to be hot-headed producer Humphrey Bogart and cute stand-in Joan Blondell.

*Joy of Living* (1938) was more screwball activity, with dashing yachtsman Doug Fairbanks, Jr., rather unconvincingly teaching repressed musical star Irene Dunne how to lighten up and enjoy herself, amid several Jerome Kern–Dorothy Fields tunes. *Trade Winds* (1938) sounded like a clever ruse by Garnett, who somehow convinced United Artists to buy his old documentary footage of Japan, China, and India; it was then spliced into a wholly set-bound production that found detective Fredric March chasing murder suspect Joan Bennett from San Francisco to the Far East, where they fall in love and clear her name. *Eternally Yours* (1939) was also a stretch, with David Niven as a work-obsessed magician whose ex-wife (Loretta Young) wants him back after she's already remarried; Garnett cast himself in a bit part as an airplane pilot at the New York World's Fair. He left romance behind to direct *Slightly Honorable* (1940), a seriocomic crime yarn starring Pat O'Brien and Broderick Crawford as lawyers on the trail of Edward Arnold, per usual playing a corrupt politician.

*Seven Sinners* (1940) offered the tantalizing combination of John Wayne and Marlene Dietrich as, respectively, a Navy lifer and Bijou, the café singer who loves him but sets him free. Dietrich looked great and got to sing two songs, while Wayne wore his officer whites and was asked to punch out a few dozen South Sea lowlifes. *Cheers for Miss Bishop* (1941) was as atypical a picture as Garnett ever essayed, a sentimental piece of Americana, with Martha Scott as a schoolteacher who devotes fifty-two years to her students to make up for the emptiness of her personal life. *My Favorite Spy* (1942) was a musicomical dud that tried to pass off bandleader Kay Kyser as a spycatcher, but Garnett was clearly more at home with the rugged heroics of *Bataan*, a superior World War II adventure whose ultra-patriotism made sense in the context of 1943; the top-notch cast included Robert Taylor, Thomas Mitchell, Desi Arnaz, and Robert Walker. *The Cross of Lorraine* (1943) was another all-male drama illumning the horrors of war; Peter Lorre plays a sadistic Nazi who tortures broken POW Gene Kelly until Jean-Pierre Aumont helps restore Kelly's fighting spirit.

*Mrs. Parkington* (1944), from the Louis Bromfield novel, was a long way from Bataan, as social climber Greer Garson marries unwitting Walter Pidgeon to give herself entrée to society, only to learn that mil-

▲ *With Gable and Beery on the set of* China Seas

lions of dollars can't buy happiness. Garnett reshot some scenes on Wesley Ruggles's *See Here, Private Hargrove* (1944), then directed Garson again in *Valley of Decision* (1945), a socially conscious soaper set in 1870s Pittsburgh, with Garson as a housemaid whose father and brother were killed in the steel mills owned by Gregory Peck, whose family now employs her.

Garnett's best film was *The Postman Always Rings Twice* (1946), a near-perfect realization of the 1934 James Cain novel; it had not been filmed yet in the United States because of censorship problems. John Garfield was perfectly cast as Frank, the drifter who can't say no to his employer's tarty wife, even when it means having to commit a murder, and Lana Turner gives the performance of her career as a far more glamorous Cora than Cain ever described. It remains one of the best noirs ever filmed, Production Code or no.

*Postman* was an enormous hit, but Garnett had never stayed at one studio for long, and his three years at MGM represented a personal record. His short-lived move to Paramount also marked the beginning of his decline. *Wild Harvest* (1947) was anything but wild, with Alan Ladd and Dorothy Lamour slogging their way through a succession of grain harvests, while *A Connecticut Yankee in King Arthur's Court* (1949) was an innocuous Technicolor remake of the 1931 Will Rogers picture; Bing Crosby supplied in voice what he lacked in native wit. *The Fireball* (1950) was a more modest enterprise in which Mickey Rooney set his sights on becoming a professional roller-skating champion, while *Cause for Alarm* (1951) found Loretta Young in jeopardy from insanely jealous husband Barry Sullivan. *Soldiers Three* (1951) was a pale remake of *Gunga Din*—Stewart Granger, Walter Pidgeon, and David Niven weren't exactly Grant, Fairbanks, and McLaglen.

Garnett didn't fare much better with the expensive Robert Mitchum Korean War pic *One Minute to Zero* (1952), awkwardly blending romance (in the form of UN envoy Ann Blyth) with two-fisted action; how this cost $2 million is anyone's guess. *Main Street to Broadway* (1953) had a succession of Broadway greats like Tallulah Bankhead, Rex Harrison, and Helen Hayes stumbling through a lame romantic subplot, while *The Black Knight* (1954) was a serviceable entry in the then-popular medieval adventure genre; Alan Ladd is up against Peter Cushing and other assorted perils. Garnett directed the Indian sequence of the documentary *Seven Wonders of the World* (1956), but didn't earn another screen credit until he made the British production *The Night Fighters* (1960), a decent yarn about the Irish Revolution starring Robert Mitchum and Richard Harris.

Garnett's final four films were spread out over the next twelve years. *Cattle King* (1963) had old MGM star Robert Taylor fighting for his grazing land with Robert Loggia, while *The Delta Factor* (1970) was a low-budget adaptation of a moronic spy novel by Mickey Spillane (although Yvette Mimieux made it almost tolerable). *The Mad Trapper* and *Timber Tramp* were shot in 1972 for a dinky company called Alaska Pictures; one shudders to think what the seventy-eight-year-old Garnett, who once directed Marlene Dietrich, Clark Gable, and Jean Harlow, felt about such a shoddy endgame.

## ● EDMUND GOULDING (1891–1959)

The exemplar of good taste during the Thirties, Edmund Goulding moved beyond the "women's pictures" which initially brought him fame to successfully explore other genres, which explains how the man who made the luxurious *Grand Hotel* could also direct the blackhearted *Nightmare Alley*. Born in London, Goulding began acting on stage at the age of twelve, gradually working his way up to playwriting and directing over the next ten years. He made his New York stage debut in 1915 and acted in a handful of silent films, but his career was interrupted by the war and he spent the next three years serving in the British Army. Returning to the United States in 1919, he wrote *Dancing Mothers*, a play that earned him an invitation to Hollywood. As a screenwriter, his silent credits included *Tol'able David*, *Fury*, and *Dante's Inferno*.

He began his directing career at MGM in 1925 with *Sun-Up* and soon was overseeing Garbo in *Love* (1927), a contemporary version of *Anna Karenina*, while continuing to write stories for the screen (*The Broadway Melody*, *Flesh*). Goulding's first talking picture was *The Trespasser* (1929), a Gloria Swanson melodrama that Swanson also produced, co-wrote with Goulding, and even sang in; she was rewarded for her efforts with an Oscar nomination as best actress. He was one of the ten directors who received credit for *Paramount on Parade* (1930), also appearing onscreen, then made *The Devil's Holiday* (1930) and *Reaching for the Moon* (1931), the latter an ur-screwball comedy starring Douglas Fairbanks, Sr., as a tipsy Wall Street millionaire who courts aviatrix Bebe Daniels aboard an ocean liner without realizing that he's gone bust. (Irving Berlin, of all people, dreamed up this yarn, which Goulding himself scripted.)

*The Night Angel* (1931) came next, but it was *Grand Hotel* (1932) that established Goulding as one of the screen's top directors. This archetypal all-star melodrama, based on Vicki Baum's novel and play, featured some of the most luminous work of Greta Garbo, John Barrymore, and especially Joan Crawford, and even ham-sters Wallace Beery and Lionel Barrymore didn't do their usual damage. It was a huge hit for MGM and won the Academy Award as the year's best picture, although neither Goulding nor any of the actors was nominated. (Nor would Goulding ever be so honored.) That triumph was followed by *Blondie of the Follies* (1932), a harmless Marion Davies vehicle distinguished by being the first film to include a scene parodying *Grand Hotel*, and *Riptide* (1934), a romantic triangle among Norma Shearer, Robert Montgomery, and (forever the third wheel) Herbert Marshall.

*The Flame Within* (1935) marked the only time that Goulding produced, directed, and wrote a film, although this tale of a woman psychiatrist who falls in love with a patient was hampered by Ann Harding's and Herbert Marshall's lack of charisma. Goulding now moved to Warners for *That Certain Woman* (1937; a remake of his 1929 film *The Trespasser*), a good showcase for the prowess of Bette Davis. *White Banners* (1938), with Claude Rains as the exploited inventor of an iceless refrigerator—now there's a story ripe for a remake!—didn't make much of a splash, but Goulding's 1938 version of *The Dawn Patrol* was a major hit. Errol Flynn has one of his best roles as the squadron leader who can't bear to see young pilots used to battle experienced German fighters, and Basil Rathbone and David Niven provide fine support. Perhaps Goulding's aerial sequences aren't quite up to those in Howard Hawks's 1930 original (although a few of those combat scenes were recycled), but his handling of the actors is markedly superior.

Returning to the more familiar terrain of the soap opera, Goulding made two superb Bette Davis pic-

tures. *Dark Victory* (1939) was an irresistible tear-jerker about a haughty socialite who learns humility as she starts to go blind from a fatal illness; both Davis and the picture earned Oscar nominations. *The Old Maid* (1939) was a period melodrama that benefited from the palpable dislike for each other of Davis and co-star Miriam Hopkins. Almost as fine was *We Are Not Alone* (also 1939), starring Paul Muni as a man accused of murdering his wife to be with governess Jane Bryan, while *'Til We Meet Again* (1940) attempts in vain to fob off shipbound George Brent and Merle Oberon as the stuff of high tragedy. But *The Great Lie* (1941) was prime Bette Davis again—except for Wyler, no director served her as well as Goulding—this time pitted against Mary Astor, who won an Oscar for her performance as a pregnant concert pianist who exploits Bette's kindness.

Goulding co-directed *Forever and a Day* (1943) with seven others, helping to make this *Upstairs, Downstairs*–like saga of a British family over several generations memorable. *The Constant Nymph* (1943), filmed twice before, was a sublime soap opera, in which Charles Boyer plays a composer whose greatest work is inspired by the love of a smitten young girl (Joan Fontaine, a bit along in years for the role). Just as emotional, if less grand, was *Claudia* (1943), a marital comedy with Robert Young and (reprising her stage role as the newlywed) Dorothy McGuire. Goulding now spent a couple of years away from Hollywood to write, produce, and direct the play *The Ryan Girl*, but he returned in 1946 to make a new version of *Of Human Bondage*; unfortunately, Paul Henreid and Eleanor Parker were hardly Leslie Howard and Bette Davis, the memory of whose incandescent performances twelve years earlier made this soggy version an embarrassment.

Goulding now moved to Fox, where he would finish his career. His first project there was another Somerset Maugham story, *The Razor's Edge* (1946); nominated for an Academy Award as best picture, it was one of Goulding's finest films. A hardened Tyrone Power was surprisingly convincing as the hero on a spiritual quest, and Power was well supported by Gene Tierney, Anne Baxter (who won an Oscar), Elsa Lanchester, and Clifton Webb (also Oscar-nominated). *Nightmare Alley* (1947) was an even more radical departure, a noirish adaptation of a harrowing novel by William Lindsay Gresham, with Tyrone Power again excellent as the carnival con man who outsmarts himself and suffers a horrendous fate. *Everybody Does It* (1949) was based on an atypically comic novelette by James Cain (filmed by Gregory Ratoff in 1939); Paul Douglas, Linda Darnell, and Celeste Holm played the bickering, aspiring singers.

*Mister 880* (1950) was an enjoyable trifle scripted by Robert Riskin, with Burt Lancaster as a Treasury agent on the trail of benign, elderly counterfeiter Edmund Gwenn, while *We're Not Married* (1952) was a Nunnally Johnson concoction with six amusing segments about couples who discover their wedding ceremony wasn't performed legally; the appealing cast included Eve Arden, Fred Allen, Eddie Bracken, Zsa Zsa Gabor, and Marilyn Monroe. The turgid *Down Among the Sheltering Palms* (1953) was a World War II soaper with William Lundigan and Jane Greer, while the "problem" picture *Teenage Rebel* (1956), despite its exploitative title, actually was a cogent drama about a mother (Ginger Rogers) who has remarried, thereby losing her daughter's trust. Goulding's last film was *Mardi Gras* (1958), an innocuous Pat Boone musical (is there any other kind?) with Tommy Sands and Sheree North.

## ● ALEXANDER HALL (1884–1968)

Another nigh-anonymous craftsman who made some fine entertainments. Originally an actor, first performing on stage at the age of four, the Boston-born Hall appeared in a number of films during the Teens, then worked his way up from editor to assistant director through the Twenties. In 1932, he made his directorial debut at Paramount with *Sinners in the Sun*, then co-directed his next four pictures, among them the George Raft crime drama *Midnight Club* (1933). Still at Paramount, he directed one of Shirley Temple's best showcases, the Damon Runyon–inspired *Little Miss Marker* (1934). That was followed by *The Pursuit of Happiness* (1934), a period yarn starring Joan Bennett, and the George Raft–Anna May Wong melodrama *Limehouse Blues* (1934). *Goin' to Town* (1935) had Mae West as a dance-hall queen who strikes oil and decides to crash society, while the 1935 *Annapolis Farewell* was a minor drama set at the U.S. Naval Academy. *Give Us This Night* (1936), a dud, featured opera star Gladys Swarthout and Polish tenor Jan Kiepura, but *Yours for the Asking* (1936), with George Raft and Ida Lupino, was a pleasant-enough romance. *Exclusive* (1937) was a crackling yarn about the newspaper biz, starring Fred MacMurray, Charlie Ruggles, and the ineffable Frances Farmer.

In 1938 Hall moved to Columbia, a less glamorous studio but the one out of which his best work would emerge. *There's Always a Woman* was an acceptable knockoff of the Thin Man films; Melvyn Douglas and Joan Blondell play a husband-wife crime-fighting team who spar in the best Powell-Loy tradition. *I Am the Law* (1938) cast Edward G. Robinson against type as a crusading D.A. in a Warners-style tale of corruption in city government, while *The Amazing Mr. Williams* and *Good Girls Go to Paris* (both 1939) used the team of Melvyn Douglas and Joan Blondell to good effect. *The Doctor Takes a Wife* (1940), with Ray Milland and Loretta Young, was a good if derivative screwball entry, but *He Stayed for Breakfast* (also 1940) was a misfire, with Melvyn Douglas reversing his role in *Ninotchka*: here he's the Russian melting under the charms of American Loretta Young. Better was *This Thing Called Love* (1941), with Rosalind Russell and Douglas (yet again!) delightful as a betrothed couple struggling to survive a three-month trial run before the nuptials.

The pinnacle of Hall's career came next. At first blush *Here Comes Mr. Jordan* (1941) seems modest enough, a whimsical tale of a sax-playing prizefighter (Robert Montgomery) who dies before his time in a plane crash, then is permitted to return to life in another body to complete his quest for the heavyweight crown. But it was nominated for a passel of Academy Awards, including best picture, direction, actor, supporting actor (James Gleason), and cinematography, and both its original story and its screenplay won Oscars. It was nicely remade in 1978 by Warren Beatty and Buck Henry as *Heaven Can Wait*, but more than fifty years later, Hall's original remains wholly enjoyable.

*Bedtime Story* (1941) wasn't in *Mr. Jordan*'s league, but it was a well-played farce, starring old pros Fredric March and Loretta Young. *They All Kissed the Bride* (1942) was more of a struggle, with ex-MGM glamour-puss Joan Crawford trying (oh, so strenuously!) to reposition herself as a light comedienne; she was supported by the ubiquitous Melvyn Douglas. *My Sister Eileen* (1942), adapted from the Broadway hit, featured a star turn by Roz Russell, but was better served in Richard Quine's 1955 musical version. Hedy Lamarr was well cast as *The Heavenly Body* (1943), but even with William Powell on hand, the film sputtered. *Once Upon a Time* (1944) was equally ridiculous, but if you can swallow Cary Grant as the owner of a dancing caterpillar, the picture isn't half bad. *She Wouldn't Say Yes* (1945) offered Roz Russell in yet another of her appealing Career Woman parts, this time as a psychiatrist who falls for patient Lee Bowman.

*Down to Earth* (1947) was a musical quasi-sequel to *Mr. Jordan*, but despite the presence of Rita Hayworth at her most beautiful as Terpsichore, the goddess of dance, the film was sunk by the weight of the earthbound Larry Parks as her romantic lead (it would bob to the surface in 1980, remade as the mega-bomb *Xanadu*). This completed Hall's tenure at Columbia, but he rebounded with the prime comedy *The Great Lover* (1949), with Bob Hope as a Boy Scout leader tempted by bombshell Rhonda Fleming. *Love That Brute* (1950) was a romance divided three ways among Paul Douglas, Cesar Romero, and Jean Peters, while *Louisa* (1950) was another triangle, with Spring Byington wooed by Charles Coburn and Edmund Gwenn (as Ronald Reagan looked on). *Up Front* (1951) was an amusing dramatization of Bill Mauldin's bestselling World War II memoir, but *Because You're Mine* (1952) was a turkey in the classic tradition, stuffed with Mario Lanza and ready for the oven. At least *Let's Do It Again* (1953), Hall's musical remake of *The Awful Truth*, with Jane Wyman and Ray Milland, had some life in it. Hall's last film was *Forever Darling* (1956), an amusing vehicle for Lucille Ball and Desi Arnaz, then at the height of their awesome popularity.

## ● HENRY HATHAWAY (1898–1985)

Known for his dozens of action films, some of which rank with the better works of Howard Hawks and John Ford, Henry Hathaway spent more than forty years behind the camera. But few of the sixty-odd films he made bear the stamp of a particular sensibility, a lack that has cost Hathaway the admiration commanded by some of his peers. And it must be admitted that a great many of his pictures could, and perhaps should, have been even better than they turned out.

Born in Sacramento, California, to an actress and a stage manager—who else would have christened him "Henri Leopold de Fiennes"?—Hathaway got a head start in show business, and by the age of ten was acting in short films. His acting career was interrupted by the First World War, in which he served. He returned to Hollywood to become an assistant director, and graduated to directing two-reel Westerns at Paramount, moving up to handle full-length "B" Westerns (some with Randolph Scott) from 1932 to 1934. Still at Paramount, he entered the mainstream in 1934 with *The Witching Hour* and *Now and Forever*, the latter with Shirley Temple sandwiched between two of the day's biggest stars, Gary Cooper and Carole Lombard. Coop was better suited to Hathaway's next film, the fine adventure *The Lives of a Bengal Lancer* (1935), which was nominated for an Academy Award as best picture and earned Hathaway the only best director nomination of his long career.

It was Gary Cooper once more in the 1935 *Peter Ibbetson*, an interesting but very peculiar romance-cum-fantasy that might have been a masterpiece in the hands of someone like Rouben Mamoulian. (The immobile Ann Harding as Cooper's long-separated love was part of the problem.) *The Trail of the Lonesome Pine* (1936), with Henry Fonda and Sylvia Sidney, was more typical Hathaway territory, while *Go West, Young Man* (1936) was a pleasant vehicle for Mae West, with Hathaway's old "B" star Randolph Scott in tow. *Souls at Sea* (1937) teamed Coop and George Raft to surprisingly good effect, and Raft returned alongside Henry Fonda for the two-fisted *Spawn of the North* (1938), a lively tale about Canadian fishermen that also gave Dorothy Lamour one of her best early roles.

That marked the end of Hathaway's tenure at Paramount. He began a brief period of freelancing by making *The Real Glory* (1939), a terrific action-fest starring Gary Cooper, set in the Philippines after the Spanish-American War. *Johnny Apollo* (1940) offered a less exotic locale, but Hathaway turned this familiar saga of a good lad (Tyrone Power) gone wrong into one of the year's better crime pictures; for those who complain that Hathaway worked well only with male actors, there was also a memorable performance by Dorothy Lamour as the bad-girl-gone-good.

*Brigham Young—Frontiersman* (1940), starring Tyrone Power and appealing new star Linda Darnell, was a fanciful biopic about the Mormon leader that totally misfired—Hathaway's worst picture since he became an "A" director and a model example of how Hollywood always manages to muck up religious history. *Shepherd of the Hills* (1941) was a sensitive drama about an Ozark community that gave John Wayne an atypical role as a conscience-racked mountaineer; both he and love interest Betty Field shone. The 1941 World War II adventure *Sundown* was exotic, and so was the gorgeous Gene Tierney—as a native of the North African desert, no less! But this elaborately mounted tale of British heroism fails to excite.

Hathaway now began his tenure as a contract director at Fox, where he would make his next twenty-five films over a period of fifteen years. First in line was *Ten Gentlemen from West Point* (1942), an enjoyable history of West Point's early days, with a neat, nasty turn by Laird Cregar. *China Girl* (1942) had Gene Tierney again, although she and George Montgomery couldn't ignite this tale of wartime espionage in the Orient. He took a detour into middle America for *Home in Indiana* (1944), a horseracing yarn that was good, old-fashioned corn, then returned to World War II action with *Wing and a Prayer* (1944), with Dana Andrews and Don Ameche uplifting as fighter pilots aboard an aircraft carrier. *Nob Hill* (1945) was a Technicolor musical that plunked George Raft and Joan Bennett down in San Francisco's saloon scene at the turn of the century, to no particular purpose. But *The House on 92nd Street* (1945) was an influential docudrama that used New York City locations and a newsreel style to tell its taut tale about Nazis trying to steal atomic bomb secrets during World War II; a number of actual FBI personnel appeared in bit parts. *The Dark Corner* (1946) was a solid noir that would have more of a reputation today if "hero" Mark Stevens had been replaced by someone with charisma, like Robert Mitchum; Lucille Ball actually holds up the film as Stevens's courageous secretary.

With *13 Rue Madeleine* (1946), Hathaway grafted noir visuals onto a Far East espionage background with fine results; James Cagney's resilient OSS agent punches across the story's tension. *Kiss of Death* (1947) is probably Hathaway's most enduring film, and even if he never made another one as good, this and the three preceding would be sufficient to secure his reputation. Filmed on location, this tale of a crook (Victor Mature) in New York City willing to turn state's evidence for the love of his girl (Coleen Gray) is best remembered for Richard Widmark's Oscar-nominated performance as a psychopathic killer who plays cat-and-mouse with Mature.

*Call Northside 777* (1948), another quasi-documentary crime yarn, starred James Stewart as a crusading reporter who risks his life to save a convicted

▲ *Hathaway (center) is flanked by Jack Hawkins and Tyrone Power on the set of* The Black Rose

killer he believes to be innocent, while *Down to the Sea in Ships* (1949) was a remake of the 1922 silent about nineteenth-century whalers, with Richard Widmark cast this time as the mentor for young Dean Stockwell. *The Black Rose* (1950) was set in thirteenth-century North Africa and was shot on location (a dream assignment for Hathaway)—but even a cast that included Tyrone Power, Orson Welles, and Michael Rennie couldn't make this overlong swords 'n' sandals pic convincing. *You're in the Navy Now* (1951) was a lame World War II comedy that wasted Gary Cooper and Jane Greer.

Mercifully, that would be Hathaway's last stab at comedy for the next twenty years, as he returned to the urban thriller form with *Fourteen Hours* (1951), another of his beloved faux-documentaries; it starred Richard Basehart and introduced Grace Kelly to moviegoers. *Rawhide* that same year was his welcome return to the Western; Tyrone Power and Susan Hayward starred in this *Petrified Forest* with six-guns and spurs. Just as exciting was *The Desert Fox*, Hathaway's fourth release of 1951, which included a splendid turn by James Mason as Field Marshal Erwin Rommel. *Diplomatic Courier* (1952) gave Tyrone Power a solid role as an American up against Red agents in Trieste, after which Hathaway contributed

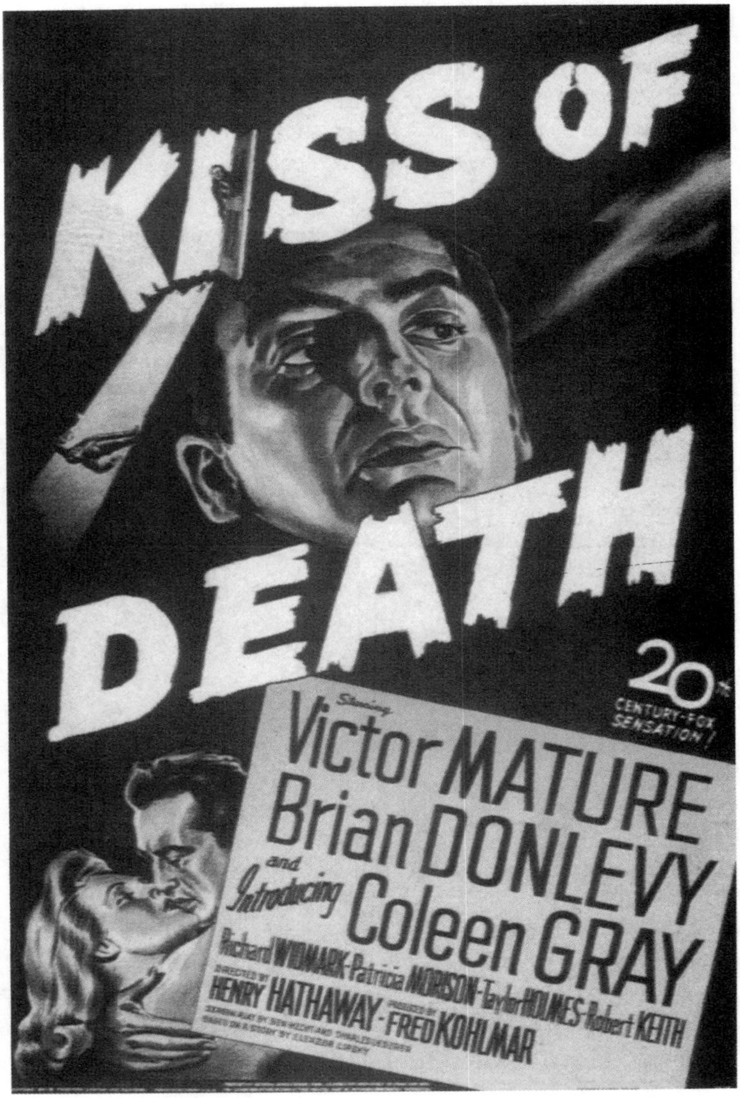

one of the five segments of *O. Henry's Full House* (1952).

*Niagara* (1953) was a pleasingly tawdry tale of infidelity and murder filmed on location at Niagara Falls, which placed second to Marilyn Monroe as the film's most spectacular natural wonder; this may well be Monroe's best dramatic film. *White Witch Doctor* (1953) was Hollywood hokum at its most labored, with Susan Hayward risking all to bring medical cures to the natives and Robert Mitchum risking nothing as he searches for hidden treasure. *Prince Valiant* (1954) *sounded* as though it would be hokum, based as it was on the famed sword-and-sorcery comic strip—but it's really pretty enjoyable, Robert Wagner as Val notwithstanding.

Eighteen-fifties Mexico was the venue for the 1954 *Garden of Evil*, but even Hathaway vets Cooper, Widmark, and Hayward couldn't jump-start the picture's leaden script. *The Racers* (1955) was shot on location in Europe, but somehow the spectacle of Kirk Douglas as a take-no-prisoners driver failed to capture the popular imagination, while *The Bottom of the Bottle* (1956) *was* the bottom of the barrel, clichéd melodrama starring Joseph Cotten as a lawyer trying to straighten out his alcoholic brother (Van Johnson). *23 Paces to Baker Street* (1956) used Van Johnson again, this time in the role of a blind playwright trying to prevent a murder. That at least offered suspense; *Legend of the Lost* (1957) placed John Wayne in the desert with Sophia Loren and Rossano Brazzi and buried them under a mountain of metaphysics. Hathaway attempted to break his slump by returning to the Western, and *From Hell to Texas* (1958) was a passable concoction, with Don Murray eluding a posse that included Dennis Hopper. *Woman Obsessed* (1959) had the advantage of Susan Hayward and the drawback of Stephen Boyd, but in the end it was just another rural soap opera.

Hathaway had not excelled during the Fifties, but as the 1960s began, he righted himself and actually enjoyed a fine decade. First came *Seven Thieves* (1960), a good caper picture set in Monte Carlo, with the tasty cast of Edward G. Robinson, Joan Collins, Rod Steiger, and Eli Wallach. That same year he made *North to Alaska*, a robust gold-rush adventure that combined John Wayne, action, and humor to create Hathaway's biggest hit—and best work—since *Niagara*. (Even Fabian was pretty good.)

That ended Hathaway's long association with Fox. He next co-directed *How the West Was Won* (1962) for MGM with John Ford and George Marshall; a sprawling Cinerama spectacular that featured appearances by everyone in Hollywood except Liberace, it remains a treat for fans of the Western. *Circus World* (1964) was almost as long, with far less purpose, although the sight of John Wayne underneath the Big Top wasn't as painful as it sounds. At least *The Sons of Katie Elder* (1965) put the Duke back where he belonged, on a saddle, and Dean Martin was fine in support. *Nevada Smith* (1966) was a section of Harold Robbins's *The Carpetbaggers* that preceded the rest of the action. Hathaway's prequel is actually better than Dmytryk's 1964 film, thanks to Steve McQueen as the Alan Ladd character at a younger age. *The Last Safari* (1967) was an unnecessary effort, with Stewart Granger as a White Hunter in need of a therapist, and *Five Card Stud* (1968) abused Dean Martin and Robert Mitchum terribly in what should have been a great team-up.

But Hathaway didn't have to suffer for long, as his next film was the irresistible *True Grit* (1969), an enormous hit (faithfully adapted from Charles Portis's bestseller) that nailed down the Duke's long-denied Oscar—supposedly a sympathy vote, but that's unfair to Wayne's great comic performance. Hathaway's last three films were the forgettable *Raid on Rommel*, *Shootout* with Gregory Peck (both 1971), and *Hangup* (aka *SuperDude*; 1974). The last was as good as most Blaxploitation pictures—but on second thought, let's not entertain the depressing thought of Henry Hathaway laboring in that genre for another instant.

## ● HOWARD HAWKS (1896–1977)

The quintessential Hollywood auteur, Howard Hawks made all of his thirty-three sound pictures without ever being under contract to a studio, although he relied almost entirely on cannily chosen studio talent. His "voice" was so distinctive that almost all his movies can be identified within moments as a Hawks film. Hawks was able to impose his style on every viable genre that was in vogue during his long career—Westerns, musicals, screwball comedies, war pictures, historical epics, romantic adventures, films noir, gangster sagas, and even science fiction; many other directors were asked to do the same, but none enjoyed Hawks's rate of success. He didn't always manage to turn out a classic, but he came close more often than any other American director, and his range far exceeded that of "rival" John Ford—Ford didn't know how (or care) to make comedies and was less reliable (and convincing) when staging romance. For those reasons alone, Hawks most fully embodies the essence of Hollywood moviemaking from 1930 to 1970.

Born in Goshen, Indiana, he moved with his family to California and attended school in Pasadena before being sent to Philips Exeter in New Hampshire. He graduated from Cornell in 1917 with a degree in mechanical engineering, but already had gotten Hollywood into his blood working for the property department of Famous Players–Lasky during summer vacations. That hobby was put on the back burner, however, while Hawks served in the First World War as a second lieutenant in the Army Air Corps. Both before and after that formative experience, he earned his living as a professional race-car driver. But at the age of twenty-two he committed himself to film, working first as a producer for directors like Allan Dwan, and then putting in a two-year stint as the head of the story department at Paramount.

In 1925 Hawks signed with Fox to direct, and while his first few efforts *(The Road to Glory, The Cradle Snatchers)* are now lost, silents like *A Girl in Every Port* (1928), with Louise Brooks, Victor McLaglen, and Robert Armstrong, and the 1928 *The Air Circus* (co-directed with Lewis Seiler, who was in charge of the last-minute talking-sequence additions) already had set in place some of the themes dearest to Hawks's heart—like the special kind of friendship two men can develop that supersedes even their rivalry over a woman *(Port),* and a young man's desire to learn how to fly a plane *(Air). Trent's Last Case* (1929), like *Air* a lost film, was made as a silent because the "talking rights" were never acquired; based on a popular mystery novel, it was never shown in the United States because the market for silents had already collapsed.

But *The Dawn Patrol* (1930), a seminal World War I adventure based on an Oscar-winning story by *Wings* author John Monk Saunders, suffered no such fate. Hawks's first true talkie, *Dawn* starred Richard Barthelmess and Douglas Fairbanks, Jr., as part of a squadron of young airmen, stationed in France, whose tenuous existence brings out the best in some while exposing the weakness of others. Although the acting is no less creaky than that in most 1930 films, the aerial footage (much of it shot from a plane piloted by Hawks himself) is first-rate, and was recycled in several films, including Edmund Goulding's 1938 remake with Errol Flynn. *The Criminal Code* (1931) was a reworking of a minor Broadway play, with Walter Huston as a prison warden whose daughter (Constance Cummings) falls for one of his prisoners (Phillips Holmes); Hawks told Peter Bogdanovich in their heralded 1962 interview that he hired ten convicts to critique the story for him so he could make it more authentic.

*The Crowd Roars* (1932) was Hawks's first opportunity to tell the screen story of his beloved world of racing; James Cagney plays a race-car driver who tries to keep kid brother Eric Linden away from the sport, with tragic results. *Scarface (Shame of a Nation)* (1932) had actually been completed before *Crowd* but was held up for several months while Hawks and co-producer Howard Hughes struggled with the censors; cameraman Lee Garmes ultimately shot the additional sequences they demanded. Arguably the best of the "big three" of early gangster epics (Mervyn LeRoy's *Little Caesar* and William Wellman's *Public Enemy* being the others), *Scarface* was, as Hawks conceived it, "the Borgias set down in Chicago," with Paul Muni as a thinly disguised Al Capone (who, Hawks maintained, loved the picture), Ann Dvorak as the sister he loves not wisely but too well, George Raft as his loyal lieutenant (whose coin-flipping routine was based on a member of the Dutch Schultz mob whom Raft used to know), and Boris Karloff as a rival mobster. (The story was "updated" in 1983 by Brian De Palma, inflated beyond all sense, with Al Pacino in the Muni role, and cocaine as the cash crop instead of booze.)

*Tiger Shark* (1932) was less sensational; Edward G. Robinson stars as a goodhearted Portuguese fisherman who helplessly watches young bride Zita Johann fall in love with fellow tuna man Richard Arlen. *Today We Live* (1933) was a World War I yarn scripted by William Faulkner from a story of his in *The Saturday Evening Post*; Hawks had read it and had the initiative to hire the author for his first Hollywood project—but MGM insisted on casting Joan Crawford among soldiers Gary Cooper, Robert Young, and Franchot Tone, even though the story had no part for her. Hawks was more than halfway through shooting *Viva Villa!* (1934), starring Wallace Beery, on location in Mexico; but when actor Lee Tracy urinated over a balcony on some soldiers parading below, the Mexican government demanded an apology before permitting filming to continue. Louis B. Mayer recalled Tracy and Hawks, who refused to apologize, and replaced them with Stu Erwin and Jack Conway, who completed the picture. Hawks received no credit, but much of his work (particularly the exterior location scenes) remains onscreen.

Hawks's résumé to this point had been weighted heavily toward action and drama, but he took a Ben Hecht and Charles MacArthur script and made *Twentieth Century* (1934), one of the enduring screwball comedies. Carole Lombard gives a classic comic performance as shopgirl Mildred Plotka, who is transformed by manic Broadway director John Barrymore into superstar Lily Garland while serving as his paramour. But when she tires of his utter control, Mildred/Lily deserts him for Hollywood. Now his fortunes dwindle, setting up their confrontation on a coast-to-coast train ride that remains a model of machine-gun repartee—this is the film that introduced Hawks's trademark overlapping dialogue—and slapstick timing. The picture wasn't really a hit, but it gave Lombard's career a new direction and Hawks the confidence to work in a new genre.

*Barbary Coast* (1935) was also written by Hecht and MacArthur, but it was just another synthetic period romance. Miriam Hopkins plays a card dealer in a notorious gambling joint who wants to escape the clutches of mentor Edward G. Robinson so she can lead a "clean" life with handsome Joel McCrea. *Ceiling Zero* (1936) was better, an exciting adaptation of a play by former pilot Frank Wead, with James Cagney as an indomitable airmail pilot and Pat O'Brien his hard-boiled (but admiring) boss. *The Road to Glory* (1936) returned to the battlefields of World War I in this Faulkner-penned drama about a

the cinema of howard hawks
by Peter Bogdanovich · The Film Library of The Museum of Modern Art

father (Lionel Barrymore) and son (Warner Baxter) who find to their dismay that they're fighting in the same unit.

The lively *Come and Get It* (also 1936), from an Edna Ferber novel, was shot primarily by Hawks, but he was canned by Goldwyn toward the end of the production and William Wyler (who received a full co-direction credit) shot the final scenes. This is probably Frances Farmer's best showcase, giving her dual roles as a mother and daughter in the nineteenth-century Pacific Northwest; Edward Arnold and Joel McCrea are also fine, and Walter Brennan won his first Oscar as Farmer's logging dad, Swede (though they were nearly the same age). It was during this period that Hawks lent his writing talents to a number of well-known pictures, including Fleming's *Captains Courageous* and *Test Pilot*, Stevens's *Gunga Din*, and even *Gone with the Wind*—though he never received a screen credit (or took one on his own pictures) for his scripting contributions.

Hawks now returned to comedy for the lunatic *Bringing Up Baby* (1938), with Cary Grant at his funniest as a hapless paleontologist trying to recover a purloined dinosaur bone; Katharine Hepburn (never more appealing) is the dotty heiress who falls for him but succeeds only in making his life miserable. Although it wasn't a success at the time—in fact, it basically bombed—*Baby* is now recognized as the definitive Thirties screwball romp. Grant served Hawks well again in *Only Angels Have Wings* (1939), a splendid romantic adventure scripted by Jules Furthman from a story Hawks cooked up about a band of mail pilots working at a remote station in South America. Their cucumber-cool leader (Grant, of course) finds his equilibrium disrupted when old flame Rita Hayworth unexpectedly turns up, and he goes into a total tailspin when stranded showgirl Jean Arthur gets under his protective covering. Those hoary romantic gambits are buttressed by some terrific interplay among the pilots (Thomas Mitchell, Richard Barthelmess, John Carroll) as they try to ply their trade under hazardous conditions that doom more than one of them. Men bravely, uncomplainingly, doing a job; grace under pressure; and the special kind of woman who endeavors to help a big lug see that his life can't be complete without a sympathetic (but equally tough) mate—these are the themes Hawks would return to again and again, the spiritual underpinnings of his most memorable pictures.

Now at the peak of his storytelling powers, Hawks reimagined the Hecht-MacArthur newspaper comedy *The Front Page* as *His Girl Friday* (1940), cannily recasting editor Walter Burns and reporter Hildy Johnson from two newspapermen (as in the 1928 play and the 1931 film version) to a once-married editor and reporter—the peerless Cary Grant and

▲ *Hawks on his cycle, circa 1943*

Rosalind Russell. With their romantic bickering added to the incisive satire of the ultra-competitive business of tabloid journalism, *Friday* is one of the funniest pictures of its era—and certainly the fastest-paced, thanks to Hawks's machine-gun pacing of the line readings.

Hawks spent a few weeks working on Howard Hughes's *The Outlaw* in 1940, finally removing himself from the production after Hughes's meddling became intolerable, then happily moved on to the Jesse Lasky production of *Sergeant York* (1941), which would become his biggest hit. A rare (for Hawks) biopic, this tale about the Tennessee pacifist who becomes one of the biggest heroes of World War I (capturing 132 Germans singlehandedly) caught the mood of pre–World War II America perfectly. Gary Cooper, rather long in the tooth for the part but York's own choice, won the best actor Oscar, and Hawks received his only Academy Award nomination for best direction; the film, screenplay, and supporting actors Walter Brennan and Margaret Wycherly were also nominated.

*Ball of Fire* (1941) was a well-conceived (but overlong) Charles Brackett–Billy Wilder romantic comedy; stuffy linguist Gary Cooper learns how to expand his vocabulary, among other things, from stripper and moll Barbara Stanwyck ("He don't know how to kiss—the jerk!"). The patriotic *Air Force* (1943) transposed Hawks's own Air Corps experience and men-at-work ethos to the frontlines, with John Garfield, Gig Young, and Arthur Kennedy part of the heroic crew of a B-17 bomber. *To Have and Have Not* (1945) permitted Hawks to indulge himself, with Humphrey Bogart and Lauren Bacall—Hawks had signed her to a personal services contract after his wife, Slim, noticed the teenager in the pages of *Vogue*—dodging the Vichy police while feinting and parrying with each other. Loosely based on the 1937 Hemingway novel, Hawks's version jettisons the book's existentialism (and most of the plot) in favor of the screenwriters' (William Faulkner and Jules Furthman) best sassy romantic dialogue. The term "screen chemistry" is still defined by what Hawks's cameras captured between Bogart and Bacall, who would marry the following year.

Hawks called on Faulkner and Furthman again, along with pulp writer Leigh Brackett, to help adapt Raymond Chandler's *The Big Sleep* (1946), a Philip Marlowe mystery that was being fashioned as the follow-up showcase for Bogart and Bacall. Even more diffuse than *To Have* in terms of story, but every bit as enjoyable in terms of romance and mayhem, its release was held up for nearly a year while Hawks complied with Warners' request to beef up the scenes between the two leads. The epic Western *Red River* (1948) was also held up for several months in post-production. Again it is the screen chemistry between two people that fuels the rather perfunctory plot, but this time the couple is John Wayne and (in his first screen work) Montgomery Clift; their interplay is oedipal, with overtones of *Mutiny on the Bounty*. Enormously expensive (over $3 million), the film has power aplenty. But an impossibly mannered performance by Joanne Dru—the "Hawks woman" at her most irritating—nearly stops the show.

*A Song Is Born* (1948) was Hawks's musical remake of *Ball of Fire*, with Danny Kaye and Virginia Mayo substituting for Cooper and Stanwyck. He oughtn't have bothered—it's a dud—although Hawks professed (in an interview with Peter Bogdanovich) never to have seen it, and to have made it only as a favor to Sam Goldwyn. No apologies were necessary for the riotous *I Was a Male War Bride* (1949), in which French Army officer Cary Grant marries WAC Ann Sheridan and has to don military drag to sneak back to the States with her. Hawks is credited only as the producer of *The Thing (from Another World)* (1951), letting longtime film editor Christian Nyby assume the directing credit—but this chilling adaptation of John Campbell, Jr.'s classic science-fiction story "Who Goes There?" plays (and, with its overlapping dialogue, *sounds*) more like a Hawks

◀ *On the set of* His Girl Friday *with Cary Grant and Roz Russell*

▲ *Cary Grant and Marilyn Monroe on roller skates for* Monkey Business

picture than does, say, *Sergeant York*; certainly Margaret Sheridan is the prototypical Hawks heroine. This was Hawks's only foray into that genre, and all he accomplished was making (okay, *overseeing*) one of the three best SF films of the Fifties.

*The Big Sky* (1952), from the A. B. Guthrie novel, had Kirk Douglas fur-trapping his way along the Missouri as pal Dewey Martin helps him fend off assorted perils, while *O. Henry's Full House* (1952) featured Hawks's "The Ransom of Red Chief," with Fred Allen and Oscar Levant, as one of its five tales (although this segment was often trimmed from the release print). The 1952 *Monkey Business* was an intermittently funny collaboration between Hawks and his favorite comic actor, Cary Grant. Written by Billy Wilder, I.A.L. Diamond, and Charles Lederer, this goofy yarn about a scientist who discovers a rejuvenation serum gave romantic idol Grant another opportunity to exhibit his proven flair for silliness, and remains the only screen teaming of Grant and rising star Marilyn Monroe (and of either of them with a chimpanzee).

Monroe may have been just window dressing in *Monkey*, but Hawks saw her comedy potential and guided her in her breakthrough vehicle, the effervescent *Gentlemen Prefer Blondes* (1953). Adapted from the 1920s Anita Loos–Joseph Fields Broadway hit, *Blondes* has the genius to set off an essentially deglamorized Monroe against sex icon Jane Russell (who was never better) without ever playing up the erotic charge of either actress, save for the musical numbers—in particular Monroe's "Diamonds Are a Girl's Best Friend," still one of the most perfect three minutes ever captured on celluloid. Continuing his genre-surfing, Hawks nearly wiped out with the biblical epic *Land of the Pharoahs* (1955), a handsome but cumbersome account of the building of the pyramids. It had all the trimmings—CinemaScope, Technicolor—except for stars: it relied on the underwhelming tandem of British actors Jack Hawkins and Joan Collins. (Hawks's comment to Bogdanovich about the stiffness of this, his own least-favorite picture: "I don't know how a pharoah talks. And Faulkner didn't know. None of us knew.")

▲ *With Rosalind Russell*

It would be several years before Hawks essayed another project, but his 1959 return to the big screen was triumphal—*Rio Bravo*, one of the best Westerns ever made in Hollywood. Scripted by Leigh Brackett and Jules Furthman, *Rio* is unusual in offering as much humor as action (as opposed to, say, *The Searchers*, *Shane*, or *High Noon*). The plot is less than original—an exact inversion of *High Noon*, as Hawks once pointed out—and Hawks spends his own sweet time spinning it out. But the cumulative effect of all those semi-improvised bits of business are more rewarding than the plot twists of more carefully constructed films. John Wayne turns in a well-rounded performance as the gruff-but-caring hero, a self-reliant sheriff who, in helping rummy Dean Martin (in his best screen performance) earn back his self-respect, learns how also to accept the helping hands extended by sultry dance-hall girl Angie Dickinson, cocky gunfighter Ricky Nelson, and cantankerous deputy Walter Brennan—quite the extended family.

*Hatari!* (1962) was even longer and more formless, but steeped in the color of big-game trapping in Africa, with Wayne as the head of the band and Elsa Martinelli as the fearless photographer who earns his grudging admiration. Some of the vignettes are more effective than others, but it looks as if the actors are having a hell of a time making the picture, particularly in the rhino-capturing sequence. *Man's Favorite Sport?* (1964) would have been a perfect comedy for Cary Grant, and still manages to suffice with Rock Hudson in the role of an expert department-store fly caster who's sent into the great outdoors by his boss, John McGiver, to enter a fishing competition—a sport he knows nothing about. Paula Prentiss is very appealing as the experienced woman who teaches the virginal Hudson a few things about rods and reels, and Hawks (who shot the film in sequence, a day per scene) expertly squeezes out what mirth the thin story possesses.

*Red Line 7000* (1965) was Hawks's disappointing return to the world of race-car driving (last visited in the 1932 *The Crowd Roars*), although then-unknown James Caan is well cast as the troubled hero. *El Dorado* (1967), with Caan, John Wayne, and Robert Mitchum, was either a sequel to, or a remake of, *Rio Bravo*, with Mitchum in Dean Martin's role and John Wayne in John Wayne's. But the sloppy *Rio Lobo* (1970)—yet another variation on the formula—found Wayne supported by an odd cast of up-and-comers and never-weres, including Jennifer O'Neill, Jorge Rivero, and (of all people) future studio head Sherry Lansing. That would prove to be Hawks's last picture, forty-five years after he completed his first, and it was not his crowning glory.

It's worth mentioning the two special film projects he never got under way—a version of *Don Quixote* with Cary Grant as the Don and Cantiflas as Sancho Panza, and *The Sun Also Rises*, which was ultimately made by Henry King in 1957. One cannot help feeling that both might have been turned into something wonderful by Hawks. Or is that stating the obvious?

## ● STUART HEISLER (1894–1979)

Born in Los Angeles, Stuart Heisler was well into his forties before he began to direct. But that doesn't mean he entered the film industry late in life. He joined Famous Players as an actor in 1913, and passed through the Sennett, Fox, and First National studios during the Teens and Twenties, before working as a film editor on such pictures as *Condemned*, *The Kid from Spain*, *Roman Scandals*, and *Klondike Annie*. In 1936, Heisler directed his first film, a Paramount "B" called *Straight from the Shoulder*. That apparently convinced John Ford to hire him as his second-unit director on *The Hurricane* in 1937, one of the year's biggest (and most popular) productions. Heisler's reward was a return to Paramount for more "B"s, including the wonderful *The Biscuit Eater*, about two Georgia boys; the perverse horror yarn *The Monster and the Girl*; and the equally demented *Among the Living* (both 1941), starring Susan Hayward and Frances Farmer.

Finally, in 1942, he was entrusted with his first "A" features. *The Remarkable Andrew*, from a fanciful Dalton Trumbo script, had Brian Donlevy as the ghost of Andrew Jackson, back to aid do-gooder William Holden. Even better was *The Glass Key*, a terse adaptation of the 1930 Dashiell Hammett novel, filmed previously in 1935 with George Raft and Claire Dodd. It was being remade so soon because of Paramount's pressing need for a worthy Alan Ladd–Veronica Lake vehicle, as they had just created a sensation in *This Gun for Hire*. The two new stars definitely had chemistry, and Heisler also benefited from a superior supporting cast that included Brian Donlevy and William Bendix. The film was a smash, and Heisler was poised to become one of Paramount's top directors. But the war interrupted his plans, and Heisler was in the service for the next three years, making a documentary called *The Negro Soldier* for the Army in 1944.

His first film upon returning to civilian life was the pleasant Gary Cooper spoof *Along Came Jones*, which Coop also produced. Heisler took over *Blue*

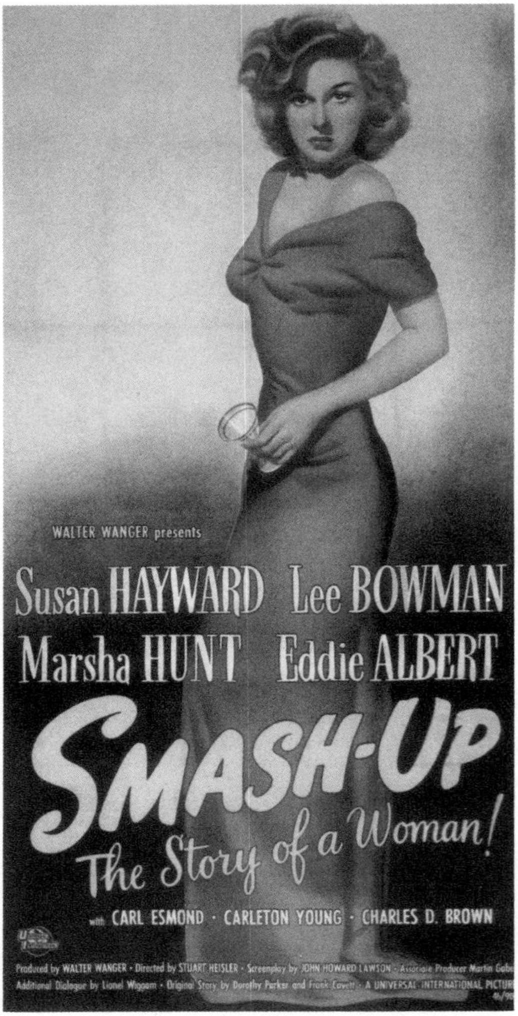
WALTER WANGER presents
Susan HAYWARD Lee BOWMAN
Marsha HUNT Eddie ALBERT
SMASH-UP
The Story of a Woman!
with CARL ESMOND · CARLETON YOUNG · CHARLES D. BROWN
Produced by WALTER WANGER · Directed by STUART HEISLER · Screenplay by JOHN HOWARD LAWSON
Additional Dialogue by Lionel Wiggam · Original Story by Dorothy Parker and Frank Cavett · A UNIVERSAL INTERNATIONAL

*Skies* (1946) after Mark Sandrich died during filming; an elaborate Irving Berlin musical with Bing Crosby, Fred Astaire, and twenty songs, its highlight was the sublime Fred Astaire–Hermes Pan production number, "Puttin' on the Ritz." *Smash-Up, the Story of a Woman* (1947), from a Dorothy Parker story (and scripted by soon-to-be Hollywood Ten victim John Howard Lawson), boasted a superb performance by Susan Hayward that earned her her first Oscar nomination. Heisler worked with her again on *Tulsa* (1949), where Hayward played an uncompromising oil woman interested in wildcat drilling first and Robert Preston second.

*Tokyo Joe* (1949), with Humphrey Bogart trying to outwit black marketeers, was formulaic to a fault, and *Chain Lightning* (1950) was probably Bogart's weakest postwar film. Next, Heisler was one of the legion of directors who toiled in vain on Howard Hughes's *Vendetta* (1950), though he remained (mercifully) uncredited. He brushed over these misfires to make another good Western with Gary Cooper, *Dallas* (also 1950), followed by the hysterical but interesting *Storm Warning* (1951)—Ginger Rogers learns that sister Doris Day has married a member of the KKK. Here even Ronald Reagan turned in a decent performance.

Heisler's subsequent pictures were a mixed bag in terms of quality. *Island of Desire* (1952), with a still-lovely Linda Darnell, didn't go anywhere, but *The Star* was a potent Bette Davis vehicle, made on a low budget in and around L.A. *Beachhead* (1954) was a perfectly adequate World War II yarn, with Tony Curtis as a hard-boiled Marine, but that was followed by the sappy *This Is My Love* (1954), the chief merit of which was the teaming of Linda Darnell and Faith Domergue. *I Died a Thousand Times* (1955) was a decent remake of *High Sierra*, with Jack Palance in the role that launched Bogie to stardom, supported by Shelley Winters.

More pleasing was Heisler's feature-length version of the popular TV series *The Lone Ranger*. But *The Burning Hills* (1960) was a pretentious Western starring Tab Hunter and Natalie Wood, teen idols not yet ready to carry this type of vehicle. Heisler's final film appeared two years later, the odd and awful *Hitler*, with Richard Basehart in the title role.

▲ *Making* The Biscuit Eater *in 1940*

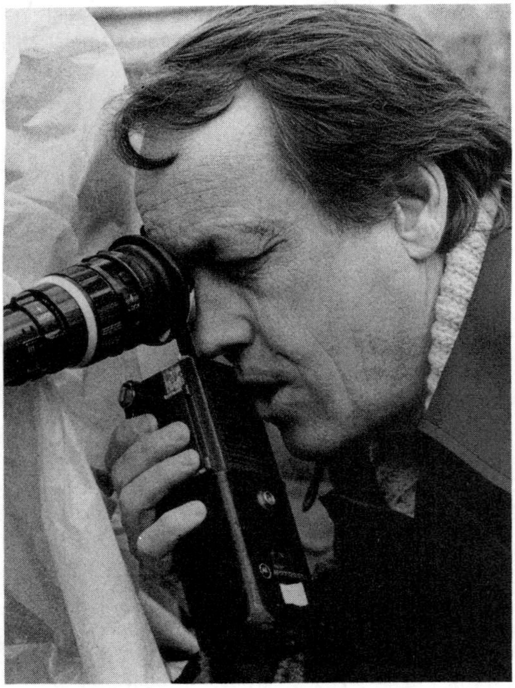

## ● GEORGE ROY HILL (1922- )

Although he would go on to direct two of the highest-grossing films in history, George Roy Hill spent the first thirty-nine years of his life working in every medium except movies. Born in Minneapolis, Minnesota, he studied music at Yale, earning his degree just before serving as a transport pilot during World War II. After the war he attended Trinity College in Dublin, where he began acting in theatrical productions. Upon returning to the States, Hill performed Off-Broadway and joined a touring Shakespearean repertory company. He became a regular on the radio soap opera *John's Other Wife* and had a supporting role in the anti-Commie film *Walk East on Beacon*, but was recalled to active duty and spent the next year as a pilot in Korea.

Hill was discharged in 1953 and immediately went to work in television. He wrote a teleplay for *Kraft Television Theater* in which he also acted, then began directing and producing for *Playhouse 90*, winning an Emmy in 1954 for writing and directing *A Night to Remember*. Hill moved back to the theater in 1957, directing such Broadway productions as *Look Homeward, Angel* and Tennessee Williams's *Period of Adjustment*. It was the latter that provided his entry to Hollywood: MGM gave him the chance to direct the screen adaptation in 1962. It turned out to be a light but pleasant romantic comedy, with Jane Fonda, Tony Franciosa, and Jim Hutton. Also via Broadway was Hill's screen version of Lillian Hellman's *Toys in the Attic* (1963), with the unlikely cast of Dean Martin, Geraldine Page, and Wendy Hiller.

*The World of Henry Orient* (1964) was Hill's first film without a theatrical origin. Based on a novel by Nora Johnson (who wrote the screenplay with her husband, Nunnally), it's a very funny—and original—comedy about two teenage groupies obsessed with pianist Peter Sellers; it's a "small" film that has aged very well. It stands in dramatic contrast to the epic *Hawaii* (1966), adapted from the mammoth novel by James Michener. Over three hours long when released, the film (begun by Fred Zinnemann before Hill was asked to replace him) meanders but is held together (barely) by leads Julie Andrews and Richard Harris. *Thoroughly Modern Millie* (1967) used Andrews again in a Jazz Age musical with Carol Channing (who was Oscar-nominated) and Mary Tyler Moore—but the film's relentless silliness eventually becomes grating, and its length is also a problem.

Hill regrouped by trying to mount *Henry Orient* as a Broadway musical in 1967, but *Henry, Sweet Henry* (as it was titled) failed. That may have been a blessing in disguise, because Hill returned to Hollywood to make *Butch Cassidy and the Sundance Kid* (1969), the legendary Western/romance/comedy that went on to earn almost $50 million in uninflated dollars, making it the fifth-biggest grossing movie of the decade. The chemistry between established star Paul Newman and newcomer Robert Redford was a large part of that success, but so was William Goldman's marvelously ironic screenplay, which won an Oscar. *Butch* was also nominated for Academy Awards for best picture and Hill earned his first nomination for best direction.

Now able to write his own ticket, Hill signed a long-term deal with Universal. His first project for them was *Slaughterhouse Five* (1971). Kurt Vonnegut's bestseller was not a book that promised to translate easily to film, with its time-traveling hero and bitterly ironic tone, and Hill was not able to wholly solve the problem; the casting of bland Michael Sacks as Billy Pilgrim certainly didn't help. Audiences didn't know what to make of it, and it ended up a financial failure. But with the help of

Redford and Newman, Hill rebounded in impressive fashion with *The Sting* (1973). An amiable caper yarn fueled by the star power of Redford and Newman, it won multiple Oscars—one for Hill and others for best picture, screenplay, and scoring. A monstrous success at the box office, the film became the eighth biggest picture of the Seventies and remains one of the highest-grossing films of all time.

With his choice of projects virtually unlimited, Hill next directed and produced *The Great Waldo Pepper* (1975), based on a story he wrote himself about a barnstorming pilot in the 1920s. Recognizing the commercial riskiness of the project, Hill hedged his bets by casting Robert Redford as Waldo and hiring William Goldman to write the screenplay. But these precautions weren't enough; the film fared poorly at the box office despite Redford and some very impressive aerial photography by Frank Tallman. (As a former pilot, Hill probably overestimated the story's appeal.) The rude, hilarious *Slap Shot* (1977) was a profane but rousing profile of a (barely) fictitious minor-league hockey team that can't win until it turns into a goon squad; it offers a riotous (and very blue) screenplay by Nancy Dowd and a fine performance by Paul Newman, but also failed at the box office (although it now has earned a cult following).

Hill and Universal parted ways, and the slump-ridden director next made the modest comedy *A Little Romance* (1979), with a very young Diane Lane as an American in Paris whose first romance is orchestrated by charming thief Laurence Olivier (in one of his better late performances). Far more ambitious was *The World According to Garp* (1982), from the picaresque John Irving bestseller that, at first blush, seemed nigh-unfilmable. Somehow Hill managed to transpose much of the book's bizarre black comedy into a (relatively) coherent story, helped immensely by the acting of Glenn Close and John Lithgow (both Oscar-nominated). But Robin Williams seems uneasy in the lead role, and the film failed to find an audience, despite generally good reviews.

*The Little Drummer Girl* (1984) was a botch of the complicated John le Carré novel, despite strenuous efforts by stars while *Funny Farm* (1988) was a bucolic Chevy Chase vehicle that was only half as amusing as it wanted to be. Hill turned to teaching drama at Yale; it remains to be seen whether he will ever direct another film.

## ● ARTHUR HILLER (1923- )

Walking proof that the *auteur* theory needn't exist, Arthur Hiller has fashioned a successful career out of making painless, smoothly impersonal commercial films. Born in Edmonton, Alberta, Hiller studied law and psychology before joining the Canadian Broadcasting Corporation, where he worked from 1950 to 1955. He broke into American television in 1956, directing series like *Playhouse 90*, *Gunsmoke*, *Alfred Hitchcock Presents*, *Perry Mason*, *Wagon Train*, and *Route 66*. In the midst of those he directed a lone feature release, the teen-angst drama *The Careless Years* (1957). But his film-directing career began in earnest in 1963 when he left TV to make Disney's live-action *Miracle of the White Stallions*, about the evacuation of Lippizan horses from Vienna during World War II, with the surprising cast of Robert Taylor, Lilli Palmer, and Eddie Albert, and *The Wheeler Dealers*, a pre-Boesky comedy that has Texas millionaires James Garner and Jim Backus playing with high-stakes investments just for the hell of it.

*The Americanization of Emily* (1964) featured Garner again as a Navy officer who is selected by superior Melvyn Douglas to be the first "victim" of D-day, thus beating out the other branches of the service for media coverage. Paddy Chayevsky's caustic script left room for a romance between Garner and Julie Andrews, but it's the satire that makes this Hiller's best film by a wide margin. *Promise Her Anything* (1966) was more typical of what filmgoers could expect from Hiller over the next three decades; a cute, snappy, sanitized sex farce starring Warren Beatty and Leslie Caron, as synthetic as its Greenwich Village locations (for which London played a poor stand-in). *Penelope* (1966) was an inept comedy that starred Natalie Wood as a bank robber, while *Tobruk* (1967) sent Rock Hudson and George Peppard into the Sahara to blow up Rommel's fuel supply, a nice idea that was vitiated by a nonstop stream of philosophical babble.

Eli Wallach kidnapped housewife Anne Jackson (his real-life wife) to make a point in *The Tiger Makes Out* (1967), but Murray Schisgal's expansion of his one-act play lumbers along for far too long. *Popi* (1969) used Alan Arkin well as a poor resident of Spanish Harlem who stages an elaborate scam to gain a better life for his two sons. *The Out-of-Towners* (1970) was Neil Simon's ode to the horrors of New York City, but Jack Lemmon and Sandy Dennis are so obnoxious as the Ohio couple stricken by an unending stream of bad luck during a twenty-four-hour visit that one cannot help rooting for New York City to chew them in its maw.

Hiller won the lottery with his second effort that year, the pop-romance classic *Love Story*, which managed to surpass even the phenomenal success of Erich Segal's novella. To say that Ryan O'Neal and Ali McGraw have never been better hardly explains why this gooey but oddly irresistible tale works as well as it does, but seven Academy Award nominations and a $50 million gross indicate that Hiller (who received one of those nominations) knew exactly what he was doing. To fully appreciate his skill, consider how many Oscar nominations Segal, O'Neal, and McGraw have totaled since then. (Of course, Hiller has yet to notch another himself.)

*Plaza Suite* (1971) was Neil Simon again, but here his adaptation of his earlier stage success (directed by Mike Nichols) worked splendidly; all three vignettes featured Walter Matthau, supported variously by Maureen Stapleton, Barbara Harris, and Lee Grant. *The Hospital* (1971) was more ambitious, a bleak black comedy via Paddy Chayevsky (who won an Oscar) that might have earned classic status had it known when to shut up for a moment here and there. Oscar-nominated George C. Scott was terrific as the weary, noble chief of surgery, and Diana Rigg as a hippie and Richard Dysart as an investment-crazed surgeon provided colorful support. But *Man of La Mancha* (1972) was an abomination, an execrable adaptation of the stage blockbuster—stars Peter O'Toole, Sophia Loren, and James Coco seem desperately in need of life preservers, not to mention singing lessons.

*The Crazy World of Julius Vrooder* (1974) was a counterculture comedy, starring Timothy Bottoms as a nutty Vietnam vet and Barbara (Seagull) Hershey as his nurse. *The Man in the Glass Booth* (1975) was a tasteful American Film Theatre production of Robert Shaw's play about a Jewish businessman (Maximilian Schell) on trial for war crimes; Schell was nominated for an Academy Award, but a displeased Shaw had his name taken off the final credits. *W. C. Fields and Me* (1976) was a fanciful account of an episode in the Great Man's life; Rod Steiger made a good Fields and Valerie Perrine played love Carlotta Monti. One of Hiller's biggest hits was *Silver Streak* (1976), a comic knockoff of Hitchcock's *The Lady Vanishes* starring Gene Wilder, Jill Clayburgh, and Richard Pryor; it hauled out every train-movie cliché in the book (some of them twice) en route to a huge gross.

*The In-Laws* (1979), written by Andrew Bergman, was genuinely, atypically (for Hiller) hilarious—an anarchic espionage spoof with over-the-top performances by Alan Arkin and Peter Falk. But the vampire-bat horror movie *Nightwing* (1979) was for the birds, despite a decent source novel by Martin Cruz Smith (who contributed to the sorry screenplay). *Making Love* (1982) was so timid as to be laughable; Hiller homogenized this homosexual romance between gay novelist Harry Hamlin and heretofore straight (and married) doctor Michael Ontkean so thoroughly it couldn't offend even your grandmother in Dubuque. *Author! Author!* (1982) featured Al Pacino's strenuously frenzied performance as a Broadway playwright whose weirdo wife walks out on him and their kids—a cute idea that Israel Horovitz's insistent script virtually jams down our throats.

*Romantic Comedy* (1983) was also about a playwright's confused state of amour, but this version of the Bernard Slade play falls flat despite the presence of Dudley Moore and Mary Steenburgen. *The Lonely Guy* (1984) was better, a funny (if uneven) expansion of the Bruce Jay Friedman premise that there's an entire universe of Lonely Guys out there, just waiting to find each other to commiserate. Steve Martin is good as the yearning protagonist, but Charles Grodin steals the picture as his worldly wise lonely pal. *Teachers* (1984) was a messy drama about the awful stuff going on in a big-city high school (Nick Nolte is the outraged protagonist who shakes things up), while *Outrageous Fortune* (1987) teamed Bette Midler and Shelley Long as rivals whose shared paramour has just kicked the bucket. *See No Evil, Hear No Evil* (1989) was a pathetic attempt to cash in on the success of the earlier Gene Wilder–Richard Pryor teamings: what they do with their Blind Man/Deaf Man shtick is painful to watch.

*Taking Care of Business* (1990) used Charles Grodin to good comic effect as an obsessive-compulsive accountant whose identity is assumed by convict James Belushi when he finds Grodin's pocket organizer, while *Married to It* (1991; released 1993) set Yuppies Beau Bridges, Stockard Channing, Ron Silver, and Cybill Shepherd loose in New York City amid a sea of clichés about friendship and love. *The Babe* (1992), a flavorful biopic of the great ballplayer, received Hiller's usual mixed reviews, this time on the grounds of wanton historical inaccuracy. But all agreed that it was a masterpiece compared to the 1948 screen debacle, and that enormous John Goodman looked more like the Sultan of Swat than William Bendix ever did. But the utterly innocuous *Married to It* (1993), with its flaccid story about three Manhattan couples (one of which is Ron Silver and Cybill Shepherd) reminds us again that Hiller can be a soporific for audiences.

▲ *James Garner takes instruction from Hiller during* The Americanization of Emily

## ● ALFRED HITCHCOCK (1899-1980)

The greatest of all directors? The most adroit? The most admired? A case can be made—indeed, *has* been made, in several book-length studies and uncountable essays—that Sir Alfred is all of the above and then some. Detractors can point to the films that simply missed by a country mile—*The Paradine Case*, *Stage Fright*, *Torn Curtain*, and *Topaz* are nobody's masterpieces—and *Lifeboat*, *The Trouble with Harry*, *Under Capricorn*, *I Confess*, *Saboteur*, and *Marnie* are among the works that in the end leave something to be desired. But then one lets those other titles trip off the tongue—*The Man Who Knew Too Much*, *The Thirty-nine Steps*, *The Lady Vanishes* (all from his pre-Hollywood period); *Rebecca*, *Shadow of a Doubt*, *Notorious*, *Strangers on a Train*, *Rear Window*, *Vertigo*, *North by Northwest*, *Psycho*, and *The Birds*—and what other word can be invoked but this: genius. The only question is, what level does the genius reach? For while Hitchcock at high tide is untoppable, Hitchcock stuck in the mire of a project gone wrong is not a pretty sight to behold.

Born in London to parents who dealt in foodstuffs, Alfred was raised in a Jesuit school, training that later would help clarify the philosophically rigorous schemes of his best pictures. He went to Salesian College and St. Ignatius College while still young, then attended the School of Engineering and Navigation in 1914. Giving in to his artistic side, Hitchcock enrolled at London University in 1917 to take drawing and design classes. His facility in that field helped land him a spot designing titles for Famous Players–Lasky's newly opened London division in 1920, and over the next two years he came to assume more responsibility. When Famous Players split off to become an independent British studio, Hitchcock was promoted to assistant director; he also worked on screenplays, a talent he would employ in Hollywood several years later.

His first released film was *Always Tell Your Wife* (1922), which he co-directed with Seymour Hicks, but solo credit didn't come for another three years, with *The Pleasure Garden* (1925). That was followed by *The Mountain Eagle* (1926), but it was really *The Lodger* (also 1926; released in America as *The Case of Jonathan Drew*) which both Hitchcock and students of the cinema would come to regard as his first "real" work. Adapted from a popular novel by Marie Belloc Lowndes, the suspenseful story introduces the structure of many Hitchcock films to come: a London man (Ivor Novello) is accused of being Jack the Ripper and finds it nearly impossible to prove his innocence. The tale is told with authority and became Hitchcock's first hit (although the 1944 sound version with Laird Cregar and George Sanders is even better).

After marrying his film editor and script supervisor, Alma Reveille, in 1926, Hitchcock made *Downhill*, *Easy Virtue*, and *The Ring* (all 1927), none of which proved to be particularly popular. *The Farmer's Wife* and *Champagne* (both 1928) were followed in 1929 by the obscure *Harmony Heaven* (which Hitch co-directed) and *The Manxman*, neither making much of an impact. It took a return to the genre that had brought him his first (and, thus far, only) box-office success for Hitchcock to find his métier.

Hitchcock's first talking picture, *Blackmail* (1929), was a thriller based on a 1928 play. One of the year's biggest hits in England, it became the first British film to make use of synchronized sound only after Hitchcock's completed silent version was post-dubbed and partly reshot. Set in London, the film starred Polish actress Anny Ondra as a would-be model who stabs artist Cyril Ritchard when he forcefully tries to make her pose nude. The murder investigation is headed by Ondra's fiancé, a Scotland Yard detective (John Longden), but she is being blackmailed for the killing and is afraid to confide in him. The film's most memorable sequence is a chase through the British Museum and across its roof, but Hitchcock builds the mood of encroaching menace nicely throughout. Only the awkward dubbing—the voice of British actress Joan Barry was used instead of Ondra's heavily accented one—and sometimes gratuitous sound effects interrupt the suspense. *Elstree Calling* (1930) was a musical parody of *The Taming of the Shrew* that Hitchcock co-directed with three others, while *Juno and the Paycock* (also 1930) adapted Sean O'Casey's popular play; neither has been widely available for viewing in many years.

But *Murder* (1930) provided Hitchcock with another opportunity to explore the imperatives of cinematic suspense. Shot simultaneously in a German-language version, it starred Herbert Marshall as Sir John Mernier, a gentleman knight and famed actor who turns amateur sleuth in order to clear convicted actress Diana Baring (played, fittingly enough, by Norah Baring) from the gallows. Though light in tone, its dramatic camerawork, colorful theatrical setting, and groundbreaking use of voice-over narration makes *Murder* one of Hitchcock's most accessible early works. Neither *The Skin Game* (1931) nor *Rich and Strange* (1932; aka *East of Shanghai*), an odd comedy starring Joan Barry and Henry Kendall, made much of an impact at the time of its release, but *Number Seventeen* (also 1932), with John Stuart and Anne Grey, offered a thrilling chase finale. *Waltzes from Vienna* (1933; aka *Strauss's Great Waltz*) was a rather feeble musical that (blessedly) would mark Hitchcock's last foray into that genre.

Signing with the Gaumont-British operation in 1933, Hitchcock paved the way for his ascension to the top rank of England's directors. *The Man Who Knew Too Much* (1934) was his first international success; its chills remain potent more than half a century later. Leslie Banks and Edna Best star as the Lawrences, a married couple on vacation in Switzerland with their daughter Betty (Nova Pilbeam); they inadvertently, and almost fatally, become enmeshed in a plot to assassinate a British diplomat when the conspirators kidnap Betty to ensure the Lawrences' silence until the deed is accomplished by the lethal Abbott (Peter Lorre in his first English-speaking role). In just seventy-five tension-racked minutes, culminating with the classic Albert Hall finale, Hitchcock established himself as the new master of the sinister.

He built on that foundation with *The 39 Steps* (1935), a crackling adaptation of a John Buchan thriller. Robert Donat is the archetypal Hitchcock protagonist: an innocent vacationer unwillingly drawn into an elaborate scheme hatched by a nest of spies who trade in murder. On the lam, handcuffed to the lovely Madeleine Carroll (the sort of droll touch Hitchcock would soon be recognized for), Donat is hunted by the misleadingly benign Godfrey Tearle and aided by a Scottish couple (Peggy Ashcroft and John Laurie) who briefly offer him refuge while the fugitives try to decipher the meaning of the film's mysterious title. This was the apotheosis of a genre Hitchcock virtually invented—the romantic thriller—and while he would equal it many times in the decades to come, neither he nor any other filmmaker ever really surpassed it. Only a hair less enjoyable, *The Secret Agent* (1936) offers Carroll, John Gielgud, and the nefarious (but wonderfully fey) Peter Lorre as undercover agents for British Intelligence, traipsing through the Swiss Alps on the trail of hostile spies. Using W. Somerset Maugham's *Ashenden* as its basis, the film subsumes romantic byplay in favor of its plentiful mordant humor—one explanation, perhaps, for its modest performance at the box office.

*Sabotage* (1936; aka *The Woman Alone*) was far less playful, as might be expected of an adaptation of a Joseph Conrad novel (*The Secret Agent*, which Hitchcock had just used as title). Sylvia Sidney is married to Oscar Homolka, a terrorist who gives Sidney's young brother (Desmond Tester) a bomb-laden suitcase to deliver without telling him of its contents; the lad dallies while delivering it and the suitcase explodes—an excruciatingly suspenseful sequence that may have been too intense for audiences of the day. *Young and Innocent* (1937), based on the Josephine Tey novel *The Girl Was Young*, was considerably more charming and still offered much in the way of suspense. The immortal Derrick de Marney stars as a young man who (need we say it?) has been unjustly accused of murder (the victim is a woman whose strangled corpse has washed up on shore); Nova Pilbeam is the teenaged daughter of the local police constable who decides to help the accused, and they quickly fall in love.

Even better was *The Lady Vanishes* (1938). This deft thriller finds Margaret Lockwood riding a train across Europe; she wonders at the sudden—and apparently unnoticed—disappearance of fellow traveler Dame May Whitty, but no one else on the train seems to remember her. Michael Redgrave, in his first major role, plays the only other passenger Lockwood manages to convince of the conspiracy, and Paul Lukas is appropriately menacing as a man with good reason to pretend that Whitty never existed. This was Hitchcock's biggest hit—in both England and the United States—since *The 39 Steps*, and its masterful synthesis of comedy and suspense earned him the New York Film Critics Circle Award for best direction. It also inspired that supreme arbiter of talent, David O. Selznick, to sign Hitchcock to a long-term contract with Selznick International.

Before moving to Hollywood, however, Hitchcock made one last picture in England, the mediocre gothic costumer *Jamaica Inn* (1939), from a popular novel by Daphne du Maurier. Charles Laughton plays (rather broadly) a country squire who secretly heads a band of cutthroat pirates; they contrive to wreck ships on the coastal rocks, the better to ransack them. The young, lovely, but obviously inexperienced Maureen O'Hara seems out of her depth as the heroine, while Robert Newton competes with Laughton for the lustiest chortles and loudest lip-smacking. (This was one of the rare times when Hitchcock's source material remained superior to his screen interpretation.)

The British film industry's loss was Hollywood's gain, as *Rebecca* (1940) made abundantly clear. The bestselling gothic mystery by Daphne du Maurier was a property Selznick had acquired at great cost to follow his production of *Gone with the Wind*, and the potentate bequeathed Hitchcock a galaxy of star power: Laurence Olivier as the brooding Maxim de Winter, Joan Fontaine as his trembling bride, Judith Anderson as the threatening Mrs. Danvers, and George Sanders, Gladys Cooper, Florence Bates, Leo G. Carroll, Nigel Bruce, and C. Aubrey Smith—half of Hollywood's British acting talent. The film was an enormous success both commercially and critically and won the Academy Award for best picture; cinematographer George Barnes also won an Oscar, and Fontaine, Anderson, and the screenplay by Robert E. Sherwood and Joan Harrison were also nominated, while Hitchcock earned his first Oscar nomination for best direction.

*Foreign Correspondent* (1940) was the only Hitch-

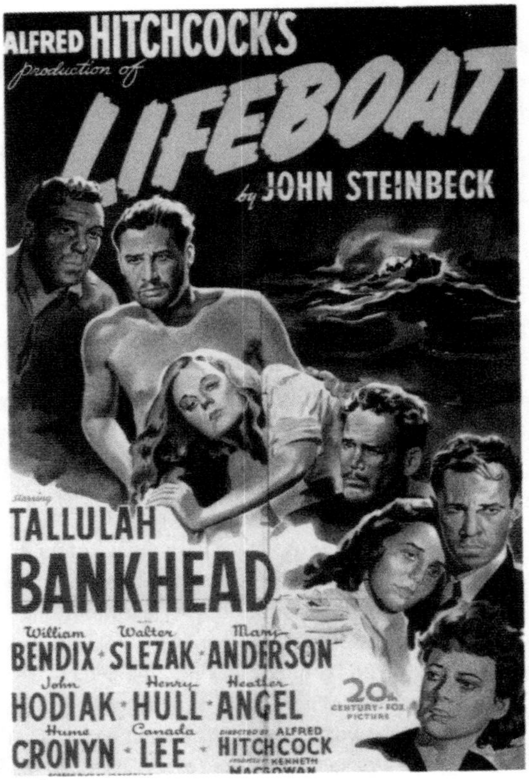

cock project in several years that didn't originate from a novel; Joan Harrison and Charles Bennett penned this peak espionage yarn, which starred Joel McCrea as a newspaper reporter who becomes involved with assassinations, Nazis, peaceniks Herbert Marshall and Laraine Day, and a kidnapped Dutch diplomat (Albert Basserman). Loaded with stunning set pieces—the umbrellas, Winchester Cathedral, and of course the windmill—the film has terrific supporting performances by the likes of George Sanders, Edmund Gwenn, and Robert Benchley. (The laconic McCrea made for a wonderfully resourceful protagonist, and it's a pity that Hitch didn't call on his services again.) Like *Rebecca*, it was nominated for an Academy Award as one of 1940's best pictures, and also earned nominations for Basserman and the screenplay, completing a remarkable one-two punch for Hitchcock.

*Mr. and Mrs. Smith* (1941) was Hitchcock's first change of pace since coming to Hollywood. For most directors this tart screwball comedy, with Carole Lombard and Robert Montgomery as the eponymous bickerers, would have seemed perfectly acceptable; for Hitch it was the equivalent of baseball legend Cy Young wasting a pitch. *Suspicion* (also 1941), from Frances Iles's thriller *Before the Fact*, seemed to promise a return to form. Joan Fontaine was provided with a meaty role as the timid wife of cad Cary Grant, who may or may not be trying to kill her. Fontaine delivered essentially the same performance here as in the previous year's *Rebecca*, when Ginger Rogers copped the best actress Oscar; this time the award went to Fontaine (although her timid-mouse shtick is enough to make anyone want to put poison in her milk). For the purposes of this Production Code–era picture, Fontaine's suspicions of Grant's murderous impulses prove to be groundless; but the film made little sense without a legitimate payoff, and Hitchcock later admitted that he hadn't played fair with his audience. Nevertheless, *Suspicion* received an Oscar nomination as best picture.

*Saboteur* (1942) was also slightly disappointing; Robert Cummings, as a patriotic factory worker framed for murder and sabotage, and Priscilla Lane, as the trusting woman who aids and abets his cross-country flight, add up to less than is needed to float the elaborate story (one Hitchcock originated) of wartime espionage and Fifth Column villainy. Still, the film has its share of exciting moments. The chilling *Shadow of a Doubt* (1943) was a far more substantial work. Hitchcock worked out the script with Thornton Wilder, basing their cold-blooded protagonist on the real-life 1920s mass murderer Earle Leonard Nelson. Joseph Cotten gives the performance of his career as the charming, utterly psychopathic Uncle Charlie, who drops in to visit his relatives in quiet Santa Rosa after murdering a woman; Teresa Wright is splendid as his devoted niece, who fights against her growing realization that her beloved uncle is the misogynistic killer of whom the entire country is terrified; Hume Cronyn is amusing as a next-door neighbor obsessed with murder; and Macdonald Carey is the detective who suspects Uncle Charlie long before Wright is ready to confront the evidence. Hitchcock was especially pleased with this picture, as well he might have been, and the story was nominated for an Academy Award.

The claustrophobic *Lifeboat* (1944) was a heavily allegorical tale about eight survivors of a ship torpedoed by a German U-boat; the passengers, each laden with his or her own symbolic baggage, were played by Tallulah Bankhead (most amusing as a

▲ *Hitch and Bergman take a break during* Notorious

mink-coated fashion journalist), John Hodiak, Henry Hull, Canada Lee, William Bendix, Heather Angel, Hume Cronyn, and, as the pompous U-boat captain whose neck they (and we) would like to wring, Walter Slezak. This *Stagecoach*-by-the-Sea alternates between expert suspense and insufferable philosophical debate; the story was written for the screen by John Steinbeck (it was scripted by Jo Swerling), who packed it with so many symbols he must have thought they were life preservers. Despite such drawbacks, Hitchcock received his second Academy Award nomination for best direction, and one went to Steinbeck as well.

Hitchcock went to England in 1944 to make two patriotic short films for the British Ministry of Information, *Bon Voyage* and *Adventure Malagache*, which were little-seen prior to their 1994 release on video. He then returned to Hollywood and Selznick to make *Spellbound* (1945). A psychological (not to say psychiatric) mystery, adapted by Ben Hecht from a Francis Beeding potboiler, it starred recent Oscar-winner Ingrid Bergman as an analyst who finds herself falling in love with the new director of the asylum, Gregory Peck, whom she begins treating after realizing that he is suffering from amnesia apparently brought on by feelings of guilt over committing murder. A clever premise, and Peck and Bergman make an attractive (if unlikely) couple, but the film's straight-faced, solemn advocacy of the healing powers of psychoanalysis (a prime concern of Selznick's) is often risible. On the other hand, the highly publicized, 2-minute Salvador Dali dream sequence—actually filmed by William Cameron Menzies after Hitchcock was told he couldn't execute the 22-minute sequence he and Dali had planned—still has a kind of goofy charm. "A manhunt story wrapped in pseudo-psychoanalysis" is how Hitchcock summarized it, which seems about right for this rather strained thriller. Amazingly, it was Oscar-nominated as best picture of 1945, and Hitchcock earned yet another nomination for best direction.

*Notorious* (1946) was a much more polished effort. Written for the screen by Ben Hecht (whose terrific screenplay was Oscar-nominated), it had something to do with espionage, a nest of Nazis in postwar Rio de Janeiro, and a hidden cache of uranium—but no mere uranium could equal the erotic energy radiated by stars Ingrid Bergman and Cary Grant. Bergman, never sexier than as the dissolute daughter of a convicted Nazi spy, is recruited by Grant and Louis Calhern, the head of a CIA-like agency, to infiltrate a Nazi stronghold in Rio by seducing and—gulp!—marrying Nazi operative Claude Rains. Grant loves her passionately but doesn't interfere when she's asked to sacrifice herself on the altar of patriotism; she loves him passionately and despairs at his callousness. It all works out in the end, but not before Rains (who deservedly received an Academy Award nomination as best supporting actor) and his viperish mother (the creepy Madame Leopoldine Konstantin) provide us with some of the most deliciously suspenseful moments in any Hitchcock movie. On the heels of that triumph, the talky, bloodless courtroom drama *The Paradine Case* (1948) seems particularly disappointing. Gregory Peck is at his stiffest as a married barrister whose ethics are compromised when he falls in love with gorgeous defendant Alida Valli, and Charles Laughton is the suspicious judge waiting to see how far Peck will go toward throwing the case.

The longueurs of *Paradine* marked the end of Hitchcock's seven-year tenure with Selznick International. Moving to Warner Bros., for whom he would make his next six pictures, he filmed *Rope* (1948), a tricked-up screen adaptation of a 1929 stage play based on the sensational 1924 Leopold-Loeb murder case; it was Hitchcock's first use of color. Jimmy Stewart stars as the vainglorious protagonist, a former professor whose dangerously amoral philosophizing has inspired John Dall and Farley Granger—well-educated, handsome, but utterly sociopathic homosexuals—to strangle a friend just to experience the thrill of the kill; they then throw a cocktail party to gloat over his corpse, which has been stuffed into a trunk standing in plain view of the guests (one, the dead boy's father). But *Rope* is not known as much for its plotting as for Hitchcock's audacious attempt to make the picture look as if it had been shot in one continuous take; in reality, he subdivided the film's eighty minutes into eight ten-minute takes, with the breaks cleverly disguised. The illusion is almost perfect, but this tour de force never manages to ignite dramatically.

*Under Capricorn* (1949) may be Hitchcock's least-remembered picture of the Forties; it was also one of his least typical, and least popular at the box office. A costume melodrama (the last he'd ever attempt) set in 1830s Australia (though shot in England), it starred Ingrid Bergman as an upper-crust Englishwoman who violates society's taboos, first by

◀ *Hitch and screenwriter Joan Harrison in 1940*

eloping with two-fisted stableboy Joseph Cotten, then by falling in love with cousin Michael Wilding. It lost a million dollars at the box office. *Stage Fright* (1950), also filmed in England, was a move back into the right genre, but otherwise was not much better. Marlene Dietrich plays an actress who may have murdered her husband; Richard Todd is her young lover, who is accused of the crime; and Jane Wyman is the plain-Jane drama student who takes a job with Dietrich in the hopes of clearing Todd, who used to be her boyfriend. The theatrical setting and Dietrich (who sings the Piaf standard "La Vie en Rose") were the best things about the picture, but the mystery itself was shockingly flat.

Hitchcock emerged from this four-year slump in impressive fashion with *Strangers on a Train* (1951), an engrossing, endlessly rewarding thriller based on a novel by Patricia Highsmith; it was adapted by Raymond Chandler (whom Hitchcock canned) and Czenzi Ormonde, an associate of Ben Hecht. The nominal star is Farley Granger, cast as unhappily married tennis pro Guy Haines, who has the bad fortune one day to be riding a train with charming psychopath Bruno Antony (Robert Walker, in the performance of his career). Bruno suggests that he and Guy "exchange" murders, so that neither can be traced to the crime. Guy humors Bruno and laughs off the proposal, little dreaming that Bruno will demonstrate his good faith by strangling Guy's wife (leaving him free to take up with mistress Ruth Roman), then demanding that Guy complete the bargain by killing Bruno's father. Stricken with guilt, Guy must try to outwit his homicidal Doppelgänger while wrestling with his sense of culpability. The homoerotic underpinnings of the story, and the fact that Bruno is ten times more appealing than the bland Guy, gives *Strangers* a nasty bite that gets under the skin.

*Stranger*'s mordant humor was sadly lacking in the Catholic guiltfest *I Confess* (1953), in which Montgomery Clift plays a priest in Quebec (where the picture was largely filmed) who is being blackmailed by a murderer whose sacrosanct confession shields him from exposure. The situation was intriguing (it originated in a 1902 play that Hitchcock somehow came across), and Clift was an expressive actor who should have been perfect as a Hitchcock protagonist—but here he seems constipated with anguish, and the overt use of guilt and expatiation is far less fun than when Hitchcock employs them as covert themes. *Dial M for Murder* (1954) was a much more commercial enterprise; originally shot in 3-D toward the end of that short-lived craze, it's a handsome if calculated adaptation of Frederick Knott's play that maintained the boundaries of the London flat presented on stage. Grace Kelly, at the peak of her beauty, stars as a straying rich wife whose jealous husband (Ray Milland) first tries to have her killed, then attempts to frame her for stabbing her would-be assassin in self-defense. Robert Cummings, late of *Saboteur*, is an odd choice to play the elegant Kelly's lover, but Milland and Kelly are well cast, and John Williams is droll as a Scotland Yard inspector.

Moving to Paramount, Hitchcock entered his third phase of sustained brilliance—one with a maturity of theme and mastery of technique that make even the great periods of 1934–38 and 1940–46 almost pale in comparison. Indisputably one of his greatest works, *Rear Window* (1954) was based on a good story by suspense master Cornell Woolrich, but Hitchcock and screenwriter John Michael Hayes enriched its genre conventions with one of the decade's sexiest screen romances, carried on by wheelchair-bound press photographer (and amateur voyeur) Jimmy Stewart and slinky, spunky girlfriend Grace Kelly; the subtext about invading the privacy of others cleverly implicates us moviegoers as a band of easily seduced voyeurs. (Hitchcock was a wicked, wicked man!) Thelma Ritter and Raymond Burr provide fine support, but it was Hitchcock who kept us staring at the screen as Stewart stared out his window at a world where the most heinous crimes are only a courtyard away. Both Hitchcock and Hayes were Oscar-nominated for their efforts. (Kelly won the best actress Academy Award, but not for either of her two Hitchcock efforts that year—rather, it was her dowdy turn in *The Country Girl* that rather inexplicably put an Oscar on her mantel.)

Kelly looked exquisite again in the bonbon *To Catch a Thief* (1955), a breathless romantic thriller that expended its oxygen on the romance and neglected the thrills—no one's in even the remotest danger of being killed (or even getting a hangnail), a plot element usually essential to Hitchcock's best pictures. Kelly is paired now with the debonair Cary Grant, who may or may not be the jewel thief that everyone's so het up about. Their fencing, as Kelly tries like hell to seduce the coy Grant, is mildly sexy, but Hitchcock flogs the scenic French Riviera setting as if he's moonlighting for the Cannes Chamber of Commerce, and the sophisticated John Michael Hayes screenplay (adapting a David Dodge potboiler) feels soft in the middle and around the edges. *Thief* never explodes like the fireworks to which Grant and Kelly make out in one famous scene, but it earned an Oscar for cinematographer Robert Burks (who had also been nominated for *Rear Window*). (Hitch would come to regret this production, however, as it was on location that Kelly met Monaco's Prince Rainier, the man who would take her away from the movies, and him, forever.) If *Thief* was lightweight, *The Trouble with Harry* (also 1955) was downright irreverent. A black comedy (written by John Michael Hayes) about a Vermont town's problems with a corpse that just won't stay buried, it had the virtues of amusing performances by Edmund Gwenn and (in her screen debut) Shirley MacLaine, plus that lovely New England fall foliage. But audiences didn't get it—at least, they didn't *go* to it.

It was back to serious business with *The Man Who Knew Too Much* (1956), Hitchcock's big-budget, VistaVision, Technicolor remake of his humble 1934 thriller. Rewritten by John Michael Hayes and Angus McPhail to incorporate an additional forty-five minutes of activity, little of it germane to the already seaworthy plot, it starred Jimmy Stewart and Doris Day as the parents (now visiting Morocco—the better to toss in several minutes of travelogue footage) whose son, Hank, is kidnapped when Stewart accidentally acquires information about some potentially lethal skulduggery. Oddly, this "opening up" of the tidy original version seems neither more nor less exciting, but the presence of Stewart and the score by

▲ *Giving Kim Novak that* Vertigo *feeling*

Bernard Herrmann are certainly assets. (As for the unspeakable "Que Sera, Sera," which won the Oscar for best song—let us be grateful it was Hitchcock's only pop-music interlude.)

The bleak *The Wrong Man* (also 1956) was based on the Kafkaesque but true (and nationally publicized) story of a debt-ridden Queens musician who was arrested in 1953 for robbing an insurance company and put through the tortures of hell trying to prove his innocence. Henry Fonda, more dour even than usual, plays the unfortunate Manny Balestrero, and Vera Miles is excellent as his wife, Rose, who cracks under the strain of his prolonged incarceration and trial. Shot in many of the New York City locales where the case unfolded, the film has verisimilitude to burn; what its overly respectful, quasi-documentary approach lacks is the sardonic wit that suffuses Hitchcock's best sagas of crime, guilt, and punishment.

Considered by many to be his masterpiece, *Vertigo* (1958) was a challenging, sometimes obscure, and, in the end, painful exploration of identity, fantasy, and compulsion. Its source was a French novel, but Hitchcock embroidered its complex plot with additional layers of symbolism, some of which only the director himself could decode. Jimmy Stewart (for the third time in five years) starred, now as a former San Francisco policeman who has taken an early retirement because of his fear of heights; a rich friend asks him to shadow his wife (Kim Novak), who's been prone to taking mysterious leaves of absence. But Stewart's detecting soon metamorphoses into a kind of voyeurism, as his observation of Novak turns first into love, then obsession, and finally agony. Although Novak isn't entirely adequate for her demanding part, in every other respect *Vertigo* is a near-perfect (and quite brave) dramatization of the themes closest to Hitchcock. Small wonder, then, that the film seemed too disturbing for the day's audiences and that it was almost entirely overlooked in the Academy Award nominations—even Bernard Herrmann's chilling score! Today *Vertigo* has come to be recognized as Hitchcock's most personal and powerful work, one that cannot be fully appreciated on a single (or even a tenth) viewing.

Hitchcock retreated from the naked trauma of *Vertigo* to make the expert, vastly entertaining *North by Northwest* (1959), a romantic thriller written for the screen by Ernest Lehman, with a nod to *The 39 Steps*. Urbane Cary Grant is back (for the first time since 1946) as the consummate Hitchcock protagonist, New York advertising executive George Thornhill, who somehow is mistaken for one George Kaplan, a government agent who has become the target of a very persistent group of international spies (headed by the equally urbane James Mason). But Thornhill/Kaplan proves to be quite resourceful himself, even with the serious disadvantage of never remotely knowing what is going on. Eva Marie Saint is acceptable (but no more) in the Bergman/Kelly role of the sensuous, worldly, but not entirely trustworthy woman who lends a hand while striving much harder than should be necessary to bed down the hero, and Martin Landau plays one of the killers with panache. Lehman was the lone member of the creative team to get an Oscar nomination; Bernard Herrmann, who contributed another wonderful score, was again overlooked.

The commercial success of *North by Northwest* emboldened Hitchcock, who now made his most shocking movie. The greatness of *Psycho* has long since become gospel, but when it was released in 1960 critics weren't sure what to make of it—moviegoers, on the other hand, took to it like Dobermans to raw meat. For the first time Hitchcock focused a movie on the killer, rather than tempering his seductive menace by placing a sympathetic protagonist in jeopardy (as was the case with Joseph Cotten and Teresa Wright in *Shadow of a Doubt*, and Robert Walker and Farley Granger in *Strangers on a Train*). In the beginning it seems that luscious Janet Leigh is our point of identification, but Hitchcock resolves her peril halfway through the picture by killing her off, leaving us alone with the lunacy of Anthony Perkins's Norman Bates. (Bates was inspired by Wisconsin mass murderer Ed Gein, who ate and otherwise recycled his victims during the 1950s; horror writer Robert Bloch based a novel on the case, from which Joseph Stefano developed his screenplay.)

The long-term effects of *Psycho* on both the grammar of the cinema and the implicit trust between an audience and a director—which the perverse Hitchcock now had forevermore compromised—were enormous. (To this day, it's a rare moviegoer who can enter the shower stall of a motel room without experiencing a frisson of terror.) So were the picture's box-office receipts: the controversy helped it become the year's second-highest grosser. (Or, as *Variety* so eloquently put it, "*Psycho* Socko!") Hitchcock received his final Academy Award nomination for best direction—losing to Billy Wilder for the now-quaint *The Apartment*—while John L. Russell's creepy black-and-white cinematography and Leigh (a sympathy vote for her excruciating demise?) were also nominated; Bernard Herrmann's classic score was, of course, ignored. The combination of the popular *Psycho* and his visibility as the host of the weekly television series *Alfred Hitchcock Presents* (1955–62) and *The Alfred Hitchcock Hour* (1962–65) gradually but inexorably converted Hitchcock into America's—perhaps even the world's—best-known director: his purring inflections and rotund silhouette made him a welcome visitor in any living room (for those who desired a longer look at him than his split-second film cameos provided).

By the time Hitchcock made *The Birds* (1963) for Universal (which would release his last six films), the media had been trained to respond to his every signal. There were cover stories in national magazines and countless features extolling Hitch's latest blond discovery, Tippi Hedren. The story itself—millions of birds settle in and finally attack the residents of the small California coastal community of Bodega Bay—was based on a novelette by Daphne du Maurier; screenwriter Evan Hunter expanded it considerably to incorporate all sorts of Freudian byplay among social butterfly Hedren, lawyer Rod Taylor (her romantic interest), schoolteacher Suzanne Pleshette (his former romantic interest), and icy Jessica Tandy, Taylor's possessive mother. To the extent that it works, *The Birds* has a sort of indelible dream logic. All too often, however, the stiff acting (and cardboard dialogue) undercut the picture's mood of supernatural menace. Although it has its detractors, *The Birds* is generally considered the last Hitchcock film for which one can at least put forth a case for greatness.

▲ *Hitch and Tippi Hedren pose during the making of* The Birds

When Grace Kelly wouldn't come out of retirement to take the part, Tippi Hedren (with whom Hitchcock apparently had become dangerously obsessed, it has since been reported) starred again in *Marnie* (1964) as a compulsive liar suffering from kleptomania because (we soon learn) she was loved neither wisely nor well during her childhood. Her handsome employer (Sean Connery) is attracted to her and wants to help her discover the roots of her emotional difficulties—including fear of sex, thunderstorms, and the color red—and so marries her, little realizing just how severely she has been traumatized. Fans of auteurism had a field day extracting the key themes and symbols underlying the rather perfunctory plot, and there's no question that Hitchcock (and screenwriter Jay Presson Allen) micromanaged every one of these 120 minutes with surgical precision; that said, the picture isn't much fun to watch, and only slightly more rewarding to ponder.

By comparison, the ponderous *Torn Curtain* (1966) made *Marnie*'s discursive approach appear a model of brevity. Paul Newman and Julie Andrews—two of the world's biggest screen stars, and as compatible as pickles and ice cream—struggle mightily to breathe life into this Cold War clunker. (Hitch had managed to ignore the first twenty years of the Cold War, so why bother with it at this juncture?) Brian Moore wrote the screenplay, which allowed Paul Newman—the handsomest nuclear scientist ever to defect to East Germany—to engage in the most brutal death struggle yet filmed; alas, there were another 115 minutes to account for. The equally inert *Topaz* (1969) was adapted from Leon Uris's bestseller by Samuel Taylor; a globe-trotting thriller about Reds having infiltrated the upper levels of the French government—yes, Cold War intrigue again—*Topaz* must be given the dubious distinction of having the least interesting cast of any Hitchcock picture over the past thirty-five years: when John Forsythe, Frederick Stafford, John Vernon, and Dany Robin are the top four names on the marquee, ushers are probably safe from being crushed by a stampede of ticket buyers.

It appeared that Hitchcock's powers had waned to the point of no return, but return they did in *Frenzy* (1972). It was the first movie he had made in England in more than twenty years, and marked a welcome, long-overdue return to the black humor and mordant suspense of his pre-Hollywood efforts of the Thirties. Jon Finch plays the hallowed role of the man wrongly accused of murder—in this case, because his ex-wife has been strangled in a particularly nasty way, as Hitchcock is pleased to share with us in all its glorious detail. Barry Foster is the sadistic "sex killer" who revels in his freedom while Finch is being hunted by Scotland Yard, and Alec McCowen is marvelously eccentric as the chief inspector. *Frenzy* is Hitchcock shorn of the big budgets, miscast stars, and fawning media attention that had combined to make him lazy and smug, and the result is his best picture in a decade. (Had Selznick not "discovered" him, Hitchcock probably would have spent a half century making films very much like this one.)

Having proven that, even fifty years and fifty films on, he still had his fastball, Hitch made the benign *Family Plot* (1976) as his swan song. Scripted by Ernest Lehman in the comic vein of *The Trouble with Harry, Plot* starred William Devane, Karen Black, Bruce Dern, and Barbara Harris as a colorful, rather endearing collection of psychic frauds, scalawags, and jewel thieves. And yet there are several moments of well-earned suspense, reminding us of the many, many thrills Hitchcock had delivered during the course of his incomparable career. It was a reminder made with a nudge and a wink—Hitchcock having his final joke. He was knighted in 1980, but it seemed a bit late to be calling this devilish genius Sir Alfred.

## ● JOHN HUSTON (1906–1987)

His bloodlines probably gave him a head start—his father was the great stage and screen actor Walter Huston—but the rest of John Huston's considerable accomplishments as a director, screenwriter, and actor were earned entirely through merit. Many of the thirty-seven films he directed are of the two-fisted variety (albeit with an existential spin), though at least half of them don't come off. Indeed, his own flamboyant life, in which Huston starred as international ladykiller, gadabout, and rebel, makes for an even more engaging tale than most of his movies. But Huston's body of work between 1941 and 1987 (the year *The Dead* was posthumously released) is as full of golden nuggets as the Sierra Madres, making him one of the most interesting (if least consistent) directors of the past sixty years.



Born in Nevada, Missouri (a town his grandfather claimed to have won in a poker game), Huston began performing on stage at the age of three and continued to perform around the country, traveling with his parents. He was a frail youth who had to spend a year in a sanatorium at the age of twelve so a diseased kidney and his enlarged heart could receive treatment. Whatever the doctors in California did, it was the right prescription, because a year later Huston was boxing, a profession he took seriously enough to win California's Amateur Lightweight Boxing Championship (his distinctive broken nose was part of his purse). In 1924 Huston moved to New York to become an actor. When nothing special materialized after a couple years of Off-Broadway and stock work, he tossed in the towel and headed for Mexico, where he earned a commission in the Mexican cavalry.

Returning to New York in 1929, Huston took a job as a reporter at the *New York Graphic* while moonlighting as a short-story writer (he had several published in *The American Mercury*). But the *Graphic* fired him, and Huston followed his father, Walter, to Hollywood, where he found work acting bit parts in a few of William Wyler's first talkies (two of which starred Walter) and writing dialogue for Wyler's *A House Divided* (1932). He moved to London in 1932 to write screenplays for Gaumont, the British studio, but apparently he was never put on salary and nearly starved. Huston moved to Paris to study painting and sold sketches to tourists for meal money, but was fortunate to be given the fare back to the States by (legend has it) a hooker who felt sorry for him. It wouldn't be the last time Huston's ability to charm a lady would bail him out of a tight spot.

Huston made another stab at acting by playing the lead in the Chicago WPA production of *Abe Lincoln in Illinois* in 1933, which led only to further scuffling. He finally made his way back to Hollywood, where in 1937 Warner Bros. signed him to a screenwriting contract. This time he stuck. Huston collaborated on the scripts for Wyler's Oscar-nominated *Jezebel*, Anatole Litvak's silly *The Amazing Dr. Clitterhouse*, and William Dieterle's ponderous *Juárez* before taking a leave of absence to direct his father in *A Passage to Bali* on Broadway in 1939. He then returned to Warners, where he co-wrote three exceptional pictures: *Dr. Ehrlich's Magic Bullet* for Dieterle, *High Sierra* for Raoul Walsh, and *Sergeant York* for Howard Hawks, the last of which earned Huston his first Academy Award nomination in 1941, for best original screenplay.

As it happened, Huston was nominated in another screenwriting category that same year for his adaptation of Dashiell Hammett's *The Maltese Falcon* (1941), which would also mark his maiden voyage as a screen director—perhaps the most impressive debut in Hollywood during the 1940s. *The Maltese Falcon* had already been filmed (indifferently) by Warners in 1931 and 1936, but Huston's proto–film noir had the advantage of Huston as the screenwriter and Humphrey Bogart as the amoral private eye Sam Spade, Mary Astor as the immoral Brigid O'Shaughnessey, and Sydney Greenstreet and Peter Lorre as those lovable cutthroats Casper Gutman and Joel Cairo. It was a genre picture, true, but the Academy recognized its merits by making it one of 1941's ten nominees for best picture (the inimitable Greenstreet was also nominated).

*In This Our Life* (1942) was a respectable (though unprofitable) pass at a "woman's film"; Bette Davis was at her villainous best as Olivia de Havilland's grasping sister, who manages to steal brother-in-law George Brent from Olivia before crashing and burning herself. That sort of high-toned soaper wasn't Huston's cup of rum, and presumably he was pleased to be handed *Across the Pacific* (1942), an espionage yarn set on the high seas. Redolent of *Falcon*, it has Bogart posing as a disgraced soldier traveling on a Japanese ship headed through the Panama Canal, the better to blow it up. The purpose of this subterfuge is to undermine Japanese agent Sydney Greenstreet and save the canal (originally the locale was Pearl Harbor!); Mary Astor comes along for the ride as a fashion designer on vacation. The film was jingoistic hooey, and Huston was relieved of completing it when he was drafted into the Special Services' Signal Corps, leaving a bewildered Vincent Sherman to pick up the pieces.

For the Army's Pictorial Service, Lieutenant Huston wrote, directed, and narrated legendary World War II documentaries like *Report from the Aleutians* (1943), *The Battle of San Pietro* (1945), and *Let There Be Light* (1945), the last a shattering record of the casualties in an Allied field hospital; its power was such that the Army suppressed it for several years. Huston was discharged in 1945 with the rank of major and awarded the Legion of Merit for making his films under perilous battle conditions. Back in the States, he dabbled in script doctoring, working on such good films as Robert Siodmak's *The Killers* and Orson Welles's *The Stranger*. Before directing a movie of his own, Huston elected to stage Jean-Paul Sartre's *No Exit* on Broadway, that hotbed of existential drama, in 1946. The New York Drama Critics gave the production an award, but it quickly closed, and Huston began preparations for his first Hollywood movie in five years.

*The Treasure of the Sierra Madre* (1948), adapted by Huston from a rather obscure novel by the mysterious writer B. Traven and shot on location in Mexico, starred Humphrey Bogart in the decidedly unheroic role of paranoid prospector Fred C. Dobbs. But as good as Bogart was in depicting Dobbs's descent into madness, acting honors had to be accorded to Walter Huston's Howard, the grizzled, sagacious prospector who tries in vain to keep greed from consuming his little band. (It was the first time that Huston had cast his father in a major role, although he'd appeared in unbilled cameos in both *Falcon* and *In This Our Life*.) *Treasure* would become one of Huston's greatest critical triumphs and remains one of the best films of its time, but its grim ending and Bogart's daring casting against type contributed to its box-office failure. Still, Huston's work was vindicated when he won dual Academy Awards for best direction and best screenplay, and the New York Film Critics Circle citation for best direction; it must have been doubly gratifying that Walter Huston was awarded the Oscar as best supporting actor. (Bogart and the film were also nominated.)

Before he knew those awards were forthcoming, Huston joined with William Wyler and screenwriter Philip Dunne in establishing the Committee for the First Amendment in response to the House Un-American Activities Committee's initial wave of investigations into the Hollywood community's past or present Communist affiliations. (Representatives Bogart and Lauren Bacall made a highly visible trip to Washington, D.C., in 1947 to publicize the committee, a junket that elicited such bad press that Bogart had to issue a press release early in 1948 distancing himself from the protest.)

Then it was back to the business of filmmaking. Bogart and Bacall starred in *Key Largo* (1948), an exciting adaptation of the Maxwell Anderson play. Deported gangster Edward G. Robinson (based on the recently deported Lucky Luciano) arrives at a hotel in the Florida Keys where Bogart, Bacall, and Lionel Barrymore are gathered, and all hell—and a hell of a storm—breaks loose. The script by Huston and Richard Brooks helps downplay the story's pretentious elements, but it's really Robinson and Claire Trevor, his abused mistress, who keep the melodrama from sinking into the Everglades. (Trevor won the Oscar for best supporting actress of 1948.) *We Were Strangers* (1949) was an atmospheric account of Cuban revolutionaries' attempt to overthrow the government; it starred Jennifer Jones, John Garfield, and Gilbert Roland. Scripted by Huston and Peter Viertel, the picture had its share of exciting moments but never really jelled. (Viertel comments in his 1992 memoir that Huston seemed more interested in fishing with Ernest Hemingway than in shooting the picture.)

W. R. Burnett had provided the source novels for such screen classics as Mervyn LeRoy's *Little Caesar* and Raoul Walsh's *High Sierra*, and now Huston acquired his hard-boiled crime story *The Asphalt Jungle* (1950). Sam Jaffe, Sterling Hayden, and James Whitmore are gang members plotting the multimillion-dollar robbery of a jewelry exchange, with Louis Calhern as the crooked lawyer who intends to fence the gems. A thrilling exercise in fatalism, *Jungle* is one of Huston's most expertly structured pictures; one can understand why he begged to be excused from *Quo Vadis* in order to make it, and why his and Ben Maddow's screenplay was nominated for an Academy Award.

Huston was less fortunate with *The Red Badge of Courage* (1951), however. An evocative staging of the classic Civil War story by Stephen Crane (co-scripted by Huston), it brilliantly cast World War II hero Audie Murphy as the young Union soldier who deserts his company, then shamefacedly returns to fight alongside them in another frightful battle. But MGM execs felt that the antiwar message was too blatant (with HUAC at its peak of influence and the Korean War raging), so they cut the picture down to 69 minutes and released it (on the lower half of double bills!) without Huston's input. What's left remains, despite the butchering (described in Lillian Ross's book *Picture*), at least a minor masterpiece.

By the time *Courage* was in the theaters, Huston was already in Africa shooting *The African Queen* (1951), his rip-roaring version of C. S. Forester's popular novel, which he adapted with James Agee. (John Collier and Peter Viertel also had a hand in the screenplay.) As everyone on the planet knows by now, it starred Humphrey Bogart as Charlie Allnut, world-class souse, and Katharine Hepburn as Rosie Sayer, the impossibly prim spinster who convinces Charlie to take her on his rattletrap steamer down the Congo River to civilization. (Books by Hepburn and Viertel among others have described the film's location miseries—and Huston's eccentric behavior on and off the set—quite fully, leading one to marvel that Huston got anything at all onscreen.) This splendid romance/comedy/adventure remains one of the most popular Hollywood movies of all time, and Huston was again nominated for dual Academy Awards—best direction and best screenplay. But it was Bogart who walked off the podium with his long-awaited Oscar.

Shot on location in France, *Moulin Rouge* (1952) was Huston's gorgeously mounted but overly sentimental biography of Toulouse-Lautrec (José Ferrer), the crippled artist who became the toast of Montmartre for his lively artworks. This was the first (but not the last) film in which Huston was able to fully indulge his exquisite painterly eye (not to mention his 1933 memories of Paris), and that eye becomes the film's saving grace. *Moulin Rouge* won Oscars for its costume design and art direction, and Ferrer, Huston, and the picture were also nominated (rather generously) for Academy Awards. After being nominated for best direction Oscars four out of the past five years, Huston would have to wait thirty-three years before the Academy nominated him again, as he entered the extended hit-or-miss phase of his career.

Now living in Ireland with his fourth wife, Huston traveled to Italy to film a delightful spoof of *The Maltese Falcon*. Written with Truman Capote and co-financed by Humphrey Bogart's Santana production company, *Beat the Devil* (1954) boasted the redoubtable cast of Bogart, Jennifer Jones, Robert Morley, Gina Lollobrigida, and Peter Lorre—a motley crew of adventurers, frauds, and con artists trying to locate a uranium mine while enduring all manner of comic disasters. Capote later admitted that they were making it up as they went along, an irreverent approach that plays well in the postmodern Nineties. But at the 1954 box office *Devil* was an utter failure, precipitating a split between Bogart ("It's a mess" was his review of the picture) and Huston after many years of fruitful collaboration.

Even Bogart wouldn't have helped Huston's epic version of *Moby Dick* (1956), although someone other than the stolid Gregory Peck might have been better cast as the fiery, obsessed Ahab. Still, Huston and Ray Bradbury captured much of the poetry of Melville in their script, and the sea storm and whaling sequences are impressively staged. Huston spent almost two years (and $5 million) on the production, and was rewarded by being cited for best direction by the New York Film Critics Circle. *Heaven Knows, Mr. Allison* (1957) was a much quieter affair, starring Robert Mitchum and Deborah Kerr at their respective best as a Marine and a nun stranded on a Pacific isle during World War II. Kerr received an Oscar nomi-

◀ *Bogart and Huston parted ways after making* Beat the Devil *in 1953*

nation as best actress, and Huston's and John Lee Mahin's screenplay was also nominated.

Huston began working on David O. Selznick's remake of *A Farewell to Arms*, but departed in favor of Charles Vidor after taking the measure of leads Rock Hudson and Jennifer Jones. But *The Barbarian and the Geisha* (1958), with John Wayne laughably miscast as America's ambassador to Japan in the late 1800s, was hardly an improvement. It was back to Africa for *The Roots of Heaven* (1958), a long-winded adaptation of a novel by Romain Gary in which Errol Flynn and Trevor Howard discuss the morality of shooting elephants while Juliette Greco, Fox boss Darryl Zanuck's pretty young mistress, poses by the campfire and pouts. But *The Unforgiven* (1960) was a return to form, with an atypically fiery Audrey Hepburn (in her only Western) as a woman raised by Indians, and Burt Lancaster and Audie Murphy as the Texas settlers who try to reclaim her.

The troubled history of *The Misfits* (1961) is another oft-told bit of Hollywood lore. Arthur Miller adapted his short story about cowboys (three portrayed by Clark Gable, Montgomery Clift, and Eli Wallach) who hunt wild horses and sell them to be slaughtered for dog food. Marilyn Monroe (Miller's then-wife, in her last screen appearance before her mysterious death) plays the divorced former stripper who joins the wranglers and argues with them about the immorality of their "profession." Monroe does not look well here, and reportedly drove Huston to distraction with a major case of JudyGarlanditis—showing up on the set late, blowing her lines, munching downers like M & Ms to offset her chronic depression. If audiences were bemused by the juxtaposition of MM's Method acting and Arthur Miller's heavy-handed allegorizing, at least Gable came across well as the gallant Gay Langland. Rather sensibly, he lets himself be convinced by Monroe's pleading to release the wild stallion he has just broken so that he and she can drive off into the sunset. (In real life, Gable died eight days before filming wrapped, the victim of a heart attack; it was widely assumed that the rugged stunts he had insisted on doing himself were the cause.)

The somber *Freud* (1962), with Huston himself narrating the tale of the founder of psychoanalysis (Montgomery Clift, who would also die shortly), seemed like a model of restraint after the misbegotten *Misfits*. It was also good to see Huston enjoying himself with the playful *The List of Adrian Messenger* (1963), as George C. Scott tries to deduce whether Frank Sinatra, Burt Lancaster, Robert Mitchum, Kirk Douglas, or Tony Curtis—all unrecognizable in period disguise—committed murder. (And all the more fun for the picture having been shot in Huston's Ireland.) But Huston stole his own thunder that year with his first screen role since 1930, appearing as Cardinal Glennon in Otto Preminger's *The Cardinal*, a

performance that earned him an Oscar nomination as best supporting actor and started him on a whole new parallel career.

*The Night of the Iguana* (1964), shot in the Mexican hamlet of Puerto Vallarta, offered the all-star assemblage of Richard Burton, Ava Gardner, Deborah Kerr, and Sue (*Lolita*) Lyon in a typical Tennessee Williams stew of psychoses, thwarted desires, and carnal confusion. It is heavy going, but occasionally rouses itself to something resembling life. Then Huston decided to make *The Bible* (1966). Filming the first twenty-two books of Genesis must have seemed like a good idea to someone somewhere, but after nearly three hours of Old Testament melodramatics with the likes of Richard Harris, Michael Parks, and George C. Scott, even the most pious viewer becomes stupefied. (Although, in fairness to director Huston, he does elicit a good performance from himself as Noah.)

Carson McCullers's 1941 novella *Reflections in a Golden Eye* was perhaps too kinky even for the cinema of 1967, but its very perversity has made it more interesting with the passage of time. Marlon Brando gives one of his classic oddball performances as the repressed homosexual Major Penderton, whose wife, Southern belle Elizabeth Taylor, understandably prefers to dally with virile Brian Keith until she is provoked into horsewhipping Brando. The film was originally released with a literally golden hue, a visual scheme intended as a play on the book's evocative title, hardly enough to forestall a frigid reception at the box office.

At least the 1967 *Casino Royale* wasn't reviled, but Huston's share of the directing—one-fifth, to be precise—could neither help nor harm this bloated circus of a movie. (Its place in history is secure, though, as it was the first time Huston and Woody Allen acted together onscreen.) Huston's descent continued with *A Walk with Love and Death* (1969), a forgettable medieval drama notable today for providing Huston's daughter Anjelica with her first lead role in a movie. *Sinful Davey* (1969), with John Hurt as a nineteenth-century highwayman and Anjelica Huston in a supporting role, was marginally more interesting, but the Cold War "thriller" *The Kremlin Letter* (1970) was a big-budget flop despite a cast that included old pros Orson Welles, Max von Sydow, George Sanders, and Bibi Andersson.

It seemed as though Huston might never make another decent (let alone popular) film, but his adaptation of Leonard Gardner's novel about small-time boxers, *Fat City*, turned into one of 1972's most affecting pictures. Stacy Keach plays a washed-up boxer in Stockton, California, a perfect purgatory of a town for losers like himself. (Apparently Brando wanted to play the part, but Huston was overruled by the suits at Columbia.) Jeff Bridges is terrific as a young loser waiting to happen, Susan Tyrrell (Oscar-nominated) is scary as the drunk with whom Keach is living, and pro boxer Curtis Cokes gives a touching performance. But it wasn't difficult for one-time lightweight John Huston to tease out the story's essence, downbeat as it surely was.

*The Life and Times of Judge Roy Bean* (1973) was Huston's entry in the newly popular genre of revisionist Westerns. Paul Newman—bearded, drunk, and crude—clearly enjoys his stint as the notorious hanging judge, whom John Milius's irreverent screenplay allows to meet all manner of peculiar folk, including Stacy Keach, Tab Hunter, Anthony Perkins, Huston himself, and (as Lillie Langtry) Ava Gardner. But *The Mackintosh Man* (1973), with Newman pitted against spy James Mason, was just more Cold War hugger-mugger, despite a screenplay by future thrill-meister Walter Hill. Huston again managed to set a new acting standard for himself in Roman Polanski's noir classic *Chinatown* (1974) as the loathsome, evil Noah Cross, a marvelously hammy turn that should have earned him (at the least) an Academy Award nomination.

*The Man Who Would Be King* (1975) was a project that Huston had been thinking about for decades. In the Fifties, he wanted Bogart and Gable to play Kipling's intrepid explorers; in the Sixties, it was to be Richard Burton and Peter O'Toole. Now Huston secured two of the Seventies' best, Sean Connery and Michael Caine, and traveled with them to Morocco, which would stand in for the story's Afghanistan locale. *King* was not particularly successful at the box office (it was the season of *Jaws*) and received respectful but restrained reviews, yet it now seems clear that the picture is one of the best of Huston's long career, a morality tale of unusual resonance, with marvelous acting by Connery as the swaggering Danny, who is taken for a god and comes to believe it himself, and by Caine, as his slightly dim sidekick Peachy. (Caine's wife, Shakira Caine, also has a key role, while Christopher Plummer is memorable as Kipling in the film's framing sequences.)

Four years passed before Huston was able to bring another favorite project, Flannery O'Connor's black comedy *Wise Blood* (1979), to the screen. Brad Dourif is well cast as the fanatical Southern evangelist who starts the Church of Truth Without Jesus Christ; gothic flavor is supplied by Harry Dean Stanton, Ned Beatty, and Huston in supporting roles. Why Huston then proceeded to make the low-budget Hitchcock ripoff *Phobia* (1981) is anyone's guess, but it probably represents the nadir of his work. Not to be confused with the Joseph Conrad story, *Victory* (1981) stars Sylvester Stallone and Michael Caine as POWs who pass up the chance to escape from their Nazi camp because they're in the midst of a soccer match. Huston completed his trifecta of tripe with his big-budget adaptation of the Broadway hit *Annie* (1982); Albert Finney makes a passable Daddy Warbucks and Aileen Quinn is as cute as necessary to play Annie. This was the first musical Huston ever directed, and mercifully, it would also be his last.

Those three efforts made it appear that the aging director was just showing up to cash his paychecks, but he somehow marshaled his forces for his last three pictures. *Under the Volcano* (1984), filmed on location in Mexico, was a valiant attempt to capture Malcolm Lowry's difficult 1947 novel, which had defied every attempt by Hollywood thus far to adapt its vivid but formless stream-of-consciousness narrative. Huston hired a young screenwriter named Guy Gallo to tackle the project, and called on Albert Finney to play the alcoholic, suicidal British consul, whose ex-wife (Jacqueline Bisset) and brother (Anthony Andrews) try their best to get him back to the States before he kills himself from drink. The result is less than wholly successful—perhaps the book truly *is* unfilmable—although Finney was nominated for an Academy Award for his gut-wrenching performance.

Far more satisfying was *Prizzi's Honor* (1985), a wonderfully stylized version of Richard Condon's loony novel (adapted by Condon and Janet Roach)

▲ *Gregory Peck, as Ahab, confers with Huston*

▲ *With the great stars of* Prizzi's Honor

about the Mafia. Jack Nicholson is at his very best as Brooklyn hit man Charlie Partanna, whose passionate romance with L.A. hit woman Irene Walker (Kathleen Turner) hits a few bumps along the way. Anjelica Huston is delicious as Charlie's possessive mistress Maerose Prizzi, and William Hickey gives a hilarious performance as her grandfather, the aged Don Corrado Prizzi. Although too darkly cynical for some tastes, *Prizzi's* was one of Huston's most warmly received films, earning him an Academy Award nomination for best direction (his first since *Moulin Rouge*); the picture, the screenplay, and Nicholson, Hickey, and Anjelica Huston were all nominated as well (and Turner should have been).

The eighty-year-old Huston celebrated that rather unexpected triumph by joining with daughter Anjelica and oldest son, Tony (whose screenplay would be Oscar-nominated), to make what would be his final movie. *The Dead* (1987) was based on James Joyce's novelette about a Dublin family who give a dinner party for the Feast of the Epiphany one night in 1904; Donal McCann and Anjelica Huston play husband and wife. Poignant, stately, and expertly acted, *The Dead* was just completed when the ailing John Huston passed away. There may have been yet a better work to serve as the epitaph for this prodigiously gifted man, lover of Ireland (and master of blarney) that he was, but *The Dead* will suffice.

## ● NORMAN JEWISON (1926- )

A former actor and writer for the BBC in London and for Canadian television, Toronto-born Norman Jewison came to the United States in 1958 to work for CBS-TV. His first assignment was to revive *Your Hit Parade*, which he did successfully. He was then put in charge of a number of musical specials that starred the likes of Judy Garland and Harry Belafonte. Jewison's first film was *Forty Pounds of Trouble* (1963), an amusing if unremarkable comedy, starring Tony Curtis as a casino boss whose life is complicated when he takes in a little girl. *The Thrill of It All* (1963) had Doris Day as a TV career woman who overlooks hubby James Garner; Carl Reiner's screenplay and performance lift this out of the ordinary just enough. Day was back in *Send Me No Flowers* (1964) and, even better, paired with Rock Hudson, here as Day's hypochondriac husband, who begs pal Tony Randall to find her a new mate when he passes on.

*The Art of Love* (1965) was a misfire, a comedy with Dick Van Dyke, Carl Reiner, and James Garner that played like a rejected skit from *Your Show of Shows*. But *The Cincinnati Kid* (also 1965) was a big step up, a suspenseful film about high-stakes poker that featured one of the great casts of the Sixties—Steve McQueen, Edward G. Robinson, Tuesday Weld, Joan Blondell, Ann-Margret, and Rip Torn. Begun by Sam Peckinpah, who was fired, the picture tried to do for poker what *The Hustler* did for pool, but came up short; Jewison's unfamiliarity with the demands of the action genre shows through in spots. He began a long association with United Artists in 1966 when he made *The Russians Are Coming! The Russians Are Coming!*, a frenetic, overly long but popular Cold War comedy (based on a Nathaniel Benchley novel) with Alan Arkin, Carl Reiner, and Jonathan Winters.

*In the Heat of the Night* (1967) was more serious business, a detective story set in the South with a racial spin. That helped it (rather unexpectedly) defeat the favored *Bonnie and Clyde* and *The Graduate* for the Academy Award as best picture; it also reaped Oscars in the categories of best actor (Rod Steiger), screenplay adaptation, and editing (by Hal Ashby), and Jewison was nominated for best direction. He squandered a bit of his momentum with *The Thomas Crown Affair* (1968), a synthetic, show-offy caper that pitted independently wealthy bank robber Steve McQueen against insurance investigator Faye Dunaway, a romance that is only intermittently believable. Far worse was the little-seen *Gaily, Gaily* (1969), a re-creation of Ben Hecht's days as a cub reporter in Chicago that was played for laughs—but there weren't any.

Jewison collected himself and made a popular version of Joseph Stein's Broadway hit *Fiddler on the Roof* (1971), with Topol as Tevye and Yiddish Theater star Molly Picon heading the boisterous cast. Originally three hours long and shown with an intermission, the film is shot through a glass darkly and has a surprisingly mediocre score. Still, the picture, Jewison, and Topol were all nominated for Academy Awards. Now in a biblical mode, Jewison went to Israel to film the Broadway (and recording) phenomenon *Jesus Christ, Superstar* (1973). It was a nervy career move, and his florid production took its share of lumps from the critics. But in retrospect, the picture—a hit—is not the embarrassment it at first seemed. *Rollerball* (1975) was a cautionary tale (based on William Harrison's *Esquire* story) about a near-future in which a handful of global conglomerates sponsor a lethal sport—the only legal expression of violence in that society. James Caan has one of his best roles as the corrupt star player who redeems himself, and John Houseman plays one of the omnipotent team owners. Too brutal for some

tastes, the film was probably just a decade ahead of its time.

*F.I.S.T.* (1978) was less defensible. An overinflated account of the rise of unionized labor, starring an overmatched Sylvester Stallone, it was one of the year's biggest bombs. Next was *. . . And Justice for All* (1979), which also went out of control; it had an alarmingly over-the-top performance by Al Pacino that somehow received an Oscar nomination (as did the hyperventilating screenplay by Barry Levinson and Valerie Curtin). Nor was *Best Friends* (1982) a reversal of form, with another problematic screenplay by Levinson and Curtin digging a hole for stars Burt Reynolds and Goldie Hawn. But Jewison got back on track with the acclaimed *A Soldier's Story* (1984), a stagy but still powerful drama about racism and murder at a black military post in 1944 Louisiana, with Howard E. Rollins, Adolph Caesar, and Denzel Washington. Adapted by Charles Fuller from his Pulitzer Prize–winning play, it was nominated for an Academy Award as best picture.

The religious mystery *Agnes of God* (1985) also originated on the stage, adapted by playwright John Pielmeyer. Again Jewison does a creditable job of opening up the production for the screen, eliciting Oscar-nominated performances from Anne Bancroft and Meg Tilly. But it took the sparkling romantic comedy *Moonstruck* (1987) to bring Jewison his first major box-office success of the Eighties. Nicolas Cage and Cher make a hugely appealing (if unlikely) couple, and she won the best actress Academy Award for her performance; Olympia Dukakis as her mother also won, as did John Patrick Shanley's terrific screenplay. Both Jewison and the film were also nominated. *In Country* (1989) was a puzzle, though, a miscalculated adaptation of the Bobbie Ann Mason novel starring an earnest but miscast Bruce Willis.

*Other People's Money* (1991) was adapted from an Off-Broadway play, with an enthusiastic but tiring performance by Danny DeVito as a Wall Street raider who wants to plunder an old New England company run by Gregory Peck and his daughter, lawyer Penelope Ann Miller. Fun, yes, but nothing a hundred other directors might not have manufactured. *Only You* (1994) was also disappointing. A romantic fable starring Robert Downey and Marisa Tomei, it lifts elements from such earlier screen lovefests as *Sleepless in Seattle* and *An Affair to Remember* without bringing anything new to the table, leaving Jewison batting 0 for the '90s.

## ● GARSON KANIN (1912- )

Better known as a writer than for his directing—and justly so—Kanin nonetheless made a handful of clever comedies (romantic and otherwise) for RKO in the late Thirties and early Forties, and they hold up quite nicely today. Born in Rochester, New York, he was forced to drop out of school when the Crash of '29 impoverished his family. He played the clarinet and sax with jazz combos and performed in burlesque as a comedian. That was enough to spur him to study at the American Academy of Dramatic Arts, and after graduating in 1933, he began acting on Broadway. By 1937 Kanin was directing stage productions, and a year after that he was ensconced at RKO, where his first project was *A Man to Remember* (1938), a tasteful "B" written by newcomer Dalton Trumbo; it was shot in two weeks for just over $100,000. Anne Shirley starred, and Kanin was able to demonstrate that he could make a little look like a lot.

*Next Time I Marry* (1938) was a screwball programmer that showed Lucille Ball to good advantage. She's an heiress who marries government construction grunt James Ellison only to qualify for a $20 million inheritance; after a cross-country chase, he convinces Ball that she actually loves him. *The Great Man Votes* (1939) was an acerbic satire on pols and pollsters, starring John Barrymore as a former professor whose obvious familiarity with the bottle is about to cost him his two wised-up kids. But just as they're about to be taken away by busybody social workers, the indigent Barrymore learns that his is the swing vote that can carry his district, and thus the mayoral election. The once-magnificent Barrymore reveled in his obvious ruination, and was well supported by William Demarest and Donald MacBride.

*Bachelor Mother* (1939) was a great popular success, as well it might have been with an "A" cast that included Ginger Rogers, David Niven, and Charles Coburn. Ginger plays a department store clerk who is mistakenly identified as the mother of an abandoned baby, leading to endless complications and a proposal from boss David Niven. One of RKO's most profitable pictures of the year, *Mother* helped launch Rogers on her solo career and earned an Oscar nomination for Felix Jackson's original story. *My Favorite Wife* (1940) was even better—in fact, it's a legitimate screwball classic—but an asterisk must go next to Kanin's name here, since the film was produced and co-written by Leo McCarey, who was severely injured in an auto accident before passing the torch to Kanin, and clearly bears his mark. Nonetheless, it's a choice reteaming of Cary Grant and Irene Dunne, who had scored a success in McCarey's *The Awful Truth* in 1937 and are equally hilarious here. Now their riotous marital mishaps involve Gail Patrick, who can't get her honeymoon with Grant consummated, and Randolph Scott, the Other Man that Dunne shared a desert isle with for seven years.

Kanin wasn't able to exercise his flair for slapstick with his next project, the high-grade soap opera *They Knew What They Wanted* (1940), from the Pulitzer Prize–winning play by Sidney Howard. Carole Lombard is a California waitress wooed by Italian grape grower Charles Laughton, who sent her a picture of his handsome hired man (William Gargan) instead of himself to encourage her to marry him. When she arrives at his vineyard she is understandably shocked—and still interested in Gargan. The adulterous characters had to be sanitized for the censors, and the film was one of the studio's biggest flops of 1940—but then, *Wife* had been its second-biggest hit. Kanin returned to more familiar territory with *Tom, Dick and Harry* (1941), a delightful comic bauble starring Ginger Rogers as a small-town telephone operator who's been proposed to by three suitors and fantasizes about life with each of them. Should she choose goofy mechanic Burgess Meredith, car salesman George Murphy, or millionaire Alan Marshal? Paul Jarrico's amusing screenplay was Oscar-nominated, and recent Academy Award–winner Rogers is more appealing here than in any of her other post-Astaire films.

Kanin now went into the service, little suspecting that his career as a Hollywood director was virtually over. He was attached to the Office of Emergency Management, where he produced and directed documentary shorts like *Night Stripes, Fellow Americans,* and *Ring of Steel.* His most visible project was *The True Glory* (1945), a feature-length documentary about D-day and Operation Overlord that he co-directed with Carol Reed; it won an Oscar. After the war Kanin chose to return to Broadway rather than Hollywood, and struck gold on his first venture, the classic comedy *Born Yesterday,* which he both wrote and directed in 1946. Over the next few years he wrote a number of screenplays for George Cukor films, including *A Double Life* (1947), *Adam's Rib* (1950), *Pat and Mike* (1952), *The Marrying Kind* (1952), and *It Should Happen to You* (1954), most in collaboration with his wife, Ruth Gordon; the first three were nominated for Academy Awards.

Kanin became fed up with the compromises that writing for the movies engendered, and stayed away from Hollywood for the next fifteen years (although he cooked up the story on which Frank Tashlin's *The Girl Can't Help It* was based). He returned in 1969 to direct a pair of screenplays he had written: *Where It's At,* a comedy set in Las Vegas with David Janssen, and *Some Kind of a Nut,* a truly awful "hip" (not!) farce with Dick Van Dyke and Angie Dickinson. Kanin also wrote the 1971 bestseller *Tracy and Hepburn,* which Hepburn reportedly did not appreciate.

Garson's brother, Michael Kanin, was also a screenwriter, and shared an Oscar with Ring Lardner, Jr., for their screenplay for *Woman of the Year*—an idea concocted by Garson that he reluctantly surrendered to Michael when he was drafted.

## ● PHIL KARLSON (1908–1986)

One of the best "B" directors of the 1950s, Phil Karlson probably had the stuff to move up to the next class but never was given the chance. Even so, a number of his films have aged better than many big-budget hits from the same period.

Born in Chicago as Philip Karlstein, he studied law at Loyola-Marymount in California before taking a job at Universal as a propman. Over the next fourteen years he slowly worked his way from assistant director to film editor to director of short subjects, until he was at last given his chance to direct his first feature in 1944, *A Wave, a Wac and a Marine*. At Monogram he continued to make programmers in a variety of genres: comedies like *G.I. Honeymoon* (1945); musicals like *Swing Parade of 1946*; series entries like the Bowery Boys' *Live Wires* (1946), *Behind the Mask* (1946) with the Shadow, and the Charlie Chan opus *Dark Alibi* (also 1946), and Westerns (*Adventures in Silverado* and *Thunderhoof*, both 1948); *Ladies of the Chorus* (1949) is of historical interest for providing Marilyn Monroe with her first major role, while *Down Memory Lane* (1949) was a compilation of classic comedy shorts by W. C. Fields, Bing Crosby, and Ben Turpin, framed by new scenes of Steve Allen acting as master of ceremonies.

Now at Columbia, Karlson made *Lorna Doone* (1951), an adequate costumer starring Richard Greene and Barbara Hale. But his first "signature" picture was *Scandal Sheet* (1952), a good crime yarn (written by Sam Fuller) about newspaper editor Broderick Crawford's attempt to cover up the murder of his ex-wife. *The Brigand* (1952) was dull swordplay involving the incompetent Anthony Dexter, but *Kansas City Confidential* (1952) was another effective noir; John Payne is well cast as an ex-con trying to clear himself of a bogus armed-robbery charge. Payne also starred in the violent *99 River Street* (1953), this time as an ex-prizefighter trying to clear himself of a trumped-up murder rap, with Peggie Castle as his dead ex and Evelyn Keyes the woman who believes in him. *They Rode West* (1954) was a Western with a pro-Indian theme, while *Hell's Island* (1955) sent old friend John Payne searching for an elusive jewel.

*Tight Spot* (1955) brought Karlson a "name" cast for the first time, with Ginger Rogers as a former moll who testifies against gangster Lorne Greene for attorney Edward G. Robinson. Even better was *Five Against the House* (1955), a terrific heist picture (based on a story by Jack Finney) in which Kim Novak, Guy Madison, and Brian Keith try to knock off a Reno nightclub. Karlson completed his finest year with *The Phenix City Story*, a two-fisted exposé of corruption in an Alabama town that was shot on location while the trial of the indicted officials was still being conducted—in fact Karlson discovered evidence while filming that helped convict them! Richard Kiley played the crusading lawyer who risks his life to see justice done, and John McIntire was the murder victim.

*The Brothers Rico* (1957), based on a Simenon novel, was another superlative crime film, with Richard Conte attempting to break up a national syndicate of hoods, while *Gunman's Walk* (1958) was a CinemaScope Western starring Van Heflin as a rancher having problems relating to sons James Darren and Tab Hunter. The fine *Hell to Eternity* (1960) was based on the story of World War II hero Guy Gabaldon; it was also Karlson's first war picture, oddly enough. *Key Witness* (1960) featured Jeffrey Hunter as a family man whose wife (Pat Crowley) has been intimidated by gangleader Dennis Hopper to keep her from testifying against him, while *The Secret Ways* (1961) starred Richard Widmark as an American mercenary hired to smuggle a famous scholar out of Communist-controlled Hungary.

*The Young Doctors* (1961) was an atypically commercial property for Karlson, a medical soap opera based on a popular novel by Arthur Hailey, with Fredric March, Ben Gazzara, Dick Clark, and (in his screen debut) George Segal as the docs who suffer sundry conflicts with work and women. Next came *The Scarface Mob* (1962), which was actually just the theatrically released version of Karlson's 1959 pilot for the long-running television series *The Untouchables*, starring Robert Stack as the tight-lipped Eliot Ness and Neville Brand an expansive Al Capone. But even recycled TV crime was preferable to the bland horrors of *Kid Galahad* (1962), an Elvis Presley vehicle and remake of Michael Curtiz's far superior 1937 original with Wayne Morris and Edward G. Robinson—although admittedly that one didn't have songs like "King (of the Whole Wide World)."

*Rampage* (1963) had the sole merit of Robert Mitchum as a big-game hunter, but *The Silencers* (1966) was the first—and best—of the Matt Helm secret-agent spoofs, based on the paperback series by Donald Hamilton. Dean Martin was at his cocky, smarmy best as the resourceful Helm, and it didn't hurt to have Stella Stevens on hand with one of her trademark goofy bombshell turns. *A Time for Killing* (1967), with Glenn Ford and Inger Stevens, was a mediocre Civil War adventure, while *The Wrecking Crew* (1969) was the abysmal final entry in the Helm series; now Dino is just going through the motions, uninspired even by the presence of Sharon Tate, Elke Sommer, and Tina Louise. (Check his pulse!) *Hornet's Nest* (1970) offered an original twist on the standard World War II actioner, with Rock Hudson enlisting a horde of kiddies to help him blow up a Nazi-held dam in Italy.

*Ben* (1972) was a poor sequel to the surprise hit *Willard*—but then, how much can one do with a boy and his rat? Karlson had been treading water for some time, but *Walking Tall* (1973) became one of the biggest (and most violent) sleepers in Hollywood history. Brilliantly promoted, it was based on the highly illegal but thrilling crusade of real-life sheriff Buford Pusser to clean up his corrupt Tennessee town using any means necessary—*The Phenix City Story* cross-bred with *Batman*. That crowd-pleasing formula made Karlson, who had a piece of the picture, a wealthy man. He went to the well once more with *Framed* (1975), in which Joe Don Baker again revenges himself on the crooked cops who sent him to prison on a trumped-up charge, then retired.

## ● PHILIP KAUFMAN (1936– )

In over a quarter century behind the camera, San Francisco–based Philip Kaufman has brought forth a mere ten films: two date from the 1960s, four from the Seventies, two from the Eighties, and two (thus far) in the Nineties. Any less prolific and he would be Terence Malick. And yet his films, based as they often are on challenging literary properties, seem to create interest and even controversy when they finally do appear, indicating that, if nothing else, he is able to make an impact out of proportion to his productivity.

Born in Chicago and educated at the University of Chicago, he completed Harvard Law School before moving to Europe to teach. He made his first film at the age of twenty-nine, the independent production *Goldstein* (1965), which he also co-produced, co-wrote, and co-directed with Benjamin Manaster. Based on a Martin Buber story, it was a satirical allegory about the prophet Elijah (Lou Gilbert) rising out of Lake Michigan only to encounter an assortment of Chicago weirdos, including obsessed sculptor Thomas Erhart and author Nelson Algren. That same year he produced, directed, and wrote *Fearless Frank*, another quasi-religious, wholly satirical fable that languished unreleased until American International picked it up in 1967. In his first screen appearance, Jon Voight plays a kid who comes to Chicago, is murdered, and then rises from the grave reincarnated as both a superhero and a super-villain.

Kaufman finally made a serious picture in 1972 with *The Great Northfield, Minnesota Raid*, which he also scripted. (He is a talented, even brilliant, screenwriter.) Robert Duvall and Cliff Robertson headed the fine cast, but Kaufman's strained demythologizing of this now-familiar bit of American outlaw history comes off second-best to Walter Hill's superior 1980 film about the James and Younger gang, *The Long Riders*. Filmed on location in northern Canada, *The White Dawn* (1974) was an overlong but beautifully photographed (by Michael Chapman) tale about whalers Warren Oates, Lou Gossett, and Timothy Bottoms stranded in the Arctic at the turn of the century, battling polar bears and taking advantage of the very Eskimos who saved them. Kaufman wrote, and started to direct, *The Outlaw Josey Wales* (1976), but was fired by star Clint Eastwood, who took over.

Kaufman's 1978 remake of *Invasion of the Body Snatchers* was an audacious and nearly successful attempt to improve on Don Siegel's 1956 classic scarefest. Kaufman expertly creates an atmosphere of mounting dread, and his cast (Donald Sutherland, Brooke Adams, Leonard Nimoy, Jeff Goldblum) has the advantage over Siegel's assemblage—but his version's additional thirty-five minutes prove to be too much for the story, which dissipates its well-earned tension before the third climax erupts. (Kaufman demonstrated his class by casting Siegel in a bit role.)

*The Wanderers* (1979) illustrated Kaufman's mastery of a quite different genre. Based on Richard Price's fine novel about a benign gang of Italian teenagers in the Bronx of 1963, the film uses the romance between Ken Wahl and Karen Allen as an emotional focal point for a wide-ranging story that somehow combines gang rumbles, sexual rites of passage, dysfunctional families, bowling, and the Marines into a moving portrait of an era. Pint-sized Linda Manz and the grotesquely huge Erland van Lidth steal the picture as a touchingly mismatched couple, while Wahl and Allen reach their respective peaks here.

After writing *Raiders of the Lost Ark* with George Lucas and Steven Spielberg, Kaufman made one of the most ambitious pictures of the Eighties, a brilliant adaptation of Tom Wolfe's impressionistic history of America's space program, *The Right Stuff*.

THE RIGHT STUFF
How the future began.

Kaufman wrote the caustic screenplay himself, facing the daunting task of compressing Wolfe's discursive epic into a cohesive narrative. He doesn't fully succeed, but the 192 minutes he puts forth are often brilliantly imagined, full of harrowing heroism, choice comic interludes, and sometimes haunting imagery. Sam Shepard makes an appropriately charismatic Chuck Yeager, while Barbara Hershey as his brave wife and Dennis Quaid, Scott Glenn, and Fred Ward as three of the original seven astronauts all register memorable performances. The picture was nominated for an Academy Award, but failed commercially—a genuine pity.

Five years would pass before *The Unbearable Lightness of Being* (1988) came to the screen. Adapted from Milan Kundera's acclaimed novel about the Soviet invasion of Czechoslovakia in 1968 (among other things), it was another boldly selected property for Kaufman, who co-wrote the intelligent, Oscar-nominated screenplay—although the near-three-hour length and arty Sven Nykvist compositions (also Oscar-nominated) take their toll after a while. Still, the performances by leads Daniel Day-Lewis, Lena Olin, and Juliette Binoche are beyond reproach. (Kaufman should also be awarded points for degree of difficulty!)

*Henry & June* (1990), written by Kaufman with his wife, Rose, was a similarly rarified effort, a recreation of the affairs among and between Henry Miller, Anaïs Nin, and June Miller in 1931 Paris that provides as much sex as any mainstream American film ever dared; unfortunately, precious little of it comes across as erotic. Fred Ward makes an adequate Henry, who is trying to write *Tropic of Cancer* in between trysts, while Uma Thurman is a convincingly predatory June and Maria de Medeiros a rather passive Anaïs. This quintessential art-house film created a bit of a stir when it was released, leading to the creation of the NC-17 rating for films too explicit to be given an "R" and too tasteful to be branded with an "X."

Kaufman moved from one extreme to the other by adapting Michael Crichton's ultra-commercial thriller *Rising Sun* (1993). Crichton and Kaufman began as collaborators on the screenplay, but Crichton angrily withdrew early on, apparently as a result of Kaufman's softening of the book's anti-Japan posturing. Crichton may have been on to something: the film loses the mild head of steam it builds up early on and never recovers. Sean Connery suffices as the elegant police captain wise (so very wise!) in the ways of the Orient, but Wesley Snipes as his hot-headed novice partner has been given a nearly unplayable part. While much was made of Kaufman's decision to change the villain of the piece, it's doubtful that this would have become markedly better merely by retaining Crichton's original plotting. Nevertheless, Kaufman managed to leach the suspense out of what had been a wonderfully tense pulp murder mystery.

## ● ELIA KAZAN (1909- )

One of the most fêted directors of the Forties and Fifties, Elia "Gadge" Kazan (né Kazanjoglov) was born in Constantinople and came to New York City at the age of four, when his parents emigrated. He was educated at Williams College, then attended Yale's famed drama department. In 1932 he joined the Group Theatre, acting in *Waiting for Lefty* and *Golden Boy* (both by Clifford Odets), and by 1935 he was directing Group productions. His first film credit was as director of *The People of Cumberland* (1937), a documentary about Tennessee miners, and he also directed a documentary about food rationing, *It's Up to You* (1941). His own acting was sporadic, but in addition to his stage roles, two of his film performances have been preserved: *City for Conquest* (1940) and *Blues in the Night* (1941), both directed by Anatole Litvak for Warner Bros.

In the early Forties Kazan made the move to Broadway, where he directed a number of classic productions, including *The Skin of Our Teeth* and *One Touch of Venus* (1943). Hollywood took note, and in 1945 Fox hired Kazan to direct his first commercial feature, *A Tree Grows in Brooklyn*, from the bestseller by Betty Smith. It was a high-profile project with which to debut, but Kazan acquitted himself in impressive fashion, eliciting Oscar-winning performances from James Dunn and Peggy Ann Garner. His follow-up, *Sea of Grass* (1947), left Spencer Tracy and Katharine Hepburn at sea in a yarn about ranching; it was probably their least successful showcase. But *Boomerang!* (1947) was a taut thriller about the arrest of an innocent man for murder; based on a true incident, it blends a theater-trained cast (Lee J. Cobb, Karl Malden, Arthur Kennedy) with Fox's implacable star Dana Andrews to good effect. Even more popular was *Gentleman's Agreement* (also 1947), Kazan's adaptation of the Laura Z. Hobson bestseller that (rather surprisingly) won him an Oscar for best direction. Fox modestly advertised it as "The Most Acclaimed Motion Picture in the History of the Screen," and it was considered a scathing assault on anti-Semitism in its day. But the film now feels tepid and conventional, with Gregory Peck posing as the world's most unconvincing Jew while rooting out injustice among the country-club set. (Ironically, a more biting treatment of anti-Semitism, *Crossfire*, appeared that same year; its director, Edward Dmytryk, lost to Kazan in the Academy Awards voting.)

Returning to Broadway, as he would do periodically throughout his career, Kazan enjoyed some of his greatest successes with *All My Sons*, *A Streetcar Named Desire* (both 1947), and *Death of a Salesman* (1949). It was during this period that he co-founded the Actors' Studio; its first star pupil was Marlon Brando. But Fox wanted a movie, so Kazan heeded their call to make another "important" film about social issues. *Pinky* (1949) was well intended, but it never recovered from its conceit of Jeanne Crain as a black woman passing for white. Still, Kazan assembled a superb cast per usual, including Ethel Waters and Nina Mae McKinney. *Panic in the Streets* (1950) was a top-notch noir about a manhunt for a criminal who doesn't know he's carrying a highly infectious plague virus. Shot on location in New Orleans, *Panic* offers great performances by Richard Widmark (a good guy this time), Jack Palance, and Zero Mostel (as a hood!).

Then came the film of *A Streetcar Named Desire* (1951). It had been a smash on Broadway, and Kazan managed to smuggle most of its cast by the powers at Warner Bros. and into the film. But he did have to concede on the exchange of Vivien Leigh for Jessica Tandy. The film was a sensation—no one had ever before seen a screen actor produce what Brando was putting onto celluloid—and Kazan was nominated again for the best direction Academy Award.

He didn't win, but most of his cast did—with the exception of Brando. Kazan and Brando teamed up the following year for *Viva Zapata!* (1952), a lively rise-to-power tale with a script by John Steinbeck and an Oscar-winning turn by Anthony Quinn. Far less accomplished was the fact-based *Man on a Tightrope* (1953), a pedestrian account of a circus troupe's escape from Communist-ruled Czechoslovakia; it starred Fredric March and Gloria Grahame.

Kazan now returned to Broadway to mount well-received productions of *Camino Real* and *Tea and Sympathy*. In 1952 he had been summoned before HUAC and named names, having the vested interest of clearing himself of his own Communist affiliation during the Thirties. Thus many critics have looked askance at *On the Waterfront* (1954) in light of that episode, particularly when the film builds its case for Brando's Terry Malloy to become a stool pigeon on ethical grounds. Fair enough; but the movie is a masterpiece anyway, one of the best of the decade in spite of its disappointing politics. Brando and Kazan both took home Oscars this time, as did six other contributors.

Kazan had always excelled with his actors, finding and nurturing talent with a success that few other directors could hope to equal. For his 1955 CinemaScope version of John Steinbeck's *East of Eden*, Kazan struck oil yet again in the person of James Dean, an actor with a short list of Broadway roles, minuscule film parts, and television credits that were no better than those of a thousand other hopefuls. Cast over the protests of the brothers Warner, Dean ignited the screen as no one had done since—well, since Kazan's *last* discovery. Again Kazan was nominated by the Academy for best direction, losing to Delbert Mann and *Marty*. (Which film would *you* rather watch tonight?) Then it was back to Broadway for *Cat on a Hot Tin Roof*, yet another triumph.

▲ *Rehearsing* A Streetcar Named Desire *in 1951*

It was beginning to appear as though Kazan could do no wrong—at least not behind the camera. *Baby Doll* (1956) was condemned by the Legion of Decency, which meant only that Kazan had succeeded in shepherding most of Tennessee Williams's story to the screen intact. Just as effective, although considerably less erotic, was *A Face in the Crowd* (1957), a cautionary tale from a Budd Schulberg script about the power of the mass media. It marked the film debuts of Andy Griffith and Lee Remick—just as Kazan's previous films had introduced Rip Torn, Eli Wallach, James Dean, Eva Marie Saint, Martin Balsam, Fred Gwynne, and Pat Hingle to film audiences.

Kazan spent the next three years on Broadway, then returned to Hollywood in 1960 to make *Wild River*. Set in Tennessee during the Depression, the film was a strong vehicle for Montgomery Clift and Lee Remick. (A pity that Kazan couldn't have worked with Clift ten years earlier.) But *Splendor in the Grass* (1961) was a hit on an entirely different scale, with Warren Beatty (in his movie debut) and Natalie Wood heating up the screen in a tale of repressed sexuality during the Twenties; it attracted a whole new generation to Kazan's work. William Inge won an Oscar for his original screenplay, although today the film seems guilty of hyperventilation.

*America, America* (1963) was a departure for Kazan, an intensely personal film based on the experiences of his Greek immigrant uncle. With its cast of unknowns and its 168-minute running time, the film had little chance of reaching a wide audience, but it undeniably has power and was a source of great satisfaction to Kazan, earning him his fifth and final Academy Award nomination. Kazan followed it by returning to Broadway to direct Arthur Miller's *After the Fall*, then spent the next few years writing his first novel. As a book, *The Arrangement* was basically high-gloss trash from the Jackie Susann school; as a film (1969), it is garbage of epic proportions, squandering its big-name cast (Kirk Douglas, Faye Dunaway, Deborah Kerr, Hume Cronyn) with a profligacy that might not have been so shocking had the Kazan name not been attached. Just as awful, though on a smaller scale, was *The Visitors* (1972), in which James Woods (in his film debut) invades the home of an old pal from 'Nam.

But Kazan pulled himself together for his swan song, the 1976 adaptation of F. Scott Fitzgerald's unfinished novel *The Last Tycoon*. Offering a fine Harold Pinter screenplay and a cast for the ages (Robert De Niro, Robert Mitchum, Jack Nicholson, Tony Curtis, Jeanne Moreau, Ray Milland), *Tycoon* was a restrained, even languid evocation of Hollywood in the Thirties. Its centerpiece was De Niro's portrayal of an Irving Thalbergesque producer who is quietly dying. It was fitting that Kazan would retire from the screen with an actors' showcase. He spent the next several years writing his autobiography, *A Life*, which was published in 1988. At 846 pages, that book may have been the only instance of Kazan letting himself run on longer than the story warranted. Then again, his remarkable accomplishments deserve at least one thick book.

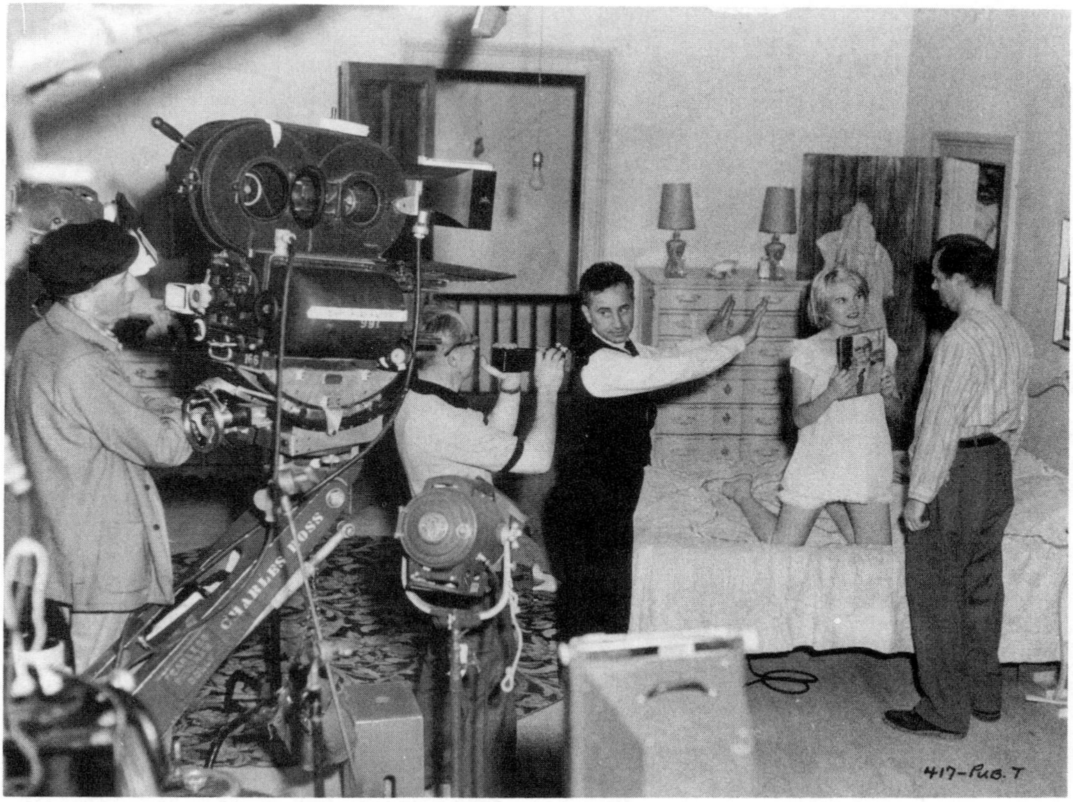


▲ *Carroll Baker and Karl Malden take direction during* Baby Doll

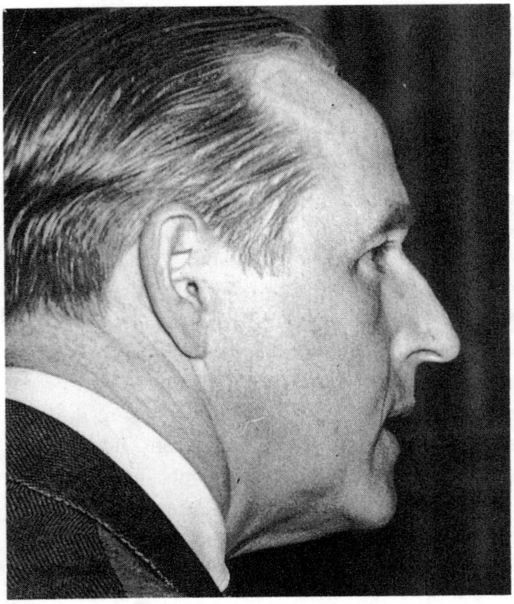

## ● WILLIAM KEIGHLEY (1893-1986)

A former actor and stage director, the Philadelphia-born Keighley was nearly forty before he directed his first film. He joined Warner Bros. in the early Thirties and remained there for the majority of the thirty-seven films he helmed. And while Keighley never ascended to the top rank (David Thompson dismisses him as "never more than one of Warners' second-string directors"), his filmography—which includes many key pictures with the studio's top stars—suggests that Warners had one *hell* of a second string.

Keighley's first Hollywood assignments were to assist William Dieterle and Michael Curtiz on some of their 1932 releases. *The Match King*, co-directed with Howard Bretherton that same year, was his first feature; an effective fable for the Depression, it offered Warren William as real-life empire builder Ivar Kreuger. *Ladies They Talk About* (1933) was another collaboration with Bretherton that featured Barbara Stanwyck, still in the temptress stage of her career, bound for San Quentin after robbing a bank. In 1934 Keighley went into high gear, making six features of varying quality. The first was *Easy to Love*, a marital comedy that starred Genevieve Tobin, who four years earlier had become Keighley's wife. *Journal of a Crime* was an inane Ruth Chatterton melodrama, while *Dr. Monica* offered long-suffering Kay Francis as a surgeon who can't retain the affections of philandering husband Warren William. *Kansas City Princess*, with Joan Blondell and Glenda Farrell as gold diggers, and *Big Hearted Herbert*, with Guy Kibbee, were comedies, while *Babbitt*, with Kibbee again in the role of Sinclair Lewis's amoral businessman, was a humdrum version of the popular novel. None of these was particularly good, but Keighley didn't yet have access to Warners' better talent.

Five films were on Keighley's slate for 1935. *The Right to Live* was another potboiler, but *"G" Men* was far better, a snappy vehicle for James Cagney (Warners' highest-paid star), with Jimmy now on the right side of the law. This box-office smash was followed by the less impressive *Special Agent*, which tried to fob off George Brent as a crimebuster in the Cagney mode. *Stars over Broadway*, a musical with Pat O'Brien, and *Mary Jane's Pa* were fodder that was here one week and gone the next. *The Singing Kid* (1936) was an Al Jolson musical with a hackneyed story line, but Jolson performs some nice Arlen-Harburg songs and Cab Calloway struts his stuff. Keighley returned to *"G" Men* territory with the excellent *Bullets or Ballots* (1936), in which undercover detective Edward G. Robinson is pitted against crime boss Barton MacLane and flunky Humphrey Bogart.

Then came the prestigious Marc Connelly musical *The Green Pastures* (1936), a black-cast retelling of the Bible, with Rex Ingram appropriately impressive as "de Lawd God Jehovah," and inspirational music by the Hall Johnson Choir. Keighley co-directed the picture with Connelly, and—unconscious racism aside—the film does possess both charm and power. But *God's Country and the Woman* (1937) was just lumberjack-in-love malarkey with George Brent. *The Prince and the Pauper* was a fine 1937 adaptation of Mark Twain; Errol Flynn's heroics and Claude Rains's villainy were heightened by Erich Korngold's terrific score.

After making *Varsity Show* (1937), a Dick Powell musical memorable only for its Busby Berkeley–orchestrated "The Finale," Keighley teamed again with Flynn, Rains, and Korngold on *The Adventures of Robin Hood*, one of 1938's biggest hits. Keighley is rarely conceded his co-credit for the film, because he was replaced halfway through the production by Michael Curtiz. The question today is whether half of what we see onscreen—and what's there is indisputably classic—is still Keighley's work, or whether Curtiz came in and started from scratch. Considering

what Keighley accomplished with Flynn in *Prince*, perhaps some of the hosannas should be his.

*Valley of the Giants* was a minor piece about deforesting, *Secrets of an Actress* a lame vehicle for the fading Kay Francis, and *Brother Rat* (all 1938) a lively version of the stage success, with Eddie Albert, Wayne Morris, and Ronald Reagan as three military cadets, one of whom is secretly married. It was back to the crime genre with *Each Dawn I Die* (1939), a good prison pic starring James Cagney, George Raft, and clouds of tear gas. (Ephraim Katz notes that Joseph Stalin told F.D.R. that this was his favorite film. Well, why not?) Two of Keighley's 1940 productions also starred Cagney: the overbaked World War I comedy-drama *The Fighting 69th* and the rollicking *Torrid Zone*, in which Cagney trades quips with Pat O'Brien and saucy singer Ann Sheridan on a plantation somewhere in Central America. Banana oil, to be sure, but of a very high grade.

*No Time for Comedy* (1940) was a change of pace for Keighley, an adaptation of the S. N. Behrman play about a pretentious playwright that happily teamed Jimmy Stewart and Rosalind Russell. *Four Mothers* (1941) was yet another soapy sequel to Curtiz's *Four Daughters*, with the Lane sisters and Claude Rains, while *The Bride Came C.O.D.* (1941) employed wishful thinking in pairing Bette Davis and James Cagney in a screwball farce. Keighley's record with comedy had been spotty, but Warners now entrusted him with one of their most expensive ($250,000) acquisitions, the Broadway hit *The Man Who Came to Dinner* (1941) by George S. Kaufman and Moss Hart. Bette Davis was nearly invisible, but Monty Woolley re-created his stage role (after John Barrymore couldn't learn his lines) with verve, and the picture was a solid hit.

Nearly as funny was *George Washington Slept Here* (1942), another Kaufman-Hart stage success; Jack Benny, Ann Sheridan, and Charles Coburn are all quite good. Absent from the screen during the war years, Keighley surfaced at RKO in 1947 with *Honeymoon*, a tepid romance starring all-grown-up Shirley Temple and Guy Madison. *The Street with No Name* (1948) was an excellent noir featuring Richard Widmark at his most menacing as a gang kingpin hunted down by the FBI. Back at Warners Keighley made *Rocky Mountain* (1950), one of Errol Flynn's least-memorable efforts, and *Close to My Heart*, (1951) a surprisingly effective weeper with Gene Tierney and Ray Milland. Keighley's final picture was *The Master of Ballantrae* (1953), a Flynn swashbuckler—fittingly, his last—shot on location in Europe. Keighley and his wife then retired to Paris.

## ● IRVIN KERSHNER (1923- )

His career seemed poised for a breakthrough all through the 1960s and '70s, and he directed some mammoth commercial successes early in the Eighties. But as of this writing, Irvin Kershner, described by Pauline Kael as "a master of visual flow," has not directed a picture since 1990, and it appears that he may never fulfill the promise of his early work.

Born in Philadelphia, Kershner attended Temple University and studied design at U.C.L.A. before serving in World War II as a flight engineer on B-24's. After the war he moved to Provincetown to paint, and in 1948 he went back to Los Angeles to study photography at U.C.L.A. By 1950 he was taking filmmaking courses at the University of Southern California while teaching photography there. Later in 1950 he was hired by the U.S. Information Service to make documentaries for them in Greece, Iran, Turkey, and Jordan.

Returning to the States in 1953, Kershner began directing the television documentary series *Confidential File*, and later in the Fifties worked on such popular series as *The Rebel*. Roger Corman hired Kershner in 1958 to direct the undistinguished hoods 'n' heroin opus *Stakeout on Dope Street*; *The Young Captives* (1959), with Luana Patten, Ed Nelson, and Dan Blocker, was another drive-in movie for the unparticular. But *The Hoodlum Priest* (1961) was a respectable piece of work, in which Don Murray plays real-life Jesuit priest the Reverend Charles Dismas Clark, who tries to save St. Louis juvenile delinquent Keir Dullea from a life of crime (he ends up in the gas chamber anyway).

*A Face in the Rain* (1963) was a competent espionage tale set during World War II, with Rory Calhoun as a spy hiding from Mussolini's minions in an Italian village. But *The Luck of Ginger Coffey* (1964) was a genuine original. Shot in Canada on a low budget and scripted by Brian Moore from his own novel, it was a sometimes grim slice-of-life study; Robert Shaw and his real-life wife, Mary Ure, are a financially strapped couple who emigrate with their rebellious teenage daughter from Dublin to Montreal hoping for a fresh start. Unfortunately, Shaw's judgment proves no better in Canada, and the family's struggles continue.

*A Fine Madness* (1966), filmed in New York City, was a tragicomedy about one man's doomed efforts to keep society and its restrictions at bay. Sean Connery is in rare form as an irreverent poet whose outbursts of violence earn him a lobotomy, and Joanne Woodward is his long-suffering wife. *The Flim-Flam Man* (1967) carried no message, but it was an often amusing profile of Southern con man George C. Scott and his unsuccessful efforts to recruit Michael Sarrazin to the trade. *Loving* (1970), a scathing and often hilarious portrait of adultery in the suburbs, starred George Segal as a commercial artist living in Connecticut and Eva Marie Saint as the cynical wife he's been chronically unfaithful to; Sterling Hayden is also memorable as the ad exec Segal is courting for a big account. This is generally considered Kershner's best work, and remains one of the most provocative American films in a year filled with iconoclastic movies.

*Up the Sandbox* (1972), from Anne Roiphe's novel, was a proto-feminist comedy a few years ahead of its time. Barbra Streisand stars as a conflicted New York City woman trying to balance the demands of motherhood with her own unfulfilled dreams, which Kershner has her enact on the screen, with mixed results. Still, it's one of Streisand's most appealing (and least strident) performances. But *S*P*Y*S* (1974) was simply a mess, with *M*A*S*H* stars Elliott Gould and Donald Sutherland trying—and failing miserably—to recapture the heights of their earlier comic triumph; here they're CIA agents ineptly overseeing the defection of Russian ballet star Zouzou.

Kershner redeemed himself somewhat with *The Return of a Man Called Horse* (1976), the bloody sequel to Elliot Silverstein's equally violent 1970 success. Every bit as fascinating as the original, it again featured Richard Harris as the Englishman who's been inducted into the Yellow Hand Sioux and heeds the call to return to his adopted tribe, whose land has been stolen from them by evil fur trappers (is there any other kind?). *Raid on Entebbe* (1977), made for television, was a well crafted and exciting account of the Israeli commando's daring rescue of hostages being held in Uganda in 1976; the powerhouse cast included Peter Finch, Charles Bronson, James Woods, Robert Loggia, and Yaphet Kotto.

The erotic thriller *The Eyes of Laura Mars* (1978) was a journey into Hitchcock–De Palma territory, with Faye Dunaway as a high-strung photographer specializing in S&M fashion layouts; when she develops a prescient ability about a series of grisly murders, police lieutenant Tommy Lee Jones finds himself involved with her as both protector and lover. (Had the plot had a less ridiculous payoff, this might have become a cult classic.) There was nothing in Kershner's résumé to suggest he should have been handed the reins to the Star Wars franchise, but *The Empire Strikes Back* (1980), the second installment of creator George Lucas's enormously popular trilogy, turned out to be the best of the three. With Lucas relegating his contribution to the basic plot, which was developed by screenwriters Leigh Brackett and Lawrence Kasdan, Kershner masterfully guides the characters through a thrilling variety of perils, culminating in an out-and-out cliffhanger of a denouement—perhaps the first time a big-budget feature has ended so indeterminately.

*Never Say Never Again* (1983) marked the long-awaited return of Sean Connery to the James Bond role he had made famous twenty years before, and while the final result was something of an anticlimax—the story is sluggish and a bit bloated, even though Connery is neither—it was still a better piece of moviemaking than most of the Roger Moore entries, and it captured a large audience. But Kershner did not work again until the 1989 made-for-cable picture *Traveling Man*, a sort of poor man's *Glengarry Glen Ross*, with John Lithgow as a traveling salesman undermined by young competitor John Glover.

Given the huge box office of the original, *Robocop 2* (1990) was inevitable, but Kershner's work extrapolates the extreme violence of Paul Verhoeven's entry to ridiculous ends. One hopes this last bit of junk will not prove the coda to Kersher's interesting career.

◄ *With star Richard Harris on the set of* The Return of a Man Called Horse

## ● HENRY KING (1888-1982)

The prolific Henry King had a career as a motion picture director that spanned a full fifty years, with nearly a hundred films to his credit, roughly half of which were made in the sound era (almost all of them at Fox). King rarely, if ever, left a "signature" on his work to personalize it, although his taste clearly ran to period stories. Although many of his films now are of little interest, his ten best pictures do comprise a mighty fine group.

Born in the plantation country of Christianburg, Virginia, King acted in road shows, in vaudeville, and on stage before making his first film appearance in 1912. Three years later, he began directing for Pathé, acting in many of his films through 1920. He moved to Mutual in the Teens, then formed Inspiration Films with actor Richard Barthelmess in 1921 to make one of his best remembered silents, *Tol'able David*. At Metro he made a star of Ronald Colman in *The White Sister* (1923), filmed on location in Italy with Lillian Gish, and between 1924 and 1926 directed Colman in *Romola*, *Stella Dallas*, *The Magic Flame*, and *The Winning of Barbara Worth*, all box-office hits.

King joined Fox in 1930 and—rather incredibly—stayed there until he retired more than thirty years later. His early sound pictures include *Lightnin'* (1930) with Will Rogers and Joel McCrea, *Merely Mary Ann* (1931) with Janet Gaynor and Charles Farrell, *Over the Hill* (1931) with James Dunn and Mae Marsh, and *The Woman in Room 13* (1932) with Elissa Landi and Myrna Loy; none enjoys much of a reputation today. *State Fair* (1933), with Will Rogers, Lew Ayres, and Janet Gaynor, is better remembered, but neither *I Loved You Wednesday* (1933) (co-directed with William Cameron Menzies) nor *Carolina* (1934), with Janet Gaynor and Robert Young, made history. *Marie Galante* (1934) was an early Spencer Tracy drama, while *One More Spring* (1935) paired Gaynor with Warner Baxter. *Way Down East* (1935) was a laughable remake of Griffith's 1920 film, with Henry Fonda in Barthelmess's old role.

But King's longueurs reversed themselves in 1936, beginning with the novelty biopic *The Country Doctor*, which starred Jean Hersholt as Dr. Dafoe, the Moosetown medic who gained a brief moment of fame when he delivered the Dionne Quints. *Ramona* (1936) was a silly but popular Technicolor romance starring Loretta Young and Don Ameche as star-crossed (and extremely unconvincing) Indian lovers. *Lloyd's of London* became one of 1936's big hits, an entertaining account of the famous British insurance firm's rise; Freddie Bartholomew grows up to become dynamic Tyrone Power (in the first of his many collaborations with King), and George Sanders (in his Hollywood debut) and Madeleine Carroll provided colorful support. *Seventh Heaven* (1937) was an inferior remake of Frank Borzage's lauded 1927 silent; James Stewart was not very convincing as a Parisian sewer worker, and Simone Simon falls short of the Oscar-winning standard of the original's Janet Gaynor.

But *In Old Chicago* (1938) was a fine period effort set in the Chicago of 1871, with Tyrone Power, Don Ameche, and Alice Faye a most appealing combination. The picture was nominated for an Academy Award, and Alice Brady (as Mrs. O'Leary) won a best supporting actress Oscar. Knowing a good thing when they saw it, Fox next assigned King *Alexander's Ragtime Band* (1938), with Power, Ameche, and Faye now joined by Ethel Merman, who handled most of the Irving Berlin songs. It, too, received an Oscar-nomination for best picture, as did Berlin's original story, while Alfred Newman's score took home an Academy Award. Now hitting his stride, King made *Jesse James* (1939), one of Tyrone Power's best vehicles and the year's third-best Western (behind *Stagecoach* and *Destry Rides Again*); its splendid supporting cast included Henry Fonda, Randolph Scott, and Jane Darwell (as Ma James). *Stanley and Livingstone* (1939) was yet another period adventure, a colorful account of reporter Stanley's (Spencer Tracy) quest through Africa to find long-lost missionary Livingstone (Cedric Hardwicke).

*Little Old New York* (1940) was less successful, a stiff account of the life of steamboat inventor Robert Fulton (a miscast Fred MacMurray) that really wanted to be a showcase for Alice Faye. *Maryland* (1940) was a harmless bit of horse-country activity starring Walter Brennan, and *Chad Hanna* (also 1940) wasted Henry Fonda, Linda Darnell, and Dorothy Lamour in a nineteenth-century circus yarn. King departed from period Americana long enough to make *A Yank in the R.A.F.* (1941), a hugely popular World War II yarn in which callow flyboy Tyrone Power in London hooks up with chorus girl Betty Grable, who obligingly sings a few songs while Power is learning about responsibility to his mates. *Remember the Day* (1942) allowed King to move back in time once more in this story about a teacher (Claudette Colbert) who inspires one of her students to grow up to become a candidate for President.

*The Black Swan* (1942) was a first-rate swashbuckler from a Rafael Sabatini novel; Tyrone Power is pitted against George Sanders for the love of Maureen O'Hara, and guess who wins? *The Song of Bernadette* (1943), adapted by George Seaton from the bestselling book, is about the nineteenth-century French girl who experiences a vision of the Virgin Mary and is ostracized by the townspeople of Lourdes when she tells them about it. Jennifer Jones won the best actress Academy Award in her feature film debut, King was nominated for the first time for best direction, and the film—an enormous moneymaker for Fox—was also nominated as best picture. But the expensive biopic *Wilson* (1944) was a major box-office disappointment, despite critical acclaim that culminated with King's second Oscar nomination and one for the year's best picture; the five Oscars it did win were all in minor categories.

*A Bell for Adano* (1945), from the John Hershey novel, was more to the tastes of the day's moviegoers. It was a sentimental but effective tale about an Army commander (John Hodiak) whose troops are occupying an Italian village with one particularly beautiful resident (a blond Gene Tierney). With *Margie* (1946), King again traveled back to a simpler time in America, using period songs to buttress the thin story about a Jazz Age teenager (Jeanne Crain)

and her friends. *Captain from Castile* (1947) was another costume epic, starring Tyrone Power as a Conquistador running afoul of Cortés (Cesar Romero); newcomer Jean Peters played his lovely wife. Though it was a half hour too long, its location photography was a feast for the eye, supported by an Oscar-nominated score by King's frequent collaborator Alfred Newman. But *Deep Waters* (1948) was a ludicrous yarn centered on fisherman Dana Andrews's romancing of Jean Peters. *Prince of Foxes* (1949), filmed on location in Italy, was a splendid account of Tyrone Power's struggle against the evil Borgias (led by a lively Orson Welles) in medieval times.

Better still was *Twelve O'Clock High* (1949), a legitimate World War II classic in the mode of *Dawn Patrol*, with top performances by Gregory Peck, Dean Jagger, and Gary Merrill. The film received an Oscar nomination as best picture, Peck was nominated as best actor, and Jagger won the best supporting actor award. King elicited another excellent performance from Peck in the downbeat Western *The Gunfighter* (1950), which probably was too nihilistic to be a box-office hit (a failure exacerbated in Darryl F. Zanuck's opinion by Peck's too-bushy mustache). *I'd*

*Climb the Highest Mountain* (1951) sent Susan Hayward to rural Georgia as the wife of preacher William Lundigan with mixed results, but Hayward had a more exotic vehicle in *David and Bathsheba* (1951), an irresistibly fulsome entry in the biblical-epic sweepstakes with Gregory Peck (about as Jewish here as he was in *Gentleman's Agreement*) hanging on to his dignity for dear life; Raymond Massey as the prophet Nathan is just one more hot dog.

*Wait 'Til the Sun Shines, Nellie* (1952) was pleasant turn-of-the-century Americana about small-town barber David Wayne finding potholes on the road to happiness. The fine *The Snows of Kilimanjaro* (1952) "opened up" Hemingway's classic story about a famous writer (Gregory Peck) who is fatally injured while hunting big game in Africa flashing back on the mistakes he made in his life (one of whom is the gorgeous Ava Gardner), while wife Susan Hayward tries to comfort him. King directed one of the segments of *O. Henry's Full House* (1952), then returned with old friend Tyrone Power to the realm of high adventure in *King of the Khyber Rifles* (1953), a rather disappointing version of Kipling. *Untamed* (1955) had Power yet again, fighting in South Africa's Boer Wars in between smootchfests with Susan Hayward.

His biggest hit of the decade was the 1955 sobfest *Love Is a Many-Splendored Thing*, a rare venture by King into contemporary romance; it used William Holden, Jennifer Jones, and a haunting theme song to earn millions at the box office and Oscar nominations for best picture, actress, cinematography, costumes, song, and score (winning in the last three categories). *Carousel* (1956) was another huge success, a handsome adaptation of Rodgers and Hammerstein's Broadway blockbuster with Gordon MacRae, Shirley Jones, and such great songs as "If I Loved You" and "You'll Never Walk Alone." Hemingway was revisited with *The Sun Also Rises* (1957), but the result was not up to *Kilimanjaro*: Ava Gardner was badly miscast as Lady Brett Ashley and Tyrone Power was too old as the tragic Jake. But Errol Flynn, in one of his final performances, was quite affecting, and the Mexico City locations helped.

*The Bravados* (1958) was one of King's rare forays into Western territory and it's a good one; Gregory Peck is atypically cast in the sort of avenger role that a decade later would be played by Clint Eastwood. But *This Earth Is Mine* (1959), with Rock Hudson and Jean Simmons, required a Douglas Sirk to make its convoluted story about California winemakers semi-plausible. *Beloved Infidel* (1959) was a disastrous attempt to dramatize F. Scott Fitzgerald's love affair with Sheilah Graham (Gregory Peck and Deborah Kerr), and Fitzgerald was no better served in *Tender Is the Night* (1962), David O. Selznick's long-planned showcase for Jennifer Jones as a mentally ill woman whose psychiatrist husband (Jason Robards) is powerless to help her. Cukor had been Selznick's first choice, but he passed, and King—who subsequently retired—might have done well to turn it down also.

▲ *On location with stars Jennifer Jones and William Holden during* Love Is a Many-Splendored Thing

## ● ZOLTAN KORDA (1895-1961)

Like his more famous older brother, Sir Alexander, Zoltan Korda is most closely identified with the British cinema. But unlike Alexander, who had been making Hungarian, Austrian, and German silents since 1915, Zoltan's directing career fell almost entirely within the sound era, and a significant number of those pictures were Hollywood productions; Alexander cleaved to England, France, and Germany for most of his sound work.

Born in Pusztaturpasto, Hungary, two years after Alexander, Korda served in the Austro-Hungarian Army during World War I. When Alexander moved his base to Germany in 1923, Zoltan followed and began working as a cameraman. In 1927 he directed his first film, the German *Die Elf Teufel*, then a few years later followed his brother to Fox, where he wrote the screenplay for Alexander's *Women Everywhere* (1930). When Alexander moved to England in 1932, Zoltan of course accompanied him. There he made *Cash* (1933), released in the United States as *For Love or Money*, a comedy with Robert Donat and Wendy Barrie, and *Sanders of the River* (1935), a glorification of the British Empire—a theme Zoltan often favored—starring Paul Robeson as a cooperative African chief and Nina Mae McKinney as his queen.

When Alexander became a partner in United Artists in 1935, Zoltan began working there as well. He shot *The Conquest of the Air* (1936), a documentary about the history of aviation, then took over direction of *Elephant Boy* (1937) after Alexander deemed the location footage shot by documentary specialist Robert Flaherty inadequate. It was the first of several Korda features starring the young Indian actor Sabu, whom Flaherty had discovered working as a stable boy for a maharajah. Despite its laughable prologue, in which Sabu addresses the moviegoer as if he is reciting the Kipling story, the film soon turns into a good jungle adventure.

*Drums* (1938), Zoltan's first color feature, was a terrific God-Save-the-Empire yarn that in many ways is superior even to *Gunga Din*, a notion that would be more widely entertained if Cary Grant and Douglas Fairbanks, Jr., had starred alongside Sabu instead of Valerie Hobson and Roger Livesey. (Raymond Massey, splendid as the evil Prince Ghul, may well have been the basis for Disney's animated Jaffar in *Aladdin.*) *The Four Feathers* (1939) had been filmed twice before and would be twice again—once by Korda himself—but this is the definitive version of the A.E.W. Mason novel about a cowardly British officer (John Clements) who redeems himself by almost single-handedly saving his captured colleagues from Sudanese rebel forces. Ralph Richardson and C. Aubrey Smith headed the fine cast.

With war on the horizon, the Kordas (including youngest brother, Vincent, the great art director) left for Hollywood. Alexander served only as a producer during this time, but Zoltan managed to eschew colonialism to make the children's classic *The Jungle Book* (1942), with Sabu a perfect realization of Kipling's Mowgli—raised by wolves, threatened by Shere Khan, the tiger, and protected by the black panther Bagheera. (A pity that the inferior 1967 animated Disney feature for many years supplanted this, but the 1994 live-action version is a worthier successor.) *Sahara* (1943) is probably Korda's best-known film, a classic World War II adventure that, unlike so many of its ilk, remains an exciting viewing experience. Based on an incident in a 1937 Soviet film, it was written by Korda with John Howard Lawson—who would pay for the film's Communistic subtext when tried before HUAC a few years later. Humphrey Bogart stars as a tank sergeant who gets cut off with his men behind enemy lines in the Libyan desert. The group, which offers the now-clichéd ethnic and political mix—a Brooklyn GI, an Italian

POW, a Southerner, a black Sudanese, etc.—is whittled down by a Nazi battalion, but a clever ruse by Bogart tricks them into surrendering, in a truly rousing finale.

*Counter-Attack* (1945) was another patriotic war yarn that leaned to the left, again adapted by John Howard Lawson from a Soviet drama. Paul Muni and Marguerite Chapman are Russian guerrillas who have captured seven Nazi soldiers in the basement of a factory and need to extract information from them in time to put it to use. Though no *Sahara*, it was a potent if stagy bit of moviemaking. Korda left the war behind to make the tense drama *The Macomber Affair* (1947), with Gregory Peck as the white hunter Joan Bennett wants to bag and Robert Preston as her cowardly husband, whom she shoots and kills in a hunting accident (maybe). Filmed on location in Baja (with second-unit footage from Africa), this remains one of the best screen adaptations of Hemingway. Just as good was *A Woman's Vengeance* (1948), adapted by Aldous Huxley from his story "The Gioconda Smile," with Charles Boyer as a congenitally unfaithful husband on trial for the murder of his wife. He didn't do it, but Korda wrings the last drop of suspense out of the question of whether he'll go to the gallows based on the damning circumstantial evidence.

Korda had spent the past ten years in Hollywood, but he returned to England to make *Cry, the Beloved Country* (1951), from Alan Paton's acclaimed novel about racial tension and reconciliation in South Africa. Sidney Poitier, Canada Lee, and Charles Carson were the principals in this tragic, still-powerful film, co-produced by Korda and Paton. Korda's final picture was *Storm Over the Nile* (1955), a downscale remake of *The Four Feathers* that he co-directed with star Terence Young; although it recycles footage from the 1939 version, having Christopher Lee and Laurence Harvey in the cast partly justified its existence.

▲ The Macomber Affair, *starring Gregory Peck and Robert Preston, was shot on location in Africa*

## ● HENRY KOSTER (1905–1988)

Yet another in the long line of nigh-anonymous moviemakers who left Germany in the Thirties for the safe harbor of Hollywood, Koster managed to turn out solid entertainments for more than thirty years without anyone ever being the wiser. The former Hermann Kosterlitz was born and educated in Berlin. He began his career in the German film industry as a screenwriter in 1925, and graduated to directing in 1932 for Universal and Terra. A year later Koster fled the Nazi tide, moving to France. Univeral's U.S. operation brought him stateside in 1936, where he immediately went to work for Joe Pasternak on the first Deanna Durbin vehicles; it was hoped that the fourteen-year-old girl could compete with Fox's number-one star, Shirley Temple. These pictures, frothy as they may have been, were desperately needed to help save the foundering studio.

Beginning with *Three Smart Girls* (1936), they did. Durbin was flanked by Nan Grey and Barbara Read as the sisters who try to reunite their estranged parents before Pop can marry a gold digger, but Deanna really was the whole show, singing pop, opera, and everything in between. *One Hundred Men and a Girl* (1937) was another smash, with Deanna trying to persuade famed conductor Leopold Stokowski to hire her out-of-work dad Adolphe Menjou (along with ninety-nine other musicians); her numbers included bits from Mozart and Verdi, and "It's Raining Sunbeams." (It's now hard to imagine, but this film was competing for the best picture Oscar of 1937.) Koster was temporarily taken off the Durbin watch to make the snappy romantic comedy *The Rage of Paris* (1938) with Danielle Darrieux and Douglas Fairbanks, Jr., but he and Deanna were reunited for *Three Smart Girls Grow Up* (1939), in which Deanna helps marry off her two older sisters.

*First Love* (1939) found orphan girl Durbin getting her first screen kiss from Robert Stack, who must have been impressed by her mastery of numbers from Puccini and Strauss, while in *Spring Parade* (1940) she was sent to a new locale and period—nineteenth-century Vienna—as a baker's assistant who wins the love of Army drummer Robert Cummings with the requisite Strauss tune. *It Started with Eve* (1941) was the sixth and last of Koster's films with Durbin, here teamed romantically with Cummings, whose rich dad (Charles Laughton, slumming) wants him to marry before he dies. Deanna keeps the old codger alive by warbling numbers based on Dvořák and Tchaikovsky.

Koster might have been relieved to direct a picture that wasn't a Durbin vehicle, but *Between Us Girls* (1942), with mom Kay Francis and daughter Diana Barrymore both tripped up by love, could have used Deanna. Moving to MGM, Koster and Pasternak recycled the Durbin formula in *Music for Millions* (1944), in which young waif Margaret O'Brien is adopted by José Iturbi's orchestra, with the help of Jimmy Durante and June Allyson. *Two Sisters from Boston* (1946) was another Pasternak musical; June Allyson and Kathryn Grayson go to work for saloon owner Jimmy Durante in turn-of-the-century New York, much to the delight of Peter Lawford. *The Unfinished Dance* (1947) offered Margaret O'Brien as a star-struck dancer who idolizes ballerina Cyd Charisse; it was the last time Koster and producer Pasternak would work as a team.

Leaving behind the light musicals which had thus far defined his career, Koster made *The Bishop's Wife* (1947): urbane angel Cary Grant comes to earth to help David Niven and wife Loretta Young raise money for their church. A feel-good Christmas fantasy, the film earned Koster his only Academy Award nomination for best direction; it was also nominated for best picture (although it was somewhat overshadowed by 1947's other big holiday heartwarmer,

*Miracle on 34th Street*). Moving to Fox, where he would spend most of the next seventeen years, Koster made the saccharine romance *The Luck of the Irish* (1948), in which reporter Tyrone Power and coleen Anne Baxter are brought together by leprechaun Cecil Kellaway. The sentimental comedy *Come to the Stable* (1949), adapted from a Clare Boothe Luce story, had Loretta Young and Celeste Holm as transplanted French nuns trying to raise money for a children's hospital in the New England town of Bethlehem. Young, Holm, and Elsa Lanchester as their patron were all nominated for Oscars.

*The Inspector General* (1949) featured Danny Kaye in a musical interpretation of the Gogol story, good enough if one has no problem with the Kaye shtick, while *Wabash Avenue* (1950) had Victor Mature and Phil Harris competing for chanteuse Betty Grable in Chicago circa 1900; just seven years earlier, audiences had enjoyed the story as *Coney Island*. The sentimental *My Blue Heaven* (1950) paired Grable with Dan Dailey as a husband-wife radio team who want to adopt a child but find the agencies unsympathetic to entertainers. Koster then made the much-anticipated *Harvey* (1950), with James Stewart in one of his best-remembered roles as Elwood P. Dowd, the souse whose best friend is an invisible six-foot rabbit. Mary Chase helped adapt her Pulitzer Prize–winning play, and Josephine Hull reprised her Broadway role as Dowd's sister, winning an Academy Award as best supporting actress.

*No Highway in the Sky* (1951) was a departure for Koster, a fine thriller (adapted from the Nevil Shute novel), with James Stewart as a scientist who believes he has discovered the cause behind a series of plane crashes; Marlene Dietrich is a fellow passenger on a plane destined for the same fate. Then it was back to the silly season with *Mr. Belvedere Rings the Bell* and *Elopement* (both 1951), an unremarkable pair of

▲ *Henry Koster is flanked by Douglas Fairbanks, Jr., and French screen star Danielle Darrieux on the set of* The Rage of Paris, *a 1938 Universal production*

Clifton Webb comedies. Koster directed an episode of *O. Henry's Full House* (1952), then made the corny but colorful 1952 biopic *Stars and Stripes Forever*, with Clifton Webb as John Philip Sousa. *My Cousin Rachel* (also 1952) was a suspenseful adaptation of the Daphne du Maurier period mystery, in which Richard Burton (who was Oscar-nominated) investigates whether or not Olivia de Havilland was responsible for the fatal poisoning of his cousin.

Koster became the first director to employ the ballyhooed CinemaScope process in *The Robe* (1953), starring Burton as the Roman centurion who presides over the crucifixion of Christ. Solemn and stodgy but not without power, the film was a record-breaking hit in its day and was Oscar-nominated as best picture; Burton was also nominated as best actor. But Koster's next costumer, *Desiree* (1954), was slow and talky; Marlon Brando played a rather goofy Napoleon, Jean Simmons his seamstress lover Desiree, and Merle Oberon a shrewish Josephine. *A Man Called Peter* (1955) was better, a stately biopic about Peter Marshall (Richard Todd), the Scottish minister who rose to the high post of chaplain to the U.S. Senate, with Jean Peters as his devoted wife, Catharine. *The Virgin Queen* (1955) cast Todd as Sir Walter Raleigh and Bette Davis as Elizabeth I (a role essayed by her previously in the 1939 *The Private Lives of Elizabeth and Essex*), while *Good Morning, Miss Dove* (1955) allowed Jennifer Jones to play Ms. Chips, as various New England townspeople affectionately look back on her long career as a schoolteacher.

*D-Day the Sixth of June* (1956) was an anomaly in Koster's career, a war movie with soap-opera overtones: American Robert Taylor and Brit Richard Todd

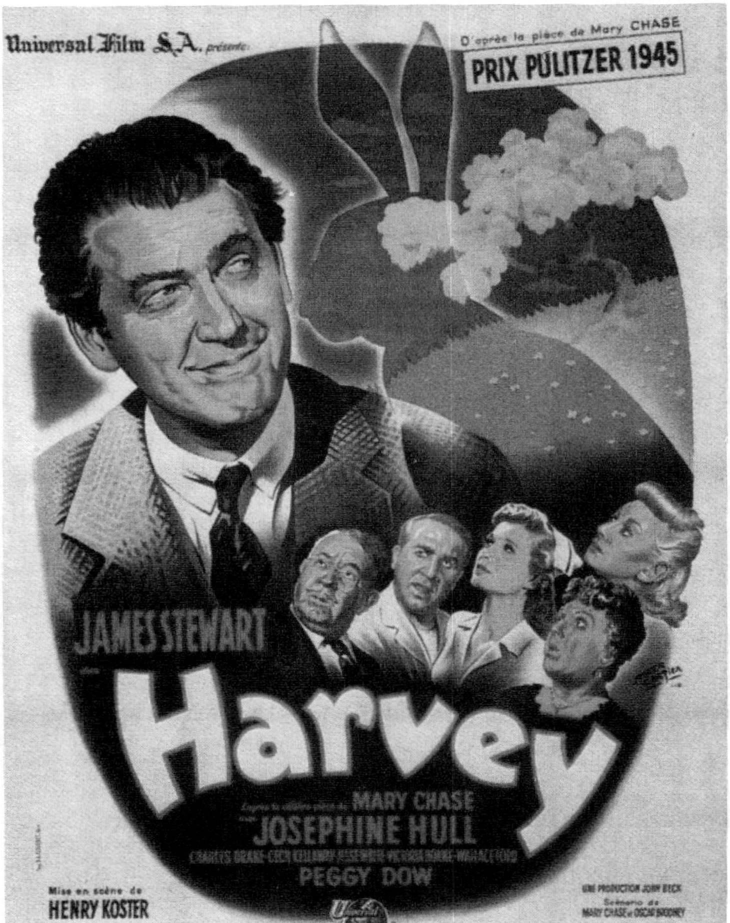

◀ *With Debbie Reynolds on the set of* The Singing Nun

muse over their competing desire for Dana Wynter while waiting for the invasion to commence. *The Power and the Prize* (1956) used Taylor again, here as an American corporate executive trying to outwit his British counterparts on a big deal. *My Man Godfrey* (1957) was an unnecessary but halfway acceptable remake of Gregory La Cava's 1936 screwball classic, although David Niven and June Allyson are pale substitutes for William Powell and Carole Lombard. *Fraulein* (1958) was a middling Cold War drama starring Dana Wynter and Mel Ferrer.

*The Naked Maja* (1959) had Ava Gardner as Goya's beauteous model for the eponymous painting, but it never overcame the miscasting of Tony Franciosa as the famed Spanish painter, while *The Story of Ruth* (1960) was another long, yawn-inducing biblical tale, with Elana Eden less than impressive in the title role. *Flower Drum Song* (1961) adapted the popular but awkward Rodgers and Hammerstein Broadway musical about romance in San Francisco's Chinatown without solving any of its problems, while *Mr. Hobbs Takes a Vacation* (1962) was a (just barely) passable comedy starring James Stewart, Maureen O'Hara, and Fabian. *Take Her, She's Mine* (1963) had Stewart again in a feeble farce (based on a Broadway hit) about his efforts to control teenaged daughter Sandra Dee while she's studying art in Paris.

Koster put Stewart through his paces once more in *Dear Brigitte* (1965), another cloying "family entertainment," with a contrived racetrack plot and the bizarre cast of Fabian, Billy Mumy, and (all too briefly) Brigitte Bardot. Last for Koster was *The Singing Nun* (1966), in which Debbie Reynolds was a guitar-wielding, record-cutting Belgian nun and Greer Garson her Mother Superior. (The fact that it was based on an actual person only made it that much more horrifying.) Still, it was nice for Koster to go out as he came in, with a wholesome box-office hit.

## ● STANLEY KRAMER (1913– )

Daring entrepreneur? Socially concerned filmmaker? Or pretentious, heavy-handed hack? Stanley Kramer has been called all of the above, and each claim carries its degree of truth. A native of New York City, he was educated at N.Y.U. and in 1933 joined Fox's research department. He worked his way up to film editor and writer, then earned his first major credits as associate producer on *So Ends Our Night* and *The Moon and Sixpence* at MGM. The war brought Kramer into the Army Signal Corps, for which he made training films.

Once he returned to Hollywood, Kramer joined forces with Carl Foreman, Sam Katz, and George Glass to form Screen Plays Inc. Their first productions were *Home of the Brave* and *Champion*, both directed in 1949 by Mark Robson. *Cyrano de Bergerac* (directed by Michael Gordon) and *The Men* (Fred Zinnemann) followed in 1950, an impressive debut for Kramer's company. But box-office receipts were not as hoped, and Kramer had to find a corporate home. Columbia made the best offer: thirty low-budget films to be produced within a five-year span.

How Kramer thought he was going to adhere to that killing schedule isn't clear, and history shows that he couldn't. *Death of a Salesman* (1951) was at least a critical success, but the Columbia productions that followed were unsuccessful (although the surreal fantasy *5,000 Fingers of Dr. T* [1953], written by Dr. Seuss, is now regarded as a cult classic). Kramer did have the satisfaction of seeing his UA production, the Zinnemann-directed *High Noon*, earn a slew of Oscar nominations in 1952. But it wasn't until 1954, when *The Wild One* and *The Caine Mutiny* came out, that a Kramer production made any money for Columbia. But it was too little too late, and Columbia canceled their joint venture.

Now a producer-director for United Artists, Kramer demonstrated the usual lapses in judgment common to the breed. *Not as a Stranger* (1955), a middling medical soap opera, was his maiden effort behind the camera; its casting—hard-boiled Robert Mitchum competing with Frank Sinatra for the affections of demure Olivia de Havilland—flirted with the preposterous. *The Pride and the Passion* (1957), on the other hand, *was* simply preposterous, with Frank Sinatra and Cary Grant battling over Sophia Loren in nineteenth-century Spain.

*The Defiant Ones* (1958) was probably the best of Kramer's message pictures—he won the New York Film Critics Circle Award for best direction and his first Academy Award nomination. Schematic it may have been, but the dramatic tension between Sidney Poitier and Tony Curtis—both Oscar-nominated as best actor—is palpable. But *On the Beach* (1959) was a ponderous meditation on the end of the world, so dignified that nary an atom of excitement from the Nevil Shute novel remained. Fred Astaire, Ava Gardner, Tony Perkins, and Gregory Peck do not embarrass themselves but typify the sort of willy-nilly assemblage of all-stars that Kramer would favor for the rest of his career.

Kramer looked to Broadway for his next project, adapting *Inherit the Wind* (1960), a dramatization of the 1925 Scopes Monkey Trial. It threatened to be another marathon course in Profundity 101—and yet it works, thanks in large part to the expert performances of Spencer Tracy (as Clarence Darrow) and Fredric March (as William Jennings Bryan). But all credit goes to Kramer for not letting its weighty issues overwhelm the drama of the tasty courtroom confrontation. (The plodding 1988 television remake with Kirk Douglas and Jason Robards demonstrated exactly how skillful Kramer had been.) *Judgment at Nuremberg* (1961) was even weightier, and at 178 minutes felt like ten tons. But once again Kramer showed that, within the confines of a courtroom, he was adept at maximizing dramatic tension even as philosophical debates raged on. It earned him his second Academy Award nomination for best direction; although he didn't win, he did receive the Irving G. Thalberg Award for the "consistently high quality" of his work.

Kramer must have heard enough criticism about his propensity for Importance, because his next film was an excruciating detour in the other direction. *It's a Mad, Mad, Mad, Mad World* (1963) was a brontosaurus of a comedy that lumbered in Cinerama for three hours. To watch half of Hollywood's working comedians search for $350,000 in stolen loot for 180 minutes was enough to make an exhausted audience beg for mercy.

So much for the madcap Kramer. *Ship of Fools* (1965), based on the Katherine Anne Porter novel, was an extravagant drama, with Vivien Leigh (in her last role), Oskar Werner (who won an Oscar), Simone Signoret, and Lee Marvin wallowing in despair. Overlong once again, but a standout in the genre of high-toned soap opera. *Guess Who's Coming to Dinner?* was one of 1967's most popular films, and probably remains the movie with which Kramer is most closely identified—which is too bad, because this object lesson in racial tolerance and etiquette was hopelessly dated even before it was released. It was the last teaming of Katharine Hepburn and Spencer Tracy (she won an Oscar) and, despite its color-by-numbers schematics, earned Kramer his third Academy Award nomination.

*The Secret of Santa Vittoria* (1969), based on a fine comic novel by Robert Crichton, was overlong but still a hoot, as Anthony Quinn and Anna Magnani try to hide a million bottles of wine from the occupying Germans during World War II. *R.P.M.* (1970) stood for "revolutions per minute," as in student revolts—the sort of torturous pun that typified the mindset of the film's bird-brained Erich Segal script. Perhaps the worst of the counterculture-clash movies—a genre with a shelf life of roughly fifteen minutes—it showed just how out of touch Kramer had grown.

*Bless the Beasts and Children* (1972), a fable about six oddball campers who band together to free a herd of buffalo, was unable to find an audience, while *Oklahoma Crude* (1973), with George C. Scott and Faye Dunaway, offered the sort of two-fisted romance that might have worked if the leads had been Clark Gable and Myrna Loy and the year was 1936. But *The Domino Principle* (1977) was a very poor thriller, badly acted by Gene Hackman and Candice Bergen, as was the unspeakable *The Runner Stumbles* (1979), in which Dick Van Dyke plays a priest accused of murdering a nun. Despite his preachiness and pretensions, Kramer deserved to go out on a better note.

◀ *Lee Marvin and Vivien Leigh, trapped on* The Ship of Fools

## ● STANLEY KUBRICK (1928- )

One of the most celebrated—and controversial—directors of the past forty years, the Bronx, New York–born Kubrick is as famed for his reclusive lifestyle in the wilds of England as for his painstaking approach to shooting and editing his (regrettably infrequent) films, the merits of which are usually hotly debated. A staff photographer for *Look* magazine at the age of seventeen, he quit the job in 1950 to make his first film, a short documentary that he sold to RKO. He repeated the process, making another short film that he sold. Thus was Kubrick able to finance his first feature, the ultra-low-budget war picture *Fear and Desire* (Paul Mazursky was one of the soldiers). It saw only limited release in 1953, but caught the attention of United Artists, which provided a modest bankroll for Kubrick's next picture, the boxing noir *Killer's Kiss* (1955), which received respectable reviews. Encouraged, UA gave Kubrick a bigger budget, enough to hire a cast of quality "B" supporting actors, including Sterling Hayden, Marie Windsor, Vince Edwards, Elisha Cook, and Timothy Carey. The result was the taut caper yarn *The Killing* (1956), one of the best late noirs and, in retrospect, one of the year's best films.

Continuing his progression up the Hollywood ladder, Kubrick was given an "A" budget by UA to shoot the antiwar drama *Paths of Glory* (1957) in Germany. Banned in France, this World War I classic offered superior acting by Kirk Douglas, Adolphe Menjou, and Ralph Meeker, with a fine screenplay by cult novelist Jim Thompson, Kubrick, and Calder Willingham. Unfortunately for Kubrick, who had waived his salary for profit participation, the film didn't fare well at the box office. He worked on developing *One-Eyed Jacks* for six months with Marlon Brando, but finally threw up his hands at Brando's vacillations and instead accepted Kirk Douglas's offer to take over *Spartacus* (1960) from Anthony Mann, who had just been fired. At 184 minutes *Spartacus* is perhaps more than even an epic truly requires, but there's no denying the virtues of its actors—particularly Douglas, Laurence Olivier, Oscar-winner Peter Ustinov, and Charles Laughton—and Dalton Trumbo's brilliant adaptation of the Howard Fast novel. *Spartacus* is probably Kubrick's most accessible film, but also his most anonymous.

Kubrick now moved to England, where his first project was adapting the controversial novel *Lolita* for MGM's British division. Overlong but provocative, this blackest of black comedies never fully solves the problem of transposing Nabokov's difficult book to the screen (although Nabokov himself is credited, perhaps spuriously, with the screenplay adaptation). But James Mason is superb as the professor who becomes obsessed with thirteen-year-old Sue Lyon, and Peter Sellers and Shelley Winters submit striking (if sometimes distracting) performances.

Kubrick's breakthrough success was the inimitable *Dr. Strangelove, or: How I Learned to Stop Worrying and Love the Bomb* (1964), a legitimate candidate for the best film of the Sixties. This wickedly nihilistic comedy about the Cold War arms race was written by Terry Southern, Kubrick, and Peter George (on whose novel *Red Alert* it was based), and had wonderfully inventive performances by George C. Scott, Sterling Hayden, and of course the brilliant Peter Sellers, who plays three roles. *Dr. Strangelove* earned Kubrick his first Academy Award nomination for best direction, and earned nominations for best picture, actor (Sellers), and screenplay; it ultimately won the New York Film Critics Circle Award as the best film of 1964.

Kubrick now sequestered himself while he spent the next four years making *2001: A Space Odyssey* (1968), a metaphysical science-fiction epic based on a haunting short story by Arthur C. Clarke. *2001* undeniably has its pretentious moments (some have argued that that would include all of its 139 minutes), sags at the most unfortunate moments, and has no acting to speak of. For all that, the film's allegorical story was accepted by audiences of the day as a quasi-religious experience. (Admittedly one that hasn't held up entirely after more than twenty-five years; even its Oscar-winning special effects now seem quaint.) But it was a (counter-) cultural phenomenon and box-office smash that gave Kubrick the latitude to make any movie he desired.

His choice was *A Clockwork Orange* (1971), which he adapted himself from a 1963 novel by Anthony Burgess set in England's near-future. Kubrick gave *Orange* an inventive visual scheme to approximate Burgess's neo-punk jargon and cast Malcolm McDowell as the murderous hoodlum who is caught and reprogrammed in horrifying fashion by the government. One of the nastiest movies in the annals of cinema, this deliberately provocative, typically (for Kubrick) nihilistic view of society and its discontented earned an "X" rating for excessive violence when released. *Orange* polarized critics more dramatically than any major studio release in memory, and its cold brilliance is sometimes subsumed by its utter repellence. Still, it was nominated for Academy Awards for best picture, best direction, and best screenplay, and Kubrick was cited by the New York Film Critics Circle as best director of 1971.

Another four years passed in the preparation of *Barry Lyndon* (1975), which Kubrick adapted himself from a Thackeray novel. One of the handsomest period films ever made, it's also long (183 minutes), slow, and oh so precious. Still, it survives the casting of Ryan O'Neal as its frustratingly passive eighteenth-century protagonist; and for once, even the device of voice-over narration works. Kubrick was nominated for an Academy Award for his fourth consecutive film, and *Barry* was also nominated for best picture, screenplay, and cinematography (John Alcott most justly won). Of course the picture didn't make a dime. Perhaps mindful of the tepid box-office reception of his last two films, Kubrick acquired the rights to an actual bestseller, Stephen King's *The Shining*. That may have been a mistake, as the liberties Kubrick took with King's schlocky but chilling horror yarn were guaranteed to antagonize the fans of the book. *The Shining* (1980) earned the

▲ *With Sterling Hayden and Peter Sellers on the set of* Dr. Strangelove

usual mixed critical reception—some argued that it was actually Kubrick's finest work—and the jury is still out on Jack Nicholson's over-the-top performance. The film has since developed a cult following—though presumably that wasn't Kubrick's objective. (Then again . . .)

It took a full seven years for Kubrick's *Full Metal Jacket* (1987) to appear. It was a potent if overly cerebral critique of the way Marines were (are?) dehumanized during basic training to operate efficiently as killing machines when sent to Vietnam. Impressive in parts, the film lets narrative take a back seat (as usual) to Kubrick's schematic game plan, resulting in a fatal lack of momentum. Still, *Jacket* boasts a solid cast that includes Matthew Modine, Adam Baldwin, and Dorian Harewood, and an Oscar-nominated screenplay by Kubrick, Michael Herr, and Gustav Hasford. (A commercial dud, *Jacket* provides an interesting contrast to Clint Eastwood's popular *Heartbreak Ridge*, also released in 1987, which has some of the same structure but allows humor and even a romantic subplot to carry some of the freight—admittedly much less weighty than the theme of *Jacket*.)

So the question remains: Is Kubrick's hermetically sealed existence in England, where he has made his (increasingly rare) films now for more than thirty years, the appropriate laboratory for his prodigious talent? Or has he fine-tuned himself into a world-class control freak who is ever less able to connect with an audience?

## ● GREGORY LA CAVA (1892–1952)

Although his reputation is based on a half dozen sophisticated comedies and dramas from the mid-Thirties, the temperamental Gregory La Cava made some twenty sound pictures (and another fifteen silents), several of which deserve a new viewing.

Born in Towanda, Pennsylvania, and raised in Rochester, New York, La Cava's artistic talents led him to the Chicago Institute of Art and New York's National Academy of Design. He started working as a cartoonist for the New York *Sunday Herald* and the *Evening World* in the Teens, and by 1917 was heading the newly formed animated cartoon division of Hearst Enterprises, which included the *Mutt and Jeff, Krazy Kat*, and *Katzenjammer Kids* animated series. He began writing and directing two-reel comedy shorts and features, signing with Paramount in 1924 and moving to Hollywood with the company in 1927. His silents, several of which he also produced, included *Running Wild* and *So's Your Old Man* with W. C. Fields, *Half a Bride* with Gary Cooper, and *Feel My Pulse* with William Powell.

La Cava left Paramount in 1929 and made *Saturday's Children* for First National before signing with Pathé, where he directed *Big News* and *His First Command* (1930). When RKO-Radio absorbed Pathé in 1931, they inherited La Cava as well, and it was there he made his first great comedies. *Laugh and Get Rich* (1931), about the goings-on in a boardinghouse, was also written by La Cava, while *Smart Woman* (1931), an early screwball farce, starred Mary Astor. *Symphony of Six Million* (1932), from the Fannie Hurst tearjerker, featured Ricardo Cortez as an upwardly mobile Jewish doctor who temporarily misplaces his ethics, until crippled Irene Dunne helps him locate them. (Gregory Ratoff, who in a few years would begin directing, made his first American screen appearance as Cortez's father.) *The Age of Consent* (1932) was less heavy going, a college romance between Richard Cromwell and Dorothy Wilson (formerly an RKO secretary).

But it was *The Half-Naked Truth* (1932) that demonstrated exactly how good La Cava could be. A rollicking screwball comedy, it offered Lee Tracy as a carnival shill who tries to turn exotic Lupe Velez into a star, transforming himself into a New York advertising whiz at the same time. It was 77 minutes of roughhouse comedy, the sort that the Code would soon extinguish. *Gabriel over the White House* (1933), made for Walter Wanger at MGM, was a Capraesque fantasy about a corrupt politician (Walter Huston) who becomes President; when a near-fatal car crash opens his eyes, he turns his back on his racketeer friends and agitates for an end to war, crime, and poverty. La Cava's last picture for RKO was *Bed of Roses* (1933), an uneven romantic drama that tried to pass off Constance Bennett as a hustler just out of reform school who is finally redeemed by her love for riverboat captain Joel McCrea.

La Cava's relationship with his bosses at RKO had been a stormy one, and he left the studio in 1933 to go freelance, turning down an attractive offer from MGM in the process. Signing a two-picture deal with 20th Century-Fox, he made *Gallant Lady* and *The Affairs of Cellini* (both released by UA in 1934). The former was a turgid soap opera about an unmarried mother (the mysteriously popular Ann Harding) who must give up her baby for adoption. But *Cellini* was a delightful costume romp, starring Fredric March as the sixteenth century's most irresistible duelist and ladies' man; Constance Bennett was the willing recipient of his affections, and Frank Morgan her unlucky husband (he earned an Oscar nomination).

*What Every Woman Knows* (1934) was a smooth adaptation of the James Barrie play; Helen Hayes repeated her stage role as the canny wife who props up her dim-bulb politician husband (Brian Aherne). *Private Worlds* (1935) was atypically grim fare for La

Cava, but he handled the story about two doctors (Charles Boyer and Claudette Colbert) who toil in a mental institution well enough to earn Colbert an Academy Award nomination. Colbert and La Cava teamed up again a few months later in *She Married Her Boss*, a so-so comedy in which Colbert learns that new husband (Melvyn Douglas) is encumbered with an impossibly obnoxious family.

Much more impressive was *My Man Godfrey* (1936), the quintessential screwball comedy and one of the most fondly remembered films of the Thirties. William Powell submits his definitive performance as the homeless man discovered by ditzy Carole Lombard on a scavenger hunt; he is then forced to take a job in her Fifth Avenue mansion. Naturally, she soon falls in love with him, and vice versa. La Cava, Powell, Lombard, and supporting players Mischa Auer and Alice Brady all received Academy Award nominations, as did the screenplay by Morrie Ryskind and Eric Hatch. La Cava trumped that triumph by returning to RKO to direct *Stage Door* (1937), a superb adaptation of the Ferber-Kaufman play about a boardinghouse for aspiring actresses. It boasted one of the decade's stellar casts: Katharine Hepburn, Ginger Rogers, Lucille Ball, Andrea Leeds, and (at his unctuous best) Adolphe Menjou. The film received an Oscar nomination for best picture, and La Cava again was Oscar-nominated for his direction (losing—ironically—to Leo McCarey for his screwball classic *The Awful Truth*). But he did win the New York Film Critics Circle Award.

Now at the top of his profession, La Cava stayed at RKO to produce and direct *Fifth Avenue Girl* (1939), a middling *Godfrey* reversal, with Ginger Rogers as a homeless waif who makes millionaire Walter Connolly hear the voice of social consciousness. *Primrose Path* (1940) starred Rogers again as a poor girl whose love for upper-crust Joel McCrea is complicated by her trashy mother (Marjorie Rambeau, who was Oscar-nominated). It was an uneasy blend of naturalism and soap opera, and the twain didn't meet. *Unfinished Business* (1941) was also

problematic, with Irene Dunne and Robert Montgomery deadly dull as a mismated couple who separate, then reconcile—but why should we care? And again, the box office was poor.

*Lady in a Jam* (1942) had Irene Dunne as a wacky (and insolvent) heiress who is convinced her neuroses will disappear if only psychiatrist Patric Knowles will marry her. Screwball it was—but funny it wasn't, despite all the huffing and puffing. La Cava's last film, *Living in a Big Way*, came five years later; his drinking had long since reached a problematic stage. This was a labored musical (from a story by La Cava) with Gene Kelly that ran way over budget and flopped at the box office. It was a premature *finis* to La Cava's once-brilliant career.

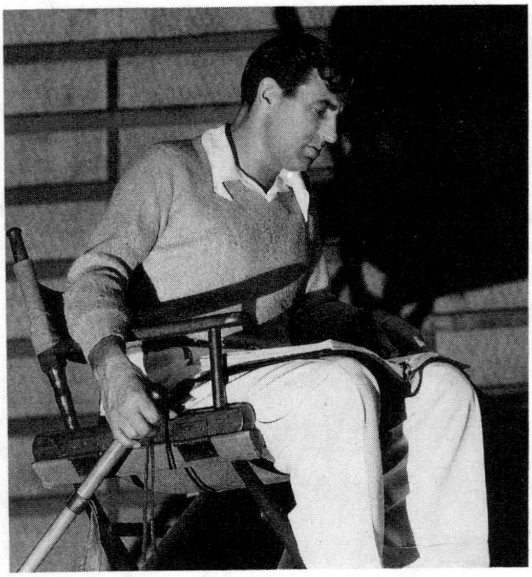

## ● SIDNEY LANFIELD (1898–1972)

Although he directed more than thirty feature films, most of them for Fox or Paramount, Sidney Lanfield's name rarely comes up when the best directors of the Thirties and Forties are listed. That is as it should be, since only a few of the pictures he helmed are likely to appear on anyone's list of all-time favorites. And yet nuggets of gold are scattered throughout his credits.

Born in Chicago and trained on the vaudeville and jazz circuits, in 1926 Lanfield went to Hollywood, where he hooked on as a gagman and screenwriter for Fox. He made his directorial debut there in 1930 with *Cheer Up and Smile*. Over the next few years he directed *Three Girls Lost* (1930) with John Wayne and Loretta Young, *Hush Money* (1931) with Joan Bennett and Myrna Loy, *Dance Team* (1931) and *Hat Check Girl* (1932) with Sally Eilers, *Society Girl* (1932) with James Dunn and Spencer Tracy, *Broadway Bad* (1933) with Joan Blondell and Ginger Rogers, and the Constance Bennett version of *Moulin Rouge* (1934); few can be seen today. *Red Salute* (1935) was a bald knockoff of *It Happened One Night*, but with an interesting twist: Barbara Stanwyck, sent down to Mexico by her military dad to get her away from her Communist-radical boyfriend (Hardie Albright), must travel back to the States with AWOL soldier Robert Young, and they fall in love along the way.

*King of Burlesque* (1935) was an Alice Faye musical, with Warner Baxter repeating his *42nd Street* role as a producer putting on a big show, while *Half Angel* (1936) was a comic murder mystery starring Frances Dee and Brian Donlevy. *Sing, Baby, Sing* (1936) was Faye's breakthrough picture, a quasi-musical, with Adolphe Menjou as a movie star, Gregory Ratoff as her nutty agent, and the Ritz Brothers for comic relief. *One in a Million* (also 1936) introduced Norwegian skating star Sonja Henie to American audiences; Don Ameche played her love interest and Adolphe Menjou the promoter who brings her to Madison Square Garden. *Wake Up and Live* (1937) had Faye as the host of an inspirational radio show who helps shy singer Jack Haley as Walter Winchell and Ben Bernie feud. Henie returned in the enormously successful *Thin Ice* (1937), now as a ski instructor romanced by disguised prince Tyrone Power, while *Love and Hisses* (1937) allowed Winchell and Bernie to continue their mock feud, with singer Simone Simon the cause of the dispute.

*Always Goodbye* (1938) was heavier going for Lanfield—a weeper in which Barbara Stanwyck gives up her illegitimate child, only to learn that his adoptive mother (Lynn Bari) is a gold digger. Far more enjoyable was *The Hound of the Baskervilles* (1939), the fondly remembered debut of Basil Rathbone as the great detective. *Second Fiddle* (1939) was an Irving Berlin tunefest, with Tyrone Power as a movie publicist who falls for Minnesota skating teacher Sonja Henie, while *Swanee River* (also 1939) was an adequate biopic of songwriter Stephen Foster; Al Jolson steals the show as minstrel singer E. P. Christy. Lanfield left Fox and made the Fred Astaire–Rita Hayworth musical *You'll Never Get Rich* (1941) at Columbia, the first of their two delightful duets, with a fine Cole Porter score. He then signed with Paramount, where his first assignment was *The Lady Has Plans* (1942), a mediocre spy farce starring Paulette Goddard and Ray Milland.

But *My Favorite Blonde* (1942) was one of Bob Hope's best vehicles: spy Madeleine Carroll takes advantage of Hope and his trained penguin, while *The Meanest Man in the World* (1943), at under an hour, did just as much for Jack Benny. The 1943 *Let's Face It* had Hope again, but he failed to jell with co-star Betty Hutton. *Standing Room Only* (1944) was a chip off *The More the Merrier*, with Fred MacMurray and Paulette Goddard hiring out as servants when they can't find living quarters—a nice premise that needed a Mitchell Leisen to carry it off. *Bring on the Girls* (1945) was a limp comedy with Eddie Bracken and Veronica Lake, while *The Well-Groomed Bride* (1946) miscast that year's Oscar winner, Olivia de Havilland, in a wedding farce with Ray Milland. *The Trouble with Women* (1947) had Milland yet again, and it was no funnier than his previous work under Lanfield. But *Where There's Life* (1947) was prime stuff, with Bob Hope crowned the head of a small country in Europe, while *Station West* (1948) was a surprisingly good, tough Western, featuring Dick Powell and Jane Greer.

*Sorrowful Jones* (1949) teamed Hope with Lucille Ball in a loose remake of Damon Runyon's *Little Miss Marker*, while *The Lemon-Drop Kid* (1951), with Hope and Marilyn Maxwell, remade another Runyon story, surpassing the 1934 version with Lee Tracy. *Follow the Sun* (1951) was a change of pace, a quasi-biography of golf great Ben Hogan starring Glenn Ford and Anne Baxter. Lanfield's last picture was *Skirts Ahoy!* (1952), a so-so Esther Williams outing with Debbie Reynolds and Vivian Blaine. He moved over to television in the early Fifties, and ended up with some two hundred shows to his credit.

◀ *Lanfield (top left) on the set of* Thin Ice *in 1937*

## ● FRITZ LANG (1890–1976)

The master of expressionistic suspense, Vienna-born Fritz Lang had already created an impressive body of work in the German cinema before coming to America in 1934. It would take Lang twenty-one years to fashion his twenty-two Hollywood pictures, hardly a prodigious output for the time. But at least half of those films are noirish masterpieces of menace, tone poems of fear and fate whose power has dissipated hardly a whit. David Thomson has stated that Lang produced the best work of the refugee directors because of his ability to fully exploit the genres in vogue in Hollywood—wartime espionage and film noir, first and foremost, but also Westerns and tawdry melodramas. His (largely) ageless body of work proves there is no expiration date for dread or desire, the legal tender of Lang's cinematic realm.

As befit the son of an architect, Lang was educated at a technical high school and at the College of Technical Sciences at the Academy of Graphic Arts in Vienna. Much later, he would avail himself of that training in the graphic arts in designing his films. But for now, Lang aspired to be an artist, and he ran away to Paris to paint before completing his studies, much to the displeasure of his family. His early success in that endeavor, however, was interrupted by the First World War, in which Lang served and was wounded four times. The last injury was quite serious, requiring a year's convalescence in a Vienna army hospital, where Lang tried his hand at writing screenplays, and once he was discharged, he began to act as well. Lang moved to Berlin in 1918 and worked as an assistant director and story editor, and just a year later was given the opportunity to write and direct his first movie, *Halbblut*, the theme of which foreshadowed such triumphs from his Hollywood period as *The Woman in the Window* and *Scarlet Street*.

Through the Twenties, Lang made ever-more ambitious films, some of them so long and dense that they were exhibited in two parts. Among the best known are *Die Spinnen* (Parts I and II), *Dr. Mabuse der Spieler* (Parts I and II)—both crime epics—and *Die Nibelungen* (Parts I and II). In 1924 he married Thea von Harbou, who had been collaborating on Lang's screenplays since 1920 and would continue to do so (sometimes solo) through 1932. Shortly after the wedding he traveled to the United States for the first time to observe moviemaking techniques in New York and Hollywood.

Lang's first project upon his return to Germany was the futuristic masterpiece *Metropolis*, which he spent most of 1925 and 1926 shooting for UFA, nearly exhausting the considerable resources of Germany's premier studio. The film's plot, about repressive society divided into exploited workers, indolent rulers, and emotionless robots, may have owed something to H. G. Wells, but the breathtaking visual scheme was like nothing ever attempted onscreen. Its color-tinted 1987 rerelease with a modern score (and a half hour trimmed) illustrated that, while inevitably dated, *Metropolis* still retains its poetic vision.

After self-producing the crime yarn *Spione* (*Spies*) in 1928, Lang returned to science fiction for the silent production *Die Frau im Mond* (known in the States as *Rocket to the Moon* and *The Woman on the Moon*; 1929), which was released without even a score. *M* (1931), a horrifying account of a child killer's compulsion (based on an actual murderer from Düsseldorf who was finally brought to bay), was Lang's greatest international success and, ultimately, his own personal favorite among his films. Anchored by Peter Lorre's chilling performance as the unhinged killer of young girls who is finally hunted down by the German underworld, *M* is one of the enduring early talkies. (Joseph Losey's 1951 remake in English pales beside it.)

Less compelling was *Das Testament des Dr. Mabuse* (1933), a political thriller that overtly was the sequel to *Dr. Mabuse der Spieler*; covertly it made a mockery of the rising Nazi tide. Joseph Goebbels, Hitler's brilliant Minister of Propaganda, was wise to Lang and politely explained in a meeting with him that *Das Testament* was banned but that Hitler himself wanted Lang to make films for the Reich. Twelve hours later, Lang (who was half-Jewish) had relocated to Paris, leaving behind his bank accounts, personal belongings, and Thea—who quickly divorced him and in short order became one of the Reich's most accomplished writers and directors of propaganda films.

Thus began the second phase of Lang's filmmaking career. He made one picture, *Liliom* (1934), while in France, then accepted David O. Selznick's offer to make a film in Hollywood for MGM. That movie turned out to be the powerful *Fury* (1936), but Lang spent over a year on abortive projects before it was made (most productively getting his U.S. citizenship papers in 1935). A moderate success at the box office, *Fury*, starring Spencer Tracy and Sylvia Sidney, was an unforgiving study of mob violence that might have been better exploited by a studio with an appetite for socially conscious controversy—say, Warner Bros. But MGM fiddled with the ending and then let Lang go.

He next found work with independent producer Walter Wanger on the equally grim *You Only Live Once* (1937), a heartrending tale of a hard-luck excon (Henry Fonda) unjustly accused of killing a man during a bank robbery. Imprisoned and sentenced to death, he busts out—unaware that he has just been pardoned—kills a well-meaning chaplain, and heads for the Canadian border, one step ahead of a nightmarish manhunt and death. Again, Sylvia Sidney is outstanding as the loving wife who is powerless to save her man—or herself—from the intractable jaws of fate. *You and Me* (1938) is less well remembered, but this eccentric tale of lovebirds (George Raft and Sylvia Sidney) who get married without realizing they both have a criminal past has certain charms, including songs by Kurt Weill that attempt to patch over the holes in the lugubrious narrative.

Lang was having difficulty finding a home at a studio sympathetic to his working methods, but after a couple of wasted years, he was signed by 20th Century-Fox. His first project there was *The Return of Frank James* (1940), a fine sequel to Henry King's 1939 success *Jesse James*, with Henry Fonda repeating his role as Frank James, now attempting to avenge Jesse's death; Gene Tierney lent emotional support in her film debut. Lang's second Technicolor Western was *Western Union* (1941), a handsome, meticulously researched staging of the company's bold expansion from Omaha to Salt Lake City. Based on a Zane Grey story, it offers a colorful cast: Robert Young, Randolph Scott, John Carradine, Dean Jagger, Chill Wills, and Slim Summerville.

Lang was fond of the American West, but made a happy return to the noir universe with *Man Hunt* (1941)—he was hired because John Ford found the subject objectionable. But Lang had no such qualms, and his version of Geoffrey Household's complicated but thrilling suspense novel *Rogue Male*, about a man who tries and fails to assassinate Hitler, became one of his masterpieces. Walter Pidgeon stars as an expert hunter who himself becomes the prey of Nazis George Sanders and John Carradine, and Joan Bennett was equally effective as the cockney prostitute who loves him and ultimately sacrifices herself to save him. But Lang was not invited to remain at Fox after clashing with Zanuck. He collaborated with

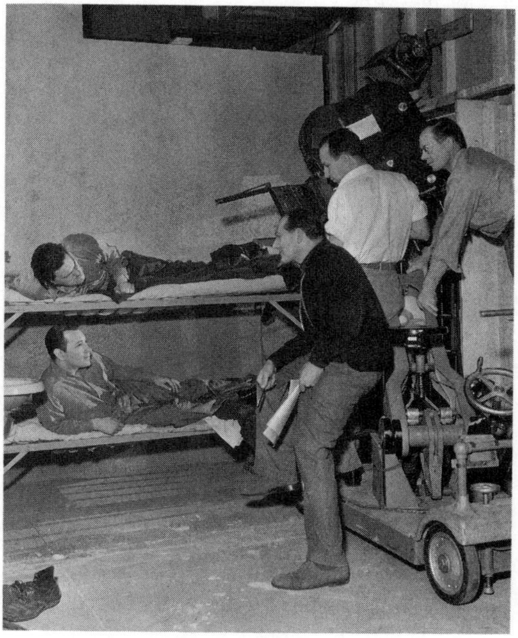

▲ *Lang (center) coaches George Raft while shooting* You and Me *in 1938*

Bertolt Brecht on the independent production *Hangmen Also Die!* (1943), an intermittently exciting but overly long account of the assassination of Czech puppet dictator Reinhard Heydrich by resistance leader Franz Svoboda (a miscast Brian Donlevy), who manages to elude the Reich's retribution until the stakes become too high.

*The Woman in the Window* (1944) was, literally, one of Lang's most nightmarish dramas. Skillfully adapted by Nunnally Johnson from an obscure novel, it stars Edward G. Robinson at his befuddled best as a married college professor who accidentally becomes involved with sultry Joan Bennett, the subject of a painting with which he has become infatuated. Bad luck leads Robinson inexorably on the path to blackmail (courtesy of the sublimely slimy Dan Duryea), murder, and the ever-tightening net of the law. *Ministry of Fear* (1944), very loosely based on the Graham Greene novel, was a gripping upgrade of *The 39 Steps*. Ray Milland is the bewildered protagonist, a man recently discharged from an insane asylum (unjustly implicated in the suicide of his wife) whose life is mysteriously endangered by as motley an assortment of spies, double agents, and bogus mediums as ever paraded across the silver screen, including Dan Duryea as a lethal tailor working for the Nazis.

Lang assembled his top actors from *Window* for *Scarlet Street* (1945), a superb remake of Jean Renoir's 1931 film *La Chienne*, with Edward G. Robinson again superb as a milquetoast department store cashier whose shrewish wife (Rosalind Ivan) denies him every pleasure except the one he finds as a weekend painter. When he falls for the two-faced "Lazy Legs" (Joan Bennett), whose true romantic interest lies with con man Dan Duryea, both Robinson and his beloved artworks are exploited by the conscienceless pair until he finally snaps. The ironic ending is morbid enough to satisfy any viewers who felt gypped by the trick denouement of *Window*.

But on the heels of that triumph, Lang's American career suddenly entered a prolonged slump. *Cloak and Dagger* (1946) was another attempt to mine the espionage genre, but this time Lang failed to sustain the necessary tension, and Gary Cooper was miscast as a college professor who agrees to serve Uncle Sam as a secret agent during a trip to Germany. Two years went by before the release of the turgid drama *Secret Beyond the Door* (1948); it was hardly worth the wait, despite the presence of the reliable Joan Bennett as a woman who fears her husband (Michael Redgrave) may be a murderer. *House by the River* (1950), made for lowly Republic, was an atmospheric Southern gothic about familial evil, with Louis Hayward menacing wife Jane Wyatt and brother Lee Bowman.

Lang was an odd choice to direct the 1950 *An American Guerrilla in the Philippines*, a rousing if conventional World War II adventure starring Tyrone Power as a stranded Navy officer leading native Filipinos in their fight against superior Japanese forces. But at RKO, the day's leading purveyor of noir, Lang was able to snap out of his six-year-long doldrums. *Rancho Notorious* (1952) was a quirky Western starring Marlene Dietrich as the hard-boiled owner (and chanteuse) of an outlaw hideout known as Chuck-a-Luck (originally conceived as the film's title, until wiser heads prevailed). Revenge-driven Arthur Kennedy wangles an invitation to the hideout from gunslinger Mel Ferrer, Dietrich's lover and partner in crime. But soon Dietrich is involved with Kennedy, and she takes a bullet meant for him during the film's climactic gunfight. The stuff of pulps, admittedly, but served up by Lang with a dash of his distinctive cynicism, which makes all the difference.

*Clash by Night* (1952) was a thick stew of human desire, based on the Broadway play by Clifford Odets that had starred Tallulah Bankhead. Here the lust is given life by its remarkable cast—Barbara Stanwyck, Robert Ryan, Paul Douglas, and, in a smaller role, Marilyn Monroe. Lang masterfully braises the actors' emotions as they paw, slap, and grind against each other from kitchen table to kitchen sink. (A pity Lang couldn't have worked more than once with the great Ryan.) *The Blue Gardenia* (1953), with Anne Baxter accused of murdering lecherous Raymond Burr, was a modest but neatly plotted little noir. *The Big Heat* that year required neither plot nor suspense—just the raw fury of Glenn Ford's rogue cop, whose wife was blown to smithereens by the mob; he swears to avenge her with the blood of unctuous boss Alexander Scourby and sadistic hoodlum Lee Marvin. But it's the wounded tenderness of doomed moll Gloria Grahame that gives the picture its moral center and peculiar resonance.

Columbia liked what Lang had wrought in *Heat* and asked him to make *Human Desire* (1954), pairing Ford and Grahame in a remake of Renoir's 1938 adaptation of Emile Zola's novel *La Bête humaine*. Lang complied, but his heart wasn't in it, and *Desire* isn't equal to Renoir's masterwork—although the five-minute train montage at the start is terrific, and Grahame is always worth murdering for. *Moonfleet* (1955) was an anomaly in Lang's oeuvre, a period picture in which buccaneer Stewart Granger crosses swords with George Sanders for the love of Viveca Lindfors.

But *While the City Sleeps* (1956) brought Lang back where he belonged, into the underbelly of New York City and a frantic manhunt for the psychopathic "Lipstick Killer" (John Drew Barrymore) by a pack of amoral journalists (Dana Andrews, Vincent Price, Thomas Mitchell, George Sanders) nearly as loathsome as he. Ida Lupino, Rhonda Fleming, and Sally Forrest take turns as the killer's prospective victims. Lang's second picture for RKO that year was *Beyond a Reasonable Doubt*, a paranoid thriller that prefigures Sam Fuller's *Shock Corridor*, with Dana Andrews pretending to be guilty of murder, only to find that he cannot extricate himself from the web of deceit he has woven. While only a middling suspenser, the film's dramatization of fate's implacable vortex was a fitting conclusion to Lang's Hollywood career.

Now the expatriate returned to Germany, weary of his struggles with the likes of Harry Cohn, Howard Hughes, and all the other studio bosses and their sycophantic underlings. He filmed a pair of related pictures in India in 1958 and 1959, which were edited into a semicoherent single film called *Journey to the Lost City* for release in America in 1960. But Lang made only one film in Germany, *Die 1000 Augen des Dr. Mabuse* (*The Thousand Eyes of Dr. Mabuse*), before retiring in 1960. That third installment of the Dr. Mabuse story should have provided Lang with a sense of closure, but he couldn't resist appearing as himself in Jean-Luc Godard's 1963 film *Contempt*. And why not? It was an emotion he had experienced many times, across two continents and five turbulent decades.

◄ *Broderick Crawford gets some slapping tips from Lang, to the dismay of Gloria Grahame, on the set of* Human Desire

## ● WALTER LANG (1898–1972)

The *other* Lang was surely less of an artist than his German counterpart, but Walter Lang's fifty-odd sound pictures—most made at 20th Century-Fox over a twenty-five-year span—were a respectable lot and then some. There were enough peaks rising over the plateaus (and occasional valleys) to show that his was a better-than-average talent.

Born in Memphis, Tennessee, Lang was trained as an illustrator, but also loved the stage, and acted in and directed stock productions shortly after World War I. He worked as an illustrator in the men's fashion field before changing careers and becoming an assistant director in the early Twenties at Hearst's Cosmopolitan Productions. He was given his chance to direct by Dorothy (Davenport) Reid, who hired him to direct her in *Red Kimono* in 1925, and over the next four years he made a number of silents at various studios, including *Money to Burn*, *The Satin Woman*, and *The Night Flyer*. Working at tiny companies like World Wide and Tiffany, Lang made a number of now-forgotten talkies in 1929 and 1930, including *The Spirit of Youth, Hello Sister, Cock o' the Walk* (co-directed with Roy William Neill), *The Big Fight*, and *The Costello Case*.

*Brothers* (1930), based on a stage play, was made at Columbia, but most of Lang's work at that time—*Hell Bound, Women Go On Forever, Command Performance*—was for companies with even less prestige, and he briefly gave up directing to move to Paris and paint. But soon he was back in Hollywood, directing Carole Lombard in *No More Orchids* (1933), a glossy melodrama, and Elissa Landi in *The Warrior's Husband* (1933), which he also co-scripted. Neither was particularly successful; nor were *Meet the Baron* (1933) and *The Party's Over* (1934). *Whom the Gods Destroy* (1934) was an overbaked melodrama featuring Robert Young and Walter Connolly, but *The Mighty Barnum* (also 1934) was an entertaining biopic about the legendary showman, with Wallace Beery's hamminess for once apropos; Adolphe Menjou made a sympathetic Bailey.

*Carnival* (1935) offered Lee Tracy as a puppeteer on the lam, with Dickie Walters as his son "Poochy" (!) and Sally Eilers and Jimmy Durante as his carny pals, while *Hooray for Love* (1935) was a backstage musical with the colorful cast of Ann Sothern, Bill Robinson, and Fats Waller. *Love Before Breakfast* (1936), a peppy screwball farce, found Carole Lombard juggling suitors Cesar Romero and Preston Foster. It was the innocuous Loretta Young soaper *Wife, Doctor and Nurse* (1937) that inaugurated Lang's term at Fox, a stay that would span thirty-four films and four decades. At Fox, Lang was given something he had never really had to work with before: frontline actors and first-rate scripts. *Wife* was followed by *Second Honeymoon* (1937), a romantic comedy that paired Young with rising star Tyrone Power as a once-married couple that decides to try it again. *The Baroness and the Butler* (1938) was a Continental *My Man Godfrey* starring William Powell, as a member of Hungary's parliament moonlighting as Annabella's butler. (Well, it makes sense if you see the movie.)

*I'll Give a Million* (1938) was a Capraesque fable about a world-weary millionaire (Warner Baxter) who disguises himself as a hobo to see whether anyone will treat him kindly without his fortune as an incentive; the woman who does will find nuptials her reward. *The Little Princess* (1939) was a handsomely mounted Technicolor version of the Frances Hodgson Burnett children's classic, starring Shirley Temple as the waif who's cruelly treated in a boarding school until father Ian Hunter returns from the Boer War to rescue her. (This is the one Shirley chose to make instead of *The Wizard of Oz.*) *Princess* was enough of a success to warrant putting her in another lavish fairy tale, but *The Blue Bird* (1940) became Shirley's first outright flop, probably because Ernest Pascal's screenplay was too heavy on the allegory and too chintzy on the fun. Lang fared better with *Star Dust* (1940), a Hollywood success story, with young Linda Darnell well cast as an aspiring actress and John Payne the newcomer who helps her make it.

The 1940 *The Great Profile* was a backstage satire about an actor whose drinking and mood swings nearly sink a show; John Barrymore, who had degenerated into a souse and a clown over the last several years, basically played himself, and bravely displayed the ruins of his once-great talent. The first of the many romantic musicals Lang directed that defined Fox in the Forties was *Tin Pan Alley* (also 1940), a period piece with the formidable cast of Betty Grable and Alice Faye (as singers, natch) and John Payne and Jack Oakie (as the struggling songwriters); Alfred Newman's score of golden oldies won an Oscar. The Technicolor *Moon over Miami* (1941) was an even bigger hit, with Grable and sister Carole Landis husband-hunting, Don Ameche and Robert Cummings were their willing prey. *Week-end in Havana* (1941) refined the formula by having shopgirl Alice Faye romanced by John Payne and Cesar Romero, while Carmen Miranda fumed on the sidelines.

*Song of the Islands* (1942) was a gorgeous trifle, with Grable and Victor Mature trying to reconcile their warring fathers against a Hawaiian backdrop. The nonmusical comedy *The Magnificent Dope* (1942) had Henry Fonda as a lazy hick whose country karma is more than a match for scheming self-help-school operators Don Ameche and Lynn Bari, while *Coney Island* (1943) was another colorful period musical, with turn-of-the-century songstress Betty Grable learning some class from George Montgomery, to the extreme displeasure of boyfriend and rival sa-

▲ *Lang takes notes, on the set of* The Baroness and the Butler

loon owner Cesar Romero. *Greenwich Village* (1944) offered Ameche as a classical composer who goes pop for William Bendix's speakeasy; Carmen Miranda makes a most colorful, if unlikely, denizen of the Twenties Village.

Lang's remake of *State Fair* (1945), a property previously directed by Henry King in 1933 with Will Rogers, starred Dana Andrews, Jeanne Crain, Dick Haymes, and Vivian Blaine putting across such Rodgers and Hammerstein tunes as the Oscar-winning "It Might As Well Be Spring" with brio (Hammerstein actually wrote the screenplay as well). *Sentimental Journey* (1946) was stickier going, a weeper about a Broadway couple (John Payne and Maureen O'Hara) who adopt a little girl, only to have mom pass away. Lang filmed another sentimental tale, *Claudia and David*, in 1946, but this sequel to the popular 1943 film *Claudia* was at least leavened with a bit of comedy, and Dorothy McGuire and Robert Young were as appealing a couple as they'd been in the original picture. *Mother Wore Tights* (1947) sent Grable back to vaudeville as half of a husband-and-wife song-and-dance team; Dan Dailey played hubby, and the film was such a success that he and Grable were teamed in three subsequent musicals.

*Sitting Pretty* (1948) was one of the year's biggest

comedy hits. Clifton Webb was in rare form as the imperious Mr. Belvedere, an author doing research on life in suburbia. To that end he offers his services as a babysitter to Robert Young and Maureen O'Hara, whose three wild young'uns have driven away every other caregiver; the film was popular enough to spawn a couple of sequels. (Webb was nominated for an Oscar, but in a minor upset lost to Laurence Olivier in *Hamlet*.) *When My Baby Smiles at Me* (1948) paired Grable and Dailey again, now as a married burlesque team that splits up when Dailey hits it big, then reunites after his alcoholism shows him how much he needs her. *You're My Everything* (1949) was another period musical; Dan Dailey is a dancer who aspires to act in silent movies but sees wife Anne Baxter gain film stardom instead.

Clifton Webb and Lang joined forces again for *Cheaper by the Dozen* (1950), a well-mounted adaptation of a popular turn-of-the-century memoir, with Webb as the stern paterfamilias of a large brood and Myrna Loy as his patient wife; it, too, would yield a sequel. *The Jackpot* (1950) was a clever satire about radio quiz shows (based on an article in *The New Yorker*), with James Stewart the "lucky" winner who now can't pay the taxes on his booty, while *On the Riviera* (1951) was a passable remake of Maurice Chevalier's *Folies Bergère*, starring Danny Kaye as a music-hall star who impersonates Gene Tierney's war-hero husband better than the husband. *With a Song in My Heart* (1952), starring Susan Hayward, was a biopic about singer Jane Froman, who'd been gravely injured in a plane crash and struggled to make a heroic comeback.

The 1953 *Call Me Madam*, a long, loud version of the Howard Lindsay–Russel Crouse Broadway hit, had Ethel Merman as the ambassador to Lichtenburg, belting out Irving Berlin songs ("It's a Lovely Day Today," "You're Just in Love") while being wooed by foreign minister George Sanders. Merman appeared again in *There's No Business Like Show Business* (1954), another Irving Berlin songfest (and schmaltzfest) that could have used less of Johnnie Ray and Mitzi Gaynor and more of Marilyn Monroe.

As Fox's top director of musicals, Lang naturally was given the challenge of adapting the classic Rodgers and Hammerstein show *The King and I* (1956) into a film; this he did, with splendid results. He had the advantage of having Yul Brynner recreate his Broadway role and Deborah Kerr star as Anna Leonowens (a part played by Irene Dunne in the 1946 nonmusical version, *Anna and the King of Siam*). The film was nominated for an Oscar as best picture, while Brynner and the score ("Getting to Know You," "Hello, Young Lovers") were among that year's winners, and Lang received his only Academy Award nomination.

*Desk Set* (1957) was hardly at that level, but it was a pleasant-enough Spencer Tracy–Katharine Hepburn romantic comedy, with its stage origins well disguised by Lang. The tart *But Not for Me* (1959) had long-in-the-tooth producer Clark Gable trying to sweep young wannabe actress Carroll Baker off her feet. But *Can-Can* (1960) failed to capture the flavor of Cole Porter's Parisian Gay Nineties stage musical, despite (or because of) Frank Sinatra and Shirley MacLaine as the leads; at least Maurice Chevalier, Louis Jourdan, Juliet Prowse, and Hermes Pan's choreography were beyond reproach. Lang adapted yet another stage property with *The Marriage-Go-Round* (1961), in which Susan Hayward is appalled by Julie Newmar's lack of morals; bookish husband James Mason is enchanted by the same.

Lang's last film was an ignominy. But what else can one say of Fox's decision to have him direct *Snow White and the Three Stooges* (1961)? It was a precipitous fall from grace, and Lang understandably stepped aside before further damage to the memory of his fine career could be inflicted.

## ● MITCHELL LEISEN (1898–1972)

A former art director whose eye for design and sense of style illuminated many of his films, Leisen was considered a "woman's director" by dint of his obvious affection for them, not because he chose material that smacked of the soap opera. But it's true that his pictures—almost all of them made at Paramount—belong to such strong female leads as Barbara Stanwyck, Paulette Goddard, Olivia de Havilland, Claudette Colbert, and Carole Lombard, who rarely were paired with an actor of equal stature (usually it was Fred MacMurray or Ray Milland, serving interchangeably). Leisen's women *were* the movie, their stories *the* story. There may not be a single fistfight in all of his work, but whatever weeping takes place therein is honestly earned.

Born in Menominee, Michigan, Leisen attended the Art Institute of Chicago and Washington University in St. Louis, where he studied art and architecture. This formal training brought him in 1919 to Hollywood, where he was hired as a costume designer by Cecil B. DeMille on *Male and Female.* He worked on such elaborate productions as *Robin Hood* and *The Thief of Bagdad*, then joined DeMille full-time as set designer and art director on *The King of Kings*, *The Squaw Man*, and *Sign of the Cross.* That last spectacular brought Leisen into the Paramount fold, where he would remain for the next twenty years.

After assisting Stuart Walker on two pictures in 1933, Leisen was given his chance to solo direct *Cradle Song*, starring Dorothea Wieck as a nun who raises an abandoned child in the convent until she is a grown woman (now Evelyn Venable) and leaves to be married. *Death Takes a Holiday* (1934) was an elegant allegory. Fredric March plays the Angel of Death, who visits a country home to observe humanity in action; he falls in love with Evelyn Venable, who willingly departs this mortal vale to be with him. *Murder at the Vanities* (1934) was less somber, a musical revue disguised as a murder mystery, with Earl Carroll's "specialty" numbers augmented by Duke Ellington's orchestra, Kitty Carlisle, and Leisen's gorgeous sets. But *Behold My Wife* (1935) was a hackneyed story about a rich lad (Gene Raymond) who marries Indian lass Sylvia Sidney and brings her home to spite his snobbish family.

*Four Hours to Kill* (1935) was an odd suspenser, with Richard Barthelmess as an escaped killer trying to revenge himself on the stoolie who sent him to the chair; the rest of the cast waits in a vaudeville theater to learn if he's been recaptured. (Leisen treated himself here to a cameo as the orchestra leader.) The fine romantic comedy *Hands Across the Table* (also 1935) was more typical of the Leisen oeuvre, with Carole Lombard at her most effervescent as a manicurist who gives up her fortune-hunting ways after falling for stone-broke playboy Fred MacMurray. MacMurray was paired with Joan Bennett in *Thirteen Hours by Air* (1936), a cut-rate *Grand Hotel* in the sky, while *The Big Broadcast of 1937* gave Leisen the chance to stage a parade of musical and comedy acts that included Burns and Allen, Jack Benny, Martha Raye, Benny Goodman, and Leopold Stokowski.

*Swing High, Swing Low* (1937) teamed Lombard and MacMurray again in a glitzy adaptation of the play *Burlesque*, with Fred as a trumpet player who lets the Broadway stars (and singer Dorothy Lamour) get in his eyes, leaving loyal wife Carole behind. She divorces the louse, he hits bottom, realizes what he lost, begs her to take him back—the rest you know. Less predictable was the 1937 comic masterpiece *Easy Living.* Preston Sturges's clever screenplay sets things in motion when irate tycoon Edward Arnold tosses a fur coat out a window; it lands on office girl Jean Arthur, changing her life from drudgery to one of obscene leisure almost against her will. Arthur has been in more famous films, but never was more radiant than she is here, making us believe unconditionally in her romance with rebellious rich boy Ray Milland.

*The Big Broadcast of 1938* was the predictable follow-up to *1937*, with Bob Hope making his screen debut and singing the Oscar-winning "Thanks for the Memory" to Shirley Ross. *Artists and Models Abroad* (1938) was also a sequel of a sort to the previous year's *Artists and Models*: Jack Benny is now in Paris with his perpetually broke theatrical troupe. *Midnight* (1939) was a more accomplished, complicated screwball comedy (scripted by Charles Brackett and Billy Wilder) that finds poor showgirl Claudette Colbert hired by wealthy John Barrymore to impersonate a Hungarian countess, while cabdriver Don Ameche pretends to be Colbert's husband; straying wife Mary Astor tries to understand it all.

*Remember the Night* (1940) was another winner. Barbara Stanwyck plays a recidivist shoplifter who gets caught at Christmas time and Fred MacMurray is the softhearted prosecutor who takes her home during the court's holiday recess to his family in Indiana, where they fall in love; the funny, slightly sappy script was by Preston Sturges. *Arise, My Love* (1940) had an Oscar-winning story, a screenplay by Brackett and Wilder, and Claudette Colbert in good form as a war correspondent covering Europe; Ray Milland plays the flier she falls for. Milland was back in a plane in the 1941 *I Wanted Wings*, with William Holden and Wayne Morris, but none of them made the slightest impression when newcomer Veronica Lake was onscreen.

*Hold Back the Dawn* (also 1941) was one of Leisen's least typical pictures, but it just might be his best. The cynical story by Brackett and Wilder offers

Romance...
Modern Style!
"HANDS ACROSS THE TABLE"

▲ *Leisen (center) is intent on stars Fred MacMurray and Carole Lombard while making* Swing High, Swing Low

Charles Boyer as a down-on-his-luck gigolo stuck in Mexico with brassy girlfriend Paulette Goddard, who sees visiting teacher Olivia de Havilland as their ticket into the United States. Boyer woos and wins Olivia, but suddenly realizes he actually loves her and, in a burst of conscience, offers to let her off the hook. The film was Oscar-nominated as the year's best picture, and de Havilland and the screenplay also received nominations. (Leisen appeared as himself, filming *I Wanted Wings* in the film's clever framing device.) *The Lady Is Willing* (1942) was a trifle in which Marlene Dietrich marries pediatrician Fred MacMurray solely to adopt a year-old orphan she is taken with. Up to that point the film made some sense, but when glamazon Dietrich falls in love with MacMurray, you know the script isn't kosher.

*Take a Letter, Darling* (1942) featured MacMurray as the male secretary (he's really a painter but needs a day job) to high-powered ad exec Rosalind Russell, who falls for him despite her better judgment. In *No Time for Love* (1943) MacMurray—yes, again—is a subway worker assisting photographer Claudette Colbert. Does she, too, fall in love with him? If you have to ask, you've never seen a Hollywood movie. Leisen next took on the Freudian musical *Lady in the Dark* (1944), an ambitious but seriously flawed attempt to transfer the inventive Broadway show by Moss Hart, Kurt Weill, and Ira Gershwin to the big screen. Leisen (or someone) unwisely dropped key songs that were clues to the neuroses of the protagonist, a magazine editor (Ginger Rogers, in over her head) who sees a psychiatrist to learn why she's near a nervous breakdown (the answer: the three men in her life). It had its moments, but someone like Vincente Minnelli might have been more appropriate as director. The 1944 *Frenchman's Creek* was an expensive costume picture, via the bestselling Daphne Du Maurier novel: eighteenth-century Englishwoman Joan Fontaine is wooed by French pirate Arturo de Cordova, who proves a distinct improvement over Basil Rathbone's rapacious nobleman.

*Practically Yours* (1944) teamed MacMurray and Colbert again—once too often?—in a farfetched Norman Krasna yarn about an Air Force pilot who sends a love letter to his dog just before he's shot down; a love-struck woman intercepts it, thinks it's for her, and—oh, never mind. Leisen made a welcome return to the eighteenth century with *Kitty* (1945), in which sly Ray Milland raises Paulette Goddard from the gutter, turning her into a duchess so she can marry into nobility and thereby make him his fortune. *Masquerade in Mexico* (1945) was Leisen's inferior musical remake of his own *Midnight*. But *To Each His Own* (1946) was a gem, a superior soaper about an unwed mother who surrenders her baby to an adoption agency during World War I, regrets it, and is separated from him for twenty years before finally locating him (now the adult John Lund). Charles Brackett's story might have turned maudlin in other hands, but de Havilland requested Leisen—a canny decision, as he directed her to her first Oscar.

That proved to be Leisen's last triumph. *Suddenly It's Spring* (1947) was a moribund marital comedy starring Fred MacMurray and Paulette Goddard as warring spouses who stubbornly refuse to divorce each other. The silly *Golden Earrings* (1947) was at least fun; Marlene Dietrich plays a gypsy recruited by Ray Milland to provide a cover for him while he searches for Hitler's poison-gas formula. *Dream Girl* (1948), from Elmer Rice's Broadway play, allowed Betty Hutton to do her best (worst?) Danny Kaye impersonation as an incessant daydreamer, while *Bride of Vengeance* (1949) recruited Leisen veteran Paulette Goddard to appear in Borgia Italy; the costumes were great, the rest spinach. *Song of Surrender* (1949) was a dull tale of farm girl Wanda Hendrix, who marries middle-aged museum curator Claude Rains circa 1900, then regrets it when MacDonald Carey turns up. But *Captain Carey, USA* (1950) paired Hendrix more happily with Alan Ladd, who is sent to a village in Italy to track down a Nazi collaborator; its theme song, "Mona Lisa," won an Oscar.

The 1950 *No Man of Her Own* was a feverish adaptation of William Irish's noir novel *I Married a Dead Man*, with Barbara Stanwyck per usual turning in a strong performance as the blackmailed protagonist, while *The Mating Season* (1951) was a tart comedy (co-scripted by Brackett) about class distinctions in America, with Gene Tierney, John Lund, and (especially) Oscar-nominated Thelma Ritter in fine form. An ancient James Barrie play was the basis for *Darling, How Could You!* (1951): teenager Mona Freeman is suspicious that mom Joan Fontaine is having an affair. It was Leisen's last film for Paramount, and perhaps understandably, it didn't have much heart.

Now a freelancer, Leisen made the 1952 *Young Man with Ideas*, starring Glenn Ford as a lawyer studying for the bar exam, and *Tonight We Sing* (1953), a musical biopic about Sol Hurok. *Bedevilled* (1955) was a weak suspense yarn, in which murder witness Anne Baxter hides out in Paris with a priest, while *The Girl Most Likely* (1958) was a musical remake of Garson Kanin's *Tom, Dick and Harry*; Jane Powell wasn't half bad in the Ginger Rogers role. Leisen had already started directing such television series as *G.E. Theatre*, and now he turned his back on moviemaking to work on episodes of *Wagon Train*, *The Twilight Zone*, and *Markham*—the last a series that starred his longtime leading man Ray Milland. In 1963 he co-directed a documentary about Las Vegas, *Spree*, which was released in 1967. Leisen then retired to return to his early love, interior design, which he practiced until his death in 1972.

## ● ROBERT Z. LEONARD (1889–1968)

One of MGM's premier directors for thirty years, Robert Z. Leonard made nearly fifty sound pictures and even more silents in a career that spanned five decades. But few of these films are particularly distinguished, while a dangerously high number flirt with mediocrity; consequently, his reputation has nearly fallen by the wayside. Born in Chicago, Leonard was acting and singing on stage early in the century and began acting in films in 1907, appearing in the likes of *The Courtship of Miles Standish* and *Robinson Crusoe*. His directorial debut was on the 1914 Universal serial *The Master Key*, in which he also acted. Leonard worked primarily for Universal and Paramount through the Teens, and many of his films during this period starred his first wife, Mae Murray. He joined Metro as the producer and director on *Peacock Alley* in 1921 and stayed there for the next thirty-four years—one of the longest continuous stints at a Hollywood studio by any director in cinema history.

*The Demi-Bride* (1926) was the first of five films he made with Norma Shearer; he also directed her last silent, *A Lady of Chance*, as well as Marion Davies in *The Cardboard Lover* (1928) and *Marianne* (1929), Davies's first sound picture. Leonard's first talkie with Shearer, *The Divorcee* (1930), was their most successful production to date: They both were nominated for Academy Awards, as was the film itself, and Shearer won her only Oscar for her performance as a sexually emancipated woman. *In Gay Madrid* with Ramon Novarro, *Let Us Be Gay* with Norma Shearer and Marie Dressler, and *The Bachelor Father* (all 1930) with Marion Davies and C. Aubrey Smith came next. *It's a Wise Child* (1931) was another Marion Davies comedy, while *Five and Ten* (1931) found Davies less successfully tackling soap opera. But *Susan Lenox: Her Fall and Rise* (1931) was a classy (if solemn) vehicle for Greta Garbo, well matched here for the first and only time with rising star Clark Gable. *Lovers Courageous* was a harmless romantic comedy, with Robert Montgomery and Madge Evans, while *Strange Interlude* (both 1932) paired Gable with Shearer in a plodding version of Eugene O'Neill's orgy of introspection. (At least it wasn't five hours long, like the original stage production!)

Leonard may have been relieved to return to comedy and Marion Davies with *Peg o' My Heart* (1933), but that modest effort was overshadowed by his other 1933 release, *Dancing Lady*. One of the biggest hits in MGM's history to that point, this backstage musical starred Joan Crawford opposite Gable, with Fred Astaire (in his film debut) added for class and the Three Stooges for comedy relief (though the sight of Joan tap-dancing with furious intensity was surely funny enough). *Outcast Lady* (1934) found Constance Bennett in the role essayed by Garbo a few years earlier in *A Woman of Affairs*; she needn't have bothered. *After Office Hours* (1935) had society dame Bennett exploited by wily newspaper editor Clark Gable to no great effect, but *Escapade* (also 1935) was more successful, a comedy set in prewar Vienna, with Luise Rainer making her impressive Hollywood debut opposite William Powell.

*The Great Ziegfeld* (1936) was Leonard's best and biggest hit, a lavish biopic of flamboyant showman Flo Ziegfeld that starred MGM's number-one team, William Powell and Myrna Loy. But it was Luise Rainer in the tear-suffused role of Flo's neglected wife, Anna Held, who stole the picture, winning the best actress Oscar. With some twenty-three songs and seven elaborate production numbers filling 170 minutes, the film won the Academy Award for best picture over nine other contenders, and Leonard was nominated for the second time. That smash was followed by *Piccadilly Jim* (1936), a merely adequate adaptation of a P. G. Wodehouse story.

Leonard was then entrusted with the career of

Jeanette MacDonald, MGM's top thrush and one of the industry's most reliable attractions at the box office. Over the next four years he made five consecutive films with her: *Maytime* (1937), an enormously popular version of the old Broadway show, with Nelson Eddy and John Barrymore dueling over opera star Jeanette; *The Firefly* (1937), which less successfully installed Allan Jones as her foil (MacDonald had asked to star without Eddy), based on the creaky 1912 stage vehicle; *The Girl of the Golden West* (1938), another revival of the hoary David Belasco show, with Eddy back on board as a most unlikely bandit; *Broadway Serenade* (1939), a rare contemporary vehicle for MacDonald (sans Eddy) that dramatically illustrated why the public wanted her in period spectaculars; and *New Moon* (1940), a passable remake of the 1930 Lawrence Tibbett–Grace Moore film set in old Louisiana, with a good Sigmund Romberg–Oscar Hammerstein score that included ''Stout-Hearted Men'' and ''One Kiss.''

Released from his bondage to MacDonald, Leonard made *Pride and Prejudice* (1940), an excellent version of the Jane Austen classic (based on a stage adaptation) with Laurence Olivier, Greer Garson, and Maureen O'Sullivan heading the fine cast. Somehow the Academy managed to ignore *Pride* in all the major categories for 1940, though it did win an Oscar for its beautiful art direction. *Third Finger, Left Hand* (also 1940) was a stab at screwball comedy that didn't quite come off; Myrna Loy and Melvyn Doug-

◀ *With William Powell and Myrna Loy on the set of* The Great Ziegfeld

las made for an uncompelling match. But Leonard was soon back in his element with *Ziegfeld Girl* (1941), an all-stops-out backstage musical that charted the rise of Judy Garland and Hedy Lamarr and the fall of Lana Turner amid much pomp and some mighty flimsy circumstances. Busby Berkeley directed the musical numbers brilliantly, and the film was an enormous box-office hit—the last Leonard could claim, though he would direct for another fifteen years.

*When Ladies Meet* (1941) was a stilted remake of the 1933 film that failed to meld the talents of Joan Crawford, Robert Taylor, and Greer Garson, while *We Were Dancing* (1942) was a labored adaptation of Noël Coward's *Tonight at 8:30* that was one of Norma Shearer's last pictures (one she chose to do over *Mrs. Miniver*—foolish woman!). Leonard made a rare foray into the war genre with *Stand By for Action* (1942), a patriotic World War II yarn featuring Robert Taylor as a Navy commander who saves a boatload of mothers and babies. *The Man from Down Under* (1943) was a heartwarming comedy starring Charles Laughton, who raises a couple of orphans in Australia; this was unfamiliar terrain for Leonard, and it showed. MGM pulled out all the stops for the soap opera *Marriage Is a Private Affair* (1944), but even the glamour of Lana Turner proved insufficient ballast to float this leaky ship.

*Weekend at the Waldorf* (1945) was a glossy but ill-advised remake of *Grand Hotel* that tried to fob off Walter Pidgeon, Lana Turner, Ginger Rogers, and Van Johnson where once Garbo, Crawford, Beery, and Barrymore had trod (yet audiences did pay to see it). Somewhat better was *The Secret Heart* (1946), an unusual drama with a gothic flair that featured June Allyson, Walter Pidgeon, and Claudette Colbert. *Cynthia* (1947), from a Vina Delmar play, was little more than an excuse for the young Elizabeth Taylor to get her first screen kiss, while *B.F.'s Daughter* (1948) was a static adaptation of the J. P. Marquand novel, starring Barbara Stanwyck and Van Heflin. *The Bribe* (1948) was Leonard's first encounter with film noir, but even Ava Gardner at her most gorgeous, Robert Taylor at his most stoic, and Vincent Price at his most hissable failed to elevate the film beyond the level of pulp.

Leonard next directed Judy Garland in *In the Good Old Summertime* (1949), an appealing musical remake of *The Shop Around the Corner* that might have been even better had Judy been paired with a more romantic figure than Van Johnson. *Nancy Goes to Rio* (1950) was a remake of a Deanna Durbin musical with a second-rate script (by Sidney Sheldon) and cast, while *Duchess of Idaho* (1950) transported Esther Williams to the slopes of Sun Valley with Van Johnson—not her best, although the singing of Lena Horne and Mel Tormé helped. *Grounds for Marriage* (1950) was a relatively painless romantic comedy about an opera singer (Kathryn Grayson) who still is interested in her ex-husband (Johnson again, whom Leonard apparently had adopted). *Too Young to Kiss* (1951) was, yes, Van Johnson, paired this time with June Allyson in the sort of blandly antiseptic romance on which MGM these days so often relied.

Leonard next directed *Everything I Have Is Yours* (1952) with Marge and Gower Champion, but even their skills couldn't energize this mundane musical. *The Clown* (1953) posited Red Skelton as an over-the-hill circus performer whose loving son still considers him a champ (and, indeed, this was a clever recycling of the 1931 sobfest *The Champ*). Skelton was moving in that, but in *The Great Diamond Robbery* (1953) he was back to being insufferable; this was his last work for MGM. *Her Twelve Men* (1954) offered Greer Garson at her most impossibly noble as a schoolteacher adored by her students, and it became *her* last MGM vehicle after fifteen often glorious years.

Leonard hadn't been given many first-rate productions to direct of late, but *The King's Thief* (1955) was his best picture in years, a good costume drama starring David Niven and Ann Blyth. That film turned out to be Leonard's swan song at MGM. His last two films were the Italian production *Beautiful but Dangerous* with Gina Lollobrigida and *Kelly and Me* (1957)—ironically, another Van Johnson musical.

## ● MERVYN LeROY (1900-1987)

LeRoy's career is a microcosm of Hollywood entire. A gag writer for one-reel comedies in the Teens, he worked as an actor in the Twenties, became a top director in the Thirties, a major producer/director in the Forties, and a busy legend through the Fifties and early Sixties. More than sixty sound pictures, many revered titles among them, and just a lone Oscar for the lot (and that for a documentary short). But subtract his forty years of moviemaking and what would you have? A gaping hole in screen history.

Born in San Francisco, LeRoy earned his first money as a newsboy; that humble skill became his entreé to show business when one of his customers helped him get a part on stage as, yes, a newsboy. Bitten by the bug, he performed in vaudeville as "The Singing Newsboy" and was hired for a gig at the San Francisco Expo of 1916. His cousin Jesse Lasky helped him get a job folding costumes at Famous Players–Lasky in 1919, and from there he made his ascent through the ranks, from lab technician to assistant cameraman. But somehow LeRoy managed a parallel career as an actor, playing juveniles in films from 1920 to 1924.

Outgrowing those parts, LeRoy moved behind the scenes, writing gags (and sometimes more) for such Colleen Moore pictures as *Sally, Ella Cinders*, and *Twinkletoes*. In 1927 Warners signed him to direct, and he commenced this most important phase of his career with low-budget efforts like *Harold Teen* (1928) and *Oh Kay!* (1928). *Naughty Baby* (1929), a comedy with Alice White, was his first sound picture, and White also starred in *Hot Stuff* and *Broadway Babies* that year and *Showgirl in Hollywood* the next; this was an inside-Hollywood yarn with portions shot in Technicolor. Also in 1930 came *Numbered Men*, shot partly on location at San Quentin, and *Top Speed*, a Joe E. Brown musical comedy with songs by Bert Kalmar and Harry Ruby. Then came *Little Caesar* (1930), the film that made LeRoy's rep, with Edward G. Robinson as a Capone-like crime czar. Based on a hard-boiled novel by W. R. Burnett, this is one of the seminal gangster pictures, along with Wellman's *Public Enemy* and Hawks's *Scarface* (although it's not as fluid as either of them).

*Gentleman's Fate, Too Young to Marry*, and the Joe E. Brown comedy *Broad-Minded* (all 1931) followed, though none had the impact of *Caesar*. But *Five Star Final* had the benefit of Edward G. Robinson again,

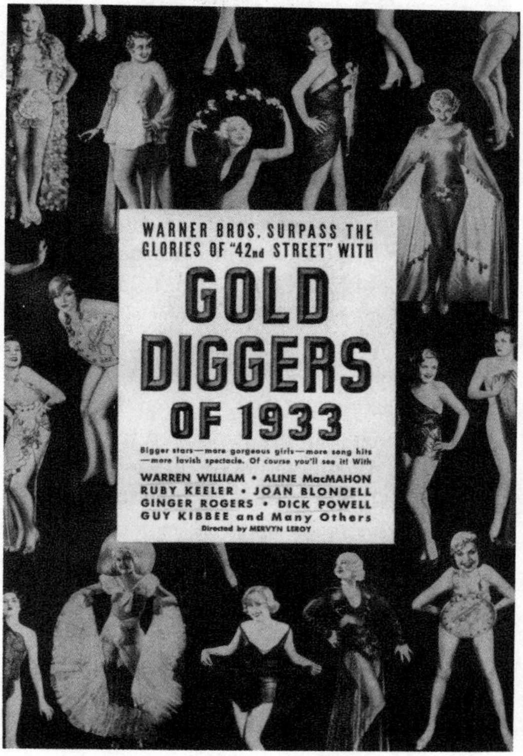

▲ *With producer Sidney Franklin (left) and Reginald Owen on the set of* Madame Curie

now as a hard-boiled newspaper editor (as if there's any other kind) whose ethics get twisted out of shape in his pursuit of higher circulation. *Local Boy Makes Good*, yet another Joe E. Brown vehicle, and *Tonight or Never* completed LeRoy's slate for 1931—six releases, an impressive figure even by the standards of the time. *High Pressure* (1932) offered William Powell in top comic form as a con man trying to find investors for his artificial rubber process, while *Two Seconds* (1932) had Edward G. Robinson playing a convicted murderer who has just moments to relive his miserable existence before the electric chair ends it all.

*Big City Blues* (1932), a modest crime yarn, starred Eric Linden and Joan Blondell, and the 63-minute *Three on a Match* was a breathless melodrama, starring Blondell, Bette Davis, and Ann Dvorak as childhood friends who reunite as adults just in time for one of them to meet a tragic fate; Warren William and, in a smaller role, Humphrey Bogart were the catalysts. LeRoy's first golden era commenced in 1932 with *I Am a Fugitive from a Chain Gang*, a blistering adaptation of Robert E. Burns's account of his horrible experiences in a Georgia prison camp. The film was nominated for an Academy Award as best picture, but it was Paul Muni's harrowing portrayal of the unjustly imprisoned con that seemed a shoo-in for an Oscar. (He lost to Charles Laughton's Henry VIII.) *Hard to Handle* (1933) hadn't an iota of social consciousness in its bones, but it remains a fine example of the Warners pre-Code comedies, with Jimmy Cagney hilarious as a press agent who'll promote anything and everything.

The 1933 *Elmer the Great* had Joe E. Brown as a very un-Ruthian home-run slugger, but it was *Gold*

*Diggers of 1933* that became a Depression classic. A hastily produced sequel to the phenomenally popular *42nd Street*, with essentially the same cast and dance director Busby Berkeley, it's memorable primarily for Ginger Rogers et al. singing "We're in the Money," Joan Blondell heading the spectacular production number "My Forgotten Man," and Dick Powell and Ruby Keeler performing the deliciously naughty "Pettin' in the Park." *Tugboat Annie* (1933) was another smash, although today exposure to the mugging of stars Wallace Beery and Marie Dressler requires a vaccination. LeRoy's fifth release of the year was *The World Changes*, a nicely done soap opera starring Paul Muni as a meat-packing tycoon and Mary Astor as his snob of a wife.

The advent of the Production Code didn't meld at first with LeRoy's strengths. *Hi, Nellie!* (1934) had Muni again, now starring in a forgettable newspaper comedy. *Heat Lightning* was a "B" murder mystery that starred second-banana Aline MacMahon—not much of an assignment for a director of LeRoy's stature—while *Happiness Ahead* (both 1934) was a semi-musical romance, with Dick Powell as a window-cleaning magnate. *Sweet Adeline* (1935), a period musical, had Irene Dunne in a Hoboken beer garden, awash in Kern-Hammerstein II songs. The 1935 *Oil for the Lamps of China* was a long, turgid drama (based on a forgotten bestseller by Alice Tisdale Hobart), in which Pat O'Brien plays an oil company executive stationed in China. But *Page Miss Glory* that same year used O'Brien to better effect as a wise-guy con man, although Marion Davies didn't add much to the frenzy surrounding the search for a beauty contestant who doesn't exist. *I Found Stella Parish* (1935) was more suds; Kay Francis played an actress trying to cover up her scarlet past.

LeRoy was finally given a prestige property with *Anthony Adverse* (1936), a hugely successful costumer based on the Hervey Allen bestseller. Fredric March starred as the globe-trotting hero, and the glittering cast included Olivia de Havilland, Claude Rains, and Gale Sondergaard, who won the first-ever Academy Award for best supporting actress. Eric Wolfgang Korngold's score also won an Oscar, and the film was nominated as best picture. LeRoy returned to the Warners mill, grinding out low-budget fare like the onetime stage hit *Three Men on a Horse* (1936) with Sam Levene and Joan Blondell and the romantic comedy *The King and the Chorus Girl* (1937), again with Blondell.

*They Won't Forget* (1937) was the first picture with a serious theme LeRoy had been given in years, and he made the most of it. Based on a novel by Ward Greene that itself dramatized the 1913 rape/murder of a fifteen-year-old Atlanta girl (played here by Lana Turner, who was under personal contract to LeRoy), the film was a powerful indictment of racism and political ambition, embodied by prosecutor Claude Rains. But then it was back to the frothy nonsense of *Fools for Scandal* (1938), with Carole Lombard badly mismatched with Fernand Gravet as lovebirds in Paris. These last three films were also produced by LeRoy, but it was becoming clear that Warner Bros. had no sense of what projects best suited him.

Thus it came as no surprise that LeRoy left Warners for the greener pastures of MGM, where he was offered an unusual deal that allowed him to function as either a producer or a director. He began by producing the films of other directors: Robert Sinclair's *Dramatic School*, W. S. Van Dyke's *Stand Up and Fight*, Eddie Buzzell's *At the Circus*, and, most enduringly, Victor Fleming's *The Wizard of Oz*. Finally, in 1940, LeRoy stepped behind the camera again. His first picture was a sanitized *Waterloo Bridge*, adapted from the Robert E. Sherwood play about a London prostitute (here a ballerina) and a soldier who fall in love during an air raid. Last filmed in 1931 by James Whale, LeRoy's glossier version starred Vivien Leigh and Robert Taylor.

*Escape* (1940) starred Taylor again, now trying to get his mother out of a Nazi concentration camp with the help of Norma Shearer, while *Blossoms in the Dust* (1941) offered Greer Garson in one of her most sentimental roles as the founder of an orphanage; naturally Walter Pidgeon was on hand to lend support. *Unholy Partners* (1941) was an offbeat period crime yarn, with Edward G. Robinson as a newspaper baron who has to make a deal with gang lord Edward Arnold to get his paper published. The crime opus *Johnny Eager* (1942) was driven by the star chemistry between Robert Taylor and Lana Turner; the acting was left to Van Heflin as Taylor's alcoholic buddy, a performance that won an Oscar.

An even bigger success was the 1942 *Random Harvest*, an irresistible weeper from the James Hilton novel. Ronald Colman—the noblest of all screen sufferers—is left with amnesia and shell shock after World War I. But his frustration melts away under the tender ministrations of dancer Greer Garson, whom he falls in love with and marries. They have a child; then a collison restores his memory and wipes out his years with Garson. But she doesn't forget him . . . There's much, much more—perhaps a bit *too* much—but suffice it to say that the film earned LeRoy his only Academy Award nomination for best direction, and the picture (a huge hit), Colman, and the screenplay were also Oscar-nominated. *Madame Curie* (1943) gave Garson a historical figure to impersonate heroically, alongside Walter Pidgeon, and the popular pair were rewarded with more Oscar nominations; it, too, was a best picture nominee.

LeRoy had been on quite a roll, and he now shifted gears for the bang-up World War II epic *Thirty Seconds over Tokyo* (1944), based on participant Ted Lawson's book about America's first bombing raid on Japan in 1942. Van Johnson stars as Lawson (well, it's *his* version of events, after all), and Robert Walker, Robert Mitchum, and Spencer Tracy are among the other fliers. Another exercise in patriotism was LeRoy's 1945 documentary short about racial tolerance, *The House I Live In*. Written by Albert Maltz, with Frank Sinatra delivering the message, it won a special Oscar for LeRoy—the only one he'd ever receive. *Without Reservations* (1946) was a pleasant romantic comedy with the offbeat pairing of John Wayne and Claudette Colbert, but LeRoy sensibly kept his name off the miserable *Desire Me* (1947), as did George Cukor and Jack Conway. *Homecoming* (1948) was an endless weeper about World War II battlefield surgeon Clark Gable and nurse Lana Turner; they'd been better served in their past teamings. LeRoy's remake of *Little Women* (1949) with Janet Leigh, Elizabeth Taylor, June Allyson, and Margaret O'Brien didn't make anyone forget the 1933 Cukor version starring Katharine Hepburn, but it has its champions (Rex Reed among them).

LeRoy hadn't had a hit since *Tokyo*, and make-work pictures like *Any Number Can Play* (1949), which featured Clark Gable as a gambler with marital problems, did nothing to re-establish him. *East Side, West Side* (1950) had the benefit of a great cast—Ava Gardner, James Mason, Barbara Stanwyck, Van Heflin—but with all that talent wrestling with marriage and temptation, this romantic drama should have been much better. MGM's foray into DeMille territory with the $7 million production *Quo Vadis?* (1951) had actually been initiated with John Huston directing in 1949, but once LeRoy took over he did a fine job ladling out the spectacle—hordes of centurions, Christians, and some 120 lions—filmed on location in Rome over six grueling months. The love affair between Robert Taylor and Deborah Kerr held the three-hour picture together, and Peter Ustinov's outrageous interpretation of Nero was inspired. Nominated for seven Academy Awards, including best picture, *Quo Vadis?* for a time became the world's second-highest-grossing picture, behind *GWTW*.

From that height, LeRoy returned to MGM's business-as-usual. *Lovely to Look At* (1952), with Kathryn Grayson, Howard Keel, and the Champions, was a handsome if unnecessary remake of *Roberta*, while *Million Dollar Mermaid* (1952), starring Esther Williams and Victor Mature, was a passable biopic about famed Australian swimmer Annette Kellerman, who became a Hollywood star in the silent era; Busby Berkeley handled the musical numbers. *Latin Lovers* (1953), however, was a gruesome semi-musical, with Lana Turner and Ricardo Montalban in

▲ *Marge and Gower Champion display their prowess to LeRoy during* Lovely to Look At

Rio, and *Rose Marie* (1954) was another inferior remake of a Thirties classic; Ann Blyth and Technicolor fail to compensate for Jeanette MacDonald's absence.

That film completed LeRoy's tenure at MGM. In a neat bit of closure he now returned to Warner Bros., where he would both produce and direct. *Strange Lady in Town* (1955) was a forgettable Western starring Greer Garson as a frontier doctor, but then LeRoy was asked to take over *Mister Roberts* (1955) from John Ford, who was ill and had been having an awful time with Henry Fonda, the star of the original Broadway success. Josh Logan, the co-author of the play and the movie's co-scripter, was reputed to have shot additional scenes, and indeed the film now plays as if too many cooks had left it on the stove too long. But it was a major box-office hit and was nominated as best picture, and Jack Lemmon won the Oscar for his Ensign Pulver.

*The Bad Seed* (1956) had also been a hit on Broadway. LeRoy's popular but slavishly faithful screen version of Maxwell Anderson's play imported most of the original cast, and Nancy Kelly, Eileen Heckart, and child actress Patty McCormack all earned Academy Award nominations. *Toward the Unknown* (1956) was a decent flyboy yarn, with William Holden and James Garner. The hit *No Time for Sergeants* (1958) captured the spirit of the Broadway show (by Ira Levin) in a way that *Mister Roberts* never did, and in the process laid the groundwork for Andy Griffith's TV career as a lovable hick. *Home Before Dark* (1958) was a well-mounted drama about Jean Simmons's efforts to readjust to a normal life after spending a year in a mental institution, while *The FBI Story* (1959) was a capsule dramatization of the agency's most famous cases (Baby Face Nelson, Dillinger, Nazi spies, the KKK), with James Stewart's agent the focus and Vera Miles as his long-suffering wife—both pictures would have profited from a half hour being trimmed.

*Wake Me When It's Over* (1960), a very funny comedy, featured Dick Shawn and Ernie Kovacs as Army pals in the Far East who have a great hustle going on the side. But *The Devil at 4 O'Clock* (1961) wasted Spencer Tracy and Frank Sinatra in a limp drama about the evacuation of a children's hospital after a volcano erupts, and *A Majority of One* (1962) was an interminable adaptation of the Broadway success; Rosalind Russell (as a Jewish divorcée) and Alec Guinness (a Japanese diplomat?!) are wildly miscast. *Gypsy* was a qualified success; Russell was better served as the frightening Rose Hovick (originally played by Ethel Merman), who drives daughters Gypsy Rose Lee (an out-of-her-league Natalie Wood) and "Baby June" Havoc halfway to the nuthouse. At least most of the Jule Styne–Stephen Sondheim songs survived.

LeRoy fished in the Broadway waters again and landed Jean Kerr's *Mary, Mary* (1963). He deliberately filmed this Debbie Reynolds–Barry Nelson marital farce as if it were still on stage, and perhaps it should have stayed there. His last credit was *Moment to Moment* (1966), a not terribly believable murder mystery with Jean Seberg and Honor Blackman. LeRoy also assisted John Wayne on *The Green Berets* (1968) before retiring. His autobiography, *Take One*, was published in 1974.

## ● JOSEPH H. LEWIS (1900– )

A talented director who remained trapped in the ghetto of "B" pictures, Joseph H. Lewis might never have become one of the greats even if he *had* been entrusted with "A" budgets, actual stars instead of has-beens and never-weres, and top studio writers. But one can't help wondering, What if . . .



Born in New York City, Lewis broke into the industry as a camera assistant at MGM, then moved to Republic, a studio known for its low-budget fare, to be a film editor. He was a second-unit director on a number of productions before co-directing (with Crane Wilbur) his first feature, *Navy Spy*, in 1937. A plethora of genre entries followed, mostly Westerns along the lines of *Two-Fisted Rangers* and *The Man from Tumbleweeds*. By 1940 he had moved to Monogram, a studio specializing in a slightly better class of programmers, where he directed the East Side Kids entries *Boys of the City* (1940) and *Pride of the Bowery* (1941) and the Bela Lugosi shocker *The Invisible Ghost* (1941). He might have taken a slight step backward by moving to PRC in 1942, where more Westerns and something called *Secrets of a Co-ed* awaited him.

At Universal he was entrusted with low-level projects like *The Mad Doctor of Market Street* (1942), with Lionel Atwill as a murderous hypnotist. But at RKO he worked on *The Falcon in San Francisco* (1945), a good entry in the series that netted him a contract with Columbia. There, for the first time, he was given properties—if not budgets—that supported better filmmaking. *My Name Is Julia Ross* (1945) was his first assignment, a good film noir in which Nina Foch is menaced by dotty Dame May Whitty and her lunatic family. *So Dark the Night* (1946) was a mystery set in the French countryside, neatly done, with one of the most obscure casts ever assembled (Steven Geray, Micheline Cheirel, Ann Codee, etc.).

*The Swordsman* (1947) sent Larry Parks and Ellen Drew to Scotland in the 1700s—a concept that had posed no problem for Michael Curtiz and Errol Flynn but which left Lewis and Parks floundering. *The Return of October* (1948), a lame comedy with Glenn Ford and Terry Moore, was equally taxing for Lewis, and its "Mr. Ed"–like story line would have defeated anyone short of Preston Sturges. But *The Undercover Man* (1949) gave Ford and Lewis a reprieve, resulting in a solid docudrama inspired by the Feds' pursuit of Al Capone for tax evasion.

His Columbia contract having expired, Lewis went to UA in 1949 to make *Deadly Is the Female*, an adaptation of MacKinlay Kantor's *Saturday Evening Post* story "Gun Crazy"; it starred John Dall, most recently seen in Hitchcock's *Rope*, and Peggy Cummins, a Welsh beauty best known for having been fired from *Forever Amber* two years earlier. The title and advertising campaign were scrapped after a brief release, and the film was overhauled into *Gun Crazy*, which in retrospect just may be the best movie of 1950. Loosely based on the Bonnie and Clyde legend (although Bonnie never looked like *that*), this delirious tale of sexual obsession and the thrill of violence was twenty years ahead of its time. The reputation Lewis now enjoys is based almost wholly on a latter-day appreciation of this poetic rendering of American bloodlust.

*Gun Crazy* was a hard act to follow, and Lewis's next film, *A Lady Without Passport* (1950), was only serviceable, although Hedy Lamarr looked great as a shady dame trying to get out of Havana. *Retreat, Hell!* (1952) was his only foray into the war picture. Frank Lovejoy starred in this downbeat but effective account of the Marines' defeat at Korea's Changjin Reservoir; it was one of the few contemporary movies about the war based on fact. At MGM there was the unremarkable *Desperate Search*, in which Howard Keel tries to find his children in the Canadian wilderness, and *Cry of the Hunted* (both 1953), a formulaic chase picture set in the Louisiana bayous. Far better was *The Big Combo* (1955), a demented crime pic starring Cornell Wilde, Jean Wallace, and Richard Conte; in it, Lewis showed off some of his personal flourishes, making this one of the last great noirs.

Lewis's final four films were Westerns, bringing him full circle. *A Lawless Street* (1955) was good Randolph Scott, falling just short of his work with Budd Boetticher, while *Seventh Cavalry* (1956) offered Scott again in the interesting role of a Little Big Horn survivor who must prove he is not a deserter, and *The Halliday Brand* (1957) had Joseph Cotten as a despotic rancher who comes to a predictable end. *Terror in a Texas Town* (1958) was the most original of the group; Sterling Hayden played a whaler (visiting his father out West) who must use his harpoon to wipe out evil oil baron Sebastian Cabot. This marked the end of Lewis's career in films, since he then moved into television, where he worked through the Sixties. He left behind a filmography that, while not imposing, shows flashes of brilliance through an eye that saw things its own idiosyncratic way.

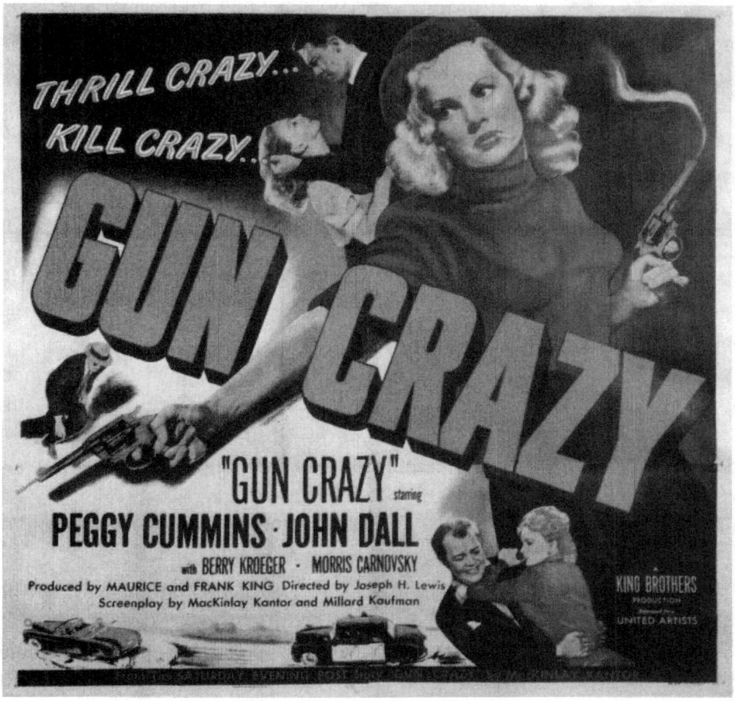

## ● ANATOLE LITVAK (1902-1974)

His Hollywood work was so diverse that it's easy to think of four other directors as having been responsible for Anatole Litvak's various phases—social realism at Warners, wartime documentaries, *films noir* and other postwar dramas, and the weighty soap operas of the Fifties. Mixed among these are some fine historical romances, leaving only comedies, musicals, and Westerns outside his purview.



Born in Kiev as Mikhail Anatol Litwak, he worked as a stagehand in a St. Petersburg theater while a teenager. Later he earned an advanced degree at a university in St. Petersburg, after which he attended the State School of Theater. A veteran of stage productions as both an actor and a director, he began working in film in 1923 at the Nordkino studios in Leningrad, and earned his first directing credit in 1925. That same year he left Russia for Germany, where he continued working as an assistant director and director until the advent of the Nazis in 1933 convinced him (a Jew) to flee to Paris. There he directed four more films, most famously *Mayerling* (1936) with Charles Boyer and Danielle Darrieux, the success of which brought him to Hollywood.

His first U.S. film was *The Woman I Love* (1937), made at RKO with Paul Muni and Miriam Hopkins; it bombed, but as a consolation prize Litvak married Hopkins. He then signed with Warner Bros., where he would make his next nine films. First came the 1937 *Tovarich*, a classy comedy about Russian émigrés working in Paris—a subject Litvak could identify with, no doubt—adapted from Jacques Deval's French play by Robert Sherwood. Charles Boyer and Claudette Colbert were excellent as former aristocrats working as domestics to make ends meet while holding on to the imperial treasure. More typical for Warners was *The Amazing Dr. Clitterhouse* (1938), an absurd but enjoyable crime pic starring Edward G. Robinson and Humphrey Bogart.

*The Sisters* (1938) was a good turn-of-the-century drama; Bette Davis is unhappily married to reporter Errol Flynn, and siblings Anita Louise and Jane Bryan have their own problems. More topical was *Confessions of a Nazi Spy* (1939), with Edward G. Robinson as an FBI agent uncovering an American Nazi *bund* headed by Paul Lukas, while *Castle on the Hudson* (1940) was a solid remake of Curtiz's 1933 gem *20,000 Years in Sing Sing*, with John Garfield and Ann Sheridan assuming the Spencer Tracy and Bette Davis roles. Litvak was next given a more prestigious production, the lavish *All This, and Heaven Too* (1940). It was adapted from a popular novel by Rachel Field, set in 1800s France, about a governess who falls in love with her nobleman employer and helps him murder his clinging wife. Bette Davis and Charles Boyer were superb as the tragic lovers, while Barbara O'Neil as the doomed wife was Oscar-nominated. The picture also received a nomination from the Academy as 1940's best, and was Warners' biggest moneymaker that year.

Litvak might have developed into another Wyler if he'd been given more properties like *Heaven*, but Warners' plans for him were different. *City for Conquest* (also 1940) was a gritty melodrama, with James Cagney as a boxer who sacrifices everything so that younger brother Arthur Kennedy can continue his career as a musician. Ann Sheridan and (in a small but colorful role) Elia Kazan also made an impact. *Out of the Fog* (1941) was an atmospheric rendering of Irwin Shaw's play *The Gentle People*, with John Garfield good in the unsympathetic role of a gangster preying on Brooklyn waterfront fishermen, while *Blues in the Night* (1941) was an ambitious but ultimately inadequate drama about the stressful lives of jazz musicians and their girlfriends, starring Richard Whorf, Priscilla Lane, and Elia Kazan (as a clarinetist).

Now an American citizen, Litvak left Warners for

Fox, but he had time to make only one picture there, the patriotic *This Above All* (1942) with Tyrone Power and Joan Fontaine, before joining the Army's Special Services Film Unit. There he worked with Frank Capra on the *Why We Fight* series of documentaries, co-directing *The Nazis Strike* (1942), *Divide and Conquer* (1943), and *The Battle of China* (1944) with Capra, and soloing on *The Battle of Russia, Operation Titanic* (both 1943), and *War Comes to America* (1945).

He returned to peacetime Hollywood and directed *The Long Night* (1947), a remake of a 1939 Marcel Carné thriller, but Henry Fonda is impossibly stiff in the Jean Gabin role as a killer under siege, and the picture was a million-dollar loser for RKO. But Litvak's production of *Sorry, Wrong Number* (1948)—inaugurating his move to producer-director—was a huge hit. Burt Lancaster starred alongside Barbara Stanwyck, who was Oscar-nominated for her intense performance as a paranoid, psychosomatically crippled heiress who overhears plans for her own murder on the telephone and then must wait in a panic for it to happen. The film was expanded from the original 22-minute radio play (which had starred Agnes Moorehead) by creator Lucille Fletcher.

*The Snake Pit* (1948) was a harrowing account of treatment in a mental institution, adapted from Mary Jane Ward's fictionalized autobiography, the rights to which Litvak bought prepublication. Olivia de Havilland, who prepared for her role for months by joining Litvak in observing a mental facility's day-to-day operations, became the second actress in a Litvak production to be nominated for an Academy Award as best actress of 1948. The film was also Oscar-nominated, as were the screenplay and the score, and Litvak received his only best direction nomination. That triumph was followed by the fine thriller *Decision before Dawn* (1951), with Oskar Werner as a double agent spying on the Nazis for the United States during World War II; Litvak used authentic German locations to lend verisimilitude to the picture.

*Act of Love* (1953) was the mundane tale of GI Kirk Douglas romancing French waif Dany Robin in Paris, while *The Deep Blue Sea* (1955), written by Terrence Rattigan, starred Vivien Leigh as a suicidal woman who has left her husband to live with another man but remains trapped in despair. *Anastasia* (1956) was Litvak's best film of the decade; Ingrid Bergman portrays the amnesiac refugee who impersonates Czar Nicholas II's long-lost daughter at the behest of Yul Brynner. It was Bergman's first U.S. film in seven years, and Hollywood made reparations of a sort for exiling her by voting her an Academy Award (her second) as best actress. Litvak then remade his *Mayerling* for a 1957 television broadcast. Brynner worked with Litvak again in *The Journey* (1959), an overlong drama set in Budapest after the 1956 takeover; he plays a Communist officer who falls in love with English noblewoman Deborah Kerr, desperate to escape to unoccupied Vienna. *Goodbye Again* (1961) offered the unlikely sight of Ingrid Bergman romancing jejune Anthony Perkins as a way of getting back at longtime flame Yves Montand. The risible *Five Miles to Midnight* (1963) was a murder yarn in which Perkins now tries to pull an insurance scam with the help of wife Sophia Loren, who kills him and then cracks up from guilt. *The Night of the Generals* (1967) was a gargantuan, overstuffed war mystery that offered such international stars as Peter O'Toole, Omar Sharif, and Christopher Plummer; in the end, its labyrinth of plots and counterplots went nowhere. Last came *The Lady in the Car with Glasses and a Gun* (1970), a kind of mod *Gaslight* that had Samantha Eggar being driven crazy by Oliver Reed.

▲ *The cemetery set of* The Long Night

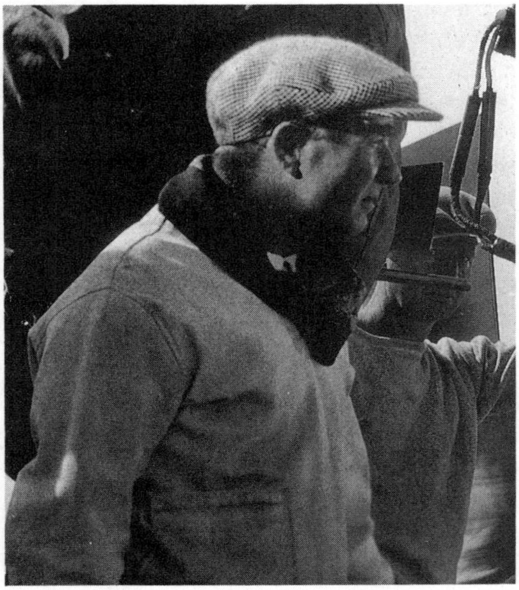

## ● FRANK LLOYD (1888-1960)

Born in Scotland, Frank Lloyd acted on the British stage until he emigrated to Canada in 1910. He moved to America in 1913, began acting in films in 1914, and by 1915 was a director. In fact, his name appears on a mind-boggling twenty-nine short films from that year, probably a record for a rookie director. His best-known early silents include *Les Miserables, Riders of the Purple Sage, Madame X, Oliver Twist* (with Jackie Coogan and, as Fagin, Lon Chaney), and *The Sea Hawk*. In 1929 Lloyd competed with himself in the Academy Awards for best direction, somehow being nominated for *Drag* and *Weary River* on the one hand and *The Divine Lady* on the other, for which he won. A largely silent account of the Lord Nelson–Lady Hamilton romance, it starred Corinne Griffith and Victor Varconi. That established Lloyd as a master of the costume picture, a label he never shed—or tried to.



His early Warners talkies are less than memorable: *Dark Streets* (1929), with Jack Mulhall playing the dual roles of twin brothers, one a cop and the other a crook; *Young Nowheres* (1929), with Richard Barthelmess as an elevator operator; *Son of the Gods* (1930), a silly drama in which Barthelmess learns he doesn't have Chinese blood; and *The Lash* (1930), with the busy Barthelmess in a costume drama that would have suited Doug Fairbanks, Sr., much better. *The Way of All Men* (1930) had Douglas Fairbanks, Jr., trapped in a Mississippi flood, while *The Right of Way* (1931) was an amnesia melodrama starring Conrad Nagel and Loretta Young. At Fox Lloyd made *East Lynne* (1930) with Nagel, Ann Harding, and Clive Brook and *A Passport to Hell* (1932) with Paul Lukas and Elissa Landi. None of these obscurities enjoys any reputation today—perhaps unjustly.

But in 1933 he made *Cavalcade*, a highly successful adaptation of a Noël Coward play about the fortunes of a British family from 1900 to the present day; it won an Academy Award for best picture and another for Lloyd for best direction (leading lady Diana Wynyard was also nominated but lost to newcomer Katharine Hepburn). *Berkeley Square* (1933) was an evocative fantasy set in 1800s England that earned Leslie Howard an Oscar nomination. After the innocuous *Hoopla* (1933) and *Servant's Entrance* (1934) with Janet Gaynor and Lew Ayres, Lloyd's term at Fox was over.

He then moved to MGM for *Mutiny on the Bounty*, the film for which he is best remembered. Considered a golden-age classic, it won the best picture Oscar for 1935, though it now seems artificial and set-bound. There's no denying the power of Charles Laughton's performance as Captain Bligh, but Clark Gable, clean-shaven as Fletcher Christian, does not hold up as well. Gable, Laughton, and Franchot Tone were all nominated as best actor, the only time three actors from the same film have been accorded that honor—but they lost to Victor McLaglen. *Under Two Flags* (1936) was a rousing Foreign Legion yarn, with the charismatic Ronald Colman alongside Claudette Colbert, while *Maid of Salem* (1937) was an interesting drama about a witchhunt in colonial Massachusetts, with Colbert on trial for her life.

*Wells Fargo* (also 1937) was Lloyd's first crack at a Western, and it was a good one; Joel McCrea plays the architect of the legendary railroad line. *If I Were King* (1938) gave Ronald Colman one of his best vehicles as the swashbuckling poet François Villon, matching wits with Louis XI (Basil Rathbone, wonderful per usual). Lloyd's only 1939 release was the long-forgotten *Rulers of the Sea*, with Douglas Fairbanks, Jr., taking the first transatlantic steamship voyage. *The Howards of Virginia* (1940) was yet another period picture, although Cary Grant looked distinctly uncomfortable in colonial attire, while *The Lady from Cheyenne* (1941) returned to the Old West, with Loretta Young good as a prototypical feminist on the range—but as with Lloyd's last few pictures, it didn't seem to connect with the tastes of the day's audiences. Neither did the 1941 *This Woman Is Mine*, a turgid historical romance featuring Franchot Tone and John Carroll as fur traders fighting over Carol Bruce—an impossibly dull cast. He worked on *Forever and a Day* (1943) with seven other directors, who among them oversaw some eighty-three British actors in a multigenerational saga.

*Blood on the Sun* (1945) was an enormous change of pace for Lloyd, an exciting tale about Japan's encroachment upon China in the mid-Thirties starring James Cagney and Sylvia Sidney. This was his best film in seven years, but Lloyd chose this juncture to retire to his ranch. He was not a young man, but in truth, changing tastes and styles in motion pictures had left him behind some time ago. Still, he came out of retirement in 1954 to direct two last films for Republic: *The Shanghai Story*, a contemporary Cold War adventure, and *The Last Command* (1955), a long but enjoyable telling of the Alamo's last days, with Sterling Hayden fine as Jim Bowie and Arthur Hunnicutt an offbeat Davy Crockett. Not exactly the sort of English drawing-room spectacle on which Lloyd built his reputation, but a colorful bit of history from a director who loved to delve into the past.

◀ *Frances Dee and Joel McCrea flank Lloyd on the set of* Wells Fargo

## ● JOSHUA LOGAN (1908–1988)

Best known as the stage director who brought such classics to Broadway as *Annie Get Your Gun*, *Charley's Aunt*, *Mister Roberts*, *South Pacific*, and *Fanny*—the last three of which he also co-authored—Josh Logan also carved out a small but significant place for himself in Hollywood during the Fifties and Sixties. Born in Texarkana, Texas, Logan attended Princeton, after which he founded the University Players, a summer-stock retinue on Cape Cod that helped launch the careers of Jimmy Stewart, Margaret Sullavan, and Henry Fonda, among others. In 1931 he was awarded a scholarship to study under Stanislavsky at the Moscow Art Theater. Logan's Hollywood career began in the mid-Thirties, when he was a dialogue coach on a pair of Charles Boyer movies. In 1938 he and Arthur Ripley co-directed *I Met My Love Again*, which reunited him with Henry Fonda. But Logan chose to return to Broadway, where he worked his way into a nervous breakdown. Recovering after a year in a psychiatric hospital—he would be plagued by depression throughout his life—Logan staged a number of the 1940s' most popular plays on Broadway, interrupted by war service in the Air Force.

It wasn't until 1955 that Logan accepted Hollywood's offer to return, stepping behind the camera to film William Inge's *Picnic*. It was a canny call; Logan got indelible, steamy performances out of William Holden and Kim Novak, and was nominated for a best direction Academy Award. Nearly as memorable was *Bus Stop* (1956), the Inge play (adapted by George Axelrod) that contains what may be Marilyn Monroe's best serious performance. *Sayonara* (1957), set during the Korean War and starring Marlon Brando, was the first of Logan's films not to have originated on stage (although he was already familiar with author James Michener's work from *South Pacific*). Red Buttons and Miyoshi Umeki won Oscars for their supporting roles as the couple whose love destroys them, while the film, screenplay, and Logan were also nominated.

Logan was now given the opportunity to film a big-budget version of Rodgers and Hammerstein's classic musical *South Pacific*, which had been a Broadway blockbuster for years. The play had been directed and co-authored by Logan (for which he had

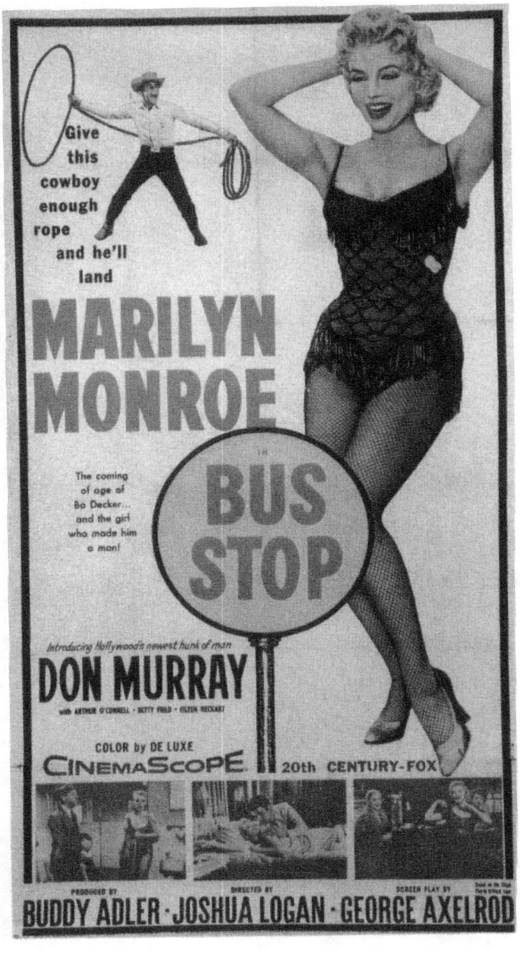

earned half of a Pulitzer Prize) and was eagerly anticipated by moviegoers. It seemed that it couldn't miss—except it did. Was it the cast? (Rossano Brazzi and Mitzi Gaynor aren't exactly Mary Martin and Ezio Pinza.) The realistic war scenes were well done but didn't blend smoothly with the great tunes. Length (almost three hours) was also a problem. Logan's next film, the romantic comedy *Tall Story* (1960), starring Anthony Perkins and Ray Walston and adapted from the Howard Lindsay—Russel Crouse play, was notable primarily for being Jane Fonda's film debut.

He returned to adapt his own stage work with his filming of *Fanny* (1961), a musical adaptation of the Marcel Pagnol trilogy, with Leslie Caron, Charles Boyer, and Maurice Chevalier; both the film and the score were nominated for Academy Awards. But *Ensign Pulver* (1964), the ill-advised sequel to *Mister Roberts*, was dreadful, with Robert Walker, Jr., now installed in Jack Lemmon's old spot. And *Camelot* (1967) endures as one of the all-time great screen misfires, a ponderous adaptation of the Alan Jay Lerner–Frederick Loewe stage success that plays out over three hours as if the Middle Ages themselves are crawling by. For the record, it starred Richard Harris, Vanessa Redgrave, and Franco Nero, and the Lerner-Loewe score won an Oscar.

Logan closed out his career with *Paint Your Wagon* (1969), a lumbering, hugely expensive ($20 million) musical Western, with unlikely co-stars Clint Eastwood and Lee Marvin time-sharing mail-order wife Jean Seberg in between songs. It sounded ominously like another overstuffed turkey waiting to be baked, but surprisingly turned out pretty well, with handsome Oregon locations, a salty script by Paddy Chayefsky, and great Lerner-Loewe songs (from the 1951 staging) including Marvin's "Wandrin' Star" and Harve Presnell's "They Call the Wind Maria." But like many big-budget screen musicals of the day, it couldn't attract a large enough audience to justify its expense. Logan then retired, the day's new tastes having passed him by.

◀ *With William Holden on the set of the smash hit* Picnic

## ● ERNST LUBITSCH (1892-1947)

The acknowledged master of romantic comedy, Ernst Lubitsch was probably the only active director ever to be made the head of production at a major studio, as he was (briefly) at Paramount. But while the lion's share of his fabled career occurred in the silent era—he made over forty German silents before he even came to America—the impact of his sound pictures (there are only nineteen) is far out of proportion to their number. Had his health not failed him while he was in his early fifties, there is every reason to believe that his legend would loom larger still.

Born in Berlin, Lubitsch became enthusiastic about acting while in high school and turned professional at sixteen, performing at night and working during the day in his father's tailor shop. In 1911 he joined Max Reinhardt's theatrical company, where over the next few years he acted in roles of ever-increasing prominence. At the same time he began appearing in, writing, and directing comedy shorts. He directed his first feature in 1918 and soon left Reinhardt to devote himself to movies full-time, directing the likes of Pola Negri and Emil Jannings. By 1922 he had been invited by Mary Pickford to make a movie with her in the States, but *Rosita* (1923) was filmed in a state of constant conflict. Lubitsch stayed on, making *Forbidden Paradise*, *The Marriage Circle*, and *Lady Windemere's Fan*, among others.

He directed Norma Shearer and Ramon Novarro in *The Student Prince* (1927), the popular operetta which, sans songs, became the play *In Old Heidelberg*. He was then given a production deal at Paramount, for whom his first film was *The Patriot* (1928), with Emil Jannings as the mad Czar of Russia, Paul I, and Lewis Stone as the country's Prime Minister. The picture was nominated for an Academy Award, as were Stone and Lubitsch. *Eternal Love* (1929) sent John Barrymore into the Canadian Rockies (standing in for the Swiss Alps), where he and illicit lover Camilla Horn were buried in an avalanche. (Sorry to give it away . . .) Lubitsch's first sound effort was the inventive 1929 musical *The Love Parade*, in which Maurice Chevalier and Jeanette MacDonald (in her film debut) find romance in the mythical land of Sylvania. With songs composed by Victor Schertzinger, this pleasant operetta was Oscar-nominated as best picture, and Lubitsch was again nominated for best direction.

After co-directing the all-star revue *Paramount on Parade* (1930) with ten other directors, Lubitsch made *Monte Carlo* (1930) with MacDonald, who memorably trills "Beyond the Blue Horizon" from a train; but she was paired with English music-hall star Jack Buchanan, whom American audiences found less compelling than the Continental Chevalier. Chevalier returned for the Oscar-nominated *The Smiling Lieutenant* (1931), flanked not by MacDonald but rather by Claudette Colbert and Miriam Hopkins; it was a major success at the box office, but Lubitsch's follow-up, the somber antiwar drama *Broken Lullaby* (1932; aka *The Man I Killed*) with Lionel Barrymore, was not. Lubitsch would not stray so far from romantic comedy again.

He returned to his tried-and-true operetta format, reuniting Chevalier and MacDonald at long last in *One Hour with You* (1932). A remake of *The Marriage Circle*, this effervescent musical was begun by George Cukor, who was unceremoniously shunted aside when supervisor Lubitsch couldn't keep his hands off the camera. Before long, Lubitsch was directing—even reshooting earlier footage—while Cukor stood to one side and fumed. When Lubitsch assigned himself sole credit, with Cukor getting an "assisted by . . . ," Cukor contested the action in arbitration. (Ultimately he waived his claim in exchange for being freed from his Paramount contract.) *Trouble in Paradise* (1932), considered by many to be Lubitsch's masterpiece, was presumably a happier enterprise.

Herbert Marshall and Miriam Hopkins play romantically involved French jewel thieves who gain employment with wealthy Kay Francis, the better to bilk her out of her fortune; but Marshall begins to fall for Francis, and complications multiply with breathtaking invention. Naughty as only a pre-Code film could be, this is also one of handsomest pictures of the decade.

Lubitsch was one of the seven directors who handled segments of the 1932 *If I Had a Million* before turning his attention to *Design for Living* (1933), another sophisticated masterpiece with an erotic tinge. An expurgated version of Noël Coward's stage success, it starred Gary Cooper and Fredric March as, respectively, an artist and a playwright who live in Paris in a ménage à trois with Miriam Hopkins. She disturbs their enlightened arrangement by marrying a square businessman, but returns to them when she realizes what she had given up. *The Merry Widow* (1934) brought Chevalier and MacDonald together again under the auspices of Irving Thalberg and MGM in a sparkling version of the Franz Lehár operetta, with new lyrics by Rodgers and Hart, among others.

Perhaps fearful that their star producer/director would permanently jump to MGM, Paramount formalized his title as head of production in 1935, an unprecedented position of power for a director. But the arrangement didn't last—he was driving the other directors crazy—and a year later Lubitsch was returned to his previous rank. He made *Angel* with Marlene Dietrich, Herbert Marshall, and Melvyn Douglas in 1937, but this romantic triangle turned into one of his most maligned commercial failures. Gary Cooper and Claudette Colbert starred in *Bluebeard's Eighth Wife* (1938), but despite a Charles Brackett–Billy Wilder script—their first together—this also fizzled. Was the master losing his vaunted touch? Paramount must have thought so, because now they did let him go to MGM.

But then came *Ninotchka* (1939) and all was well once more. Positioning the famously solemn Garbo as a comedienne for the first time (the poster's tag line was "Garbo Laughs!"), Lubitsch—with the help of screenwriters Brackett, Wilder, and Walter Reisch—concocted one of her most enduring films. Garbo is an icy Communist official dispatched to Paris by commissar Bela Lugosi to retrieve the Czar's old crown jewels after her emissaries have failed; she finds them, but also waiting is urbane count Melvyn Douglas, and like her subordinates she is soon seduced by the pleasures of Western decadence. Garbo, the film, the screenplay, and the original story by Melchior Lengyel were all nominated for Academy Awards (and in a year of less awesome achievements, Lubitsch surely would have been as well). Better still was *The Shop Around the Corner* (1940), starring James Stewart and Margaret Sullavan as co-workers in Frank Morgan's Budapest notions shop; they detest each other, little knowing they have already fallen in love through their anonymous correspondence. Perhaps Lubitsch's warmest film, *Shop* boasted a typically lovely screenplay by Samson Raphaelson. It may have failed to earn even a single Oscar nomination in its day (this wasn't one of the ten best pictures of 1940?!), but it endures as a classic romantic comedy.

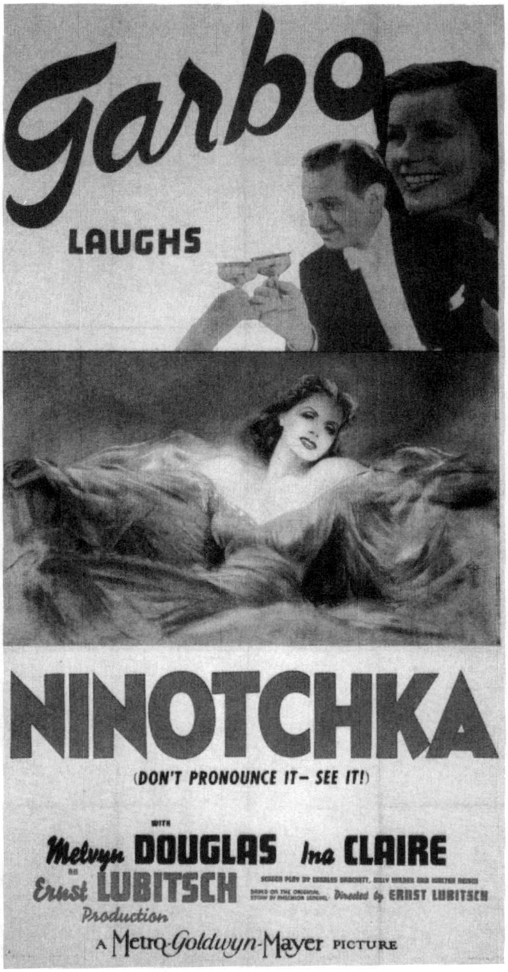

*That Uncertain Feeling* (1941) was something of a comedown after Lubitsch's two previous triumphs. A remake of his 1925 comedy *Kiss Me Again*, it starred Melvyn Douglas and Merle Oberon as an unhappily married couple who consider divorce but finally learn to appreciate each other. In between was indiscriminate craziness, embodied by Burgess Meredith as an obnoxious pianist. The daring political comedy *To Be or Not to Be* (1942), from a story by Lubitsch and Lengyel, was another high-water mark for Lubitsch. Husband-wife actors Jack Benny and Carole Lombard are the stars of a Polish theatrical troupe in 1939 Warsaw; forced to stage *Hamlet* after their anti-Nazi play is censored, they risk their lives to collaborate with the Polish Resistance. Unappreciated in its day for dealing lightly with the Nazis, portrayed here as buffoons, the picture's success was also undermined by Lombard's death in a plane crash just before the film's release. Today those concerns have receded, and *To Be* can be fully appreciated for its razor-edged satire.

*Heaven Can Wait* (1943), Lubitsch's first picture under a new producer/director contract with Fox, was a bittersweet period comedy in which ladykiller Don Ameche reviews a lifetime of romantic overindulgence for a skeptical Devil (Laird Cregar) as he awaits admittance to hell. A less serious *Citizen Kane*, this charming but rueful fantasy was graced with a clever screenplay by Sam Raphaelson and the presence of lovely Gene Tierney. Lubitsch finally received another Oscar nomination for his direction, but he was unable to savor it in the wake of a massive heart attack that nearly took his life. While recuperating, he started *A Royal Scandal* (1945), with Tallulah Bankhead as Catherine the Great, but had to hand over the reins to Otto Preminger; the finished work was inferior to the 1924 *Forbidden Paradise*, on which it was based.

Lubitsch eventually regained enough strength to complete *Cluny Brown* (1946), a charming period romance between Czech refugee Charles Boyer and maid Jennifer Jones, set on an English estate just before World War I. He was awarded a special Oscar for his lifetime achievements in 1946, then commenced work on *That Lady in Ermine* (1948), scripted by Sam Rafaelson. But after just eight days of filming, Lubitsch (who always inhaled his ever-present cigars) was struck down by his fifth heart attack, and again Preminger was summoned to finish the movie. A musical set in a mythical kingdom, *Ermine* harked back to Lubitsch's early pictures with Chevalier and MacDonald. But before it was released he suffered his sixth and final heart attack, and the Lubitsch touch was sheathed forever.

► *Lubitsch clowns with Maurice Chevalier on the set of* The Love Parade

## ● SIDNEY LUMET (1924- )

Although Sidney Lumet was one of the most respected directors of the Seventies and early Eighties, his work—thirty-eight films' worth—has been strangely unreliable since 1983, although he's worked with the same top level of talent he was accustomed to in his earlier, better work. This alarming decline could be reversed at any moment—and if it is, it won't be a moment too soon.

Born in Philadelphia, Lumet was acting in New York's Yiddish Theater at the age of four, following in the footsteps of his father. He continued acting as a juvenile on Broadway (he was in the original production of *Dead End*), performed on radio series, and even appeared in one film as a teenager, the socially conscious *One Third of a Nation* (1939). After serving in the Army Signal Corps during World War II, Lumet founded an Off-Broadway acting group, of which he was the director. In 1950 he was invited to work for CBS-TV, originally as an assistant director. The following year he was put in charge of the adventure series *Danger*, which he directed for three years, and also worked on a season's worth of *You Are There* episodes. He graduated to CBS's dramatic anthology series *Playhouse 90*, *Kraft Television Theatre*, *Omnibus*, and *Studio One*, where he alternated with the likes of George Roy Hill, Franklin Schaffner, Martin Ritt, Delbert Mann, and Robert Mulligan.

Reginald Rose's drama *12 Angry Men* had been a live television production, and Lumet was asked by star and producer Henry Fonda to direct the 1957 film version, which Rose would adapt. Lumet did it well enough to be nominated for an Academy Award, as was the film itself—an impressive achievement for a first-time movie director. *Stage Struck* (1958) tried to capitalize on Lumet's theatrical experience, but this remake of the 1933 *Morning Glory* only proved that Henry Fonda and Susan Strasberg were not Adolphe Menjou and Katharine Hepburn. *That Kind of Woman* (1959) was a sophisticated tale about a furtive romance between Sophia Loren and Tab Hunter, similar in plot to *The Shopworn Angel*, while *The Fugitive Kind* (1960) was a mediocre transposition of the Tennessee Williams play *Orpheus Descending*, starring Marlon Brando as the sexy drifter who shakes up a Southern town. *A View from the Bridge* (1961) was a well-realized version of Arthur Miller's drama on the Brooklyn waterfront, with Raf Vallone and Maureen Stapleton as an unhappily married couple.

It was *Long Day's Journey into Night* (1962), though, that brought Lumet his best notices to date. A lengthy, deliberately theatrical adaptation of O'Neill's classic play, *Night* offered great performances by Katharine Hepburn (Oscar-nominated), Jason Robards, Dean Stockwell, and Ralph Richardson. Lumet next moved far afield with the nuclear-crisis thriller *Fail-Safe* (1964), an adaptation of the bestseller about America on the brink of nuclear warfare, starring Henry Fonda and Walter Matthau; it was overshadowed by Stanley Kubrick's brilliant *Dr. Strangelove*, which had been released earlier that year.

*The Pawnbroker* (1965) was a grim but powerful account of a concentration-camp survivor's efforts to sublimate his memories of that terrible time while he runs his business in Harlem (shot on location); Rod Steiger was Oscar-nominated for his performance as pawnbroker Sol Nazerman. The 1965 *The Hill* was an in-your-face tale about the hard cases in a British military stockade; it really needed a Robert Aldrich at the helm. It featured Sean Connery, Ossie Davis, and a primarily British cast whose utterings were often difficult to decipher.

*The Group* (1966) was a somewhat sanitized version of the sexy Mary McCarthy bestseller about eight women who keep in touch after graduating in 1933 from their Ivy League college; Candice Bergen, in her film debut, led the pack, which also included Jessica Walter, Shirley Knight, and Elizabeth Hartman. *The Deadly Affair* (1967) was a good spy yarn starring James Mason and Simone Signoret, based on a novel by John le Carré, while *Bye Bye Braverman* (1968) was an uneven black comedy about four friends (including George Segal and Jack Warden) who freak out on their way to a funeral. Lumet filmed *The Sea Gull* (1968) in England with James Mason, Vanessa Redgrave, and Simone Signoret with mixed results, then made the glossy but empty soaper *The Appointment* (1969) with Omar Sharif and Anouk Aimee.

*Last of the Mobile Hot-Shots* (1970) was no better than its title, an awkward transposition of Tennessee Williams's *Seven Descents of Myrtle*, with James Coburn and Lynn Redgrave making a very odd couple. Lumet co-directed the Oscar-nominated documentary *King: A Filmed Record . . . Montgomery to Memphis* (1970) with Joseph Mankiewicz, then made the ultra-commercial *The Anderson Tapes* (1972), an elaborate caper flick based on a Lawrence Sanders thriller; it offered enjoyable star turns by Sean Connery and Dyan Cannon. *Child's Play* (1972) was a confused version of a Robert Marasco play, with James Mason and Robert Preston as college professors at odds with each other, while *The Offense* (1973) cast Sean Connery against type as a British police detective who kills a suspect in a rage, then must examine his motives.

The much-admired 1973 *Serpico* became Lumet's biggest hit to date, and still may be his best film. A terrific adaptation of the Peter Maas book about real-life undercover cop Frank Serpico's efforts to stay alive after agreeing to testify before the Knapp Commission about corruption among New York City police, it starred Al Pacino (in the performance of his career) as the embattled cop. Pacino should have won that year's Academy Award, but Lumet wasn't even nominated.

*Lovin' Molly* (1974) was perhaps too radical a departure—Lumet never was able to capture the flavor of the Larry McMurtry source novel *Leaving Cheyenne*—and the foolish casting of Anthony Perkins and Beau Bridges as the cowboy rivals didn't help matters. *Murder on the Orient Express* (1974) was a box-office hit, a clever adaptation of the vintage Agatha Christie mystery that seemed to employ half the stars in America and England; Ingrid Bergman received a best supporting actress Oscar, and for his Hercule Poirot, Albert Finney also received a nomination. *Dog Day Afternoon* (1975), highly praised at the time, was a frenetic, fact-based story about a pair of amateur crooks (Al Pacino and John Cazale) who try to hold up a Brooklyn bank. The whole thing now seems overcooked, but it was nominated for Academy Awards for best picture, actor (Pacino), supporting actor (Chris Sarandon as Pacino's boyfriend, who desires a sex-change operation), and screenplay (an Oscar for Frank Pierson); and Lumet was nominated for his direction.

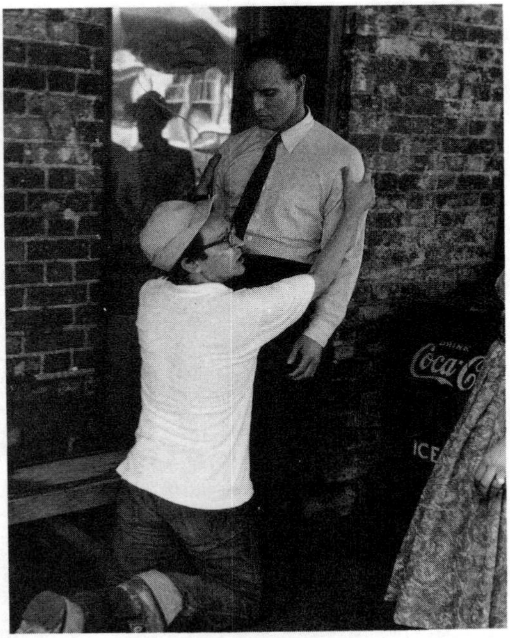
▲ *Lumet implores Brando to give his best during the filming of* The Fugitive Kind

*Network* (1976) was even more enthusiastically received, though it bears both the defects and the virtues of Paddy Chayefsky's thundering screenplay about TV's rampant philistinism. Lumet, who thrived when working with a New York City locale, helped three of his actors—Peter Finch (who died after filming this), Faye Dunaway, and Beatrice Straight—win Oscars for their performances; Lumet, William Holden, Ned Beatty, and the film itself also received nominations. On the heels of these back-to-back smashes, Lumet made one of his most disappointing films: *Equus* (1977) adapted Peter Shaffer's Broadway success but literalized the play's highly stylized symbolism, robbing the drama of much of its impact. But Lumet's unique rapport with his actors still elicited a pair of Oscar-nominated performances, by Richard Burton (as the psychiatrist) and Peter Firth (as the disturbed youth).

If *Equus* was a noble failure, *The Wiz* (1978) was an ignoble one, a ludicrous version of the black-cast Broadway show, with the wanton miscasting of Diana Ross as Dorothy merely the most obvious of the film's many problems. But Lena Horne made a wonderful Glinda. *Just Tell Me What You Want* (1980) looks better now than it did at the time; Alan King is surprisingly effective as a loutish businessman who tries to win back the affections of mistress Ali McGraw after driving her away. But the police-corruption drama *Prince of the City* (1981) was hardly a patch on *Serpico*, in part due to Treat Williams's lack of charisma, in part to the rather formless screenplay (co-written by Lumet and Jay Presson Allen) that makes the film at least an hour too long. Still, Lumet's eye for New York City and the fine supporting cast make it worth at least one viewing. *Deathtrap* (1982) was theatrical artifice (based on Ira Levin's Broadway play) that tried to capture the success of 1972's *Sleuth* but came off a distant second-best, although Michael Caine, Dyan Cannon, and Christopher Reeve do their best.

*The Verdict* (1982) was a widely acclaimed courtroom drama, with a powerhouse performance by Paul Newman as an alcoholic, shyster lawyer who rediscovers his pride—and his talent—when he takes on an unpopular case. Lumet, Newman, and the film were all Oscar-nominated, as were David Mamet's potent screenplay and James Mason's indelible turn as Newman's diabolically crafty opponent. *Daniel* (1983) was a moving adaptation of E. L. Doctorow's docu-novel about the Rosenbergs, *The Book of Daniel*, starring Timothy Hutton and Mandy Patinkin, while *Garbo Talks* (1984) tried to blend whimsy and sentiment with mixed results. *Power* (1986), however, was an unmitigated disaster; Richard Gere was totally at sea as a political spin doctor. *The Morning After* that same year wasted Jane Fonda and Jeff Bridges in a clumsily told story of an alcoholic actress who wakes up one morning to find a dead man in her bed.

*Running on Empty* (1988) was far better, a heartfelt account of the difficulties faced by a family on the run from the FBI for radical acts the parents performed when they were students seventeen years earlier. Judd Hirsch and Christine Lahti as the parents and River Phoenix and Martha Plimpton as their long-suffering children are uniformly excellent, and Phoenix and the screenplay were nominated for Academy Awards. But the peculiar *Family Business* (1988) was a strangely ineffective heist picture; a flabby adaptation of a Vincent Patrick novel, it at least offered good performances by Sean Connery, Dustin Hoffman, and Matthew Broderick. Lumet himself wrote the screenplay for *Q & A* (1990), adapting the tough Edwin Torres novel about a young assistant D.A. (Timothy Hutton) who refuses to soft-pedal his investigation of a brutal but respected police detective (Nick Nolte). It starts off promisingly, especially when drug lord Armand Assante is introduced, but Hutton is unappealing and Nolte's character is so revolting that the picture (a half hour too long) finally implodes.

Lumet's erratic track record was extended with the risible *A Stranger Among Us* (1992); Melanie Griffith was wildly miscast as an undercover cop who penetrates the Hasidic community of Brooklyn, while *Guilty as Sin* (1993), with Don Johnson as a slick killer and Rebecca DeMornay as his guileless attorney, was a competent if shamelessly derivative thriller. Clearly, Lumet's strength has not been his ability to select material—at least, not for the *first* forty years of his career. His book, *Making Movies*, was published in 1995.

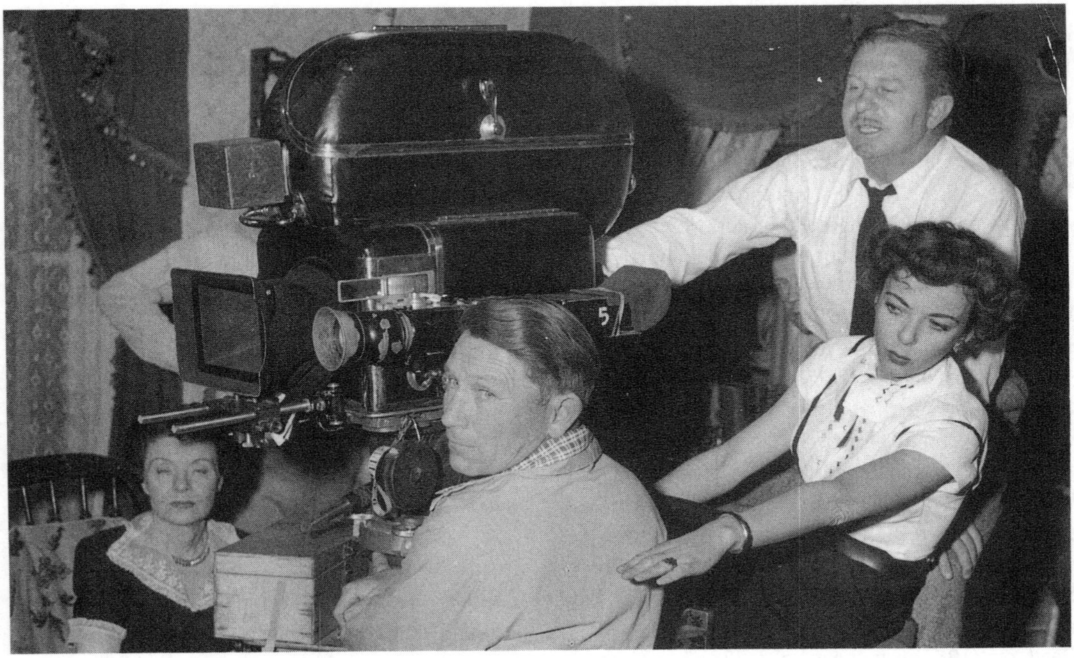

## ● IDA LUPINO (1918–1995)

She was endlessly fascinating as an actress, particularly in her hard-boiled characterizations for Warner Bros. in the 1940s and her portrayals of neurotic, damaged women in RKO films of the Fifties. But London-born Ida Lupino, daughter and granddaughter of professional actors and the 1942 winner of the New York Film Critics Circle best actress award (for *The Hard Way*) also aspired to direct. In the end she made only a handful of low-budget but effective genre pictures, most dating from the early Fifties, before turning her energies toward the fecund fields of television.

Lupino wed Columbia Pictures executive Collier Young in 1948, and a year later they founded The Filmakers (sic) production company. Their first project was the unwed-mother drama *Not Wanted* (1949), which Lupino produced and co-scripted with Young. Director Elmer Clifton, a one-time leading man for D. W. Griffith who had been toiling in Poverty Row serials for decades, fell ill midway through the production, and Lupino stepped in and completed it. She became Hollywood's first credited female director since the 1943 retirement of Dorothy Arzner with *Never Fear* (1950), a low-budget drama in which *Not Wanted* star Sally Forrest plays a young dancer stricken with polio. Filmakers now signed an agreement with RKO to be their distribution arm. Their first joint venture was *Outrage* (1950), a socially conscious but rather strident tale about the devastating aftereffects of a rape on a young woman (Mala Powers); Lupino and Young co-scripted, with Young producing.

Although Lupino and Young divorced in 1950, they continued their professional relationship. The Filmakers' next venture was the inaccurately titled *Hard, Fast and Beautiful* (1951), which sounded like a steamy Jane Russell lovefest but proved to be an oddly prescient drama about a teenaged tennis star (Sally Forrest) shamelessly exploited by her greedy mother (Claire Trevor, terrific as always). Lupino's direction was deft, but the picture this time missed Young's and her scripting talents. Nicholas Ray cast her as the lonely blind woman who helps heal the psychic wounds of police detective Robert Ryan in his potent crime yarn *On Dangerous Ground* (1951). But she again found herself behind the camera (in an uncredited capacity) when the despondent Ray, whose marriage to actress Gloria Grahame had just come to a shocking end, suffered a nervous breakdown; fortunately for RKO, she was able to take over until Ray was well enough to go back to work.

Lupino's masterpiece was probably the grim noir *The Hitch-Hiker* (1953), 71 minutes of unabated tension, with William Talman as a vicious psychopath who holds vacationing businessmen Frank Lovejoy and Edmond O'Brien hostage as he cuts a swathe through Mexico toward Central America and (he hopes) freedom. Lupino and Young now parted ways with RKO. She directed herself for the first and only time in *The Bigamist* (1953), an occasionally maudlin but not unaffecting soaper with Edmond O'Brien as a goodhearted fellow who just happens to love—and marry—two women (Lupino and Joan Fontaine).

Lupino would not direct another theatrical film for thirteen years. She plunged back into acting with juicy roles in *Women's Prison*, *The Big Knife*, and *While the City Sleeps*, while directing episodes of television series like *Have Gun, Will Travel*, *The Donna Reed Show*, *Mr. Novak*, and *Dr. Kildare*. But more of her time was spent acting, starring with new husband, Howard Duff, in the television sitcom *Mr. Adams and Eve*; she also appeared in countless television shows as a guest star. In 1966 she directed one last motion picture, the innocuous but pleasant comedy *The Trouble with Angels*: rebellious teen Hayley Mills makes life difficult for Mother Superior Rosalind Russell at a convent school in Pennsylvania. Lupino never directed again, although she remained in demand as a television and film actress. After 1975 a series of health problems impaired her ability to work, and she was forced to retire. In retrospect, her modest filmography as a director belies what she probably could have accomplished in another, later era.

## ● LEO McCAREY (1898-1969)

A premier director and writer of silent comedy during the Twenties, Leo McCarey developed into one of Hollywood's most versatile talents in the Thirties and Forties, winning two Academy Awards for best direction. Although his filmography includes a mere twenty-three sound features, a third of them have attained classic stature—some are among the best comedies ever made.

Born in Los Angeles, McCarey attended law school, but was unable to make a go of his practice in either L.A. or San Francisco. He made himself useful at Universal in the late Teens, tracking script revisions and finally becoming an assistant to Tod Browning. By 1923 he was directing Charley Chase two-reelers and writing gags for the *Our Gang* series, and soon was supervising a hundred comedy shorts a year for the Hal Roach studios as vice president of production. An impressive level of activity, to be sure; but it took pure, unadulterated genius to pair dour English comic Stan Laurel with the plump American funny man Oliver Hardy in 1926—pair them and then oversee every aspect of the movies they made over the next four years, from the writing of the stories to the editing and previewing of the finished films. For this alone, McCarey would warrant inclusion in the cinema's hall of fame.

But in 1929 he turned to directing features, making two for Pathé before signing with Fox in 1930. There he made *Wild Company*, a hell-in-a-handbasket account of heedless youth that starred Frank Albertson; it's of interest today only for Bela Lugosi's role as a nightclub owner. Next came *Part-Time Wife*. *Let's Go Native* (1930) shipwrecked Jeanette MacDonald, Kay Francis, and Jack Oakie on a tropical isle, where they whiled away the day in song—a safer pastime on the whole than sampling the Gloria Swanson antique *Indiscreet* (1931), a creaking romantic drama (with dashes of comedy) that unwisely allowed Gloria to warble two songs. *The Kid from Spain* (1932) was better, a lavish Eddie Cantor vehicle with songs, slapstick, the Goldwyn Girls (including Lucille Ball and Betty Grable), and Busby Berkeley's inventive dance sequences.

McCarey now signed with Paramount, where he spent four productive years. His first project there was the sublime *Duck Soup* (1933), arguably the Marx Brothers' best film and less arguably one of the year's best pictures—although audiences of the day didn't think so, to judge from the poor box-office receipts. (It took the Marxes a full eighteen months to gain another screen sponsor, which turned out to be Irving Thalberg and MGM.) As with most of the work the Marxes did onscreen, *Duck Soup* incorporated material that had been given a dry run, in this case on their NBC radio series *Flywheel, Shyster & Flywheel*, which ran for twenty-six weeks in 1932 and 1933. But McCarey must be given full credit for overseeing their purest, most enduring vehicle.

*Belle of the Nineties* (1934) had Mae West as a New Orleans singer involved with three men; not her best film by a long shot, but it was enlivened by Duke Ellington and his orchestra (if not by male leads Johnny Mack Brown and Roger Pryor). The 1934 *Six of a Kind* featured the intriguing mix of W. C. Fields, George Burns and Gracie Allen, and Mary Boland and Charlie Ruggles—a concentrated dose of comic talent in a plot as mad as a hatter. *Ruggles of Red Gap* (1935) was a splendid comedy set in the Old West, with Charles Laughton as a butler won in a poker game by hard-tack rancher Charlie Ruggles and his pretentious wife, Mary Boland. Laughton was never better, although his sublime comic performance was overshadowed by his thundering Captain Bligh that same year. *The Milky Way* (1936) was Harold Lloyd's best sound picture, a fanciful tale of a meek milkman who ends up fighting for the middleweight boxing championship (remade ten years later with Danny Kaye as *The Kid from Brooklyn*).

*Make Way for Tomorrow* (1937) was a radical departure for McCarey, an unabashed tearjerker about an impoverished elderly couple (Beulah Bondi and Victor Moore) whose selfish children aren't willing to house them, so they must live apart. It was just this side of too much, but McCarey showed a hitherto unrevealed facility for dramatizing serious emotion, which he would call on more frequently in the future. He went to Columbia to make his most celebrated comedy, *The Awful Truth* (1937). It had been filmed twice before, but never with Cary Grant and Irene Dunne as the bickering couple whose divorce becomes unstuck when their courting of prospective new mates drives them back into each other's arms. A screwball masterpiece, *Truth* displayed Cary Grant's comic skills in full bloom, carrying him to the next level of stardom. Dunne and Ralph Bellamy were Oscar-nominated, as were the film and Vina Delmar's screenplay. But it was McCarey who ultimately won an Academy Award, for best direction; that he won for a comedy is even more impressive.

This triumph was followed by the ultra-romantic *Love Affair* (1939), in which Charles Boyer and Irene Dunne fall in love during a cruise, only to have their reunion disrupted when Dunne is struck by a car, crippling her. McCarey worked on the script with his writers even as shooting was progressing, and the result was a four-hankie classic that was nominated for an Academy Award, as were Dunne and Maria Ouspenskaya, who played Boyer's grandmother. (McCarey would remake the picture eighteen years later as *An Affair to Remember* and had a hit all over again.) The frenetic comedy *My Favorite Wife* with Cary Grant and Irene Dunne was written by McCarey; he was slated to begin directing it when a near-fatal car crash forced him to hand the reins over to Garson Kanin, who turned it into one of 1940's comic gems.

*Once Upon a Honeymoon* (1942), a witless comedy/drama/romance—it never made up its mind *which* it wanted to be—starred Cary Grant as a radio reporter who has to save Ginger Rogers from her Nazi husband (Walter Slezak) as they're honeymooning across war-torn Europe; it was a major misfire for McCarey, who hadn't made a picture this bad since his first talkies. It ended his tenure at RKO, but Paramount was happy to obtain McCarey's services, particularly after they tabulated the grosses on *Going My Way* (1944), a shamelessly sentimental yarn—from McCarey's own story—about priest Bing Crosby, whose good works earn the ire of superior Barry Fitzgerald until Bing can prove his unorthodox methods are indeed kosher. Somewhat freakishly, *Going My Way* became the year's biggest hit and nearly swept the Academy Awards to boot, winning for best picture, best direction, best actor, best supporting actor, best story, best screenplay, and best song ("Swinging on a Star"). Such a smash—so McCarey sensibly decided to replicate it with *The Bells of St. Mary's* (1945), a flabby orgy of sentimentality; Bing is now at loggerheads with Mother Superior Ingrid Bergman. Once again, the Oscar nominations poured down from heaven; McCarey, Crosby, Bergman, and the film itself were all cited, though none was a winner this time.

Three years elapsed before *Good Sam* (1948), and this feeble comedy was hardly worth the wait. Gary Cooper plays a compulsive doer of good deeds, a trait that drives his long-suffering wife crazy (Ann Sheridan, who submits the film's only decent performance). Another extended period of inactivity followed, culminating in 1952 with the absurd *My Son John*, a rabid anti-Communist tract with Robert Walker as a seditious (not to mention impolite) son whom loony mother (a wildly over-the-top Helen Hayes) cannot save, even with the power of her love. Incredibly, McCarey's Red-baiting story was nominated for an Oscar.

His powers were clearly on the wane, but McCarey pulled himself together five years later for *An Affair to Remember* (1957), a remake of *Love Affair* that today is better remembered than its predecessor, though it's not as good. (That's what Technicolor and Cary Grant can do for you; too bad Warren Beatty had only the Technicolor for his ill-fated 1994 remake.) McCarey even co-wrote the lyrics to the Oscar-nominated title tune, sung by Vic Damone in the film. *Rally 'Round the Flag, Boys!* (1958), starring Paul Newman, Joanne Woodward, and Joan Collins, was McCarey's first comedy in ten years and it had scattered moments of proficiency, but on balance it failed to capture the madcap humor of Max Shulman's bestselling book. McCarey's final film, *Satan Never Sleeps* (1962), was a hopelessly dull, inexcusably long anti-Communist yarn about two intractable priests (William Holden and Clifton Webb) who refuse to give ground when the Chinese Communists overrun them. It was *My Son John* meets *Going My Way*, and a rather sad ending to the career of this once-great talent.

▲ *On the set of* The Awful Truth *with Cary Grant and Irene Dunne*

## ● NORMAN Z. McLEOD (1898–1964)

A former fighter pilot with the Royal Canadian Air Force, Michigan-born Norman Zenos McLeod broke into the film industry after the war as an animator and gagman, skills that would serve him well on the many comedies he directed over the course of thirty years. His big break came when he was hired to assist director William Wellman on *Wings*, overseeing the aerial sequences. He then co-wrote the story for *The Air Circus* (1928), which Howard Hawks directed with Lewis Seiler. That same year McLeod made his directing debut at Fox with *Taking a Chance*, after which he moved to Paramount, where he made eighteen comedies and musicals between 1930 and 1937.

McLeod co-directed his first two sound pictures, minor affairs with Leon Errol and Buddy Rogers, but his third was *Monkey Business* (1931), the classic Marx Brothers farce written by S. J. Perelman, Arthur Sheekman, and (uncredited) Nat Perrin. Much of the activity was improvised by the Marxes, who for the first time were not adapting one of their stage vehicles, and the result was 77 minutes of unadulterated madness. *Touchdown* (1931) was a comedown, an inane football melodrama with Richard Arlen and Jack Oakie, while *The Miracle Man* (1932) was a remake of an old silent, with director-to-be Irving Pichel as the faith healer and Sylvia Sidney his reluctant subject.

The Marxes' 1932 *Horse Feathers* was, if anything, even funnier than *Monkey Business*, capped by a hilarious football game that parodied films like *Touchdown*; Thelma Todd returned as the token sane person. *If I Had a Million* (1932) offered Paramount's galaxy of stars—W. C. Fields, Gary Cooper, George Raft, Charles Laughton, et al.—in an eight-episode anthology, one of which McLeod directed. *A Lady's Profession* and *Mama Loves Papa* (both 1933) were minor comedies that have failed to survive the passing of six decades. But *Alice in Wonderland* (1933) was an elaborate (perhaps *too* elaborate) production that used every star on Paramount's lot to bring Lewis Carroll's two fantasies to life. Unfortunately, the novelty of having Cary Grant as the Mock Turtle, Gary Cooper as the White Knight, W. C. Fields as Humpty Dumpty, and Edward Everett Horton as the Mad Hatter was squandered by their being virtually unrecognizable behind their storybook costumes and masks.

*Melody in Spring* (1934) was an indifferent musical, starring the pallid Lanny Ross, a radio crooner who (deservedly) is now the answer to a trivia question. But *Many Happy Returns* (1934) survived on the strength of George Burns and Gracie Allen; Gracie wrecks a department store and a movie studio in blissful ignorance, and Guy Lombardo supplied the painless tunes. The 1934 *It's a Gift* had W. C. Fields at his very best in a remake of his silent *It's the Old Army Game*; he plays a hapless grocer who decides to change his luck by hauling his family out West. (McLeod may not have been a genius, but when he was given chicken to work with, he *always* delivered chicken salad.)

*Redheads on Parade* and *Here Comes Cookie* (both 1935) brought McLeod back to earth, although the latter at least offered the talents of Burns and Allen, with Gracie as a screw-loose heiress who turns her father's Fifth Avenue mansion into a sanctuary for unemployed vaudeville performers. *Coronado* (1935) was another tossed-off musical, this time with Jack Haley and Eddy Duchin, while *Early to Bed* (1936) had Charlie Ruggles as a sleepwalker who becomes embroiled with gangsters. After such fare McLeod was probably relieved to be loaned to Columbia with Bing Crosby in 1936 to make *Pennies from Heaven*, a treacly effort that might have been insufferable if not for its Oscar-nominated song and the musical skills of Louis Armstrong. *Mind Your Own Business* (1937), another Charlie Ruggles showcase, concluded McLeod's Paramount career in unspectacular fashion.

Moving to MGM, McLeod was immediately made welcome by being handed *Topper* (1937) as his first project. This sublime comedy, from the Thorne Smith novel, offered Cary Grant and Constance Bennett as a just-deceased society couple who return as ghosts to advise henpecked Roland Young how to improve his quality of life; it's the good deed that will get them into heaven. *Topper* remains one of the most effervescent concoctions of the Thirties, with Young's Oscar-nominated performance just one of its many virtues. *Merrily We Live* (1938) may have been a chip off *My Man Godfrey*, but at least it was a capable one; Constance Bennett was again excellent in the role of a spoiled society girl who learns about life's true values from new butler Brian Aherne.

*There Goes My Heart* (1938) was just as brassy about recycling *It Happened One Night*; Virginia Bruce had Claudette Colbert's role as the runaway heiress and Fredric March had Gable's as the reporter who tames her. *Topper Takes a Trip* (1939) was the inevitable sequel to McLeod's earlier success and it wasn't bad, even though Roland Young had to carry on this time without the benefit of Cary Grant's *bon mots*. The forgotten *Remember?* (1939) was Greer Garson's unimpressive follow-up to *Mr. Chips*, a quasi-screwball comedy—co-written by McLeod—in which she was badly miscast, while *Little Men* (1940) was a treacly version of Louisa May Alcott that demonstrated again why McLeod was best known as a director of comedies.

*The Trial of Mary Dugan* (1941) was McLeod's brief foray into the courtroom thriller, with new star Laraine Day re-creating the part played to better effect in 1929 by Norma Shearer. *Lady Be Good* (1941) returned McLeod to the more comfortable territory of the musical, with top-line players like Eleanor Powell, Ann Sothern, Red Skelton, and Robert Young on hand and Busby Berkeley staging the impressive dance numbers. But *Jackass Mail* (1942) was a formula Western starring Wallace Beery and Marjorie Main, hardly the sort of thing a valued director would be given. *Panama Hattie* (also 1942) was a barely passable version of the 1940 Cole Porter stage success; Ann Sothern was a pale (if game) substitute for Ethel Merman, although the singing of Lena Horne and the dancing of the Berry Brothers provided some compensation. *The Powers Girl* (1943) was another labored musical—fashion photographer George Murphy makes Carole Landis into a top model while losing his heart to her sister (Anne Shirley); the tunes were by Benny Goodman, and the girls were actual Powers Agency models. The 1943 *Swing Shift Maisie* was an entry in Ann Sothern's popular series, pleasant enough but strictly a "B" production. McLeod never made another film for MGM.

After the war he found himself at RKO, where he made two of Danny Kaye's better pictures. *The Kid from Brooklyn* (1946) recycled Harold Lloyd's 1936 *The Milky Way*—a milkman accidentally becomes a professional boxer—while *The Secret Life of Walter Mitty* (1947) was a self-conscious but handsome production that used the James Thurber story about a daydreaming wimp (Kaye) as a point of departure. McLeod then moved to Paramount, where he did good work with Bob Hope, Bing Crosby, and Dorothy Lamour on *The Road to Rio* (1947), and with Hope and Jane Russell on *The Paleface* (1948), the latter buoyed by a Frank Tashlin script. But *Isn't It Romantic?* (1948) was just an uninspired period ro-

mance set in Indiana (it was Veronica Lake's last film for Paramount).

*Let's Dance* (1950), an adequate Fred Astaire–Betty Hutton musical, had some good Frank Loesser tunes and a couple of Fred's eye-opening dance inventions to patch over the tired plot. Then it was Hope again in *My Favorite Spy* (1951), a surprisingly nimble Cold War spoof, with Hedy Lamarr providing some extra oomph. McLeod made his last few pictures as a freelancer. *Never Wave at a Wac* (1953) found socialite Rosalind Russell enlisting in the armed forces with predictably silly results, while *Casanova's Big Night* (1954) set Bob Hope down in eighteenth-century Venice, with colorful support from heavies Basil Rathbone, Vincent Price, and Raymond Burr. *Public Pigeon No. 1* (1957) was a feeble Red Skelton vehicle, but McLeod was able to wrap up his career on a high note with *Alias Jesse James* (1959), a late but lively Bob Hope entry; Rhonda Fleming provides some appealing love interest.

## ● ROUBEN MAMOULIAN (1897–1987)

Dividing his professional life between Hollywood and the theater, Rouben Mamoulian directed a mere sixteen films between 1929, when he made *Applause*, and 1957, when he returned from a long hiatus to make *Silk Stockings*. In between he enjoyed an active career as one of Broadway's leading directors. And yet so stylish, deft, and imaginative are most of those sixteen movies that it seems unimportant that Mamoulian's filmography is only a third as extensive as those of most of his contemporaries.

Born in Tiflis, in the Russian province of Georgia, to Armenian parents, Mamoulian attended the Moscow Art Theater, after which he toured England with the Russian Repertory Theater. He then studied drama at the University of London and, soon after, began directing plays. In 1923 he accepted an offer from the George Eastman Theater in Rochester, New York, to direct operas, and worked there for three years. His next stop was Broadway, where he directed plays for the Theatre Guild, including its 1927 staging of *Porgy*; years later Mamoulian would again direct the play in its new incarnation as Gershwin's *Porgy and Bess*.

The dawning of the sound era in motion pictures made successful Broadway directors a hot commodity, and Mamoulian accepted an offer from Paramount to direct *Applause* (1929) on location and at its Astoria, New York, studio. The film preserves one of the few major performances of the great torch singer Helen Morgan, who plays Kitty Darling, a burlesque star beset by love, alcohol, and family problems.

*City Streets* (1931) was written by Dashiell Hammett and offered rising star Gary Cooper as a carnival worker who falls for racketeer's daughter Sylvia Sidney. One of the better early gangster pictures, its visual presentation was light-years beyond such more celebrated contemporaries as *Little Caesar*, *The Public Enemy*, and *Scarface*. Even more impressive was *Dr. Jekyll and Mr. Hyde* (1932), the first sound version of the classic Robert Louis Stevenson story (John Barrymore had made a well-received silent version in 1920). Fredric March garnered his first Oscar (sharing the best actor award with Wallace Beery) for his performance, and Mamoulian also elicited the best performance of Miriam Hopkins's career as the doomed prostitute Ivy. *Love Me Tonight* (1932) was based on a play, but in Mamoulian's hands it expands into an inventive musical comedy that ranks with the very best of Lubitsch. Maurice Chevalier and Jeanette MacDonald have never been better, and sexy, sardonic Myrna Loy is another delight, as are the great Rodgers and Hart tunes like "Isn't It Romantic," "Lover," and "Mimi."

*Song of Songs* (1933) was Mamoulian's last film for Paramount as producer-director; a failure at the box office, even its strong Marlene Dietrich performance cannot lift it beyond trite melodrama. He redeemed himself at MGM with *Queen Christina* (1933), which had an exquisite performance by Garbo at its center; alas, he and Garbo were never again able to work together. *We Live Again* (1934) was a ponderous stab at Tolstoy, with Fredric March and Russian actress Anna Sten unable to breathe life into this adaptation of *Resurrection*. Better was *Becky Sharp* (1935), another costumer, which had the novelty of being the first Technicolor feature release; Mamoulian (who took over the film when original director Lowell Sherman died) seems more at ease with Thackeray's comedy of manners (adapted from the novel *Vanity Fair*) than with Tolstoy. Still, the film simply isn't that good, and neither is Miriam Hopkins, who somehow was nominated for an Academy Award.

Mamoulian left Hollywood briefly to stage his acclaimed version of *Porgy and Bess* on Broadway, but he was back in 1936 to film *The Gay Desperado*, a strenuously whimsical comedy with the insufferable tenor Nino Martini, although Leo Carillo (in the title role) and Ida Lupino are good. The spectacle of *High, Wide, and Handsome* (1937) was more pleasing, as Irene Dunne, Randolph Scott, and Dorothy Lamour battle in the oil fields of nineteenth-century Pennsylvania when not belting out the Jerome Kern–Oscar Hammerstein score. Clifford Odets's proletarian drama *Golden Boy* (1939), a smash for the Group Theater in 1937, seemed an unlikely project for Mamoulian, just as Columbia was an unlikely studio for him (he had traded projects with Frank Capra). But this sentimental story of a boxing violinist (William Holden, in his screen debut) torn between the inimical demands of two careers and his love for Barbara Stanwyck somehow works, despite the clichés (which at the time weren't quite so familiar). Of course, they had to cop out on Odets's original suicide ending.

*The Mark of Zorro* (1940) was a classic swashbuckler, with Tyrone Power better served than in any other film he would make. It also offered the incandescent Linda Darnell as his love interest and the inimitable Basil Rathbone as his *bête noire*. Almost as fine was *Blood and Sand* (1941), which reunited Power and Darnell and added a fearsomely beautiful Rita Hayworth for good measure. Though its pace is too leisurely, the film still has an indelible effect. Mamoulian's third effort for Fox was the less successful *Rings on Her Fingers* (1942), a Henry Fonda–Gene Tierney romantic comedy with a plot that bore an uncanny resemblance to Sturges's earlier *The Lady Eve*. Tierney and Mamoulian were set to work again in *Laura*, but he was pulled off the project by Zanuck and replaced by Otto Preminger; some of his extensive work on the script may have remained.

The *Laura* experience understandably soured Mamoulian on Hollywood, but he probably was just as happy to return to Broadway, where he directed the enormous hits *Oklahoma!* (1943) and *Carousel* (1945). He made just two more films, both for MGM: the charming *Summer Holiday* (1948), a lively musical reworking of Eugene O'Neill's play *Ah, Wilderness!*, and *Silk Stockings* (1957), a musical version (via Cole Porter) of *Ninotchka* starring Fred Astaire; it might have topped Lubitsch's great original if Cyd Charisse had had Garbo's talent. In between, he shot some new scenes for the American release of Michael Powell's 1952 *The Wild Heart*. Mamoulian was slated to direct the film version of *Porgy and Bess* in 1958, but was replaced again by Preminger. And he had actually started *Cleopatra* for Fox when Zanuck fired him yet again: creative differences, of course. (Imagine what he might have wrought with *that* spectacle!) And so we are left to wonder why a director with Mamoulian's credits was never even nominated for an Academy Award.

## ● JOSEPH L. MANKIEWICZ (1909–1993)

One of the great writer/directors, Mankiewicz had already been a producer for over a decade, and a screenwriter for nearly twice as long, when he was summoned by Fox in 1946 to direct his first film. This most literate of directors was the younger brother (by twelve years) of successful screenwriter Herman J. Mankiewicz (who won an Oscar for his contribution—the larger part, some contend—to the screenplay of *Citizen Kane*). Born in Wilkes-Barre, Pennsylvania, raised in New York City, and educated at Columbia, Joseph joined his brother in Hollywood at the end of the silent era, working at Paramount as a writer on such projects as *Skippy*, *If I Had a Million*, and the 1933 production of *Alice in Wonderland*. Moving to MGM, he co-wrote *Manhattan Melodrama* and soon after was promoted to producer status, in charge of such major releases as *Fury*, *The Gorgeous Hussy*, *Mannequin*, *The Philadelphia Story*, and *Woman of the Year*.

In 1943 he signed a contract with 20th Century-Fox, where he was to work as both a producer and a screenwriter. When Ernst Lubitsch became too ill to oversee *Dragonwyck* (1946), Mankiewicz was asked to direct as well as script the gothic mystery, which featured Gene Tierney, Vincent Price, and Walter Huston. No sooner had he completed that than he was assigned to direct *Somewhere in the Night*, a passable film noir that suffered a bit from uncharismatic leads John Hodiak and Nancy Guild and its complicated but formulaic plot. *The Late George Apley* (1947) was a more typical Mankiewicz project, a comedy of manners that preserves the literary flavor of the J. P. Marquand novel on which it is based; Ronald Colman plays a Boston blueblood concerned only with his social standing. *The Ghost and Mrs. Muir* (1947) was a classic romantic fantasy, with Gene Tierney at her most lovely as a widow courted by the ghost of sea captain Rex Harrison, and there was an appropriately haunting score by Bernard Herrmann.

*Escape* (1948) was less memorable, although the location photography (it was made in England) and Rex Harrison's performance as a wrongfully incarcerated man raised it above the norm. But *A Letter to Three Wives* announced that Mankiewicz had truly arrived. This tale of three married women whose husbands have been targeted by a predatory female boasted a complicated but witty Mankiewicz screenplay and deft performances by Linda Darnell, Jeanne Crain, Ann Sothern, Thelma Ritter, and Paul Douglas. It was nominated for an Academy Award as the best picture of 1949, and won Oscars for best screenplay and best direction—the first time a director had won in both categories simultaneously.

Mankiewicz would repeat that remarkable accomplishment a year later, but first he made *House of Strangers*, a potent if somewhat heavy-handed drama about a Machiavellian businessman (well played by Edward G. Robinson) who exploits his own sons. *No Way Out* (1950) was an excellent noir co-scripted by Mankiewicz, with a searing performance by Richard Widmark as a racist killer whom Linda Darnell and Sidney Poitier must outwit. But *All About Eve* is the film with which Mankiewicz is most closely associated; it is an acerbic comedy of manners, with some of the best dialogue ever set to celluloid and a handful of performances to match, notably those by Bette Davis, George Sanders, and Thelma Ritter. The film received a record fourteen Oscar nominations, winning in six categories: best picture, supporting actor (George Sanders), direction, writing, costume design, and sound. (Those dual Oscars for writing and directing in consecutive years were the moviemaking equivalent of pitcher Johnny Vander Meer's consecutive no-hitters: something that probably will never happen again.)

The chatty *People Will Talk* (1951) featured Cary

Grant as a long-winded doctor with opinions on everything under the sun, and some beyond it; Jeanne Crain does most of the listening. (Of course, listening to reams of Mankiewicz dialogue isn't the most unpleasant task in the world.) *Five Fingers* (1952) was a World War II espionage yarn that offered the usual great performance by James Mason; it earned Mankiewicz his third Oscar nomination—and his first loss. (That disappointment was perhaps mitigated by his being invited to direct *La Bohème* for the Metropolitan Opera.) His contract with Fox now up, Mankiewicz formed his own production company, Figaro Inc., whose first release was *Julius Caesar* (1953), a model adaptation of the play with a cast for the ages: Marlon Brando (Oscar-nominated for his Marc Antony), John Gielgud, James Mason, Deborah Kerr, Louis Calhern, Greer Garson. Produced by John Houseman, the film was nominated for an Academy Award as best picture.

*The Barefoot Contessa* (1954) was another splendid entertainment, a caustic dissection of Hollywood myth-making, with Humphrey Bogart as a cynical director who makes a star out of ravishing but naïve Spanish dancer Ava Gardner with the help of unscrupulous press agent (or is that redundant?) Edmond O'Brien, who won an Oscar as best supporting actor; Mankiewicz was nominated for his story and screenplay. *Guys and Dolls* (1955) has been widely reviled, but it's really not bad, even with an admitted lack of chemistry among its stars and a bloated running time. *The Quiet American* (1958) was a bowdlerized version of Graham Greene's Vietnam novel, with a dour Audie Murphy finding himself in Saigon, knee-deep in murder.

But *Suddenly Last Summer* (1959) was prime Mankiewicz; Gore Vidal adapted the Tennessee Williams play, and Elizabeth Taylor, Katharine Hepburn (both Oscar-nominated), and Montgomery Clift were all superb. The debacle of *Cleopatra* (1963) would require an entire book to tell the tale; suffice it to say that Darryl F. Zanuck's replacing Rouben Mamoulian with Mankiewicz did not save this famously ill-fated venture. *The Honey Pot* (1967), with Rex Harrison and Susan Hayward, was an intermittently clever reworking of *Volpone*, while *There Was a Crooked Man* (1970) was a fascinating (if overlong) Western in which Kirk Douglas plays a McMurtryesque prisoner of progressive warden Henry Fonda. After co-directing the 1970 documentary *King* with Sidney Lumet, Mankiewicz topped off his splendid career by filming *Sleuth* (1972); playwright Anthony Shaffer adapted his inordinately clever murder mystery, and there were Oscar-nominated performances by Michael Caine and Laurence Olivier and a final best direction nomination for Mankiewicz—which made him the only director ever to retire on such a note.

◀ *Mankiewicz shares a laugh with Marlon Brando and Sam Goldwyn on the set of* Guys and Dolls

M

## ● ANTHONY MANN (1906-1967)

A poet of action and retribution in the Old West, Anthony Mann has long been recognized as a textbook example of the kind of director auteurists love: one who offers stories with recurring themes, whose protagonists share a common psychology, and whose visual techniques are recognizable as his signature. But the sublime 1950s Westerns that earned him his stripes in the "pantheon" are supplemented by an array of films in other genres, revealing Mann's résumé to be as varied as most of his peers'—sometimes to the detriment of his popular reputation.

Born Emil Anton Bundsmann in San Diego, California, he moved to New York City as a child and entered the theater as an actor and stagehand after high school. He became production manager at the Theatre Guild in the Thirties, and later directed *Thunder on the Left*, among other plays. Later in the decade he was a director for the Federal Theatre Project, where he came to the attention of David O. Selznick, who hired him in 1939 to direct screen tests, scout for talent, and help with casting. Once in Hollywood, he changed his name to Mann and began working as an assistant director at Paramount. A few years later he was given the chance to direct his first feature, the low-budget mystery *Dr. Broadway* (1942). He made the innocuous musical *Moonlight in Havana* at Universal, then signed in 1943 with "B" specialist Republic Studios. Of the five films he made there, the most interesting was probably *Strange Impersonation* (1946), an eerie mystery that had Brenda Marshall conducting dangerous experiments.

This led him to a contract with RKO, where he made *Two O'Clock Courage* (1945), another mystery starring Tom Conway as an amnesiac who is aided by newcomer Bettyjane Greer (who soon would become plain "Jane"). *The Bamboo Blonde* (1946) was a humdrum Frances Langford musical disguised as a war movie—or maybe it was vice versa—but *Desperate* (1947) was a terrific little noir about a truck driver (Steve Brodie) who runs afoul of gangster Raymond Burr and his fur thieves and has to run for his life; Mann co-wrote the original story. Just as good was *Railroaded* (1947), the first of four fine pictures Mann directed for tiny Eagle-Lion; here Hugh Beaumont plays a tough cop who tries to save Sheila Ryan from lowlife hood John Ireland, and again, Mann needed only seventy-odd minutes to tell his tale. *T-men* (1947) was more ambitious, a first-class noir with Dennis O'Keefe as a treasury agent going undercover to nail counterfeiter Charles McGraw. Even in a year revered for its wealth of great films noir, this one stands out.

*Raw Deal* (1948) was as raw as they come, a positively nasty yarn about con Dennis O'Keefe breaking out of prison to nail Raymond Burr, who had framed him; John Ireland, Claire Trevor, and Marsha Hunt complete the excellent cast. *Reign of Terror* (1949; aka *The Black Book*) was a change of venue, with Robert Cummings and Arlene Dahl caught in the midst of the French Revolution.

Mann's fine work now brought him to the attention of MGM, which signed him and then assigned him to the 1949 *Border Incident*. It was a hard-as-nails account of the wetback-smuggling industry, with Ricardo Montalban as a Mexican pawn in an illegal enterprise run by perennial villain Howard da Silva. *Side Street* (1949) was a taut noir with the appealing duo of Farley Granger and Cathy O'Donnell, fresh off their success in Nicholas Ray's *They Live by Night*. Here Granger, a bank clerk, finds $30,000 in stolen loot and foolishly tries to keep it, putting his life in jeopardy.

But it was the Universal production *Winchester '73* (1950), Mann's first Western, that signaled the beginning of a new phase in both his career and that of star James Stewart. The plot was simple but sturdy: Stewart must hunt down his brother, who has stolen his hard-won rifle—but when he catches up to him, the rifle has passed into other hands, and Stewart's quest begins anew. Finally, after much blood and sweat, the Winchester returns to Stewart's hands. *The Furies* (1950), a Freudian Western written by Niven Busch, wasn't as big a commercial success, perhaps because Mann allowed Barbara Stanwyck and her cattle-baron dad Walter Huston to talk for far too many of its 109 minutes. *The Devil's Doorway* (1950) boldly cast erstwhile matinee idol Robert Taylor as an Indian who returns to his tribe after serving in the Civil War, only to find that his kinsmen have been exploited by evil whites.

*The Tall Target* (1951) was a suspenseful tale set on a train (in 1861) carrying President Lincoln, with Dick Powell as the detective who must find would-be assassin Leif Erickson before it's too late. Mann and Stewart were teamed again in *Bend of the River* (1952), with Stewart as the leader of a wagon train traveling to Oregon that is about to be robbed by his former outlaw partner, Arthur Kennedy; the story rambled a bit, but the Pacific Northwest locations were stunning. The very best of Mann's Westerns was *The Naked Spur* (1953), with Stewart now as a bounty hunter tracking killer Robert Ryan through the Rockies; the strong supporting cast included Janet Leigh and Ralph Meeker, but the film's special resonance can be credited to Stewart's obsessive, emotionally repressed protagonist. As usual, the location photography in the Rockies was superb.

Mann and Stewart deviated from their standard Wild West venue for *Thunder Bay* (1953), a contemporary adventure starring Stewart and Dan Duryea as oil drillers who understandably upset the local

▲ *With Walter Huston on the set of* The Furies

shrimp fishermen when they start blasting off the Louisiana coast. The film had its moments, but wasn't up to the level of their previous collaborations. The biopic *The Glenn Miller Story* (1954) was a well-mounted production flavored too heavily with saccharine as it dramatized (and idealized) the late bandleader's life and music. Stewart was acceptable as Miller, but June Allyson made for a dull wife; still, it was great to see the likes of Gene Krupa and Louis Armstrong performing, and the picture was an enormous moneymaker. Stewart and Mann got back to business with *The Far Country* (1955), a tale of two cattlemen (Stewart and Walter Brennan) who drive their herd to an Alaskan gold-rush town, only to have it seized by the despotic sheriff who runs the place (John McIntire). Stewart makes a satisfying transformation from a good-natured cowboy to a man thirsting for vengeance after Brennan is bushwhacked, and Mann devises some good byplay between romantic rivals Ruth Roman and Corinne Calvet.

*Strategic Air Command* was about a ballplayer (Stewart, of course) who is recalled to active service in the Air Force to test atomic jets; June Allyson was again cast as his wife, and again they made a less-than-compelling couple; nevertheless, the film was Paramount's biggest moneymaker of 1955. That year Mann collaborated one final time with Stewart on *The Man from Laramie*, another fine tale of retribution that sent Stewart on a hunt in search of the men who indirectly caused his brother's death; next came *The Last Frontier* (1956), a Western with every element in place except James Stewart—and that absence kept the film from rising above the ordinary. *Serenade* (1956) represented a major departure, but unfortunately Mann's adaptation of James M. Cain's great 1936 novel was a complete botch. The casting of Mario Lanza as Cain's bisexual, two-fisted opera singer was an utter failure, although Vincent Price makes an impression as the manipulative impresario (here shorn of the predatory homosexuality he had in the book).

He got back on track with *Men in War* (1957), a good if familiar Korean War tale with Robert Ryan, Vic Morrow, and Aldo Ray heading the top-notch cast. *The Tin Star* (1957) used polar opposites Henry Fonda and Anthony Perkins to good effect as, respectively, a seasoned bounty hunter and a greenhorn sheriff who's in over his head and knows it. Mann's version of Erskine Caldwell's bestseller *God's Little Acre* (1958) was strengthened by the presence of Robert Ryan, Aldo Ray, and especially Tina Louise as the Georgia crackers waiting out the Depression on their unfarmed farm, although much of the flavor of the funny but profane novel was leached out to satisfy the censors. There was no compromising on the 1958 *Man of the West*, a brutal but superbly staged drama (scripted by television's Reginald Rose), starring Gary Cooper as a former bank robber who is held hostage, along with dance-hall singer Julie London, by his old gang (headed by sadistic Lee J. Cobb). A kind of *Petrified Forest* of the Old West, *Man* was not a box-office success, but now it is recognized as Mann's last great Western. *Cimarron* (1960) was a remake of the 1931 Academy Award–winning epic, and although it was better on various technical levels and had a more impressive cast, Mann's 147-minute version of the Ferber novel never caught fire.

*Spartacus* was to be his next project, but Mann fell out with producer-star Kirk Douglas and was replaced by Stanley Kubrick. Instead, he made the splendid *El Cid* (1961), with Charlton Heston in one of his best roles as the liberator of eleventh-century Spain; Sophia Loren was a cause worth dying for. Made for the Samuel Bronston Company, this three-hour spectacle remains one of the best historical epics of that genre's golden period. *The Fall of the Roman Empire* (1964), another Bronston production, might have been as memorable but for leading man Stephen Boyd, the only liability in a great cast that includes Sophia Loren, James Mason, Alec Guinness, and Christopher Plummer. *The Heroes of Telemark* (1965) had large-scale World War II action, with Kirk Douglas and Richard Harris saving Norway almost single-handedly. Mann started *A Dandy in Aspic* (1968) but died in the midst of production, and it was completed by, and credited to, star Laurence Harvey.

◀ *James Stewart and Mann on location for* The Man from Laramie

## ● GEORGE MARSHALL (1891-1975)

A smoothly functioning cog in the Hollywood factory who only occasionally was able to raise his work above the merely satisfactory, George Marshall spent more than forty years making every conceivable kind of movie, with comedies, musicals, and Westerns dominating his résumé. But if only a few of his seventy-three sound pictures have attained the status of minor classics, most reward at least one viewing.

Born in Chicago, he started his film career by working as an extra in the early Teens. By 1916 he had already begun directing Westerns, but his career was put on hold for a stint overseas during World War I. He picked up where he had left off when he returned, directing serials like *The Adventures of Ruth* with Ruth Roland and *Haunted Valley* for Pathé. He also made Westerns for Fox, where he both shot and supervised shorts through much of the Twenties, including some Laurel and Hardy two-reelers and Bobby Jones How-To's on golf. In 1932 he returned to feature work, co-directing the Laurel and Hardy feature *Pack Up Your Troubles* with Raymond McCarey.

Signing with Fox in 1934, Marshall made the Western *Wild Gold* with Claire Trevor and *She Learned about Sailors* with Alice Faye and Lew Ayres. *365 Nights in Hollywood* (1934) was a romantic comedy with Faye and James Dunn, while *Life Begins at Forty* (1935) was one of Will Rogers's best vehicles, with Will as a small-town newspaper editor. After making *Ten Dollar Raise* (1935) with Edward Everett Horton, Marshall directed Rogers again in his last film before his untimely death, *In Old Kentucky* (1935). *Music Is Magic* (1935) was short on both magic and music; Alice Faye plays an up-and-coming chorus girl who replaces fading star Bebe Daniels in a new movie. But the 1935 *Show Them No Mercy!* was a superior gangster picture starring Bruce Cabot and Cesar Romero as kidnappers brought to bay by the FBI, with the aid of comely Rochelle Hudson.

*A Message to Garcia* (1936) used an actual incident from the Spanish-American War as its springboard; John Boles was the message bearer from President McKinley, and Wallace Beery and Barbara Stanwyck his companions during his trek through Cuba's jungle. *The Crime of Dr. Forbes* (1936), a "B" thriller about euthanasia, was years ahead of its time in theme if not execution, while *Can This Be Dixie?* (also 1936) was a musical set in the cotton-pickin' South, with Jane Withers and Slim Summerville. Marshall was kept on a small budget for *Nancy Steele Is Missing* (1937), a crime yarn with an interesting twist that featured Victor McLaglen and Peter Lorre as former cellmates, while *Love Under Fire* (1937) was a junior league *Desire*: Loretta Young is accused of being a jewel thief and Don Ameche is the Scotland Yard inspector who tracks her to Spain, clears her, then falls in love with her.

Marshall was loaned out to make *The Goldwyn Follies* (1938), a rather awful variety showcase for the Ritz Brothers, Kenny Baker, Zorina (who was choreographed by George Balanchine), and Edgar Bergen and Charlie McCarthy. Back at Fox he directed *Battle of Broadway* (1938) with Gypsy Rose Lee, Victor McLaglen, and Brian Donlevy, followed by the riotous political satire *Hold That Co-Ed* (1938), with John Barrymore in good form as a Huey Long-ish demagogue. This completed Marshall's tenure at Fox, and he spent the next few years freelancing. *You Can't Cheat an Honest Man* (1939) was a typically mad W. C. Fields hallucination, although veteran Eddie Cline actually directed Fields while Marshall handled cast members Edgar Bergen, Constance Moore, and Eddie Anderson. Even more successful was the wonderful comic adventure *Destry Rides Again* (1939), based on a Max Brand novel that had been filmed "straight" in 1932 with Tom Mix. Now it's James Stewart as the pacifist sheriff who outsmarts a town's worth of lowlifes without ever raising his voice, and in the bargain wins the heart of saloon singer Marlene Dietrich, the ineffable "Frenchy." John Ford's *Stagecoach* may have been the year's most important Western, but *Destry* was by far the most fun, and it remains the high-water mark of Marshall's long career.

*The Ghost Breakers* (1940) was an excellent Bob Hope comedy/chiller set in a haunted house in Cuba; Paulette Goddard, his co-star in the previous year's popular *The Cat and the Canary*, again provides the romantic interest, with Noble Johnson as a very creepy zombie. The 1940 *When the Daltons Rode* was an exciting account of the legendary brothers, with Brian Donlevy and Broderick Crawford facing off against hero Randolph Scott. James Stewart teamed with Paulette Goddard in *Pot o' Gold* (1941), but the results were instantly forgettable (Stewart once claimed this was his worst picture). *Texas* (1941) was much better, as William Holden competes with Glenn Ford for the favors of Claire Trevor, but *Valley of the Sun* (1942) was less convincing: corrupt government agent Dean Jagger stirs up unrest among the Indians until James Craig and Lucille Ball set things right.

Marshall now signed with Paramount, where he would stay for the next twelve years. *The Forest Rangers* (1942) had Susan Hayward and Paulette Goddard battling over ranger Fred MacMurray—lucky dog!—while *Star Spangled Rhythm* (also 1942) served up Bing Crosby, Bob Hope, Veronica Lake, Dorothy Lamour, Paulette Goddard, and most of Paramount's other stars in a frothy concoction that included the standard "That Old Black Magic." *True to Life* (1943) was a pleasant comedy in which soap-opera writer Dick Powell moves in with Mary Martin's family to get material about "the common folk" for his show. But *Riding High* (1943) was a below-par musical that starred Dorothy Lamour as a burly-Q stripper who catches silver miner Dick Powell's eye.

*And the Angels Sing* (1944) offered Lamour and Betty Hutton as singing sisters discovered by bandleader Fred MacMurray, while *Murder, He Says* (1945) demonstrated MacMurray's flair for slapstick—he's an insurance pollster whose foray into hillbilly territory lands him in the lap of Marjorie Main's family of killers. Betty Hutton starred as the eponymous *Incendiary Blonde* (1945), a biopic about vaudeville singer Texas Guinan, the best part of which was Hutton's rendition of "It Had to Be You." Marshall went blond again with Veronica Lake as a jewel thief courted by millionaire kleptomaniac Eddie Bracken in the 1945 *Hold That Blonde*.

After this steady diet of fluff, Marshall must have savored making Raymond Chandler's *The Blue Dahlia* (1946), a typically convoluted noir that featured Paramount's top box-office team of Alan Ladd and Veronica Lake: he's a war vet suspected of killing his sluttish wife (Doris Dowling), she's the woman who helps keep him out of the cops' hands until he can turn up the actual killer. But Chandler reportedly wrote the screenplay for producer John Houseman while on a two-week bender, and the plot can induce a hangover. *Monsieur Beaucaire* (1946) in its own way was more accomplished, a hilarious costumer set in the court of Louis XV, with Bob Hope as a barber who accepts a suicide mission to avoid the guillotine and winds up with Joan Caulfield; the wild sword-fight sequence was directed by Frank Tashlin.

The purported screen biography of silent serial star Pearl White, *The Perils of Pauline* (1947), had some good Frank Loesser songs to make up for the trademark overexuberance of star Betty Hutton, and

also featured a host of silent movie stars in cameos, Chester Conklin, William Farnum, and Creighton Hale among them. *Variety Girl* (1947) was yet another collection of skits, featuring Bob Hope, Bing Crosby, and every other Paramount headliner and second-stringer, plus cameos by directors Cecil B. DeMille, Mitchell Leisen, and Marshall himself. *Hazard* (1948) was a minor romantic mystery starring Paulette Goddard as a girl on the run and MacDonald Carey as the detective who tracks her down, while *Tap Roots* (1948) transported Van Heflin and Susan Hayward to antebellum Mississippi, where lurked Indian medicine man Boris Karloff.

Marshall's adaptation of the popular radio series *My Friend Irma* (1949) starred statuesque Marie Wilson as the dizzy Irma, but the film is memorable today chiefly for marking the screen debut of the Dean Martin/Jerry Lewis combo, who would make millions for Paramount in the next decade. *Fancy Pants* (1950) was a creditable remake of the 1935 *Ruggles of Red Gap*, with Bob Hope inheriting the Charles Laughton role as the English valet and Lucille Ball as his new owner, but *Never a Dull Moment* (1950)—a precursor to TV's *Green Acres*—was a middling comedy based on the premise of Park Avenue songwriter Irene Dunne moving to a ranch in Wyoming after marrying rodeo cowboy Fred MacMurray (who gives one of his least appealing performances).

Marshall and MacMurray fared better with *A Millionaire for Christy* (1951), a screwball romp in which engaged radio entertainer Fred is the marital target of secretary Eleanor Powell after he inherits a fortune. *The Savage* (1952) was the first Western Marshall had made in many a moon; Charlton Heston was in good form as a white raised by Indians who is torn between the two cultures when a war breaks

▲ *On the set of* Houdini *with newlyweds Janet Leigh and Tony Curtis*

out. *Off Limits* (1953) was a medium-funny yarn, with Bob Hope as a reluctant MP in the service who discovers the boxing skills of Mickey Rooney and decides to manage him. The 1953 *Scared Stiff* was Marshall's remake of his own *The Ghost Breakers*, with Martin and Lewis now installed in the Bob Hope role and Lizabeth Scott the owner of the haunted mansion; regrettably, songs replace the chills in this goround (although Carmen Miranda has a neat cameo).

*Houdini* (1953) offered athletic Tony Curtis as the legendary escape artist—real-life mate Janet Leigh played his wife—while *Money from Home* (also 1953) was an unimpressive 3-D version of the Martin and Lewis act. *Red Garters* (1954) was a half-serious musical Western with Rosemary Clooney and Guy Mitchell. After that, Marshall and Paramount parted ways. Now freelancing, he jumped at the opportunity to handle two-fisted action again in the 1954 *Duel in the Jungle*, with Dana Andrews as an insurance investigator who suspects David Farrar of not being quite as dead as he's supposed to be. At Universal Marshall remade *Destry* (1954) with Audie Murphy and Mari Blanchard; while adequate, it hardly came up to his 1939 version. *The Second Greatest Sex* (1955) was a sodden musical—"What Good Is a Woman without a Man?" The title tune was as limp as stars George Nader and Jeanne Crain.

*Pillars of the Sky* (1956) was a decent Western that starred Jeff Chandler as a cavalry scout trying to rebuff an Indian attack while building a fort and romancing married settler Dorothy Malone, and *The Guns of Fort Petticoat* (1957) trod similar ground; Audie Murphy plays an Army deserter who teaches a contingent of women how to rebuff an attack by hostile Indians. *Beyond Mombasa* (1957) sent Cornel Wilde and Donna Reed trekking through the African jungle in search of a uranium mine. Marshall then worked with a solo Jerry Lewis for the only time in the 1957 *The Sad Sack*, a lame expansion of the minimalist comic strip by George Baker. It was back to the Old West for the lively *The Sheepman* (1958), with Glenn Ford and Leslie Nielsen competing for both Shirley MacLaine and grazing territory.

Ford starred less successfully in *Imitation General* (1958), a rank World War II comedy, but *The Mating Game* (1959) got its share of laughs—tax agent Tony Randall falls for bucolic client Debbie Reynolds despite opposition from dad Paul Douglas. *It Started with a Kiss* was typical Fifties fluff, with Army officer Glenn Ford and kookie wife Debbie Reynolds stationed in Spain, but the pair worked better in *The Gazebo* (1960), a comic mystery that has some of the flavor of Alfred Hitchcock's *The Trouble with Harry.* Ford starred again for Marshall in the sentimental *Cry for Happy* (1961) as a Navy photographer who falls for a geisha girl, while *The Happy Thieves* (1962) tried to recapture past glamour by having Rita Hayworth and Rex Harrison attempt a museum theft in Spain.

Marshall's last Western was his portion of *How the West Was Won* (1963), a Cinerama epic that starred John Wayne, James Stewart, and Gregory Peck (the other segments were directed by John Ford and Henry Hathaway). *Papa's Delicate Condition* (1963) was an offbeat biopic, with Jackie Gleason as silent film star Corinne Griffith's lush of a dad and the great tune "Call Me Irresponsible" (by Jimmy Van Heusen and Sammy Cahn). After the French-Italian *Dark Purpose*, Marshall made the Civil War comedy *Advance to the Rear* (1964) with Glenn Ford and Stella Stevens and *Boy, Did I Get a Wrong Number!* (1966), an appalling farce starring Bob Hope and Phyllis Diller. *Number!* was matched in ineptness by Hope and Diller's reteaming in the following year's *Eight on the Lam*—surely these marked the nadirs of Marshall's long career. Almost as laughless were *The Wicked Dreams of Paula Schultz* (1968) with Elke Sommer and *Hook, Line, and Sinker* (1969), one of Jerry Lewis's last and least efforts. Fortunately, Marshall then called it a career.

## ● ARCHIE MAYO (1891-1968)

Most closely associated with the sound pictures he made at Warner Bros. between 1929 and 1937, Archie Mayo was never much more than an able craftsman, and sometimes fell below that standard. Still, his name appears on a number of interesting pictures, both from the Warners period and after, and he worked effectively with most of the day's major male stars.

Born in New York City, young Archibald acted on stage before entering films as an extra in 1916. He graduated to directing comedy shorts a year later, but was not entrusted with features until 1926, when he directed *Money Talks* for MGM. In 1927 Mayo moved to Warners, where he made a half dozen silents before helping the studio enter the sound era with *State-Street Sadie* (1928), an early Myrna Loy crime drama, and *My Man* (also 1928), which featured Fanny Brice singing the title tune as well as "Second Hand Rose." *Sonny Boy* (1929) was a transparent—but successful—attempt to cash in on the popularity of child actor Davey Lee, whose deathbed scene in the previous year's *The Singing Fool* had left America awash in tears, while *Oh! Sailor Behave* (1930) was an Olsen and Johnson vehicle based on the Broadway hit.

*Doorway to Hell* (1930) was marginally more interesting, with sixth-billed James Cagney supporting a miscast Lew Ayres in a melodrama about the perils of bootlegging. *Illicit* (1931) had a promising title and Barbara Stanwyck going for it, but it was really just standard soap-opera fare about love gone wrong, while *Svengali* (1931) was a rather creaky version of the George du Maurier tale, despite an effective performance by John Barrymore in the title role. *Bought* (1931) was another "woman's picture," starring Constance Bennett—then Hollywood's highest-paid actress—as a woman born illegitimate who tries to fit into society. The majority of the five features Mayo released in 1932 were also weepies, including *Street of Women* with Kay Francis, *Two Against the World* with Constance Bennett, and *Under Eighteen* with Marian Marsh. Only *Night after Night* stood out, and that was because it marked Mae West's screen debut; alas, co-star George Raft wasted most of the picture romancing Constance Cummings.

But Mayo drew a more interesting slate in 1933, thanks to *The Life of Jimmy Dolan*, with Doug Fairbanks, Jr., a boxer fleeing a murder rap (he ends up helping a group of crippled children) and *The Mayor of Hell*, a prime Cagney showcase that found Jimmy helping abused boys in a reform school, with Frankie Darro as the leader of the hard-boiled lads and Dudley Digges the corrupt superintendent. (Warners would remake both pictures later in the decade.) *Ever in My Heart* was soap opera once again, and even Barbara Stanwyck as the DAR wife of German turncoat Otto Kruger was not able to disguise the proceedings as anything but outlandish. *Convention City* was pleasant foolishness about a salesmen's annual gathering, with Adolphe Menjou, Dick Powell, and Joan Blondell among the proficient cast members, while *Gambling Lady* (1934) gave Stanwyck still more tears to wade through as an aboveboard gambler whose unsavory profession creates problems with upper-crust hubby Joel McCrea and his snooty family.

*The Man with Two Faces* (1934) was a melodrama adapted from a play by crimebusters George S. Kaufman and Alexander Woollcott, with Edward G. Robinson as a hammy actor who has to murder his sister's husband (Mary Astor and Louis Calhern) before he drives her insane—a plot that didn't resemble many others, it must be said. After *Desirable* (1934), a minor but entertaining soap opera with George Brent and Jean Muir, Mayo made the near-classic *Bordertown* (1935), an overheated but compelling drama starring Paul Muni as a Mexican lawyer who tries (but fails) to fend off the advances of his rich boss's wife—Bette Davis, over-the-top but terrific. (If Davis hadn't won the Oscar that year for *Dangerous*, she could have taken it home for this performance.) *Go Into Your Dance* (1935) teamed real-life husband and wife Al Jolson and Ruby Keeler in a backstage musical that managed to combine a gangster subplot with such Harry Warren–Al Dubin tunes as "A Latin from Manhattan," while *The Case of the Lucky Legs* (also 1935) was a passable Perry Mason yarn, played largely for laughs, with Warren William as Erle Stanley Gardner's crack detective—here a bit hungover, no doubt a nod to Nick Charles.

*The Petrified Forest* (1936) was Mayo's most prestigious project to date, an adaptation of Robert E. Sherwood's Broadway success that imported original cast members Leslie Howard and (at Howard's insistence) Humphrey Bogart, with Bette Davis added for the box office. Considered by many a bona fide Thirties classic, the film really isn't very good; Bogart as killer Duke Mantee is almost painful to watch, snarling and stiffly shambling around the café where he's holding everyone hostage, and Sherwood's dialogue is drenched in purple. Still, it gave Bogart his chance, for which we shall be forever grateful. Mayo's other 1936 productions were less impressive: *I Married a Doctor* was a remake of Sinclair Lewis's *Main Street*, while *Give Me Your Heart* interspersed Kay Francis's tears for her illegitimate baby with loving shots of her fabulous wardrobe, the latter clearly closer to her heart.

After the success of *Forest*, Mayo and Bogart were teamed again on *The Black Legion* (1937), a surprisingly bold indictment of the KKK and its offshoots, inspired by racist incidents that had taken place in Detroit the year before; Bogart had his best role of the decade as a factory worker seduced by the supremacist party line of his co-workers before coming to his senses. *Call It a Day* (1937) gave Mayo an innately silly premise and he wasn't able to improve on it, but *It's Love I'm After* (also 1937) was a first-rate screwball romance starring Leslie Howard, Bette Davis, and Olivia de Havilland, none of whom was ever again as funny. Mayo demonstrated a lightness of touch here absent from most of his work to date; perhaps Casey Robinson's screenplay was the key element. This confection proved to be his final work for Warners, severing their eleven-year connection.

Mayo's first freelance project was *The Adventures of Marco Polo* (1938) for UA, a tongue-in-cheek account (by Robert E. Sherwood) of the thirteenth century's greatest explorer. Gary Cooper, Sigrid Gurie, Alan Hale, and Basil Rathbone headed the players, and all but the last were horribly miscast. *Youth Takes a Fling* (1938) was, if anything, worse—a stupid romantic comedy with New York shopgirl Andrea Leeds in hot pursuit of transplanted hick Joel McCrea. But *They Shall Have Music* (1939) was *sui generis*, with classical violinist Jascha Heifetz presented as the savior of Walter Brennan's East Side music school. This sentimental earful was written by John Howard Lawson and nurtured by Sam Goldwyn, whose pet project it was. Mayo was probably happy to return to the dirty dealings of *House across the Bay* (1940), a Walter Wanger crimefest with the top-notch cast of George Raft, Walter Pidgeon, Joan Bennett, and Gladys George.

*Four Sons* (1940), the first of eight consecutive films Mayo directed for 20th Century-Fox, was a timely remake of John Ford's 1928 silent, but with the Nazi menace instead of World War I as its backdrop. *The Great American Broadcast* (1941) was an imaginative account of the rise of the radio industry; Alice Faye and John Payne handle the romantic duties and the Four Ink Spots the singing. *Charley's Aunt*

(1941) had Jack Benny in drag per the requisites of the Broadway play (filmed in 1930 with Charlie Ruggles and in 1925 with Syd Chaplin), while *Confirm or Deny* (also 1941) had Don Ameche and Joan Bennett romancing each other among the air-raid shelters. Mayo took over for Fritz Lang on *Moontide* (1942), a downbeat but affecting tale in which suicidal Ida Lupino is saved from herself by no-nonsense seaman Jean Gabin. A more commercial project was the 1942 *Orchestra Wives*, which combined the music of Glenn Miller (''Serenade in Blue'') and the dancing of the Nicholas Brothers with an affecting story about the band's neglected wives (Carole Landis, Lynn Bari, Ann Rutherford).

*Crash Dive* (1943) sent Tyrone Power and Dana Andrews off to fight the Germans in a sub, although they seemed to spend the bulk of their time competing for Anne Baxter. Mayo returned to the musical milieu with the 1944 *Sweet and Low-Down*, which used Benny Goodman and his smokin' band to anchor an elementary romance between trombonist James Cardwell and Fox's reigning beauty, Linda Darnell. Mayo then spent a year out of work before hooking on with United Artists, where he made his final two films in 1946. *A Night in Casablanca* had the Marx Brothers outwitting Nazi spies in their penultimate picture; Frank Tashlin collaborated on the script. The uneven *Angel on My Shoulder* starred Paul Muni as an agent of Satan (a typically effective Claude Rains) sent back to earth for evil purposes; he's transformed by the love of Anne Baxter into a do-gooder, and Rains meets defeat. Not a bad little fantasy, but—like so much of Mayo's work over the years—it just missed the mark.

## ● PAUL MAZURSKY (1930– )

This keen-eyed satirist, who always seems poised to become the next Woody Allen before backsliding with an ill-fated picture or two, was born in Brooklyn as Irwin Mazursky. After attending Brooklyn College, in 1951 he moved to Greenwich Village, where he began working as an actor while studying under Lee Strasberg and Paul Mann. While performing in clubs, he made connections that helped him break into live television. He also had a part in Stanley Kubrick's low-budget debut *Fear and Desire* in 1953, which helped him land a role in the more prominent *The Blackboard Jungle*. But his acting career failed to take off and soon he was writing for television, including a long stint on *The Danny Thomas Show* with collaborator Larry Tucker.

He and Tucker were part of the creative team that launched *The Monkees* series in 1966, after which they co-wrote the screenplay for *I Love You, Alice B. Toklas!* (1968), in which Peter Sellers discovers the counterculture. That success positioned Mazursky to direct his first film, *Bob & Carol & Ted & Alice* (1969). This comedy about est and sexual experimentation among two pairs of friends (Robert Culp and Natalie Wood, Elliott Gould and Dyan Cannon) was considered a boundary breaker, although today it would barely pass muster for a Fox sitcom; still, it was a box-office hit and earned Oscar nominations for Gould, Cannon, and the screenplay by Mazursky and Tucker. Their Hollywood in-joke *Alex in Wonderland* (1970) fared less well, with Donald Sutherland as a compulsively fantasizing film director and Ellen Burstyn as his supportive wife; Federico Fellini and Jeanne Moreau appeared as themselves, and Mazursky and his daughter Peg also took roles. If not exactly $8^1/_2$, it was at least a solid 7.

It took Mazursky three years to get *Blume in Love* (1973) made, this time without Tucker as his collaborator. A penetrating marital farce, the film stars George Segal as an L.A. divorce lawyer whose wife (Susan Anspach) leaves him for laid-back musician Kris Kristofferson. Segal's frenetic, pathetic efforts to reclaim her are the film's glue, but Mazursky lets the story travel pretty much where it will, reaping some quirky comic benefits along the way. (Mazursky cast himself in a bit part.) *Harry and Tonto* (1974) was a road-trip yarn with a twist: its protagonist is a seventy-two-year-old retired college professor (Art Carney). He sets off with his cat on a cross-country bus trip to visit daughter Ellen Burstyn in Chicago and son Larry Hagman in L.A. Carney gave an Oscar-winning performance as the lonely but spirited Harry (winning over whippersnappers Dustin Hoffman, Jack Nicholson, and Al Pacino); Mazursky's and Josh Greenfield's screenplay was also nominated.

Mazursky's autobiographical comedy *Next Stop, Greenwich Village* (1976), based on his adventures as a struggling actor in the early Fifties, starred Lenny Baker (who died at an early age of cancer), who's positively splendid as Larry Lapinsky, taking Method-acting lessons and waiting for a callback from a studio that's casting for a Juvenile Delinquents pic; Shelley Winters as his hysterical mother, Ellen Greene as his girlfriend, and Christopher Walken as a proto-beat poet also are fun to watch. Mazursky then took a rare acting assignment outside his own projects, as the manager in the awful 1976 remake of *A Star Is Born*. His biggest hit to date was *An Unmarried Woman* (1978); Jill Clayburgh starred as a wife deserted by her cowardly husband (Michael Murphy) who suddenly must fashion a new life for herself. Mazursky's script was unsparing and well-observed, and Alan Bates was a standout as the lover with whom Clayburgh may or may not settle down. Clayburgh and the film were both nominated for Academy Awards, and Mazursky was nominated twice, for best direction and for best screenplay.

With a mainstream popular and critical success

▲ *With Kris Kristofferson on the set of* Blume in Love



under his belt, Mazursky might have been expected to consolidate his position as one of Hollywood's top director/producer/writers. But his next project was *Willie and Phil* (1980), a loose transposition of *Jules and Jim* to Greenwich Village and California, with Ray Sharkey and Michael Ontkean as the friends who both fall in love, and alternately pair off, with Margot Kidder. It wasn't Truffaut, but it had its own charms; still, ticketbuyers were few and far between. *Tempest* (1982) was an uneasy updating of Shakespeare, with John Cassavetes as a world-weary New York architect who chucks it all and takes his family to a small Greek isle, where magic and mirth await —sort of. Susan Sarandon, Gena Rowlands, Raul Julia, Molly Ringwald, and of course Mazursky himself make for an appealing cast, but as scripted, the film is so fraught with the Meaning of Life that it's impossible to be moved—or amused—by it for long.

*Moscow on the Hudson* (1984) played ever so much better, with Robin Williams well cast as a sax-playing, homesick Soviet defector who tries to adjust to New York City, which (despite its plentiful supply of toilet paper) is not the paradise he had envisioned. As with most of Mazursky's work, this bittersweet comedy lets its heart roll down its sleeve more often than it should, and its best moments seem to happen on the periphery of the plot. But somehow the film sticks with you. The same is true of *Down and Out in Beverly Hills* (1986), but this time Mazursky and writing partner Leon Capetanos leave out the sentiment and shovel on the laughs. A reworking of Renoir's 1931 film *Boudu Saved from Drowning*, this merciless lampoon of the California lifestyle among the rich and nonfamous may be Mazursky's best movie, with Nick Nolte in top form as the derelict who by degrees takes over the family of clothes-hanger mogul Richard Dreyfuss—including wife Bette Midler, daughter Tracy Nelson, maid Elizabeth Pena, and even dog Mike. It was also Mazursky's biggest hit, earning $28 million.

*Moon Over Parador* (1988) again starred Richard Dreyfuss, now as an actor imported to Latin America to impersonate a dictator whose death is being hushed up. It's funny enough, and you can't argue with a cast that includes Jonathan Winters, Charo, and Sonia Braga, but Mazursky needed someone like Andrew Bergman as co-scripter to take this over the top. Eschewing such silliness, Mazursky now co-

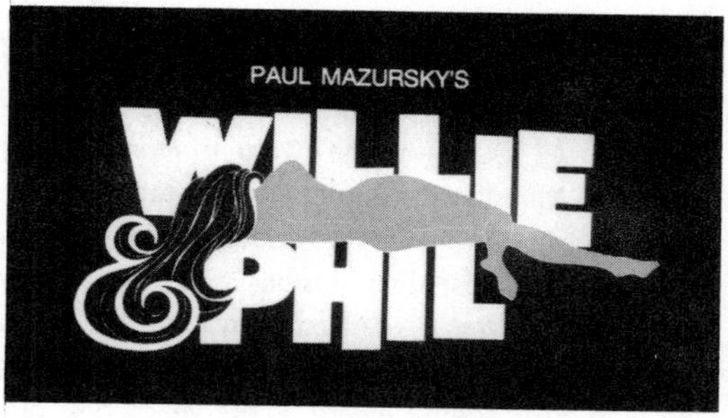


adapted a work by ironic eroticist Isaac Bashevis Singer. *Enemies: A Love Story* (1989) starred Ron Silver as a Holocaust survivor who is living in Coney Island in 1949 with wife Margaret Sophie Stein, who saved him from the Nazis. Even as he's carrying on an affair with Lena Olin (who is also married), first wife Anjelica Huston—thought deceased—turns up, further complicating the lucky (but guilt-stricken) fellow's life. Emotionally profound (though populated by characters whose behavior is often maddening), *Enemies* earned universally glowing reviews.

But *Scenes from a Mall* (1991) didn't. In fact, it was a near-disaster, an inert comedy starring Woody Allen and Bette Midler as a couple who unravel while celebrating their anniversary with a day at the mall. *The Pickle* (1993) would have been considered another disappointment, had anyone been able to see it. But this inside-Hollywood farce, written per usual by Mazursky, barely earned a release. Danny Aiello is an egotistical movie director whose downhill slide can be reversed only by a major hit. Dozens of stars have cameos, but there the film's resemblance to *The Player* ends. For another director, this might have been a damaging setback, but in the context of Mazursky's roller-coaster career, it only meant business as usual.

## ● LEWIS MILESTONE (1895–1980)

One of the premier directors when sound pictures were in their infancy, Lewis Milestone was still working in Hollywood when his greatest triumphs were some twenty years behind him. But the first half of his filmography contains such a high proportion of masterpieces and near-classics that his more pedestrian late work can easily be forgiven.

Born near Odessa in the Ukraine with the family name Milstein, Milestone emigrated to America in 1913 and served in the First World War as an assistant director on training films for the Army. Back in the States, he changed his name to Milestone and became a U.S. citizen. His Hollywood career began in 1920 as an assistant cutter for Henry King. By 1925 he had graduated to directing at Warner Brothers, with *Seven Sinners* his debut. Just two years later Milestone won the first (and only) Academy Award for best direction in the Comedy division for *Two Arabian Knights* (1927), produced by the twenty-two-year-old Howard Hughes. (The following year the Comedy Picture and Dramatic Picture categories were merged.)

Another of his silents of historical interest is *The Racket* (1928), an adaptation of a hit Broadway play (originally featuring Edward G. Robinson), also produced by Hughes, that was a best-picture nominee in the Oscars' first year. *Betrayal* was one of Gary Cooper's 1929 releases, but it's another one (*The Virginian*) that is now remembered. *New York Nights* (1929) was Norma Talmadge's disastrous talkie debut, but *All Quiet on the Western Front* (1930) cemented Milestone's reputation as a top-flight director. This antiwar classic about seven German schoolboys who lose their illusions (and lives) as they fight in World War I, adapted from the Erich Maria Remarque novel, was one of the year's biggest hits and won an Academy Award as the year's best picture; Milestone received his second Oscar for best direction.

Back at United Artists, where he was promoted to head of production, Milestone made a sparkling version of the Ben Hecht–Charles MacArthur play *The Front Page* (1931) for Howard Hughes, with Pat O'Brien and Adolphe Menjou as the fast-talking, cynical newspapermen. It became another box-office success, earning a best picture nomination and Milestone's final Oscar nomination. *Rain* (1932) seemed like a sure-fire attraction—star Joan Crawford was cast as Somerset Maugham's fallen woman Sadie Thompson (played four years earlier by Gloria Swanson) and Walter Huston was the island missionary she leads into temptation—but moviegoers of 1932 had enough problems without watching such a depressing tale, and the picture failed. *Hallelujah, I'm a Bum* (1933), an inventive musical drama starring Al Jolson as the "mayor" of Central Park's hoboes, may have been a little *too* different for audiences of the day, who stayed away, while *The Captain Hates the Sea* (1934) was a bizarre comedy that tried in vain to blend such disparate elements as John Gilbert, Leon Errol, and the Three Stooges.

Now at Paramount, Milestone made *Paris in Spring* (1935), a halfhearted stab at screwball comedy with Ida Lupino, while *Anything Goes* (1936) was a very loose adaptation of the hit play; it transported Ethel Merman from Broadway, but foolishly neglected to bring most of Cole Porter's score with her. *The General Died at Dawn* (also 1936) was one of the year's best pictures, a grand adventure set in turbulent China, with Gary Cooper a soldier-of-fortune trying to wrest money for a shipment of guns out of the hands of a bandit warlord (Akim Tamiroff, in a juicy, Oscar-nominated turn). Clifford Odets's screenplay edged into deep purple at times, but Victor Milner's cinematography gave the film a great look, and it plays better today than many more famous members of the class of '36.

After a couple years of directing in the theater, Milestone returned to Hollywood in 1939 to make the obscure *The Night of Nights* and *Of Mice and Men*, a powerful adaptation of the Steinbeck novel, with Lon Chaney, Jr., and Burgess Meredith; it was nominated for an Academy Award as the best picture of 1939, a year rich with great movies. But *Lucky Partners* (1940) was a feeble comedy that wasted Ronald Colman and Ginger Rogers, and the 1941 *My Life with Caroline* (also with Colman) wasn't much better. Milestone next collaborated with Soviet director Joris Ivens to make *Our Russian Front* (1942), a pro-Russia documentary (narrated by Walter Huston) that was made to spur support for Russian war relief. *Edge of Darkness* (1943) was a top-notch war picture, with Errol Flynn, Ann Sheridan, and Walter Huston nicely teamed as leaders of the Norwegian resistance against the Nazis.

*The North Star* (1943) was an overtly pro-Soviet tale of Russian peasants (headed by village doctor Walter Huston) heroically rising up against the Nazi invaders, who are led by a wonderfully civilized Eric von Stroheim. Dana Andrews, Anne Baxter, and Farley Granger lent able support, but Lillian Hellman's preachy script gave the picture a political tone of the sort that would land Hollywood's filmmakers in hot water with HUAC a few years later (however politically correct at the time). At Fox Milestone made the excellent *The Purple Heart* (1944), a stirring tale (co-written by Darryl Zanuck) about an Air Force crew (Dana Andrews, Richard Conte, Farley Granger) shot down over Tokyo and tried for war crimes by the Japanese. *A Walk in the Sun* (1945) was a stylistically adventurous war yarn, adapted brilliantly by Robert Rossen from the fine novel by Harry Brown. The film focuses almost entirely on the states of mind of GIs Dana Andrews, Richard Conte, John Ireland, etc., as they try to knock out a Nazi-held farmhouse in Italy, rendering their battle experiences impressionistically; the effect is closer to *All Quiet*'s antiwar message than to the gung-ho heroics of most World War II pictures.

*The Strange Love of Martha Ivers* (1946) was a departure for Milestone, who had spent the war years making nothing but war movies; this was an effective noirish melodrama starring Barbara Stanwyck, Lizabeth Scott, and (in his film debut) Kirk Douglas. *Arch of Triumph* (1948), adapted from the Remarque novel and co-scripted by Milestone, was an overlong romance between Ingrid Bergman and Charles Boyer set in wartime France, while *No Minor Vices* (1948) was an ill-advised comedy featuring the stolid Dana Andrews. *The Red Pony* (1949) seemed an odd project to attract Milestone's interest, but his adaptation of Steinbeck's short novel is nicely handled; it's a "little" story about a boy who bonds with his horse, with appealing performances by Myrna Loy and Robert Mitchum. More typical for Milestone was *The Halls of Montezuma* (1950), a rousing if conventional World War II picture buttressed by an exceptional cast—Richard Widmark, Jack Palance, Karl Malden, and Jack Webb.

Having testified as an unfriendly witness before HUAC, Milestone dramatically reduced his working options without ever quite reaching the blacklist stage. (Those earlier pro-Soviet films couldn't have helped.) He made *Kangaroo* (1952); it was an adventure with Maureen O'Hara and Peter Lawford shot on location in Australia but otherwise of little interest, and remade *Les Miserables* (1952), a respectable version of the Victor Hugo tale, though not up to the 1935 version (Michael Rennie and Robert Newton are hardly Fredric March and Charles Laughton). *Melba* (1953) was a biopic about Australian opera singer Nellie Melba, made in England, while *They Who Dare* (also 1953) was another war picture, shot for low-budget Allied Artists with a largely British cast. A further indication that Milestone was having difficulties came in the form of *The Widow* (1955), an Italian-French soap opera about a woman who falls for a race-car driver—an absurd project for someone of Milestone's stature to take on. Seeing the writing on the wall, he worked in television for the next few years.

But toward the end of the decade his graylisting

was lifted. He filmed *Pork Chop Hill* (1959), a hard-boiled Korean War movie with an outstanding cast headed by Gregory Peck, Rip Torn, and Woody Strode, followed by *Oceans 11* (1960), the first "Rat Pack" picture and the only one that's not a total joke (though it's now hard to watch Frank Sinatra, Dean Martin, Joey Bishop, and Sammy Davis, Jr., cavort without giggling a bit). Milestone's last credited work was the epic remake of *Mutiny on the Bounty* (1962), which he took over from Carol Reed. A sumptuous, sometimes interesting (though ridiculously long) version of the famous story, it was scuttled by Marlon Brando's deliberately irritating interpretation of Fletcher Christian. Milestone began work on *PT 109* (1963), a bit of JFK hagiography that was completed by Leslie Martinson; he also was replaced during the filming of the Italian production *The Dirty Game* (1966) by Terence Young, an embarrassing end to a career that had spanned five decades.

► *Milestone confers with Gregory Peck while making* Pork Chop Hill

## ● VINCENTE MINNELLI (1903–1986)

"Stylish" is the adjective that is inevitably invoked whenever the work of Vincente Minnelli is discussed. Whether he was working on movie musicals—the genre with which he is most closely associated—comedies, or melodramas, he always managed to impart so many distinctive flourishes that even those who reject the auteur theory of directing must acknowledge that there is something about his work—the good, the bad, and the magnificent—that bespeaks the Minnelli "touch."

Born to conductor Vincent Charles Minnelli and singer Mina Le Beau in Chicago, he was given the less exotic name of Lester Anthony Minnelli; later in life he adopted his father's name, adding the final e as a flourish. The Minnelli Brothers Tent Theatre was an attraction that traveled throughout the Midwest, and so little Lester was virtually "born in a trunk," performing on stage with them as soon as he could stand on his own two feet. Later he was taken in by relatives in Chicago and Delaware, Ohio, so that he could attend school on a regular basis while his parents worked the vaudeville circuit. Eventually his mother and father settled in Delaware, but Lester moved back to Chicago as soon as he graduated from Delaware High School, hoping to find work as an artist.

His first job was helping to design window displays at Marshall Field's, the giant department store, while attending the Chicago Art Institute at night. Minnelli next worked as a society photographer's assistant, always sketching to fine-tune his sense of design. Those talents finally landed him the position of chief costume designer with the Balaban and Katz movie chain, Chicago's biggest exhibitor. The weekly revues he mounted to entertain the crowds in between screenings quickly helped establish Minnelli as a rising star in his field, and in 1931 he was summoned to New York to work as a costume designer for Paramount.

Moonlighting for *Earl Carroll's Vanities*, Minnelli displayed adventurous designs to the jaded New York crowds, and in 1933 the newly established Radio City Music Hall hired him to costume its spectacular live shows. Soon he had graduated to art director, staging ever more elaborate and inventive revues. Perhaps it was inevitable with that sort of exposure that Minnelli would catch the eye of the Shuberts, who signed him in 1935 to both produce and design three Broadway musical revues for them over the next eighteen months. His first, *At Home Abroad*, featured the likes of Ethel Waters, Eleanor Powell, comedienne Beatrice Lillie, and Eddie Foy, Jr., with songs by Howard Dietz and Arthur Schwartz. It received terrific notices, as did Minnelli's second effort, the *Ziegfeld Follies of 1936*, with a star-studded roster that included Josephine Baker, Bob Hope, Eve Arden, and the tap-dancing Nicholas Brothers; songs by Vernon Duke and Ira Gershwin; and two ballets by George Balanchine.

Minnelli's third revue, *The Show Is On*, was another smash hit, and Hollywood took note. In 1937 Paramount Pictures approached him with a heady offer: Come West and work for us as a producer/director. Six months later Minnelli came crawling back to the Shuberts, his time in tinseltown a total waste. But the shows he put together for them failed to capture an audience, making Minnelli receptive to MGM producer Arthur Freed's offer to join the studio in 1940 as a special consultant. He would receive a modest salary in return for helping to stage and co-direct musical numbers, and could elect to return to Broadway any time he wanted. As it turned out, he never did.

Minnelli used this extraordinary on-the-job training to aid the Freed Unit on individual numbers in such high-profile musicals as *Strike Up the Band, Babes on Broadway*, and, more extensively, *Panama*

*Hattie*, a Norman McLeod project that MGM asked Roy Del Ruth and Minnelli to reshoot extensively. Although the final result was still disappointing, the MGM brass liked what Minnelli had wrought with the musical numbers—particularly those featuring the lovely young Lena Horne, who had just signed with MGM after working in the black-cast film industry—and decided to launch Minnelli as a solo director.

*Cabin in the Sky* (1943), made for the Freed Unit for well under a million dollars, was an extraordinary first effort, a highly stylized, vibrant adaptation of the Broadway show that Minnelli had worked on in 1940. Original stars Ethel Waters (whom Minnelli had directed in *At Home Abroad*) and Rex Ingram were both retained for the film version; Dooley Wilson, though, was replaced by the popular Eddie "Rochester" Anderson, sidekick to radio and movie star Jack Benny. The first important (i.e., major studio) black-cast film since Marc Connelly's 1936 production of *The Green Pastures* (Connelly was sensibly hired to help with the adaptation), *Cabin* also featured many of the day's top black performers: Lena Horne (replacing the stage version's Katherine Dunham as the temptress Georgia Brown), Louis Armstrong, and the Duke Ellington Orchestra. Roger Edens and Busby Berkeley, Freed's top song-and-dance directors, helped oversee the musical numbers, some of which (like the Oscar-nominated "Happiness Is a Thing Called Joe") were newly penned for the film by the crack team of Harold Arlen and Yip Harburg, augmenting such gems from the John Latouche–Vernon Duke score as "Honey in the Honeycomb."

*Cabin* was greeted with a mixed response from both black and white audiences upon its release. Indeed, its embrace of the conventions of Southern "folklore" steers a course perilously close to racism, a charge leveled against the picture from certain quarters even in 1943. Nevertheless, it was a profitable venture, and when all was said and done, it provided a rare showcase for the great Waters and Horne, too few of whose performances have been preserved on film. *I Dood It* (1943), a flavorless musical with Red Skelton and Eleanor Powell, entailed far less controversy: both critics and audiences concurred that it simply wasn't very good (save for brief musical interludes featuring Lena Horne and songstress Hazel Scott).

Minnelli then landed the plum assignment of directing *Meet Me in St. Louis* (1944), a lavishly mounted, big-budget adaptation of Sally Benson's autobiographical *New Yorker* stories about a family in St. Louis circa 1903. The picture starred Judy Garland as Esther Smith, the teenaged daughter whose romance with the boy next door (the fatally dull Tom Drake) serves as the fulcrum for a sentimental but lovingly rendered tale of family togetherness that, in the midst of World War II, was embraced by nostalgic American moviegoers. Garland's sprightly "The Trolley Song" was nominated for an Oscar, and for years afterward remained a popular part of her repertoire, but it was the heartbreaking "Have Yourself a Merry Little Christmas" that best captured the film's bittersweet nostalgia. *Meet Me* provided Garland with the role that smoothed her transition to adult roles, and the on-set romance that bloomed between her and Minnelli seems to saturate every lamp-lit frame of the film.

According to Stephen Harvey in his essential study, *Directed by Vincente Minnelli, The Ziegfeld Follies* (1944), a $3 million all-star Metro revue with studio luminaries Fred Astaire, Gene Kelly, Judy Garland, Lucille Ball, Lena Horne, and Red Skelton, had initially been under George Sidney's direction. But when Sidney's first three months of footage were found wanting, Minnelli was called in to take control. As it turned out, Minnelli directed about half the production numbers, including the Fred Astaire–Lucille Bremer showstopper "Limehouse Blues" and Judy Garland's witty parody of MGM *grande dame* Greer Garson, "A Great Lady Has an Interview." Sidney's spots with Red Skelton and Lucille Ball (the S&M hoot "Bring on the Beautiful Girls") were preserved, although entire routines by the likes of Jimmy Durante, Fanny Brice, Lena Horne, and even Astaire were ultimately scrapped. This was the closest Minnelli ever came to re-creating one of his Thirties Broadway revues—one of which had been *The Ziegfeld Follies of 1936*—on film. But as a whole this extremely costly ($3.4 million) picture is distinctly underwhelming.

Minnelli had barely completed *Follies* (which would linger in editing limbo until released in 1946) when he was asked by Freed to take over the direction of *The Clock* (1945). This wartime, homefront romance originally was to have been directed by old MGM hand Jack Conway, and when he took ill, young Fred Zinnemann was handed the reins. But Garland didn't take to the reserved émigré from Austria and insisted that Minnelli—who was not dat-

ing her at that moment—replace Zinnemann. This would be his first nonmusical picture, and Minnelli thought long and hard before finally agreeing.

The tale is simple: Robert Walker is a hayseed corporal on a two-day leave in New York City before shipping out to fight in the war, and Garland is the wised-up New Yorker he meets, pals around with for a day, and falls desperately in love with. The film's marvelously sustained tension is generated by the segment in which the young lovers are accidentally separated, without either knowing how to contact the other. Shot entirely on some of the most convincing New York City sets ever built, *The Clock* remains one of the most charming of Hollywood's World War II romances and one of Garland's most enduring dramatic vehicles. Minnelli and Garland celebrated their successful collaboration by marrying on June 15, 1945, three weeks after the picture had wrapped.

*Yolanda and the Thief* (1945), with Fred Astaire and Lucille Bremer, is generally considered one of Minnelli's lesser musicals. Today it is difficult indeed to wade through the picture's 108 minutes of wildly stylized ballets (staged by Eugene Loring), and its farfetched plot is no help—Astaire as an American con man visiting the mythical Latin American country of Patria, with an eye to fleecing convent-raised orphan Bremer by posing as the guardian angel to whom she has been praying for guidance. Even the songs by the usually reliable Arthur Freed and Harry Warren are sub-par, save for the jitterbugging classic "Coffee Time." Astaire and Bremer were adequate as a team in the short ballet "Limehouse Blues" in *Ziegfeld Follies*, but they lacked the chemistry to carry a full-length production, let alone one as arch and artificial as this belabored (and expensive) fantasy. Its patronizing take on Pan-Americanism aside, *Yolanda* simply didn't work for audiences of the day. Technicolor MGM production values or not, it became Minnelli's first flop.

*Undercurrent* (1946) was a melodrama starring Katharine Hepburn as a New England spinster who falls in love with suave, filthy rich Robert Taylor, only to learn after marrying him that he's mentally unbalanced and jealous of his black-sheep brother (the reliably laconic Robert Mitchum). There wasn't an original bone in the film's body, and its ballyhooed suspense was just wishful thinking on the part of the studio ad flacks; nevertheless it was a box-office hit. *Till the Clouds Roll By* (1946) was a (barely) passable biopic about the great songwriter Jerome Kern, officially credited to house director Richard Whorf—although the likes of Busby Berkeley, Henry Koster, and George Sidney reportedly worked on it at one time or another. Minnelli was brought on board specifically to direct the three numbers that featured Judy Garland (now four months pregnant with Liza) as Twenties Broadway star Marilyn Miller, singing such Miller signature tunes as "Look for the Silver Lining," "Who?," and "Sunny"—easily the best things in an otherwise forgettable film.

Minnelli's next project was to be an adaptation of the 1942 Lunt and Fontanne stage success *The Pirate* (1948), from the play by S. N. Behrman, with a score by Cole Porter. But it was put on hold for nearly a year while he and Judy enjoyed their newborn Liza. *The Pirate* finally went before the cameras in February of 1947, with Gene Kelly as the dashing Serafin, a not-so-humble street minstrel, and Judy as the wide-eyed Manuela, who imagines him to be Macoco, the scourge of the Caribbean and the lusty rogue of her dreams.

Six months later the film was finished, but it was a long way from being ready for release. Garland had backslid into a dependence on barbituates, a problem that had plagued her since her *Oz* days, and the combination of Minnelli's complex vision and her own inability (and, at times, simple reluctance) to go back to work proved disastrous. Minnelli tinkered with the picture for another six months, reshooting sequences, deleting two of Judy's solo numbers, and running its staggering cost up to more than $3.7 million—almost what *Gone with the Wind* had cost eight years earlier. But *The Pirate* was to prove no such box-office bonanza; it ended up losing over $1.5 million, the biggest flop of Garland's (and, for that matter, Minnelli's) career. She never forgave him entirely for that and, in fact, had Minnelli taken off what would have been their next film collaboration, *Easter Parade*, ostensibly on the advice of her psychiatrist (Charles Walters ended up directing it).

With his marriage now beginning to crumble, Minnelli spent a year in near-total inactivity (he actually spent the bulk of his time on the lot directing screen tests) before taking on the challenging assignment of adapting Gustave Flaubert's *Madame Bovary* (1949). Jennifer Jones was cast as the pretentious, adulterous heroine, Van Heflin as her cuckolded husband, and Louis Jourdan as her seducer; James Mason played Flaubert himself, on trial on obscenity charges, in a framing sequence. The erotically charged ballroom sequence was Minnelli at his expressive best, but fans of the novel complained then (as now) that the tale had been hopelessly Hollywoodized. Perhaps it had, but Minnelli's necessary compressions are intelligent ones, and he used Jones's slightly blank beauty to better effect than any other director ever would. Shot far more quickly and for much less money than his last few ventures, *Madame Bovary* at least managed to turn a profit and restored the studio's faith in him.

The delightful *Father of the Bride* (1950) was a departure for Minnelli in both its contemporary domestic setting and its absence of stylistic flourishes (not that it required any). It's a deft bit of work that feels lighter than what had come before. Spencer Tracy gives one of his great comic performances as the shell-shocked dad who finds his daughter's impending nuptials spiraling out of all control, and Joan Bennett is the mother who delivers her dry antidotes to his hysteria with superb timing. Elizabeth Taylor, then just seventeen (but already married to Nicky Hilton), has rarely looked more beautiful, although her performance as the spoiled bride is merely adequate. One of 1950's biggest hits, *Bride* remains Minnelli's funniest movie, one that holds up quite nicely today (and is far superior to the 1991 remake with Steve Martin).

*An American in Paris* (1951) was developed by Freed from an orchestral suite written some years back by the Gershwins. It would soon become one of Minnelli's biggest hits, but just as important to Minnelli was the wide acclaim the picture received, which culminated in eight Academy Award nominations and wins for best picture, story, and screenplay (Alan Jay Lerner), color cinematography, art direction, musical score, and color costume design. Minnelli garnered his first nomination for best direction but lost to George Stevens (as did Elia Kazan, John Huston, and William Wyler—what a field!).

Gene Kelly, who also served as the film's choreographer and unofficial assistant director, exhibited his trademark exuberance as Jerry Mulligan, an American artist studying in Paris who allows himself to be supported by wealthy patron Nina Foch, only to fall in love with young dancer Leslie Caron (whom Kelly suggested for the part after seeing the teenager perform in the Ballets des Champs-Elysées). The peerless Oscar Levant adds some much needed humor to the picture as Kelly's cynical pal. Shot almost entirely on MGM's Culver City sound stages, *An American in Paris* offered such Gershwin gems as " 'S Wonderful," "I'll Build a Stairway to Paradise," and "I Got Rhythm." But it was the film's spectacular concluding number, a 17-minute ballet that cost a half-million dollars and four weeks to film, that ultimately transported moviegoers (and probably cinched those six Oscars).

As Harvey reveals in *Directed by Vincent Minnelli*, *Father's Little Dividend* was actually filmed during a break in the making of *An American in Paris*, taking a mere twenty-three days from start to finish. While not up to the sublime satire of *Father of the Bride* (which itself was shot in a month), this amusing sequel about Tracy and Bennett's impending grandparenthood does not embarrass itself, Minnelli, or Taylor. After working for Freed on pre-production for the never-filmed musical version of *Huckleberry Finn* and filming (without credit) the elaborate closing number in Mervyn LeRoy's *Lovely to Look At*, Minnelli made the short film "Mademoiselle," the central segment of *The Story of Three Loves* (1953), an anthology about the varied miseries of romance. New star Leslie Caron was featured as the pretentious governess of a young American visiting Rome (Ricky Nelson); under the spell of sorceress Ethel Barrymore, the lad is transformed into a handsome adult (Farley Granger), who immediately falls in love with Caron. It took Minnelli three weeks to film "Mademoiselle"—Gottfried Reinhardt directed the other two episodes—and another year for MGM to release the finished picture, which ultimately lost nearly a million dollars.

In the meantime, the newly divorced Minnelli devoted himself to a far weightier project. *The Bad and the Beautiful* (1952) was a Hollywood gothic, a searing exposé of the industry's peculiar dreams and nightmares. Kirk Douglas stars as the manipulative movie producer (based rather obviously on David O. Selznick) who ruins the lives of those around him in his quest for screen perfection; he has an affair with unproven star Lana Turner to give her confidence, then dumps her as soon as her performance is in the can. On-the-money portraits of various archetypes—Dick Powell as a disillusioned screenwriter, Gloria Grahame as his unfaithful wife, Gilbert Roland as a randy Latin actor, and Barry Sullivan as an exploited director—add verisimilitude. Minnelli indulged himself with a florid, expressionistic camera style that mirrored the violent emotions of the characters to great effect. One of the classic "inside" Hollywood yarns, *The Bad and the Beautiful* was nominated for six Oscars, including Douglas for best actor, Grahame for supporting actress, Charles Schnee for best screenplay, Robert Surtees for black-and-white cinematography, black-and-white art direction, and costume design; all but Douglas won.

Minnelli now was on a roll, and he capped this most fruitful period of his career with the all-time terrific musical *The Band Wagon* (1953), a hilarious skewering of Broadway's pretensions, scripted by Betty Comden and Adolph Green, with a sensational score by Howard Dietz and Arthur Schwartz. Fred Astaire stars as Tony Hunter, a washed-up movie-musical star—a role uncomfortably close to Astaire's own dim screen status at the time—whose desperation reluctantly lands him in a ridiculously overstuffed musical about Faust, engineered by pompous theatrical "genius" Jeffrey Cordova (British music-hall star Jack Buchanan, in a role apparently based on the recent pretentious stage efforts of José Ferrer, though redolent of Orson Welles's excesses as well).

Oscar Levant and Nanette Fabray are appealing analogues for Green and Comden, while Cyd Charisse—painfully stiff except when dancing—is Astaire's love interest, haughty ballerina Gaby Gerard. Michael Kidd's choreography illuminates the wonderful production numbers—"That's Entertainment," "Dancing in the Dark," "A Shine on Your Shoes," and the clever parody of Mickey Spillane's hard-boiled detective novels, "The Girl Hunt Ballet"—amid which Astaire and Charisse play out their less-than-compelling romance. *The Band Wagon* wasn't nominated for many major awards at Oscar time (and left empty-handed), but over the years its reputation has soared, and many now consider it a leading candidate for the best screen musical of all time.

*The Long, Long Trailer* (1954) was a rather long descent from the artistic heights of Minnelli's last

◀ *High hilarity pervades the set of* The Long, Long Trailer

several efforts, but it became one of his biggest commercial successes. It's a slapstick vehicle crafted for television superstars Lucille Ball and Desi Arnaz (on summer hiatus from their top-rated *I Love Lucy* series), who play a husband and wife traveling across the United States in their forty-foot New Moon trailer. The film had its share of laughs and an undeniable energy, but could have been filmed by any director worth his salt.

*Brigadoon* (1954) was much more of a challenge for Minnelli, one that he (and his collaborators) ultimately failed to conquer. A hit in the 1946–47 Broadway season, this Lerner and Loewe musical about a mythical land that materializes once every hundred years in the Scottish highlands was originally scheduled to be filmed on location. But the MGM brass made Minnelli shoot it in Culver City (and, perversely, in CinemaScope), giving it an artificial, tacky mien. A strident Gene Kelly stars as the visiting New Yorker who falls in love with one of the village's time-traveling residents (the lovely but inert Cyd Charisse), and Van Johnson is his cynical pal. Although it has its moments, *Brigadoon* failed to recreate the magic that was the essence of its story, ensuring that Minnelli would never again attempt a dance-oriented musical film—or (just as tellingly) ever work again with Gene Kelly.

He spent much of 1954 scouting South American locations for an adaptation of *Green Mansions*, but never got the project off the ground (Mel Ferrer finally filmed it in 1959 with his wife, Audrey Hepburn, as Rima). Minnelli next turned to *The Cobweb* (1955), a star-studded, hyperventilating psychodrama set in an institution, about as far removed from the Scottish highlands as a motion picture could get. Produced by John Houseman, it featured Richard Widmark, Lauren Bacall, Gloria Grahame, Lillian Gish, and—as the cream of the jest—that Babe Ruth of celebrity neurotics, Oscar Levant. There is dramaturgy and anguish aplenty, but the material in the end is formless—a condition perhaps exacerbated by its having a half hour hacked out without Minnelli's input.

The hoary *Kismet* (1955) was based on a 1953 Broadway musical that offered now-classic songs like "Stranger in Paradise" and "Baubles, Bangles and Beads" and a great deal of Oriental hooey. Filmed previously in 1920, 1930, and 1944, it seemed unlikely to interest Minnelli after the near-disaster of *Brigadoon.* But Freed and Dore Schary twisted his arm until Minnelli agreed to direct it, a chore he executed in two months flat. Howard Keel, Ann Blyth, and crooner Vic Damone head the hopelessly unappealing cast, which also passes off benign Sebastian Cabot as the villain of the piece. It would have had to have been twice as bad to be any fun, or twice as good to be simply half-bad. Presumably no one at MGM twisted Minnelli's arm again.

His mind had been on making *Lust for Life* (1956), a biography of the tormented artist Vincent

Van Gogh, all along. Based on a 1934 bestseller by Irving Stone, which over the years had defeated the many other filmmakers who had tried in vain to bring it to the screen, it was the project about which Minnelli felt most passionately. To play Van Gogh, a fragile genius who put everything into his work while an unheeding world spun on, the expressive Kirk Douglas was the logical choice, while Anthony Quinn drew the key role of Van Gogh's friend and mentor, Paul Gauguin. From the dozens of meticulously re-created canvases to the location filming in Paris, Amsterdam, Belgium, and Provence—including scenes shot at the original asylum in St.-Rémy where Van Gogh had recovered from a psychotic episode—no effort or expense was spared (much to the dismay of MGM's bookkeepers). The oceans of sweat and inspiration expended upon the film earned *Lust for Life* critical accolades, including a best actor Academy Award nomination and the New York Film Critics Circle Award for Douglas and a best supporting actor Oscar for Quinn (who was onscreen for all of eight minutes!)—but the picture did indifferent business, being too high-toned for the madding crowd.

*Tea and Sympathy* (1956), from the play by Robert Anderson, had been directed on Broadway by Elia Kazan. Now Minnelli inherited its stars, Deborah and John Kerr, along with a wheelbarrow full of censorship difficulties. The final result was a limp, bowdlerized drama about a boy (in the original wrestling with his homosexuality) who is seduced by the older wife of his instructor (Leif Erickson) heavily rewritten by Anderson himself over a period of years to comply with Code standards—a degree of compliance unthinkable by today's standards. *Designing Woman* (1957), conceived as a latter-day Spencer Tracy–Katharine Hepburn love-and-slugfest, with Grace Kelly and Jimmy Stewart as the leads and Josh Logan directing, ended up in Minnelli's lap after Kelly's retirement from the screen in 1956. He finally drew Gregory Peck and Lauren Bacall as his leads—competent professionals, to be sure, but short on the romantic spark that ignited pictures like *Woman of the Year* (to which this bears more than a passing resemblance). But even with Bacall's brittle, jealous designer and Peck's bland sportswriter at its flawed center, the picture boasts wonderful sets and Minnelli's meticulously re-created world of high fashion, warts and all.

*Gigi* is probably the Fifties film with which Minnelli is most closely associated, largely because of the way it dominated the Academy Awards for 1958: best picture, screenplay (Alan Jay Lerner), song ("Gigi" by Lerner and Loewe), score (André Previn), costume design (Cecil Beaton), color cinematography (Joseph Ruttenberg), and editing. It also won Minnelli his lone Oscar for best direction, at long last—one of only two times he was nominated during his long and brilliant career. Based on a novella by Colette about a French teenager raised by courtesans and trained in the art of being a proper mistress to a gentleman, *Gigi* had been adapted by Anita Loos into a Broadway play starring the then-unknown Audrey Hepburn in 1951. Five years later Freed had been green-lighted to put it into production, but Hepburn turned down the role when it was offered to her. Second choice, and a more logical one, was Leslie Caron, who had played the part in a British production. She was supported by Maurice Chevalier (in just his second major role in a Hollywood production since the mid-Thirties), Louis Jourdan, and Hermione Gingold.

Filmed on location in Paris (until the money ran out and MGM summoned one and all back to California to complete their work), *Gigi* offered songs nearly on a par with those Lerner and Loewe had crafted for their recent stage success, *My Fair Lady*, including the title track, "Thank Heaven for Little Girls," and "I Remember It Well." A few retakes shot by Charles Walters in Culver City aside, the picture is as distinctively Minnelli as anything he had ever made or ever would make. It may not be Minnelli's most inventive musical, but despite occasional slow patches, *Gigi* surely ranks among his three or four masterworks, a triumphant last gasp of the studio system that had alternately nurtured and restricted his soaring vision.

*The Reluctant Debutante* (1958) may seem like a humble production compared to the lavish *Gigi*, but this English comedy of manners, from a popular West End play by William Douglas Home, actually was a fairly expensive proposition. That it proved a box-office failure said more about American audiences (these were the days before Anglophilia took over) than it did about the perils of working without a superstar cast. The newly wed Rex Harrison and Kay Kendall were joined by Angela Lansbury to provide Minnelli with a high talent quotient around which to disguise the presence of Sandra Dee (as Rex's daughter!!) and John Saxon as her beatnik boyfriend; Minnelli clearly had a ball with the picture's class satire. *Some Came Running* (1959) was more mainstream entertainment, drawn from James Jones's massive (and rather disappointing) follow-up to his acclaimed first novel, *From Here to Eternity.* Proto Rat Packers Frank Sinatra and Dean Martin starred with starlet Shirley MacLaine in a tale about the return of prodigal son and ex-GI Sinatra to his stagnant Indiana hometown. Most critics felt Minnelli had improved on his source material, and the film was a solid commercial success as well. *Some* earned a best actress Oscar nomination for MacLaine and, in supporting categories, Martha Hyer and Arthur Kennedy.

*Home from the Hill* (1960) was one of Minnelli's most ambitious melodramas, and while only moderately popular at the time, it stands today as one of his strongest "serious" films. Shot in Texas and Oxford, Mississippi, it stars Robert Mitchum as boozing patriarch Wade Hunnicutt, whose battles with neurotic wife Eleanor Parker are punctuated by bouts of catting around, a hobby that finally gets him killed. Recent Actors Studio grad George Peppard is his rakish illegitimate son, and a young George Hamilton is the timid, "good" son who needs to survive a rite of passage—hunting down and shooting a lethal wild boar—for his father to consider him a true man of Texas. Mitchum gives one of his greatest performances, keeping the long, depressing, but potent saga of this dysfunctional family afloat.

*Bells Are Ringing* (1960), adapted from the 1956 Broadway hit by Betty Comden and Adolph Green, with songs by Jule Styne, was tailored for the talents of Judy Holliday; no one could have suspected at the time that this would prove to be her last film. Holliday plays Brooklynite Ella Peterson, an operator for the Susanswerphone answering service who can't resist playing Cupid for her customers, while original cast member Jean Stapleton was joined by Dean Martin (then at the peak of his popularity) as, of all things, a blocked playwright. Few of the tunes —which included "It's a Perfect Relationship," "I'm Going Back," "The Party's Over," and "Do It Yourself"—became standards, but as delivered by Holliday and/or Martin, they efficiently propel the merely functional plot. *Bells* also marked Minnelli's final collaboration with Arthur Freed, after their efforts to film *Camelot* and *My Fair Lady* came to naught. Thus ended an era, and the last great creative burst of Minnelli's career.

The problems surrounding the making of *The Four Horsemen of the Apocalypse* (1962) are limned in all their gruesome detail in Harvey's book; suffice it to say that this ill-advised remake of the 1921 Rex Ingram silent classic took four years and almost $8 million to foist upon the public. In a moment of corporate madness, stolid Glenn Ford was cast as the (noticeably overage) Argentinian playboy essayed by the young, vital Rudolph Valentino in the original film. The disastrously unimaginative casting involved not only Ford—way out of his league in this antiwar parable—but also Lee J. Cobb, Ingrid Thulin (famed for her work with Ingmar Bergman), Paul Henreid, Yvette Mimieux, and Paul Lukas. The Paris location work predictably clashes with the sections of the film shot on the MGM backlots, just as Thulin's dubbed line readings (Angela Lansbury was summoned for the awkward task) can never disguise their synthetic nature. This was easily the worst movie of Minnelli's career, and became one the decade's certified bombs—an eloquent argument for why the studio system deserved to become extinct.

*Two Weeks in Another Town* (1962) was a rather more noble failure. Very loosely based on an Irwin Shaw novel about the travails of a movie crew filming on location in Rome, it starred Kirk Douglas as a former actor summoned by his onetime favorite director (Edward G. Robinson, wonderful as usual) to help salvage a troubled production; Claire Trevor, Cyd Charisse, and George Hamilton headed the supporting players. The story must have seemed ripe with irony for Minnelli, who had just suffered through an excruciating location shoot with *Four Horsemen* and who ten years earlier had directed Douglas in another inside-Hollywood opus, also scripted by Charles Schnee. But the magic that infused *The Bad and the Beautiful* failed to visit *Town*, and despite its merits—and there were a few—the film lost a shocking $3.6 million for MGM, almost as much as its scorned predecessor.

Surprisingly, even after digesting such staggering losses, MGM still was willing to offer a new contract to Minnelli and his newly formed Venice Productions. Venice's first project was *The Courtship of Eddie's Father* (1963), a harmless, almost charmless romantic comedy about a widower (Glenn Ford, less miscast than in *Four Horsemen*) whose exuberant son (Ron Howard, in perhaps his best screen performance) helps him choose among three prospective stepmothers (Shirley Jones, Dina Merrill, and the always delightful Stella Stevens, here a redhead to signal her inappropriateness as marriage material). Despite the picture's smug mediocrity, it was something of a relief to see Minnelli leave behind his recent obsession with psychodrama, marital misery, and tawdry losers to construct a bit of good, old-fashioned junk. But it gives one pause to admit that the television sitcom by the same name that ran on ABC from 1969 to 1972 may have been superior to Minnelli's feeble effort.

*Goodbye, Charlie* (1964), a 20th Century-Fox production, became Minnelli's first project outside the confines of MGM—he had foolishly held out for a better deal after Jack Warner offered him a flat fee to direct *My Fair Lady.* We'll never know what Minnelli would have wrought with the Lerner and Loewe classic—one can speculate that it might have become a more interesting, inventive picture than the one directed by George Cukor—but the smarmy farce that was *Charlie* was hardly a feather in Minnelli's cap. Based on George Axelrod's play, it featured Tony Curtis as a sensitive hood who falls for Debbie Reynolds, not realizing that his recently deceased gangster buddy has been reincarnated within her. This sort of sex-change comedy would reach the screen in later years in the form of Blake Edwards's *Switch* and Carl Reiner's *All of Me*, but Minnelli's version was the first. Alas, it was also the least, a smirking concoction with the mindset of a 1964 issue of *Playboy*.

*The Sandpiper* (1965) became not only the final Venice production but the last picture Minnelli would make at MGM, ending over twenty years of (more often than not) mutually beneficial collaboration. *The Sandpiper* also turned out to be one of the biggest hoots of the Sixties, with Elizabeth Taylor cast as the world's unlikeliest beatnik—an artist, no less, complete with eye shadow and an exquisite wardrobe (the diamond she managed to leave home)—and Richard Burton the married clergyman she falls in love with amid the scenic wonders of Big Sur. The film made millions, but at an unthinkable cost: Minnelli was now revealed to be the hack that changing times and tastes had obliged him to become. Retreating to the stage he had left a quarter-century ago, he directed the bomb *Mata Hari*, which closed out of town in 1967 without ever making it to Broadway.

Minnelli spent the next two years licking his wounds, then pounced on the opportunity to direct the screen version of Alan Jay Lerner's Broadway musical *On a Clear Day You Can See Forever*, which in 1965 had been a modest success. Now it was transformed into a star vehicle for Barbra Streisand, with Yves Montand as Dr. Chabot, the psychologist who hypnotizes Barbra's ungainly college student back into her previous life as a notorious nineteenth-century adventuress accused of murder. Sixth-billed Jack Nicholson as her hippie brother and a raft of Lerner-Lane songs ("Come Back to Me," "Love with All the Trimmings," "He Isn't You") are the chief pleasures of the film, which works best when Barbra is visiting 1812; the contemporary New York scenes are an embarrassment, and show how far out of touch Minnelli was with the times. But he reportedly got on well with the demanding Streisand—no small feat, considering she won her Oscar for *Funny Girl* in the midst of production—who certainly understood that he was throwing her the picture.

*Clear Day* became a moderate success, but it didn't lead to any new offers to direct. Minnelli spent the next five years trying to launch a variety of abortive projects and writing his autobiography, the 1974 *I Remember It Well*. It was during this time that daughter Liza won her best actress Academy Award for *Cabaret*, which surely must have been a satisfying moment for her father. Vincente and Liza finally fulfilled their dream of making a film together when exploitation movie king Samuel Z. Arkoff's American-International Pictures (AIP) agreed to finance the period fantasy *A Matter of Time* (1976). Shot on location in Rome and Venice, the film also starred Ingrid Bergman as the Countess for whom Liza's chambermaid toils and, in a bit part, old friend Charles Boyer.

Whether Minnelli might have created a latter-day masterpiece with *Time* will never be known, because the picture—which does have its striking moments and images—was taken out of his hands in post-production and edited with a heavy hand by Arkoff. Martin Scorsese led a protest when Hollywood became aware of the situation, and Minnelli refuted the final-release version. In any case, the picture is an utter disaster, a depressing end to a career that had soared so high for so very long. Minnelli's final decade was plagued by serious illness. When he died in 1986, the eulogies were delivered by Gregory Peck and Kirk Douglas.

## ● ROBERT MULLIGAN (1925– )

Best remembered as the Oscar-nominated director of *To Kill a Mockingbird*, Robert Mulligan has been making movies for more than thirty-five years. Yet even Mulligan's best work—some of which is very good indeed—can't be said to bear a personal stamp. But while he's no auteur, Mulligan's craftsmanship can—at times—be impressive. But that work appears less and less frequently.

Born in the Bronx, New York, he originally had set his sights on the priesthood. War service interrupted his studies, and when he returned, Mulligan got a job at *The New York Times*. He then moved into television, starting at CBS as a messenger. Within a few years he was directing for the prestigious live-drama showcases *Playhouse 90* and *Suspense*. Hollywood beckoned, and in 1957 Mulligan made his first film, *Fear Strikes Out*, with Tony Perkins as Red Sox outfielder Jimmy Piersall, who suffered a nervous breakdown in the early fifties. Like many of his future pictures, it was produced by Alan J. Pakula.

Mulligan returned to TV for a few years, then filmed *The Rat Race* (1960) with Tony Curtis and Debbie Reynolds, based on a Garson Kanin play. Curtis joined Mulligan again for *The Great Imposter* (1961), a biopic about Ferdinand Demara's remarkable life; it should have been much better. *Come September* (1961) was a sprightly if totally irrelevant romantic comedy, with Rock Hudson and Gina Lollobrigida squaring off against youngbloods Bobby Darin and Sandra Dee. But that was ambrosia compared to the painfully earnest *The Spiral Road* (1962), which at 145 minutes was about two hours too long.

Then came *To Kill a Mockingbird* (1962), and all was forgiven. Sensitively adapted from Harper Lee's Pulitzer Prize–winning novel by Horton Foote, the film won Oscars for Foote and Gregory Peck, and earned nominations for best picture and best direction. Few Hollywood films from the Sixties have aged as well as *Mockingbird*, which was the first official release from Pakula-Mulligan Productions. Shot on location in New York, *Love with the Proper Stranger* (1964) was a downbeat Steve McQueen–Natalie Wood hepster-meets-straight-chick romance, while *Baby, the Rain Must Fall* (1965) was another showcase for perennial drifter McQueen, who was paired with Lee Remick to good effect. Again Mulligan tapped Horton Foote for the screenplay, which Foote adapted from his own play; the theme song was also terrific.

But with *Inside Daisy Clover* (1966) Mulligan was out of his element—this needed to be a far trashier exposé of 1930s Hollywood. Still, Natalie Wood and Robert Redford made a handsome couple. Safe as a dish of vanilla ice cream was *Up the Down Staircase* (1967), Mulligan's adaptation of Bel Kaufman's best-seller about a teacher's trials and tribulations in the New York City school system. Sandy Dennis does her neurotic best, but the film conveys as much tension as an episode of *Welcome Back, Kotter*.

Mulligan's next project—the last under the aegis of Mulligan-Pakula Productions—reunited him with Gregory Peck. But *The Stalking Moon* (1969) was an uninventive retelling of the old captivity narratives, with Eva Marie Saint rescued from the Apaches who raised her by Army scout Peck. *The Pursuit of Happiness* (1971) had some juice to it, not to mention Barbara Hershey, but this tale of the legal injustice visited upon wiseguy Michael Sarrazin played to miniscule audiences. But no one overlooked *Summer of '42* (1971), a nostalgic tale of first love that would have been laughably sentimental if it weren't so damnably effective. Manipulative, yes—but *Summer of '42* tapped into something that audiences responded to (maybe it was just that Oscar-winning score by Michel Legrand) and became Mulligan's biggest hit since *Mockingbird*.

The creepy *The Other* (1972) was quite a change of pace, a tale of supernatural possession adapted from his bestseller by Tom Tryon. But *The Nickel Ride* (1975), with Jason Miller a fence for the mob's stolen goods, completely stiffed, and *Bloodbrothers* (1978), with Richard Gere, Tony Lo Bianco, and Paul Sorvino, failed to capture the full flavor of the tangy Richard Price novel on which it was based. The 1978 *Same Time, Next Year* delivered the wistful charm of the Bernard Slade play, and Alan Alda and Ellen Burstyn are splendid as the two lovers whose affair has been renewed annually for twenty-six years. Once again, a superior theme song proved a good-luck charm for Mulligan.

The hapless *Kiss Me Goodbye* (1982) was a ghostly romance that needed much more than James Caan and Sally Field for star chemistry, while *Clara's Heart* (1988), with Whoopi Goldberg as a Jamaican maid working in Maryland for yuppies, was well intentioned but awful. The surprisingly touching *The Man in the Moon* (1991), however—a young love/coming-of-age piece set in 1957 Louisiana—indicated that Mulligan could still fashion a winner given the proper material.

FEAR STRIKES OUT
HE'S DYNAMITE—READY TO EXPLODE!
Here's the whole heart-story of today's mixed-up kids!
ANTHONY starring KARL
PERKINS · MALDEN
Tony Perkins—Tremendous in his first starring role!
PRODUCED BY ALAN PAKULA · DIRECTED BY ROBERT MULLIGAN · SCREENPLAY BY TED BERKMAN and RAPHAEL BLAU
VISTAVISION® Based on a Story by Jimmy Piersall and Al Hirshberg · A Paramount Picture

● JEAN NEGULESCO (1900–1993)

A master of Forties film noir, Jean Negulesco reinvented himself into a director of big-budget, glossy musicals and epic-scaled romantic melodramas—but the results were not always happy. Negulesco was born in Romania as the century was turning. He made his reputation as a stage designer and painter in Paris during the Twenties, and came to the United States in 1927 to exhibit his work. Staying on, he made his way to Hollywood, where he began as an assistant producer and second-unit director on "B" pictures during the Thirties. Negulesco directed his first feature for Warners in 1941, *Singapore Woman*; a remake of the studio's 1935 hit *Dangerous*, it wasn't very good, and he had to wait several years for his second chance.

That turned out to be the excellent *The Mask of Dimitrios* (1944), starring Warners' best character actors, Peter Lorre and Sydney Greenstreet, along with Zachary Scott; the film was adapted from the exciting Eric Ambler novel with style and authority. *The Conspirators* (1944) again used bad boys Lorre and Greenstreet, with Hedy Lamarr along for scenic value, while *Nobody Lives Forever* (1946) was based on a good hard-boiled novel by W. R. Burnett: it gave John Garfield a showy role as a petty crook who cons, then falls for, rich widow Geraldine Fitzgerald. *Three Strangers* (1946) was an off-beat yarn pairing Lorre and Greenstreet with Fitzgerald as joint holders of a sweepstakes ticket, while *Humoresque* (1947) was a step up in class; John Garfield and Joan Crawford were well matched as a violinist who hungers for success and the wealthy—but hysterical—patroness who falls for him.

*Deep Valley* (1947), with Ida Lupino as an isolated woman and Dane Clark the gangster who energizes her too-quiet life, was a perfectly adequate melodrama. But it was Negulesco's last film for Warners, the 1948 drama *Johnny Belinda*, that became his greatest triumph. It starred Jane Wyman as a deaf-mute Canadian farm girl who is raped, finds she is pregnant, and bonds with sensitive doctor Lew Ayres. A major box-office success, the film was nominated for an Academy Award as best picture, and also earned nominations for Ayres, Charles Bickford, Agnes Moorehead, and Negulesco. Incredibly, Jack Warner disliked the picture so much that he canned Negulesco before it was released, a move he quickly came to regret. Negulesco moved on to Fox, where he made *Road House* (1948), a good noir with a terrific cast, notably Richard Widmark at his most unbalanced and Ida Lupino at her most sultry (she sings "Again," probably the best song introduced in a film that year); Cornel Wilde and Celeste Holm were also on hand.

Negulesco hadn't faltered in five years, but that streak came to a crashing halt with the British production *The Forbidden Street* (1949), a Victorian melodrama with Maureen O'Hara that required Dana Andrews not only to play a period role but also to take on dual parts—rampant optimism. *Under My Skin* (1950), based on the Hemingway story "My Old Man," was better but lacked unity, despite another good Garfield performance. But *Three Came Home* (1950) was a triumph, easily the best of Claudette Colbert's later work and a model of how to adapt a strong literary property. The 1950 *The Mudlark* had a dash of British class, good of its kind; Irene Dunne was effective as Queen Victoria, as was Alec Guinness as Disraeli. But *Take Care of My Little Girl* (1951) was just foolish, a heavy drama about sorority life on campus that offered the hapless cast of Jeanne Crain, Jeff Hunter, George Nader, and Mitzi Gaynor.

The suspenseful *Phone Call from a Stranger* (1952) had a great gimmick and Negulesco played it for all it was worth, with Bette Davis and Gary Merrill heading the good cast. *Lydia Bailey* (1952) returned Negulesco to the uncomfortable (for him) waters of historical adventure; certainly, having Dale Robertson as the weak lead didn't help. *Lure of the Wilderness* (1952) was an uninspired remake of Renoir's *Swamp Water* with Jeff Hunter and Jean Peters. Negulesco completed the year by directing "The Last Leaf" episode of *O. Henry's Full House*, then made the big-budget *Titanic* (1953) with Barbara Stanwyck, Clifton Webb, Robert Wagner, and Thelma Ritter (the story won an Oscar).

The CinemaScope *How to Marry a Millionaire* (1953) became Negulesco's biggest hit in years. Although the film offers Marilyn Monroe at her peak alongside Lauren Bacall and Betty Grable, the comic premise now creaks dangerously. *Scandal at Scourie* (1953) was forgettable Greer Garson and Walter Pidgeon, but *Three Coins in the Fountain* (1954) was a smash, thanks as much to its Rome locations and Oscar-winning theme song (by Jule Styne and Sammy Cahn) as anything supplied by Clifton Webb, Jean Peters, Dorothy McGuire, or Louis Jourdan. And yet it was nominated for an Academy Award as best picture of 1954.

*Woman's World* (1954) was another glossy production, with the archetypal "all-star" cast—June Allyson, Van Heflin, Fred MacMurray, Lauren Bacall—but venomous Clifton Webb made it work. Fred Astaire almost put over *Daddy Long Legs* (1955), a bloated remake of the oft-filmed drama about a rich playboy who secretly puts a poor kid (Leslie Caron) through school. It had nice music by Johnny Mercer, but it cried out for the Minnelli touch. *The Rains of Ranchipur* (1955) was Negulesco's color remake of the 1939 *The Rains Came*, but leads Lana Turner, Richard Burton, and Fred MacMurray were so ill matched that it never had a chance. *Boy on a Dolphin* (1957) offered the spectacle of Sophia Loren as a skindiver searching for treasure off the Greek isles—but Alan Ladd was getting too old for this sort of thing.

Negulesco had long since abandoned the tight, stylish little dramas that had been his calling card a decade earlier. Now his lack of discrimination in choosing his projects reached alarming proportions. *The Gift of Love* (a remake of *Sentimental Journey*), *A Certain Smile* (both 1958), and *Count Your Blessings* (1959) were all sappy, clumsily executed works. *The Best of Everything* (1959) at least had the courage of its trashy convictions, and remains one of the most enjoyable "exposés" of the New York City publishing game ever set to celluloid. For the first time in a while Negulesco had a cast with pizzazz, including Joan Crawford, Suzy Parker, Martha Hyer, Hope Lange, and mogul-in-waiting Robert Evans.

▲ *On the set of* Woman's World *with Cornel Wilde and June Allyson*

But *Jessica* (1962) was another misbegotten drama that asks us to swallow Angie Dickinson as an Italian midwife and Maurice Chevalier as the village priest. At least *The Pleasure Seekers* (1964), Negulesco's musical remake of *Three Coins*, now set in Spain, had the virtue of being a representative Sixties' girl-fest, with Ann-Margret, Pamela Tiffin, and Carol Lynley. Quiet for several years, Negulesco came out of his unofficial retirement in 1970 to make two last films. *Hello-Goodbye* was unspeakable, but the Iranian-made actioner *The Invincible Six* actually has its moments—a gang headed by Stuart Whitman helps harassed villagers defeat a bandit horde. Negulesco's sprightly autobiography, *Things I Did . . . and Things I Think I Did*, was published in 1984.

## ● MIKE NICHOLS (1931– )

One of Broadway's most honored directors, Mike Nichols's first two films earned him a pair of Academy Award nominations (and one Oscar) for best direction. While he has had difficulty sustaining that initial burst of brilliance, his name still carries a great deal of weight in Hollywood. Whether that reputation is still merited, however, is an open question.

Born Michael Igor Peschkowsky in Berlin, he emigrated to the States with his family in 1938, and became a citizen six years later. After graduating from the University of Chicago, he studied acting with Lee Strasberg in 1954, then in 1955 returned to Chicago, where he helped found the Compass Players improvisational troupe with Elaine May, Alan Arkin, and Barbara Harris; their venue was the Compass restaurant-cabaret. In 1957 he and May took to the road, ending up on Broadway a few years later in *An Evening with Mike Nichols and Elaine May*.

Nichols directed his first Broadway show, Neil Simon's *Barefoot in the Park*, in 1963, and a year later won a Tony for his direction of *Luv*. He won the award again in 1965 for Simon's *The Odd Couple*, then made his film directing debut with *Who's Afraid of Virginia Woolf?* (1966), a corrosive adaptation of Edward Albee's 1962 play. A sensation upon release due to its shocking language (it was initially denied a Production Code seal), it was a box-office hit and received an Academy Award nomination for best picture; Nichols was also Oscar-nominated, as were stars Elizabeth Taylor (who won) and Richard Burton, George Segal, Sandy Dennis (who won as best supporting actress), Ernest Lehman's screenplay, and Haskell Wexler's cinematography (another winner). Nichols had rehearsed the actors for three weeks before commencing filming, a strategy that obviously paid off.

His second film made an even greater impact. *The Graduate* (1967), based on an obscure but very funny novel by Charles Webb, starred a then-unknown New York actor named Dustin Hoffman as the college graduate at loose ends who enters into a sordid affair with one of his parents' friends (Anne Bancroft as the rapacious Mrs. Robinson), then finds himself in love with her daughter (the delectable Katharine Ross). The film spoke to the youth culture in a way that none had since *Rebel Without a Cause*, and it became the seventh-biggest-grossing movie of the decade. Nichols won the Oscar for his direction —a flashy turn that borrowed intelligently from several European directors—and the picture, Hoffman, Bancroft, Ross, Robert Surtees's cinematography, and the screenplay by Buck Henry and Calder Willingham were also nominated.

Nichols then returned to Broadway to direct Neil

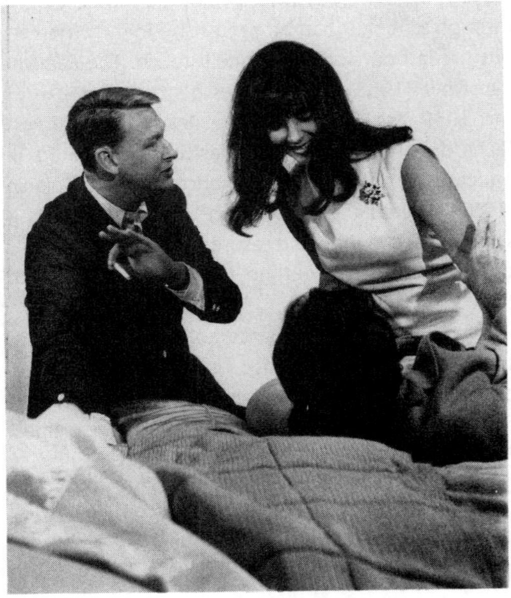

▲ *Liz Taylor is not yet in character as she rehearses her Oscar-winning role in* Who's Afraid of Virginia Woolf?

Simon's *Plaza Suite*, for which he won the 1968 Tony Award. His next film project was adapting Joseph Heller's 1961 antiwar cult classic, *Catch-22*. Perhaps expectations for Nichols's $18 million screen version were unrealistically high, but it bombed, failing to please either fans of the novel or casual moviegoers, who may have been put off by the picture's surfeit of surrealistic black humor. This despite (or because of?) an almost all-oddball cast that included Alan Arkin as Yossarian, Anthony Perkins, Orson Welles, Art Garfunkel, Bob Newhart, Buck Henry (who wrote the episodic screenplay), and Charles Grodin.

The brilliant but equally depressing *Carnal Knowledge* (1971) did win many critics back to Nichols's side, but it, too, was controversial. A trenchant but painfully sad portrait of the sexual and emotional failings of two former college buddies, it starred Jack Nicholson and Art Garfunkel as the pals and Ann-Margret, Candice Bergen, Carol Kane, and Rita Moreno as the women who try to love (or at least please) them. It was a hard film to warm up to, and might have found a wider audience had its protagonists not been quite so loathsome (Nicholson) and pathetic (Garfunkel).

After earning yet another Tony Award in 1971 for directing Neil Simon's *The Prisoner of Second Avenue* on Broadway, Nichols moved on to the big-budget *The Day of the Dolphin* (1973), which starred George C. Scott as a scientist who lends his trained dolphins to the CIA to help foil an assassination attempt. A politically correct thriller, or ecological exploitation? But it was fun to hear a dolphin with screenwriter Buck Henry's voice telling George C. Scott, "Fa loves Pa!" Nichols fared even less well with the frenetic comic caper *The Fortune* (1975), which featured Jack Nicholson and Warren Beatty as a pair of 1920s con artists who first romance, then kidnap heiress Stockard Channing, only to learn that she's been disinherited. The stars did demonstrate some talent for slapstick, but this wasn't the type of showcase audiences wanted to see Beatty and Nicholson in.

Five years elapsed before Nichols's next film, *Gilda Live* (1980), made it to the screen. A cheerful recording of Gilda Radner's Broadway show, it served up several of her popular skits and characters from NBC-TV's *Saturday Night Live* show, here in unexpurgated form. But it was *Silkwood* (1983) that marked Nichols's return to form. Meryl Streep stars as Karen Silkwood, the courageous lab worker who died under mysterious circumstances in 1974 trying to blow the whistle on the Kerr-McGee nuclear power plant in Oklahoma for gross safety violations. Streep, Cher (in a supporting role), the screenplay, and Nichols also received Academy Award nominations, with Nichols staging the mounting paranoia as if it were the work of vintage Alan Pakula.

*Heartburn* (1986) was less weighty material, but Nichols did well by Nora Ephron in this filming of her quasi-autobiographical bestseller about a woman who learns her husband is cheating on her while she's pregnant. Meryl Streep and Jack Nicholson stood in for Ephron and Carl Bernstein, her then-husband, who had already been played onscreen (more flatteringly) by Dustin Hoffman. *Biloxi Blues* (1988) was Nichols's first filming of a play by his longtime stage collaborator Neil Simon, who here adapts his popular laughfest into a more naturalistic period piece about a Simonish young man (Matthew Broderick) who grows up while undergoing basic training in Mississippi in the 1940s. As his clever, cruel drill sergeant, Christopher Walken was superb alongside Corey Parker and Penelope Ann Miller.

*Working Girl* (1988) was Nichols's biggest hit in some time, a longish but generally effective romantic drama. Melanie Griffith plays as a rough-edged Staten Island girl who takes a job as a secretary at a New York brokerage house and survives the exploitative maneuvers of her icy boss (Sigourney Weaver, in a nice comic turn) to rise to account executive, landing handsome arbitrageur Harrison Ford in the

▲ *With Orson Welles on the set of* Catch-22

bargain. Griffith won an Academy Award as best actress (to the surprise of many), while Nichols also was rewarded for his work with a nomination. *Postcards from the Edge* (1990), adapted by Carrie Fisher from her acerbic novel, starred Meryl Streep as a royally screwed-up actress who has to endure first drug rehabilitation, then probation with her alcoholic, domineering mother (Shirley MacLaine) before finally getting her life under control. Although Nichols's portrait of Hollywood is pleasingly venomous, both Streep and MacLaine are miscast, a problem that constantly threatens to capsize the film—although Streep, who gets a chance to show off her vocal talents, was Oscar-nominated for the umpteenth time.

If *Postcards* divided the critics with its uneven tone, *Regarding Henry* (1991) united them in the common cause of contempt. Perhaps the year's least-admired movie, it starred Harrison Ford as a successful lawyer and reprehensible human being whose life becomes a clean slate when a gunshot wound leaves him amnesiac, childlike, and near-helpless. His return to the love of his family (Annette Bening and Mikki Allen), physical and intellectual competency, and the practice of law is detailed by Nichols with a laughable disregard for reality—unavoidable, perhaps, given twenty-four-year-old Jeffrey Abram's jejune screenplay.

Nichols's much-hyped, expensive *Wolf* saw its release delayed for several months in 1994, despite the tantalizing prospect of Jack Nicholson as a rather meek book editor who, once bitten, is fated to turn into a werewolf. Nicholson and Michelle Pfeiffer made an appealing romantic combo, but Nichols's staging is often clumsy, and the film's early scenes satirizing New York's publishing scene are sorely missed when they are replaced by the inevitable—but inexcusably hackneyed—horror-pic set pieces. Neither fish nor fowl, *Wolf* lost money and left the open question: Why had Nichols taken it on in the first place?

## ● ALAN J. PAKULA (1928– )

One of the Seventies' most interesting and influential directors, Alan J. Pakula has since fallen into a longueur that has lasted for an alarmingly long time. But he continues to draw prestige projects that at least provide him with opportunities to escape his lengthy slump. Born in New York City, he attended Yale Drama School, after which he worked briefly in Warner Brothers' cartoon division. Jobs at MGM and Paramount as a production assistant followed.

Interestingly, Pakula experienced success as a movie producer long before he attempted directing, beginning in 1957 with Robert Mulligan's first film, *Fear Strikes Out.* Pakula then formed a production company with Mulligan, the first fruit of which was *To Kill a Mockingbird*; it received a passel of Academy Award nominations, including best picture, and earned Gregory Peck his only Oscar. Pakula and Mulligan then collaborated on *Love with the Proper Stranger*; *Baby, the Rain Must Fall*; *Inside Daisy Clover*; *Up the Down Staircase*; and *The Stalking Moon*. In 1969, Pakula decided to direct one of his productions for the first time. *The Sterile Cuckoo* was based on a touching novel by John Nichols and featured Liza Minnelli in an Oscar-nominated performance as the kooky Pookie, who first wins, then loses, the love of college student Wendell Burton.

Pakula's second directorial effort remains one of his best, the superb thriller *Klute* (1971). Jane Fonda is neurotic call girl Bree Daniels, who against her will becomes emotionally involved with a reserved detective (Donald Sutherland, underplaying brilliantly) who is trying to save her from her self-destructive tendencies, as well as a psychotic killer (a wonderfully creepy turn by Charles Cioffi). Fonda won a well-deserved Oscar for her searching performance, and Pakula should have been nominated as well. *Love and Pain (and the Whole Damn Thing)* (1973) was a smaller, less commercial enterprise, with Maggie Smith and Timothy Bottoms in a September-May romance that begins cute and ends in tears.

More impressive was *The Parallax View* (1974), a masterpiece of paranoia in which Warren Beatty plays an investigative reporter who uncovers evidence about a group of political assassins; he infiltrates their organization, but so sophisticated are their evil machinations that no one believes they exist, despite an ever-increasing stack of dead witnesses. *View*'s uncompromisingly downbeat ending may have hurt the film's commercial prospects, but it remains a classic of Watergate-era malaise. *All the President's Men* (1976) was a striking adaptation of Bob Woodward and Carl Bernstein's bestselling book about how they singlehandedly (well, not *exactly*) brought down the Nixon administration by tumbling to the Watergate break-in and cover-ups. Applying the techniques he developed in *Klute* and *Parallax* to create an atmosphere of mounting dread, Pakula came up with a peerless real-life political thriller without so much as a single fistfight, car chase, or murder attempt to hype the plot. *Men* received an Academy Award nomination for best picture and Pakula earned his only best direction nomination; unfortunately, they ran into John Avildsen's *Rocky* express (although Pakula garnered the equivalent award from the New York Film Critics Circle). Oscars went to William Goldman's screenplay and Jason Robards's salty impersonation of Ben Bradlee.

On the heels of a critical and financial success like *Men*, Pakula's *Comes a Horseman* (1978) seemed a major disappointment. As pretentious as its title, it was an excruciatingly slow (if beautifully photographed) psychological Western set in postwar Montana. Jason Robards is fine as a crusty rancher who tries to buy out rival rancher Jane Fonda, who is assisted in her struggle by James Caan and twinkle-eyed Richard Farnsworth (Oscar-nominated). *Starting*

*Over* (1979), adapted from Dan Wakefield's novel, was a mildly pleasant romantic comedy; Burt Reynolds is at his most appealing as a divorced professor in Boston whose affair with Jill Clayburgh keeps getting derailed by the frantic reconciliation attempts of ex-wife Candice Bergen. But *Rollover* (1981) was a disaster, an incoherent "thriller" about high finance starring Jane Fonda and Kris Kristofferson that should have been stamped "insufficient fun" before release.

*Sophie's Choice* (1982), adapted by Pakula from William Styron's award-winning novel, was overlong and respectful to a fault to its source. But the film did feature Meryl Streep's Oscar-winning performance as the Holocaust survivor whose postwar life in Brooklyn has been irrevocably damaged by her concentration-camp experiences; Pakula's screenplay, Nestor Almendros's cinematography, and Marvin Hamlisch's score also were nominated by the Academy.

After an absence from the screen of several years, Pakula returned in 1986 with the underwhelming *Dream Lover*, a clumsy psychological thriller with Kristy McNichol and Ben Masters that garnered withering reviews and worse box office. The little-seen *Orphans* (1987) was an intriguing "small" drama, adapted from his own play by Lyle Kessler; Albert Finney is a rich drunk shanghaied by a pair of orphaned brothers (Matthew Modine and Kevin Anderson) to their Newark home, where he slowly but steadily changes their lives.

No one much saw *See You in the Morning* (1989), either, but in this case there wasn't much to miss. Jeff Bridges and Alice Krige embark on their second marriage (the first with each other), but their exes and kids (Farrah Fawcett, David Dukes, Macaulay Culkin, and Drew Barrymore) conspire to make the transition a bumpy one. With *Presumed Innocent* (1990), Pakula selected Scott Turow's vaunted bestseller, a murder mystery/legal thriller. Harrison Ford stars as an attorney charged with the murder of his former assistant, a beauty with whom he'd had an affair. The usually dashing Ford is relentlessly dour and sports one of the most unfortunate haircuts in cinema history, while Gordon Willis's dark, dank palette quickly wears out its welcome. But Pakula (who co-wrote the screenplay) allows the clever plot to unravel effectively, and the work of the supporting cast (Bonnie Bedelia, Brian Dennehy, Raul Julia, Greta Scacchi) is a joy to observe.

If *Presumed* was something of a comeback film for Pakula, *Consenting Adults* (1992) frittered away that goodwill with an implausible tale: sociopathic mastermind Kevin Spacey frames Kevin Kline for the murder of his (Spacey's) wife (Rebecca Miller) after first arranging to have Miller sleep with Kline, whose own wife (Mary Elizabeth Mastrantonio) then turns against him; when Kline is sent to prison, Spacey conspires to—oh, skip it; life is too short.

Nor did the enormously popular *The Pelican Brief* (1993) restore Pakula's critical reputation. A handsome but vacuous adaptation of John Grisham's bestseller, it opens with brilliant law student Julia Roberts tumbling to the plans of a ruthless cartel that has just assassinated two Supreme Court Justices; when the conspirators realize she knows why they did it, they kill off the entire supporting cast and make her their next target. The intrepid (and always perfectly groomed) Roberts eludes the killers by using disguises as sophisticated as pinning back her hair, aided by fearless investigative journalist Denzel Washington. With its Washington, D.C., locations and inevitable parking garage shoot-out, *Pelican* might have been *Parallax View* meets *All the President's Men*, but those earlier films are light-years beyond this movie, which huffs and puffs until it blows itself down. But flaccid conclusion or no, the picture still took in $140 million—so why should Pakula worry?

## ● SAM PECKINPAH (1925–1984)

Cinema's self-appointed poet laureate of violence, Sam Peckinpah made only fourteen films in his directorial career, of which fewer than a half dozen stand out. Yet such was his impact during his heyday that the Peckinpah name became synonymous with a new genre, one that gloried in the kind of brutality from which the camera had previously averted its eyes. It was a brash style of filmmaking—one that surely would have been born without him—but it was Peckinpah who dragged it, kicking and screaming, into the 1970s.

Born in Fresno, California, Peckinpah enlisted in the Marines as an eighteen-year-old, then attended Fresno State College before earning his master's in drama from U.S.C. in 1950. He was the director-producer in residence at Huntington Park Civic Theatre in 1951, then became a stagehand at KLAC–TV in Los Angeles. After working as an editor at a CBS station in 1954, he assisted Don Siegel on films like *Riot in Cell Block 11* and *Invasion of the Body Snatchers*, in which Peckinpah also had a small part as a meter man. By 1957 he had broken into television as a writer for the top-rated show *Gunsmoke*, an experience that inspired him to create the popular series *The Rifleman* in 1958 and *The Westerner* in 1960; he wrote and directed the pilots as well as several episodes of each.

His first film, *Deadly Companions* (1961), was a low-budget Western that starred Brian Keith as a former cavalry officer who pays penance for an accidental killing by escorting the funeral procession through hostile Indian territory. The elegaic, lovely *Ride the High Country* (1962) was about two former lawmen who find their paths have diverged when a shipment of gold tempts one of them. Western icons Joel McCrea and Randolph Scott were supported by Warren Oates, L. Q. Jones, James Drury, and Edgar Buchanan—memorably cast as an assortment of dangerous lowlifes—and Mariette Hartley (so very charming) was the high-spirited girl the lawmen reluctantly take under their wing. The film's visual splendor (cinematography by Lucien Ballard) and wry script make it a near-perfect eulogy for McCrea and Scott, who then retired.

Peckinpah's future looked bright, but after a year of working for Disney—not a match made in heaven—he began directing *The Cincinnati Kid*, a movie about a cocky card shark (Steve McQueen). But Peckinpah was fired early in the production, and Norman Jewison replaced him. Then came the ill-fated *Major Dundee* (1965), with Charlton Heston as Amos Dundee, the officer in charge of a New Mexico prisoner-of-war camp filled with Rebs, criminals, and deserters. To avenge an Apache massacre and reclaim three children kidnapped by Apache chief Sierra Charriba, Dundee assembles a ragtag group (including Richard Harris, Jim Hutton, Ben Johnson, James Coburn, and Warren Oates) to follow him into Mexico. This Western *Dirty Dozen* held vast promise, but Peckinpah was fired by producer Martin Ransohoff during a bitter postproduction battle; the rambling two-hour-plus version finally released was intermittently powerful but frequently confused, and Peckinpah publicly disowned it. How much his own editing might have improved the film will never be known.

That contretemps kept Peckinpah out of the movie industry for several years. He did direct the drama *Noon Wine* for ABC-TV in 1966, then wrote the screenplay for *Villa Rides!* (1968) with Robert Towne. Finally Warner Brothers gave him the chance to get behind a camera again, and the result was *The Wild Bunch* (1969), a stylistic breakthrough that revitalized and reshaped the Western (as *Bonnie and Clyde* had recently done for the gangster film). Peckinpah contributed to the Oscar-nominated screenplay, but the story—a gang of long-in-the-tooth outlaws mosey into Mexico in 1914 to hijack an arms

McQUEEN/MacGRAW
THE GETAWAY
STEVE McQUEEN/ALI MacGRAW IN "THE GETAWAY" A FIRST ARTISTS PRESENTATION
CO-STARRING BEN JOHNSON · AL LETTIERI AND SALLY STRUTHERS AS "FRAN"
SCREENPLAY BY WALTER HILL · FROM THE NOVEL BY JIM THOMPSON · MUSIC BY
QUINCY JONES · A SOLAR/FOSTER-BROWER PRODUCTION · PRODUCED BY
DAVID FOSTER AND MITCHELL BROWER · DIRECTED BY SAM PECKINPAH
FILMED IN TODD-AO 35 · TECHNICOLOR®
A NATIONAL GENERAL PICTURES RELEASE
PG
PARENTAL GUIDANCE SUGGESTED

shipment as their last big score, with fatal results—paled alongside Lucien Ballard's seductive cinematography and the gritty performances of William Holden, Robert Ryan, Warren Oates, Ben Johnson, and the rest of the splendidly bedraggled cast. Now embraced as a landmark, *Bunch* was released in 1969 at 134 minutes, but in 1995 was given a limited re-release that restored about ten minutes of footage, including a bordello sequence that explains a key plot point about the split between former compadres Holden and Ryan.

*The Ballad of Cable Hogue* (1970) was also set out West, but there the resemblance to *Bunch* ends. A quirky, ironic, and self-indulgent parable about the passing of the Old West, it starred Jason Robards and the Peckinpah stock company, as well as the underrated Stella Stevens, with Lucien Ballard's typically stunning photography—but it never transcended its minor key. But *Straw Dogs* (1971) was another violent, boundary-breaking assault. Dustin Hoffman starred as a mild-mannered American mathematician who has moved to rural England with his wife (Susan George), a native of the area. When she is raped by one of her old suitors, Hoffman is forced to defend her, his home, and himself from an onslaught of vicious locals by becoming even more ruthless than they. A harrowing and visceral cinematic experience, it was the year's most controversial movie (sorry, *Dirty Harry*), with few critics agreeing as to its merits—or even whether any existed.

*The Getaway* (1972) was based on a 1958 paperback novel by Jim Thompson (expertly adapted by Walter Hill), and Peckinpah used its superb plotting, the star power of Steve McQueen, and the pouting

▲ *Rehearsing Jason Robards and Stella Stevens in* The Ballad of Cable Hogue

◀ *Tough times during* The Getaway, *Peckinpah's biggest hit*

of Ali McGraw to fashion an exciting thieves-fall-out chase picture, jettisoning Thompson's bleak ending in favor of one more attuned to the box office. This was Peckinpah's biggest commercial success, with enough jarring moments to keep it from being just another genre exercise. (The 1994 remake with Alec Baldwin and Kim Basinger upped the sexual intensity but strictly adhered to the original's choreography of action.) *Junior Bonner* (1972) used McQueen again, this time as a rodeo performer past his prime who makes a farewell appearance in his hometown in front of his parents (Ida Lupino and Robert Preston), who detest each other. It's a kinder, gentler Peckinpah we find here, and one wishes he had made other films in this quasi-comic vein.

*Pat Garrett and Billy the Kid* (1973) was a self-conscious demythologizing of the Billy the Kid legend; it suffered somewhat from the casting of Kris Kristofferson as Billy and, in a thankfully minor role, Bob Dylan as a cryptic onlooker (though his score does deliver the killer "Knockin' on Heaven's Door"). Still, James Coburn makes an interesting Pat Garrett, and such Peckinpah regulars as L. Q. Jones and Jack Elam look fine alongside iconic Western performers like Katy Jurado, Chill Wills, and Slim Pickens. The film's narrative weakness has since been explained as post-production fiddling by MGM, and a restored video release has nineteen additional minutes and even some resequencing, which helps enormously.

*Bring Me the Head of Alfredo García* (1974) went even further; it was a laconic, ultra-violent exercise that featured Warren Oates as an erstwhile piano player who becomes a remorseless bounty hunter, with Kris Kristofferson as a motorcycle-riding rapist and Gig Young as a classy hood. But *The Killer Elite* (1975) didn't offer even *García*'s black humor as a saving grace. James Caan plays a CIA agent who is mortally wounded when his partner (Robert Duvall) betrays him; he survives, undergoes a grueling martial-arts training program, then wreaks his revenge on Duvall's mercenary cartel of assassins. The film was more than faintly ridiculous, but Peckinpah filled every one of its 122 minutes with action. *Cross of Iron* (1977) was Peckinpah's only foray into the war genre, and it's good enough to make one wish he had tried again. James Coburn, Maximilian Schell, and James Mason star as German soldiers fighting on the Russian front in 1943.

Based on a pop song by C. W. McCall that had freakishly become a number-one crossover smash, *Convoy* (1978) featured Kris Kristofferson as an interstate trucker who refuses to kowtow to corrupt cop Ernest Borgnine and leads a horde of sympathetic eighteen-wheelers across the Southwest, crashing through roadblocks and drinking lots of bad coffee as thousands of cruisers follow in hot pursuit. It was dumb, it was antiauthoritarian, and it had Ali McGraw with a terrible haircut—so how'd it become one of the year's surprise hits? *The Osterman Weekend* (1983) was devoid of *Convoy*'s good-natured idiocy, but its intricate Cold War plot, courtesy of the Robert Ludlum bestseller, did have moments of coherence, and the cast (Burt Lancaster, Dennis Hopper, Rutger Hauer, John Hurt) was good enough to patch things over when it stopped making sense. And so we are left with an inconclusive ending to a career filled with periods of genuine brilliance, but undercut by a self-destructive streak a mile wide.

## ● ARTHUR PENN (1922- )

Nominated for best direction Academy Awards three times in the 1960s, Philadelphia-born Arthur Penn has little to show for his last twenty years of sparingly issued films. Yet while his muse seems to have departed, on the basis of that one great decade Penn will maintain a spot in the history of Hollywood moviemaking for his innovative early work.

Penn's high-school acting interest led him to form a drama group when he was stationed in South Carolina during World War II, and while serving in France in 1945, he joined the Soldiers Show Company. After the war, he acted in Joshua Logan's stage company and later studied at the L.A. branch of the Actors' Studio. He started in television in 1951, working as floor manager on *The Colgate Comedy Hour*, and soon graduated to writing and directing dramas for such prestige programs as *Gulf Playhouse* and *Philco Television Playhouse*. In 1956 he directed *The Miracle Worker* for *Playhouse 90*, and in 1958 staged his first Broadway play, *Two for the Seesaw*. That same year he made his screen directing debut with *The Left-Handed Gun*, a psychoanalytic version of the Billy the Kid legend, from a play by Gore Vidal, with Paul Newman rendering a Method-drenched performance (building off his earlier interpretation of the role in a 1955 *Philco Playhouse*). Although Newman was a rising star, the film (taken out of Penn's hands in postproduction) was a box-office failure.

Penn returned to Broadway, where he triumphed with *The Miracle Worker* in 1959 and *Toys in the Attic* and *All the Way Home* in 1960. Hollywood beckoned again, and in 1962 Penn directed the acclaimed screen version of *The Miracle Worker*. Patty Duke and Anne Bancroft repeat their stage roles as Helen Keller and Annie Sullivan, the blind teacher who broke through Keller's world of blindness and deafness so successfully that Keller was able to graduate magna cum laude from Radcliffe, write her autobiography, lecture, and co-found the ACLU. Bancroft won the best actress Oscar and Duke the best supporting actress Award, while Penn received his first nomination for best direction. Penn then began work on the 1963 war movie *The Train* but was fired by producer/star Burt Lancaster, who replaced him with John Frankenheimer.

He returned to Broadway in 1964 to direct Sammy Davis, Jr., in the hit musical *Golden Boy*, then made his second film, the ambitious, portentous (and, many critics complained, pretentious) *Mickey One* (1965), in which Warren Beatty plays a nightclub comedian undergoing delusions of persecution by the mob: he assumes a new identity, but finds that his problems remain a part of him. A far more commercial enterprise was *The Chase* (1966), a long, bloody, punch-drunk version of a 1952 Horton Foote novel (adapted by Lillian Hellman); Marlon Brando starred as a Texas sheriff nominally in charge of a town overrun with nymphomaniacs, drunks, and assorted bullies, all of them waiting for the return of escaped convict Robert Redford. Jane Fonda, E. G. Marshall, and Janice Rule also appeared, but even with their talent, the film was a mess.

Which made the accomplishment of *Bonnie and Clyde* (1967) all the more surprising. Now recognized as one of the decade's best—and most influential—movies, it originally was something of a sleeper. Star Warren Beatty also functioned as producer and chose Penn to direct (earlier candidates had been Truffaut and Godard), and Penn gave the picture his own New Wave vision: richly comic moments alternate with scenes of shocking brutality. But mixed reviews and Warners' ineffective marketing campaign made it a slow starter, and it wasn't until Beatty interceded with Warners that the film got a second wind (and was even rereviewed in several national publications). It went on to become the studio's second-highest grosser to date ($23 million) and earned nine Academy Award nominations, including best direction, picture, actor, actress (Faye Dunaway at her most delectable), supporting actress (Estelle Parsons, who won the Oscar), supporting actor (Gene Hackman), screenplay (Robert Benton and David Newman), and cinematography (Burnett Guffey, the only other winner). It was a stunning vindication for Beatty, and made Penn a bankable director.

He chose to follow *Bonnie* with the kinder, gentler *Alice's Restaurant* (1969), the plot of which was based on Arlo Guthrie's eighteen-minute-long counterculture narrative. Penn, who co-wrote the screenplay, captured the flavor of that rambling ode well—perhaps too well, as the film now has faded to the same embarrassing pallor as an old tie-dyed T-shirt. Nevertheless, Penn was rewarded with another Oscar nomination. (Guthrie's acting, however, was overlooked by the Academy.)

*Little Big Man* (1970) was erected on a sturdier foundation, Thomas Berger's picaresque novel. Penn reimagined it brilliantly, turning it into a parable about Vietnam. Although the 150-minute running time is more than needed, the film is a genuine original, comprised in equal parts of burlesque and tragedy. In the process it depicts and then debunks most Western movie conventions, including captivity narratives, gunfighter myths, medicine shows, and historical debacles like Little Big Horn. Dustin Hoffman gives an inventive performance as bewildered protagonist Jack Crabbe, and Chief Dan George (who was Oscar-nominated) and Faye Dunaway provide colorful support—although Richard Mulligan's Custer is too broad to be palatable.

Penn spent five years away from the screen, then returned with the carefully crafted but extremely downbeat noir *Night Moves* (1975); Gene Hackman plays a former football player whose mundane practice as a private detective is complicated by both his broken marriage to Susan Clark and a case involving a runaway teenager (Lolita-like Melanie Griffith) that leads to a smuggling cartel and, of course, murder most foul. *The Missouri Breaks* (1976) was ever so controversial—an eccentric, big-budget Western with the tantalizing combo of megastars Jack Nicholson and Marlon Brando. Brando's outrageously

WARREN BEATTY
FAYE DUNAWAY
They're young... they're in love
...and they kill people.
BONNIE AND CLYDE
CO-STARRING
MICHAEL J. POLLARD · GENE HACKMAN · ESTELLE PARSONS
Written by DAVID NEWMAN and ROBERT BENTON · Music by Charles Strouse · Produced by WARREN BEATTY · Directed by ARTHUR PENN
TECHNICOLOR® FROM WARNER BROS.-SEVEN ARTS

showy, postmodern turn as a hired killer toying with a gang of rustlers formerly led by Nicholson essentially capsizes the production, although on one level it's fun to watch Brando stretch the envelope. The digressive screenplay by Thomas McGuane had its moments, and the Montana locations were gorgeous—but much more than pretty vistas was expected of Penn, who let this one slip away.

After another five-year hiatus, Penn returned with the underwhelming *Four Friends* (1981), an impressionistic account of America in the Sixties as seen through the eyes of Yugoslavian immigrant Craig Wasson, based on an obviously personal screenplay by Steve Tesich. Again, narrative problems contributed to the picture's failure, but even more critical were the deficiencies of the no-name cast, who simply couldn't tote the story's heavy baggage. *Target* (1985) was the third teaming of Penn and Gene Hackman, but unlike their first two collaborations, magic was noticeably absent. The disjointed tale offered Hackman and Matt Dillon as a father and son on vacation in Europe who are suddenly thrust into a world of menace when Hackman's wife is kidnapped; the film aspired to Hitchcockian thrills, but simply couldn't deliver.

*Dead of Winter* (1987) was better, an uncredited remake of Joseph Lewis's 1945 noir *My Name Is Julia Ross*, with the always interesting Mary Steenburgen as the woman being kept prisoner in a spooky mansion by oddball Roddy McDowall. *Penn & Teller Get Killed* (1989) was a cult movie by definition, and thus not for every taste—but fans of the subversive comedian-magicians insist that Penn (Arthur, that is) got it right with this marriage of black humor and violence. Penn's television film *The Portrait* (1993) was a fine adaptation of Tina Howe's play *Painting Churches*, starring Gregory Peck and Lauren Bacall as the icons who agree to be painted by their daughter (Peck's real daughter, Cecilia). It brought Penn full circle to where his career began; but will he ever reenter Hollywood's mainstream? With each passing year, it seems less likely.

## ● SYDNEY POLLACK (1934- )

One of Hollywood's most reliable commercial directors for almost twenty years, Sydney Pollack emerged in 1993 from seven years of famine to prove that he was not yet ready to relinquish his hard-earned reputation as a hit maker of tasteful projects. Yet even his best-executed films leave the viewer hungering for just a bit more, as if his efficient packaging of all the story elements has inadvertently leached out their deeper meaning.

Born outside South Bend, Indiana, Pollack entered the film industry in the manner typical to so many of his generation: taking acting classes in New York (under Sanford Meisner); acting on Broadway (in *A Stone for Danny Fisher*) and on television (in a variety of *Playhouse 90* dramas); and, after serving in the Army during the Elvis years, moving to Los Angeles to direct episodes of TV series like *Ben Casey* and *Shotgun Slade*. He had a role in the 1962 Korean War movie *War Hunt*, which also marked the screen debut of Robert Redford, then supervised the English dubbing of Luchino Visconti's *The Leopard* (1963).

His first credit as a film director was *The Slender Thread* (1965), in which hot-line volunteer Sidney Poitier keeps sleeping-pill-overdose victim Anne Bancroft talking on the phone (and thus, awake) until an ambulance can reach her. That modest effort was sufficient to get Pollack his first prestige production, *This Property Is Condemned* (1966), an extremely loose expansion of Tennessee Williams's one-act play—basically, they kept the title and made up the rest. The plot: tubercular Natalie Wood falls in love with drifter Robert Redford and ends up an adulterous slut in a Mississippi town. *The Scalphunters* (1968) was a lively Western starring Burt Lancaster, Ossie Davis, and Telly Savalas; it would have worked even better if Pollack had jettisoned the heavy-handed lessons about racial equality and stuck to the comedy.

*Castle Keep* (1969) was a bust of a World War II adventure, despite the presence of Burt Lancaster, Peter Falk, and Bruce Dern, but *They Shoot Horses, Don't They?* (1969) was a powerful adaptation of Horace McCoy's 1935 existential novel about a dance marathon that ends tragically for several of its desperate contestants. Three of the four principal actors—Jane Fonda, Susannah York, and Gig Young—were nominated for Academy Awards (with Young winning), and Pollack received his first nomination for best direction. He followed this downbeat ode with the metaphysical Western *Jeremiah Johnson* (1972), a beautifully photographed (on location in Utah) account of the life of a misanthropic 1800s mountain man who survives the perils of nature, Indians, and even cavalry soldiers. Robert Redford successfully sacrificed his golden-boy persona to underplay his cryptic character; it was an approach that may not have benefited the picture, which unfolds at too leisurely a pace. Even thus muted, however, the film was a hit.

But Pollack got the matinee-idol Redford next in *The Way We Were* (1973), an enormously popular, unremittingly nostalgic, pitilessly shmaltzy love story—the kind Hollywood would make every week of the year if it could patent the formula. It was adapted by Arthur Laurents from his own novel, and co-starred dynamo Barbra Streisand as a strident Jewish radical who becomes apolitical Redford's conscience as he moves (declines?) from writing novels to writing screenplays to writing for television. Streisand may wear on nonfans, but she received a best actress nomination from the Academy, and the title song and Marvin Hamlisch score won Oscars. Pollack moved far afield from that romantic blockbuster with *The Yakuza* (1975), a flavorful (if long) post-noir about Japanese gangsters written by Paul Schrader and Robert Towne; Robert Mitchum plays a private

▲ *On the set of* This Property Is Condemned *with a young Robert Redford and Natalie Wood*

eye who must challenge the *Yakuza* organization on their home turf to rescue a kidnapped American girl.

*Three Days of the Condor* (1975) was a more commercial venture, an exciting adaptation of a James Grady novel (which takes *six* days to unwind). Robert Redford stars as a CIA researcher who inadvertently survives a massacre of his co-workers that was meant to include him; now hunted by his own agency, he takes refuge with a photographer (Faye Dunaway) until he can figure out how to counterattack, which he does most ingeniously. A post-Watergate conspiracy thriller that is very much a product of its time, *Condor* would be Pollack's last excursion into the suspense genre for many years. *Bobby Deerfield* (1977), with Al Pacino as a race-car driver in love with dying heiress Marthe Keller, was an unmitigated disaster, an interminable and very bad movie of the sort that eventually earns a cult following of those who admire ineptitude on an epic scale.

But Pollack climbed right back into the saddle with *The Electric Horseman* (1979), a slick updating of 1962's *Lonely Are the Brave*, with an animal-rights spin. Robert Redford is an erstwhile rodeo champion reduced to being a walking (or riding) endorsement for a breakfast cereal in Las Vegas. When he learns that the company's $12 million steed is scheduled for the glue factory, he rides off with it, leading his high-tech, corporate pursuers on a merry chase; in an obvious box-office concession, Jane Fonda plays a reporter covering the story who falls in love with Redford. Naturally he frees the horse in the wild and returns a media star. *Absence of Malice* (1981) was considerably more weighty, a well-plotted exploration of the boundaries of journalistic ethics, with Sally Field as a newspaper reporter duped into acting irresponsibly and Paul Newman as the man whose life is ruined by her story. The measured pace of the picture was a beat too slow, but at least it was *about* something. Newman, Melinda Dillon, and writer Kurt Luedtke (a former newspaperman) all earned Academy Award nominations.

*Tootsie* (1982) is the highlight to date of Pollack's career, a magical blend of romance and comedy built around the talents of Dustin Hoffman (although, let's face it, he doesn't make a very convincing woman); it also draws on a lovely performance by Jessica Lange and fine work by Bill Murray, Dabney Coleman, Teri Garr, and Charles Durning (not to mention Pollack's own neat turn as Hoffman's skeptical agent). The film, Pollack, Hoffman, and the screenplay were nominated for Academy Awards, but 1982 was the year of the *Gandhi* juggernaut and only Lange took home an Oscar. (At this writing, *Tootsie* was among *Variety*'s all-time top-twenty-five grossers.)

*Out of Africa* (1985), a life of Karen Blixen with Meryl Streep as the Danish émigré who gained fame as author Isak Dinesen, was Pollack's most lauded film. But in many ways it is one of his worst, an expensive coffee-table book emblematic of the problems that afflict even his best work. It's an hour too long (instead of the usual twenty minutes), too ponderous, and too predictable; even the beautiful vistas of antelope running through the Nairobi veldt begin to run together after the tenth go-round. And then there is the problem of Robert Redford, whose presence probably added $15 million to the film's grosses but whose laughable miscasting as British adventurer Denys Finch-Hatton fatally compromises the picture's legitimacy. That said, let it be noted that the film won the Academy Award as the best picture of 1985, that Pollack was honored for best direction, and that five more Oscars followed (though not to Streep or the deserving Klaus Maria Brandauer). It even made a pile of money.

Many of those same flaws surfaced in *Havana* (1990), and this time Pollack was lambasted—to a degree that was perhaps unfair. Robert Redford is at least acceptable as the Rick Blaine of Havana's gambling scene circa 1958, but love interest Lena Olin doesn't strike sparks, and the wholesale borrowing of *Casablanca* (which was thirty-eight minutes shorter) only serves to underline *Havana*'s bloatedness. Still, if the picture hadn't been the year's biggest loser at the box office, one wonders if critiques of it would have been as heated. (Backlash for the critics having gone overboard on *Africa?*) Pollack licked his wounds for a few years, then redeemed his reputation as a premier producer/director with the box-office smash *The Firm* (1993). An efficient adaptation of John Grisham's overrated thriller, it runs too long—no surprise there—and makes unnecessary changes in the plot. But Tom Cruise carries his weight as the hunted lawyer, and Holly Hunter as a helpful Memphis secretary, David Strathairn as his convict brother, and Ed Harris as a hard-ass FBI contact are all superb—a reminder of Pollack's ability to use actors inventively when their name isn't Redford.

▲ The Firm, *Pollack's comeback hit*

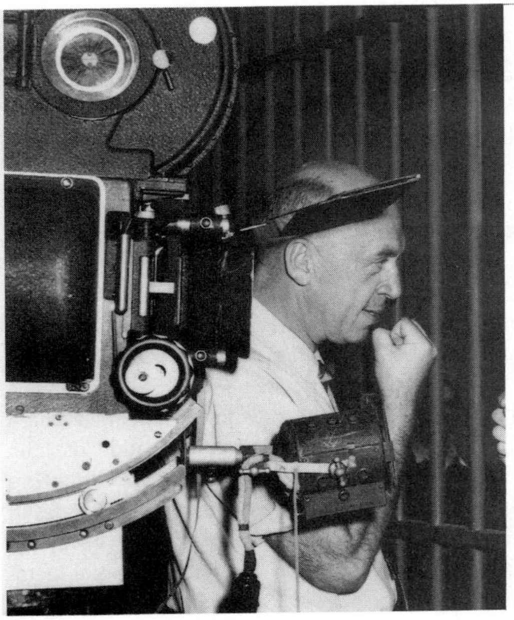

## ● OTTO PREMINGER (1906–1986)

Andrew Sarris described Otto Preminger in 1994 as "the most maligned, misjudged, misunderstood and misperceived American filmmaker." It's probably not as bad as all that—Preminger's name usually comes up whenever a list of Hollywood's best directors is compiled—but it is true that his deliberately provocative works have been re-evaluated so many times as tastes have changed that it is difficult to get a fix on whether he was truly great or merely very good. Probably the latter.

Growing up in Vienna, Preminger was prepared for a career in law, following in the footsteps of his attorney-general dad. He went so far as to earn his doctor of law degree, but his love of acting and the theater won out. He worked at Max Reinhardt's Theater in der Josefstadt in Vienna, both producing and directing plays, and in 1931 directed his only non-English film, *Die Grosse Liebe*. He was invited to direct one of his Vienna plays on Broadway (in English), then made his way to Hollywood, where he worked on a couple of "B"s at Fox. But Darryl F. Zanuck fired him during the early stages of *Kidnapped* in 1937, and he had to return to the stage to find work. On Broadway he directed *Margin for Error*, in which he also cast himself as a Nazi.

His performance must have been terrific, because he was invited back to Hollywood in 1942 to act in Irving Pichel's Oscar-nominated *The Pied Piper*, again as a Nazi. Then he was asked to re-create his stage role in the film version of *Margin for Error* (1943); he agreed on the condition that he also direct. It was a poor film (and Preminger's performance smacked of ham), but at least he was back behind the camera, albeit without the absent Zanuck's knowledge. The tepid Jeanne Crain soaper *In the Meantime, Darling* (1944) was next, but then came the sublime *Laura* (1944). Preminger originally was set to produce and direct this inventive murder mystery (based on a Vera Caspary novel), but Zanuck was steamed at Preminger for working behind his back as a director and handed the reins to Rouben Mamoulian, who began working on the screenplay. But when Zanuck didn't like the early rushes, he fired Mamoulian and reinstated Preminger. The result is one of the great films of the Forties, with Dana Andrews as an implacable police detective who falls in love with the portrait of lovely Gene Tierney, the reports of whose death turn out to have been greatly exaggerated. Preminger received his first Academy Award nomi-

nation for best direction, and Clifton Webb was nominated for his acidulous Waldo Lydecker, while Joseph LaShelle's glowing camerawork won an Oscar.

The commercial and critical success of *Laura* gave Preminger leverage, and Zanuck had to give him a long-term contract. *A Royal Scandal* (1945) had been started by Lubitsch, but when he fell ill, Preminger completed it; a silly biography of Catharine the Great as impersonated by Tallulah Bankhead, it was the first of many Preminger-directed costume pictures that failed to click. The nasty *Fallen Angel* (1945) was a first-rate noir: gold digger Dana Andrews marries rich Alice Faye, then finds he's accused of murdering Linda Darnell, whom he'd been seeing on the side. *Centennial Summer* (1946) was a bland if colorful musical set at the Philly Expo of 1876, with Jeanne Crain, Linda Darnell, and Cornel Wilde, but *Forever Amber* (1947), with a blond Linda Darnell, captured little of the naughtiness (though much of the length) of the scandalous bestseller and ended up an expensive box-office bomb.

Paroled from costumer hell, Preminger made *Daisy Kenyon* (1947), a good romantic melodrama with the unusual combination of Joan Crawford, Henry Fonda, and Dana Andrews. Then it was on to Victorian England for *The Fan* (1949), adapted from an Oscar Wilde comedy of manners. George Sanders almost saved it, but the miscasting of Jeanne Crain as Oscar Wilde's heroine Lady Windemere proved fatal—another example of how the studio system, with its reliance on stars under contract, could compromise a project before so much as a foot of film had been shot. Zanuck must have finally conceded that Preminger's talents lay in another direction, as his two 1950 releases were the sort of inventive thrillers that would become his trademark. *Whirlpool* (1949) had mad hypnotist José Ferrer jeopardizing Gene Tierney, while the 1950 *Where the Sidewalk Ends* reunited Tierney with her *Laura* co-star Dana

▲ *Big Bob Mitchum visits the set of Carmen Jones, to the amusement of Dorothy Dandridge and Harry Belafonte*

▲ *On location with Paul Newman during* Exodus

Andrews for the first time; both pictures were well scripted by Ben Hecht. *The 13th Letter* (1951) served up more suspense, with Linda Darnell the victim of poison-pen letters; it was her fourth picture working for Preminger.

His contract with Fox having expired, Preminger happily struck out on his own. He directed plays on Broadway, acted up a storm as the Nazi commandant in *Stalag 17*, and made the underrated thriller *Angel Face* (1953) at RKO with Robert Mitchum and Jean Simmons. He then acquired the rights to F. Hugh Herbert's stage success *The Moon Is Blue* and produced it himself for United Artists. Starring William Holden and Maggie McNamara, it became the scandal of 1953 when Preminger released it without Code approval. The sex chat seems harmless enough now—quaint, even—but the controversy made it a box-office smash, and McNamara was nominated for an Academy Award. Preminger returned in triumph to Fox in 1954 to make *River of No Return*, a lively if conventional CinemaScope Western that happily teamed Robert Mitchum and Marilyn Monroe. *Carmen Jones* (1954) was a well-mounted modernizing of the Bizet opera, now set in Florida with an all-black cast that featured Pearl Bailey, Harry Belafonte, and the great Dorothy Dandridge, who deservedly received a best actress nomination; unfortunately, many of the actors had their Oscar Hammerstein II song lyrics dubbed.

Nineteen fifty-five was another good year for Preminger. He produced and directed *The Man with the Golden Arm*, for which Frank Sinatra received his first Academy Award nomination in the best actor category, then made *The Court-Martial of Billy Mitch-*

*ell*, a fact-based courtroom drama about the soldier who predicted the Pearl Harbor attack sixteen years before it happened; it starred Gary Cooper and Rod Steiger. But *Saint Joan* (1957) was a near-disaster; newcomer Jean Seberg (at age eighteen) was unable to carry this ambitious adaptation of Shaw's play. *Bonjour Tristesse* (1958) was a better showcase for the charismatic Seberg, who here tries to keep David Niven from making Deborah Kerr her stepmother, amid much gorgeous scenery on the French Riviera.

With *Porgy and Bess* (1959), Preminger displaced Mamoulian as a project's director for the second time, but this time less successfully. This black-cast production boasts great actors (Dandridge, Sammy Davis, Jr., Sidney Poitier, Pearl Bailey) and wonderful Gershwin music ("I Got Plenty o' Nothin'," "Summertime")—but Mamoulian, who directed it on Broadway, might have served up the drama with a lighter hand. The 1959 *Anatomy of a Murder* was a potent courtroom drama with a sexually explicit subject matter that made it controversial at the time. Ben Gazzara is superb as the lout who kills a man for "raping" his promiscuous wife (Lee Remick at her come-hither best), and Jimmy Stewart is the attorney who must defend him (while despising him) from crafty prosecutor George C. Scott. All this and a score by Duke Ellington, too. Preminger, who also produced, saw the film receive Academy Award nominations for best picture, actor (Stewart), screenplay, and cinematography.

*Exodus* (1960), a 213-minute epic about the struggle to found Israel, was adapted by Dalton Trumbo from Leon Uris's bestseller; it could have lost an hour of running time without anyone protesting, and earnest leads Paul Newman and Eva Marie Saint were miscast. *Advise and Consent* (1962) was a busy version of the Allen Drury novel about political gamesmanship in Washington; it had also been dramatized on Broadway in 1960. The film boasted one of the most interesting casts in many a moon: Henry Fonda, Charles Laughton, Lew Ayres, Burgess Meredith, Franchot Tone. (Reportedly Preminger offered the Reverend Martin Luther King, Jr., an acting role, but he turned it down, alas.)

What *Advise* did for politics, *The Cardinal* (1963) tried to do for religion. But after nearly three hours it was clear that Preminger had contracted Stanley Krameritis, a disease he had been able to avoid in the past. Still, it's hard not to like a film that gives you Dorothy Gish, John Huston, Chill Wills, *and* Ossie Davis. Rather surprisingly, Preminger was Oscar-nominated for best direction. The excruciating *In Harm's Way* (1964) was a World War II would-be epic that tried mightily to blend John Wayne, Kirk Douglas, and Henry Fonda, to name but a few of the cast's big names. But the film seemed as long as the war in the Pacific. Preminger's alarming tendency toward gigantism was arrested with the distasteful thriller *Bunny Lake Is Missing* (1965): Carol Lynley's little girl is kidnapped and Noël Coward and Laurence Olivier are suspected. Reviled by many, it has since developed a cult following. The laughable *Hurry Sundown* (1967) was problematic in an entirely different way, with Michael Caine chewing up the Deep South scenery as a greedy landowner contending with haughty Jane Fonda. Preminger's decline, if in doubt, was certified by the hopeless *Skidoo* (1968), a gangster comedy with a crazy-quilt cast (Groucho Marx, Jackie Gleason, Frankie Avalon, George Raft) guaranteed to bore late-Sixties audiences.

These four failures were followed by the offbeat *Tell Me That You Love Me, Junie Moon* (1970), a fable about love and friendship that connected with the Zeitgeist as surely as *Skidoo* had missed it; Liza Minnelli was superb as the outwardly scarred girl who holds the group together. Not a commercial success, the film at least earned back some respect for Preminger. *Such Good Friends* (1971) was a witty black comedy scripted by Elaine May, but *Rosebud* (1975) was that rarity, a film without a single redeeming quality. Preminger's last picture was *The Human Factor* (1979), a passable adaptation of Graham Greene's espionage novel starring Derek Jacobi and Nicol Williamson.

## ● BOB RAFELSON (1935- )

For about ten minutes at the beginning of the Seventies, Bob Rafelson was considered one of Hollywood's brightest, hottest directors. But he's made five movies over the last twenty years, each more disappointing than the last. Born in New York City, Rafelson was off to see the world as soon as he was able, performing in rodeos out West, shipping out on an ocean liner, and playing jazz with a combo in Acapulco—all before he was out of his teens. He began his studies at Dartmouth but dropped out, serving a hitch with the Army in Japan, where he was the deejay at a military radio station. His drifting days over, he went to work after his discharge for David Susskind's television series *Play of the Week* in New York as a story editor, and other TV work followed. Rafelson's television breakthrough was *The Monkees*, a zany comedy fashioned after Richard Lester's Beatles films, *A Hard Day's Night* and *Help!* Rafelson co-created the series for ABC, helped choose the band members, and directed several episodes.

This led directly to his first feature film, *Head* (1968), a cheerfully off-the-wall, psychedelic celebration of the Monkees with Annette, Frank Zappa, Teri Garr, and Jack Nicholson; Rafelson and Nicholson produced and wrote it. *Head* considered itself cutting edge and very far out, but it's now as quaint as a memento of the era as *Laugh-In*, Donovan, and bongs. Rafelson and Nicholson next collaborated on the more weighty *Five Easy Pieces* (1970), an alternately profound, hilarious, and pretentious portrait of drifter Bobby Dupea (Nicholson), an erstwhile classical pianist whom we first meet working as an oil rigger in Texas. When his waitress girlfriend (Karen Black) tells him she's pregnant, he takes to the road (during which the celebrated "hold the chicken salad" sequence takes place) and heads back to see his wealthy family in Washington State. There the psychodrama flows like molten lava, until Nicholson bugs out and hitches a ride on a logging truck bound for Alaska. The film, Nicholson, and Black all received Academy Award nominations, as did Rafelson and Carole Eastman's ("Adrien Joyce") screenplay. Although he didn't receive an Oscar nomination for his direction, Rafelson was chosen best director by the New York Film Critics Circle.

The impact of *Pieces* was such that Rafelson probably could have made any film he wanted; unfortunately, his choice was the ponderous *The King of Marvin Gardens* (1972), from a story he wrote with Jacob Brackman. Jack Nicholson stars as an FM deejay with a taste for metaphysics and purple ponderings, and Bruce Dern is his slightly askew, ex-con brother, who dreams of buying a tropical isle with long-suffering girlfriend Ellen Burstyn's life savings. Beautifully photographed (by *Pieces*'s Laslo Kovacs) on location in Atlantic City, the film is well acted but a downer, smug and deliberately opaque. It befuddled both audiences and critics.

*Stay Hungry* (1976) appeared four years later. Rafelson's adaptation of the novel by Charles Gaines turned out to be a perceptive and often funny film about the world of bodybuilding. Jeff Bridges is an upper-class Alabaman who aids health-club members Arnold Schwarzenegger and Sally Field in their battle against the hostile takeover his boss is orchestrating. It was the first time Rafelson worked from someone else's concept, and the book's structure seems to have benefited the film. Not to be overlooked is Schwarzenegger's very successful performance, paving the way for a career that within ten years would find him an industry giant.

Rafelson's career, however, was moving in the opposite direction. He started filming *Brubaker* with Robert Redford, but after a week was fired. He moved on to *The Postman Always Rings Twice* (1981), and while his remake of MGM's 1946 hit with John

Garfield and Lana Turner did succeed in restoring James Cain's earthy, tawdry sexuality, he and screenwriter David Mamet lost the fatalistic narrative thrust that made the 1934 novel so irresistible in the first place. Jack Nicholson and Jessica Lange do their best as the rutting lovers who murder to stay together, but somehow they don't look right, and neither does the film, which flopped.

Six years elapsed before Rafelson's next project, *Black Widow* (1987), saw the light of day. An intermittently interesting variation on *Double Indemnity*, it stars the always intriguing Theresa Russell as a female Bluebeard who slays her husbands one after the other for their money; Debra Winger is the dogged investigator who's on to the scam but finds herself oddly attracted to Russell. Unfortunately, Rafelson once again lets the narrative meander just when it most needs to focus, and he doesn't sustain the tension this neo-noir requires.

*Mountains of the Moon* (1990) was a beautifully filmed adaptation of William Harrison's mammoth novel about the great explorer Sir Richard Burton. Scripted by Rafelson with Harrison, in many ways this is his most cohesive work; it has an authenticity of detail that shames the infinitely more popular *Out of Africa*. Granted, Patrick Bergin is not Robert Redford—but he is more believable as Burton than Redford ever was as Denys Finch-Hatton. Had Rafelson opted for two big stars and a gauzy central romance, perhaps *Moon* could have drawn audiences; without them, the picture failed, however unjustly.

But injustice had nothing to do with the inadequacies of *Man Trouble* (1992), Rafelson's abysmal attempt to drag screwball comedy kicking and screaming into the Nineties. Jack Nicholson (teamed with Rafelson for the fourth time) is a guard-dog trainer hired by opera singer Ellen Barkin to upgrade her security. A romantic comedy that is neither romantic nor comic, this misses the mark by an alarmingly wide margin. To think that it was written by Rafelson and Eastman, the same team that conjured up *Five Easy Pieces*, is too depressing for words.

## IRVING RAPPER (1898– )

A Warners' house director for much of his career, Irving Rapper's best work tended to be adapted from the stage. He was born in London but moved with his family to New York City early in the century. He began working on theatrical productions while attending N.Y.U., and made his way to Broadway in the 1920s. Warners invited him to Hollywood in 1935, and he served as assistant director and/or dialogue coach on such top releases as William Dieterle's *The Story of Louis Pasteur*, *The Life of Emile Zola*, and *Juárez*, and Michael Curtiz's *Four Daughters*. He was promoted to director in 1941 for *Shining Victory*, a stately version of A. J. Cronin's play about a research psychologist (James Stephenson) whose dedication blinds him to the love of his assistant (Geraldine Fitzgerald). Even better was *One Foot in Heaven* (1941), a nicely mounted bit of Americana, with Fredric March as a minister who struggles with the problems of church and state.

*The Gay Sisters* (1942) was a leaden soap opera starring Barbara Stanwyck, Geraldine Fitzgerald, and Nancy Coleman as siblings whose affairs of the heart involve George Brent and Gig Young. But the 1942 *Now, Voyager*, from an Olive Higgins Prouty novel, was suds of a much higher grade. Bette Davis had one of the defining roles of her career as the repressed Bostonian whom psychiatrist Claude Rains teaches how to love; married Paul Henreid is the suave recipient of her newly awakened affections. Both Davis and Gladys Cooper (as her tyrannical mother) received Academy Award nominations, and Max Steiner's throbbing score won an Oscar. "Schlock classic," as some critics view it, or no, *Voyager* remains one of the Forties' most fondly remembered cinema romances.

*The Adventures of Mark Twain* (1944) was a rather plodding take on the great writer's life; Fredric March plays Clemens and Alexis Smith the love of his life, his wife, Olivia. *The Corn Is Green* (1945) had been a hit on Broadway with Ethel Barrymore, and although Bette Davis was really too young to play Miss Moffat, the English teacher who dedicates her life to the impoverished students of a Welsh mining town circa 1890, she essayed the role with conviction.

Rapper was on less steady ground with *Rhapsody in Blue* (1945), a well-meaning biopic (aren't they all?) of the Gershwin brothers—Robert Alda as George, Herbert Rudley as Ira, and Oscar Levant as himself. The wonderful music and guest performances by such greats as Hazel Scott and Paul Whiteman almost compensated for the film's fanciful embroidering of the facts. (If nothing else, it was less absurd than Cary Grant's hopeless impersonation of Cole Porter in *Night and Day*.) *Deception* (1946) was a florid melodrama with Bette Davis, Claude Rains, and Paul Henreid—yes, that *Now, Voyager* gang—and just may be Rapper's best picture. Davis plays the frustrated mistress of egomaniacal composer Rains, who knows she really loves cellist Henreid and torments the poor fellow into a nervous breakdown, a selfish act that earns him a bullet. It's all great fun.

*Voice of the Turtle* (1947), from John van Druten's Broadway play, was a rare romantic comedy for Rapper, but a good one; Ronald Reagan is unusually appealing as a soldier on leave with whom Eleanor Parker falls in love, and Eve Arden and Wayne Morris are excellent as support. (To date, nearly half of Rapper's films had been based on plays, a source that played into his strengths as a former stage director.) Rapper now let his contract with Warners expire, and while he would work for the studio again, he never reached the modest heights he attained as their employee.

His first freelance project was *Anna Lucasta* (1949), with Paulette Goddard as the Brooklyn waterfront prostitute trying to make a better life for herself. It was a role originated by an all-black cast in Philip Yordan's 1944 Broadway production (casting that would be restored for the 1958 film version), but Goddard was deglamorized fairly convincingly. Rapper's version of Tennessee Williams's *The Glass Menagerie* (1950) was a prestigious assignment; it was a respectable if uninventive transcription of the stage success, with Jane Wyman as Amanda, the crippled recluse, Gertrude Lawrence her Southern-belle mother, and Kirk Douglas the suitor who tries to bring Wyman into the real world, with disastrous results.

*Another Man's Poison* (1951), also a stage vehicle, presented Bette Davis in one of her campiest roles as a lusty mystery writer living on a Yorkshire farm and married to a crook whose no-account pal involves her in blackmail. Filmed in England, this overripe suspenser co-starred Bette's then-husband, Gary Merrill. *Bad for Each Other* (1953) was another heavy-breathing melodrama; Charlton Heston was cast against type as a noble surgeon, and Lizabeth Scott was totally *in* type as the sulking society girl who covets him. Rather better was *Forever Female* (1953), a sprightly comedy (scripted by the Epstein *frères*), with Ginger Rogers as a mature stage actress who reluctantly admits that young Pat Crowley is more appropriate for the ingenue role they both covet. Rapper's knowledge of the theater (and its temperamental stars) supplies the film with its considerable verisimilitude, although it still must take a back seat to *All About Eve*.

*Strange Intruder* (1956) provided a showy role for Ida Lupino, who plays a widow menaced (she believes) by Edward Purdom, her dead husband's old pal. *The Brave One* (also 1956) was a sentimental but effective tale of a Mexican boy whose love for his bull, Gitano, cannot save the noble animal from the bullfighting arena. Filmed in Mexico, it was written by the then-blacklisted Dalton Trumbo under the pseudonym of Robert Rich—he couldn't take possession of the Oscar his script was awarded for almost twenty years.

Rapper's biggest project in some time was his version of *Marjorie Morningstar* (1958), Herman Wouk's bestselling novel about a New York girl (Natalie Wood) who dreams of an acting career but ends up mowing the lawn in the 'burbs—until she has a fling with a charismatic theatrical producer (Gene Kelly) in the Catskills. Again Rapper was able to capitalize on his own background to authenticate the story's summer-stock setting. *The Miracle* (1959), based on an earlier stage production by Max Reinhardt, was a wholly absurd period drama set in 1800s Spain, with Carroll Baker trying to decide between the nunnery and soldier Roger Moore (an elementary decision, when you really think about it)—and a statue of the Virgin Mary comes to life in the midst of all the activity.

Over the next ten years all Rapper added to his résumé were two Italian productions, a rather precipitous fall for a director who had been so recently handling bestselling properties. Finally, in 1970, Rapper returned to Hollywood to make *The Christine Jorgensen Story*, a laughable, predictably tawdry account of the world's most famous sex-change case, with John Hansen as the trailblazing Christine. Eight more years passed before Rapper made his final picture, the insufferable *Born Again* (1978). A feeble dramatization of the religious conversion of convicted Watergate felon Charles Colson (Dean Jones), Nixon's loathsome former special counsel, it was not exactly the story all America had been breathlessly awaiting.

## ● NICHOLAS RAY (1911–1979)

The bard of expressionism in the postwar American cinema, Nicholas Ray enjoys a reputation based on a half dozen exceptional works; the rest of his output hovers in the middling range. But novelists have sustained their following for a hundred years and more with fewer than six masterpieces, so why not a Hollywood director?

Born Raymond Nicholas Kienzle in La Crosse, Wisconsin, Ray studied architecture at the University of Chicago under Frank Lloyd Wright, among others, as well as theater. After graduating, he became the resident director of Wright's Taliesin Playhouse, then worked as a touring stage actor in the Theater of Action troupe. In 1938 he joined John Houseman's Phoenix Theatre Company in New York, shortly after which he suffered an accident that cost him the use of his right eye. Houseman named him War Information Radio Program Director in 1942, an office that required him to write and direct propaganda dramas. His debut as a Broadway director came a year later, and in 1944 he agreed to accompany Elia Kazan to Hollywood to be his assistant on *A Tree Grows in Brooklyn.*

After adapting *Sorry, Wrong Number* for television in 1946, Ray began work on his first film under John Houseman's aegis at RKO, adaptating Edward Anderson's 1937 novel *Thieves Like Us*; Farley Granger and Cathy O'Donnell played the young couple whose naïve flirtation with crime spells their doom. It was completed in 1948 and given a test release as *The Twisted Road*, but sat on the shelf for over a year before appearing nationally as *They Live by Night* late in 1949. A seminal noir, it ranks as one of Hollywood's most impressive directorial debuts. *A Woman's Secret* (1949) was a Herman J. Mankiewicz project that became a serviceable vehicle for Ray's new wife, Gloria Grahame, whose role as the shooting victim of Maureen O'Hara is explained in a series of elaborate flashbacks. Released before *They Live by Night*, the film was a huge money loser for the studio.

Ray's next two films were made for Humphrey Bogart's Sanatana production company. *Knock on Any Door* (1949), from Willard Motley's bestselling novel about juvenile delinquency, starred Bogart as a socially conscious attorney who defends his murderous punk of a client (John Derek) on the grounds that his slum background never gave him a fair shot. Earnest and stilted, the film bore none of Ray's stylistic flourishes and today is a chore to watch. But *In a Lonely Place* (1950) was a triumph, a penetrating study of a screenwriter's compulsively self-destructive behavior; it may well contain Bogart's finest performance. Very loosely based on Dorothy Hughes's novel about a psychopath who isn't aware that he has committed a murder, *Place* also featured Gloria Grahame as the starlet whose love Bogart tragically rejects. The subcurrent of paranoia verging on mental illness that makes Bogart so convincing echoed the chronic depression with which Ray himself had to wrestle throughout his life.

*Born to Be Bad* (1950) was Ray's silliest film; Joan Fontaine was simply absurd as a conniving civet whose transparent machinations make worldly Robert Ryan and Zachary Scott jump through hoops. *Flying Leathernecks* (1951) was typical World War II grist, starring John Wayne as a hard-as-nails major and Robert Ryan a bleeding-heart officer who wants him to lighten up on the recruits; their dispute is amicably resolved when Ryan admits he was dead wrong. Ryan was permitted to be far more interesting in the unsettling *On Dangerous Ground* (1951) as a sadistic, frustrated cop on the verge of a nervous breakdown who brutalizes one suspect too many. When his superiors ship him upstate on a murder investigation, he falls for blind girl Ida Lupino, whose love ultimately saves Ryan from himself.

(Ironically, Lupino had to save Ray as well—he was too ill to work for extended periods, and she pinch-hit for him by directing several scenes.)

After reshooting parts of Joseph von Sternberg's *Macao*, with which Howard Hughes was typically tinkering, Ray directed *The Lusty Men* (1952), a rodeo yarn built around good old-fashioned bronco-busting and adultery, not necessarily in that order. Robert Mitchum was at his best as the seen-it-all, done-it-twice ex-champ who teaches his skills to eager novice Arthur Kennedy while eyeing Kennedy's underappreciated wife, Susan Hayward, who eyes him back. It ended with Mitchum making a noble but rather preposterous sacrifice, an unconvincing climax that may have been shot by Robert Parrish, filling in for the depressed Ray, whose marriage to Grahame now was dissolving. Their divorce—precipitated by Ray's finding Grahame in bed with his teenage son Tony (whom she married several years later)—coincided with his split from RKO.

Ray went to humble Republic Pictures for his next project, the perverse Freudian Western *Johnny Guitar* (1954), which contained enough repressed sexual pathology to keep Krafft-Ebing occupied for months. Joan Crawford as a brassy saloon owner was the titular star, but it was Sterling Hayden as the guitar-wielding Johnny and, most especially, Mercedes McCambridge as a bloodthirsty virago with

SUSPENSE MOUNTS STEADILY
with every second and every word.
the Bogart picture with the surprise finish!
Humphrey BOGART
In A Lonely Place
with GLORIA GRAHAME
FRANK LOVEJOY · CARL BENTON REID · ART SMITH · JEFF DONNELL · MARTHA STEWART
Screen Play by Andrew Solt · A SANTANA PRODUCTION
Produced by ROBERT LORD · Directed by NICHOLAS RAY · A COLUMBIA PICTURE

her own peculiar agenda who stole the picture. The 1955 *Run for Cover* was more mundane; James Cagney is a new sheriff manipulated into robbing a train by young pard John Derek—decidedly one of Ray's minor efforts.

*Rebel Without a Cause* (1955), however, was a watershed, the *Potemkin* of the Juvenile Delinquent film. A CinemaScope drama of youthful alienation that rendered teen rituals like "chicken" racing and switchblade duels with a gravity hitherto reserved for biblical epics, the film was fueled by James Dean's incandescent performance as an anguished, screwed-up kid whose basic goodness is invisible to adult society. Natalie Wood and Sal Mineo also gave indelible performances, but it was Dean's Method-saturated turn—one of the screen performances most emblematic of the Fifties—that transformed the film into something mythic. If *Rebel* was Ray's masterpiece, *Hot Blood* (1956) was nothing but a preposterous tale about gypsy life—set in Los Angeles, of all places—with Jane Russell and Cornel Wilde as a couple who had no say in their betrothal arrangement but who conveniently fall in love anyway.

Ray fared much better with the 1956 *Bigger than Life*, starring James Mason as a teacher (and part-time cabbie) who becomes addicted to cortisone and finds himself growing increasingly violent toward

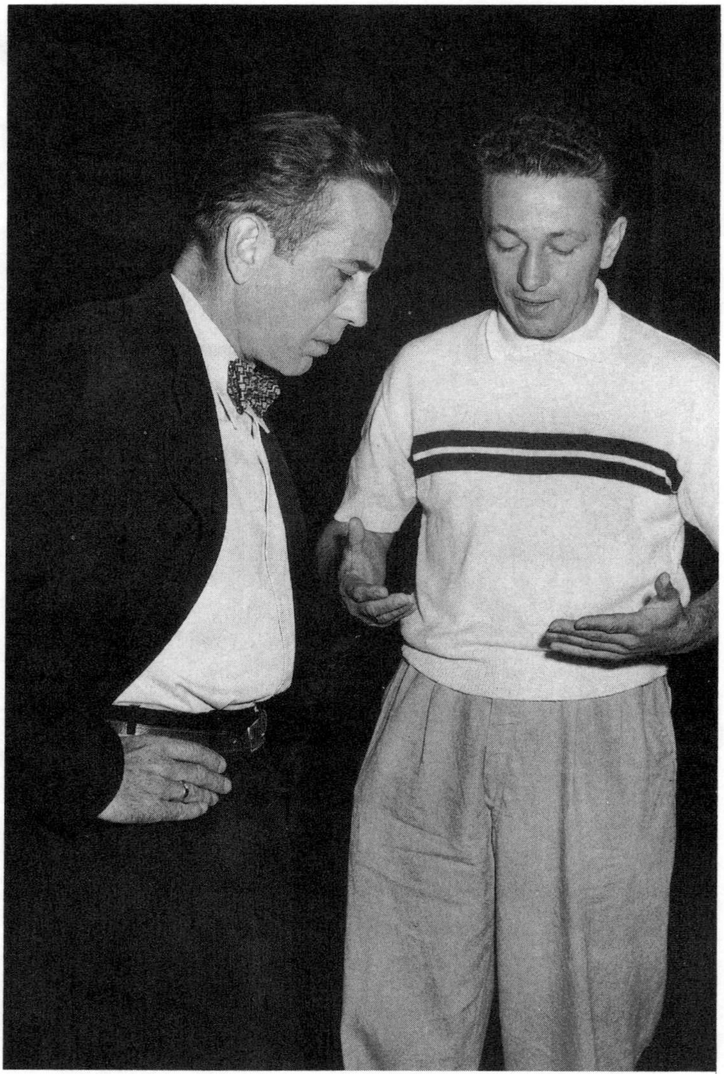

► *Bogie concentrates on Ray's advice during the filming of* Knock on Any Door

his co-workers and family. A harrowing indictment of the banal hell of suburban existence, it uses CinemaScope brilliantly to show Mason's tortured state of mind, making it one of the Fifties' most powerful—and unusual—films. Not so *The True Story of Jesse James* (1957), a pallid retelling of the legend, with Robert Wagner and Jeffrey Hunter proving no threat to the memory of the 1939 version's James brothers, Tyrone Power and Henry Fonda.

*Bitter Victory* (1957) was more ambitious, a French-English production that starred Curt Jurgens, Richard Burton, and Ruth Roman against a World War II backdrop. *Wind Across the Everglades* (1958) was an offbeat collaboration with writer-producer Budd Schulberg that featured Christopher Plummer as a game warden in the early 1900s whose efforts to save the Everglades' bird life from poachers are compromised by his love of the bottle and loose women. *Party Girl* (1958) was a return to the crime genre, with Cyd Charisse as a 1920s Chicago showgirl who questions her ties to syndicate boss Lee J. Cobb when mob lawyer Robert Taylor wants her to make a break with him. Charisse was fine in her dance numbers but had trouble keeping up with Taylor and the flamboyant Cobb in the dramatic scenes; still, it's a flavorful picture that has come to be appreciated after failing initially.

*The Savage Innocents* (1960) was a bold departure for Ray, an international production shot in Greenland, Canada, and (for studio shots) England that chronicled the struggles of an Eskimo (Anthony Quinn) to keep his family alive under the most challenging conditions imaginable. Its documentary approach and leisurely pace kept it from appealing to a wide audience, but it was an audacious and, on its own terms, successful enterprise. *King of Kings* (1961) was Ray's 168-minute entry in the biblical sweepstakes, and in many ways it was the best of the lot. Jeffrey Hunter made a surprisingly effective Christ and Robert Ryan a great John the Baptist, and the sweep of CinemaScope combined nicely with Orson Welles's narration to impart a sense of grandeur and lyric tragedy.

*55 Days at Peking* (1963) was also given the full epic treatment, with Charlton Heston, Ava Gardner, and David Niven fighting against the tide of the Boxer Rebellion. Ray walked off the set before filming was completed (Andrew Marton finished the picture) and kept right on walking until he landed in Paris, where he resided for the rest of the decade. He never directed another film, although he worked on one with his students at S.U.N.Y. in the Seventies. Just before his death Ray made himself available to Wim Wenders for *Lightning over Water* (1979), a moving record of his last months, after taking a small part as the general in Milos Forman's *Hair*. Earlier he had acted alongside Sam Fuller in Wenders's *The American Friend* (1977), a fine adaptation of Patricia Highsmith's diabolical thriller *Ripley's Game*; in it he played a master forger. If it was a joke, it was a good one. As Ray once observed, "If it's all in the script, why make the picture?" That attitude explains why so many of his films became something special.

## ● MICHAEL RITCHIE (1938– )

For a time in the Seventies, Michael Ritchie was a rising director with a nice satiric touch and a number of hits under his belt. His decline since 1980 has been just this side of alarming. Born in Waukesha, Wisconsin, he began directing plays while at Harvard, including the first production of the eventual Broadway hit by Arthur Kopit, *Oh Dad, Poor Dad, Mama's Hung You in the Closet and I'm Feelin' So Sad* in 1959. He then was hired to work on the television series *Omnibus*, and later directed installments of *Profiles of Courage, The Man from U.N.C.L.E.*, and *Dr. Kildare*, as well as the pilot film for *The Outsider*. Ritchie's impressive first feature was *Downhill Racer* (1969), with Robert Redford in fine form as the arrogant, talented star of an Olympic ski team coached by Gene Hackman.

*Prime Cut* (1972) was an excellent neo-noir, much in the fashion of John Boorman's 1967 *Point Blank*, with which it shares Lee Marvin, again as a professional killer up against the mob. Here Gene Hackman runs a booming white-slave trade in Kansas, and Sissy Spacek (in her film debut) is one of the girls Marvin rescues. Far less lurid was *The Candidate* (1972), a documentary-flavored satire on situation ethics in politics. Robert Redford stars as an incorruptible candidate for the Senate who turns out to be as seduced by power as his venial opponents, and the screenplay by Jeremy Larner won an Oscar. *Smile* (1975) was a much broader and in many ways more interesting satire (set in Santa Rosa) on another facet of American life, the teenage beauty pageant. The targets Ritchie nails dead center include Bruce Dern's smarmy pageant judge, Barbara Feldon's megalomaniacal director, and (especially) Michael Kidd's over-the-hill choreographer; Joan Prather, Colleen Camp, and Annette O'Toole stand out among the contestants, whom Ritchie salted with actual beauty pageant aspirants. But as good as it was, the film didn't draw an audience.

Ritchie got his box-office smash with his next picture, however. *The Bad News Bears* (1976) was a salty comedy about a hapless juvenile baseball team that learns how to overcome its limitations, thanks to beer-swigging coach Walter Matthau and foul-mouthed star pitcher Tatum O'Neal. The film also featured a nice villainous turn by Vic Morrow, and went on to inspire two (inferior) sequels and a television series. A semi-hit, *Semi-Tough* (1977) was a genial but flabby adaptation of Dan Jenkins's hilarious novel about the world of pro football. Burt Reynolds and Kris Kristofferson were fine as the Miami Bulls teammates who both love rich Jill Clayburgh, and the supporting cast was strong, but the meandering screenplay spent too much of the film satirizing the est movement and not enough skewering pro football, squandering most of Jenkins's prime material. *An Almost Perfect Affair* (1979), set against the madness of the Cannes Film Festival, was a "small" romance, with Keith Carradine as a young director who gets in over his head with Monica Vitti, the wife of a high-powered Italian producer.

Every director endures a disaster of major proportions sooner or later, and for Ritchie it was *The Island* (1980), a horrible version of Peter Benchley's crummy but bestselling thriller (adapted by Benchley) starring Michael Caine and David Warner. At least *Divine Madness!* (1980) did what it was supposed to, which was present a Bette Midler concert in all its loony glory—although next to similar efforts by Martin Scorsese (The Band) and Jonathan Demme (The Talking Heads), it seems at best adequate. *The Survivors* (1983) was yet another loser, with unemployed Robin Williams and Walter Matthau preparing for an attack by a criminal (Jerry Reed) they have seen commit a robbery. It may just be the confused script, but when Ritchie aims for satire here, his scattershot approach nails only squirrels.

*Fletch* (1985) was even worse, because it was adapted from a suspenseful detective novel (by Gregory McDonald) that generated high expectations. But what we get is a lame Chevy Chase vehicle, with the book's clever plot buried under a virtual compost heap of dumb jokes (thank adapter Andrew Bergman) and Chevy's inane disguises. *Wildcats* (1986) was better, an unsurprising but efficient comedy that has Goldie Hawn coaching a gang of football players (they aren't exactly a team) at an inner-city high school, with Wesley Snipes, L. L. Cool J., and Woody Harrelson just part of the lively supporting cast. But the moronic 1986 *The Golden Child* returned Ritchie to purgatory; Eddie Murray is at his most insufferable as he rescues magical child J. L. Reate from kidnappers. Wretched the film may have been, but Murray's fans helped it gross $40 million.

*The Couch Trip* (1988) relied on the promising cast of Walter Matthau, Charles Grodin, and the husband-wife team of Dan Aykroyd and Donna Dixon to float the comic premise about an escaped mental patient (Aykroyd) who sets up shop as a shrink in Beverly Hills and soon has his own radio talk show, while *Fletch Lives* (1989) sent Chevy Chase to Louisiana, where he proceeded to make an even bigger ass of himself than in the 1985 original. But *Diggstown* (1992) was a surprise, a modest but clever boxing-sting yarn in which James Woods plays an ex-con con man who teams up with old pal Lou Gossett to fleece Georgia millionaire Bruce Dern. It has a total of two surprises, but the gears mesh smoothly and it's a pleasure to watch an actual plot unfold properly; unfortunately, it landed at the box office with a resounding thud.

Ritchie fared better with the well-received black comedy *The Positively True Adventures of the Alleged Texas Cheerleader-Murdering Mom*, made for HBO in 1993. Holly Hunter is as funny as she's ever been as a homicidally overprotective mother, and Beau Bridges and Swoosie Kurtz also submit nifty performances. But *Cops and Robbersons* (1994) was as deft as a kick to the groin, and just as funny—in short, another Chevy Chase cowpie. The baseball comedy *The Scout* (1994) failed to capitalize fully on Albert Brooks's gift for comic self-delusion. Not a home run, then, but a solid single up the middle. Ritchie's book *Please Stand By: A Prehistory of Television* was published to good reviews that year, and he had a co-writing credit on the sleeper hit of 1994, *Cool Runnings.*

## ● MARTIN RITT (1920–1990)

Martin Ritt began his career as a neo-realist with a social conscience, and while his visual technique changed from film to film, his Marxist underpinnings make themselves felt in much of his best work. Born in New York City, Ritt attended DeWitt Clinton High School before attending St. John's University, where he met Elia Kazan. In 1937 Ritt joined the Group Theater, where over the next five years he acted in a number of productions, including *Golden Boy*. He joined the Air Force in 1942, taking time out to act in both the stage and the film versions of the play *Winged Victory*. After the war he began directing Off-Broadway productions, and soon moved into television, working as both a director and an actor.

But the bottom fell out for Ritt in 1951, when Laurence Johnson, a Syracuse, New York, grocer reported him for donating money to Communist China. Ritt was blacklisted from television and spent the next five years directing theater (including the acclaimed *A View from the Bridge*) and teaching at the Actors' Studio. He finally was able to break into films in 1957, when he directed *Edge of the City*, a superbly gritty adaptation of Robert Alan Arthur's *Playhouse 90* drama *A Man Is Ten Feet Tall*. The film featured top-notch performances by Sidney Poitier (who had also acted in the TV version), John Cassavetes, and Jack Warden. *No Down Payment* (1957) was a surprising follow-up, a glossy soap opera set in the suburbs that must have had Ritt gritting his teeth as he filmed it, while *The Long Hot Summer* (1958) was a labored adaptation of Faulkner's novel *The Hamlet*, with Ritt's former pupil Paul Newman and Joanne Woodward teaming onscreen for the first time.

Ritt was even less fortunate with *The Sound and the Fury* (1959), a doomed attempt to film the unfilmable—and the miscasting of Yul Brynner, Joanne Woodward, and Stuart Whitman didn't help. *The Black Orchid* (1960) had a simpler tale to tell, but it signified nothing in the end, despite an appealing turn by Sophia Loren. She was needed in, but absent from, *Five Branded Women* (1960), a farfetched World War II yarn that somehow required the cooperation of three nations (Yugoslavia, Italy, and the United States) to be made. Far better was *Paris Blues* (1961), an interesting story about expatriate jazzmen Paul Newman and Sidney Poitier wooing tourists Joanne Woodward and Diahann Carroll, marinated in good jazz via Duke Ellington and Louis Armstrong. *Hemingway's Adventures of a Young Man* (1962) probably seemed like a good way to avoid the Faulkner jinx, but Ritt was behind the eight ball as soon as Richard Beymer was installed as the lead. The film is an hour too long, but it probably wouldn't have worked at any length.

Based on that disaster, the prospects for *Hud* (1963), an adaptation of Larry McMurtry's trim novel *Horseman, Pass By*, might not have seemed especially promising. But it turned out to be the apex of Ritt's career, with a marvelously nasty performance by Paul Newman and Oscar-winning turns by Melvyn Douglas and Patricia Neal. Ritt was nominated for an Academy Award, and the indelible cinematography by James Wong Howe won an Oscar. *The Outrage* (1964) was a misguided attempt to transform *Rashomon* into a Western; it was the fourth consecutive appearance by Newman in a Ritt film, but both of them probably regretted this one. Ritt bounced back, however, with *The Spy Who Came in from the Cold* (1965), a grim but effective transposition of the popular John le Carré novel with Richard Burton in one of the best performances of his career as the burned-out agent whose last assignment proves fatal; the rest of the international cast (Claire Bloom, Oskar Werner, Cyril Cusack) was also superb.

With *Hombre* (1967), Ritt and Paul Newman returned to the old West via an Elmore Leonard story, with Richard Boone memorable (per usual) as the villain. *The Brotherhood* (1968), starring Kirk Douglas and Susan Strasberg, preceded *The Godfather* by several years and in some ways resembles its more celebrated kin. *The Molly Maguires* (1970) had Sean Connery and labor disputes set in nineteenth-century Pennsylvania coal mines, but a confusing script squandered its potential. Ritt's unsurprising version of *The Great White Hope* (1970), adapted from the Broadway play about the remarkable life of boxing great Jack Johnson, was able to use the original cast stars James Earl Jones and Jane Alexander, who at times seemed still to be playing to the back row—but both were nominated for Academy Awards, so why quibble?

The noisy racial theme of *The Great White Hope* was turned on its ear in the elegant, elegaic *Sounder* (1972), one of the most fondly recalled films of the Seventies. Ritt elicits lovely performances from Cicely Tyson and Paul Winfield, who are well supported by John Alonzo's evocative photography and a great Taj Mahal score that evokes the feel of 1930s rural Louisiana. *Sounder* was Oscar-nominated as best picture, and Tyson, Winfield, and the screenplay also received nominations. *Pete 'n' Tillie* (1972), based on a Peter De Vries novel, was an uneasy blend of comedy and tragedy, but it at least offered a nifty ham-on-wry turn by Walter Matthau. *Conrack* (1974) was more satisfying; based on a memoir by Pat Conroy, it starred Jon Voight as an idealistic teacher at a poor black school off the Carolina coast.

Ritt next had a rare opportunity for payback, although *The Front* (1976) couldn't possibly do as much damage to blacklisters as they had done to Ritt—and much of the picture's cast—back in 1951. Woody Allen is terrific as a part-time bookie hired by a group of blacklisted television writers to affix his name to their work so it can be sold, Zero Mostel gives a harrowing performance as a comic who can't get work, and Walter Bernstein's screenplay was nominated for an Academy Award. But *Casey's Shadow* (1978) was an innocuous showcase for Walter Matthau, who plays a horse trainer whose wife has left him alone with their three sons.

Then came *Norma Rae* (1979), one of Ritt's most popular pictures. A classic "feel-good" movie, its centerpiece was Sally Field's role as real-life textile worker Crystal Lee Sutton, who led the fight to unionize a North Carolina cotton mill in 1973. Jane Fonda had turned the part down, thus enabling Fields to earn an Academy Award as best actress. Ron Liebman and Beau Bridges provided good support, and the film was Oscar-nominated for best picture, as were the screenplay and the winning song "It Goes Like It Goes." Field and Ritt teamed again on *Back Roads* (1981), but the result was immediately forgettable, while *Cross Creek* (1983) was a charming (if fanciful) biopic about author Marjorie Kinnan Rawlings (Mary Steenburgen), with Oscar-nominated performances by Rip Torn and Alfre Woodard. Ritt and Field tried again with *Murphy's Romance* (1985), an earnest effort to produce an adult romance; it earned James Garner his first Academy Award nomination. (No wonder actors loved to appear in Ritt's pictures—half of them ended up in line for an Oscar.)

But *Nuts* (1987) was deeply problematic, a small play (by Tom Topor) overpowered by Barbra Streisand's acting, producing, scoring, and (probably) ticket-taking. Much quieter, but in the end no more successful, was *Stanley & Iris* (1990), a sincere but stilted love story about blue-collar recluse Robert De Niro, whose illiteracy is conquered by grieving widow Jane Fonda. An honorable failure, but not the film one might have wished as the capstone to Ritt's career. Alas, he died shortly after its completion.

## ● MARK ROBSON (1913–1978)

One of the many Hollywood directors whose early career, fashioned under the restrictions and support of the studio system, outshone his lengthier second act, Montreal-born Mark Robson attended U.C.L.A. before entering the film industry in 1932 as a property boy at Fox and moving over to RKO in 1935 to become a cutter. It took him five years to rise up the ladder, but he finally became an editor in 1941, coediting (with Robert Wise) Orson Welles's first two films, *Citizen Kane* and *The Magnificent Ambersons* (although he worked on them without a credit). His name finally appeared as sole editor on the atmospheric *Journey into Fear*, another Welles RKO project (nominally directed by Norman Foster).

With Welles having worn out his welcome at RKO, Robson had to find a new unit, and was assigned along with Wise to Val Lewton's low-budget production company. Immediately Robson was named editor on Jacques Tourneur's *Cat People*, a phenomenally successful "B" horror picture. Robson was rewarded by being assigned to direct Lewton's next production, *The Seventh Victim* (1943), an eerie tale of witchcraft set in Greenwich Village. Robson then directed Lewton's *The Ghost Ship* (1943), with Richard Dix, which had its creepy moments. Lewton's next task for Robson was quite a change of pace: *Youth Runs Wild* (1944), a teenagers-running-amok problem-pic torn right from the headlines. The ponderous *Isle of the Dead* (1945) and *Bedlam* (1946), about an eighteenth-century insane asylum desperately in need of reform, both starred Boris Karloff; these were two of his best Forties vehicles.

Robson didn't direct again until 1949, when he directed two pictures for Stanley Kramer's newly formed Screen Plays Inc. *Champion* had Kirk Douglas as a cruel boxer who destroys everyone in his path; still considered a classic by many, Douglas's sneering, Oscar-nominated performance now seems overwrought (Arthur Kennedy was also nominated, as was Carl Foreman's screenplay). Next came Robson's adaptation of Arthur Laurents's play *Home of the Brave*, with James Edwards as a black soldier whose fellow GIs ostracize and abuse him. Its unforgiving (if strident) exploration of racism was daring for its time and garnered critical hosannas. He returned to RKO for the more modest *Roughshod* (1949), an excellent Gloria Grahame Western that remains one of her best showcases, and the sentimental romance *My Foolish Heart* (also 1949)—the only film ever made from a work by J. D. Salinger (his story "Uncle Wiggily in Connecticut"). It was quite a year for Robson, one that would have looked good on the résumé of any Hollywood director.

*Edge of Doom* (1950) was his first outright failure, a melodramatic study of Farley Granger's religious angst. Granger was better in the small-town drama *I Want You* (1951), a Korean War *Since You Went Away* starring Dana Andrews and Dorothy McGuire, while *Bright Victory* (also 1951) offered an Oscar-nominated performance by Arthur Kennedy as a blinded soldier who has to adjust to civilian life. But *Return to Paradise* (1953) had Gary Cooper sleepwalking his way through a James Michener story, and *Hell Below Zero* (1954) found Alan Ladd aboard a whaling vessel in search of revenge. The 1954 *Phffft!* was a rare comedy outing for Robson; Jack Lemmon and Judy Holliday are in fine form as a couple that begin to rue their recent divorce, and Kim Novak and Jack Carson lend support to this George Axelrod farce. *The Bridges at Toko-Ri* (1954), from the James Michener novel, was a popular, occasionally exciting Korean War tale starring William Holden as a Navy bomber pilot recalled to active duty, to the dismay of wife Grace Kelly. *A Prize of Gold* (1955) had Army sergeant Richard Widmark stealing a shipment of gold from a Berlin airlift to help repatriate a group of war orphans.

*Trial* (1955) was a socially conscious courtroom drama; Glenn Ford defends Katy Jurado's son from a murder charge that has Red-baiting overtones. The caustic *The Harder They Fall* (1956) was Robson's excellent version of Budd Schulberg's boxing exposé; Humphrey Bogart (in his final film) is superb as the cynical sportswriter who sells out to shady promoter Rod Steiger to make a killing with talentless behemoth Mike Lane, then discovers his conscience at the last moment. But *The Little Hut* (1957) was coy titillation, with Ava Gardner, David Niven, and Stewart Granger stranded on a desert isle. *Peyton Place*, the *Gone with the Wind* of small-town soap operas, was probably the most eagerly awaited film of 1957. Well adapted by John Michael Hayes from the multimillion seller by Grace Metalious, it was filmed on location in Camden, Maine, and did not disappoint the book's legions of fans. Its nine Oscar nominations (none of which came in a winner) went to Robson, the film, Lana Turner, Arthur Kennedy, Russ Tamblyn, Hope Lange, Diane Varsi, the screenplay, and the cinematography.

*Inn of the Sixth Happiness* (1958), with Ingrid Bergman as an English missionary leading a group of children out of China just before World War II, was a fact-based inspirational adventure; it was perilously long, but Robson found himself nominated again for best direction. But *From the Terrace* (1960), with Paul Newman and Joanne Woodward, was glossy junk (via John O'Hara) that committed the cardinal sin of being boring, except for Myrna Loy's turn as a bitter drunk. *Lisa* (1962) was a reasonably effective chase picture shot on location in Europe, while *Nine Hours to Rama* (1963) was an ambitious but portentous speculation about the events leading up to Gandhi's assassination. *The Prize* (1963), with Paul Newman, Elke Sommer, and Edward G. Robinson, managed to deliver the meat of Irving Wallace's trashy bestseller about the Nobel Prize ceremonies without pretension, and *Von Ryan's Express* (1965) was one of the better Frank Sinatra vehicles, a well-paced World War II adventure about an escape from a POW camp. *Lost Command* (1966) was a big, exciting tale of the French-Algerian war in North Africa, starring Anthony Quinn, George Segal, and Claudia Cardinale.

Then came *Valley of the Dolls* (1967). A runaway disaster of the sort that only happens once every ten years or so, *Dolls* today is relished as camp watershed, with wonderfully over-the-top performances by Patty Duke, Barbara Parkins, Sharon Tate, Susan Hayward, and Joey Bishop. Whether that was Robson's intent is another matter—although Jacqueline Susann's novel wasn't exactly *Middlemarch* to begin with. *Daddy's Gone a-Hunting* (1969), a small and rather nasty suspenser, hardly mattered, while *Happy Birthday, Wanda June* (1971) was a clever rendition of Kurt Vonnegut's black comedy, with Rod Steiger and William Hickey in fine fettle. *Limbo* (1972), a Vietnam drama with Kate Jackson, was at least well intended, but the box-office smash *Earthquake* (1974) was profoundly stupid even for a disaster picture. Still, the special effects won an Oscar, and it boasted an all-star cast—Ava Gardner, Charlton Heston, and the inevitable George Kennedy. Robson's final film, *Avalanche Express* (1979), was another hoot, a Cold War yarn with an international cast that blended as smoothly as Jell-O and broken glass (Joe Namath and Maximilian Schell?!). But Robson's late disasters need not eradicate the very decent work he did in so many genres during the Forties and Fifties.

## ● HERBERT ROSS (1927– )

A former choreographer and Broadway director, Herbert Ross has been making glossy, highly professional, but somewhat empty movies for twenty-five years. Few of his films are essential, but many of them have been popular, and a few can even be considered good.

Born in New York City, Ross first worked in the theater as an actor and a dancer. In 1954 he enjoyed his first burst of success, directing *House of Flowers* on Broadway and choreographing Otto Preminger's film *Carmen Jones*. His best-known Broadway work includes *Finian's Rainbow* (1960) and *I Can Get It for You Wholesale* (1962), while his choreography has been seen in such films as *Doctor Dolittle* (1967) and *Funny Girl* (1968), among others. Ross directed his first movie in 1969, the profoundly awful musical version of *Goodbye, Mr. Chips*: two and a half hours of tedium punctuated by lousy songs, with an overmatched Petula Clark opposite Peter O'Toole (whose Chips actually wasn't bad).

But Ross got something going in his adaptation of the Broadway play *The Owl and the Pussycat* (1970). Barbra Streisand and George Segal were delightful in this frenetic comedy about a prostitute who wants to be tutored by an uptight egghead, with the two finally falling in love. *T. R. Baskin* (1971) was a painless Finding Yourself drama with some light touches, starring Candice Bergen, while *Play It Again, Sam* (1972) was an excellent adaptation of Woody Allen's play about a schlub who is coached in his love life by the ghost of Humphrey Bogart (Jerry Lacy). This was Woody's first film with Diane Keaton, and they're both great, while hilarious turns were also submitted by Susan Anspach and Tony Roberts. *The Last of Sheila* (1973) didn't do much at the box office, but this intricate murder mystery has a cult following and a game cast that includes James Coburn, Raquel Welch, James Mason, and Dyan Cannon.

Ross had worked on the choreography for William Wyler's *Funny Girl*, so it made sense to assign him to direct its sequel, *Funny Lady* (1975). Although it wasn't quite up to the first film (which itself was no masterpiece), it managed to avoid disaster, even if James Caan made a most unlikely Billy Rose. *The Sunshine Boys* (1975), with the benefit of Neil Simon's Broadway-honed script, was much better, a prime comic vehicle for George Burns and Walter Matthau as a pair of ancient vaudevillians coming out of retirement to make a television special. Burns won a best supporting actor Oscar, and Matthau received a best actor nomination.

*The Seven Percent Solution* (1976) was a near-perfect adaptation of Nicholas Meyer's bestselling Sherlock Holmes pastiche. Nicol Williamson made a flamboyant Holmes, Robert Duvall a pleasingly dim Watson, Alan Arkin a charismatic Sigmund Freud, and Laurence Olivier a worthy Moriarty. Ross's next film was one of his most successful, and it was also his most personal. *The Turning Point* (1977), from a story by Arthur Laurents (who co-produced with Ross), was about two former prima ballerinas whose lives diverged many years before. Shirley MacLaine is fine as the housewife whose daughter (Leslie Browne) is ready for her debut, and Anne Bancroft is convincing as the imperious former star who may deign to become her teacher. Mikhail Baryshnikov is also on hand as Browne's dance partner and, eventually, lover. Highly praised when released, the film ladled on suds rather heavily; nonetheless, it was nominated for ten Academy Awards (winning none). The four principal actors each received nominations, as did the film, Laurents's screenplay, and Ross. (Because Ross was formerly the resident choreographer at the American Ballet Theatre and was married to ballet dancer Nora Kaye, such recognition was no doubt doubly gratifying.)

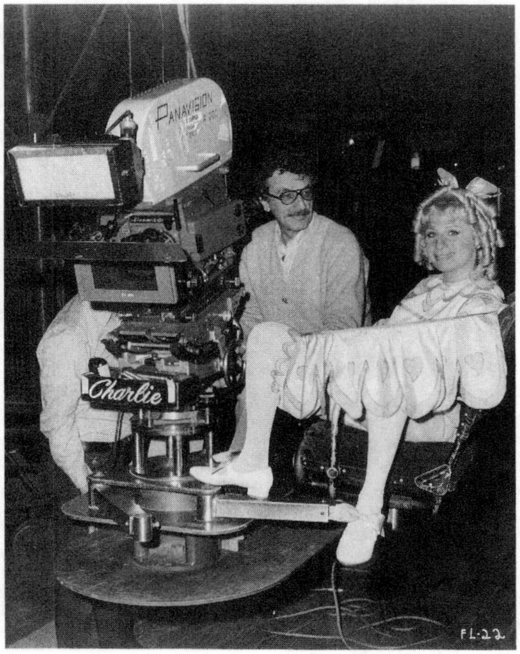


▲ *On the set of* Funny Lady *with Barbra Streisand in 1975*

*The Goodbye Girl* (1977) was an even bigger commercial success, a slick adaptation of Neil Simon's play, with Richard Dreyfuss and Marsha Mason meeting cute as unwilling roommates in a New York City apartment. Both were nominated for Oscars, as was scene-stealer Quinn Cummings and the picture itself. Thus, Ross had a total of seven actors and two films to root for in the 1977 Academy Awards, a quandary few directors ever have been so fortunate as to find themselves in. (Dreyfuss was the lone winner of the group, for a performance some found insufferable.) *California Suite* (1978) was middling Neil Simon, although some of its four skits were much weaker than others; Maggie Smith, as an actress about to lose in the Academy Award competition, won a real-life Oscar. *Nijinsky* (1980) tried to tap into the success of *The Turning Point*, but this biopic about the legendary ballet dancer (George De La Pena) and his impresario lover (Alan Bates) did not convince—surprising for one with Ross's background.

*Pennies from Heaven* (1981) was an ambitious adaptation of Dennis Potter's acclaimed BBC series, with Steve Martin daringly cast as the desperately unhappy sheet-music salesman whose fantasies—envisioned as glorious musical numbers in the style of the Astaire-Rogers pictures—briefly relieve him of the Depression's grim realities. Probably no one short of Astaire at his peak could have carried this off (although Bob Hoskins did just fine in the BBC version). Still, the production numbers are impressive, and there's something compelling about the film's morbid tone. But *I Ought to Be in Pictures* (1982), with Walter Matthau and Dinah Manoff, and *Max Dugan Returns* (1983), with Jason Robards and Marsha Mason starring as father and daughter, were second-rate Neil Simon.

Ross's biggest box-office hit was *Footloose* (1984), a teen musical that would have benefited from more dancing—what there is is great—and less emoting. Still, it's not as dumb as *Flashdance* and Kevin Bacon is quite good as the toe-tapping hero. But *Protocol* (1984) was a lame Goldie Hawn comedy, and *The Secret of My Success* (1987) a resistible vehicle for Michael J. Fox. The little-seen *Dancers* (also 1987) was an unfortunate reteaming of Leslie Browne and Baryshnikov, hackneyed beyond belief. *Steel Magnolias* (1989), on the other hand, was a valid expansion (by Robert Harling) of the play with a terrific cast, and *My Blue Heaven* (1990) a funny (if vastly unpopular) Steve Martin showcase, written by Nora Ephron.

In 1991 Ross directed *True Colors*, a middling drama starring John Cusack and James Spader as former law-school pals whose careers diverge. That had the advantage over *Undercover Blues* (1993), a hopeless spy farce with secret agents Kathleen Turner and Dennis Quaid trying to keep their baby safe while battling the bad guys. (Why do so many of these lame projects end up in Ross's lap?) *Boys on the Side* (1995) was a decent stab at forging a female buddy picture, with Whoopie Goldberg, Drew Barrymore, and Mary-Louise Parker; a little gummy in the center, it garnered decent reviews and attracted an audience, accomplishments few of Ross's recent pictures could claim. After Nora Kaye's death in 1987, Ross married Lee Radziwill.

## ● ROBERT ROSSEN (1908-1966)

Another talented filmmaker whose career was interrupted—and damaged—by the blacklist, New York–born Robert Rossen didn't direct his first film until 1947. Before breaking into Hollywood as a screenwriter in 1936, he had directed and stage-managed in the theater for several years. But Rossen wasted little time once he set up shop at Warner Bros., writing (or co-writing) some of their very best films of the Thirties, including *Marked Woman*, *They Won't Forget*, *Dust Be My Destiny*, and *The Roaring Twenties*. (It was during this period that he became a member of the Communist Party.) In the Forties he worked on *The Sea Wolf*, *Out of the Fog*, and *Edge of Darkness* at Warners, but topped those after he left the studio to script the World War II classic *A Walk in the Sun* and *The Strange Love of Martha Ivers*; he also contributed (uncredited) to the screenplay of John Huston's *The Treasure of the Sierra Madre*.

His first two directorial efforts were the competent Dick Powell noir *Johnny O'Clock*, which he also wrote, and the boxing classic *Body and Soul* (both 1947); arguably John Garfield's finest performance, it earned Garfield his only Oscar nomination. James Wong Howe's trailblazing cinematography and a potent script by Abraham Polonsky provided Rossen with unusually strong support. Rossen ascended to the top rank of Hollywood directors with *All the King's Men* (1949), which he produced himself and also scripted, adapting the Pulitzer Prize–winning novel by Robert Penn Warren. It was an enormous critical and commercial success, winning Academy Awards for best picture, best actor (Broderick Crawford), and best supporting actress (Mercedes McCambridge); Rossen was nominated for best direction and best screenplay (losing on both counts to Joseph Mankiewicz).

*The Brave Bulls* (1951) was Rossen's peculiar choice to follow such a triumph. Shot in Mexico, its story about a matador had limited commercial appeal, particularly with the no-star cast Rossen (who also produced) assembled. But he had little time to concern himself with that film's prospects, as he was called before the 1951 session of HUAC after his name had been mentioned by others who testified that he had been a member of the Party. (He had broken with it in 1945.) Rossen took the Fifth, and of course was promptly blacklisted. He twisted in the wind for two years, then contacted HUAC and, in a special closed session, recanted and named names.

Rossen was free to work again, but he could not bear to remain in Hollywood. He made *Mambo* (1954) in Venice with Shelley Winters, Vittorio Gassman, and Silvana Mangano. *Alexander the Great* (1956), with a blond Richard Burton, was a handsomely mounted account of the legendary Greek's remarkable conquests, but *Island in the Sun* (1957) was the first time in many years that Rossen neither produced nor scripted one of his own films, and it suffered from his absence. Too bad, because the cast—Dorothy Dandridge, Joan Collins, James Mason, Harry Belafonte—was intriguing. The 1959 *They Came to Cordura* set Gary Cooper and Rita Hayworth during the days of Pancho Villa in Mexico; not a bad film, but its failure at the box office haunted Rossen for years.

Based on his post-blacklisting work, it did not appear that Rossen would ever regain his former stature. But he did in 1961, the year *The Hustler* was released. Based on Walter Tevis's superb novel, the film was produced and co-written (with Sidney Carroll) by Rossen, and it earned him his first Academy Award nomination for directing since 1949. (He didn't win, but he was cited by the New York Film Critics Circle.) Easily one of the year's best films, it holds up today as well as ever, and contains what may be the best work of Paul Newman's career (superior even to his Oscar-winning performance in Scorsese's 1986 sequel, *The Color of Money*).

The success of *The Hustler* might have signaled the start of a whole new career for Rossen, one in which he could again work regularly in Hollywood. But he would make only one more movie. *Lilith* (1964), shot in England, was a mixed success; Warren Beatty plays a therapist-in-training at a Maryland asylum who falls in love with mentally ill patient Jean Seberg, only to lose his own hold on reality. Rossen produced and co-wrote the screenplay, which was laden with more than its share of psychobabble. But it was a work to take seriously, and indicated Rossen had more to give. Time ran out, though, when he died two years later, his best years having been spent in self-imposed exile.

▲ *With Jean Seberg and a self-conscious Warren Beatty on the set of Lilith, Rossen's last film*

## ● WESLEY RUGGLES (1889–1972)

A former Keystone Kop who began directing in 1917, Los Angeles–born Wesley Ruggles grew up just as the film industry was moving West. His screen-acting career began in 1914, and a year later he was working in such Chaplin shorts as *The Bank* and *Police*. The younger brother of actor Charlie Ruggles, he moved naturally into directing comedies soon after, and eventually took on dramas as well—long-forgotten productions like *The Leopard Woman* and *The Remittance Woman*, as well as the first screen version of Edith Wharton's *The Age of Innocence* (1924). He directed a series of Laura La Plante farces for Universal in the late Twenties, then tried (unsuccessfully) to usher her into the sound age with *Scandal* (1929). *Girl Overboard* with Mary Philbin was another part-talkie, while *Street Girl* (both 1929), a musical with Jack Oakie and Betty Compson, was RKO-Radio's first official release and a profitable one at that. At Paramount, Ruggles directed *Honey* (1930), a musical comedy with Nancy Carroll that had been a hit on Broadway years earlier; its high point was the "Sing, You Sinners" number by the legendary Lillian Roth.

The earliest Ruggles work that maintains any sort of reputation today is *Cimarron* (1931), which in its day was one of the most expensive films ever made: $1.43 million, more than most hit pictures then were grossing. Based on Edna Ferber's bestselling novel about the settling of Oklahoma, it was an enormous smash and ended up winning the Academy Award as the best picture of 1931, with Ruggles and leads Richard Dix and Irene Dunne also nominated for their work. (It would prove to be the only Western to win a best picture Oscar until 1992's *Unforgiven*.) Ruggles collaborated with writer Howard Estabrook again on the socially conscious *Are These Our Children?* (1931), a cautionary tale of a youth (Eric Linden) who lets liquor and fallen women lead him into committing a murder, for which he is sentenced to death.

*Roar of the Dragon* (1932) brought Richard Dix to war-torn Manchuria, much to the disinterest of America's moviegoers, but *No Man of Her Own* (1932) was a good romance, with Clark Gable and Carole Lombard (prior to their own real-life romance)—the only time they acted together onscreen. *The Monkey's Paw* (1933) was an appropriately creepy staging of the classic supernatural tale by W. W. Jacobs; C. Aubrey Smith plays the owner of the cursed thing.

Ruggles now moved to Paramount, where he would spend the remainder of the decade, first making the silly but endurable musical comedy *College Humor*, with Bing Crosby and Burns and Allen. The fine Mae West vehicle *I'm No Angel* (also 1933) was one of her best films and doubly enjoyable for the presence of the young Cary Grant, while *Bolero* (1934) was a wonderfully effective teaming of George Raft and Carole Lombard as professional dancers (Sally Rand also performed a number).

Ruggles demonstrated a sure hand with romantic business in *The Gilded Lily* (1935), a pleasant triangle involving Claudette Colbert, Fred MacMurray, and Ray Milland, while *Accent on Youth* was a passable comedy with Sylvia Sidney and Herbert Marshall. *The Bride Comes Home* (also 1935) reteamed Colbert and MacMurray; this time Robert Young was the rich fly-in-the-ointment. It also marked the beginning of Ruggles's six-year stint as a producer/director. *Valiant Is the Word for Carrie* (1936) was an unusual assignment, considering that Ruggles's strength lay in comedy, but he did a creditable job with this unabashed tearjerker, based on a popular novel of the day. Gladys George was Oscar-nominated for her performance, and Arline Judge, Ruggles's wife, was also in the cast.

*I Met Him in Paris* (1937) was the sort of romantic froth with which Ruggles was more familiar; Claudette Colbert is almost too precious as an American fashion designer visiting the Continent and torn between Melvyn Douglas and Robert Young. *True Confession* (1937), on the other hand, is probably the most disliked screwball comedy of the Thirties—but what's not to like about Carole Lombard as a pathological liar? (The film also boasts a very funny turn by John Barrymore.) *Sing, You Sinners* (1938) offered Bing Crosby and Fred MacMurray as brothers divided by Crosby's gambling addiction (not that it's called that in the film), a nice blend of sentiment, comedy, and songs. *Invitation to Happiness* (1939) had the fearsome Fred MacMurray as a boxer with blood in his eye and upscale wife Irene Dunne in his heart, inimical interests that the film reconciles after ninety-five minutes or so.

Moving to Columbia, Ruggles directed *Too Many Husbands* (1940) with Jean Arthur, Melvyn Douglas, and old friend Fred MacMurray; it was a perky comedy that reversed the hoary plot device employed by its contemporary, Garson Kanin's *My Favorite Wife*. *Arizona* (1940) sent Arthur out West to tame the territory and William Holden, but this self-conscious effort to recapture the glory of *Cimarron* was too long and formulaic. *You Belong to Me* (1941) had Henry Fonda and Barbara Stanwyck committing screwball romance—but compared to that year's *The Lady Eve* with the same stars, it's alarmingly flat. Marginally better was the glossy wartime romance *Somewhere I'll Find You* (1942), with Clark Gable and Lana Turner well matched. But the dim comedy *Slightly Dangerous* (1943) didn't give Lana either Gable or a decent script to work with.

MGM entrusted Ruggles with the sure-fire military comedy *See Here, Private Hargrove* (1944), from a bestselling memoir about life in the Army, and the film was a popular success. Somewhat surprisingly, that proved to be Ruggles's last Hollywood work. He made a picture called *London Town* in 1946 for a British studio, then retired from filmmaking. It was a rather sudden end to a career that, if not exactly illustrious, at least had provided a few of the brightest—and funniest—moments in the cinema of the Thirties.

# ● MARK SANDRICH (1900-1945)

He will always be known as the man who directed *Top Hat*, but Mark Sandrich's too-brief career extended beyond such beloved musicals. A native of New York City, Sandrich attended Columbia University before taking his first job in the movie business as a prop man. By 1927 he was directing comedy shorts with Lupino Lane, and a year later he made *Runaway Girls*, a melodrama about a manicurist who takes up with evil companions. He wrote as well as directed *The Talk of Hollywood* (1929) before being demoted back to shorts with the coming of sound. But when one of his RKO shorts, *So This Is Harris*, won an Oscar in 1933, he again was entrusted with features.

His first was *Melody Cruise*, followed by *Aggie Appleby—Maker of Men* (both 1933). Neither enjoys a reputation today, although Sandrich did stage some elaborate, Busby Berkeleyish numbers in the former. *Hips, Hips, Hooray* and *Cockeyed Cavaliers* (both 1934) were Bert Wheeler and Robert Woolsey comedies featuring the delightful Thelma Todd, the first also offering a rare performance by songstress Ruth Etting. But it was *The Gay Divorcee* (1934) that put Sandrich on the map. The first of the Fred Astaire–Ginger Rogers vehicles (they had been featured performers in *Flying Down to Rio* the year before), it was a huge hit and established the formula that would carry Astaire and Rogers (sometimes kicking and screaming) through the decade. *Gay* was nominated for an Academy Award for best picture, but won the Oscar only for its song "The Continental" (which wasn't even its best tune).

Producer Pandro S. Berman wasn't about to break up a winning combination, and so Sandrich was back behind the camera for *Top Hat* (1935), which was even better than *Divorcee*. How much of the credit should be laid at Sandrich's doorstep is open to question—Berman, Astaire, and co-choreographer Hermes Pan surely had as much to do with the best parts of the film as did Sandrich—but what cannot be questioned is *Top Hat*'s status as a classic. The most profitable film of the decade for RKO, it, too, was nominated for the best picture Academy Award—but this time didn't win even for Irving Berlin's music (the sublime "Cheek to Cheek" lost to "Lullaby of Broadway"). *Follow the Fleet* (1936) was next, and if Astaire in a sailor suit couldn't compare to him in a white tie and tails, it still was fine entertainment, with more great Berlin songs ("Let's Face the Music and Dance," "Let Yourself Go").

A second Astaire-Rogers picture was scheduled

for 1936, but—oddly—*Swing Time* was given to George Stevens; instead, Sandrich made *A Woman Rebels* with Katharine Hepburn. A proto-feminist period piece that failed to attract an audience, this was but one of Hepburn's string of mid-Thirties commercial failures, most of which seem quite good today. Sandrich was reunited with Astaire and Rogers on *Shall We Dance?* (1937), and while the formula was beginning to fray around the edges just a bit, its Gershwin tunes ("They All Laughed," "They Can't Take That Away from Me") were possibly the best yet. *Carefree* (1938) offered Irving Berlin's songs ("Change Partners") and Fred Astaire as a psychiatrist treating zany Ginger Rogers; a minor plot departure, but it helped.

This would prove to be Sandrich's last picture for RKO. He moved to Paramount, where his first project was *Man About Town* (1939), an inconsequential Jack Benny musical with Dorothy Lamour and Betty Grable. *Buck Benny Rides Again* (1940) held together better, but Sandrich's next Jack Benny showcase was a strained concoction about his feud with fellow radio star Fred Allen, *Love Thy Neighbor* (1940). *Skylark* (1941) was infinitely better, a deft romantic comedy starring Claudette Colbert and Ray Milland that was swamped in the wake of the year's more substantial productions. Sandrich finally got Astaire back, along with Bing Crosby, for the bucolic musical *Holiday Inn* (1942), an enormous box-office success and the source of Irving Berlin's Oscar-winning "White Christmas."

*So Proudly We Hail!* (1943) was quite a change of pace, a grimly patriotic drama about a group of nurses stationed in the Pacific during the war. The fine cast included Claudette Colbert, Paulette Goddard, and Veronica Lake; Goddard was nominated for an Academy Award, and Lake should have been.

▲ *Sandrich tweaks the nose of Virginia Dale, co-star of* Holiday Inn

*Here Come the Waves* (1944) explored the more familiar territory of musical comedy with Bing Crosby and Betty Hutton, though it's one of those films that must have gone down easier fifty years ago. Sandrich's last completed film was *I Love a Soldier* (1944), a plodding wartime soap opera with Paulette Goddard and Sonny Tufts (oh, those contract players!), who are having marital difficulties.

He began work on the musical *Blue Skies*, a good pairing of Astaire and Crosby, but passed away during production at the far-too-young age of forty-five; Stuart Heisler completed the film and was director of record. With his career truncated as it was, Sandrich's name will deservedly be forever linked with those classic Astaire-Rogers films.

## FRANKLIN J. SCHAFFNER (1920–1989)

Long before Franklin Schaffner made his first film he had conquered the television medium, winning a Peabody for *The United Nations Telecast* (1950), back-to-back Emmys for directing *12 Angry Men* (1954) and *The Caine Mutiny Court-Martial* (1955), another Emmy for an episode of *The Defenders* in 1962, and a special Emmy for his documentary *Tour of the White House*, hosted by Jackie Kennedy. Indeed, Schaffner was associated with many of television's most prestigious drama showcases, including *Studio One*, *Playhouse 90*, and *The Kaiser Aluminum Hour*. But it is his film work for which he is best remembered.

Born in Tokyo to missionary parents, Schaffner was raised in Japan until he was sixteen. He then came to the United States and Columbia University, where his law studies were interrupted by the outbreak of World War II. He served in the Navy, after which he became an assistant director on the *March of Time* shorts. In 1949 Schaffner went to work for CBS, where he remained for much of the next thirteen years. In 1960 he directed *Advise and Consent* on Broadway, a production for which he won the New York Drama Critics Award. His first film was *The Stripper* (1963), based on a William Inge play. It was oddly cast, with Joanne Woodward as the Older Woman and Richard Beymer over his head as the wide-eyed teenager; the film was taken out of Schaffner's hands for editing, which may have inflicted damage. *The Best Man* (1964) was a knowing dissection of political conventions and the bartering of power. Based on the Gore Vidal play, it featured Henry Fonda and Cliff Robertson as presidential candidates.

Schaffner obviously knew his way around the political arenas of the day, but *The War Lord* (1965), a medieval drama starring Charlton Heston and Richard Boone, proved to be a stretch. *The Double Man* (1967) was an espionage misfire, with Yul Brynner in a dual role as an American and an East German spy. Schaffner's first big commercial success was *Planet of the Apes*, which may have been only the second-best science-fiction movie of 1968 (*2001* also was released that year). Still, it was an immensely enjoyable adventure/parable, imaginatively adapted from Pierre Boulle's novel; it gave Charlton Heston one of his best roles in many years. *Patton* (1970) was Schaffner's most lauded film, the Oscar-winning best picture that earned him an Academy Award for best direction. A box-office and critical smash—alarmingly, it was Richard Nixon's favorite movie—*Patton* may have been a bit overrated in its time (as was George C. Scott's scenery-chewing performance, for which he famously declined the best actor Oscar), but it certainly was one of the year's outstanding pictures. (Remember, the Academy *could* have voted for best-picture nominees *Love Story* or *Airport*.)

The gorgeously mounted historical epic *Nicholas and Alexandra* (1971) was a victim of a three-hour-plus running time and uncharismatic leads Michael Jayston and Janet Suzman. Even so, it was nominated for a best picture Academy Award. *Papillon* (1973) was also too long (and too unpleasant by half), but it at least had the benefit of Steve McQueen's last great performance; but Dustin Hoffman's carefully crafted turn finally seems too fussy. *Islands in the Stream* (1977) was an ambitious attempt to render Ernest Hemingway's sprawling (unfinished) novel into a cohesive film; Schaffner didn't succeed, but the picture certainly has its moments, and George C. Scott is even better than he was in *Patton*. *The Boys from Brazil* (1978) was a crass thriller (as was the Ira Levin bestseller from which it was adapted), a genre Schaffner had little experience with—and it showed. But Laurence Olivier was fun as the Nazi-hunting

Jewish survivor of the death camps, in an Oscar-nominated performance frighteningly similar to the one he submitted in *The Jazz Singer* two years later; Gregory Peck fared less well as Mengele, who's trying to clone Hitler.

To this point Schaffner's work had been of a generally high level, even when the box-office response was indifferent. But in the Eighties that would all change. *Sphinx* (1981), from the Robin Cook best-seller, was an idiotic suspense yarn with Lesley-Anne Down chased by Frank Langella through the pyramids, while the mere mention of *Yes, Giorgio* (1982) is enough to bring tears of laughter to the eyes of any moviegoer who survived—unfortunately, the film was not intended as a comedy. It took Schaffner five years to recover, with *Lionheart* finally being released—sort of—in 1987. This off-beat Crusades adventure with Eric Stolz and Gabriel Byrne was actually Schaffner's best work in ten years, but it did not receive national distribution. *Welcome Home* (1989) did, but this variation on *Enoch Arden* was too sappy for words—a precipitous fall for an Oscar-winning director. Schaffner died shortly after its release.

## ● JOHN SCHLESINGER (1926– )

London-born John Schlesinger was a star of the British New Wave in the 1960s before making his mark in Hollywood, where he won an Oscar for his first American picture.

Schlesinger's career in show business began during the Second World War, when he entertained British troops with a magic act while still in his teens. In 1945 he enrolled at Oxford, where he joined the Dramatic Society and trod the boards. But even while thriving as an actor, Schlesinger was laying the groundwork to become a director, making short films like *Black Legend* (1948) and *The Starfish* (1950). He earned his bread and butter acting, however, playing bits in films as of 1952 and on television beginning in 1956. But in 1957 Schlesinger was offered a post at BBC-TV as a director. He made more than twenty documentaries for the programs *Tonight* and *Monitor*, while serving as an interviewer on a popular series about Winston Churchill, *The Valiant Years*. *Terminus*, his documentary about the bustle of Waterloo Station in London, won first prize in its category at the 1961 Venice Film Festival.

Schlesinger's first feature films were British productions. *A Kind of Loving* (1962) was a low-key but effective drama out of the kitchen-sink school, with Alan Bates forced to marry pregnant June Ritchie. Even more accomplished was *Billy Liar* (1963), a less whimsical version of "The Secret Life of Walter Mitty," with Tom Courtenay as a young funeral-home worker who relies on his fantasy life to help him escape from the drudgery of his job. Based on a stage drama which starred Albert Finney, *Billy* later spawned a stage musical and a television series, but is most notable for featuring Julie Christie in her screen debut. Christie was moved to center stage for *Darling* (1965), a corrosive portrait of an amoral tart who changes professions (model, actress, countess) as often as she changes lovers (Dirk Bogarde, Laurence Harvey, José Luis de Villalonga). Although this ironic exponent of the British New Wave now seems quite dated, one can see how Christie—astonishingly beautiful—and screenwriter Frederic Raphael won Academy Awards for their work, and why the film and Schlesinger were nominated for Oscars.

*Far from the Madding Crowd* (1967) was Schlesinger's big-budget payoff for the success of *Darling*. Made for MGM's British division, it cast Julie Christie as the beleaguered heroine and Alan Bates, Peter Finch, and Terence Stamp as the troika of men who try to worship, abase, or simply possess her. Scripted by Frederic Raphael and photographed (gorgeously) by Nicholas Roeg, this long but rewarding take on Thomas Hardy's epic novel is surely one of Schlesinger's best, though its name rarely comes up when period classics are mentioned.

But *Midnight Cowboy* (1969), Schlesinger's first Hollywood picture, made the film world sit up and take note. Waldo Salt adapted James Leo Herlihy's novel about small-time New York City hustlers Ratso Rizzo (Dustin Hoffman) and Texas transplant Joe Buck (Jon Voight), who unexpectedly bond in the course of living their marginal, rather nauseating existences. Schlesinger's gritty mise-en-scène was (at the time) so shockingly raw that the Motion Picture Association of America penalized the picture with an "X" rating—certain death for most mainstream releases, but the publicity served only to pique interest. (The film was soon re-evaluated and given an "R," permitting a broader audience to see it.) It fared even better at Academy Awards time, winning for best picture, with Schlesinger getting the Oscar for best direction and Salt for best screenplay; Voight and Hoffman, each nominated for best actor, canceled each other out. (In 1994 *Cowboy* was given a twenty-fifth-anniversary rerelease to widespread acclaim.)

*Sunday, Bloody Sunday* (1971) was Schlesinger's

perversely uncommercial follow-up, with Londoners Glenda Jackson and Peter Finch unhappily sharing the sexual favors of bisexual Murray Head (whose lack of charisma nearly sinks the enterprise); Schlesinger, Finch, Jackson, and scenarist Penelope Gilliatt were all nominated for Academy Awards. After directing the marathon segment of the 1972 Olympics documentary *Visions of Eight* (1973), Schlesinger returned to Hollywood to film Nathanael West's peerless Hollywood fable, *Day of the Locust* (1975). The film attempts—too strenuously—to distill West's inimitable dark humor, but despite the best efforts of screenwriter Waldo Salt and the good work of actors Burgess Meredith, Karen Black, Donald Sutherland, and Geraldine Page as its eccentric characters, *Day* remains mushy at its center. Casting bland William Atherton as Tod, the wide-eyed protagonist, was certainly a mistake, but Schlesinger's ham-fisted staging of the novel's satirical set pieces is an even bigger problem.

Needing a hit, Schlesinger wisely chose William Goldman's foolproof espionage yarn *Marathon Man* (1976) as his next project; it was adapted by Goldman himself. Although grossly manipulative and in parts clumsy, the film is carried by its clever plot and its stars: Dustin Hoffman plays an innocent Jewish graduate student who by degrees finds himself matching wits with Laurence Olivier's surpassingly evil Nazi-in-hiding, who has slain Hoffman's brother, rogue CIA operative Roy Scheider. Save for the impossibly gruesome torture-through-better-dentistry sequence, *Man* is a compelling thriller, with Olivier's over-the-top performance earning the sly old pro an Oscar nomination.

But that box-office triumph would be Schlesinger's last for many, many years. *Yanks* (1978) was an irritatingly sappy World War II romance set in England, with Richard Gere and Lisa Eichhorn as the charmless lovers who find the air raids interfering with their affair, while *Honky Tonk Freeway* (1981) was an unmitigated dud, a satire of American culture that was as subtle as a landfill; a large cast of largely wasted character actors (Hume Cronyn, Jessica Tandy, Teri Garr, William Devane, Beverly D'Angelo, Beau Bridges) was unable to lend coherence to the story. *An Englishman Abroad* (1983), with Alan Bates and Coral Browne, was an elegant, well-received drama made for the BBC. But *The Falcon and the Snowman* (1985) was another disappointing effort, lacking the tension of Robert Lindsay's probing nonfiction account of two California kids (Timothy Hutton and Sean Penn) who sell government secrets to the Russians out of half-baked idealism. Penn's wacky take on pothead Daulton Lee intermittently brings the tale to life, but Hutton's monotonously somber Christopher Boyce is simply inert.

The little-seen *The Believers* (1987) was a creepy, even ghoulish contemporary horror story about a boy drafted into New York's Santeria cult; Martin Sheen plays the widowed dad who doesn't at first realize the danger his son is in. Schlesinger made a television movie of *Separate Tables* in 1987, then received his best reviews in quite some time for *Madame Sousatzka* (1988), an indelible character sketch of a quirky London piano teacher (Shirley MacLaine) who helps her gifted fifteen-year-old Indian student (Navin Chowdhry) realize his full potential. Schlesinger and Ruth Prawer Jhabvala skillfully adapted Bernice Rubens's novel, but MacLaine's studied portrayal of the dotty, autocratic teacher is at once the film's greatest strength and (when she isn't under control) its greatest drawback.

The thriller *Pacific Heights* (1990) was a bid for a wider audience. It featured Melanie Griffith and Matthew Modine as a young married couple who buy a lovely old house in San Francisco but find their lives in peril from their new boarder, an ever-more-menacing Michael Keaton. It was formula and it was violent, but done well. *A Question of Attribution* (1991), made for BBC television, dramatized a meeting between Sir Anthony Blunt (James Fox) and the Queen (Prunella Scales); few saw *The Innocent* (1994), though, leaving Schlesinger without a box-office success since 1976.

▲ *The once-shocking kiss between Peter Finch and Murray Head in* Sunday, Bloody Sunday

## ERNEST B. SCHOEDSACK (1893–1979)

Specializing in the fantastic, Ernest Beaumont Schoedsack made only a handful of movies, most of the important ones in collaboration with Merian C. Cooper. But those few films have taken on such a patina of legend that he can no more be ignored than can a ten-ton gorilla.

Born in Council Bluffs, Iowa, he ran away from home in his teens and eventually found work as a surveyor in the San Francisco area. His brother Felix helped him get a job as a cameraman with Mack Sennett in 1914, a skill that he put to use when he enlisted during World War I and served as a cameraman in the Signal Corps in France, eventually rising to the position of captain in the Red Cross photographic unit. After the war ended, he remained in Europe as a newsreel cameraman.

The Russian Revolution led him to Poland to cover the invasion of 1919; it was there he met Merian C. Cooper, another adventurous soul interested in exploring the possibilities of film. Cooper got him a job as a cameraman on a world cruise sponsored by *The New York Times*, after which they collaborated on the making of *Grass* (1926), a documentary about the migratory tribes of Iran, and *Chang* (1927), a quasi-documentary filmed in the jungles of Thailand (then Siam) about a family menaced by man-eating tigers and leopards; its "star" was a baby elephant. No trick photography was used, and the herd of stampeding elephants that climaxes the film nearly flattened Schoedsack and his cameraman. It was at this time that Schoedsack married Ruth Rose, a former stage actress who had joined the expedition to Siam for *Chang* and later would collaborate on several Cooper-Schoedsack productions.

With Cooper (and Lothar Mendes, who shot additional studio footage without their knowledge) Schoedsack directed the silent *The Four Feathers* (1929), with Richard Arlen, William Powell, and Fay Wray. Schoedsack wrote, produced, and directed *Rango* (1931), a mostly silent quasi-documentary set in Sumatra about a pet orangutan who sacrifices himself to save a boy from a killer tiger, after which the family's water buffalo gores the tiger to death. Cooper and Schoedsack then produced the suspense gem *The Most Dangerous Game* (1932); Schoedsack co-directed with Irving Pichel, who was in charge of the dialogue. Based on the classic short story by Richard Connell, *Game* is barely an hour long, but makes the viewer feel he too is being chased through the jungle by the crossbow-wielding madman Count Zaroff and his bloodthirsty pack of hounds (comedian Harold Lloyd's Great Danes!).

Even as Schoedsack was shooting *Game*, Cooper was using much of its cast, sets, and technicians to simultaneously shoot *King Kong*, a story Cooper had nurtured for several years. (Edgar Wallace, who is also credited for the story, died of pneumonia before actually working on it.) Its characters were based on Cooper, Schoedsack, and Rose herself, but it was the wonderful special effects (including but not limited to Willis O'Brien's and Marcel Delgado's stop-motion models) that set *Kong* apart from any other film of its time—indeed, they have yet to be equaled. Credit for the film's brilliance should also be spread among composer Max Steiner, whose score is one of the most innovative of the decade; Ruth Rose and James Creelman's screenplay; and such actors as Fay Wray, Robert Armstrong, and Noble Johnson, all of whom were also involved with *Game*. (Once *Game* had wrapped, Schoedsack worked on *Kong* with Cooper full-time.)

The spectacular success of *Kong* upon its release in March of 1933 convinced RKO executives that a sequel should follow as quickly as possible, and Schoedsack and Cooper immediately began working on it. Schoedsack directed solo and Ruth Rose wrote the screenplay, drawing once again on her experiences as a member of the Cooper-Schoedsack expeditions; six months later *The Son of Kong* (1933) was completed. More modest in every way than *Kong*, due primarily to a budget half that of the original, *Son* relied on some whimsical comedy to make up for its relative lack of sheer thrills. As a companion piece to its more ambitious predecessor, *Son* offers its own modest pleasures. As if 1933 hadn't been full enough for Schoedsack and Rose, they also collaborated on the obscure *Blind Adventure*, with Robert Armstrong and Helen Mack (the leads in *Son*) paired as amateur detectives in London's West End. (Cooper wasn't involved; his career as a director was over, although he would continue to produce films successfully for another two decades, including a number in collaboration with John Ford and John Wayne.)

*Long Lost Father* (1934) was another strained comic adventure that remains one of John Barrymore's least-remembered efforts. Schoedsack took a stab at DeMille-style spectacle with *The Last Days of Pompeii* (1935), with Cooper again producing, Ruth Rose writing the screenplay, and Willis O'Brien handling the special effects. But even that formidable creative team couldn't breathe life into this moribund epic, set in the days of Christ, and it was a major box-office failure. Schoedsack was reduced to making two low-budget Jack Holt adventures at Columbia, *Trouble in Morocco* and *Outlaws of the Orient* (both 1937), before getting another chance at a grade-A fantasy with *Dr. Cyclops* (1940). While it didn't turn out to be another *King Kong*, it could claim the distinction of being Hollywood's first Technicolor excursion into the realm of science fiction, with smooth-pated Albert Dekker one of the screen's most memorable mad scientists.

Whatever else Schoedsack might have achieved behind the camera was permanently interrupted by a serious eye injury he suffered while testing photographic equipment at a high altitude for the Air Force during World War II. He directed only one more film, the benign *Mighty Joe Young* (1949)—a kind of *King Kong*–lite co-produced by Merian Cooper from his own story, with a screenplay by Ruth Rose, a supporting role by Robert Armstrong, and Oscar-winning special effects by Willis O'Brien and Ray Harryhausen. It was almost old home week for the gang that had made cinema history many years before, and a worthy enterprise with which Schoedsack wrote finis to his abbreviated career. He took a curtain call by directing the prologue for *This Is Cinerama* (1952), a Cooper co-production, without credit.

▲ *Schoedsack and Fay Wray during the making of* King Kong

## ● MARTIN SCORSESE (1942- )

Ambitious, bold, and brilliant, Martin Scorsese has created a body of work over the past twenty-five years unsurpassed by any of his contemporaries. But even his most popular films are demanding, sometimes unpleasantly intense dramas that have enjoyed relatively little commercial success; thus Scorsese bears the not totally undeserved mien of a cult director who just happens to work with big budgets and Hollywood's most desirable stars. Yet he may be today's most respected Hollywood director—in terms of artistry, if not box-office grosses.

Born in Flushing, New York, he was raised in a tenement in Little Italy—a sickly child beset with pleurisy and asthma who watched endless movies, sketching out his favorite sequences afterward. He attended a seminary after graduating high school, but gave up his dreams of the priesthood for a more secular passion, enrolling at N.Y.U. in 1960. There he was able to indulge his love of films fully by making shorts like *What's a Nice Girl Like You Doing in a Place Like This?* (1963) and the award-winning *It's Not Just You, Murray* (1964), which starred Scorsese's mother and several of his fellow students.

After graduating from the N.Y.U. Film School in 1966 with an M.A., Scorsese stayed on as an instructor while working on his own projects. He made the gruesomely comedic six-minute short *The Big Shave* (1967), then finished his first feature-length picture, at various junctures titled *I Call First* and *Bring on the Dancing Girls* but released in 1968 as *Who's That Knocking on My Door?* Harvey Keitel, in his screen debut, starred as Scorsese's alter ego, a streetwise but sensitive Italian-American Catholic kid plagued by guilt over his sexual relationship with girlfriend Zina Bethune. *Knocking* earned Scorsese encouraging reviews, but his best job offer turned out to be the key position of assistant director and supervising editor on *Woodstock*, which translated into converting the one hundred-plus hours of raw concert and crowd footage into the three-hour, four-minute masterpiece that won an Academy Award as 1970's best documentary.

Scorsese directed the less widely seen documentary *Street Scenes* (1970), which played at the New York Film Festival, and he was no more visible working as an editor on the rock concert film *Medicine Ball Caravan* and the lame *Elvis on Tour*. But Roger Corman invited him to direct *Boxcar Bertha* (1972) for AIP, a sequel to Corman's dunderheaded account of Ma Barker and her sons, *Bloody Mama*. Scorsese easily outshone him and made the most of the opportunity with an exciting if ultimately empty yarn about train robbers David Carradine, Barbara Hershey, and Bernie Casey wreaking havoc through the Depression-era South.

Far more significant was the boundary-breaking *Mean Streets* (1973), co-scripter Scorsese's reworking of the themes introduced in *Knocking*. Harvey Keitel stars as a small-time collector for the mob in Little Italy, stricken with Catholic guilt over his affair with epileptic Amy Robinson and frustrated by his inability to control his friend (and Robinson's brother), the dangerously unhinged Robert De Niro. The moving, often hilarious improvisations of Keitel and De Niro are as much responsible for igniting this low-budget ($500,000) masterpiece as Scorsese's atmosphere-drenched locations (some neatly faked by L.A.), shockingly frank language, explosive violence, and showy camera technique.

A hit at the New York Film Festival, *Mean Streets* inspired Pauline Kael to lead the nation's film critics in championing a prodigious new talent, an outpouring of support that didn't help the downbeat picture at the box office but did enable Scorsese to gain entrée to Hollywood through the front door. After making the 48-minute documentary *Italian-american* in 1974, Scorsese went to work on his first mainstream picture, the tame *Alice Doesn't Live Here Anymore* (1975), which at first seems a bit disappointing after the pyrotechnic invention of *Streets*. But in its own subdued way, *Alice* is a fairly effective drama about a widow (Ellen Burstyn) who strikes out from New Mexico to California after the death of her abusive husband to make a new life for herself and her adolescent son (Alfred Lutter). Harvey Keitel makes an impact as a deceptively charming beau with an unexpected violent streak, and Kris Kristofferson gives a likable performance as the rancher who awkwardly tries to court Alice while she's working as a waitress. But it was Burstyn's Academy Award for best actress that helped convince the Hollywood establishment that Scorsese could bring more than his maverick talent to the table. (It's still hard to believe that this dark soap opera was transmogrified into the cheery TV sitcom *Alice* a year later.)

Having proven that he could hew to a fairly conventional agenda, Scorsese then shocked filmgoers with *Taxi Driver* (1976), a hellish tour of a disturbed Vietnam vet's peculiar madness. Brilliantly written by Paul Schrader, photographed by Michael Chapman, and scored by Bernard Herrmann, this unsettling work is as fascinating as it is horrifying; it has a hallucinatory quality never before displayed in a mainstream American film. De Niro gives what may prove to be his definitive performance as the pathetically alienated but dangerously unhinged Bickle, and Harvey Keitel exudes menace in the small but key role of the seductive pimp Sport, who keeps twelve-year-old Jodie Foster in thrall. Perhaps the most controversial, and certainly the creepiest, Academy Award nominee for best picture to date, *Taxi Driver* also earned Oscar nominations for De Niro (who lost to Sylvester Stallone!), Foster, and Herrmann. The New York Film Critics Circle was more appreciative, naming Scorsese (who cast himself in a small but telling cameo as a murderously jealous husband) best director and De Niro best actor, while the film was awarded the Golden Palm at Cannes. And it made money.

Scorsese had pushed the envelope and been vindicated, but his status as Hollywood's newest *enfant terrible* lasted only until the release of *New York, New*

▲ *Amy Robinson and Harvey Keitel in* Mean Streets, *Scorsese's breakthrough film*

York (1977), a daring but fatally self-indulgent rethinking of the Fifties Hollywood musical. Deliberately stylized to evoke past screen triumphs by Vincente Minnelli and George Cukor, it features De Niro as the cocky Jimmy Doyle, a novice sax player who sublimates his love of jazz in order to work in a big band behind singer Francine Evans (Liza Minnelli), a hugely talented but utterly conventional singer in the mode of the early Doris Day. Their torrid love affair proves as impossible to reconcile as their musical tastes, and the vain, self-destructive Jimmy drifts away from domestic bliss with the pregnant Francine to submerge himself in the reefer-hazed world of black music and bebop. Although Jimmy's self-pity becomes wearing, De Niro is wonderful in a basically unsympathetic part, and Minnelli reincarnates her mother (circa 1946) with frightening authority. Then there's the great, if now overly familiar, title tune. But after its mesmerizing start, the film becomes flabby during the mercilessly prolonged second act, even though its two and a half–hour release print was ninety minutes shorter than Scorsese's original cut. (Cut even further for general release, the film was restored in 1981 to include the twelve-minute "Happy Endings" number, a spectacularly uninteresting riff on MGM's big golden-age showstoppers.) While critical opinion was mixed, ticketbuyers voted thumbs-down.

Stung by the rejection, Scorsese turned to editing his footage of The Band's November 1976 farewell concert, which he and several cinematographers shot while Scorsese was still in the midst of *New York, New York*. It became the well-received rockumentary *The Last Waltz* (1978), with unparalleled performance footage of Bob Dylan, Joni Mitchell, Van Morrison, Muddy Waters, Eric Clapton, and other of the day's musical luminaries. Next came *American Boy* (1978), the second of Scorsese's mid-length documentaries about his family.

Scorsese then made the brutal but beautiful *Raging Bull* (1980). Loosely adapted from the memoir of former middleweight boxing champ Jake LaMotta by Paul Schrader and Mardik Martin, this vitriolic essay on the pleasurable pain of violence is immediately impressive for its stunning black-and-white cinematography by Michael Chapman—richer than any color palette—and for its meticulous re-creation of 1940s New York City. The acting is also first-rate, particularly that of Joe Pesci as Joey, Jake's loyal brother, and Cathy Moriarty as Vickie, Jake's abused trophy of a wife. But it is Robert De Niro's towering, Oscar-winning performance as the self-destructive LaMotta, a proud but foolish man undone by forces he can neither understand nor control, that unifies this pitiless psychodrama. Scorsese and the film were both nominated for Academy Awards but lost to the tasteful discretion of Robert Redford and *Ordinary People*; even so, this remains the standard by which all subsequent efforts by Scorsese (and, for that matter, De Niro) have been measured.

Scorsese had gone as far in deconstructing violence as he (or anyone working in Hollywood) possibly could, and *The King of Comedy* (1983) was a drastic but entirely logical change of pace. Here De Niro gives yet another wholly original performance as Rupert Pupkin, a self-styled, wannabe stand-up TV comedian. Blissfully unaware of his profound lack of talent, Rupert lives serenely in his parents' basement rec room in Queens, where he practices his pathetic comedy routines to no avail. Finally he is goaded by the equally unhinged Sandra Bernhardt to kidnap reigning late-night TV star Jerry Langford (a sublimely arrogant Jerry Lewis) in exchange for a ten-minute stint on his program. Paul Zimmerman's corrosive, darkly comedic screenplay cleaved a bit too closely to the truth about America's obsessive approach to celebrity, and the film (which sat on the shelf for over a year before being released) bombed.

*After Hours* (1985) was a minor but amusing diversion, with Griffin Dunne as a mild-mannered, Upper East Side office worker who finds himself imperiled by a colorful variety of lunatics (Rosanna Arquette, John Heard, Teri Garr) one long, strange night in SoHo. Written by Columbia University film student Joseph Minion and shot on location by cinematographer Michael Ballhaus for a song ($3.5 million), this is an exhilarating (and rare) illustration of what a Scorsese movie can be like when his only mission is fun.

But it was back to business with *The Color of Money* (1986), a supercharged but superficial adaptation (by Richard Price) of Walter Tevis's fine sequel to his earlier novel *The Hustler.* Paul Newman, reprising his Oscar-nominated role as "Fast Eddie" Felsen, is now retired from competition and a promoter of young players. He smells raw talent in callow pool shark Tom Cruise and takes him under his wing, sharing all his hard-earned knowledge about the game. But they part ways, and (predictably) end up facing each other at an Atlantic City tournament for all the marbles. Snappy, tough, and lovely to look at, this is Scorsese at his most commercial and least interesting. Still, it's a professional job that won Newman his long-denied Academy Award (though he, too, has done much more interesting work) and reminded Hollywood that Scorsese could deliver a hit of at least modest proportions when he tried.

*The Last Temptation of Christ* (1988) was, but for a brief burst of protest from conservative Christians prior to its release, a well-received version of Nikos Kazantzakis's epic novel (adapted by reformed heretic Paul Schrader) about the self-doubts of Jesus as he carries out his mission. Willem Dafoe was well cast as Jesus and David Bowie made for a fine Pontius Pilate, but some critics had problems with Harvey Keitel as Judas, Barbara Hershey as Mary Magdalene, and Harry Dean Stanton as Saul and Paul. (Scorsese had some fun casting director Irvin Kershner as Zebedee.) But the evocative cinematography by Michael Ballhaus and the neo-traditional score by Peter Gabriel do much to enliven this longish, demythologized account of the Gospel, which earned Scorsese his second Academy Award nomination.

His vivid "Life Lessons" segment of the *New York Stories* (1989) triptych, scripted by Richard Price, was neither as perfectly crafted as Woody Allen's nor as dispensable as Coppola's. Nick Nolte is in his element as a middle-aged, bearish slob of a downtown action painter, desperate to keep restless paramour/disciple Rosanna Arquette from moving out to see a younger man. To his surprise, though, Nolte finds that his art has been re-energized when she does depart—a lesson that somehow feels profound, as if Scorsese were giving himself a pep talk.

Another kind of New York story—the kind that

helped fashion Scorsese's reputation—was the basis of the acclaimed *Good Fellas* (1990). Adaptated from Nicholas Pileggi's excellent *Wiseguy*, this knowing portrait of small-time Brooklyn mobster Henry Hill's life and crimes (scripted by Pileggi and Scorsese) feels more authentic than any Scorsese film since *Raging Bull*. Robert De Niro, too old to play the part of Hill, had to defer to Ray Liotta, who has his moments but ultimately leaves a void where the De Niro or Keitel of *Mean Streets* would not have. But Paul Sorvino, Joe Pesci, and De Niro are terrific in their supporting roles, as is Lorraine Bracco as Hill's wife. Funny, violent, and pungent, the picture—which does falter in the home stretch—keeps Scorsese wholly involved (as, say, *Money* did not) and inspires him to display his mastery of the medium in new and unexpected ways. Scorsese was again nominated by the Academy for his direction, although it was Joe Pesci who took home an Oscar.

This triumphant return to form led to the commercially successful but surprisingly unsubtle *Cape Fear* (1991), a hyped-up, ultra-violent remake of the suspenseful 1962 film (based on a John D. MacDonald novel) that starred Gregory Peck as a Southern lawyer whose family is terrorized by ex-con Robert Mitchum, who blames Peck for his prison conviction and seeks revenge. Now it's a lean, buffed De Niro playing the demented Max Cady, with Nick Nolte as the attorney who has to confront the murderous ex-con when the police refuse to take his threats seriously. Screenwriter Wesley Strick's script complicates the premise of the original by making Nolte's character culpable on several levels, from his framing of Cady fourteen years earlier to his current infidelity to wife Jessica Lange. But while Nolte's cowardice adds moral complexity to the story, Strick and Scorsese up the ante too far on Cady, turning him into a cartoon villain complete with ten-inch stogies, jailhouse tattoos, and a psycho swagger that in real life would get him busted the moment he walked down the street (although De Niro is plenty convincing when trying to seduce Juliette Lewis, Nolte's teen-

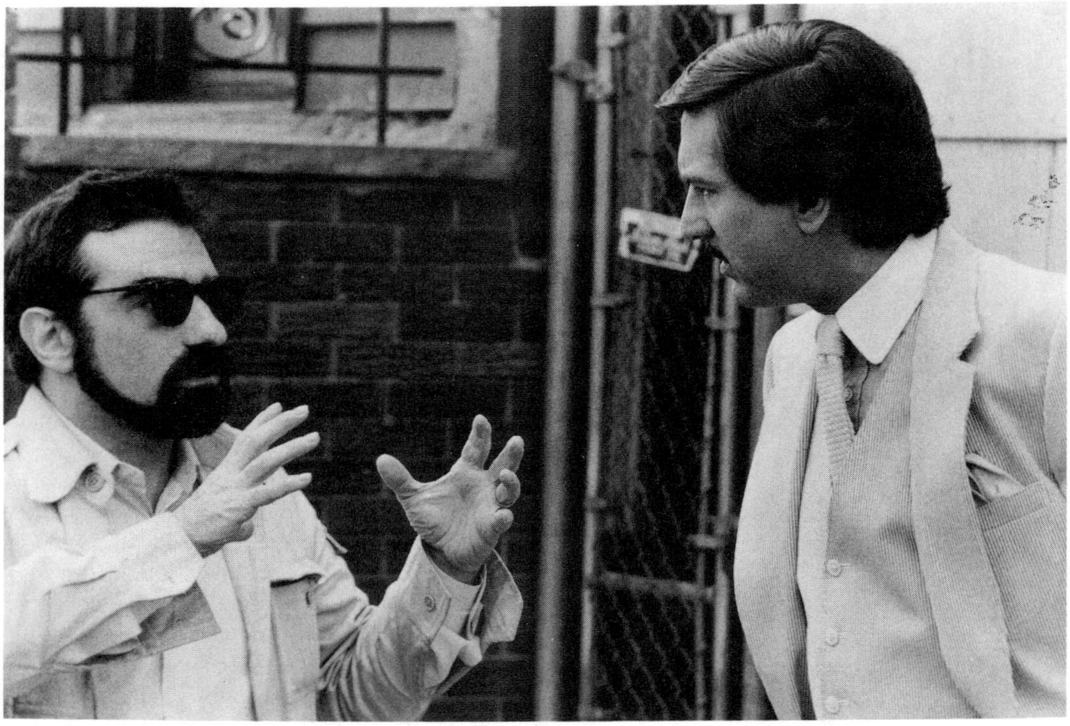

▲ *De Niro as Rupert Pupkin in* The King of Comedy, *a commercial failure for Scorsese*

aged daughter). By the lightning-drenched, bloody finale, we know we're in *Straw Dogs/Fatal Attraction* territory.

Scorsese's box-office success with *Cape Fear* enabled him to attract the big budget he desired for his exquisite version of Edith Wharton's *The Age of Innocence* (1993), a lovingly rendered, subtly acerbic portrait of New York City's upper crust in the late nineteenth century. The story revolves around the unconsummated love affair between Daniel Day-Lewis's sensitive barrister Newland Archer and Michelle Pfeiffer's Countess Ellen, whose separation from her brutish husband and general flouting of convention is a scandal proper society cannot tolerate. In a more subtle role, Winona Ryder does well as Archer's deceptively vapid fiancée May, who understands far more than she lets on.

Eyebrows were raised when Scorsese announced that he was venturing into Merchant-Ivory territory, and raised higher when the $40-million-plus production had its early 1993 release delayed nine months for additional editing. But with his most fluid camerawork yet, Scorsese demonstrated that his sensibility—thought too coarse for such period themes and nuances—had more range than he was given credit for. While he acquitted himself triumphantly on the artistic front, however, there was no realistic way *Age* could have succeeded at the box office with its huge budget (a take of $100 million would have been necessary). To add insult, Scorsese was neglected in the Academy Award nominations for best direction, his slot usurped (many felt) by Andrew Davis, whose crowd-pleasing *The Fugitive* was the year's second-biggest hit. But that wound, too, will be healed with time.

## ● VINCENT SHERMAN (1906– )

A good hand at melodrama who spent the first half of his directorial career at Warner Bros., Georgia-born Vincent Sherman first worked in Hollywood as an actor, appearing in such early-Thirties films as William Wyler's *Counsellor-at-Law.* By the end of the decade he was working at Warners as a screenwriter on Bogart crime pictures like *King of the Underworld.* Already in place, he made the transition to directing in 1939 with *The Return of Doctor X*, perhaps Bogart's silliest "B" (he plays a vampire!). *Saturday's Children* (1940) was a step up, a serious (for Warners) drama based on a Maxwell Anderson play; John Garfield and Ann Shirley starred as struggling young marrieds.

*The Man Who Talked Too Much* (1940) was a decent courtroom drama with such stock players as George Brent and Brenda Marshall, while *Flight from Destiny* (1941) was an interesting story about a dying man (Thomas Mitchell) who decides to spend the last months of his life helping out a young couple (Geraldine Fitzgerald and Jeffrey Lynn). *Underground* (1941) was an early anti-Nazi picture with Philip Dorn and Jeffrey Lynn, while *All Through the Night* (1942) was an atypically comical Bogart adventure in which Bogey makes fools out of Nazi saboteurs Conrad Veidt and Peter Lorre. Sherman's first important movie was the 1942 *The Hard Way*, a gritty show-business melodrama with fine performances from Ida Lupino, Joan Leslie, and Jack Carson. *Old Acquaintance* (1943) was a delight, an extended cat fight between real-life rivals Bette Davis and Miriam Hopkins as writers who feud with each other for twenty years. (George Cukor remade this as *Rich and Famous* in 1981, but it wasn't as good.)

*In Our Time* (1944) tried to make Ida Lupino and Paul Henreid into Bergman and Bogart, but this romance, set in Poland just before the war, never takes

Loving her once is once too often!
IF YOU WERE NORA PRENTISS WOULD YOU KEEP YOUR MOUTH SHUT?
Ann Sheridan
as
"NORA PRENTISS"
THE NEW WARNER SENSATION
CO-STARRING
KENT SMITH · BRUCE BENNETT
WITH ROBERT ALDA · ROSEMARY DECAMP
DIRECTED BY
VINCENT SHERMAN
SCREEN PLAY BY N. RICHARD NASH
FROM A STORY BY PAUL WEBSTER &
JACK SOBELL · MUSIC BY FRANZ WAXMAN

off. *Mr. Skeffington* (1944) was much more fun—a trashy soap opera in which Bette Davis and Claude Rains are stuck in a horrendous marriage, allowing Davis to indulge her most florid tendencies. But *Pillow to Post* (1945) was nonsense, a feeble patch off *The More the Merrier*, with Ida Lupino struggling to find the humor in all the hubbub. *Nora Prentiss* (1947) allowed Sherman to return to the more fertile territory of lives in misery; Ann Sheridan is appealing as a "bad girl" nightclub singer who ruins physician Kent Smith's marriage. Sheridan was well used again in *The Unfaithful* (1947), a loose remake of Somerset Maugham's *The Letter*, adapted by David Goodis and James Gunn; Lew Ayres and Zachary Scott provide good support.

Sherman next tried his hand at swordplay, and *The Adventures of Don Juan* (1949) proved to be a fine vehicle for Errol Flynn (who was an old thirty-nine when filming began), although Flynn's unreliability made the picture run fatally over budget. *The Hasty Heart* (1949) was a quiet adaptation of John Patrick's play, filmed in England, with Richard Todd (who was Oscar-nominated), Patricia Neal, and Ronald Reagan. But *Backfire* (1950) was a trite noir, with Virginia Mayo and Gordon MacRae, while *The Damned Don't Cry* (1950) cast Joan Crawford as a poor woman who aspires to become a gangster's moll—a bit ridiculous for the forty-four-year-old Joan at this stage of her career. That year Crawford and Sherman went as a package to Columbia, where they filmed *Harriet Craig*, a good remake of Dorothy Arzner's 1936 *Craig's Wife*; Wendell Corey plays her long-suffering husband. They collaborated once more on *Goodbye, My Fancy* (1951), an adaptation of a Broadway romantic comedy that optimistically cast Joan against type as a congresswoman.

This ended Sherman's association with Warner Bros., and he began freelancing, making the Clark Gable–Ava Gardner Western *Lone Star* and *Affair in Trinidad* (both 1952), the latter marking Rita Hayworth's return to the screen after "retiring" three years earlier to marry Prince Aly Khan; Glenn Ford, her *Gilda* co-star, was in tow. Sherman didn't work again in Hollywood for five years, making a lone Italian film during that time. His next credit was *The Garment Jungle* (1957), a tough exposé of corruption in New York's dressmaking union; it actually was 90 percent Robert Aldrich's work—Sherman mopped up after Aldrich was fired by Columbia for not cutting certain scenes. *The Naked Earth* (1959) was a poor British production that went down in flames because of star Juliette Greco, but *The Young Philadelphians* (1959) was an engaging soap opera starring Paul Newman as a lawyer on the rise.

*Ice Palace* (1960), from the Edna Ferber novel, was an ambitious period adventure set in Alaska, with Richard Burton and Robert Ryan trading dogsleds and fisticuffs throughout the years. *A Fever in the Blood* (1961) was a courtroom drama that wasted Angie Dickinson by pairing her with TV star Efrem Zimbalist, Jr., while *The Second Time Around* (1961) was a pleasant little Western, with Debbie Reynolds as a sheriff courted by Andy Griffith.

Sherman never made another picture in Hollywood. After a long absence, he capped his career with a half dozen made-for-TV pictures, including *The Last Hurrah* (1977), *Women at West Point* (1979), the poor biopic *Bogie: The Last Hero* (1980), and *The Dream Merchants* (1980), a bland version of Harold Robbins's bestseller about the rise of Hollywood; Morgan Fairchild and Morgan Brittany co-starred for the first and, alas, only time.

## ● GEORGE SIDNEY (1916– )

One of MGM's most reliable directors of musicals during the Forties, George Sidney was a former child actor whose father was an executive with Loew's–MGM in New York. He joined MGM as a messenger boy while in his teens and soon had advanced to the position of film editor. By 1935 Sidney was working as a second-unit and assistant director, and a year later he started conducting many of the studio's screen tests. He also began directing one-reel shorts for Pete Smith, one of which won an Academy Award in 1940; in 1941, his "Passing Parade" short *Of Pups and Puzzles* won another.

Sidney was now promoted to directing features, the first of which was *Free and Easy* (1941), a pleasant "B" with Robert Cummings and Ruth Hussey. *Pacific Rendevous* (1942) and *Pilot No. 5* (1943) were patriotic programmers, but *Thousands Cheer* (1943) was a Technicolor extravaganza, using the old "let's put on a show!" premise to highlight such top MGM players as Mickey Rooney, Judy Garland (singing "The Joint Is Really Jumpin'"), Lena Horne, Red Skelton, Gene Kelly, and, well, thousands more. Sidney's facility with this all-star production earned him a shot at a musical, and *Bathing Beauty* (1944), Esther Williams's first starring vehicle, became a success, aided by Red Skelton, Xavier Cugat, Harry James, and a climactic water ballet of Olympian dimensions.

*Anchors Aweigh* (1945) was equally popular; Gene Kelly and Frank Sinatra are a couple of sailors on leave who take turns singing to and with Kathryn Grayson. Kelly's dancing duet with Jerry, the animated mouse, was a state-of-the-art special-effects triumph (dusted off in recent years for a Paula Abdul video and, of course, *Roger Rabbit*). *The Harvey Girls* (1946) was Sidney's most prestigious assignment to date, a period musical about a restaurant chain that tames the Old West; top star Judy Garland was well supported by Ray Bolger, Angela Lansbury, and John Hodiak. The film was a major box office hit and won an Oscar for "On the Atchison, Topeka and the Santa Fe," a Johnny Mercer–Bert Warren composition. *Holiday in Mexico* (1946) was a so-so musical comedy, with sixteen-year-old Jane Powell trying to find a spouse for dad Walter Pidgeon, while glamorous Ilona Massey sings her way into his heart.

Sidney departed from his métier to direct *Cass Timberlane* (1947), a glossy adaptation (by Donald Ogden Stewart) of the Sinclair Lewis novel—but stars Spencer Tracy and Lana Turner were ill matched. Lana was better served by *The Three Musketeers* (1948), a lively (but now seldom seen) version of the Dumas classic in which she played Lady DeWinter alongside Gene Kelly, Van Heflin, Gig Young, and Vincent Price. *The Red Danube* (1949) was another unlikely project for Sidney, a plodding Cold War melodrama that featured Janet Leigh as a ballerina hiding in Vienna from Russian agents, while *Key to the City* (1950) was a forgettable romantic comedy in which long-ago real-life lovers Loretta Young and Clark Gable feign interest in each other.

But the 1950 *Annie Get Your Gun* was a hugely popular adaptation of the Irving Berlin musical, which suffered only slightly from the casting of Betty Hutton in what was intended to be a role for Judy Garland (who actually began filming under the direction of Busby Berkeley in 1949 before suffering a nervous breakdown). *Show Boat* (1951) was a colorful version of an Edna Ferber story, last filmed by James Whale in 1936. Again, Judy Garland was supposed to be one of the principals (as Julie), but Ava Gardner ended up with the role; the cast also featured Howard Keel, Kathryn Grayson (who's a bit much), William Warfield, and Marge and Gower Champion. The production was lavish and well mounted, and not surprisingly became one of MGM's more popular Fifties musicals. *Scaramouche* (1952) was, in its own way, even better, a top-notch swashbuckler; Stewart Granger was quite effective in the kind of role made famous (but no longer playable) by Flynn.

Granger laid down his sword in *Young Bess* (1953), which again demonstrated Sidney's skill with costume pictures; Charles Laughton appeared as Henry VIII, the role he'd won an Oscar for twenty years earlier, and Jean Simmons (Granger's real-life wife) was Elizabeth I. The 1953 *Kiss Me Kate* (originally released in 3-D) was an inventive filming of the stage hit, with its terrific Cole Porter score (a generous fourteen songs including "Too Darn Hot") nearly intact; the appealing cast included Ann Miller, Howard Keel, Kathryn Grayson, and Keenan Wynn. It was on to ancient Rome for the ill-advised *Jupiter's Darling* (1955); Esther Williams was unhappily cast as a fleshpot who uses her wiles to distract Hannibal (Howard Keel) from attacking the empire.

This concluded Sidney's long stay at MGM, and he moved to Columbia to make *The Eddy Duchin Story* (1956). Rich in detail and full of Thirties music, this overlong biopic of the Golden Age pianist needed the Tyrone Power of a decade earlier to energize it. *Jeanne Eagels* (1957) was another period picture, with Kim Novak as the tragic stage actress, but as with *Duchin*, the restrictions of the screen biography—and the limitations of Ms. Novak—didn't play to Sidney's strengths. *Pal Joey* (1957) also starred Novak, but it worked much better, in part due to the quality of the 1940 Rodgers and Hart stage production on which it was based (though here predictably laundered). Its classic tunes included "The Lady Is a Tramp" and "My Funny Valentine," and it didn't hurt having Frank Sinatra and Rita Hayworth on hand.

*Who Was That Lady?* (1960) was patently ridiculous, although Dean Martin and Tony Curtis proved to be an amusing team. *Pepe* (also 1960) was a three and a quarter–hour disaster, however, and Mexican superstar Cantinflas wasn't saved by Zsa Zsa Gabor, Joey Bishop, and Sammy Davis, Jr., a few of the legions of stars with cameos. *Bye Bye Birdie* (1963) was a lively version of the Broadway blockbuster (inspired by Elvis's Army induction), starring bombshell Ann-Margret and Dick Van Dyke. A-M also helped elevate *Viva Las Vegas* (1964) far above the usual Elvis musical; the King awakens from his screen slumber to actually shake his thing for the first time in years for "C'Mon Everybody" and the great title tune.

In between those was *A Ticklish Affair* (1963), a by-the-numbers romantic comedy starring Gig Young and Shirley Jones, and even Ann-Margret couldn't rescue the inherent phoniness of *The Swinger* (1966). Last came the willing but hopelessly lame *Half a Sixpence* (1967), an overextended British musical that required a cast, book, and score transplant to work; none was forthcoming. But at least Sidney's final work had been a musical, his favorite genre.

◄ *Photographing Ava Gardner on the set of* Show Boat

## ● DON SIEGEL (1912–1991)

A master of the action film, Don Siegel had an unlikely background for his future vocation. Born in Chicago, he was educated in England at Jesus College, Cambridge University, then attended London's Royal Academy of Dramatic Art as preparation for a career on stage. But acting and Siegel couldn't make their peace, and he returned to the States. Soon he found himself in Hollywood at Warner Bros., where in 1933 Hal Wallis got him a job at their film library. He rose to cutter, then headed Warners' montage department, where he contributed second-unit work of a high caliber to *Casablanca*, *Yankee Doodle Dandy*, and *City for Conquest*, among others.

Siegel's first solo efforts were the short films *A Star in the Night* and *Hitler Lives?* (both 1945), which won Oscars and showed Warners that he was ready to graduate to features. His first was *The Verdict* (1946), a Scotland Yard period piece with Sydney Greenstreet and Peter Lorre. *Night unto Night* was shot in 1947 but not released until 1949, which was just as well for stars Ronald Reagan and Viveca Lindfors (who was now Siegel's wife). Moving to RKO, he made *The Big Steal* (1949), a lighthearted crime yarn that reunited Robert Mitchum and Jane Greer, the stars of Jacques Tourneur's noir classic *Out of the Past*. Although not up to that level, *Steal* showed Siegel's facility with hard-boiled action, the genre in which he would eventually make his reputation.

But first Siegel had to struggle through *Duel at Silver Creek* (1952), an uninspired Audie Murphy Western. Not much better were *No Time for Flowers* (1952), a Cold War comedy with Lindfors that failed to amuse, and the farfetched melodrama *Count the Hours* (1953), in which Macdonald Carey takes the fall for a murder he didn't commit so wife Teresa Wright can have their baby in peace. Siegel returned to action with *China Venture* (1953), a decent World War II yarn that pitted a Marine commando group headed by Edmond O'Brien against the Japanese Navy. Better still was *Riot in Cell Block 11* (1954), an exciting prison drama that Siegel made for Walter Wanger; after forty years, the picture remains gripping and is the first of Siegel's "signature" efforts. Almost as exciting was *Private Hell 36* (1954), a late noir that featured the great Ida Lupino as lead actress, screenwriter, and co-producer (with husband Collier Young; her next husband, Howard Duff, was also in the cast).

The crime film seemed to be Siegel's forte, but his next picture was the mawkish *An Annapolis Story* (1955); suffice it to say that John Derek and Diana Lynn were the leads. But *Invasion of the Body Snatchers* (1956) was a quantum leap forward. One of the two or three best science-fiction movies of the decade, *Snatchers* triumphed over its low-wattage cast and minuscule budget (this was, after all, an Allied Artists film) to become a classic of paranoia. (It has been remade twice, by Philip Kaufman in 1979 and by Abel Ferrara in 1993, neither of which topped Siegel's original for pure chills.) *Crime in the Streets* (1956) adapted a 1955 Reginald Rose TV drama, using original cast members John Cassavetes, future director Mark Rydell, and Will Kuluva as disaffected teens, with Sal Mineo (hot off *Rebel Without a Cause*) added for star power. Siegel's fourth and final AA project was *Baby Face Nelson* (1957), an appropriately violent look at the infamous gangster that offered Mickey Rooney one of his few decent roles of the Fifties.

*Spanish Affair* (1958) was, fittingly, a Spanish production that sent Richard Kiley off to Iberia in search of romance—except for the Chamber of Commerce, who cared? *The Lineup* (1958) put Siegel back on track with a feature-length version of the TV series; it offers Eli Wallach and Richard Jaeckel among its hard-boiled pleasures. *The Gun Runners* (also 1958) was the third screen version of Hemingway's *To Have and Have Not*, but it was the least convincing. With *Hound-Dog Man* (1959), Siegel performed the minor miracle of making teen idol Fabian's screen debut palatable and then some. *Edge of Eternity* (1959) was a contemporary Western, with deputy Cornel Wilde chasing down killer Mickey Shaughnessy. *Flaming Star* (1960) was a real surprise: Elvis Presley is totally convincing as a half-breed Kiowa whose allegiances are divided, and Dolores Del Rio plays his mother. This is far and away Elvis's best nonmusical film, and a solid work by any standard.

*Hell Is for Heroes* (1962) was a hard-as-nails World War II picture that had it all: a top cast (Steve McQueen, Fess Parker, Nick Adams, James Coburn), a great script (by Robert Pirosh), and of course Siegel at the helm. He now moved into television, primarily shooting pilots; *The Killers* (1964), with Ronald Reagan, Lee Marvin, and Angie Dickinson, was supposed to be shown as a TV original, but it was deemed too violent for America's living rooms and got a theatrical release after all. His next TV film, *The Hanged Man* (1964), was a passable remake of the 1947 *Ride the Pink Horse*, while *Stranger on the Run* (1967) was a suspenseful Reginald Rose tale with the fine cast of Henry Fonda, Anne Baxter, Sal Mineo, and Dan Duryea.

At this point it wasn't clear where Siegel was going with his career—many film directors had entered television without ever returning to feature work—but his next two projects answered that question with authority. *Madigan* (1968) was simply the best cop movie of the Sixties, with a great Richard Widmark performance at its center, and excellent work by Henry Fonda and Inger Stevens. *Coogan's Bluff* (1968) established Clint Eastwood with American audiences after his years of working overseas with Sergio Leone; here he's a laconic Arizona deputy tracking a killer to New York. Both films were spun off into TV series (the latter as *McCloud*), but Siegel was staying with motion pictures. *Death of a Gunfighter* (1969) featured Widmark again, but it was codirected with Robert Totten and released with the credit "Allen Smithee"—the standard pseudonym for work disowned by its director.

*Two Mules for Sister Sara* (1970) was a rather whimsical pairing of Clint Eastwood and Shirley MacLaine, from a Budd Boetticher story—perhaps it was a bit *too* cute—after which Eastwood and Siegel teamed up again for *The Beguiled* (1971), an unusual psychological drama set just after the Civil War. The film is slow and too long, but a cult following has grown around it. That was also the year of *Dirty Harry*, probably Siegel's best-known picture (though not necessarily his most admired); a huge popular success, it catapulted Clint Eastwood to superstardom as the Seventies' quintessential anti-hero and led to four profitable (but inferior) sequels (none directed by Siegel). Critics carped about the violence, but its very nastiness is what has kept it from dating (much), and the action sequences remain without peer. Siegel served as producer on his next project (as he had on his previous two). *Charley Varrick* (1973) turned out to be a top-notch thriller; a caper movie in reverse, it has Walter Matthau running from a legion of Mafia hit men, who want the money that Matthau (unwittingly) stole from them.

*The Black Windmill* (1974) was shot in the United Kingdom and starred Michael Caine, but Siegel appeared uneasy with its espionage background and the payoff is disappointing. *The Shootist* (1976), how-

ever, was an elegaic gem—the last film made by John Wayne, who, like the character he plays here, was dying of cancer. The cast—Jimmy Stewart, Lauren Bacall, Richard Boone, Hugh O'Brian, John Carradine—is a dream, and some call this Siegel's finest achievement. *Telefon* (1977) was not in the same league, but Siegel (who took over from Peter Hyams) did better than expected with this complicated espionage yarn, which offers a memorable performance by Charles Bronson as a Russian agent.

*Escape from Alcatraz* (1979) was stronger, a prime vehicle for Clint Eastwood based on real-life inmate Frank Morris's 1962 escape, which led to the closing of the "escape-proof" institution. A bit longer than necessary, the film gains power from its very starkness. (By working with him so often, Siegel was also able to tutor Eastwood in the art of directing, lessons Eastwood has often acknowledged, and put to good use.)

Siegel's last two films were, to put it bluntly, failures. *Rough Cut* (1980) was the less disastrous of the two, a blithe caper pic in which Burt Reynolds is out of his league as a suave jewel thief; Siegel was its fourth and last director, and the mismosh is all too evident. *Jinxed!* (1982) is self-explanatory, a painfully unfunny combination of singer Bette Midler, blackjack dealer Ken Wahl, and Las Vegas. Siegel retired thereafter, and one can only hope he was able to expunge those last unfortunate works from his memories, if not his otherwise splendid résumé.

▲ *Siegel and protégé Clint Eastwood during the filming of* Dirty Harry

## ● ROBERT SIODMAK (1900–1973)

A number of great directors fled Germany in the 1930s to work in the United States, but Robert Siodmak was surely the only one to have been born in Memphis, Tennessee. (His father, a Leipzig banker, was on a business trip in the States with his wife when Robert was born.) Siodmak's first brush with show business was as an actor in a German repertory company, but eventually he went into banking. Failing at that, in 1925 he gained entrée to the film industry by accepting a job as a translator for silent films imported from the United States. He advanced to film editor, and by 1929 was co-directing his first feature with Edgar G. Ulmer, a documentary entitled *Menschen am Sonntag* (*People on Sunday*). Siodmak directed a number of thrillers at UFA, but with the rise of the Nazi movement he fled Germany in 1933 for the safety of Paris. In 1940, when Paris was about to become occupied, he hurriedly departed for Hollywood at the invitation of Paramount, which tendered a two-year contract.

Siodmak's first films were "B"s of every description: inspirational dramas like *West Point Widow* (1941), spy thrillers like *Fly by Night* (1942), romantic comedies like *The Night before Divorce* and *My Heart Belongs to Daddy* (both 1942), domestic dramas like *Someone to Remember* (1943). But in 1943 Siodmak found a home at Universal, where he signed a seven-year contract. His first effort there was the stylish *Son of Dracula* (1943), in which Lon Chaney, Jr., conducts a reign of terror as "Count Alucard," in a gothic Southern setting. *Christmas Holiday* (1944) was a moody melodrama, with Gene Kelly and Deanna Durbin cast against type, while *Cobra Woman* (1944) was a florid Maria Montez vehicle that somehow seemed better (if no less silly) than most of her other Technicolor extravaganzas—she plays twins, one evil, one pure of heart, and both hot for Jon Hall.

But Siodmak's first triumph was *Phantom Lady* (1944), a top-notch adaptation of William Irish's *roman noir*, with Alan Curtis as the amnesiac protagonist, Ella Raines his faithful secretary, and Franchot Tone his ostensibly loyal pal. *The Suspect* (1945) was a period thriller, starring Ella Raines and Charles Laughton (as a sympathetic murderer), who play cat-and-mouse in Victorian London. *(The Strange Affair of) Uncle Harry* (1945), adapted from a Broadway play, was a psychological thriller with the appealing Raines now paired with urbane George Sanders, whose affections for her are thwarted by his insanely possessive sister (Geraldine Fitzgerald).

Nineteen forty-six would become Siodmak's banner year, with three near-classic works. The best may be Mark Hellinger's production of *The Killers*, which took the original Hemingway short story as its opening point and developed it in an elaborate series of flashbacks; the film earned Siodmak his only Oscar nomination for best direction and launched the career of Burt Lancaster in dramatic fashion. (Ava Gardner also has her first major role here, and she is positively worth dying for.) Equally memorable was the gothic thriller *The Spiral Staircase*, in which crippled victim Dorothy McGuire heads a superb cast that includes Ethel Barrymore and Elsa Lanchester. Finally, there was *The Dark Mirror*, which offered Olivia de Havilland as twin sisters, one of whom is a murderer.

Siodmak never had another year like that one—but then, few directors do. His lone production for 1947, *Time Out of Mind*, was a dull period piece with Raines and Phyllis Calvert, but *Cry of the City* (1948) was a welcome return to the noir universe, with good performances by Victor Mature and Richard Conte as childhood pals who grow up on opposite sides of the law. *Criss Cross* (1949) was even better; Burt Lancaster plays a bitter, none-too-bright bank guard who becomes enmeshed in an armored-car robbery planned by gangster Dan Duryea, currently

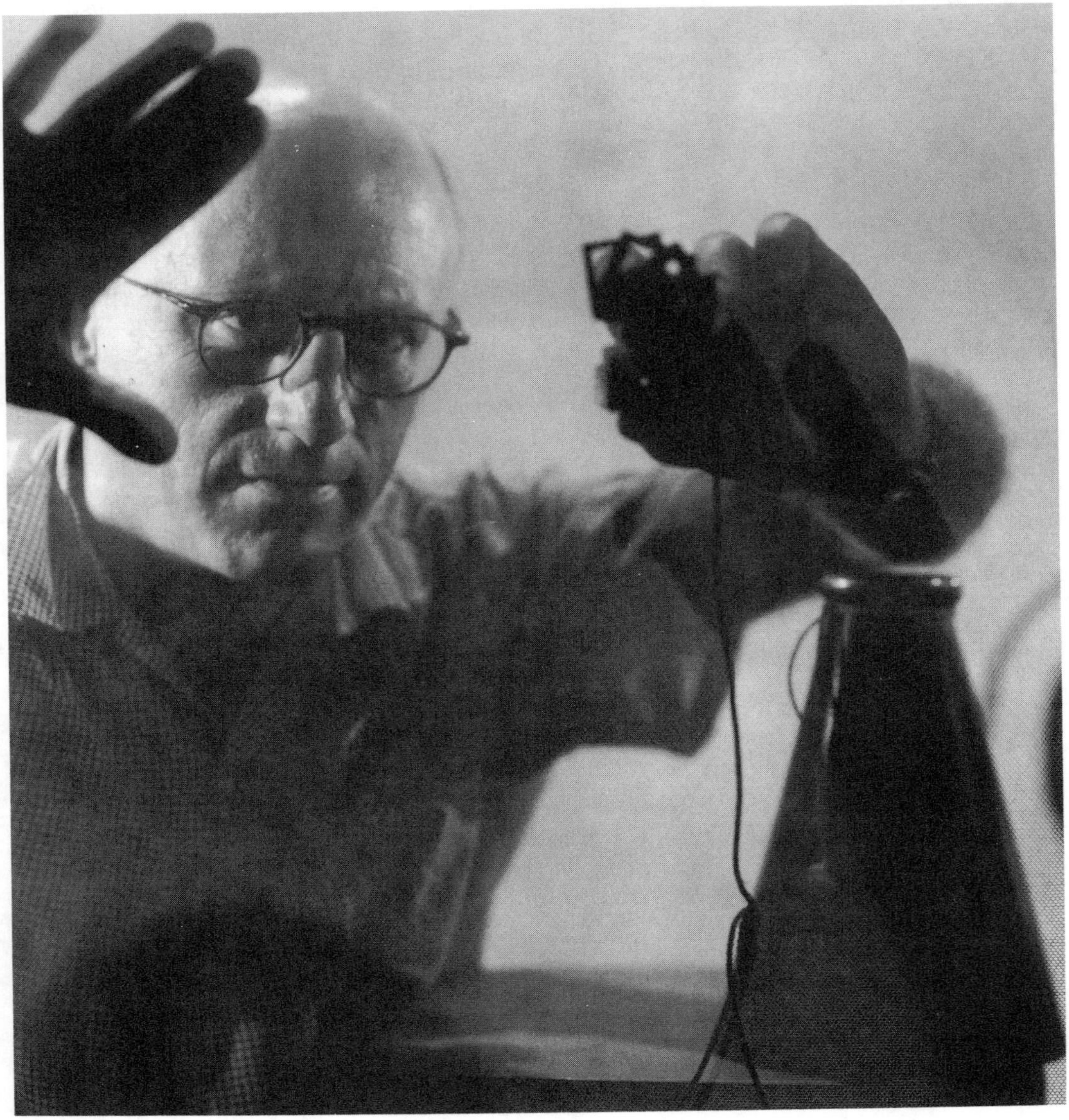

the boyfriend of his ex-wife (Yvonne De Carlo), for whom Lancaster is still carrying a torch. De Carlo was a tad out of her depth, but the complicated tale (written by Daniel Fuchs) had atmosphere and resonance, and remains one of the best—and bleakest—noirs from that classic era.

*The Great Sinner* (1949) had Gregory Peck, Ava Gardner, and MGM's patented gloss, but somehow this story of a couple infected by gambling fever sounded more promising than it played. Siodmak was on more familiar turf with the noirish *(The File on) Thelma Jordan* (1949), a flavorful crime yarn in which Barbara Stanwyck is suspected of murder; Wendell Corey plays the D.A. who falls for the jailbird anyway. *Deported* (1950), with Jeff Chandler, was a hard-boiled yarn inspired in part by Lucky Luciano's deportation to Italy in 1946, while *The Whistle at Eaton Falls* (1951) was an interesting story about plant layoffs in New Hampshire, filmed in semi-documentary fashion.

Siodmak's last Hollywood movie of the Fifties was one of his most enjoyable. *The Crimson Pirate* (1952) was an energetic spoof of swashbucklers that owed its good nature to Burt Lancaster's charismatic, wonderfully athletic performance; the location photography on the pleasing Mediterranean island of Ischia didn't hurt, either. Despite its success, *Pirate* was essentially Siodmak's farewell to Hollywood. In 1953 he moved back to France, and a year later he completely reversed his exile by returning to Germany, where he directed more than a dozen films over the next fifteen years.

During that time he made just three English-language movies. *Portrait of a Sinner* (1959), filmed in England, was a seamy tale of an amoral tart (Nadja Tiller) who corrupts William Bendix and everything else that crosses her path wearing pants, while *Escape from East Berlin* (1962) was the fact-based Cold War saga of an enterprising East German (Don Murray) who tunnels under the Wall to help his family and girlfriend (Christine Kaufmann) escape to the West. Finally, there was the Cinerama production *Custer of the West* (1968), an iconoclastic portrait of the infamous general, played here by Robert Shaw; the interesting cast also included Mary Ure (Shaw's wife), Robert Ryan, Jeffrey Hunter, and Lawrence Tierney. It was the only Western Siodmak ever made—an interesting postscript to a career all too briefly set in the environs of Hollywood.

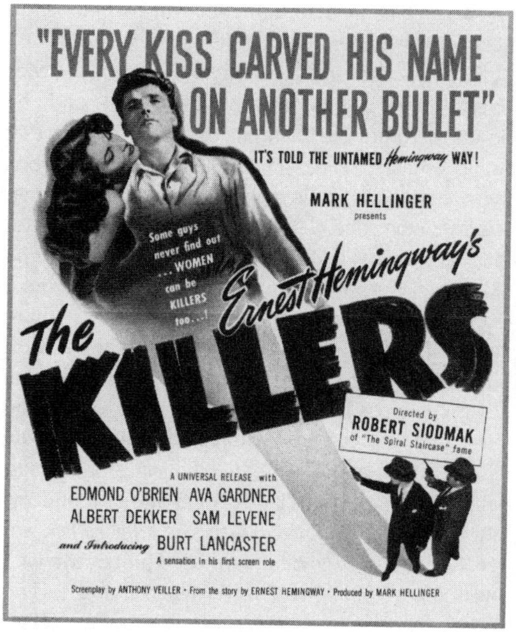

## ● DOUGLAS SIRK (1900–1987)

He was perhaps the greatest, and surely the most stylish, of Hollywood's melodramatists. Born in Denmark as the century turned, Claus Detlev Sierk was raised in Copenhagen but moved to Hamburg, Germany, while still young. He changed his name to Hans Sierck when his acting career in Germany commenced, and spent most of the Twenties directing theater productions in Berlin. In 1934 he received an offer from UFA to make motion pictures, and over the next three years he directed nine films under its aegis. But the specter of Nazism convinced Sierck that he had to leave his adopted homeland, and he emigrated first to France, then to South Africa, Switzerland, and Holland.

Warner Bros. contacted him in 1939, and soon he was headed to the States and a career in Hollywood. Now working as Douglas Sirk, he spent the better part of the next three years waiting for his career to commence. In 1942 he took a job with Columbia as a writer, but even that didn't pan out. Finally Sirk aligned himself with a group of German émigrés to make two independent productions. The first was *Hitler's Madman* (1943), an effective low-budget thriller about Nazi commandant Reinhard Heydrich (John Carradine) that was distributed by MGM; the second, *Summer Storm* (1944), was a sensitive adaptation of Chekhov's *The Shooting Party*, with George Sanders and Linda Darnell. *A Scandal in Paris* (1946; aka *Thieves' Holiday*) was a breezy adventure about a French con man played to perfection (as usual) by George Sanders. That was followed by *Lured* (1947), a gothic thriller in which Lucille Ball is menaced by both Sanders and Boris Karloff.

*Sleep My Love* (1948) was a stylish knockoff of *Gaslight*, with Don Ameche cast against type as the husband trying to drive wife Claudette Colbert insane. Ameche returned to more familiar turf in *Slightly French* (1949), an amiable musical in which Dorothy Lamour is passed off as a star of the Paris stage. *Shockproof* (1949) was a great-looking film noir (written by Samuel Fuller) that explored the dark side of human nature, as evinced by gorgeous-but-evil parolee Patricia Knight and bewitched parole officer Cornel Wilde (her real-life husband).

Sirk now returned to Germany, but his stay was brief; Universal-International beckoned, and he signed a contract with them that kept him at that studio until he retired in 1959. But his first efforts there gave little indication of what was to come. *Mystery Submarine* (1950) was perhaps a bit better than its title, but this tale of a sub commander who kidnaps a German scientist need not be exhumed. Nor were Sirk's four 1951 releases of much more import. *The First Legion* was the best of the lot, with Charles Boyer as a Jesuit priest who must determine if a miracle has occurred. *The Lady Pays Off* was an inane romantic comedy, with Linda Darnell's beauty its lone asset, and *Thunder on the Hill* a mildly suspenseful drama, with Claudette Colbert as a nun trying to unravel a murder. *Weekend with Father* was yet another variation on the oft-used plot of two widowers (Van Heflin and Patricia Neal) trying to find romance while their kids try to gum up the works.

*No Room for the Groom* was more foolishness, with Tony Curtis and Piper Laurie, while *Has Anybody Seen My Gal?* (both 1952) was a Twenties period piece of no particular distinction, although Charles Coburn was his usual droll self and Rock Hudson and Piper Laurie at least *looked* good. (From such assignments, one must assume that the Universal executives who hired Sirk were totally unfamiliar with his previous work.) *Meet Me at the Fair* (1953) was cut from the same nostalgic cloth, with Dan Dailey selling patent medicine at a sideshow, while *Take Me to Town* at least offered some star chemistry in its story of nineteenth-century saloon singer Ann Sheridan and preacher Sterling Hayden. On first blush, *All I*

*Desire* (also 1953) seemed just another period piece. But while it suffers a bit from unequal leads (Richard Carlson is hardly a match for Barbara Stanwyck), Sirk presents the soap-opera elements of the story with a conviction and flourish uncommon to the genre.

Released in 3-D for about fifteen minutes before being issued in the standard format, *Taza, Son of Cochise* (1954) was a nominal sequel to Universal's 1952 *Battle of Apache Pass*; a raven-tressed Rock Hudson starred as the eponymous hero in a familiar yarn that was most memorable for its location shooting in Utah. But *Magnificent Obsession* (1954) represented Sirk at his grandest—here was a broad canvas and an emotionally rich romance with which to work. A remake of the fine John Stahl version from 1935, this is the film that made a star of Rock Hudson (who compares favorably to the original's Robert Taylor) and made Sirk a bankable director. Jane Wyman was Oscar-nominated for her performance as a rich woman blinded in a car accident caused by a drunken playboy (Hudson), who then puts himself through medical school to learn how to restore her vision.

That whopping box-office success was followed by the risible *The Sign of the Pagan* (1954), a florid tale of Rome under attack by Attila the Hun (Jack Palance)—an absurd assignment for Sirk after the tasteful *Obsession*, it would seem, but under the studio system the later film was probably completed before the results of the earlier one had been tabulated. *Captain Lightfoot* (1955) transported Rock Hudson and Jeff Morrow back to nineteenth-century Ireland; Sirk shot it on location (though his best work emerged from studio sets). *There's Always Tomorrow* (1956) gave him a contemporary romance to work with, although this passionate affair between Fred MacMurray and Barbara Stanwyck didn't prove to be another *Double Indemnity*. *All That Heaven Allows* (1956) was more like it, a glossy, set-bound reteaming of Hudson and Wyman as, respectively, a lowly gardener and the wealthy widow who falls for him. It afforded Sirk plenty of room for his carefully heightened embellishments, the better to tug on the heartstrings.

*Written on the Wind* (also 1956) was an all-stops-out melodrama with a great cast (Rock Hudson, Robert Stack, Lauren Bacall, and Dorothy Malone); it may well be Sirk's masterpiece. Malone won a best supporting actress Academy Award for her splendidly vulgar performance as a nymphomaniac who hates her wealthy family, and Stack (as her playboy brother) was also nominated. *Battle Hymn* (1957) was another vehicle for Rock Hudson and not a bad one—although as a priest training fighter pilots in Korea, Rock was pushing the envelope. *Interlude* (1957) was an adequate remake of the 1939 Dunne-Boyer soap opera *When Tomorrow Comes*, hampered by the low star wattage of June Allyson and Rossano Brazzi, but *The Tarnished Angels* (1958) provided Sirk with old favorites Rock Hudson, Dorothy Malone, and Robert Stack, and he made the most of the opportunity. An adaptation of Faulkner's 1931 novel *Pylon* about barnstorming pilots, it was grandly dramatic, full of Sirk's signature touches.

*A Time to Love and a Time to Die* (1958) was somewhat less successful, a World War II love story (from the Erich Maria Remarque novel) that could have used more impressive leads. *Imitation of Life* (1959) provided Sirk with Lana Turner in a potent updating of the 1934 tearjerker that outshines John Stahl's formidable original. It's Sirk's longest film, yet hardly a moment exists that does not support his expressionistic scheme. Both Juanita Moore and Susan Kohner received Academy Award nominations in the supporting actress category, and the film was one of the year's biggest hits—and the biggest ever for Universal up to then.

Still at the peak of his creative powers, Sirk seemed poised to enter the Sixties as one of America's premier directors. But health considerations forced him into early retirement, and he moved back to Germany, robbing moviegoers of an untold number of delights. As it is, *Imitation* may be the best—and most lucrative—final film ever submitted by a Hollywood director.

## ● STEVEN SPIELBERG (1947– )

The reigning *Wunderkind* of the American cinema, Steven Spielberg already has (at this writing) fifteen theatrical features to his credit at the age of forty-eight. For a time he was perceived as a card-carrying phenomenon, although a few recent stumbles—of the same epic dimension as his successes—nearly reduced him to mortal dimensions. Then came *Jurassic Park* and *Schindler's List*, and the epithet "genius" was bandied about once more.

Born in Cincinnati, Ohio, Spielberg was raised outside Los Angeles, a locale geographically and spiritually proper for one who would soon dedicate his life to filmmaking. At the age of thirteen, he won first prize in a contest for his 40-minute war movie, *Escape to Nowhere*. He spent most of his sixteenth year working on *Firelight*, a feature-length science-fiction yarn, which was followed by an accomplished short about hitchhikers called *Amblin'*. Universal got a look at *Amblin'* and tendered a contract to Spielberg, who began by working in their television film division. His first credit was the Joan Crawford episode of the pilot for *Night Gallery* in 1969, an impressive debut that was followed by work on top TV series like *Columbo*, *Marcus Welby*, and *Owen Marshall*. Then came *Duel* (1971), a taut, almost claustrophobic exercise in paranoia that was strong stuff indeed for television (it was released theatrically in Europe). Although Spielberg permitted star Dennis Weaver to register a one-note impression of sweaty terror throughout, his handling of the action sequences with the homicidal truck was masterful, staged and executed with the nerveless bravado soon to be seen in *Jaws*.

His next TV movies, *Something Evil* (1972), a good haunted-house yarn, and *Savage* (1973), a so-so pilot for a ne'er-born series about a pair of investigative reporters (husband-wife actors Barbara Bain and Martin Landau), weren't quite at that level. But Spielberg's first theatrical release (which he also co-wrote), *The Sugarland Express* (1974), demonstrated that he was ready to step up to the big leagues. A chase picture with deft accents of comedy but an inexorable movement toward tragedy, it was anchored by a fine performance by Goldie Hawn. But the proficiency of *Sugarland* could hardly have prepared anyone for the mega-success of *Jaws* (1975), one of the highest-grossing films of all time and the suspense movie by which all others have been measured since. Improving on the portentous bestseller by Peter Benchley, *Jaws* was Oscar-nominated as best picture: apparently it was decided that sophomore director Spielberg would have to bide his time for similar recognition.

That came with his very next opus, the mystical science-fiction tale *Close Encounters of the Third Kind* (1977), which Spielberg also wrote. Richard Dreyfuss was cast as the lead, and submitted the best performance of his career as a simple telephone lineman who experiences the numinous in the Indiana skies and struggles obsessively to understand what it is that has moved him so. Incredibly, the film was not in the running for an Academy Award as best picture—this was also the year of *Star Wars* and the Academy must have decided that one SF picture was enough—but Spielberg received his first nomination for best direction. Vilmos Zsigmond's stunning cinematography earned the film's only Oscar, and Spielberg became the second director in history to score back-to-back $100 million grosses. (George Lucas turned the trick that same year.)

Based on the phenomenon of those consecutive blockbusters, Spielberg's expensive *1941* (1979) was expected to be another smash. It wasn't, for the simple reason that it was awful: a bloated, frighteningly unfunny comedy about L.A.'s undergoing a non-invasion by the Japanese right after Pearl Harbor. The equally bloated cast included John Belushi, Dan Aykroyd, Ned Beatty, and John Candy, all of whom sank into the morass. Spielberg pulled himself together for *Raiders of the Lost Ark* (1981), a loving, expert (if slightly redundant) tribute to the old adventure serials conceived by Spielberg, co-producer George Lucas, and Philip Kaufman. A couple of hundred million dollars later, no one remembered *1941* and Spielberg received his second Academy Award nomination for best direction; the film was also a best picture nominee.

Few wagered that Spielberg would top *Raiders* with his very next try, but he did. *E.T. The Extra-Terrestrial* (1982) was a moving exploration of First Contact that cleverly eschewed the epic scale of *Close Encounters* for the microcosm of its effect on a single California family. Henry Thomas is positively brilliant as the boy who discovers and befriends the stranded alien, and Dee Wallace makes an enviably sympathetic Mom. As with most Spielberg films to this juncture, the special effects were a large part of the movie's appeal—in this case, the wonderfully articulated E.T.—but it was Spielberg's mastery of human (and alien) emotion that made this the most successful motion picture release of all time. Both Spielberg and the film were nominated for Academy Awards, as were Melissa Mathison's screenplay and Allen Daviau's cinematography, and the score by John Williams won an Oscar.

Spielberg acted as executive producer on the frightening ghost tale *Poltergeist* that same year; it was a position he would assume on a number of films directed by others. It was whispered that he had stepped in and reshot the work of director Tobe Hooper; in any case, someone made a heck of a movie. He directed just one of the four episodes in *Twilight Zone—The Movie* (1983), although his probably was the weakest of the lot (George Miller, Joe Dante, and John Landis directed the other segments). *Indiana Jones and the Temple of Doom* (1984) was the inevitable (and deafening) sequel to *Raiders*, and like most sequels, it didn't measure up to the original—except in terms of dollars grossed. Otherwise, it was inferior in terms of cast, story, stunts, and pacing, with some decidedly unpleasant sequences lending a sour taste to the whole overcalculated affair.

Spielberg appeared to be in a rut, but he extricated himself by boldly choosing to adapt Alice Walker's Pulitzer Prize–winning novel *The Color Purple* (1985). The film moves from 1909 to 1950 while exploring one black woman's almost unbearably harsh, yet ultimately fulfilling, life. *Color* was roundly criticized for downplaying the novel's lesbian element, for perpetuating stereotypes about black men, and for sentimentalizing what life in the Deep South was like; nevertheless, it found an audience that appreciated the fine cast (including Whoopi Goldberg, Margaret Avery, and Oprah Winfrey), literate script (by Menno Meyjes), and superb score (by co-producer Quincy Jones), all of which were Oscar-nominated. So was the film—but Spielberg was not, a slight that created a small scandal at the time. The Directors' Guild softened the blow by giving him their top award that year, but the insult lingered. More important, Spielberg had made one of the few commercially successful films about the black experience, paving the way for like projects to be greenlighted.

He must have liked the taste he got of literary adaptation, as Spielberg chose another critically acclaimed book as the basis of his next film. *Empire of the Sun* (1987) was a long (too long!), lovingly detailed re-creation of the World War II prison-camp milieu of J. G. Ballard's autobiographical tale (scripted by Tom Stoppard). But where *Color* was able to punch across some emotional truth, *Empire* almost lets the story about its young protagonist (Christian Bale) drown under a wave of pyrotechnics. A box-office failure, *Empire* is worth seeing for its first half, and mourning for its second. *Indiana Jones and the Last Crusade* (1989) turned out to be a kinder, gentler Indiana Jones blockbuster; Sean Connery was cannily cast as Indy's resourceful but emotionally distant dad, and the graphic gore that marred *Temple* was blessedly absent. But the formula had become threadbare by this time. (*Another* magical religious artifact to help the Nazis conquer the world? Why not the Golden Fleece, while we're at it?)

Since he hadn't had luck basing his films on prize-winning books or making sequels to his own movies, Spielberg next adapted the 1943 *A Guy Named Joe*, a chestnut from Hollywood's golden era. It's a passable entertainment, but *Always* proves only that Richard Dreyfuss isn't Spencer Tracy and that 1989 isn't 1943 in terms of an audience's willing suspension of disbelief. (Holly Hunter deserves a more compelling romantic lead—someone like Kevin Costner might have made the sentimental medicine go down easier.) *Always* was nothing to be ashamed of, but the same cannot be said of *Hook* (1991), a bloated, clanking, overendowed mess of a movie that gave revisionism a bad name. Parceling out the blame for this expensive dud is not difficult—certainly Robin Williams is miscast, but is that his fault? Misconceived from the first to the last of its 144 minutes, *Hook* damaged the Spielberg aura as no other film had.

To his credit, he licked his wounds—and wounds there must have been—and salvaged his reputation in dramatic fashion with not one but two enormously popular 1993 releases. The first, *Jurassic Park*, was a triumph on the mechanistic front, proving that Spielberg could still be counted on to haul in $400 million (the most a movie has ever grossed) when given the right property—in this case, Michael Crichton's multimillion-selling novel about dinosaurs re-created and running amok on a remote isle. To be sure, the film could have been even better—some of the dinosaur encounters, and indeed some of the dinosaurs themselves disappoint (snot from a brachiosaurus?), and the scenes of peril are less deftly blended with character-focused downtime activity than in, say, *Jaws*. But the technology is dazzlingly employed, and there are enough potent shocks to indicate that Spielberg still has his fastball.

*Jurassic* made so much money that the grosses for *Schindler's List* are almost irrelevant (although it has already passed the $70 million). What matters is that *Schindler's* was overwhelmingly acknowledged as the artistic triumph Spielberg had never really been credited with, for all his past success. Considering the film's uncommercial subject matter (the Holocaust), technique (black-and-white cinematography, quasi-documentary presentation), cast (just marginal stars Liam Neeson and Ben Kingsley), and scope (three-hours-plus running time), that was surely his primary concern. That, and the Oscar he was finally awarded for best direction in the 1993 Academy Awards, which also cited *Schindler's* for best picture, screenplay, cinematography, and score—total vindication at last.

The news that Spielberg had joined with multimedia moguls Jeffrey Katzenberg and David Geffen in October 1994 to found the new studio DreamWorks had the industry abuzz—the implications were mind-boggling, as if Babe Ruth, Lou Gehrig, and Walter Johnson had somehow contrived to buy their own baseball team back in 1925. If Spielberg makes movies as late into his life as Hitchcock did, we have another thirty years of wonder to look forward to.

▶ *Henry Thomas is coached by Spielberg during the filming of* E.T. The Extra-Terrestrial

## ● JOHN M. STAHL (1886-1950)

The Thirties' preeminent director of "women's pictures," John M. Stahl was born in New York City and began acting on stage while a teenager. He appeared in some bit parts in films in 1913, then turned to directing in 1914. Some of his early work has been lost, but he made some twenty silents at First National and MGM, including *Suspicious Wives*, *Why Men Leave Home*, *The Gay Deceivers*, and *Lovers?*, the last a Ramon Novarro drama. He spent a few years at the Tiffany studio as a producer, then began the sound era at Universal by directing the weeper *The Lady Surrenders* (1930), the genre in which he would specialize. *Seed* (1931) was a soap opera set in the world of publishing, with John Boles as a clerk who leaves his wife and five children for an editor he hopes might publish his writings, while *Strictly Dishonorable* (1931) was an adaptation of the Preston Sturges stage comedy, with Paul Lukas and Sidney Fox as the would-be lovers.

Stahl next made the seminal weeper *Back Street* (1932), with Irene Dunne pining for John Boles; it was a huge hit. That was followed by *Only Yesterday* (1933), which more nearly resembled *Letter from an Unknown Woman* than the popular history from which it took its name; Margaret Sullavan made her screen debut here as an unwed mother forgotten by one-night-stand John Boles. *Imitation of Life* (1934) was a well-mounted adaptation of Fannie Hurst's drama about a light-skinned black girl (the lovely Fredi Washington) who passes for white, breaking her mother's (Louise Beavers) heart; the subplot has employer Claudette Colbert trying to come to grips with the fact that she and daughter Rochelle Hudson are competing for the same man. *Magnificent Obsession* (1935) required just as many handkerchiefs. Irene Dunne suffers splendidly as a woman who is blinded after her car is smashed into by irresponsible playboy Robert Taylor; he then spends six years learning medicine so that he can operate on Dunne and restore her sight, winning the Nobel Prize in the bargain. (Both this and *Imitation* were remade in glorious Technicolor by Douglas Sirk in the Fifties, but Stahl's versions still hold their own.)

Stahl went to MGM in 1937 to make the debacle *Parnell* with Clark Gable, then returned to Universal for *Letter of Introduction* (1938), starring Andrea Leeds as a would-be actress who refuses to draw on her estranged actor dad's well-known name to break into the biz. *When Tomorrow Comes* (1939) reteamed Charles Boyer and Irene Dunne in another weeper following their hugely popular *Love Affair*, while *Our*

*Wife* (1941) was a standard screwball comedy, with Melvyn Douglas and Ruth Hussey. *The Immortal Sergeant* (1943), the first of nine films Stahl would make for Fox, was an adequate war pic, with Henry Fonda learning what it takes to earn his stripes. Much better was *Holy Matrimony* (1943), a rare comedy for Stahl and nicely carried off, with the considerable aid of Monty Woolley. *The Eve of St. Mark* (1944) was more wartime inspiration, with a good performance by Anne Baxter. But it was *The Keys of the Kingdom*, from the A. J. Cronin novel, that gave Stahl an epic canvas on which to work. This tale of a missionary's event-filled life was overlong and a bit too earnest, but it launched Gregory Peck to stardom and was one of the year's big hits.

Stahl's next film for Fox was quite possibly the best of his career. *Leave Her to Heaven* (1945) was based on a bestseller by Ben Ames Williams and featured the pride of the Fox stable, including the radiant Gene Tierney, Vincent Price, Cornel Wilde, and Jeanne Crain. Drenched in Technicolored tragedy, *Heaven* became one of the year's biggest hits—a feverish, operatically emotional delight which earned Tierney her only Oscar nomination. But *The Foxes of Harrow* (1947), in which Rex Harrison and Maureen O'Hara suffer for each other in 1820s New Orleans, and *The Walls of Jericho* (1948), with Cornel Wilde and Linda Darnell stuck in Kansas, were dull misfires.

The genial *Father Was a Fullback* (1949) was better; Fred MacMurray played a college football coach whose losing season embarrassed daughters Natalie Wood and Betty Lynn, while the period musical *Oh, You Beautiful Doll* (1949) featured "Cuddles" Sakall as songwriter Fred Fisher, with June Haver as his talented daughter and Mark Stevens his collaborator. Less than a year after completing these films, Stahl died. His legacy is a handful of films that provide us with some of the best work by Irene Dunne, Claudette Colbert, and Gene Tierney, stars who became great actresses in his hands.

## ● GEORGE STEVENS (1904–1975)

Few filmmakers have amassed a lifetime of work that runs the cinematic gamut as completely as did George Stevens. Cutting his directing teeth on modest "B" comedies, he slowly but surely ascended through musicals, period adventures, screwball comedies, soap operas, and war documentaries to ambitious but increasingly gargantuan productions that oozed taste and "excellence"—even as they threatened to crush moviegoers with their sheer bulk.

Born in Oakland, California, to professional actors, he began performing on stage at the age of five, and remained in his father's theatrical troupe as an actor and, eventually, a stage manager. He began working as an assistant cameraman at age sixteen, and by 1927 had become a full-fledged cameraman with Hal Roach, for whom he worked on a number of Laurel and Hardy shorts. In 1930 Roach made him a director of two-reel comedies, and in 1934 he directed his first "B" feature for Universal, *The Cohens and Kellys in Trouble*. That year at RKO, he also made the low-budget romantic comedy *Bachelor Bait* with Stu Erwin and Rochelle Hudson, while *Kentucky Kernels* was a Bert Wheeler–Robert Woolsey farce with Spanky McFarland, Noah Beery, and Margaret Dumont. In *The Nitwits* (1935), the comic duo puzzled out a murder mystery with the help of Betty Grable.

*Laddie* (1935) was nostalgic Americana, Indiana style, with John Beal and Gloria Stuart. But it was *Alice Adams* (1935) that signaled RKO's willingness to promote Stevens. A sensitive adaptation of Booth Tarkington's Pulitzer Prize–winning novel, it starred Katharine Hepburn as a social-climbing small-town girl with delusions of grandeur; Fred MacMurray is her unsuspecting, upper-class beau and Hattie McDaniel her hilariously unprepared "maid." The film was one of 1935's ten best-picture nominees for the Academy Award, and Hepburn was also nominated as best actress. *Annie Oakley* (1935), with Barbara Stanwyck as the legendary markswoman and Preston Foster as her sharpshooting sweetie, was a tasty if fanciful swipe at history. *Swing Time* (1936) was sublime Astaire and Rogers; "The Way You Look Tonight," "Bojangles of Harlem," and the other Jerome Kern–Dorothy Fields tunes alone make it fully the equal of *Top Hat*, and Stevens handled the courtship scenes expertly.

*Quality Street* (1937) brought Stevens back to earth. A tasteful but bland filming of the James Barrie play (which MGM made in 1927 with Marion Davies), it starred Hepburn as a spinster who cleverly tricks old beau Franchot Tone into falling in love—another nail in Hepburn's "box-office poison" coffin. Better was *Damsel in Distress* (1937), which despite the absence of Ginger Rogers offered some prime Fred Astaire numbers (via the Gershwins), including the Oscar-winning "Fun House" (directed by Hermes Pan) and "Nice Work If You Can Get It." George Burns and Gracie Allen were also in rare form, but Joan Fontaine as a stuffy (and dull) British heiress bogged things down. Stevens then drew Rogers solo in *Vivacious Lady* (1938); Ginger plays a nightclub singer who marries professor James Stewart, who dreads telling his family, and Charles Coburn and Beulah Bondi provide good comic support.

*Gunga Din* (1939), originally slated for Howard Hawks to direct, was one of the best films in a year laden with great motion pictures; it was also the most expensive movie RKO had ever made. Cary Grant, Victor McLaglen, and Douglas Fairbanks, Jr., are British soldiers and bosom buddies stationed in India; when the fanatic Thuggee sect threatens the Empire's beneficent rule, the lads risk all for God and country to quell the uprising. Sam Jaffe was memorable as the groveling Din, and the three stars were in top form. *Vigil in the Night* (1940), from an A. J. Cronin novel, featured Carole Lombard as a nurse who dedicates her life to the poor denizens of a remote hospital ward after her sister's negligence causes a patient's death. Grim stuff, and not the way the public wanted to see Lombard; it was a box-office disaster, despite its uplifting conclusion.

Stevens now departed RKO, which he felt didn't appreciate him, and went to Columbia to make *Penny Serenade* (1941), a four—no, make that six—handkerchief weeper, scripted by Morrie Ryskind. Cary Grant and Irene Dunne, recently teamed in screwball comedies like *My Favorite Wife*, here play a couple who adopt a baby after Dunne miscarries, then endure the pain of the child's death six years later. The film came very, very close to drowning in its own tears, but Stevens steered it past the perilous shoals of bathos. *The Talk of the Town* (1942) had Grant again, now a fugitive—falsely accused, of course—hiding out in Jean Arthur's home alongside boarder Ronald Colman, a vacationing law professor about to be appointed to the Supreme Court. He and Grant debate the niceties of law while they compete for Arthur's affections, and she tries to decide which of them she prefers. Provocative, intelligent, and funny (credit Irwin Shaw and Sidney Buchman's Oscar-nominated screenplay), *Talk* received an Academy Award nomination as best picture.

Stevens hadn't made an out-and-out comedy for years, but now he made two for the ages. *Woman of the Year* (1942) was the first teaming of Spencer Tracy and Katharine Hepburn, and it has some claim to being their best vehicle. Garson Kanin came up with the original notion of having a gruff sportswriter woo and marry an upper-crust political columnist (guess who plays whom), but when Kanin was drafted he handed the concept over to his brother Michael and Ring Lardner, Jr. Their deft screenplay earned them an Oscar, and Hepburn was nominated as best actress, the least she deserved after enduring the indignity of that riotous breakfast scene. Just as funny (and romantic) was *The More the Merrier* (1943). Jean Arthur stars as a government worker who patriotically rents half her small home to Charles Coburn to help out during Washington's wartime housing crunch—but Coburn has rented half of his half to handsome soldier Joel McCrea, and the sexual tension the new arrangement generates is thick enough to cut with a knife. Its screwball flair helped *More* earn an Academy Award nomination for best picture; Stevens, Arthur, Coburn (the lone winner), the story, and the screenplay also were nominated.

But by Awards time Stevens was already serving in the Army Signal Corps, where he was quickly made head of the Special Motion Pictures unit. One of his assignments was to film the D-day invasion and, more disturbingly, the liberation of the Dachau inmates for the National Archives. He returned covered in glory but shaken by what he had seen—too shaken to work. After a period of inactivity, he was invited by Frank Capra to join him and William Wyler (like Stevens, all ex-Army colonels) in forming Liberty Films; Stevens eagerly accepted the chance for independence from studio interference.

"Why are nice men such dopes?"
It's about a blonde lovely who had a spare room to rent in Washington!...A gay and glorious romance that puts laughter on your lips... love light in your eyes...and a tender glow in your heart!
Only "The MORE THE MERRIER" has a DINGLE!
No other motion picture can make this claim!
JEAN ARTHUR · JOEL McCREA · CHARLES COBURN
in GEORGE STEVENS'
The More The Merrier
Screen Play by Robert Russell and Frank Ross, Richard Flournoy and Lewis R. Foster · Story by Robert Russell and Frank Ross
Directed by GEORGE STEVENS · A COLUMBIA PICTURE

After two years of development hell, Stevens loaned himself out to RKO to make *I Remember Mama* (1948). Based on the nostalgic stories of Kathryn Forbes about her Norwegian immigrant family's struggle to adjust to life in turn-of-the-century San Francisco, which had been successfully dramatized

▲ *With Barbara Bel Geddes on the set of* I Remember Mama

on Broadway in 1943 by John Van Druten, this longish but well-observed (and extremely expensive) film starred Irene Dunne as the rock to which family members Barbara Bel Geddes and Ellen Corby cleave. All three actresses were nominated for Oscars, as was hambone Oscar Homolka, who plays the eccentric Uncle Chris.

With Liberty now sold to Paramount, Stevens went there (somewhat reluctantly) as a producer/director for three films. The first was a remake of Theodore Dreiser's classic novel *An American Tragedy*, which had been filmed by Josef von Sternberg in 1931. *A Place in the Sun* (1951) tends to bank too heavily on the heavenly beauty of stars Montgomery Clift and Elizabeth Taylor, presenting their romance on a gargantuan scale that soon becomes intrusive. Yet *Place* was an enormous popular and critical success, earning Academy Award nominations for best picture, actor, actress (Winters, not Taylor), screenplay, and cinematography. It won Oscars in the last two categories, and Stevens won his first Academy Award for best direction over a very tough field: Vincente Minnelli, John Huston, William Wyler, and Elia Kazan.

*Something to Live For* (1952) is Stevens's forgotten film, a pedestrian melodrama in which alcoholic Joan Fontaine tries to wrest AA member Ray Milland away from wife Teresa Wright—but he weans her from the demon rum and stays home. Now Stevens turned his sights on a once disreputable genre for a more ambitious project. *Shane* (1953) suffers from some of the elephantitis that afflicted *Place*, but with the Western's mythic structure to support it, the picture manages to carry its epic load. Alan Ladd, whose taciturn persona serves him well for once, is an erstwhile gunslinger who becomes a ranch hand for the Starrett family (Jean Arthur, Van Heflin, and Brandon de Wilde). But when Jack (Don't Call Me "Walter") Palance rides into town as a regulator for greedy cattle baron Emile Meyer and starts killing ranchers, Ladd realizes he will have to strap on his guns once more, ending his peaceful interlude. (Ladd's attraction to Arthur, and vice versa, would have made his staying on at the ranch impossibly tense anyway.) And so after winning the climactic gun battle with Palance—a high point in the annals of the Western—the mortally wounded Ladd bids farewell to the adoring de Wilde and rides off into the Wyoming mountains. In postproduction for over a year, converting to the Wide-Screen process, *Shane* received six Oscar nominations: best picture, direction, supporting actor (de Wilde and Palance), screenplay (A. B. Guthrie, Jr.), and cinematography (Loyal Griggs, the lone winner). Stevens received the Irving G. Thalberg Memorial Award, a nice consolation prize for losing to Fred Zinnemann.

If *Shane* was as big as all outdoors, *Giant* (1956) was, well, as big as creation, and probably longer in the making. Based on an epic novel by Edna Ferber, it starred Rock Hudson as a wealthy cattle rancher, Elizabeth Taylor as his new Virginia bride, and James Dean as all hell breaking loose. A colorful array of characters played by Mercedes McCambridge, Dennis Hopper, Sal Mineo, and Carroll Baker help fill up the canvas, which covers two generations' worth of feuding, wildcatting, and brawling. Although it has several effective set pieces, at 200 minutes—enough for two features, a short subject and a cartoon—*Giant* is simply too long and diffuse. And Hudson and Dean, both of whom were nominated for Academy Awards, might as well be acting in two different movies. The picture, McCambridge, the screenplay adaptation, and Dimitri Tiomkin's score were also nominated, but the only winner was Stevens, who took his second Oscar over an unusually weak field.

▲ *A conference during the shooting of* A Place in the Sun

*The Diary of Anne Frank* (1959), adapted from the acclaimed Broadway show, was Stevens's first attempt to deal onscreen with the horrors of war he had witnessed firsthand. The claustrophobic setting is effective, all right, but at nearly three hours the film feels even longer than *Giant*. And to put it bluntly, Millie Perkins as Anne is barely adequate. Joseph Schildkraut as her father and Shelley Winters and Ed Wynn as fellow attic dwellers are fine, however, and the film does possess a cumulative power that comes across almost in spite of itself. Stevens was again nominated by the Academy for best direction, and the picture, Wynn, Winters, and cinematographer William Mellor were also nominated, with the last two winning Oscars.

*The Greatest Story Ever Told* (1965) rode in on the wave of biblical spectacles that had been popular since the Fifties, but the tide had already gone out and Stevens ended up with a beached whale. Originally exhibited at a whopping four hours and twenty minutes, it was pared by an hour for general release (and by another hour for rerelease). But this stupefying spectacle, which managed to combine Charlton Heston, Max Von Sydow (as Christ), Sidney Poitier, Ed Wynn, John Wayne, and Telly Savalas in one of the most unintentionally hilarious actors' stews ever served onscreen, was widely ridiculed, and Stevens never recovered from the embarrassment. He practically tossed off his final film, *The Only Game in Town* (1970), adapted by Frank Gilroy from his play. Yet it is this relatively modest picture, with Warren Beatty and Elizabeth Taylor most appealing as small-time Las Vegas entertainers who try (and fail) to keep their affair casual, that belatedly returned Stevens to his old virtues of unadorned storytelling.

▲ *Making* Shane *in 1953 with Van Heflin*

## ● ROBERT STEVENSON (1905–1986)

After spending the first eight years of his career at such British studios as Gaumont and General Film, directing the likes of *Nine Days a Queen* (1936), *Non-Stop New York* (1937), and the Paul Robeson version of *King Solomon's Mines* (1937), the London-born Stevenson was put under contract by David O. Selznick and brought to Hollywood in 1939. Typically, Selznick never used Stevenson himself, instead lending him out over the next ten years to Universal, RKO, and United Artists. *Tom Brown's School Days* (1940) was a colorful adaptation of the popular novel, with Freddie Bartholomew and Jimmy Lydon, which Stevenson followed with a fine remake of the sturdy weeper *Back Street* (1941), with Charles Boyer and Margaret Sullavan as the illicit lovers.

*Joan of Paris* (1942) was one of the best early World War II actioners, starring Michele Morgan, Paul Henreid, and Laird Cregar, while *Forever and a Day* (1943) was a classic *Upstairs, Downstairs* saga with a galaxy of British stars in its cast; Stevenson directed one of its eight installments. The well-mounted *Jane Eyre* (1944), with Joan Fontaine and Orson Welles (whose hand hovers over this atmospheric production), also featured Margaret O'Brien and the young Elizabeth Taylor, but *Dishonored Lady* (1947) was a fairly awful mystery starring Hedy Lamarr as an art director accused of murder. *To the Ends of the Earth* (1948), an especially good Dick Powell opus about the international heroin trade, ranks with the best hard-boiled films of the day.

Stevenson now signed with RKO, for whom he had done most of his work to date. One of his best films was the frenetic and underrated *I Married a Communist/The Woman on Pier 13* (1949) with Robert Ryan, Laraine Day, and Janis Carter as victims of the insidious Red network. *Walk Softly, Stranger* (1950) was a moody love story in which thief Joseph Cotten turns over a new leaf after he falls in love with a crippled girl (Valli), while *My Forbidden Past* (1951) was a so-so drama featuring Robert Mitchum and Ava Gardner in nineteenth-century New Orleans. *The Las Vegas Story* (1952) was simply foolishness, with Victor Mature and Vincent Price competing for the formidable Jane Russell.

Stevenson didn't work for a few years, but he joined Disney's Buena Vista division in 1956, where he was kept busy making several of the best children's pictures of that era. *Johnny Tremain*, about a youth's adventures during the Revolutionary War, and *Old Yeller* (both 1957), a wonderful, heartbreaking yarn about a boy (Tommy Kirk) and his dog set in 1850s Texas, are fondly recalled by millions of baby boomers. The whimsical fantasy *Darby O'Gill and the Little People* (1959) featured a young Sean Connery and some spooky special effects. Stevenson's version of *Kidnapped* (1960) was nothing special, despite a top-notch cast that included Peter Finch, Peter O'Toole, and James MacArthur, but *The Absent-Minded Professor* (1961) was a spectacular success at the box office and holds up as one of Disney's better live-action efforts; it starred Fred MacMurray as the pixilated inventor of Flubber.

*In Search of the Castaways* (1962) failed to capture

the flavor of the Jules Verne novel, while *Son of Flubber* (1963) was a cut below the original—though it was probably good enough to pass muster with an audience of eight-year-olds. *The Misadventures of Merlin Jones* (1964), with Tommy Kirk as a brilliant inventor, was thin stuff (although it made enough money to require Stevenson to direct the sequel, *The Monkey's Uncle*, a year later). But 1964 was also the year of *Mary Poppins*, the most popular thing to come out of England since the Beatles. One of the decade's biggest hits, it won Academy Awards for Julie Andrews (whose first film this was, having been passed over for the screen version of *My Fair Lady*) as well as for best song, best score, and best visual effects (rather creaky by today's standards); it also earned Stevenson his only best direction nomination. Today its primary flaw seems the same as in 1964: 140 minutes is just too damn long for a children's movie!

Stevenson's last ten pictures never again reached that level, but most of them had merit. *That Darn Cat* (1965) was the best of the group, with Hayley Mills appealing per usual as the plucky heroine who aids FBI agent Dean Jones, while *The Gnome-Mobile* (1967) offered Walter Brennan as a cantankerous businessman who tries to keep gnomes he has discovered in a forest from being exploited. *Blackbeard's Ghost* (1968) was enlivened by the casting of Peter Ustinov as the eponymous pirate, but it was *The Love Bug* (1969) that was the sleeper hit of the year; Dean Jones plays the bewildered owner of Herbie, a VW that can think. *Bedknobs and Broomsticks* (1971) was also quite popular, with Angela Lansbury in fine fettle as a witch who decides to help the Allied cause during World War II.

*Herbie Rides Again* (1974) was one of three sequels inspired by *Bug*, while *The Island at the Top of the World* (1974) starred David Hartman as the leader of an Arctic expedition that stumbles across a tribe of lost Vikings. Finally, there was *One of Our Dinosaurs Is Missing* (1975), a surprisingly inept spy comedy about a bunch of English nannies trying to recover stolen secrets hidden in a dinosaur bone. *The Shaggy D.A.* (1976), a follow-up to the popular *The Shaggy Dog*, completed Stevenson's career on a high note. There may never be a Stevenson retrospective, but in essence, he *was* Disney's live-action franchise for some twenty years—an accomplishment that exists now in virtual obscurity.

## ● JOHN STURGES (1911– )

A proficient director of Westerns and war pictures who excelled during the Fifties and Sixties, John Sturges spent over ten years in the film business before getting the chance to direct a feature. Ultimately, he would make more than forty motion pictures, several of which are revered as action classics.

Born in Oak Park, Illinois, Sturges attended a junior college in California, which gave him access to the film studios. In 1932 he joined the RKO art department, where his brother worked, and moved from blueprints to production assistant for David O. Selznick to film cutter to editor. When the war intervened, Sturges served as a captain in the Army Air Corps, where he directed more than forty documentaries, most famously the feature length *Thunderbolt* (1945), on which he shared the credit with Lieutenant Colonel William Wyler. Once the war had ended, Sturges found himself much in demand and signed a contract with Columbia, where he was put to work on a number of genre pieces. *The Man Who Dared*, *Shadowed*, and *Alias Mr. Twilight* (all 1946) were low-budget crime yarns of no particular distinction, while *For the Love of Rusty* and *Keeper of the Bees* (both 1947) were child-driven human-interest stories of the sort that would have had no difficulty playing in Peoria.

*The Best Man Wins* (1948) was based on Mark Twain's "The Jumping Frog of Calaveras County," starring Edgar Buchanan as the peripatetic gambler, while *Sign of the Ram* (1948) featured a wheelchair-bound Susan Peters (who had been crippled in a real-life accident) in a *Leave Her to Heaven*–flavored melodrama. *The Walking Hills* (1949) was the first of Sturges's many Westerns; Randolph Scott and Ella Raines search for buried gold in Death Valley, alongside an untrustworthy band that includes John Ireland and Edgar Buchanan. *The Capture* (1950) was a decent little detective story set in the West, with Lew Ayres and Teresa Wright on the trail of Victor Jory. Moving to MGM, where he would stay for the next seven years, Sturges made *Mystery Street*, about a murder at Harvard (partly filmed on location), with Ricardo Montalban and Elsa Lanchester. *Right Cross* (also 1950) was a boxing picture with a love triangle among Montalban, Dick Powell, and June Allyson as its dramatic focus, while *The Magnificent Yankee* (1950) was a solid biopic about Oliver Wendell Holmes, starring Louis Calhern and Ann Harding.

*Kind Lady* (1951) had good period suspense; Ethel Barrymore is in jeopardy from Maurice Evans and Angela Lansbury, via the play that had been filmed before in 1936. *The People Against O'Hara* (1951), adapted from an Eleazar Lipsky novel, found lawyer Spencer Tracy struggling with his conscience during a murder trial. Sturges then contributed one of the seven episodes in the epic production *It's a Big Country* (1951). *The Girl in White* (1952) was a modest but well-done biography of New York City's first woman doctor, Emily Dunning—although casting sunny June Allyson as the hard-nosed pioneer who worked in a slum hospital at the turn of the century was quite a stretch. Sturges was on more familiar ground with *Jeopardy* (1953), a thriller that found Barbara Stanwyck menaced by killer Ralph Meeker.

*Fast Company* (1953) was a mismatch of director and material, a musical comedy about a quirky race horse that drives Howard Keel and owner Polly Bergen to distraction. The 1953 *Escape from Fort Bravo* was better, a solid cavalry-vs.-Indians yarn set in Arizona during the Civil War, with William Holden and Eleanor Parker. Sturges's breakthrough film was *Bad Day at Black Rock* (1955), a taut psychological Western, filmed in CinemaScope, with the superb cast of Spencer Tracy, Robert Ryan, Ernest Borgnine, Lee Marvin, and Dean Jagger. Sturges received his only

Academy Award nomination for best direction for it, and Tracy and the Millard Kaufman screenplay were also nominated. But *Underwater!* (1955) was just deep-sea foolishness, inflated by Jane Russell's skin diving for treasure in a bikini while Richard Egan and Gilbert Roland watch appreciatively. *The Scarlet Coat* (1955) told the story of Benedict Arnold, with Cornel Wilde suitably dashing as a colonial spy, sword in hand; then it was back to the Wild West with *Backlash* (1956), as Richard Widmark tries to elude a posse hunting for buried gold.

*Gunfight at the O.K. Corral* (1957), a major success, was an epic presentation of the Wyatt Earp–Doc Holliday legend (scripted by Leon Uris); Burt Lancaster and Kirk Douglas make a charismatic team as they face down Clantons John Ireland, Dennis Hopper, and Lee Van Cleef. *The Law and Jake Wade* (1958) was a kind of precursor to Sam Peckinpah's *Ride the High Country*; outlaw Richard Widmark forces old pal Robert Taylor to lead him to buried treasure and soon they're at each other's throats. Sturges took over for Fred Zinnemann on the prestige project *The Old Man and the Sea* (1958)—but despite the presence of his frequent star Spencer Tracy, he failed to capture the flavor of the novella by Hemingway (another alumnus of Oak Park, Illinois). *Last Train from Gun Hill* (1959) was a better use of energy, a crackling Western in which Kirk Douglas is at his best as an uncompromising sheriff sworn to deliver at any cost the man who raped and killed his wife. *Never So Few* (1959) offered the tangy combination of Frank Sinatra, Steve McQueen, and Gina Lollobrigida against the backdrop of World War II.

Beginning an eight-year tenure at United Artists, Sturges directed *The Magnificent Seven* (1960), a remake of Akira Kurosawa's 1954 classic *The Seven Samurai*, now transposed to a small town in Mexico. Since most American audiences were unfamiliar with the earlier film, *Magnificent* seemed perfectly fresh, with a two-fisted cast that included Steve McQueen, Yul Brynner, Charles Bronson, James Coburn, and—as the craven villain—Eli Wallach. Just as important as any of those noble gunslingers was Elmer Bernstein's rousing score, which soon would become known as the "Marlboro theme." (After seeing Sturges's work, Kurosawa presented him with a sword.) *By Love Possessed* (1961) was hardly in that league, but as glitzy Lana Turner soap operas go, it held its own. Sturges was next given the unenviable task of remaking *Gunga Din* as a Western with Frank Sinatra's Rat Pack; the sight of Sammy Davis, Jr., as the uprooted DIn may induce hysterical laughter, but that was *Sergeants 3* (1962).

*A Girl Named Tamiko* (1963) was a soaper as smug as its smarmy protagonist, Eurasian photographer Laurence Harvey, who uses his oily charm to sucker an American (Martha Hyer) into marrying him so he can become a U.S. citizen. But that misfire was quickly erased with the success of *The Great Escape* (1963), one of the decade's top action pictures and a grand entertainment that still holds up. James Clavell and W. R. Burnett scripted this World War II thriller about Allied POWs who undertake an excruciatingly elaborate escape plan, which is partially successful. Sturges is masterful in his pacing of this mammoth production (shot on location in Germany) and in handling the enormous cast—Steve McQueen (his definitive performance), James Garner, Charles Bronson, James Coburn, Richard Attenborough—every one of whose characters we come to care for.

And Elmer Bernstein's score nearly rose to the level of his work on *Magnificent*.

Sturges went in another direction with the suspense drama *The Satan Bug* (1965): George "Route 66" Maharis teams with Anne Francis to track down flasks of a deadly virus stolen by nut-case Richard Basehart. *The Hallelujah Trail* (1965) was an absurdly overinflated, would-be-comic treatment of a clever idea: cavalry colonel Burt Lancaster tries to deliver forty wagonloads of whiskey to miners in the face of stiff opposition from temperance activists led by hell-cat Lee Remick. *Hour of the Gun* (1967), a ponderous sequel to *Gunfight at the O.K. Corral*, starred James Garner as Wyatt Earp, Jason Robards as Doc Holliday, and Robert Ryan as vengeance-obsessed Ike Clanton, while *Ice Station Zebra* (1968), like *Gun*, featured an all-male cast (headed by Rock Hudson, Jim Brown, and Ernest Borgnine) on a submarine bound for the North Pole as a Cold War crisis looms. *Marooned* (1969) was as slow and unyielding as molasses, with astronauts James Franciscus, Richard Crenna, and David Janssen drifting through space for what seems like light-years.

*Joe Kidd* (1972) was Sturges's best film since *Escape*. It was a typically violent Clint Eastwood Western with a good Elmore Leonard screenplay, and Robert Duvall made a worthy antagonist. For the Italian production *Chino* (1973; U.S. release 1976), Charles Bronson became a horse rancher whose livelihood is threatened by the usual lowlifes, while in *McQ* (1974) Sturges was at last teamed with John Wayne; alas, the Duke was long past his prime and way out of his venue, at sea in this contemporary cops 'n' hoods story. But *The Eagle Has Landed* (1977) showed flashes of Sturges's old prowess; based on a Jack Higgins bestseller about Nazis plotting to kidnap Winston Churchill, the film is an old-fashioned nail biter, with an expert cast that includes Michael Caine, Robert Duvall, Donald Sutherland, and Anthony Quayle, and effective location photography. It was a strong picture to sign off with, and this Sturges did.

▲ *On location in Utah with Frank Sinatra for* Sergeants Three

## ● PRESTON STURGES (1898–1959)

One of Hollywood's great writer/directors, Preston Sturges possessed a dizzying talent; his twelve films are—mostly—masterpieces of comic invention and timing. And he might have contributed a dozen more cinematic gems had not his turbulent life mirrored the kind of absurd chaos he subjected so many of his characters to. As it is, he compressed five years of peak artistry into a spectacular (if highly eccentric) career.

Born as Edmund Biden in Chicago, he was adopted by Solomon Sturges, Mary Desti's second husband and a wealthy socialite. Educated in private schools across the United States and Europe, at the age of sixteen he was managing a branch of the family's cosmetics business in Normandy. The First World War found him enlisting in the American Air Corps, and when it was over, he moved back to the States, where he continued in the cosmetics field, inventing a kiss-proof lipstick that caught on in a big way. A prolonged hospital stay allowed him to dabble at playwriting, and—incredibly—his second effort turned into a Broadway smash in 1929. *Strictly Dishonorable* was subsequently filmed in 1931 (and again in 1951), which helped convince Sturges that he, too, belonged in Hollywood—particularly after his next couple of plays failed. Of course, he was absolutely correct.

Sturges had already contributed dialogue to *The Big Pond* and *Fast and Loose* at Paramount in 1930, but he made his first impression as a screenwriter on William K. Howard's *The Power and the Glory* (1933), employing a theme and elaborate flashback structure that are reminiscent of *Citizen Kane*. He scripted *We Live Again*, *The Good Fairy*, and—most recognizably—*Easy Living*, Mitchell Leisen's 1937 screwball comedy with Jean Arthur and Ray Milland, and one of the best in that hallowed genre. It was made for Paramount, and Sturges begged them to let him direct his screenplay for *The Great McGinty*. Happily they did, and the result was one of 1940's most original comedies, with Brian Donlevy submitting a sly performance as a hobo who is used as a stooge by political boss Akim Tamiroff, until Donlevy capsizes the machine by going honest. Sturges won an Oscar for his screenplay, and he was on his way.

After writing the snappy (if atypically sentimental) screenplay for Mitchell Leisen's *Remember the Night*, Sturges directed *Christmas in July* (1940), a 67-minute, low-budget masterpiece of comic confusion. Crafted impeccably by Sturges from his own story,

it's about a lowly clerk who goes on a mad shopping spree after mistakenly thinking he's won $25,000 in a contest. It starred Dick Powell, who responded to the fresh material by giving his best performance in years. *The Lady Eve* (1941) was a step up in cast and budget—in fact, it was Sturges's first "A" production—and he was equal to the task, creating a tart romantic comedy classic that has aged better than most of its peers. Barbara Stanwyck positively glows as a con artist who first fleeces, then falls for naïve herpetologist Henry Fonda, to the horror of mentor Charles Coburn. The slapstick elements actually are the weaker part of the film, which contains just the right blend of cynicism and stardust. (And how much more convincing Stanwyck's love scenes are with Fonda than those she plays opposite Gary Cooper in Howard Hawks's *Ball of Fire*, for which she was Oscar-nominated that same year.)

*Sullivan's Travels* was Sturges's other 1941 release, and to many it remains his greatest work. Certainly the first half of the film, with its merciless satire of the movie industry and prickly romance between self-important film director Joel McCrea and Veronica Lake, is without peer. The second half veers into the melodrama of McCrea being mugged by a hobo while in his tattered disguise, beaten by a railyard dick into a state of amnesia, and sent to a brutal prison farm for his own murder—a bit too much, really, and one begins to long for the breezy observations of the early scenes. Sturges supposedly wrote the part specifically for McCrea, and he is terrific, while Lake was at her most appealing (even though she reportedly drove Sturges crazy during the filming). He turned to McCrea again for *The Palm Beach Story* (1942), a zany romp that, unlike *Sullivan's*, never takes itself seriously for an instant. Sturges elicits a warm, knowing performance from Claudette Colbert, and the fine supporting cast is enriched by a splendid (and rare) comic turn by Mary Astor.

▲ *Directing Joel McCrea and Claudette Colbert on the set of* The Palm Beach Story

*The Miracle of Morgan's Creek* was actually filmed right after *Palm Beach*, but problems with the censors withheld it from release until 1944. A boldly conceived farce, it depicts the unusual problem faced by Trudy Kockenlocker (Betty Hutton), who gives birth to sextuplets exactly nine months after spending a drunken evening at a wild party populated by GIs and hasn't the foggiest notion who the father might have been. Frazzled suitor Eddie Bracken eventually steps up to make her "respectable," but with Sturges it's never quite as simple as that. *McGinty* veterans Brian Donlevy and Akim Tamiroff also appeared in what may be Sturges's purest dissection of American mores.

Or should that honor be ascribed to *Hail the Conquering Hero* (1944), his incisive satire on America's propensity for hero worship? Eddie Bracken was again superb as the 4-F Marine wannabe who doesn't dare to disabuse his hometown pals, girlfriend (the lovely Ella Raines), and family of their notion that he was wounded heroically at Guadalcanal. Sturges's original screenplays for *Miracle* and *Hail* competed against each other for Academy Awards (a feat unique to a director until Francis Ford Coppola turned the trick in 1974). He had yet another release in 1944, but with *The Great Moment* that vaunted touch finally deserted Sturges. This erratic biopic about the Boston dentist who discovered the benefits of ether as an anesthetic had been kicking around Paramount since being completed in 1942, when it was taken out of Sturges's hands for re-editing. (The same fate had almost befallen *Hail*.) Joel McCrea and the Sturges stock company did their best with the picture's wild fluctuations of tone, but

it needed a William Dieterle to synthesize the material into a narrative that would attract an audience—and this didn't.

Bidding farewell to Paramount and the triumphs he had enjoyed there, Sturges went into the marketplace as a very valuable commodity. But his decision to sign with Howard Hughes, who assured Sturges that as a producer/director he would enjoy almost total autonomy, was like taking out a lease on a viper's den. His first project for Hughes was the screwy *The Sin of Harold Diddlebock*, starring erstwhile silent star Harold Lloyd; after being given a limited release in 1947, it was shelved by Hughes, and it sat until given a general release in 1950 as *Mad Wednesday*. Under either title it was a box-office flop, though its quotes from Lloyd's silent masterpiece *The Freshman* added flavor. At Fox Sturges made his last great film, that blackest of black comedies, *Unfaithfully Yours* (1948). Rex Harrison starred as a symphony conductor who suspects his wife (lovely Linda Darnell) of cheating on him, and as he is conducting he imagines three scenarios in which he exacts his revenge upon her. Too grim for the day's audiences (and even for some of *today's* viewers), *Unfaithfully* was a dark masterpiece that thumbed its nose at the conventions of Hollywood's typically pasteurized comedies—which is why it was a box-office flop. (The 1984 remake fared no better, and was only half as good.)

*The Beautiful Blonde from Bashful Bend* (1949) was another financial failure, but this Western farce still shows flashes of brilliance, and the colorful cast—Betty Grable, Hugh Herbert, Rudy Vallee, Cesar Romero—is handled expertly. Hughes now gave Sturges his second RKO assignment, the abysmal *Vendetta* (1950), a period melodrama that was as far from Sturges's métier as earth is from Pluto. It starred Hughes's new protégée Faith Domergue, so when push came to shove, it was Sturges whom Hughes pushed out the door. (Three other directors were involved in making this claptrap, which finally was released in 1950 with Mel Ferrer credited for direction.)

Sturges moved to France in 1949 and settled down, although he was broke and probably brokenhearted at the sudden decline he had suffered. After seven years of silence he made *Les Carnets du Major Thompson* with Jack Buchanan and Martine Carol. It was released in the United States as *The French, They Are a Funny Race* (1957)—a great title but not a very good movie. Sturges saw some of his earlier triumphs remade into inferior pictures—*The Miracle of Morgan's Creek* became *Rock-a-Bye Baby* for Frank Tashlin and Jerry Lewis, while *The Lady Eve* was turned into *The Birds and the Bees* with George Gobel, of all people—but no one was knocking on his door for new material. Sturges dropped dead in his room at the Algonquin Hotel in 1959—a classy way to check out, come to think of it.

## ● FRANK TASHLIN (1913-1972)

A comic innovator who began as an animated cartoonist, Frank Tashlin was able to transpose that medium's elasticity to the films he wrote and directed, including many popular vehicles for Bob Hope, Dean Martin and Jerry Lewis, and Jayne Mansfield. Born in Weehawken, New Jersey, Tashlin dropped out of high school and by 1928 was working for animation pioneer Max Fleischer as an errand boy and assistant. In 1930 he went to RKO to work on Paul Terry's *Aesop's Film Fables* series, moonlighting as a magazine cartoonist. In 1933 Tashlin moved on to Warner Bros., where he animated some of the early *Looney Tunes* and *Merrie Melodies*, remaining there through much of the decade except for a brief stint at MGM for their "Flip the Frog" series.

In 1939 Tashlin was hired by Disney as a story editor, and for the next two years he handled most of the Mickey Mouse and Donald Duck cartoons. He joined Columbia's cartoon division in 1941 as an executive producer, but returned to Warners and Bugs Bunny in 1942. For Frank Capra's film unit of the Army Signal Corps he created the instructional cartoon series *Private Snafu*. With his understanding of how to construct a visual gag, it was only natural that he would enter the world of "real" films in 1944, when he co-scripted the Jane Powell comedy *Delightfully Dangerous*. After a year as Eddie Bracken's gagman for his CBS radio show, Tashlin began to work full-time as a screenwriter, earning credits on *Variety Girl*, the Bob Hope classic *The Paleface*, *The Fuller Brush Man* with Red Skelton, and *Love Happy*, the Marx Brothers' final film.

In 1949 and 1950 Tashlin wrote a number of good comedies for Lloyd Bacon, including *Miss Grant Takes Richmond* with Lucille Ball, *Kill the Umpire*, *The Good Humor Man*, and *The Fuller Brush Girl* (Ball again). It was while another of his scripts, *The Lemon-Drop Kid* (1951), was being filmed that star Bob Hope asked him to take over for Sidney Lanfield. Although his work behind the camera was not credited, the experience encouraged Tashlin to become a writer-director. He began working at NBC-TV in 1952, the same year he teamed with Hope on *Son of Paleface*. *The First Time* (1952), with Bob Cummings and Barbara Hale enduring tribulations as new parents, and *Marry Me Again* (1953), with Cummings and Marie Wilson, were pleasant marital farces, while *Susan Slept Here* (1954), starring Dick Powell and Debbie Reynolds, might have been as funny if Tashlin had also worked on the script.

Tashlin's classic period began with *Artists and Models* (1955), a nifty Dean Martin–Jerry Lewis vehicle, with Dino as a cartoonist who uses Jerry's dreams as the basis for his comic strip, provoking the interest of enemy agents. (You can be sure Tashlin helped write *this* one!) Shirley MacLaine, Eva Gabor, and Anita Ekberg provided the dancing and pulchritude. After the mediocre *The Lieutenant Wore Skirts* (1956) with Tom Ewell and Sheree North, Tashlin directed (but did not write) Martin and Lewis's swan song as a team, *Hollywood or Bust* (1956), a passable comedy that used Anita Ekberg as set decoration; but the two stars orbited through the film like separate planets—as thereafter they would in fact become.

*The Girl Can't Help It* (1956) was an inspired, wildly exaggerated comedy with the wildly exaggerated Jayne Mansfield as gangster Edmond O'Brien's girlfriend; Tom Ewell was the press agent charged with making her a star. Using Mansfield as a three-dimensional cartoon, *Girl* combined broad comedy with legendary rock 'n' roll performances by Little Richard, Fats Domino, Gene Vincent and His Blue Caps, and The Platters. Tashlin then produced, directed, and adapted George Axelrod's Broadway play *Will Success Spoil Rock Hunter?* (1957), which had launched Mansfield to stardom in 1955 (and for which she won a Tony). A clever satire of a Marilyn Monroesque bombshell whose endorsement of a lipstick will make or break the career of adman Tony Randall, it contains Mansfield's best work and remains a classic of its kind. (Without Tashlin, where would Jayne's film career have gone?)

*Rock-a-Bye Baby* (1958) was Tashlin's first project with the now-solo Jerry Lewis; a variation on Preston Sturges's *The Miracle of Morgan Creek*, it has Marilyn Maxwell as a secretly married movie star who has triplets and Jerry as the babysitter she entrusts them to. Lewis and Tashlin teamed again on *The Geisha Boy* (1958), with Jerry playing a clumsy magician who visits Japan and Korea to entertain the troops; somehow he becomes saddled with a little boy. (This pair of films, produced by Lewis, more or less established the sentimental formula he would maintain when he began directing himself in 1960.) *Say One for Me* (1959) was Tashlin's first real misfire, a blah comedy that starred Bing Crosby as a priest (now where have we heard that one before?) and Debbie Reynolds and Stella Stevens as chorus girls. But then, Tashlin didn't write it.

*Cinderfella* (1960) was a little better; Jerry Lewis re-enacts the Cinderella legend, with the help of fairy godfather Ed Wynn's magic and Anna Maria Alberghetti's singing. *Bachelor Flat* (1962) was a creepy comedy, with Tuesday Weld trying to seduce visiting Brit Terry-Thomas. But the 1962 *It's Only Money* was a strong Lewis vehicle, with Jerry as a TV repairman who aspires to be a private detective like idol Jesse White; the film substituted mystery for sentiment and was the better for it. *The Man from the Diner's Club* (1963) relied on Danny Kaye, who was not even Jerry Lewis. (And screenwriter William Peter Blatty, the future author of *The Exorcist*, was no Frank Tashlin, either.) But *Who's Minding the Store?* (also 1963) presented Jerry as a department-store clerk with a crush on elevator girl Jill St. John, whose mother (Agnes Moorehead) despises him (as well she might).

*The Disorderly Orderly* (1964) was the last of the Tashlin-Lewis collaborations and it was a pretty good one; Jerry takes a job in a nursing home after medical school has rejected him—more's the pity for the patients. *The Alphabet Murders* (1966) tried to pass off Tony Randall as Agatha Christie's Hercule Poirot, with mixed results, while *The Glass-Bottom Boat* (1966) was an enormously successful Doris Day–Rod Taylor comedy in which she's mistaken for a Russian spy. *Caprice* (1967) was Day spying again, but this time it didn't take. *The Private Navy of Sgt. O'Farrell* (1968), though, was a hideous Bob Hope–Phyllis Diller megaton bomb—an unfortunate film with which to conclude a decent little career.

## ● NORMAN TAUROG (1899–1981)

There aren't many Oscar-winning directors with more than seventy "A" pictures to their credit who are less recognized today than Norman Taurog. It's not as if the movies themselves have been forgotten—there are several good Mickey Rooney and Judy Garland pictures (both together and individually), as well as some of the better Martin and Lewis and solo Jerry Lewis movies. Taurog spent his last decade primarily on Elvis Presley vehicles; modest though they were, could they have negated his achievements of the previous thirty years?

Born in Chicago, Taurog acted on stage when he was a child and still wasn't shaving when he broke into films as a juvenile at the Ince studios. In 1919 he became a director of two-reel comedies at Vitagraph, working with Lupino Lane and Larry Semon. It took him almost ten years to break into features, but Taurog was given his chance in 1929 at Tiffany, where he co-directed *Lucky Boy* with Charles Wilson. Three more Tiffany productions followed before he caught the eye of Paramount, who signed him in 1930 to direct *Follow the Leader*, a gangster comedy with Ed Wynn, Ginger Rogers, and Ethel Merman.

Taurog co-directed the Leon Errol–ZaSu Pitts farce *Finn and Hattie* (1931) with Norman Z. MacLeod before hitting the jackpot with *Skippy* (1931), an adaptation of an innocuous comic strip. Jackie Cooper, Taurog's nephew, starred as a resourceful lad endeavoring to raise three dollars to spring his pooch from the pound. A surprise smash, *Skippy* earned a slew of Academy Award nominations, including best picture and actor, and Taurog actually won for best direction over Josef von Sternberg, Lewis Milestone, Wesley Ruggles, and Clarence Brown—one of the great Oscar upsets of the century. *Newly Rich* (1931) was a minor comedy about a child actor visiting London, while the 1931 *Huckleberry Finn* was a clunky version of the children's classic; Junior Durkin and Jackie Coogan repeated their roles as Huck and Tom from the 1930 *Tom Sawyer*.

*Sooky*, Taurog's fifth film of 1931, was a sequel to *Skippy*, with Cooper now helping his pal Sooky (Robert Coogan) get over his mother's death, while *Hold 'Em Jail!* (1932) was a typical Bert Wheeler and Robert Woolsey comedy. The musical *The Phantom President* (1932) was a box-office failure, in spite of George M. Cohan's Hollywood debut and the work of Claudette Colbert and Jimmy Durante. Taurog contributed an episode to the 1932 anthology *If I Had a Million*, then directed *A Bedtime Story* (1933), with Maurice Chevalier as (what else?) a Parisian playboy who unwillingly adopts a baby (Baby LeRoy); it was a musical remake of Chevalier's silent *A Gentleman of Paris*. *The Way to Love* (1933) had Chevalier again in a passable musical comedy, again set in Paris with Ann Dvorak (who replaced the AWOL Sylvia Sidney) as his love interest.

*We're Not Dressing* (1934) was one of Taurog's best efforts at Paramount, a somewhat naughty musical comedy starring Bing Crosby as a singing sailor who helps trim the sails of a bunch of shipwrecked upper crusters that included Carole Lombard, Ethel Merman, and Burns and Allen. *Mrs. Wiggs of the Cabbage Patch* (1934), yet another screen version of the venerable book and stage success, was one of the few times W. C. Fields was cast as a sex symbol—or so he appeared to ZaSu Pitts—while *College Rhythm* (1934) had Jack Oakie and Joe Penner in competition both during and after their school days. *The Big Broadcast of 1936* (1935) was a typical all-star showcase, which here translated into Bing Crosby singing a song by Dorothy Parker, Burns and Allen joking, and Bill Robinson and the Nicholas Brothers dancing. All this and Ethel Merman, Amos 'n' Andy, and the Vienna Boys Choir to boot. (So why did it flop?)

*Rhythm on the Range* (1936) was Taurog's last pic-

ture for Paramount after seven generally successful years; if not a classic, at least it had the talents of Bing Crosby, Frances Farmer, and Martha Raye to keep it from dry gulch. But *Strike Me Pink* (1936) was a simply awful Eddie Cantor vehicle, while *Reunion* (1936) was another excuse to trot out the Dionne Quints to satisfy the curiosity of the masses. Taurog fared a bit better with *Fifty Roads to Town* (1937), a screwball comedy featuring Don Ameche and Ann Sothern as snowbound companions, and *You Can't Have Everything* (1937) was top-of-the-line Alice Faye, accompanied by Ameche, the Ritz Brothers, and Gypsy Rose Lee. Taurog got a second crack at Twain with the Selznick production of *The Adventures of Tom Sawyer* (1938); it remains the best screen version of that tale despite an underwhelming cast that featured Tommy Kelly, Jackie Moran, and May Robson.

*Mad about Music* (1938) was one of Deanna Durbin's wildly popular vehicles; Herbert Marshall played her faux-father and Gail Patrick her bitchy mom. Taurog now signed with MGM, for whom he would work exclusively through 1951. His very first film there was also his biggest success, the treacly but effective *Boys Town* (1938), with Mickey Rooney as the bad kid who just needs a firm but loving hand and Spencer Tracy as the Father who supplies it. Based on the true story of Father Edward Flanagan, the founder of Indiana's Boys Town, the film was nominated for numerous Academy Awards, including best picture, screenplay, and direction, while Spencer Tracy won the best actor Oscar for the second year running. (Rooney and Durbin, Taurog's last two juvenile stars, were also awarded special Oscars.)

*The Girl Downstairs* (also 1938) was a total non-event, with Hungarian import Franciska Gaal making her third (and, happily, last) Hollywood appearance as a maid who wins Franchot Tone's heart, while *Lucky Night* (1939) proved only that Myrna Loy and Robert Taylor were not a match made in heaven; it may have been MGM's worst "A" release from that fabled year. But *Young Tom Edison* (1940) was energized by the presence of Mickey Rooney, and *Broadway Melody of 1940* had the felicitous teaming of Fred Astaire and Eleanor Powell as well as a top Cole Porter score that included "Begin the Beguine." *Little Nellie Kelly* (1940) was a passable musical with "Singin' in the Rain," Judy Garland, and George Murphy (based on a 1922 George M. Cohan play), while the 1941 *Men of Boys Town* was the inevitable sequel to Taurog's earlier smash, with Rooney and Tracy back for more bonding; like most sequels, it didn't make anyone forget the original, but neither was it an embarrassment. (Newt Gingrich, take note.)

*Design for Scandal* (1941) is a little-remembered comedy featuring Rosalind Russell as a judge and Walter Pidgeon as a reporter who is penning an embarrassing profile of her. Taurog made the irrelevant *Are Husbands Necessary?* (1942) with Ray Milland and Betty Field on loan-out to Paramount, then returned to helm the equally banal *A Yank at Eton* (also 1942), with Mickey Rooney supposedly teaching Freddie Bartholomew a few things about American know-how (before the Brits deported him, no doubt). *Presenting Lily Mars* (1943) promised to be at least pleasant; Judy Garland is Booth Tarkington's stage-struck heroine. Although Judy looked and sounded great, the picture played flat.

Taurog broke out of his prolonged slump when he inherited the 1943 *Girl Crazy* from Busby Berkeley, who was canned early on but had already staged the "I Got Rhythm" finale. (Charles Walters staged such other musical gems by the Gershwins as "Embraceable You" and "But Not for Me.") This last teaming of Mickey and Judy is in many ways their best, a credit to both Taurog and the quality of the original 1930 stage hit (which had starred Ethel Merman). *The Hoodlum Saint* (1946), Taurog's first postwar project, offered William Powell in an overly familiar guise as a con man whose fraudulent charity operation becomes genuine thanks to the good offices of Esther Williams.

*The Beginning or the End?* (1947) was a compelling drama about the development of the A-bomb, with Brian Donlevy, Hume Cronyn, and Robert Walker among the scientists struggling with their consciences; F.D.R., Truman, and Einstein are portrayed by various actors. But *Big City* (1948) was a shameless tearjerker: Margaret O'Brien is adopted by—would that it were a joke!—a reverend, a cantor, and an Irish-Catholic cop. *The Bride Goes Wild* (1948) was another misfire: June Allyson and Van Johnson played cute while Butch Jenkins refereed. The 1948 *Words and Music* did its best to pass off Tom Drake and Mickey Rooney as famed composers Rodgers and Hart (oh, how Hart would have winced!); there were nineteen songs (including Lena Horne's great "The Lady Is a Tramp") and another seventeen musical interludes, the best of which was Gene Kelly's eight-minute "Slaughter on Tenth Avenue," a brilliant set piece.

*That Midnight Kiss* (1949), a Joe Pasternak production, featured Mario Lanza in his screen debut as a singing truck driver who whisks Kathryn Grayson off her feet. *Please Believe Me* (1950), with Deborah Kerr, Peter Lawford, and Robert Walker, was a romantic comedy of little distinction, while *The Toast of New Orleans* (1950) again entrusted Taurog with Lanza (now a singing fisherman) and Grayson, and again he delivered a box-office hit, with Lanza's "Be My Love" becoming a smash on the pop charts as well. *Mrs. O'Malley and Mr. Malone* (also 1950) was a mystery played for laughs, while *Rich, Young and Pretty* (1951) had Jane Powell visiting Paris, being romanced by Vic Damone and Fernando Lamas, and meeting mom Danielle Darrieux for the first time.

This brought down the curtain on Taurog's long stay at MGM. Although his successes there over the past thirteen years were not plentiful, it was a golden age compared to his next thirteen years. Following the pleasant *Room for One More* (1952), with Cary Grant and Betsy Drake as a couple who keeps adopting underprivileged orphans, Taurog returned to Paramount for a second stint. First up was a pair of the studio's enormously popular Dean Martin and Jerry Lewis vehicles. *Jumping Jacks* had the duo paratrooping at Fort Benning, Georgia, while *The Stooge* (both 1952) was a semibathetic period piece, with vaudeville star Dino jealous as his antic partner increasingly becomes the focus of the act. (Sound like anyone we know?)

The silly *The Stars Are Singing* (1953) had Anna Maria Alberghetti as a Polish illegal alien (nice casting, guys!) with operatic ambitions and Rosemary Clooney as her pal—her "Come On-A-My House" became the year's biggest pop hit. Then it was back to the Martin and Lewis watch, with *The Caddy* (1953; "That's Amore" and not much else), *Living It Up* (1954; a decent remake of *Nothing Sacred*), and *You're Never Too Young* (1955; *The Major and the Minor* again, with Jerry disguised as a twelve-year-old) in rapid succession. Taurog continued recycling comedy classics by trying to turn *The Lady Eve* into *The Birds and the Bees* (1956), but George Gobel and Mitzi Gaynor were hardly Henry Fonda and Barbara Stanwyck. For the 1956 *Pardners*, Taurog stole from himself, remaking his *Rhythm on the Range*, with Martin and Lewis in their penultimate appearance as a screen team.

*Bundle of Joy* (1956) was yet another remake, this time of Ginger Rogers's 1939 hit *Bachelor Mother*; "America's Sweethearts," Debbie Reynolds and Eddie Fisher, play the confused couple. *The Fuzzy Pink Nightgown* (1957) wasn't a remake, but perhaps it should have been; this flimsy vehicle for Jane Russell—as a blonde, yet—was one of her least memorable outings. *Onionhead* (1958), an unofficial sequel to the smash *No Time for Sergeants*, had amiable hick Andy Griffith doing his wide-eyed shtick for the Coast Guard. *Don't Give Up the Ship* (1959) reunited Taurog with Jerry Lewis, and it represented their best work in years. They fared less well with *Visit to a Small Planet* (1960), Gore Vidal's clever fantasy about an alien visitor, here overwhelmed by Lewis's goofy shenanigans.

*G.I. Blues* (1960) was the first of nine Elvis Presley musicals that Taurog would helm, and it probably was the best of the lot; Elvis is stationed in Germany (as he had been for the past two years), where he meets cabaret dancer Juliet Prowse. *All Hands on Deck* (1961) was another military musical comedy, with Pat Boone and Buddy Hackett doing the sailor routine. Then came an Elvis triptych: *Blue Hawaii* (1961), with the signature tune "Can't Help Falling in Love with You," *Girls! Girls! Girls!* (1962), with "Return to Sender," and *It Happened at the World's Fair*

(1963), with the King at the Seattle World's Fair and nary a good tune to be found.

It only got worse for Taurog. The 1963 *Palm Springs Weekend* attempted to pass off Robert Conrad, Troy Donahue, Connie Stevens, and other twenty-somethings as starry-eyed teens, while *Tickle Me* (1965) sent Elvis to a dude ranch populated entirely by gorgeous gals. *Sergeant Deadhead* (1965) was a further step down, with Frankie Avalon as an astronaut who is launched with a chimp, while *Dr. Goldfoot and the Bikini Machine* (1966), with Frankie trying to stop the mad plans of Vincent Price, was absolutely the nadir. By contrast, the four enervated Elvis musicals that completed Taurog's career—*Spinout* (1966), *Double Trouble* (1967), *Speedway* (1968), and *Live a Little, Love a Little* (1968)—seemed the second coming of *Top Hat*. After his retirement, Taurog taught film studies at U.C.L.A.

▲ *On the set of* The Caddy *with Dean Martin and Jerry Lewis*

## ● JACQUES TOURNEUR (1904-1977)

Born in Paris, Jacques Tourneur had the inestimable advantage of having as his father one of the French cinema's preeminent directors, Maurice Tourneur, who helmed some ninety pictures, nearly half of which were made in Hollywood between 1914 and 1926. Jacques emigrated to America with his father in 1913, working as a script boy on many of Maurice's films and acting in a number of silents as well. He returned to Paris with his father in 1928, continuing to function as Maurice's film editor until 1933 and directing his own first movies there. But in 1934 he returned to Hollywood, where he would work for the next thirty years.

His first credits were as second-unit director for such MGM projects as *The Winning Ticket* and Jack Conway's *A Tale of Two Cities.* He then directed twenty-odd shorts, mostly for MGM, before he was given his first features, *They All Came Out* and *Nick Carter—Master Detective* (both 1939). These were capable if unremarkable "B"s, as was his next Nick Carter entry, *Phantom Raiders* (1940). But Tourneur was ready for more, and he got his chance when he left MGM for Val Lewton's new unit at RKO.

Tourneur's very first project was the 1942 *Cat People*, a modest production that relied on suggestion to create a sense of unspeakable horror about to descend on star Simone Simon. It was one of the year's surprise hits, and today is recognized as a classic. Even better to some tastes was his follow-up, the macabre *I Walked with a Zombie* (1943), which despite its lurid (if accurate) title was one of the most atmospheric and haunting dramas ever produced by Hollywood—all accomplished in just 69 minutes of screen time. And while *The Leopard Man* (1943), starring Dennis O'Keefe and Margo, was more routine, Tourneur had clearly proven his was a talent that could not be restricted to "B"s.

His reward was to direct RKO's ballyhooed production *Days of Glory* (1944), in which Gregory Peck made his screen debut as a heroic Russian peasant fighting the Nazis to preserve his homeland. It was timely, it was earnest, and it was boring beyond belief. Far better was *Experiment Perilous* (1944), a *Gaslight* knockoff featuring Hedy Lamarr that provided Tourneur with plentiful opportunities to demonstrate his mastery of shadowy menace. He then was loaned to Universal to direct *Canyon Passage* (1946), a capable Western starring Dana Andrews and Susan Hayward.

He came back to the present with *Out of the Past* (1947), which was based on a complicated Geoffrey

Homes novel entitled *Build My Gallows High*; it fit squarely into the postwar vogue for bitter, cynical films noirs. Tourneur's technique also was suited to that genre, and the result was a brooding masterpiece, a candidate for the best noir ever made and the film that launched Robert Mitchum to stardom. Oddly, it would be one of the few times Tourneur worked with such material, despite his obvious proficiency. *Berlin Express* (1948) was a flavorful spy yarn set on a train, as the always excellent Robert Ryan tries to outwit the Nazi underground with the help of the Russians. *Easy Living* (1949) was an adroit drama about a football star who can't get on with his life after his playing days end. Victor Mature, Lizabeth Scott, and Lucille Ball all turned in fine performances in this adaptation of an Irwin Shaw story.

Tourneur's first project as a freelancer was *The Flame and the Arrow* (1950), a good swashbuckler with Burt Lancaster. He then made the atypically sensitive *Stars in My Crown* (1950), with Joel McCrea as a nineteenth-century minister. *Circle of Danger* (1951), a British production, returned Tourneur to the more familiar terrain of crime and punishment, but it was merely adequate. The same indifference permeated *Anne of the Indies* (also 1951), although the spectacle of Jean Peters as a remorseless pirate at least had the virtue of novelty. The Gene Tierney–Rory Calhoun adventure, *Way of a Gaucho* (1952), wasn't much better.

Tourneur seemed to have lost his way, and he never really found it again. He spun his wheels over the next thirteen years, making a variable assortment of genre pieces: *Appointment in Honduras* (1953) with Glenn Ford and Ann Sheridan; *Stranger on Horseback* and *Wichita* (both 1955), a pair of decent Joel McCrea Westerns; and *Great Day in the Morning*, a Civil War drama with Robert Stack, Virginia Mayo, and Ruth Roman. Better than these were *Nightfall* (1956), a trim noir from a David Goodis novel, and *Curse of the Demon* (1957), a superb adaptation of M. R. James's classic supernatural story "Casting the Runes" starring Dana Andrews; it makes one wonder what Tourneur might have accomplished had he stayed with Val Lewton.

*The Fearmakers* (1958) found adman Dana Andrews uncovering Commies in his office, while *Timbuktu* (1959) sent Victor Mature and Yvonne De Carlo into African revolt. By the end of the Fifties Tourneur was working in television, returning only to make horror films like AIP's tongue-in-cheek *Comedy of Terrors* (1963), featuring horror-pic icons Karloff, Price, Lorre, and Rathbone, and *War Gods of the Deep* (1965), with Vincent Price and Tab Hunter—some combo!—fending off an invasion of gill-men. Small wonder Tourneur then retired.

## ● EDGAR G. ULMER (1904-1972)

The poet of Poverty Row, the supreme stylist of the "B" (and lesser grade) movie, Edgar Ulmer did more with the little he was given than any other Hollywood director of his time. It is not exaggerating to say that the time and money a George Stevens spent on one of his 1950s spectaculars—and the millions of feet of footage he would expose while making it—would have kept Ulmer afloat for ten years and thirty films. He claimed to have directed well over a hundred pictures, many of which were shot in a week and made on a minuscule budget; no one seems to have kept track.

Born in Vienna, Ulmer studied architecture while designing sets at the Burg Theater. Max Reinhardt hired him in 1919 to design his stage productions, and soon Ulmer was also working as an assistant director. In 1923 he traveled with Reinhardt to New York, and signed on with Universal as a set designer. Two years later he returned to Germany, where he assisted F. W. Murnau on *The Last Laugh* and *Faust*. When Murnau went to Hollywood in 1927 to make *Sunrise*, Ulmer followed; he also assisted on *City Girl* and *Tabu*. Ulmer co-directed the 1929 documentary *Menschen am Sonntag* (*People on Sunday*) with Robert Siodmak. He then returned to Hollywood as an art director at MGM.

Ulmer's first American films were the exploitation entry *Damaged Lives* and *Mr. Broadway* (both 1933), the latter featuring Ed Sullivan and former heavyweight champ Jack Dempsey. But his first major release was *The Black Cat* (1934), made at Universal in between the first two Frankenstein pictures. Boris Karloff plays a Satanist and necrophiliac who lives in an expressionistic mausoleum that must have been designed jointly by Dr. Caligari and Frank Lloyd Wright. One of his grim souvenirs is scientist Bela Lugosi's ex-wife, now pickled and floating in a tank; when Karloff tries to sacrifice Lugosi's daughter as well, Lugosi skins him alive. Barely an hour long, the film was written by Ulmer with Peter Ruric (aka Paul Cain) and is truly one of the most striking—and morbid—horror movies from that classic period.

Most directors' careers would have been launched by such a success, but after re-creating Germany in his set design for Frank Borzage's *Little Man, What Now?*, Ulmer disappeared into a morass of Westerns (directed under the name John Warner), Yiddish-language dramas shot in New York, public-health documentaries (*Let My People Live*, about tuberculosis among blacks), and even the black-cast film *Moon over Harlem* (1939), a tale about the numbers racket, with music by the great jazz clarinetist Sidney Bechet. Ulmer finally surfaced in 1942 at the humble PRC studio, where he set about making hour-long dramas like *Tomorrow We Live* with Jean Parker and Ricardo Cortez and *Prisoner of Japan* (story credit only, though he has since claimed to have co-directed it).

Nineteen forty-three was a busy year for Ulmer at PRC. The boxing comedy *My Son, the Hero* was followed by *Girls in Chains*, in which Arline Judge struggles to improve conditions in a girls' reformatory. *Isle of Forgotten Sins* was an "epic" (86-minute) pearl-diving adventure with John Carradine and Gale Sondergaard, based on Ulmer's original story, while *Jive Junction* was a musical with clever Dickie Moore organizing an all-girl swing band to perform for servicemen. *Bluebeard* (1944), a handsome presentation of the famous story, featured John Carradine as a puppeteer in 1800s Paris who murders women as a sideline; Jean Parker is one of his prospective victims. *Strange Illusion* (1945) was a murder mystery with Warren William and Sally Eilers, and *Club Havana* (1945) starred low-rent lothario Tom Neal. A week after wrapping *Havana* Ulmer and Neal made *Detour*, a terrific noir that was shot on the PRC lot in six days. Neal plays a musician whose hot temper gets him fired, spurring him to hitchhike to California; he is picked up by a genial businessman, but when the driver drops dead, Neal decides to keep the car until he reaches L.A. Along the way he picks up conniving Ann Savage, who turns Neal's life into a living hell until he accidentally strangles her. Even then, he isn't free. Dark and fatalistic, *Detour* is a threadbare masterpiece that is now Ulmer's best-remembered film.

*The Wife of Monte Cristo* (1946) was a fanciful extension of the Alexandre Dumas tale, with the immortal Leonore Aubert continuing her husband's fight for justice in his disguise, while *Her Sister's Secret* (1946) was pure soap opera, with unmarried Nancy Coleman letting her married sister, Margaret Lindsay, adopt her baby. Ulmer finally ascended to a major studio when he was hired by producer Hunt Stromberg in 1946 to direct the expensive melodrama *The Strange Woman* at United Artists—Hedy Lamarr raises havoc among the men of 1800s Bangor, Maine. *Carnegie Hall* (1947) shoehorned appearances by classical music giants Arthur Rubinstein, Jascha Heifetz, Lily Pons, Risë Stevens, and Leopold Stokowski into a contrived story about pushy Marsha Hunt and her pianist son.

*Ruthless* (1948) was an enjoyably noirish yarn, with Zachary Scott using and abusing Diana Lynn, Lucille Bremer, Martha Vickers, and even formidable tycoon Sydney Greenstreet. *The Pirates of Capri* (1949) was a swashbuckler set in Sirocco starring Louis Hayward, while *St. Benny the Dip* (1951) was a minor comedy with Dick Haymes, Lionel Stander, and Roland Young as con men disguised as priests in New York City. Far more interesting was *The Man from Planet X* (1951), an evocative science-fiction "B" set on the Scottish moors. Reportedly made in under a week, this cult favorite is a thoughtful First Contact tale that just misses being in the league of its bigger-budgeted contemporaries *The Thing (From Another World)* (Howard Hawks–Christian Nyby) and *The Day the Earth Stood Still* (Robert Wise).

Ulmer's last picture for UA was the dumb *Babes in Bagdad* (1952) with once-self-respecting stars Paulette Goddard and Gypsy Rose Lee. *Murder Is My Beat* (1955), an ultra-low-budget noir, starred fading bombshell Barbara Payton, while *The Naked Dawn* (1955) was a decent crime yarn with Arthur Kennedy. *The Daughter of Dr. Jekyll* (1957), featuring John Agar and Gloria Talbott, was crummy even by horror picture standards, while *Hannibal* (1960) sent Victor Mature across the Alps with his horde of pachyderms. *The Amazing Transparent Man* and *Beyond the Time Barrier* (both 1960) were middling science-fiction quickies; they proved to be Ulmer's last work in the United States. He made two pictures in Europe before retiring in 1965.

## ● W. S. VAN DYKE (1889–1943)

Woodbridge Strong Van Dyke II was never a stylist; in fact he was so uninterested in the nuances of film-making that he became known in the industry as "one-take Woody." This proclivity must have made the studio accountants happy, but it also lent a hit-or-miss quality to even his best pictures at MGM (where he made all his sound pictures over a fifteen-year span), sometimes compromising the finished work. Still, he made as many important pictures at that studio as any other director through the Thirties, and many of them hold up splendidly sixty years later.

Named for a father who died before he was born, Van Dyke also had a mother who was a touring vaudeville actress—perhaps foreordaining that the Seattle-born youth would enter the show business world. At the age of three he did just that, appearing on stage in San Francisco. As he grew older he alternated music-hall appearances with work as a miner and, while still a teenager, as a soldier of fortune in Mexico. After touring with his mother's theatrical company, he broke into films as an assistant on D. W. Griffith's *Intolerance* in 1916, and began working as an assistant director on Westerns at Essenay Pictures of Chicago. That led to work directing serials for Pathé, including the fabled *Daredevil Jack* with heavyweight boxing champ Jack Dempsey, *The Avenging Arrow*, and *White Eagle*.

Van Dyke carved out a niche as a director of two-fisted tales through the Twenties, primarily Westerns, and continued making Westerns even after joining tony MGM in 1926. He accompanied documentary pioneer Robert J. Flaherty to the Marquesas Islands in the South Pacific in 1928 to make a melodrama called *White Shadows of the South Seas*, but when Flaherty threw in the towel, Van Dyke was asked to complete what became the studio's first sound film. From that point he was given quality material, beginning with *The Pagan* (1929), another on-location South Seas adventure, with beefcake Ramon Novarro singing "Pagan Love Song" to Renee Adoree. *Trader Horn* became even more of an event, requiring seven months of arduous on-location filming with a cast and crew of 200 in the jungles of Africa, and another year of postproduction to make sense of the tons of footage Van Dyke had shot. But when the film was finally released in 1931, it became one of MGM's biggest hits and was nominated for a best picture Academy Award.

*Guilty Hands* and *Never the Twain Shall Meet* (both 1931) were less accomplished melodramas, the former with Lionel Barrymore as a pompous killer, the latter memorable only as stage actor Leslie Howard's first picture for MGM. The 1931 *Cuban Love Song* demonstrated that Van Dyke's métier was not the musical, and in fact it became star Lawrence Tibbett's Hollywood swan song after its box-office failure was evident. But with *Tarzan, the Ape Man* (1932) Van Dyke returned to the African jungle setting he loved so much—not literally, though, as he simply blended unused *Trader Horn* footage (of which there was plenty) with studio-set work. But *Tarzan* made stars of Olympic swimmer Johnny Weissmuller and Maureen O'Sullivan and presented screengoers with something fresh and exciting. (*Tarzan* also happens to be one the best screen adaptations of a famous book ever committed to celluloid.) The picture was a gold mine for MGM, both as one of 1932's smash hits and as the basis for a long-running, lucrative series of sequels.

*Night Court* (1932) was hardly up to that standard, but as a crooked judge who frames an innocent girl for prostitution, Walter Huston gives an enjoyably hammy performance. *Penthouse* (1933) was a change of pace for Van Dyke: a snappy screwball-crime hybrid, with William Powell as a lawyer who requires the help of call girl Myrna Loy to nail mobster C. Henry Gordon. Loy and Powell worked so well together that they would become an

MGM staple for the remainder of the decade, and most of their classic performances were rendered under Van Dyke's guidance. *The Prizefighter and the Lady* (1933) used heavyweight boxing contender Max Baer as the lug who fights his way to the top, only to turn his back on those who helped him get there, in this case Myrna Loy and Walter Huston. The boxing finale between Baer and six-foot-seven Primo Carnera, the reigning champ whom Baer would dispatch for real the following year, was especially well done.

*Eskimo* (1933) was Van Dyke's most ambitious project to date; he and his crew traveled on a whaling schooner to the northern tip of Alaska, where the ship was iced until the spring thaw. Van Dyke used a native Inuit cast, whose dialogue was translated into subtitles—not the most commercial enterprise, and paying audiences were less enthusiastic than the critics, who admired the spectacular location photography (which won an Oscar). *Laughing Boy* (1934) was a rather laughable version of the quaint Oliver La Farge tale, with Ramon Novarro and Lupe Velez valiantly attempting to maintain their dignity while decked out in silly Indian garb. But Van Dyke had another big hit with *Manhattan Melodrama* (1934), a rare team-up of Clark Gable and William Powell that tells the now-familiar tale of a charismatic gangster (Gable) whose boyhood friend (Powell) is now the D.A. who will prosecute him and also end up with the girl they both love (Myrna Loy).

*The Thin Man* (1934) was Van Dyke's deft version of Dashiell Hammett's popular detective novel; it wisely downplayed the book's rather haphazard detective work in favor of warm byplay between Powell and Loy, cannily cast as society doyens Nick and Nora Charles. Yet another box-office success, the film earned Van Dyke his first Academy Award nomination for best direction, with other nominations going to Powell, the screenplay, and the film itself. *Hide-Out* was another crime comedy, light on the crime; Robert Montgomery is a gangster who retires to the country to recover from a gunshot wound and ends up falling in love with hick Maureen O'Sullivan. *Forsaking All Others*—Van Dyke's fifth release of 1934—paired Joan Crawford and Clark Gable in a plodding adaptation of a Broadway comedy, while *Naughty Marietta* entrusted Van Dyke with the first teaming of Jeanette MacDonald and Nelson Eddy. It

was based on Victor Herbert's 1910 operetta, and Van Dyke survived the experience, "Ah, Sweet Mystery of Life" and all. In fact, the Academy nominated it for best picture of 1935.

*I Live My Life* (1935) was romance between debutante Joan Crawford and archaeologist Brian Aherne, the sort of synthetic dud that must have had Van Dyke longing for Africa, the Arctic—anyplace but Culver City. *Rose Marie* (1936) was the second Eddy-MacDonald musical; it was an even bigger hit than the first and perhaps the best of their showcases. *San Francisco* proved that MacDonald could hold her own opposite the studio's biggest star, Clark Gable, in a primarily dramatic role. It became MGM's most profitable release of 1936 and was rewarded with a best picture Oscar nomination; Van Dyke received his second nomination and Spencer Tracy his first.

Van Dyke was on a roll, but it came to a screeching halt with *His Brother's Wife* (1936), a turgid weeper, with Barbara Stanwyck and Robert Taylor as lovers who nearly let each other get away. *The Devil Is a Sissy* (1936) had the successful gimmick of teaming young stars Mickey Rooney, Freddie Bartholomew, and Jackie Cooper as lads from differing backgrounds who end up attending the same school in New York, while *Love on the Run* (also 1936) featured Gable and Franchot Tone as foreign correspondents and Joan Crawford as the woman they both desire. (Guess who gets her.) It was fluff, but never was intended to be more.

*After the Thin Man*, Van Dyke's sixth release of 1936, may have been even better than the popular original, although the story was concocted without the aid of Dashiell Hammett this time. He finally had the opportunity to direct Jean Harlow in *Personal Property* (1937), but it was one of her weaker vehicles, due in part to the inadequacies of co-star Robert Taylor, while *They Gave Him a Gun* (1937) was a rare foray into social consciousness for Van Dyke (and MGM), with Franchot Tone as a meek clerk who goes a little gun crazy after serving in World War I despite the best efforts of pal Spencer Tracy to save him from a life of crime. Then it was back to the MGM-musical salt mines with *Rosalie* (1937), a labored Nelson Eddy–Eleanor Powell concoction that became tolerable only during the Cole Porter songs—and then just barely. *Marie Antoinette* (1938) was overlong but did offer Norma Shearer as the former Austrian princess who becomes Queen of France, and Robert Morley was terrific as Louis XVI; both were nominated for Oscars.

*Sweethearts* (1938) had Eddy and MacDonald once again, but the formula was showing signs of wear, despite the lavish Technicolor production values, the Victor Herbert score, and the screenplay by Dorothy Parker and Alan Campbell. *Stand Up and Fight* (1939) was Van Dyke's first Western in many a moon and he seemed to have lost his knack in the interim, submitting a formulaic railway-vs.-stagecoach yarn, with Robert Taylor and Wallace Beery as the stubborn antagonists. *It's a Wonderful World* was a screwball comedy chipped off the block of *It Happened One Night*, with James Stewart as a fugitive on the run and Claudette Colbert a runaway poet (rather than a runaway heiress, as in her earlier triumph). A creditable farce, the film wore its wackiness on its sleeve a bit too obstreperously, but its character actors—Edgar Kennedy, Guy Kibbee, Hans Conreid, Nat Pendleton—kept it afloat.

*Andy Hardy Gets Spring Fever* (1939) wasn't a very prestigious project for a director of Van Dyke's stature, but his track record at MGM had been extremely spotty the last year or two, and perhaps this was an attempt to get him back on track. But it was no better than most of Mickey Rooney's "Andy" vehicles, and not as good as some of the others in the series. *Another Thin Man* (1939) was a more likely project, and Van Dyke spun an enjoyable confection out of three murders on a Long Island estate and Nick and Nora Charles's new baby, Nick Jr.

*I Take This Woman* (1940) subjected the mismatched Spencer Tracy and Hedy Lamarr to a cloying story of unappreciated sacrifice, while *Bitter Sweet* sent Jeanette MacDonald and Nelson Eddy through their paces once more, this time in the Noël Coward musical that had worked considerably better in its 1933 British incarnation with Anna Neagle. *I Love You Again* (1940) provided Van Dyke with his favorite team of Powell and Loy and the results were splendid—a screwball contrivance as funny as many better-known Thirties classics.

He took over *Rage in Heaven* (1941) from Robert Sinclair, but this was the dark side of James Hilton, and perhaps no director could have made the grim story work; even so, with Ingrid Bergman and Robert Montgomery in the cast, the picture was a disappointment. *Shadow of the Thin Man* (1941) seemed like another sure thing, and if not quite up to the level of the three earlier entries in the series, the reliable Powell-Loy chemistry still came through. *The Feminine Touch* (also 1941) was a passable marital farce, with Rosalind Russell, Don Ameche, and Kay Francis all fine in their somewhat underwritten roles, but *Dr. Kildare's Victory* (1942) was a definite comedown for Van Dyke, a programmer starring Lew Ayres (in his last appearance as the good doctor) fighting a hospital zoning problem, of all things.

*I Married an Angel* (1942) was the last of the Eddy-MacDonald musicals, a supremely uninteresting bit of whimsy, with Jeanette gently seducing playboy Nelson away from his retinue of showgirls; the Rodgers and Hart tunes (''Spring Is Here,'' etc.) sounded as tired as the movie played. *Cairo* (1942) wasn't any better, demonstrating only that Jeanette MacDonald wasn't any more of a draw playing at espionage with Robert Young than performing in operettas with Nelson Eddy (although it's worth seeing for supporting players Dooley Wilson and Ethel Waters).

Van Dyke's final work was the 1942 *Journey for Margaret*, a surprisingly appealing exercise in World War II sentimentality, with five-year-old Margaret O'Brien irresistible as a survivor of the London blitz who is adopted by Robert Young and Laraine Day. Van Dyke was fifty-one when he was called to active service by the Marines after Pearl Harbor, and he died early in 1943 without ever making another film.

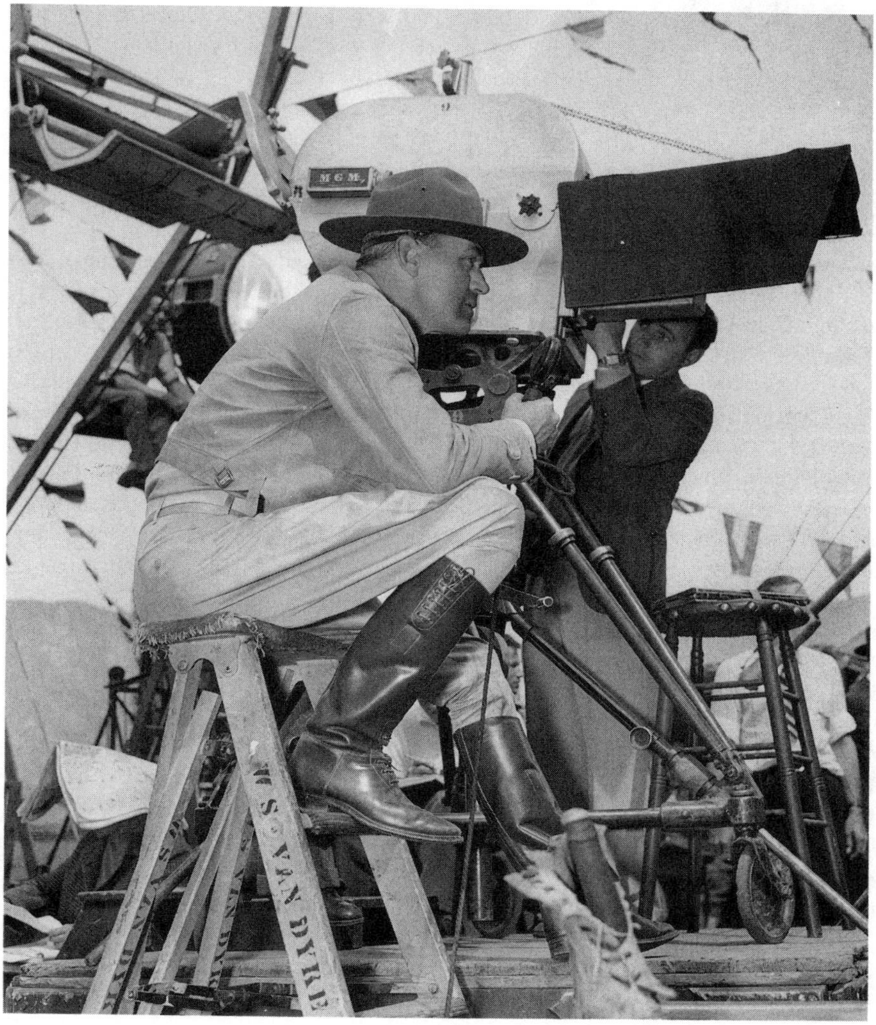

## ● CHARLES VIDOR (1900-1959)

Born in Budapest as the century turned, Charles Vidor spent his teenage years fighting in the First World War, where he rose to the rank of lieutenant. He worked at the UFA studio in Berlin in the Twenties, then came to the United States. But he did not gravitate to Hollywood immediately, instead becoming an opera singer for a time. Once in Hollywood, he wrote screenplays, edited film, and worked as an assistant director. He co-directed (uncredited, with Charles Bralin) the kitsch classic *The Mask of Fu Manchu* (1932), with Boris Karloff as the evil Fu and Myrna Loy as his wonderfully depraved daughter.

The next seven years were spent directing a number of nearly forgotten "B"s. *Sensation Hunters* was made at Monogram and *Double Door* (both 1934) at Paramount, the latter an adaptation of a stage show set in a gothic mansion with Anne Revere. At RKO he made *The Arizonian* (1935) with Richard Dix, *Strangers All* (1935), a domestic drama with May Robson, and *His Family Tree* (1935), a bit of blarney with James Barton. *Muss 'em Up* (1936) was a gangster yarn, with Preston Foster as a tough detective Tip O'Neil, while *A Doctor's Diary* (1937) was a story about negligence at a hospital, featuring George Bancroft. *She's No Lady* (1937) exposed the insurance fraud racket with the help of Ann Dvorak, and *The Great Gambini* (1937) boasted a juicy performance by Akim Tamiroff.



Moving to Columbia in 1939, Vidor made *Romance of the Redwoods. Blind Alley* was an early attempt to blend psychoanalysis with the crime picture, with Ralph Bellamy and Chester Morris. *Those High Grey Walls* (1939) was a prison picture starring Walter Connolly, while *The Lady in Question* (1940), one of Rita Hayworth's first decent showcases, was an adaptation of a 1937 French film. (She and Vidor would eventually make several pictures together, some of them quite important.) *Ladies in Retirement* (1941) was a good gothic melodrama with Ida Lupino and Elsa Lanchester, while *New York Town* (1941) was a cute Mary Martin vehicle in which Fred MacMurray helps her locate Gotham's eligible males. *The Tuttles of Tahiti* (1942) was a wholly original comedy; Charles Laughton was at his best as the patriarch of an island family that has devoted itself to avoiding work entirely. *The Desperadoes* (1943) was an action-packed Western with Glenn Ford, Randolph Scott, and Claire Trevor.

Vidor's next assignment was the prestigious *Cover Girl* (1944), an elaborate Rita Hayworth–Gene Kelly musical with songs by Jerome Kern and Ira Gershwin. The film's reputation is inflated—the supporting cast of Eve Arden, Phil Silvers, and Jinx Falkenburg is really the best thing about it—but it was a major box-office success and established Vidor as a bankable director. He used that momentum to film *Together Again* (1944), a sweet romantic comedy starring Charles Boyer and Irene Dunne, and *A Song to Remember* (1945), one of the preeminent examples of elevated Forties schmaltz—although Merle Oberon makes a surprisingly effective George Sand. *Over 21* (1945), from a Ruth Gordon play, was a funny if minor wartime farce starring Alexander Knox, Irene Dunne, and the always delightful Charles Coburn.

To this point Vidor's reputation stood on comedies and musicals for the most part, so who could have anticipated the impact that *Gilda* (1946) would have? But it was a sensation, one of the big hits of the year and a film that continues to fascinate and perplex audiences. Rita Hayworth, then at the peak of her popularity, was hurled into the unfamiliar context of the film noir: hard-boiled dialogue, menacing shadows suffusing everything and everyone (shot by Rudolph Maté), bursts of sudden violence, a sense of treachery informing every turn of the utterly incomprehensible plot.

But *Gilda* offered another element that had been

sublimated in most noirs up to that point, and that was the sexual gamesmanship motivating the principals. It was present in Billy Wilder's *Double Indemnity*, to be sure, but *Gilda* did the James Cain story one better by making the competition a triangle—a second man, her twisted husband (George Macready), was the wild card. (How different the film would have been had Rita Hayworth and another woman been competing for Glenn Ford!) Vidor caught that *frisson* and massaged it, delivering a palpable erotic tension rare for films of that era.

Vidor should have been in his glory, but it was then that he chose to enter into a most peculiar *contretemps* with Harry Cohn. Cohn was a notoriously abusive studio boss, though probably not that far outside the industry norm. But Vidor took him to court on the grounds of excessive profanity in the workplace. Vidor lost and was forced to crawl back to Columbia and return to work. Cohn threw him a bone and allowed him to produce as well as direct *The Loves of Carmen* (1948), yet another teaming of Rita Hayworth and Glenn Ford. This was Bizet sans music, and it was far less successful than *Gilda*.

Vidor finally bought out his contract for $75,000—one can only imagine what his working conditions had been like since the litigation—and went freelance. But his name did not appear on another film for three years. When it did, it was as one of the six directors who contributed to the pro-Americana *It's a Big Country* (1951). That one wasn't Vidor's fault, but he *was* responsible for *Hans Christian Andersen* (1952), an elaborate piece of malarkey with Danny Kaye; it did, however, boast some nice Frank Loesser tunes. *Thunder in the East* (1953) was synthetic adventure, with Alan Ladd as a gunrunner in India opposite Deborah Kerr. With *Rhapsody* (1954) Vidor returned to the world of romance and music, but even a radiant Elizabeth Taylor couldn't elevate the humdrum story.

But *Love Me or Leave Me* (1955) was an excellent biopic of singer Ruth Etting, with Doris Day as Etting and James Cagney as her gangster boyfriend (in an Oscar-nominated performance). *The Swan* (1956), a pleasant fantasy of romance among royalty, was Grace Kelly's farewell to moviemaking, while the biopic *The Joker Is Wild* (1957) offered Frank Sinatra in good form as alcoholic nightclub comic Joe E. Lewis. Less happy was Vidor's 1957 remake of *A Farewell to Arms*, starring Rock Hudson and Jennifer Jones—but the bathos weighed a ton. Vidor died during the filming of *Song without End* (1960), a biopic about composer Franz Liszt; George Cukor completed it. How appropriate that Vidor finished his career making a film about the world of music.

● KING VIDOR (1894–1982)

One of Hollywood's most innovative and—for a time—most powerful directors, King Vidor was responsible for as many classics (and near-misses) as anyone who worked in the Twenties and Thirties. Among his formidable achievements are such widely admired works as *The Big Parade*, *The Crowd*, *Hallelujah*, *The Champ*, *Our Daily Bread*, *Stella Dallas*, and *The Citadel*. Unfortunately, the erratic quality of his later work has marred his reputation more than seems fair.

Born in 1894 in Galveston, Texas, Vidor fell in love with the movies at an early age; one of his first jobs was as ticket taker and back-up projectionist at a local nickelodeon. Once he had his own camera, Vidor shot newsreel footage which regional exchanges would purchase. Encouraged by this taste of show business, he and his bride, the former Florence Arto, set out for Hollywood in 1915 to make their fortunes. As it happened, Florence found hers first. Within a year's time she was appearing in major productions, and by 1917 had signed with Famous Players–Lasky as a featured lead. She went on to enjoy a full decade of stardom, but by 1923, when Florence Vidor and he separated, King's own star was also on the rise.

Working at Metro, which a year later would be merged into the entity known as MGM, Vidor had graduated from directing two-reelers to direct, produce, and sometimes write more than a dozen features (some of which starred Florence). But in 1925 he hit the jackpot with the antiwar masterpiece *The Big Parade*, which became MGM's biggest moneymaker to date and vaulted lead John Gilbert to the pinnacle of stardom. Indeed, the film was such a success that it was rereleased just two years later. Vidor had another success with *The Crowd* (1928). Based on his original story, it starred Eleanor Boardman (whom Vidor had married in 1926) and James Murray as a struggling couple. *The Crowd* earned Vidor the first of his five Oscar nominations for best direction in the initial year of the Academy Awards. He next made a pair of comedies with Marion Davies, a genre he would rarely return to. *The Patsy* (1928) gave Davies a showcase for her imitations of several of Hollywood's top female stars, while *Show People* (1928) was a thinly disguised account of Gloria Swanson's rise, with stars like William S. Hart, John Gilbert, and Norma Talmadge making cameo appearances (as did Vidor himself).

Although the coming of sound had finished the careers of many performers—including Florence Vidor—to King it was a challenge quickly mastered. His *Hallelujah*, shot as a silent on location in Arkansas and Tennessee and then made into a talkie in postproduction, may have been the best picture of 1929, and remains one of the seminal films of that transitional period. MGM was concerned about booking a "black cast" film into many of its theaters, though, so Vidor was obliged to invest his own salary in the production to get Irving Thalberg's green light. ("For several years I had nurtured a secret hope," Vidor explained in his 1954 autobiography, *A Tree Is a Tree*. "I wanted to make a film about negroes, using only negroes in the cast. The sincerity and fervor of their religious expression intrigued me, as did the honest simplicity of their sexual drives.") The film starred Daniel Haynes as Zeke, a cotton picker who becomes a preacher but who loses his way when entranced by the charms of "loose woman" Chick, memorably played by Nina Mae McKinney. The critics loved Vidor's blend of melodrama and music, but American audiences weren't quite ready to embrace such a bold departure, and the film was a box-office failure.

If Vidor was disappointed, he didn't let it affect

his next projects. *Not So Dumb* (1930), adapted from a George Kaufman–Marc Connelly Broadway play, was another effervescent comedy with Marion Davies, but the ballyhooed, 70mm "Realife" release of *Billy the Kid* (1930), with Johnny Mack Brown and Wallace Beery, creaks by today's standards. Not so the inventively naturalistic *Street Scene* (1931), from Elmer Rice's Pulitzer-winning play; it was a moving drama that provided Sylvia Sidney with one of her best roles. *The Champ* (1931) was an unabashedly maudlin—but wildly popular—tale of father-son love, with Jackie Cooper tugging at the heartstrings of Depression audiences. It won an Academy Award for Wallace Beery (shared with Fredric March), who should have been arrested for mugging the camera; Vidor was nominated again for best direction, but lost for the second time to Frank Borzage.

*Cynara* (1932) was a mediocre drama about a straying husband starring Ronald Colman and Kay Francis, while *Bird of Paradise* (also 1932) had Joel McCrea and (as an unspoiled native girl) Dolores Del Rio, in a fanciful but unconvincing gambol on an island utopia. *The Stranger's Return* (1933), with Lionel Barrymore, Miriam Hopkins, and Franchot Tone, is a little-remembered drama about the merits of returning to one's bucolic roots. That theme was explored with a different slant in what became Vidor's biggest artistic gamble, *Our Daily Bread* (1934). An unapologetically didactic picture (heavily influenced by Sergei Eisenstein and other Soviet filmmakers) about the rewards of communal living, it argued (rather clumsily) that the way to Paradise is paved not with gold but, rather, by humbly toiling on the land for the good of the group. But even with its uplifting finale, *Bread* wasn't found satisfying by the day's entertainment-starved audiences, and Vidor—who had once again invested his own money to get the production off the ground—reaped a major financial loss. (The no-name cast didn't help its prospects, and the film fared no better when rereleased as *Hell's Crossroads*.)

"SURE I LIKE A GOOD TIME!"
STELLA DALLAS
They called her a party wife. They said she "wasn't fit to be a mother." But *you'll* recognize Stella Dallas as one of the greatest, finest characters on the screen!
SAMUEL GOLDWYN
STELLA DALLAS
BARBARA STANWYCK
JOHN BOLES - ANNE SHIRLEY
Directed by KING VIDOR


The elaborate romance *The Wedding Night* (1935) was made for Samuel Goldwyn; leading man Gary Cooper was fine, but Vidor was stumped by the leaden emoting of Anna Sten (in her third American movie), whom Goldwyn had dreamed (in vain) of turning into the next Garbo. *So Red the Rose* (1935) was a passable Civil War drama starring Margaret Sullavan and Randolph Scott, while *The Texas Rangers* (1936) was an unpretentious, well-paced Western, with Fred MacMurray and Jack Oakie on the trail of outlaw Lloyd Nolan.

One of Vidor's best-remembered efforts is *Stella Dallas* (1937), a remake of the 1925 hit. Barbara Stanwyck essayed the role of the self-sacrificing mother who defers her own happiness for that of her class-conscious daughter (Anne Shirley), and both tear-stained actresses were nominated for Oscars. Nearly as popular was Vidor's 1938 adaptation of A. J. Cronin's novel *The Citadel*, with Robert Donat as the once-idealistic doctor seduced by fame and wealth, despite the pleas of wife Rosalind Russell. Filmed in England, its outstanding cast also boasted Rex Harrison and Ralph Richardson, earning Vidor his fourth Academy Award nomination.

Although he was not credited with any releases in 1939, that grandest of movie years, Vidor did have a hand in *The Wizard of Oz*, shooting a few scenes when Victor Fleming was ill. Vidor was then entrusted with two of MGM's most prestigious productions of 1940: *Northwest Passage*, a rousing adaptation of Kenneth Roberts's bestseller about Rogers' Rangers, with Spencer Tracy, Robert Young, and Walter Brennan, and *Comrade X*, a strained romantic comedy that starred Clark Gable and Hedy Lamarr; it bore more than a passing resemblance to

Ernst Lubitsch's *Ninotchka*, a hit for MGM a few months earlier. These would be Vidor's last box-office successes for more than six years.

One of Vidor's great strengths to this point had been his ability to adapt popular fiction and make it work on screen. The 1941 *H. M. Pulham, Esq.*, from a John P. Marquand story, featured Robert Young, Hedy Lamarr, and Ruth Hussey and boasted a literate script by King and third wife Elizabeth Hill. Nevertheless, its box office was weak. Now Vidor submerged himself for the next three years writing, producing, and directing *An American Romance* (1944), an ambitious, expensive epic about a steelworker (Brian Donlevy) who rises beyond his class to become a leader of industry. A less cynical (but less interesting) take on the *Citizen Kane* myth, it was met with deafening indifference by wartime moviegoers. As with *Our Daily Bread*, Vidor's decision to bypass bankable stars in favor of cheaper actors (here a cast headlined by Brian Donlevy, Ann Richards, and Walter Abel) surely compromised the film's chances. In any case, Vidor's long association with MGM was over.

But if he had temporarily lost his way in Hollywood's commercial mainstream, Vidor returned with a vengeance in one of the decade's most controversial projects, David O. Selznick's *Duel in the Sun* (1946). Selznick was desperate to re-create the national excitement that *Gone with the Wind* had enjoyed, and also needed a spectacular showcase for the object of his obsession, Jennifer Jones (who had won an Academy Award as best actress for *The Song of Bernadette* in 1943). Vidor was asked to take Selznick's fevered screenplay (and its attendant neuroses) and shape it into an epic masses would adore, with Selznick peering over his shoulder at every moment. Begun in 1944, this laughably horny Western was completed (with 1.5 million feet of exposed film) twenty months later—Vidor quit two days before the final wrap. (He had patiently stood by as Selznick trucked half the directors in Hollywood through to reshoot his work; a partial list includes Josef von Sternberg, William Dieterle, and William Cameron Menzies.)



Jennifer Jones has her limitations as an actress, but here she's more than adequate as the tempestuous half-breed Pearl, who makes life miserable both for herself and for the two brothers who want her (Joseph Cotten and Gregory Peck—some brothers!). A monument to Selznick's ego and censored in several major cities, *Duel* was still one of the year's big hits (grossing an impressive $12 million), and remains fun to watch for those willing to check their brains at the door. But its lone Academy Award nomination was for Lillian Gish in a supporting role, a crushing blow for Selznick—and perhaps for Vidor as well.

*On Our Merry Way* (1948), co-directed with Leslie Fenton, had a cloying premise: Burgess Meredith plays a reporter interviewing stars like Fred MacMurray and Paulette Goddard about their feelings toward children. The trashy *Beyond the Forest* (1949) was somewhat better than that, though primarily enjoyable for Bette Davis's over-the-top portrayal of a small-town slattern. *The Fountainhead* (1949) was prestigious enough, but somehow Ayn Rand's best-selling doorstop of a novel (which she adapted herself) resisted Vidor's attempts to translate it to the screen. A less-than-dynamic Gary Cooper as the driven, brilliant architect Howard Roark was part of the problem, and even a good turn by Patricia Neal as Dominique, his domineering mistress, was not enough to make Rand's pontificating palatable. Still, the sexual pathology was fun.

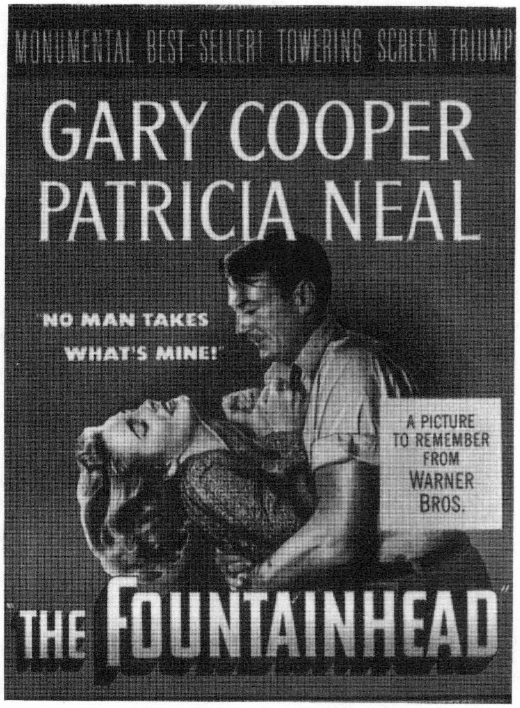

▲ *Vidor cracks the whip on the set of* Solomon and Sheba *with star Gina Lollobrigida*

Vidor's decline was now evidenced by the projects he undertook. *Lightning Strikes Twice* (1951), a murder melodrama with Ruth Roman and Richard Todd, and *Japanese War Bride* (1952), the title of which is self-explanatory, were the sort of near-"B"s that would have been inconceivable for someone of his stature a decade earlier. *Ruby Gentry* (1952) had Jennifer Jones as a Southern vixen with hot pants (her most reliable screen persona) for Charlton Heston, with Karl Malden as the eternal cuckold. Vidor then waited three years for his next project, which turned out to be the modest (although enjoyable) Kirk Douglas Western *Man without a Star*.

Perhaps tired of expending his efforts on such lightweight fodder, Vidor signed on to direct nothing less than one of the world's great works of literature. But his three and a half–hour version of *War and Peace* (1956) never jelled, a victim of a hodgepodge international cast (including Audrey Hepburn, Mel Ferrer, Vittorio Gassman, Anita Ekberg, and a visibly uncomfortable Henry Fonda), six screenwriters (one of whom was Vidor), and its status as a U.S.–Italian co-production. Incredibly, Vidor received an Academy Award nomination for best direction (although the battle scenes, the film's best parts, were actually directed by Mario Soldati).

His last production was the 1959 *Solomon and Sheba*, an entry in the biblical-epic sweepstakes that was snakebit from the start. Tyrone Power died of a heart attack in 1958 during filming in Madrid and was replaced by Yul Brynner, who refilmed the extant footage. The result was quite acceptable, but the film was swamped in the wake of *Ben-Hur*, convincing Vidor to retire from the business. On April 9, 1979, King Vidor was given an honorary Oscar for "his incomparable achievements as a cinematic creator and innovator." Fittingly, it was awarded in the year of *The Deer Hunter* and *Coming Home*—two of the decade's best antiwar films. That must have pleased the maker of *The Big Parade*. Just before he died, Vidor took a small role in James Toback's *Love and Money* (1982).

## JOSEPH VON STERNBERG (1894–1969)

One of the screen's great stylists, his name must forever be linked with that of Marlene Dietrich, whom he loved, lost, and filmed indelibly eight times. Indeed, the seven other sound pictures he made in Hollywood pale beside his body of work with Dietrich. In the meantime, she fared relatively well under the direction of others, working for another twenty-five years and sometimes even attaining greatness. But is there anyone of sound mind who would trade her eight von Sternberg collaborations for the rest of her oeuvre?

Born in Vienna as Josef Sternberg, he emigrated with his family to New York when he was seven, but was sent back to Vienna to complete his high-school years. Returning to the States at seventeen, he got a job patching film for the World Film Company in Fort Lee, New Jersey, and rose through the ranks there as cutter, writer, and assistant director. But in 1917 he was drafted into the Army, where he served in the Signal Corps and made any number of training films. For the next five years he traveled widely, working as an assistant director to Harold Shaw and Lawrence Windom, among others.

By 1924 he had settled in Hollywood. Soon he was given the unusual opportunity to direct his own screenplay for *The Salvation Hunters* (1925), financed by the British stage actor George K. Arthur, who was looking for a screen vehicle. It was an evocative portrait of the dockside underclass that von Sternberg rendered in what would become his trademark shadowy style. (Around this time the "von" was added to his name, supposedly without his knowledge, to make him sound more prepossessing.) Douglas Fairbanks, Sr., was impressed by the film's original style and had United Artists pick it up for distribution. Von Sternberg co-directed his next two pictures, then made the never-released *A Woman of the Sea* (1926) for UA before signing with Paramount, where most of his great (and near-great) triumphs would be made.

*Underworld* (1927) was his initial project there, a seminal gangster drama that made the many others that followed possible. George Bancroft starred as the remorseless mobster. Clive Brook was his mouthpiece, and Evelyn Brent his moll; Ben Hecht won an Academy Award for the story. *The Last Command* (1928) came from an interesting idea by Ernst Lubitsch, with Emil Jannings giving an Oscar-winning performance as a Russian emigré who ends up working in Hollywood for a sadistic director (William Powell), his former rival in the old country. *The Dragnet* (1928) teamed Bancroft and Brent again in a tale about an ex-cop who loses himself in the bottle before being redeemed; Powell again was cast as the villain of the piece.

*The Docks of New York* (1928) revisited the territory of *Salvation Hunters*, with George Bancroft as a ship stoker who saves Betty Compson from killing herself; he marries her first as a kindness, then falls in love with her. It was von Sternberg's most enduring silent, and some argue that it is his masterwork. Less impressive was the costume drama *The Case of Lena Smith* (1929), with Esther Ralston as an Austrian peasant who is seduced and abandoned by a soldier. *Thunderbolt* (1929), his first talkie, had Bancroft as a convict on death row who is planning one more murder from inside the walls. It earned Bancroft an Oscar nomination and laid to rest whatever fears there were that von Sternberg would have trouble adapting to sound.

To this point, von Sternberg had established himself as a major presence in Hollywood. It came as something of a surprise, then, that he agreed to make his next picture at UFA in Germany at Emil Jannings's request. But *The Blue Angel* (1930), filmed simultaneously in German and in English, was such a raw portrait of sexual degradation that American audiences might never have had the opportunity to see it had it not been for the discovery of Marlene Dietrich, whose appeal, von Sternberg was betting, would cross all national boundaries. Before *The Blue Angel* ever played in America, he exported her to Paramount, where they made the classic 1930 romantic adventure *Morocco.* Here she benefits from the high-voltage charisma of co-star Gary Cooper, then at the peak of his beauty. (He may have been the only actor capable of wresting the camera's loving eye away from her; maybe she didn't mind, as they enjoyed an affair during the filming.) Both Dietrich and von Sternberg were nominated for Academy Awards, as was Lee Garmes's gorgeous cinematography.

*Dishonored* (1931) was a disappointment, with a stiff script, a hackneyed premise (cooked up by von Sternberg himself), and a disastrous lack of chemistry between Dietrich and co-star Victor McLaglen, who is badly miscast as a dashing spy. (As if she would sacrifice herself to a firing squad for this big lug!) Von Sternberg wasn't able to fit Dietrich into his rather flat adaptation of Theodore Dreiser's bestseller *An American Tragedy* (1931), which Sergei Eisenstein was originally scheduled to direct. Sylvia Sidney does fine as the factory girl fated to die at the hands of lover Phillips Holmes, but the material clearly eluded von Sternberg, who may have been pining away for Marlene. (Dreiser ended up suing Paramount for distorting his novel.)

Von Sternberg and Dietrich were reunited with memorable results on *Shanghai Express* (1932), a wonderfully erotic, extravagantly lovely adventure that never could have been made after the Code. Although co-star Clive Brook lacks the stature and sex appeal Coop would have provided (as he did in the similar *The General Died at Dawn* a few years hence), Marlene is glorious as Shanghai Lily, "the White Flower of the Chinese Coast." Warner Oland's warlord and Anna Mae Wong's prostitute add still more exotica, and Jules Furthman's jaded screenplay and Lee Garmes's Oscar-winning cinematography are beyond reproach. It was a box-office hit—one of the few von Sternberg could claim—and was nominated for an Academy Award as best picture; von Sternberg received his second (and last) nomination for best direction.

The awful *Blonde Venus* (1932) may have been too silly for words, but not for film. Despite the unforgettable, startlingly surreal "Hot Voodoo" dance sequence (Marlene in an ape suit), this is woman's-magazine stuff, as signaled by the casting of Herbert Marshall as the sickly husband for whom Dietrich sacrifices her honor to cad Cary Grant. *The Scarlet Empress* (1934) submerged Dietrich's Catherine the Great beneath an ocean of stylistic flourishes and ornate art direction, leaving the viewer either hypnotized or brain dead—maybe both. But whether loved or loathed, the film is what the term "self-indulgent" was coined for. Despite its obvious expense, *Empress* landed at the box office with a resounding thud, a fate that might have been mitigated if the leading man had been someone of Dietrich's stature rather than future politico John Lodge.

The final collaboration between von Sternberg and Dietrich, *The Devil Is a Woman* (1935), takes the once symbiotic relationship between the two into a realm that can only be described as perverse. Where once Dietrich had suffered the slings and arrows of misfortune in film after film for von Sternberg, now she again assumed the role of the dominant, taunting manipulator of men whom audiences saw in *The Blue Angel*; here she emasculates the pride of nineteenth-century Spain—Lionel Atwill and Cesar Romero—but was the picture also redolent of their own love affair? (Von Sternberg took a cinematography credit on this, with Lucien Ballard noted as "assistant.") Dietrich hereafter would be delivered into the care of Ernst Lubitsch, who summarily fired von Sternberg from Paramount, essentially ending his career as a first-string Hollywood director.

Von Sternberg found a temporary home with Harry Cohn and Columbia, where his first film was nothing less than *Crime and Punishment* (1935). Shot by Lucien Ballard, the film is stamped with their signature flourishes, but its budget was not Paramount-esque and the constraints show around the edges. Also, the cast is uneven—Peter Lorre is interesting as Raskolnikov, Edward Arnold passable as Porfiry—but Marian Marsh as Sonya, the prostitute? Oy! And the screenplay resembles typing more nearly than it does Dostoevsky. The operetta *The King Steps Out* (1936) was set in the court of Austrian Emperor Franz Josef (Franchot Tone), with Grace Moore and Frieda Inescort as sisters who can't decide which one should become Empress; if nothing else, it allowed von Sternberg to stage a visit to the land of his birth.

He went to England to script and direct the legendary *I Claudius* for Alexander Korda and UA. Today it exists only in fragments; production was shut down after a traffic accident to Merle Oberon badly cut her face, and the film was never completed. A pity, because from the existing evidence this might well have rehabilitated von Sternberg's reputation; one craves the entirety of Charles Laughton's Claudius. Instead, he languished for a couple of years until MGM asked him to direct *Sergeant Madden* (1939), a maudlin drama with Wallace Beery as a lovable slob of a cop estranged from son Tom Brown.

*The Shanghai Gesture* (1941) at least permitted von Sternberg to return to his favored domain of exotic depravity, but here he was undone by impossible casting: Texas beauty Gene Tierney is a Eurasian lured into a gambling den (a bordello in John Colton's play) populated by the likes of Victor Mature and Mike Mazurki in fezzes. The atmospherics are there, but the other elements that made *Shanghai Express* work ten years earlier are regrettably (even laughably) absent. It would be eleven years before von Sternberg's name was credited to another feature production, although he made the propaganda short *The Town* in 1943 and occasionally pinch-hit on productions like the Selznick/Vidor *Duel in the Sun* (1946).

Finally he went to work for Howard Hughes at RKO. The fruits of his labors were the Cold War romance *Jet Pilot* with John Wayne and Janet Leigh—shot in 1950 but tinkered with by Hughes for the next seven years before being released—and *Macao* (1952), a handsome if uninventive noir starring Jane Russell and Robert Mitchum (Nicholas Ray reportedly was called in for major surgery before it was released). Von Sternberg's most interesting project during this period was the 1953 Japanese *Ana-Ta-Han* (*The Saga of Anatahan*), a film he wrote, produced, directed, photographed, and (for the English-language version) narrated. It was based on a bizarre but true World War II incident, and David Thomson has pronounced it "a masterpiece."

Whether he realized that it would be the last film he would ever make is unclear. But von Sternberg's 1965 autobiography, *Fun in a Chinese Laundry*, leaves little doubt that he saw his life after Dietrich as a series of disappointments, betrayals, and ill fortune. The thought lingers that von Sternberg might have accomplished so much more had he been a bit less willful and much less proud.

● RAOUL WALSH (1887–1980)

Long acknowledged as one of the great directors of the action film, Raoul Walsh still is not accorded the respect given such peers as John Ford and Howard Hawks. That his talent was above average none would dispute; the question is, was he merely a skilled craftsman or a bona fide (if primitive) genius? (Not that he would have cared much for the question, let alone the answer.) Most of his best work falls within the boundaries of the genre film, and his forays into comedy and romance were rarely memorable. But if his range was less ambitious than Ford's, and boasted fewer colorful quirks than Hawks's, Walsh clearly excelled within his self-prescribed territory.

One of the few Hollywood directors whose own life rivaled his screen characters' for drama, color, and worldliness, Walsh was born in New York City, but ran away while in his teens to ship out to Cuba; later he learned to wrangle and ride in Mexico and Montana. A stint at Seton Hall was followed by several years of working a variety of jobs out West, one of which was undertaking. His acting career began in 1910, when he performed on stage in San Antonio, and by 1912 he was playing cowboy roles in silent films. He began working for D. W. Griffith at Biograph, first as an actor and then as an assistant director. When the company moved to Hollywood, Griffith sent Walsh to Mexico to shoot footage of Pancho Villa, which was incorporated into *The Life of General Villa* (1914), with Walsh both co-directing and playing the part of the young Villa. In *Birth of a Nation*, Walsh was John Wilkes Booth. But he spent most of his energy directing, racking up ten credits alone in 1915. A contract with Fox followed, which lasted twenty years.

Walsh's best-known silents include the 1924 version of *The Thief of Bagdad* with Douglas Fairbanks, Sr., one of the decade's enduring classics, and *What Price Glory?* (1926), a seriocomic treatment of World War I with Victor McLaglen and Edmund Lowe as the boisterous duo Flagg and Quirt, rollicking and wenching their way through France whenever the gunfire abates. (John Ford's 1952 remake with James Cagney and Dan Dailey isn't as much fun, or as convincing.) Nearly as famous was *Sadie Thompson* (1928), which Walsh wrote the screenplay for and also starred in as the rowdy Sergeant Tim O'Hara, opposite the constipated Lionel Barrymore and, as the eponymous trollope, Gloria Swanson. He was also going to direct and act in *In Old Arizona* (1929), a Cisco Kid yarn (based on an O. Henry story) that would have been his first talkie. But Warner Baxter ended up as Cisco when a jackrabbit smashed through the windshield of Walsh's car early in the production, leaving him with his trademark eyepatch. (Irving Cummings had to finish directing the film—and got an Oscar nomination.)

*The Cockeyed World* (1929) was the popular sequel to *What Price Glory?*, with McLaglen and Lowe now frolicking in the South Seas with island temptress Lily Damita; it was long and slow, but grossed a million for Fox, back when that was big box office. *Hot for Paris* (1929) with Victor McLaglen and Fifi D'Orsay came next, but it was *The Big Trail* that became one of 1930's biggest hits, an epic with young John Wayne in his first starring role as the head of a wagon train heading from Independence, Missouri, to Oregon City—"Twenty thousand pioneers in a magnificent migration, vanquishing Indian, bear, buffalo, blizzard," as the ad proclaimed. *Women of All Nations* (1931) was yet another go-round with Marines Flagg and Quirt (McLaglen and Lowe again), this time reveling in a Turkish harem, while *The Man Who Came Back* (1931) featured the popular box-office team of Janet Gaynor and Charles Farrell.

*The Yellow Ticket* (1931) was set in Romanoff Russia, with a fresh-faced Laurence Olivier pitted against evil Secret Police officer Lionel Barrymore for the love of Jewish peasant Elissa Landi. *Me and My Gal* (1932) was a romantic crime yarn, starring Spencer Tracy as a policeman who falls for waitress Joan Bennett, only to learn that her family is embroiled with gangsters, while *Sailor's Luck* (1933) involved the popular team of James Dunn and Sally Eilers in a quasi-screwball romance, an uncommon property for Walsh to handle. *The Bowery* (1933) returned Walsh to the familiar turf of his childhood, with George Raft and Wallace Beery in bowlers as rival saloon owners tussling over beer rights, Fay Wray, and orphan lad Jackie Coogan in 1890s New York City. On loan to MGM, he made *Going Hollywood* (1933), a frothy musical comedy with Bing Crosby and Marion Davies, followed by the perky *Baby Face Harrington* (1935), a minor parody of gangster pictures that starred Charles Butterworth.

Walsh now moved to Paramount, where his projects perversely ran exactly contrary to his strengths. *Every Night at Eight* (1935) offered George Raft in the unlikely role of a radio-show bandleader who transforms three factory girls (Alice Faye, Frances Langford, and Patsy Kelly) into singing stars; its one enduring element was the debut of "I'm in the Mood for Love." *Klondike Annie* (1936) was more up Walsh's alley; it was set in the funky confines of a tramp steamer bound for Alaska and carrying fugitive Mae West, who has killed her lover and now employs her wiles on worthy opponent Victor McLaglen. There were songs, there were wisecracks, and Mae got away with as much as the Code would allow—and then some. *Big Brown Eyes* (1936) set Walsh up with rising stars Cary Grant and Joan Bennett, but the resulting "Thin Man" knockoff was less than convincing. The same could be said of *Spendthrift* (1936), a high-society love story starring Henry Fonda as a polo-playing featherhead whose wife soaks him for all he's worth after he falls in love with a girl from the "lower class."

Walsh now took the unusual step of traveling to England in 1937 to make his next two pictures for British companies, *O.H.M.S.* for Gaumont and *Jump for Glory* for Criterion. Back in the States he made the screwball musical *Artists and Models* (1937) with Jack Benny, Ida Lupino, and Martha Raye—about as unlikely an assignment as he would ever carry out. *Hitting a New High* (1937) and *College Swing* (1938) were also musical comedies, the former with Lily Pons, the latter with the formidable cast of Burns and Allen, Bob Hope, Martha Raye, and Betty Grable; Preston Sturges worked on the script and Frank Loesser on the songs for *Swing* without noticeable impact. *St. Louis Blues* (1939) was at least half serious; Dorothy Lamour played a showgirl specializing in an exotic act who runs away from Broadway and ends up on a Mississippi riverboat, where everybody loves her for herself. This completed Walsh's tenure at Paramount, for which he probably breathed a sigh of relief.

Walsh had made twenty-two films thus far in the Thirties, but none equaled his last of the decade, *The Roaring Twenties* (1939), which also happened to be his first for Warner Bros. Replacing Anatole Litvak, Walsh turned out a crisp mini-epic (based on a Mark Hellinger story) spanning fifteen years in the life of a smart cookie—James Cagney at the top of his form—who is forced into racketeering in order to survive after World War I, and then develops a taste for it. (This may not have been *Once upon a Time in America*, but it was about as close as a studio product was likely to get in 1939.) *They Drive by Night* (1940) began as a flavorful adaptation of A. I. Bezzerides's story of two brothers' struggles in the trucking business (Humphrey Bogart and George Raft, surprisingly well matched), but shifted gears halfway through to become a remake of the 1935 film *Bordertown*, with Ida Lupino inheriting Bette Davis's famed courtroom crack-up scene.

Walsh slipped over to Republic to make the 1940 *Dark Command*, a lively telling of the Quantrill's Raiders tale starring John Wayne and Claire Trevor (who had recently teamed in *Stagecoach*) battling renegade Walter Pidgeon, as Roy Rogers and Gabby Hayes look on. That was good fun, but with *High Sierra* (1941) Walsh enjoyed a breakthrough, as did star Humphrey Bogart, who lucked out when Paul Muni and George Raft both turned down the part of sensitive killer Mad Dog Earle. Walsh would remake it as a Western eight years later, but it is this version of the W. R. Burnett novel that is considered a classic, thanks in no small part to the fine support of Ida Lupino. *The Strawberry Blonde* (1941) was lighter fare, but again Walsh had a top cast—James Cagney, Olivia de Havilland, Rita Hayworth, Jack Carson—and their ensemble work (and the Epstein brothers' screenplay) made this box-office hit even better than the 1933 original with Gary Cooper, *One Sunday Afternoon*.

*Manpower* (1941) pitted power linemen Edward G. Robinson and George Raft against each other for the prize of café hostess Marlene Dietrich, who warbles a couple of tunes and looks great, while *They Died with Their Boots On* (also 1941), starring Errol Flynn as a highly sanitized George Armstrong Custer, completed an extraordinary year for Walsh. Flynn preferred working with Walsh to Warners' other top action director, Michael Curtiz, and they teamed again twice in 1942: *Desperate Journey* was an exciting tale of five Allied pilots (Ronald Reagan among them) who are shot down over Germany and try to make their way back to England, while *Gentleman Jim* was an excellent biopic of boxing champ Jim Corbett (Ward Bond was a memorable John L. Sullivan); set during the days of Walsh's youth in New York, it was clearly a special project for him, and it was Flynn's favorite role as well.

*Background to Danger* (1943), from Eric Ambler's novel of World War II espionage, sent George Raft into the fray in Turkey, where Sydney Greenstreet and Peter Lorre provided suitable menace. Then it was Flynn again with more patriotic derring-do in *Northern Pursuit* (1943), as a Mountie tracking downed Nazi flyer Helmut Dantine across the Canadian wilderness. Walsh and Flynn inherited less trustworthy material in *Uncertain Glory* (1944), resulting in a turgid account of a Resistance fighter who must make the supreme sacrifice. But *Objective, Burma!* (1945) was one of the decade's best—and grittiest—war movies, with Errol Flynn leading fifty paratroopers into battle against the Japanese. (Alvah Bessie's jingoistic screenplay was Oscar-nominated, but apparently wasn't patriotic enough to keep him from being jailed as one of the Hollywood Ten a few years later.) *Objective, Burma!* still has the courage of its (outdated) convictions when viewed today, and contains Flynn's best performance of the Forties.

*The Horn Blows at Midnight* (1945) wasn't nearly as successful at the box office, but this oddball fantasy at least was original—Jack Benny is a trumpet player who falls asleep and dreams he is an angel sent to destroy the world by blowing on Gabriel's horn (it was a film that Benny detested). *Salty O'Rourke* (1945) returned Walsh to Paramount and safer ground with a pleasant yarn about racetrack con man Alan Ladd falling for schoolteacher Gail Russell. He helped David Butler on *San Antonio* (1945), then made *The Man I Love* (1947), a great vehicle for Ida Lupino, who plays a feisty nightclub singer harassed by gangster boss Robert Alda.

*Pursued* (1947) was Walsh's first Western in many years and it was a good (if talky) one, with new star Robert Mitchum tracking down his father's killers while suffering disturbingly Freudian dreams. *Cheyenne* (1947) was less adventurous; an obviously uncomfortable Dennis Morgan and Jane Wyman try (but fail) not to look ridiculous. *Silver River* (1948) had the merits of Errol Flynn and Ann Sheridan, if not much else. This would prove to be Walsh's final project with Flynn, ending a very fruitful collaboration.

*Fighter Squadron* (1948) continued Walsh's slump with an overly familiar tale of Air Force pilot Edmond O'Brien and his struggle to win World War II singlehandedly, while the 1948 *One Sunday Afternoon* was a pallid Technicolor musical remake of his own *The Strawberry Blonde*, starring the underwhelming tandem of Dennis Morgan and Janis Paige. In a remake mood, Walsh now mined *High Sierra* for the raw materials of *Colorado Territory* (1949), which worked well as a Western with Joel McCrea, Virginia Mayo, and Dorothy Malone. But it was *White Heat* (1949) that showed Walsh once more at the peak of his powers; James Cagney had one of his greatest roles as Cody Jarrett, a psychopathic yet pathetically tortured killer whose mother complex would have kept Freud busy for decades. Typically, Walsh eschewed the conventions of the then-popular film noir to make this a virtual homage to the studio's crime pictures of the early Thirties.

After lending a hand on Ray Enright's *Montana* (1950), Walsh shot *Along the Great Divide* (1951), a conventional Western strengthened by some good location photography—although Kirk Douglas was less than compelling as a U.S. marshal on a manhunt. Walsh had one of his biggest hits with *Captain Horatio Hornblower* (1951), a well-mounted version of the C. S. Forester novels, that starred Gregory Peck at his most stalwart as the British naval commander who conquers all during the Napoleonic Wars. *Distant Drums* (1951) recycled the story structure from *Objective, Burma!*, transposing the struggle into the Florida Everglades, with a nearly somnabulent Gary Cooper pitted against the Seminole Indians and a bunch of unscrupulous gunrunners. This ended Walsh's twelve-year term at Warner Bros., where so much of his best moviemaking had taken place.

Now a freelancer, Walsh made his next seven films at five different studios. His lone MGM picture was *Glory Alley* (1952), a better-than-average boxing yarn with Ralph Meeker and Leslie Caron, set in the New Orleans of Louis Armstrong, who makes an appearance. *The World in His Arms* (1952) sent Peck back to sea, this time as the captain of a sealing schooner who somehow ends up in Alaska romancing runaway Russian countess Ann Blyth while fending off poacher Anthony Quinn. Walsh moved another century back in time for the 1952 *Blackbeard the Pirate*, but Robert Newton tendered a ripe performance that would have made even Wallace Beery blush, although co-star Linda Darnell was, as always, an ornament to the production.

*The Lawless Breed* (1953) had Rock Hudson as legendary gunman John Wesley Hardin—his first starring role, and a surprisingly good effort—but *Sea Devils* (1953) used Hudson less well as a smuggler circa 1800 who gets mixed up with spy Yvonne De Carlo. A more serious enterprise was *A Lion Is in the Streets* (1953), and while this thinly disguised Huey Long drama finally didn't deliver on its promise, it offered mesmerizing performances by James Cagney as the demagogue and Anne Francis as a temptress named Flamingo. *Gun Fury* (also 1953) was originally shot in 3-D, but even without that novelty its story of depraved lowlifes Lee Marvin and Neville Brand kidnapping Rock Hudson's bride-to-be (Donna Reed), complemented by stunning Arizona location photography, made this more than an ordinary Western. *Saskatchewan* (1954) permitted Walsh to explore the topography of the Canadian Rockies, but the story—Alan Ladd as a Mountie raised by Indians who tries to keep the Sioux and Cree tribes from an uprising—left something to be desired.

He inaugurated his fortieth year behind the camera with the prestigious *Battle Cry* (1955), a two and a half–hour ode to the Marines of World War II that remained as faithful as was then possible to Leon Uris's epic novel, aided by Uris's own screenplay adaptation. It was Walsh's first CinemaScope production, and starred Van Heflin, Aldo Ray, Tab Hunter, and—for some much-needed sex appeal—Dorothy Malone as a frustrated wife. *The Tall Men* (1955) had the cast to excel, but somehow this cattle-drive soap opera squandered the possibilities suggested by Clark Gable, Robert Ryan, and Jane Russell. Walsh used Russell again in *The Revolt of Mamie Stover* (1956), showcasing her as a saloon singer in prewar Honolulu to good advantage.

*The King and Four Queens* (1956) was a mediocre Western that asked Clark Gable to play the morally dubious role of a con man who gyps a rancher (Jo Van Fleet) and her four daughters out of a fortune in gold, while in *Band of Angels* (1957) Gable and Walsh teamed in a compromised version of a Robert Penn Warren novel: Rhett Butlerish Gable buys a mulatto beauty (Yvonne De Carlo) from slave traders, makes her his mistress, and falls in love with her, all in antebellum New Orleans. Walsh tackled his most daunting literary source with *The Naked and the Dead* (1958), Norman Mailer's prize-winning novel about a platoon of American soldiers trying to capture an island in the Pacific during World War II. It kept just the bare bones of the action—but enough to fill over two hours of screen time—and jettisoned the other 75 percent of Mailer's searing tale, as was to be expected from a Hollywood production in 1958. *Naked* compares favorably with the other "big" war pictures of the Fifties.

His final five films were a humdrum lot. *The Sheriff of Fractured Jaw* (1959) was made in England with Jayne Mansfield, and the most remarkable thing about this downscale comedy is that it wasn't half bad. *A Private's Affair* (1959) was another lightweight product, with Sal Mineo and Barbara Eden mounting an Army revue for TV, Rooney-Garland style. Few Hollywood directors managed to avoid the Great Bible Stories derby of the Fifties, and Walsh's contribution turned out to be *Esther and the King* (1960), a U.S.–Italian co-production that starred Joan Collins and Richard Egan as two of the big screen's least likely incarnations of Old Testament principals. *Marines, Let's Go!* (1961) at least returned Walsh to the relative safety of the Korean War; unfortunately, it was no better than *Esther*, with Tom Tryon and David Hedison laboring mightily to impersonate leathernecks fighting and playing hard.

Walsh was able to partially redeem these disappointments with *A Distant Trumpet* (1964), a rather familiar tale of the cavalry battling Indians in 1883 Arizona. It managed to echo some of his earlier Western triumphs without equaling them, in part because stars Troy Donahue and Suzanne Pleshette were hardly Flynn and de Havilland. But Walsh himself was suffering from physical difficulties, primarily fading sight in his one good eye, and had to retire after this. His legacy of sixty-nine sound pictures (and scores of earlier silents) remains among the most impressive bodies of work submitted by any Hollywood director, past or present. Walsh's delightful autobiography, *Each Man in His Time*, was published in 1974.

◀ *Making* The Lawless Breed *with Rock Hudson*

## ● CHARLES WALTERS (1911–1982)

A former dancer, the Brooklyn-born Charles Walters directed such Broadway musicals as *Banjo Eyes* and *Let's Face It* in 1941 before moving to MGM as a choreographer. There he was associated with some of the best musical films of the decade, including *DuBarry Was a Lady*, *Girl Crazy*, *Meet Me in St. Louis*, *The Harvey Girls*, and *Ziegfeld Follies*—clearly Vincente Minnelli relied on him. He directed a short, *Spreadin' the Jam*, in 1945, then choreographed Rouben Mamoulian's *Summer Holiday* in 1947. That same year he was given his first feature to direct, the bubbly *Good News*, an updated version of the 1930 show that starred up-and-comers June Allyson and Peter Lawford. It did well, and Arthur Freed rewarded Walters with a major assignment, the Irving Berlin period piece *Easter Parade* (1948). It was a huge success for the studio and pleasant enough as a spectacle, with seventeen Berlin tunes—although Fred Astaire (replacing an injured Gene Kelly) and Judy Garland look a bit strained as a duo.

Walters next inherited Astaire and his original screen partner, Ginger Rogers, for *The Barkleys of Broadway* (1949), which boasted a nice Betty Comden–Adolph Green screenplay and some great tunes, including Fred's ageless "They Can't Take That Away from Me." *Summer Stock* (1950) was a happy pairing of Garland and Gene Kelly, in some ways even better than what they accomplished for Minnelli in *The Pirate*, with able comic support from Eddie Bracken and Phil Silvers; Judy's "Get Happy" became a standard for her. But *Three Guys Named Mike* (1951) was a precipitous fall from grace; Jane Wyman and Van Johnson demonstrate the talent gap between them and Walters's previous star leads. It was also Walters's first nonmusical, which may have contributed to its inadequacy.

*Texas Carnival* (1951) *was* a musical, but it wasn't much better, despite a cast that included some of MGM's top talent: Esther Williams, Howard Keel, and Ann Miller. He put Fred Astaire and Vera-Ellen through their paces in the Gay Nineties musical *The Belle of New York* (1952); it was passable entertainment, but the songs were tepid and no sparks were struck between the leads. More popular was the sentimental *Lili* (1953), adapted from a Paul Gallico story by Helen Deutsch. Leslie Caron is heartbreaking as a French waif and Mel Ferrer is the bitter puppeteer who loves her. Walters and Caron were both nominated for Academy Awards, but only Bronislau Kaper's score (which included "Hi-Lili, Hi-Lo") won an Oscar.

*Dangerous When Wet* and *Easy to Love* were mediocre Esther Williams vehicles, but *Torch Song* (all 1953) was a great deal more interesting; Joan Crawford plays a tough Broadway star who falls for blind pianist Michael Wilding. A wee bit absurd, it still was one of Crawford's better Fifties movies, and Walters himself made a rare appearance as her dance partner in the opening number. *The Glass Slipper* (1955) reunited Walters with Caron in a Cinderella-like fable with enchanting songs and dances, while in *The Tender Trap* (1955) Walters showed at last that he could mount a good romantic comedy that wasn't a musical (although Frank Sinatra's rendition of the title tune was Oscar-nominated). *High Society* (1956) relied on Sinatra again; it was a musical remake of *The Philadelphia Story*, with great Cole Porter songs. But Sinatra, Bing Crosby, and Grace Kelly could never be Jimmy Stewart, Cary Grant, and Katharine Hepburn (though the Philadelphia-born Kelly, at least, was well cast).

*Don't Go Near the Water* (1957), a "comedy" set in World War II starring Glenn Ford and Eva Gabor, was a total disaster, while *Ask Any Girl* (1959) was an antiseptic looking-for-love-in-the-big-city yarn that needed Doris Day but instead had Shirley MacLaine.

Walters *did* draw Day for his next picture, a lively adaptation of Jean Kerr's play *Please Don't Eat the Daisies*, and it became one of 1960's most popular films. With *Two Loves* (1961), though, it was back to Shirley MacLaine as leading lady, and she was no better as a New Zealand spinster than she had been as an innocent in New York City. (Why Walters was selected to direct this remains an open question.) The musical *Jumbo* (1962) was an overlong circus spectacle that had been staged on Broadway by Billy Rose during the Thirties; Doris Day, Jimmy Durante, and Martha Raye are used to their best advantage (with the help of Busby Berkeley's choreography), but it's the Rodgers and Hart tunes that are the stars of the show.

*The Unsinkable Molly Brown* (1964) allowed Walters to adapt a more current Broadway musical and he made the most of it, getting the performance of Debbie Reynolds's career (and her only Oscar nomination). His final film was *Walk, Don't Run* (1966), a surprisingly pleasant remake of George Stevens's *The More the Merrier* that must be cherished as Cary Grant's last film performance. Made for Columbia, it was the only motion picture Walters had worked on in almost twenty-five years that wasn't an MGM production.

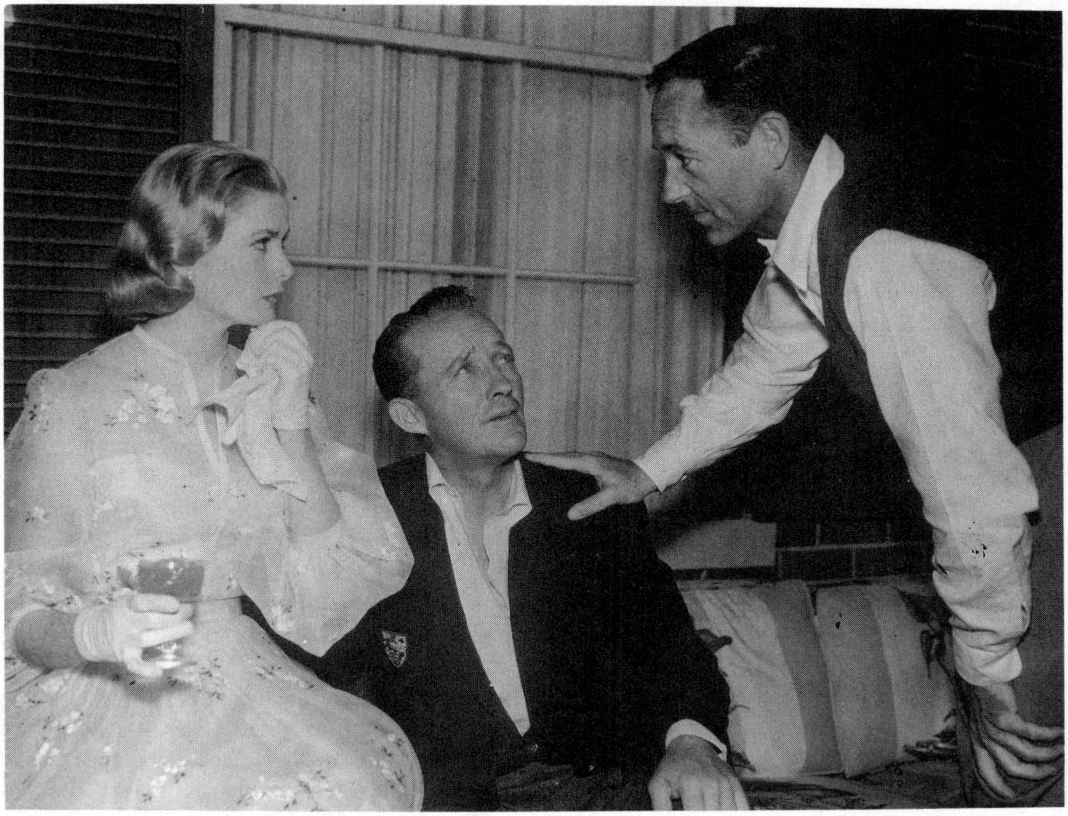

▲ High Society *stars Grace Kelly and Bing Crosby confer with Walters*

## ● ORSON WELLES (1915-1985)

*Enfant terrible*, genius, showman, megalomaniac, fraud—one could fill a page with the adjectives, superlatives, and accusations (each with its own grain of truth) that describe Orson Welles. To think that so much fuss extended over some four decades about a man who completed fewer than a dozen films! However, some of those works, uncompleted in his lifetime, have since seen limited release, in response to the mystique that grew up around them.

He was born George Orson Welles in Kenosha, Wisconsin, to a mother who was a concert pianist and a father who was a successful inventor. With those bloodlines, it's small wonder that George quickly established himself as a pint-sized prodigy, adept at the piano, acting, drawing, painting, and writing verse; he also entertained his friends by performing magic tricks and staging mini-productions of Shakespeare. The family moved to Chicago, but his mother died when he was eight, and George spent the next few years traveling around the world with his father.

In 1926 they returned to Illinois, and young Welles entered the exclusive Todd School in Woodstock. There his gifts found fertile ground, and he dazzled the teachers and students with stagings of both modern and classical plays. His father passed away just a year later, and Welles became the ward of a family friend, Chicago doctor Maurice Bernstein. At sixteen he graduated from Todd, but instead of attending college (several had pursued him), Welles traveled to Dublin, where he somehow convinced the head of the Gate Theatre that he was an established New York director.

After a year of directing at the Gate, Welles tried to get work on the stages of London and New York, but found their doors closed to him. Instead, he traveled for a year, settling in Spain for a time. In 1933 he returned to the States, and this time was hired to act with Katharine Cornell's road company. That experience gained him entrée to Broadway, where he made his debut in 1934 as Tybalt in Cornell's production of *Romeo and Juliet*. That same year he also made his first film, a four-minute opus called *The Hearts of Age*, in which he acted alongside his new wife, Chicago actress Virginia Nicholson. He was all of seventeen.

When Welles met another young dynamo by the name of John Houseman, the two theater lovers took to each other immediately. They worked together in Houseman's Phoenix Theatre Group, then moved on to mounting and directing productions for the Federal Theater Project; their most (in)famous effort there was the proletarian drama *The Cradle Will Rock*. In 1937 they formed the Mercury Theatre Group, one early success of which was an avant-garde production of *Macbeth*; performed in Harlem, it was set in Haiti and had an all-black cast. By 1938 Welles was on the cover of *Theatre* magazine, as befit a nationally famous *Wunderkind* of the stage.

But the theater wasn't big enough to contain Welles. He and Houseman branched into radio with *The Mercury Theatre on the Air*, which boldly reinvented a number of classic dramas. This forum led to what would prove Welles's most outrageous stunt: a live broadcast of H. G. Wells's *The War of the Worlds* on Halloween in 1938. Scripted by Howard Koch and narrated feverishly by Welles, the broadcast set the scene of the alien invasion at Grovers Mills, New Jersey. Although the show was periodically interrupted with the explanation that this was a fictional drama, many New Jerseyans panicked, some even evacuating their homes. The national coverage that resulted from this *faux*-crisis brought Welles's name before Hollywood, which had long been in the habit of poaching top talent from radio and the stage.

It was RKO which first approached Welles, and in 1939 he signed a contract with them that would

guarantee him near-total autonomy on any film he made. It was an extraordinary offer to make a twenty-three-year-old—especially one whose only screen-directing experience was a 40-minute featurette called *Too Much Johnson*, a comedy via William Gillette; it was intended to be shown in tandem with a stage production of the play, but as it turned out, the short film was never shown in public, and no copies survive. RKO asked Welles to choose a property to film, and he selected Joseph Conrad's *Heart of Darkness*. The prospect of Welles as the burned-out Kurtz remains exciting to contemplate, but unfortunately the film never got off the ground. He narrated the 1940 version of *Swiss Family Robinson* while waiting for another project to evolve. Finally, one did—the film that would transform Orson Welles overnight into a Hollywood star.

*Citizen Kane* (1941) is arguably the greatest movie ever to come out of Hollywood, and surely is the most impressive tour de force by a novice director. Welles, then just twenty-five, also produced and co-scripted the film; he originally represented himself as the sole author of the terrific screenplay, but guild arbitration installed Herman J. Mankiewicz, the older brother of Joseph Mankiewicz, as its co-author—and some critics (notably Pauline Kael) have built a pretty convincing case that Mankiewicz actually wrote the lion's share. That imbroglio notwithstanding, Welles submits a joyfully energetic performance as Charles Foster Kane, the newspaper magnate (clearly based on zillionaire William Randolph Hearst) who rises from a privileged but dull background to amass uncountable millions—none of which he is able to enjoy, thanks to his epic ambitions and increasingly bizarre compulsions. It's a confident job of acting that at times even overshadows Welles's dynamic (if show-offy) direction.

*Kane* (which originally was to have been titled *John Citizen, U.S.A.*) featured an ensemble cast in support of Welles, comprised mostly of such Mercury Players as Joseph Cotten, Agnes Moorehead, Everett Sloane, Paul Stewart, and Ruth Warrick. Shot with an array of classic and experimental techniques by Gregg Toland, evocatively scored by Bernard Herrmann, and edited brilliantly by Robert Wise (with an assist from Mark Robson), *Kane* is a flat-out masterpiece of moviemaking. Welles made it on a modest budget, but was contractually allowed by RKO to do essentially whatever he wanted. (This may have been the last time Welles made a Hollywood movie that reached the screen intact.)

While it initially received rave reviews, *Kane* was effectively quashed by Hearst, who marshaled all the vaunted power of his newspaper chain to hamstring its commercial prospects. In this Hearst succeeded: *Kane* was not a financial success. But the film did garner Academy Award nominations for best picture, actor, direction, scoring, original screenplay, cinematography, art direction, editing, and sound. Only the Mankiewicz-Welles screenplay won an Oscar, but it's to the credit of the Academy that they dared nominate the work of this brash newcomer in so many categories despite the pressure from Hearst. (Still, by today's lights, giving Gary Cooper an Oscar for his pattycake performance as Alvin York in *Sergeant York* over Welles's bravura turn seems either cowardly or stupid.)

*The Magnificent Ambersons* (1942) was produced, written, and directed by Welles, and to some critics represents the peak of his artistry—even though it was taken out of his hands by RKO after poor test screenings and assigned to Robert Wise for reediting that involved some heavy trimming (43 minutes were lopped off), with a new ending tacked on. (If the studio system did indeed possess "genius," as André Bazin maintained in his famous 1957 commentary, then how to explain these frequent outbreaks of idiocy?) *Ambersons* was adapted by Welles from a novel by Booth Tarkington about the declining fortunes of a wealthy nineteenth-century Indianapolis family whose smugness (and inability to comprehend the significance of the industrial revolution) leads to their downfall. The ensemble cast features Tim Holt as the spoiled scion whose arrogance finally earns him a well-deserved comeuppance that nonetheless carries the weight of tragedy. Mercury Players (and *Kane* veterans) Joseph Cotten, Agnes Moorehead, and Ray Collins are all wonderful, while erstwhile silent star Dolores Costello and young Anne Baxter demonstrate Welles's affection for, and attention to, his female actors.

Photographed brilliantly by Stanley Cortez, who was nominated for an Oscar, *Ambersons* was one of the year's ten nominees for the best picture Academy Award, and also earned a nomination for Agnes Moorehead. But, as with so much of Welles's work, it remains a classic case of "what might have been"; the film's occasional longueurs and disappointing conclusion he might well have been corrected by Welles had he not been banished from postproduction; and what about that 43 minutes, anyway? We'll never know, unless someone finds the footage in a garage someday.

Even while Robert Wise was taking a scissors to *Ambersons*, Welles was deeply involved in filming his quasi-documentary *It's All True* (1942), a trilogy set in South America about its indigenous peoples. It was intended as pro–Pan American propaganda. But what could its commercial prospects have been? Limited at best—a fact that apparently occurred to RKO, which pulled the plug on the project midway, leaving Welles and his Mercury Players stranded in Rio. But Welles hung on to the footage of the three short films—"Samba," about Rio's annual Carnival; "My Friend Benito," about bullfighting; and "Jangadieros," about four humble fishermen who become national heroes after a daring voyage. In 1993 the legendary project, never released, resurfaced when the mostly extant footage was assembled, edited, and scored by Richard Wilson, Bill Krohn, and Myron Meisel. When their effort, entitled *It's All True: Based on an Unfinished Film by Orson Welles*, premiered at the New York Film Festival, it was greeted as an intriguing, if ephemeral, part of the Welles canon. (It's now available on video.)

Welles had started work on *Journey into Fear* (1942) before leaving for Brazil, and he came back to find that RKO had begun meddling with it, as they had with *Ambersons*. This time, though, Welles was able to intercede, and the threat of a lawsuit pressured the studio into letting him shoot additional scenes and restore at least some of the brutal editing (it was released at a "B"-length 70 minutes). *Fear* was officially credited to Norman Foster, a journeyman director who also assisted Welles on *It's All True*, but it was produced, co-scripted, and acted in by Welles, who played the supporting part of Colonel Haki of Turkish intelligence.

Since there's not much in Foster's oeuvre to suggest how he suddenly might have been stricken with an attack of genius on this one project, the hand of Welles is clearly evident—although Welles told Peter Bogdanovich in a 1961 interview that he "designed the film but can't properly be called its director." A gripping (if sometimes confusing) adaptation of Eric Ambler's thriller about espionage and munitions smuggling, *Fear* starred Welles's then-paramour, Dolores Del Rio, as the mysterious Josette, while *Kane* veterans Cotten (who co-wrote the screenplay), Ruth Warrick, Agnes Moorehead, and Everett Sloane enhance the production enormously. But RKO was unimpressed—they kicked Welles and his Mercury Productions off the lot.

Welles spent the rest of the year wooing (and winning the hand of) Rita Hayworth, then agreed to perform one of his magic acts onscreen—as the Great Orsino, sawing Marlene Dietrich in half!—in the patriotic revue *Follow the Boys* (1944). He was splendid as the mysterious Rochester in Robert Stevenson's *Jane Eyre* (1944) opposite Joan Fontaine; his performance impressed the critics, and the film looks as though Welles might have given Stevenson a few tips on creating gothic atmosphere. But none of the studios was rushing to sign him as a director. He starred opposite Claudette Colbert in Irving Pichel's weeper *Tomorrow Is Forever* before finally being given a chance by producer Sam Spiegel.

*The Stranger* (1946) was a suspenseful but, in the end, rather conventional thriller about a Nazi (Welles, in another marvelous performance) hiding out as a schoolteacher in a small New England town; his impending nuptials with Loretta Young are interrupted when FBI war-crimes investigator Edward G. Robinson tracks him down, then waits for Welles to give himself away. Welles was underwhelmed by the job he did directing—he was trying to adhere to a strict schedule and budget to repair his reputation and so could ill afford any of his trademark

▲ *Welles in character as Macbeth in 1948*

flourishes—but any other director would have been proud to add this to his résumé.

Harry Cohn, the truculent head of Columbia Pictures and thus Rita Hayworth's boss, was impressed enough with what Welles had wrought to hire him to produce, direct, write, narrate, and act in a thriller opposite Rita. It was a decision Cohn, who had never forgiven her for marrying Welles in the first place, would come to deeply regret. *The Lady from Shanghai* (1948) began shooting in 1946, when the Welles-Hayworth marriage, though recently blessed by the birth of a daughter, was already threatening to disintegrate in the face of Welles's neglect (it did, after filming wrapped in 1947). Based on a potboiler by Sherwood King, the story was reimagined by Welles as a feverishly intricate meditation on the nature of evil, with Welles as the philosophic windbag of a protagonist, Michael O'Hara, Rita as the treacherous Elsa Bannister, and Mercury veteran Everett Sloane as her crippled but poisonous husband, the corrupt lawyer Arthur Bannister.

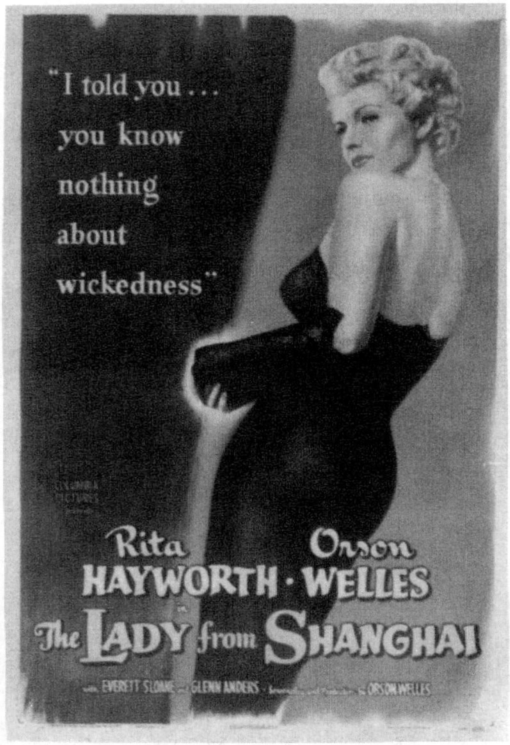
"I told you...
you know
nothing
about
wickedness"
Rita
HAYWORTH
Orson
WELLES
The LADY from SHANGHAI

In a typical display of mordant humor, Welles had Rita shorn of her lovely red tresses and dyed a platinum blond, a transformation dutifully covered in the fan magazines; predictably, it made Cohn apoplectic (a response Welles may well have anticipated). Shot in a variety of colorful Mexican locations, one of which was off the coast of Acapulco on board Errol Flynn's yacht, this frighteningly expensive (and rather incomprehensible) picture bombed. Today *Lady* is regarded as one of Welles's masterpieces, a triumph of style over substance—even though Welles was unable to oversee its final, truncated cut.

Welles continued his career devolution by hauling himself and Mercury Productions over to genre factory Republic Pictures, where he surprised everyone but himself by making (in twenty-three days!) a loose but strikingly original version of *Macbeth* (1948). Welles, as usual, best summarized his low-budget achievement by describing it to Peter Bogdanovich as "for better or worse, a kind of violently sketched charcoal drawing of a great play . . . I am not ashamed of the limitations of the picture." One of those limitations is Jeanette Nolan's Lady Macbeth, and while Welles is reliably entertaining as Shakespeare's tragic hero, Roddy McDowall, Dan O'Herlihy, and Edgar Barrier make up a decidedly unprepossessing (if not untalented) cast. Using brilliantly stylized sets to support his vision, Welles boldly takes the liberties he must with the text to make it live on the screen. (Originally released at 107 minutes, the film was for many years seen only in a redubbed 89-minute version; it was recently restored on video, now offering the actors with Scots accents.)

There was nothing now for Welles in Hollywood, so he moved to Europe, eager to hire himself out as an actor to earn funds to mount his next production. In 1949 he was Cagliostro in Gregory Ratoff's *Black Magic*, helping with the directorial chores (sans credit); then a colorful Cesare Borgia in Henry King's *Prince of Foxes*; and (most famously) the enigmatic, amoral Harry Lime in Carol Reed's classic thriller *The Third Man*. Highly paid by producers Alexander Korda and David O. Selznick for this role (for which he employed no makeup, a rarity), Welles supplied his kibbitzing to Reed at no extra charge (and Reed was smart enough to put at least some of his suggestions to use). Welles next played a thirteenth-century warlord to perfection in Henry Hathaway's 1950 release *The Black Rose*.

By now he had raised enough to commence *Othello* (1952), which he started filming in Morocco;

over the next three years Welles fitfully continued filming it on location in Italy and in a Rome studio, stopping whenever funds ran low to take on another acting assignment. The result of his Herculean labor was shown at Cannes in 1952, winning a prize, but was not given a U.S. release until 1955. The nigh-unknown cast—aside from Welles as the Moor, it starred Suzanne Cloutier as Desdemona and Michael MacLiammoir of the Abbey Theatre as Iago—ensured that its commercial prospects would remain modest. Still, this is a brave and brilliant cinematic thrust that takes what it wants of Shakespeare's poetry and creates what it needs to with the camera. Stitched together like Frankenstein's creation (not all the actors were able to remain on call for three years!), this is the work that some argue is Welles's greatest achievement—particularly if extra points are given for overcoming obstacles.

*Mr. Arkadin/Confidential Report* (1955), based on an original story by Welles and financed by half of Europe, has never been seen in the form Welles intended—Warner Bros., its distributor, cut it so extensively as to make it unrecognizable even to Welles. It's a *Kane*-like story with a different but equally tragic ending: a wealthy, powerful financier hires a shady young American to reassemble his past history, which the tycoon claims to have forgotten, but fears will be so rife with scandal that his beloved daughter will turn away from him in horror. Released in England in 1955 as *Confidential Report* and retitled *Mr. Arkadin* for its U.S. release in 1962, the film employed an elaborate flashback structure that moviegoers saw only in a reshuffled, chronological format. As with so many of Welles's later works, the picture's merits wrestle fiercely with its pretensions, pitfalls, and production deficiencies; but its possibilities—now never to be entirely realized—tantalize.

Nineteen fifty-five was also the year Welles commenced work on *Don Quixote*, a never-completed contemporary reworking of the Cervantes tale that he also produced, narrated, and co-scripted; in addition, Welles gave himself a role as—himself. *Quixote* surfaced in 1994 in fragmented form at the Edinburgh Film Festival and the Museum of Modern Art in New York. Rough though it was, the sample whet the appetites of his admirers, who speculated anew on what the master might have achieved if only the funds had been made available to him. Welles continued to accept as many acting assignments as he could get—in movies originating in England (*Trent's Last Case*, *Three Cases of Murder*), France, and Italy. American audiences saw him in John Huston's *Moby Dick*, well cast as Father Mapple; less so as a rancher in Jack Arnold's Western *Man in the Shadow*; and as the imposing Varner in Martin Ritt's *The Long Hot Summer*. He then returned to Hollywood for the first time in ten years to make what is now considered one of his finest, and most personal, films.

*Touch of Evil* (1958) was based on a Whit Masterson detective novel; Welles took its plot about a crooked police chief and embroidered it with the themes close to his heart (guilt and redemption, situation ethics vs. morality, relative vs. utter evil), abetted by some of his most dazzling camerawork to date (the picture's opening tracking shot is one of Welles's most famous). Charlton Heston and Janet Leigh star as Americans caught in a maze of corruption just over the Mexican border, but it's really Welles as the gross Hank Quinlan and Marlene Dietrich as a hard-boiled madam who steal the show. (Henry Mancini's score was another asset.) Welles delivered a 108-minute cut to Universal, but the studio predictably fiddled with it, adding a few minor new scenes and (more damagingly) cutting more than 13 minutes of Welles's character exposition. This footage has now been restored on video, and makes a great film that much greater.

Now it was back to acting for Welles: as Cy in *The Roots of Heaven*, attorney Jonathan Wilk in the Leopold-Loeb drama *Compulsion*, and King Saul in *David and Goliath*, among other roles. Next he made *The Trial* (1962) in Europe, most of it shot on a shoestring budget in a deserted train station in Paris. Kafka's 1925 novel of existential dread would seem to be a good match for Welles's baroque pessimism, and indeed, Welles himself considered the film his best work. But while Anthony Perkins (convincingly anguished as Joseph K.), Welles (formidable as Hastler, the advocate), Jeanne Moreau, and Romy Schneider certainly make for an exceptional cast, the picture doesn't build upon its effective early scenes.

*Chimes at Midnight/Falstaff* (1966) is probably Welles's last great film. Casting himself as Shakespeare's buffoon Falstaff, and borrowing elements from *Henry IV (Parts I and II)*, *Henry V*, *Richard II*, and *The Merry Wives of Windsor*, Welles assembled an impressionistic, very cinematic, and often moving tribute to the grandeur of Shakespeare. More may have

▲ *Orson Welles oversees wife Rita Hayworth's makeover for* The Lady from Shanghai, *the film that essentially ended his career as a Hollywood director*

been attempted here than the minuscule budget could bear—a stunning Battle of Shrewsbury toward the film's end has power aplenty, but some of the other staging is awkward, and much of the picture is poorly dubbed—but Welles makes the most of his Spanish locales and a terrific cast that includes John Gielgud (as Henry IV), Margaret Rutherford, Jeanne Moreau, and Fernando Rey. But it is Welles's shambling, stumbling Falstaff who is rightly the film's centerpiece, and justice is done to his tragic fate.

After roles in *Is Paris Burning?*, *A Man for All Seasons* (splendid as Cardinal Wolsey), and *Casino Royale*, the 1967 James Bond spoof, Welles made *The Immortal Story* (1968), an hour-long film for French TV. Many more acting appearances followed, including roles in John Huston's *The Kremlin Letter*, Mike Nichols's *Catch-22* (as General Dreedle), *Treasure Island*, and Brian DePalma's *Get to Know Your Rabbit*. More and more, he put that famous, mellifluous baritone to work narrating films—it had served him on Nicholas Ray's *King of Kings*, and he employed it now on the documentary *Directed by John Ford* and, of all things, *Bugs Bunny, Superstar*, as well as on a popular series of wine commercials.

His final theatrical release would not appear until 1975. *F Is for Fake*, scripted by Welles, was based on documentary footage shot by François Reichenbach, whose subjects were art forger Elmyr de Hory and *faux*-biographer Clifford Irving. It was a caustic and rather profound meditation on the nature of truth in art, an irresistible topic for Welles, who always appreciated a good joke, even when it was at his own expense. That same year Welles received the American Film Institute's Life Achievement Award; just before his death, the Directors' Guild of America would proffer their highest honor, the D. W. Griffith Award. In between, he accepted acting jobs in such potpourri as *Voyage of the Damned*, *History of the World, Part I*, and, most delectably, the trashy 1981 version of James Cain's *Butterfly*, opposite Pia Zadora. (Now *there* was a screen duo for the ages.)

Among Welles's unfinished works is *The Other Side of the Wind*, a 1970 project about a director who struggles to get his films financed and produced. John Huston was set to play the hard-luck protagonist; if Welles had been ten years younger, he surely would have elected to cast himself. But then, finishing it might have meant finishing himself, and Orson Welles had always specialized in art that would face eternity incomplete.

▲ *Coaching the hoods who attack Janet Leigh in* Touch of Evil

## ● WILLIAM WELLMAN (1896–1975)

William Wellman has been ranked by some as another John Ford or Howard Hawks. That assessment seems overly generous, but a survey of his sixty-odd sound pictures clearly indicates that his talent was not ordinary, particularly when it was applied to the action picture. But "Wild Bill" Wellman was also infamous for his nastiness to his actors and his familiarity with the bottle, traits which may have stemmed from his boyhood days in Massachusetts (he was born in Brookline), where he was known as something of a juvenile delinquent, stealing cars and dropping out of school to join a semi-pro hockey team in 1914.

But World War I might have saved him. Originally he enlisted as an ambulance driver for the French Foreign Legion, then became a pilot for the Lafayette Escadrille when America entered the war, winning the Croix de Guerre when his plane was shot down. After the Armistice, Wellman became a stunt flyer and crash-landed on the estate of Douglas Fairbanks, Sr., whom he quickly imposed on to help him break into the industry. Fairbanks found him a job as an actor and, when that didn't work out, helped him hook on with Goldwyn Pictures as a messenger boy.

By 1923 Wellman had worked his way up to directing Westerns at Fox, and in 1926 signed with Paramount. His third picture for them was *Wings* (1927), an aviation drama written by former pilot John Monk Saunders and starring Clara Bow (Gary Cooper had a bit part); it won the first Academy Award for best picture. He and Saunders collaborated again on *Legion of the Condemned* (1928), a tale about the Lafayette Escadrille that featured Gary Cooper, while *Ladies of the Mob* (1928) had Clara Bow and Richard Arlen fending off gangsters. *Beggars of Life* (1928), which offered a few lines of dialogue to make it (just barely) Wellman's first sound picture, starred Louise Brooks (disguised as a man) and Richard Arlen as tramps on the lam from the law. A succession of underworld dramas and romances followed (*Chinatown Nights*, *The Man I Love*, and *Woman Trap* in 1929; *Dangerous Paradise* and *Maybe It's Love* in 1930) before Wellman could make the aviation yarn *Young Eagles* (1930) with Buddy Rogers and Jean Arthur—but it didn't repeat *Wings*'s success.

In 1931 Wellman moved to Warner Bros., where he would direct fifteen pictures over the next three years (and two more for other studios). The first, *Other Men's Women*, has long been forgotten, but Wellman took one of its young actors, New York transplant James Cagney, and starred him in *The Public Enemy* (1931). A last-minute replacement for Archie Mayo, Wellman turned this low-budget, high-violence gangster saga into one of the year's biggest hits and in the process launched Cagney on the road to stardom. *Night Nurse* (1931) was also good, unwholesome fun, starring Barbara Stanwyck as a fearless nurse who stands up to murderous blackmailer Clark Gable, even after he punches her out. *Star Witness* and *Safe in Hell* (both 1931) kept Wellman in the realm of the underworld, while *The Hatchet Man* (1932) found *faux*-Orientals Loretta Young and Edward G. Robinson in the tong wars of San Francisco's Chinatown.

Wellman switched gears with *So Big* (1932), a truncated version of Edna Ferber's bestselling novel that starred Barbara Stanwyck as the Illinois teacher who triumphs over many tribulations. *Love Is a Racket* was Douglas Fairbanks, Jr., as a Broadway heel, while *The Purchase Price* (both 1932) featured Barbara Stanwyck again—she was Wellman's favorite actress—this time as a torch singer who flees her gangster boyfriend and improbably ends up as the mail-order bride of North Dakota farmer George Brent. Wellman was imported to RKO to make the epic *The Conquerors* (1932), a bald-faced remake of Wesley Ruggles's 1931 hit *Cimarron*; Richard Dix returned to scowl his way through fifty more years of glory and disaster, accompanied by stoic Ann Harding. Barbary Coast melodrama was the setting of *Frisco Jenny* (1933), a Ruth Chatterton three-hankie job that bore a passing resemblance to her 1929 smash *Madame X*.

*Central Airport* (1933) was an aviation soap opera after Wellman's own heart, with Richard Barthelmess as a stunt pilot who loves but refuses to marry parachutist Sally Eilers, who then marries his brother (Tom Brown) out of spite, amid plenty of aerial action. *Midnight Mary* (1933) was an interesting melodrama that starred Loretta Young as a gang girl on trial for murder, flashing back on what brought her to such an end. Wellman used Barthelmess again in the farfetched *Heroes for Sale*, a socially conscious but contrived drama about a former soldier and drug addict who becomes a millionaire, only to find himself sympathizing with his striking workers. That was a nice companion piece to the pre-Code gem *Wild Boys of the Road* (also 1933), a message picture in the best Warners tradition about three Depression-ravaged kids who become hoboes while seeking a better life. But *Lilly Turner* was a patently ridiculous yarn, starring Ruth Chatterton as the unhappy wife of a carny magician, and *College Coach* (both 1933), with Pat O'Brien as the driven coach, was an outright embarrassment, especially for whoever cast crooner Dick Powell as the star halfback.

Those seven 1933 releases ended Wellman's association with Warner Bros., and he began a very successful period as a freelancer. *Looking for Trouble* (1934) was a bit of a mess, although Spencer Tracy (whom Wellman punched out during filming for some long-forgotten reason) was fun to watch as a telephone linesman, while *Stingaree* (1934) was a flamboyant romantic adventure set Down Under, starring Richard Dix and Irene Dunne. *The President Vanishes* (1935) was a political cautionary tale that is memorable today chiefly for providing Rosalind Russell's first screen appearance, but *Call of the Wild* (1935) was a major box-office success; Clark Gable is his most magnetic as Jack London's Yukon-conquering hero and Loretta Young is an appealing love interest (offscreen as well as on, it was rumored). *The Robin Hood of El Dorado* (1936) was a lively but inconsistent biopic about Mexican bandit Joaquin Murietta, while *Small Town Girl* teamed Robert Taylor and Janet Gaynor in a corny love story that must have been hard to swallow even in 1936.

Wellman embarked on his most creative period with *A Star Is Born* (1937), David O. Selznick's remake of the 1932 Cukor film *What Price Hollywood*. Cukor had declined to direct on the second go-round, but Wellman proved to be a fine second choice, collaborating on the story with Robert Carson and winning an Oscar for that piece of work. He also received an Academy Award nomination for best direction, and stars Fredric March and Janet Gaynor and the film received nominations as well. (Although Cukor's 1954 musical remake with Judy Garland is more familiar today, Wellman's version still plays very well indeed.) Just as outstanding in its own right was *Nothing Sacred* (1937), a scathing screwball comedy that features what may be Carole Lombard's best performance and a terrific (and frighteningly modern) screenplay by Ben Hecht about media manipulation, and vice versa. *Men with Wings* (1938) was a Technicolor account of the development of aviation written by Wellman and Robert Carson—but it was undone by its overly mythopoeic treatment and the problematic casting of genial Fred MacMurray and Ray Milland as the heroic pilots.

*Beau Geste* (1939) was a spectacular remake of the 1926 silent, with Gary Cooper, Ray Milland, and Robert Preston as the brothers who stake their honor against the cruelty of their Foreign Legion commander (Oscar-nominated Brian Donlevy). That was high adventure at its best, but *The Light That Failed* (1939) succeeded on very different terms. It was a sensitive adaptation of a Rudyard Kipling story, starring Ronald Colman as the soldier/artist who goes blind and Ida Lupino as the cockney girl who becomes his final portrait. *Reaching for the Sun* (1941) was an odd misfire, a whimsical story with Joel McCrea that might have worked in the hands of a Preston Sturges. *Roxie Hart* (1942), on the other hand, a loud and labored comedy with Ginger Rogers, years later became the basis for the Broadway musical *Chicago*. *The Great Man's Lady* (1942) used McCrea and Barbara Stanwyck as the fulcrum of a saga about oil and the Old West; it covered several decades, yet in the end went nowhere.

Wellman wasn't cut out for such trifles, but a return to the theme of flying—even with the war as a backdrop—wasn't enough to make *Thunder Birds* (1942), a yarn about Army flight instructors starring Gene Tierney and Preston Foster, more than grist for Hollywood's patriotic mill. The Oscar-nominated *The Ox-Bow Incident* (1943), however, was a fine piece of work, a telling indictment of mob rule (based on the Van Tilburg Clark novel) that occasionally slipped into portentousness; Dana Andrews was unusually good as one of the trio unjustly accused of rustling. The murder mystery *Lady of Burlesque* (1943) was far lighter fare, with Barbara Stanwyck most enjoyable as author Gypsy Rose Lee's alter ego.

*Buffalo Bill* (1944) featured Joel McCrea as the Wild West's most flamboyant showman, with Linda Darnell, Maureen O'Hara, and Chief Thundercloud providing good support, while *This Man's Navy* (1945) was a standard actioner about sub-chasing Tom Drake and Wallace Beery. Until *Navy* Wellman hadn't had much truck with military stories, but in *The Story of G.I. Joe* (1945) he made one of the best World War II pictures. Robert Mitchum was great as the battle-weary 18th Infantry captain, and Burgess Meredith also shone as war correspondent Ernie Pyle. Mitchum and the screenplay both received Oscar nominations; unfortunately, Pyle died before he could see how good a job Wellman had done adapting his memoir.

*Gallant Journey* (1946) permitted Wellman another foray into the roots of aviation, with Glenn Ford developing the first gliders in the late 1800s, but as with *Men with Wings*, this history lesson failed to take off. *Magic Town* (1947) was considerably better, a choice satire on Middle America (written by longtime Capra collaborator Robert Riskin) in which James Stewart plays a pollster who locates the exactly average American town, with disastrous results. But the leaden *The Iron Curtain* (1948) could have used some of its predecessor's deftness. This Cold War drama, based on a 1945 scandal involving a Canadian scientist and a Member of Parliament, made the least of stars Dana Andrews and Gene Tierney's chemistry—*Laura* this most definitely was not. But *Yellow Sky* (1948) was an exciting Western in which Gregory Peck and Richard Widmark are well matched as opponents.

Wellman now moved to MGM, a studio not obviously suited to his talents but where he nonetheless made some of his more interesting films. First up was *Battleground* (1949), a solid but unremarkable account of the Battle of the Bulge that was a major box-office hit; Wellman, who had had many more deserving works overlooked, was Oscar-nominated for his direction. *The Happy Years* (1950) was turn-of-the-century Americana about a boy's prep school—the sort of sanitized *Saturday Evening Post* fare that Wellman had successfully avoided for most of his career. At least *The Next Voice You Hear* (1950) was original: God decides to talk to America over the radio, understandably changing the lives of James Whitmore and Nancy Davis.

*Across the Wide Missouri* (1951), with Clark Gable in buckskins, was a more typical Wellman undertaking—but something went wrong with this expensive Technicolor Western (shot on location in Colorado) and drastic cutting took place before it was released. He directed the Van Johnson segment of the ill-fated *It's a Big Country*, then made *Westward the Women* (also 1951) with Robert Taylor, from a story written by Frank Capra. *My Man and I* (1952) was a hothouse romantic triangle between Ricardo Montalban, Claire Trevor, and Shelley Winters, while *Island in the Sky* (1953) was an overly talky World War II aviation drama that starred John Wayne, with whom Wellman tussled but (sensibly) didn't come to blows with. *The High and the Mighty* (1954) was adapted from a bestseller, and this time Wellman remembered to put in some action. The prototypical airplane disaster movie, it was a huge hit and boasted a mouth-watering cast that included John Wayne, Robert Stack, Claire Trevor, and Jan Sterling; Oscar nominations went to Wellman, Sterling, Trevor, and the Dimitri Tiomkin score (which won).

The 1954 *Track of the Cat*, starring Robert Mitchum, was an ambitious attempt to do something more with a genre picture, but its overly deliberate schematics—color cinematography rendered as though black-and-white—finally overwhelmed the production. *Blood Alley* (1955) pitted John Wayne and Lauren Bacall against the Chinese Communists, while *Good-bye, My Lady* (1956) was Southern-fried sentimentality about a young boy and his dog. Now Wellman returned to his roots with the World War II opus *Darby's Rangers* and *Lafayette Escadrille* (both 1958), a superficial drama about Wellman's actual World War I unit that suffered from the deficiencies of lead Tab Hunter. Still, it was a fitting way for the feisty old ace to say goodbye.

▲ *On location in the Rockies for* Across the Wide Missouri

## ● JAMES WHALE (1896-1957)

One of the most distinctive filmmakers of the early Thirties, James Whale cut short his Hollywood career to become a painter. But his abbreviated filmography contains as many high points as those of many directors who toiled three times as long. Born in Dudley, England, he was captured by the Germans during World War I and began acting while in a prisoner-of-war camp. After he was released, Whale continued acting on stage, eventually becoming a set designer and, later, a director. His London play *Journey's End* (1928) was his calling card to Hollywood, where he was invited in 1930 to prepare a film version for the Tiffany studio.

Howard Hughes then asked him to assist on *Hell's Angels* (1930), after which Whale was hired by Universal's Carl Laemmle, Jr., to direct *Waterloo Bridge* (1931), an adaptation of the Robert E. Sherwood tearjerker about a London streetwalker (Mae Clarke) who nobly gives up her soldier lover so that he won't be disgraced. (Mervyn LeRoy's glossy 1940 version with Vivien Leigh as a Code-approved ballet dancer is the better remembered today.) *Frankenstein* (1931) was scheduled to be directed by Robert Florey, but when Bela Lugosi decided he didn't want to be typecast after starring in *Dracula*, Whale was assigned to the picture; it was he who cast a little-known British actor named Boris Karloff to play the monster. Though much more cinematic than, say, *Dracula*, the film is awkward in spots; still, it has the power to shock. An enormous popular success, *Frankenstein* launched Whale as the preeminent director of the horror film, a much more reputable genre then than it is today.

Whale's next picture was *The Impatient Maiden* (1932), a romance of the sort they just don't make anymore: surgeon Lew Ayres wins the love of secretary Mae Clarke by performing an appendectomy on her. After that embarrassment, Whale was undoubtedly relieved to be assigned to *The Old Dark House* (1932), a hugely enjoyable chiller starring Charles Laughton, Boris Karloff, Raymond Massey, and Ernest Thesiger, who take turns chewing the moldering scenery. *The Kiss Before the Mirror* (1933) was a bizarre but interesting romantic mystery set in Vienna, with a highly colorful cast: Paul Lukas, Nancy Carroll, Frank Morgan, Jean Dixon, Gloria Stuart, and Walter Pidgeon. (Whale himself would remake it five years later.)

*The Invisible Man* (1933) returned Whale to the realm of the macabre, and he made the most of it in this splendid version of H. G. Wells's Victorian science-fiction story. Claude Rains—or at least his voice—is wonderful in his debut as a scientist distintegrating into madness, a part Karloff turned down. *By Candlelight* (1934) was merely a creaking romantic comedy, with Paul Lukas and Elissa Landi, an antique before the camera even started rolling. But *One More River* (1934) was a treat for Anglophiles based on a John Galsworthy novel chronicling the dissolution of a marriage; its cast included Diana Wynyard (fresh from her Oscar-nominated turn in *Cavalcade*), Colin Clive, and Lionel Atwill.

Though to some the wildly inventive *The Bride of Frankenstein* (1935) can never be more than a genre film, it is a brilliantly imagined and executed bit of cinema, perhaps the year's best and surely Whale's masterpiece. A stylishly decadent effort, it demonstrated how far Whale's artistry had progressed in just four years. Stars Karloff, Ernest Thesiger, Elsa Lanchester, and Colin Clive are all superb, as is Franz Waxman's soaring score. (Needless to say, not one of them was so much as nominated for an Academy Award.)

*Remember Last Night?* (1935) was a minor but satisfactory comedic mystery in the *Thin Man* vein, though Edward Arnold and Constance Cummings were not exactly Powell and Loy. *Show Boat* (1936) had been made in 1929 and would be again in 1951, but Whale's version of the Oscar Hammerstein–Jerome Kern musical (via the Edna Ferber novel) just may be the best; Irene Dunne is a surprisingly strong lead, and she has peerless support from Paul Robeson and Helen Morgan. A big hit at the box office, the film came too late to save the Laemmle regime from toppling at Universal. *The Road Back* (1937) was a sequel to *All Quiet on the Western Front*, with the surviving German soldiers finding their homecoming rather rockier going than expected; it must have seemed like a good idea at the time, but the film quickly veered into soap opera and ended up trivializing Erich Maria Remarque's original story.

Whale next made *The Great Garrick* (1937) while on loan to Warners; the theatrical background of the story was well suited to his talents. But *Sinners in Paradise* (1938) was a (very) poor man's *Grand Hotel*, a feeble melodrama about a group of plane crash survivors stuck on a mysterious island, each of them carrying a dark secret. Universal was now deep into its austerity program, so remaking *The Kiss before the Mirror* as *Wives under Suspicion* in 1938 was another obvious cost-cutting move, although only so much could be done with Warren William and Gail Patrick. *Port of Seven Seas* (1938), MGM's attempt to film *Fanny* with Wallace Beery and Maureen O'Sullivan, failed in spite of Preston Sturges's script. Whale finally was given a first-rate property to work on at United Artists, where he made the Dumas classic *The Man in the Iron Mask* (1939). It starred Louis Hayward in a dual role and Joan Bennett; what it needed was Errol Flynn and Olivia de Havilland, but it was a good swashbuckler nonetheless, complete with cameo appearances by D'Artagnan and the Three Musketeers.

*Green Hell* (1940) sent George Sanders, Vincent Price, and Douglas Fairbanks, Jr., into the Brazilian jungle to no good purpose, but it was a masterpiece compared to *They Dare Not Love* (1941), a ridiculous melodrama set in war-torn Europe, starring George Brent as a noble Austrian prince who sacrifices himself to the Nazis. This was enough to send Whale into retirement, where he spent the next fifteen years painting. He was found dead in his swimming pool in 1957, a grim ending for a talent that Hollywood only intermittently used wisely or well.

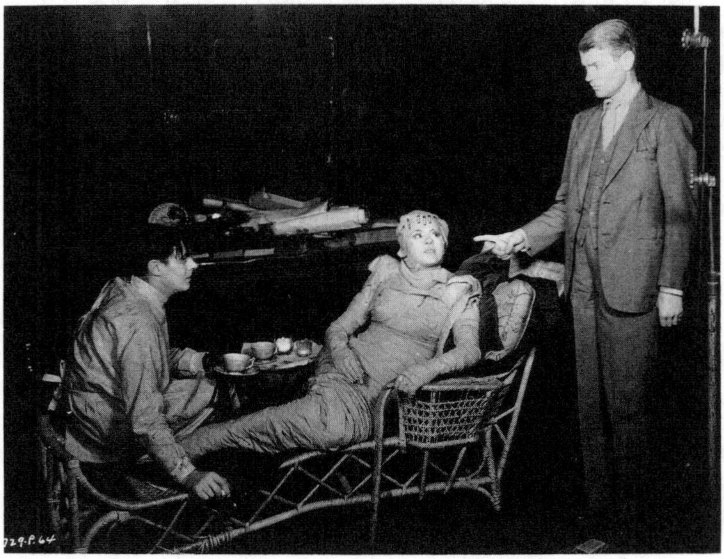


◀ *With stars Colin Clive and Elsa Lanchester on the set of Whale's greatest movie,* The Bride of Frankenstein

## ● BILLY WILDER (1906– )

Was there any director in Hollywood who made more great movies during the Forties and Fifties than Viennese transplant Billy (né Samuel) Wilder? Has there ever been a director who was as good a writer for as long a time? John Huston may be the closest contender, but he hung up his typewriter in mid-career. (Oliver Stone? Please!)

The crown prince of cynicism, Wilder was raised in Vienna and attended the University of Vienna as a pre-law student. But after a year he dropped out to work as a reporter on a Vienna newspaper. A major paper in Berlin hired him away in 1926 to cover the crime beat, experience that would serve him well in his subsequent career. But already Wilder was looking beyond journalism and got his first screenwriting credit working on the Edgar Ulmer–Robert Siodmak *Menschen am Sonntag* (*People on Sunday*) in 1929. More scripts for a variety of German films followed over the next four years, but when the Nazis took power in 1933, Wilder, like so many other Jews in the arts, fled. In Paris he co-directed *Mauvaise Graine* with Alexander Esway before continuing on to the United States, after a brief stopover in Mexico.

Wilder's first years in Hollywood were not pretty. He could speak little English and roomed with Peter Lorre while trying to eke out an existence as a screenwriter who understood only German. By collaborating with writers who could translate his contributions, he accumulated credits on scripts for fluff like *Music in the Air* and *Lottery Lover*. But in 1937 he was signed by Paramount and assigned to work with Charles Brackett, a bit of luck that improved not only his own life but those of moviegoers everywhere. The Brackett-Wilder team debuted on Ernst Lubitsch's *Bluebeard's Eighth Wife* in 1938 and continued through such romantic comedy gems as Mitchell Leisen's *Midnight*, Lubitsch's *Ninotchka*, and Howard Hawks's *Ball of Fire*. For Wilder, his most personal work during this period was probably Leisen's *Hold Back the Dawn* (1941), a compelling drama about a suave European refugee (Charles Boyer) stranded in Mexico who uses his wiles to entice an American schoolteacher (Olivia de Havilland) into marriage so that he can gain entry to the United States. Boyer's underlying desperation is captured well by the hard-boiled screenplay.

In 1942 Wilder and Brackett entered into a brilliant arrangement: Wilder would direct, Brackett would produce, and both would write their subsequent projects. Their first picture made in this manner was *The Major and the Minor* (1942), a clever farce in which Ginger Rogers masquerades as a twelve-year-old to avoid paying full fare on a train bound for her hometown in Iowa; Ray Milland is the engaged Army major who can't quite figure why he's so attracted to a young girl. (He finds out about ninety minutes later.) *Five Graves to Cairo* (1943) was suspenseful wartime espionage, with stranded British soldier Franchot Tone impersonating a double agent to trick Field Marshal Rommel (a perfectly cast Eric von Stroheim) into revealing military secrets while the two are holed up in a Sahara hotel run by Akim Tamiroff and sultry Anne Baxter.

*Double Indemnity* (1944) is one of the most searing of the early films noirs, and it just may be the best. Masterfully adapted by Raymond Chandler and Wilder from James M. Cain's 1936 novella, it had been deemed too hot for Hollywood's Production Code at the time (as had Cain's previous book, *The Postman Always Rings Twice*). But by 1944 war-wise America was ready to take its entertainment medicine straight, and Wilder was happy to give them a bitter dosage. Genial Fred MacMurray is cast against type as Walter Neff, a skilled but jaded insurance salesman who's the apple of boss Edward G. Robinson's jaundiced eye. But when Barbara Stanwyck, the sexy wife of a prospective client, comes on to him,

MacMurray surprises himself by buying the package she proposes: insure her husband without him knowing it, kill him, collect the money, and spend it together. Told in flashback, the film was nominated for an Academy Award—a rarity for this genre—as was Stanwyck, whose icy, calculating Phyllis Dietrichson shocked moviegoers used to her romantic-comedy persona. Wilder received the first of his seven Academy Award nominations for best direction, and another nomination for his and Chandler's screenplay.

Wilder had arrived. He actually managed to equal the success of *Double Indemnity* with *The Lost Weekend* (1945), a stark, harrowing portrait of one man's descent into alcoholism, from the novel by Charles R. Jackson. Ray Milland gives the performance of his career as Don Birnam, who is struggling with writer's block and relies on the bottle to help him blot out his misery; he then nearly blots himself out of existence during a weekend binge. (The Bellevue footage was shot on location, and Third Avenue makes a strong cameo appearance.) So powerful was the film for the time that Paramount was initially afraid to release it. But once they did, both critics and (more surprisingly) audiences embraced the grim cautionary tale. At Oscar time *Lost Weekend* won as the year's best picture and Milland as best actor; the Brackett-Wilder screenplay also won an Academy Award, and Wilder was cited for best direction by both the Academy and the New York Film Critics Circle.

He now was probably the hottest director in Hollywood, but he never got the chance to parlay his back-to-back hits into a trifecta. Uncle Sam beckoned, and it would be three years before Wilder directed another film. In the meantime, he became a colonel in the Psychological Warfare Division of occupied Berlin—an interesting assignment, and one that, typically, Wilder would put to good use in a future project. But his first movie after his Army stint was the hopelessly corny *The Emperor Waltz* (1948), a Bing Crosby–Joan Fontaine musical set in back-lot Austria—it must have been entrusted to Wilder because of his birth certificate rather than his sensibility.

The Brackett-Wilder team was better represented a few months later with *A Foreign Affair*, a wonderfully cynical romantic comedy set in the same occupied Berlin that Wilder had just departed, starring Jean Arthur as a prim congresswoman from Iowa on a fact-finding mission and John Lund as the wheeler-dealer Army captain who's afraid of the facts she'll find—namely, his well-paid mistress (Marlene Dietrich, in one of her last great screen roles). Arthur and Lund wouldn't make anyone forget Ingrid Bergman and Humphrey Bogart, but even if the gimmick of their ersatz romance turning to gold is never entirely convincing, Dietrich's Erika von Schlutow is, singing in her smoky cabaret and philosophically conceding Lund to her strait-laced rival. *Affair* also illuminates the workings of the postwar armed services with a candor entirely unique for the day.

Brackett and Wilder collaborated on just one more film before going their separate ways, but it may be their best. *Sunset Boulevard* (1950) is the caustic tale of out-of-work screenwriter Joe Gillis (William Holden), who agrees to move in with former screen actress Norma Desmond (Gloria Swanson), an eccentric recluse who wants Joe to script her comeback vehicle (an impossibly archaic version of *Salome*). The story is narrated by Joe's corpse, which we see floating facedown in Norma's swimming pool in the film's indelible opening scene. It's a testament to Wilder and Brackett's storytelling prowess that our interest in the perverse fable—still the greatest Hollywood story of them all—never flags. Holden gives the first important performance of his career as the kept Joe, who despises himself for his willingness to sell out even while pitying his self-deluded benefactress, and Erich von Stroheim is utterly superb as Max, Desmond's butler, former husband, and director (von Stroheim actually did direct Swanson in the uncompleted silent *Queen Kelly*, a segment of which is shown here—just one of Wilder's many devilish in-jokes). But all praise to Swanson (Wilder's fifth choice for the role!), whose electrifying, deliberately over-the-top performance as the tragic Norma is truly *sui generis*. She was nominated for an Oscar but lost to Judy Holliday—though for once a best actress award may have been inadequate, anyway. Wilder and the picture were also nominated for Academy Awards, but it was the Wilder–Brackett–D. M. Marshman, Jr., screenplay and the grand Franz Waxman score that ultimately won Oscars.

Why Wilder and Brackett split after this, one of their greatest achievements, seems puzzling, but apparently it took place without rancor. *Ace in the Hole* (aka *The Big Carnival*; 1951) was Wilder's first endeavor as both producer and director, and it would prove to be his first box-office failure. A corrosive account of New York tabloid reporter Kirk Douglas's amoral manipulation of a New Mexico mining tragedy to artificially extend its run on the front pages *Ace* ladled on the acid with too heavy a hand. But even lacking nuance (a criticism that also applies to Douglas's performance), it was an acerbic drama that benefited from its location photography and a memorable performance by Jan Sterling, the twenty-minute egg of hard-boiled blondes, as the victim's tawdry wife. The screenplay earned Wilder a share of another Oscar nomination.

*Stalag 17* (1953) was far more successful on every front. Based on a Broadway play about the dynamics of a Nazi POW camp written by two former internees, it starred William Holden as a clever but reviled bunkhouse entrepreneur who has been framed as leaking inside dope to the camp commandant (Otto Preminger, in a brilliant von Stroheimesque turn). The black humor and suspense are adroitly handled by Wilder, who again was nominated for an Academy Award, but it's really Holden's show, and he delivers an Oscar-winning performance. (The picture was trivilized a decade later as the popular television sitcom *Hogan's Heroes*.)

Wilder mined Broadway once more and found Samuel Taylor's play *Sabrina Fair* there for the taking, but *Sabrina* (1954) lacked the customary Wilder bite—although as a workable romantic comedy it passed muster with the day's audiences. Humphrey Bogart and William Holden portray wealthy Long Island brothers with inimical lifestyles—Bogart is stable and responsible, Holden a dissolute playboy—who both fall for chauffeur's daughter Audrey Hepburn after a Continental makeover makes her a prize worth winning. The star power was high, as the healthy box-office returns attested, but the baloney was piled even higher, and the payoff feels faked.

◀ *On location in New Mexico with Kirk Douglas for* Ace in the Hole

Nevertheless, Wilder, Hepburn, and the screenplay were all nominated for Academy Awards.

George Axelrod's Broadway hit *The Seven Year Itch* (1955) became Wilder's next unremarkable adaptation. Axelrod collaborated with Wilder on the screenplay, and *Itch* starred Marilyn Monroe at the peak of her sex-bomb phase; Tom Ewell is the book publisher whose wife and son are away for the summer, leaving him free to fantasize about his nubile upstairs neighbor. But this leering version of "Walter Mitty" plays now as a one-joke embarrassment. At least *The Spirit of St. Louis* (1957), with James Stewart as Charles Lindbergh, had the merits of history, with Lindbergh's 1927 New York–to–Paris solo flight the set piece around which Wilder constructs a first-rate biopic (the only time he would choose to work in this genre).

*Love in the Afternoon* (1957) found Wilder with a new writing partner, I.A.L. Diamond—but this take-off on the play *Ariane* (and homage to Ernst Lubitsch's sophisticated Continental comedies) would not prove to be the apex of their joint ventures. Gary Cooper, looking uncomfortable and far older than his fifty-six years, is at times painful to watch as an American playboy living in the Paris Ritz who develops an interest in schoolgirl Audrey Hepburn and unwittingly hires her own private-eye dad (Maurice Chevalier) to investigate her. Shot on location, *Love* has some charming moments, but it's a half hour too long, the artifice of the romance feels forced—and Coop sometimes looks as though he'd like to doff his tux, don his buckskin gear, and ride off to hunt buffalo.

Wilder's third release of 1957, the brilliantly structured courtroom drama *Witness for the Prosecution*, based on Agatha Christie's long-running play, was cannily "opened up" by Wilder. London barrister Charles Laughton, suffering from a variety of ailments, is about to retire on the advice of his doctors; then murder suspect Tyrone Power (in his last screen appearance) begs him for help, and Laughton wheezes his way to the courtroom to defend him. Marlene Dietrich, as Power's loyal but inscrutable wife, basically steals the picture, but she has to earn it with the likes of the Oscar-nominated Elsa Lanchester and Laughton on the boards. Wilder and the film were also nominated for Academy Awards.

Although he hadn't had much luck with comedies of late, Wilder now made one of the decade's best—*Some Like It Hot* (1959), a riotous sex farce (written with I.A.L. Diamond) that served Marilyn Monroe (who was pregnant during filming and reportedly a nightmare to work with) far better than *Itch* had. Set during Prohibition, it starred Jack Lemmon and Tony Curtis as Chicago musicians on the lam from the mob after accidentally witnessing the St. Valentine's Day Massacre. They don women's clothes to join Sugar Kane (Monroe) and her all-girl band, bound for a gig in Florida. The rest of the picture alternates between Curtis's efforts to woo the luscious but vulnerable Monroe while disguised as an impotent yachtsman with Cary Grant diction, and Lemmon's gradual surrender to his feminine side, which ends with his accepting a marriage proposal from millionaire Joe E. Brown. *Hot* was a box-office smash (the biggest hit of Monroe's career) and earned Wilder yet another Oscar nomination for best direction and (with Diamond) best screenplay.

Just as daring in its way was *The Apartment* (1960), with Jack Lemmon in fine fettle as a milquetoast business executive who, hoping for a promotion, lets his S.O.B. of a boss (Fred MacMurray, cast against type again with splendid results) use his apartment to conduct an extramarital affair with neurotic elevator operator Shirley MacLaine. When MacMurray dumps her for fresh game, MacLaine tries to commit suicide; Lemmon nurses her back to health, falling in love with her in the process. The payoff comes when Lemmon finds his courage and tells off MacMurray in no uncertain terms. Like most moralistic tales, *The Apartment* is very much a product of its time—sort of an antidote to Hugh Hefner's "Playboy Philosophy"—and seems a bit quaint today. But in 1960 this was bold stuff, and the film won Academy Awards for best picture, best direction, and best screenplay (by Wilder and Diamond); the New York Film Critics Circle also made Wilder's direction and screenplay their choice as the year's best.

*One, Two, Three* (1961), shot on location in Germany, was a frenetic Cold War comedy, starring James Cagney as a Coca-Cola executive in West Berlin whose neck is on the line when his boss's visiting daughter (Pamela Tiffin) falls for and marries an East German Communist (Horst Buchholz). Cagney went into retirement after this; he probably was exhausted from delivering his lines at the speed of sound. The naughty *Irma La Douce* (1963) was a flabby, two and a half–hour adaptation of the 1956 French (and later Broadway) musical, sans music; Shirley MacLaine

and Jack Lemmon were reunited as, respectively, a philosophical Parisian streetwalker and the self-righteous constable who tries to shut down her operation but manages only to get himself fired. MacLaine (who was again Oscar-nominated as best actress) and Lemmon give their all, but the material defeats them—although *Irma* was one of the year's biggest hits.

The coarse *Kiss Me, Stupid* (1964) is considered by many to represent the nadir of Wilder's storied career, and it's still hard to envision what Wilder and Diamond were after here. Dean Martin plays an egotistical pop singer (appropriately named "Dino") visiting Climax, Nevada; local songwriter Ray Walston believes he might be given a shot at the big time if he lends Dino his wife for a night, and so he hires party girl Polly the Pistol (Kim Novak) to sub for his real wife. The film was condemned by the Legion of Decency, but since no one felt particularly compelled to see it in the first place, its poor box office was probably foreordained. Wilder and Diamond bounced back, however, with one of their tartest comedies, *The Fortune Cookie* (1966). Jack Lemmon is a cameraman covering pro football who is accidentally trampled by running back Ron Rich. Although his injuries are minor, Lemmon lets brother-in-law Walter Matthau, a shyster lawyer referred to by his peers as Whiplash Willie, talk him into suing the Cleveland Browns for a million dollars. It's a great premise, and Matthau holds up his end of the picture (winning a best supporting actor Oscar in the process), but Wilder again demonstrates a certain laziness not found in his earlier work, and the

picture doesn't hit on all six cylinders. Still, the screenplay earned another Oscar nomination.

Absent from the screen for the next four years, Wilder returned in 1970 with *The Private Life of Sherlock Holmes*, a generally underrated bit of revisionism (co-scripted with Diamond) that blessedly forgoes the stridency of Wilder's last several movies in favor of a more subdued, even contemplative approach to the Sherlock Holmes legend. Made in England and cut to two hours (from three and a half) for its release, the picture hadn't much chance at the U.S. box office with obscure actors like Robert Stephens as Holmes and Colin Blakely as Watson, and in the year of *Patton* and *Love Story* it came and went without making much of a ripple. (A restored version is now available on video.) *Avanti!* (1972) fared no better commercially, although once again that was more a function of Wilder being out of step with the times than any deficiency in the work itself. Jack Lemmon stars as a millionaire who travels to Italy to bury his father, only to quickly fall in love with Juliet Mills, the lovely daughter of Pop's mistress. An atypically gentle (but all too typically overlong) romantic comedy, this film deserves rediscovery.

Audiences actually turned out to see Wilder's noisy remake of the Ben Hecht–Charles MacArthur play *The Front Page* (1974), although if truth be told it ran a weak third to both Lewis Milestone's 1931 original and Howard Hawks's 1940 version, *His Girl Friday*. Lemmon and Matthau are paired as editor Walter Burns and reporter Hildy Johnson, but neither they nor Wilder (and Diamond, who again co-scripted) bring anything new to this satirical chestnut. In its own esoteric way, the little-seen, German-financed *Fedora* (1978), with producer William Holden trying to bring Garbo analogue Martha Keller out of retirement, is more interesting (and much less loud).

But *Buddy, Buddy* (1981), adapted by Wilder and Diamond from the French farce *A Pain in the A——*, was a fitting (if imperfectly sounded) note for Wilder to close out his fine career. Matthau and Lemmon are teamed one last time under Wilder's auspices as a hit man trying to carry out his assignment and the nosy stranger who keeps interfering with the job. The slapstick timing was off by a beat (or three), but watching Wilder execute his gags was as nostalgic a pastime as going to Dairy Queen for a frappe—devoid of redeeming qualities and almost sickeningly sweet, but what the hell?

◀ *With Kim Novak and Dean Martin on the set of* Kiss Me, Stupid

## ● ROBERT WISE (1914– )



Robert Wise has been labeled by some as a chameleon for the variety of forms in which he has worked—musicals, horror, film noir, science fiction, Westerns, war stories, period adventures, contemporary romance—but why be pejorative about it? He succeeded at least once in each of those genres, demonstrating a flexibility that at the least should compensate for his lack of a consistent style or theme.

Born in Winchester, Indiana, Wise traveled to Hollywood in 1933 after he ran out of money for college, taking a job as an assistant editor at RKO, where his brother David was an accountant. He rose to the rank of full editor in 1939, working on such films as *Bachelor Mother*, *The Hunchback of Notre Dame*, and *My Favorite Wife*. Most famously, he edited *Citizen Kane* and *The Magnificent Ambersons*, the latter after RKO had taken it out of Welles's hands. He got his chance to direct when Val Lewton needed someone to step in as a replacement on *The Curse of the Cat People* (1944), which was running behind schedule. The result was an eerie, touching film about a young girl dangerously prone to fantasizing; the lovely screenplay was by DeWitt Bodeen, who also had authored the more horrific *Cat People* two years earlier.

Wise stayed with the Lewton unit for two more films: *Mademoiselle Fifi* (1944), a loose adaptation of Guy de Maupassant's story of a courageous laundress (Simone Simon) who frees her village from the specter of the Prussian invaders in 1870s France, and *The Body Snatcher* (1945), a superior "B" based on a Robert Louis Stevenson story about a doctor (Henry Daniell) who hires a graverobber (Boris Karloff) to supply him with cadavers for his teaching experiments. Bela Lugosi, originally cast in Daniell's role, was also on hand for this minor classic of the macabre. But *A Game of Death* (1946) was merely a by-the-numbers remake of RKO's 1932 success *The Most Dangerous Game*, with an inferior cast and uninspired direction by Wise, while *Criminal Court* (1946) was a dull mystery starring Tom Conway and Martha O'Driscoll. *Born to Kill* (1947), though, was something special, a pitiless noir in which tough-guy Lawrence Tierney plays a sociopathic killer who tries to marry his way into respectability. Claire Trevor and Elisha Cook provide good support in this sometimes shockingly brutal adaptation of James Gunn's *Deadlier Than the Male*.

*Mystery in Mexico* (1948) was just a standard detective yarn, with William Lundigan as an insurance investigator, but *Blood on the Moon* (1948) was the first noir Western, with Robert Mitchum and Robert Preston stalking each other through the shadows as Barbara Bel Geddes waits breathlessly. Even better was *The Set-Up* (1949), a terrific noir (set in "real" time, a device later employed in *High Noon*) about an over-the-hill boxer who refuses to take a dive and pays a frightful price for his decision. Robert Ryan was at his best as the prideful fighter, at least as deserving of an Oscar-nomination as Kirk Douglas was that year for the more ballyhooed *Champion*. *Two Flags West* (1950) was a formulaic Civil War tale hobbled by its haphazard casting, but *Three Secrets* (1950) was a suspenseful soap opera in which Ruth Roman, Eleanor Parker, and Patricia Neal wait to hear which one's child was the lone survivor of a plane crash.

*The House on Telegraph Hill* (1951) was a noirish spy story that starred Richard Basehart and Valentina Cortese, but it was *The Day the Earth Stood Still* that captured the imagination of that year's moviegoers. Based on a humble 1930s pulp novelette by Harry Bates called "Farewell to the Master," it was made as an "A" production (unlike the majority of contemporary SF films). *Day* was also distinguished by its superior acting (Michael Rennie, Patricia Neal, and Sam Jaffe, among others), Edmund North's philosophical screenplay, and an evocative Bernard Herrmann score, making it a candidate for the best science-fiction movie of the decade. *The Captive City* (1952) was considerably more mundane, but its account of a crusading newspaper editor (John Forsythe) mounting a one-man campaign against his town's corrupt government did have its moments.

*Something for the Birds* (1952), though, was a typically fanciful MGM concoction, hardly an area that played to Wise's strengths (and why cast Victor Mature in a romantic comedy?). *The Desert Rats* (1953) was a strong sequel to Hathaway's 1951 *The Desert Fox*, with James Mason repeating his role as Field Marshal Rommel, pitted against Richard Burton. The 1953 *Destination Gobi* was a good companion piece, a World War II tale starring Richard Widmark, who enlists Pacific island natives against the Japanese. Wise shifted gears once again for *So Big* (1953), the third time Edna Ferber's Pulitzer Prize–winning novel had made it to the screen; here Jane Wyman stars as the country teacher, with Sterling Hayden as her husband and Steve Forrest her overly beloved son. *Executive Suite* (1954) was based on a slick bestseller about a big-business power struggle, with William Holden, Fredric March, Barbara Stanwyck, and Walter Pidgeon jockeying for position while June Allyson and Shelley Winters root them on.

*Helen of Troy* (1955), an elaborate Italian-French production, was devoid of interest, except for an early appearance by Brigitte Bardot, but *Tribute to a Bad Man* (1956) was a good, tough Western in which James Cagney is well cast as a hard-as-nails rancher.

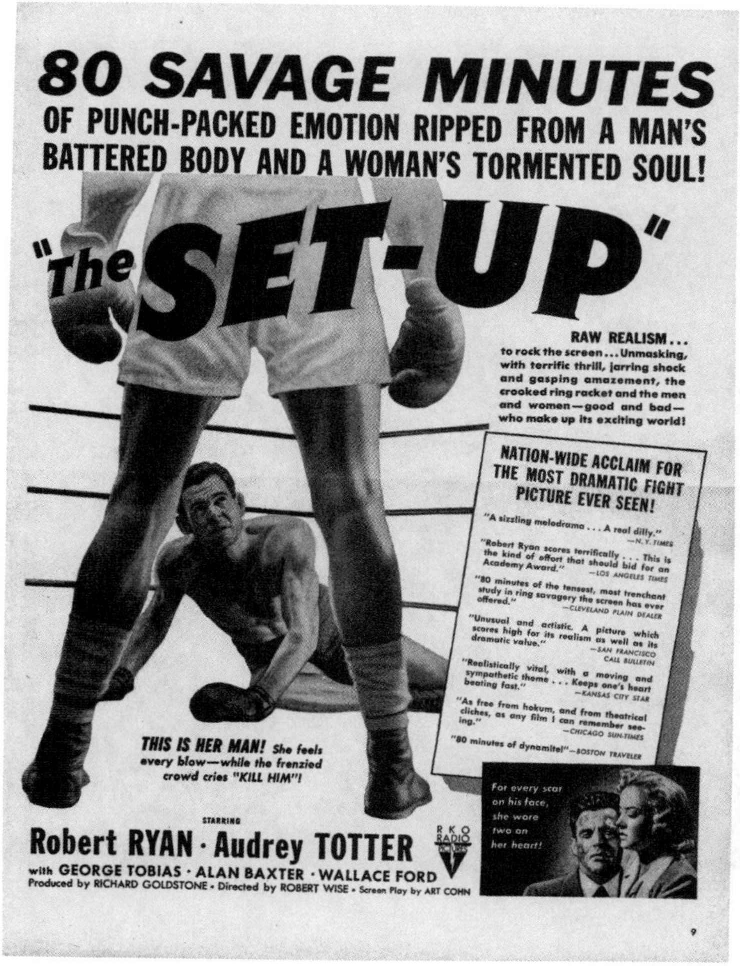

*Somebody Up There Likes Me* (1957) was a first-rate biopic about the life of boxer Rocky Graziano, with Paul Newman quite appealing as the eventual middleweight champ (a role originally targeted for James Dean). Jean Simmons starred in *This Could Be the Night* and *Until They Sail* (both 1957), the first a comedy about a strait-laced teacher working for gangster Paul Douglas, the second a courtroom drama set in New Zealand, with Paul Newman and Sandra Dee among her (oddly cast) compatriots.

Moving to UA in 1958, Wise made the suspenseful submarine-warfare drama *Run Silent, Run Deep* with Burt Lancaster and Clark Gable. But *I Want to Live!* (1958) attracted more attention. A sterling dramatization of the Barbara Graham murder case that made no bones about where the filmmakers' sympathy lay, it starred Susan Hayward, who earned her only Oscar for her portrayal of the haughty, hard-boiled hooker railroaded (the film maintains) into a death sentence; Wise received his first Academy Award nomination for best direction. *Odds Against Tomorrow* (1959) was a fine late noir, with Robert Ryan, Harry Belafonte, and Ed Begley most effective as bank robbers doomed because of Ryan's racism.

*West Side Story* (1961), which Wise co-directed with choreographer Jerome Robbins, marked his biggest hit to date. It was an enormously popular adaptation (filmed on West Sixty-fourth Street in New York) of the long-running Broadway show, itself a clever contemporization of *Romeo and Juliet*. Artistically there were some problems—Natalie Wood was no Chita Rivera, Richard Beymer made for a hopelessly bland Tony, and Leonard Bernstein's score had enough syrup for a truckload of pancakes. But the film won a whopping ten Oscars, including one for

▲ *Shooting* Two for the Seesaw *with Robert Mitchum and Shirley MacLaine*

best picture and another for Wise, and its $11 million take made it the year's biggest-grossing picture. *Two for the Seesaw* (1962), from William Gibson's romantic comedy, was considerably less successful, although the unlikely team of Robert Mitchum and Shirley MacLaine managed not to embarrass themselves. Wise went to England to make *The Haunting* (1963), a suggestive version of Shirley Jackson's tale of the supernatural, starring Julie Harris and Claire Bloom; it remains one of the best ghost stories captured on celluloid.

*The Sound of Music* (1965) may have won only half as many Academy Awards as *West Side Story*, but it's not likely anyone connected with the film was too disappointed. Based on the real-life story of the Von Trapp family, who escaped Nazi-held Austria in 1938, it starred Julie Andrews, who replaced the Rodgers and Hammerstein stage blockbuster's Mary Martin. Wise turned this swollen songfest into the top-grossing movie to that point in history (unseating *Gone with the Wind*) and, in the process, won his second Oscar for best direction; the film also won as best picture. *The Sand Pebbles* (1966) was even more ambitious: an epic, three-hour-long adventure, it stars Steve McQueen, who's at his very best as a sailor on an American gunboat in 1926 China. *Pebbles* sprawled too much for its own good; even so, it was an Oscar nominee for best picture, and McQueen was nominated as best actor. Wise then returned to the big-budget musical with *Star!* (1968), but three hours proved to be way too much (it usually is onscreen). Julie Andrews tries mightily but fails to capture the electricity of stage star Gertrude Lawrence.

*Star!* may not have *lost* quite as much money for Fox as *Sound made*, but it was the year's biggest flop, and Wise and the studio parted ways. He filmed a so-so version of Michael Crichton's bestselling thriller *The Andromeda Strain* in 1971, then directed the glossy weeper *Two People* (1973) with Peter Fonda and Lindsay Wagner. The disastrous disaster picture *The Hindenburg* (1975), starring George C. Scott, Anne Bancroft, and a pile of 1937 newsreel clips was another bomb. But *Audrey Rose* (1977), based on Frank DeFelitta's bestseller about a reincarnated girl, was a popular chiller; Anthony Hopkins plays a distraught dad and Marsha Mason and John Beck the girl's disbelieving parents.

There was nothing wrong with the cast of *Star Trek—The Motion Picture* (1979), but this $45 million extravaganza was hobbled with a script that was weaker than many of the TV series' weekly episodes (one of which provided its basis). Still, it grossed as much as *Rocky*, and demonstrated that there was an audience for Captain Kirk and Mr. Spock on the big screen. (Subsequent entries in the series were made for much less, and proved highly profitable.) Wise took a ten-year hiatus, then filmed *Rooftops* (1989), a gritty, nonmusical variation on *West Side Story* with a no-name cast, which failed to find an audience; it now appears that this will prove to be his last effort behind the camera.

## ● SAM WOOD (1883-1949)

Sam Wood is a classic example of the unobtrusive (some might add, uninspired) hand that can guide diverse productions to a high level of accomplishment without ever making them more than they might have been. To this extent he was an obvious beneficiary of the studio system. But over thirty years, Wood did manage to oversee a dozen or so near-classics among his forty-odd sound pictures—not a startling ratio, perhaps, but one which must be respected (even if Wood's noxious, ultraconservative politics need not).

Born in Philadelphia, Wood moved to Los Angeles at the age of twenty after failing to find gold in Nevada and soon was dealing in real estate. In 1908 he was invited to make his acting debut for the Famous Players Company, but he found himself uncomfortable in front of the camera and within a few years was assisting Cecil B. DeMille behind it. After a five-year stint as an apprentice and director of two-reelers, Wood was given his chance to handle features by Paramount in 1920, a year in which he directed seven films. One of the stars he worked with most frequently was Gloria Swanson—he directed her in several silent melodramas, including *Under the Lash*, *Beyond the Rocks*, *Her Gilded Cage*, and *Bluebeard's Eighth Wife*.

Moving to MGM in 1927, Wood was assigned to *The Latest from Paris* (1928) with Norma Shearer, *Telling the World* (1928) with William Haines, and *The Fair Co-ed* (1927) with Marion Davies, among other projects. *So This Is College* (1929) and *Sins of the Children* (1930), both with Robert Montgomery, were among his nearly forgotten early sound pictures; he also directed such similarly obscure fare in 1930 as *Within the Law*, *Way for a Sailor* (a John Gilbert flop), *They Learned about Women* (co-directed with Jack Conway), and *The Girl Said No*, with Haines and Marie Dressler. *Paid* (1930) was a popular Joan Crawford melodrama, and *A Tailor-Made Man* (1931) was another light comedy with William Haines. *The Man in Possession* (1931) starred Robert Montgomery again, a Wood favorite, while *The New Adventures of Get-Rich-Quick Wallingford* (1931) featured Haines with Broadway sensation Jimmy Durante.

*Huddle* (1932) was an inane football drama starring Ramon Novarro, but *Prosperity* (1932) was a funny teaming of popular screen duo Marie Dressler and Polly Moran (their last). *Hold Your Man* (1933) was a calculated showcase for the charismatic Clark Gable and Jean Harlow team, which audiences had embraced several months earlier in *Red Dust*; this one was almost as good as long as it stuck to bantering, but then it took a left turn and bogged down into a women's-prison melodrama. *The Barbarian* (1933) served up Myrna Loy and Ramon Novarro in a romantic bonbon written by Anita Loos, while *Christopher Bean* (1933), from a Sidney Howard play, proved to be Marie Dressler's last film before her death. Myrna Loy starred in *Stamboul Quest* (1934) as a German spy—not an antiheroic role by Hollywood standards of the day.

*Let 'em Have It* (1935) was a valentine to J. Edgar Hoover's G-men, with Richard Arlen on the trail of scar-faced Bruce Cabot, but it's that year's *A Night at the Opera* that today's audiences continue to enjoy. This was the Marx Brothers' sixth film, but their first for MGM; to many tastes, it remains their best. (At Irving Thalberg's suggestion, their material had been road-tested before filming, smoothing out the rough edges of anarchist humor that can be savored in Leo McCarey's *Duck Soup*.) *Whipsaw* (1935) was another now-forgotten Myrna Loy vehicle, this time offering her as a jewel thief who can't quite shake persistent detective Spencer Tracy, while *The Unguarded Hour* (1936) was a complicated but stagy mystery starring Franchot Tone and Loretta Young. *A Day at the Races* (1937) was more prime Marx

Brothers, only an iota under the heights of lunacy reached in *Opera*; its material was polished through 140 performances before live audiences prior to filming.

*Navy Blue and Gold* (1937), with thirtyish Robert Young and James Stewart gussied up as Annapolis cadets, was a mass of clichés, but *Madame X* (1937) was a fine remake of the 1929 Ruth Chatterton vehicle, with Gladys George now the mother who sacrifices her own welfare to ensure the success of son John Beal. *Lord Jeff* (1938), a showcase for MGM's two boy wonders, Mickey Rooney and Freddie Bartholomew, had little Peter Lawford helping Freddie get straight at a naval academy. The equally unnecessary *Stablemates* (1938) ended up as a protracted mugging contest between Mickey Rooney and Wallace Beery; its racetrack setting was left awash in tears.

To this point Wood had hardly distinguished himself as more than a competent director, and if his career had ended then, his name would warrant only a footnote in motion-picture history. But suddenly he entered a new phase, one which found him mysteriously possessed of a keener eye and a surer hand. The turning point was *Goodbye Mr. Chips* (1939), a faithful adaptation of James Hilton's sentimental novel about a selfless teacher and schoolmaster whose generations of students love him without reservation. Why MGM entrusted Wood with this prestigious bit of Anglophilia in the first place is a bit of a mystery, but the result was one of the year's Academy Award nominees for best picture, with Robert Donat's interpretation of Chips earning him the best actor Oscar in one of the toughest fields ever. Other nominations went to Greer Garson, the screenplay, and Wood.

*Chips* was Wood's last credited picture for MGM, but he spent considerable time co-directing *Gone with the Wind* in place of the ill Victor Fleming (although Fleming alone took home the Oscar that year). Whether it was that experience that decided Wood to leave MGM and go freelance is not clear, but his fortunes now continued to rise. *Raffles* (1940), starring David Niven, was a decent version of the oft-filmed adventures of a gentleman thief, although it didn't quite come up to the 1930 version with Ronald Colman. But *Our Town* was a great piece of Americana, a well-handled adaptation of the Thornton Wilder play that used half the Broadway cast, including Martha Scott, who was Oscar-nominated; the film became one of the year's ten best picture nominees. *Rangers of Fortune* was a minor Western with the unexciting cast of Fred MacMurray, Albert Dekker, and Gilbert Roland, but *Kitty Foyle* (also 1940) was a huge hit for RKO, a high-class soap opera about a noble working-class girl (Ginger Rogers) whose trials and tribulations would have tested Job. The ripe role made erstwhile glamour girl Rogers a surprise winner of the best actress Academy Award; the film, Wood, and Dalton Trumbo's screenplay were also nominated.

*The Devil and Miss Jones* (1941) was lighter fare, and all the better for it. Jean Arthur was at her zenith as a spirited department-store clerk who unwittingly teaches her millionaire boss (Charles Coburn at *his* zenith) some hilarious but sage lessons about how the "common people" live. *Kings Row* (1942), a sanitized adaptation of the sensational bestseller, is probably Wood's finest work, a sprawling canvas of a Midwestern town's hidden life in the early 1900s. Warner contractees Ann Sheridan, Ronald Reagan, and Claude Rains were joined by Charles Coburn and

▲ *American League Rookie-of-the-Year Gene Bearden takes direction from Wood on the set of* The Pride of the Yankees

Betty Field to good effect, although some of the book's more shocking aspects had to be toned down to meet Code standards. Nominated as best picture by the Academy, the film earned Wood his third best direction nomination in four years.

At the Academy Awards ceremony Wood's loyalties were divided, however, because his next film, *The Pride of the Yankees*, was also a best picture nominee. This biopic about Yankee great Lou Gehrig was perhaps too much of a good thing, with Gary Cooper aw-shucks-ing his way into sainthood with barely a change in expression and even fewer moments of baseball action—but that didn't stop him and co-star Teresa Wright from receiving Oscar nominations as well. *For Whom the Bell Tolls* (1943) became Wood's highest profile project when he replaced Cecil B. DeMille—his old mentor. But after nearly three hours of paralyzingly slow running time, it becomes clear that the film offers the epic scope of Hemingway's most popular novel without capturing its sensibility. Still, *Bell* was an enormous box-office success and was nominated for an Academy Award, as were stars Gary Cooper, Ingrid Bergman, Akim Tamiroff, and Katina Paxinou (who won).

Bergman and Cooper worked again with Wood on *Saratoga Trunk* (1945), but this adaptation of an Edna Ferber novel had its release delayed for nearly two years for reasons that become evident upon a viewing—not a moment of it is convincing, and it takes forever to go nowhere. *Casanova Brown* (1944), a more modest undertaking, was a recycling of an earlier "B" comedy about ex-mates whose baby becomes a point of contention (Gary Cooper and Teresa Wright are pleasantly reunited), while *Guest Wife* (1945) was a romantic comedy starring Claudette Colbert and Don Ameche, who didn't make a particularly compelling team. *Heartbeat* (1946) was an utter bomb, a lame remake of a French comedy about a pickpocket (Ginger Rogers) and a diplomat (Jean-Pierre Aumont) who somehow end up in a nuptial state. Quite a losing streak, but Wood fared better with *Ivy* (1947), a decent suspenser in which Joan Fontaine is cast against type as a murderess.

A rabid anti-Communist who had helped found, and became president of, the watchdog Motion Picture Alliance for the Preservation of American Ideals, Wood took time out in 1947 to testify against half of Hollywood before the House Un-American Activities Committee (as did pal Gary Cooper) before returning to MGM to make his last three pictures. *Command Decision* (1948) was a solid version of a William Wister Haines play; Clark Gable is quite good as a conscience-racked flight commander, and Walter Pidgeon, John Hodiak, and Van Johnson are among the fliers he deals with. *The Stratton Story* (1949) was a fine biopic about the baseball player who overcame the loss of one leg, with James Stewart and, as Stratton's wife, June Allyson. Finally, there was *Ambush* (1949), an adequate cavalry-vs.-the-Indians exercise with Robert Taylor and Chief Thundercloud. But before the film was released, Wood suffered a fatal heart attack. Alarmingly, his will specified that his heirs had to sign a loyalty oath before receiving their inheritance.

## ● WILLIAM WYLER (1902–1981)

One of the most honored of Hollywood directors, William (né Willy) Wyler was sometimes excoriated by exhausted actors (and budget-conscious studio executives) for his painstaking methods on the set, which earned him the nickname "Ninety-take Wyler." Those same actors won a plethora of Oscars for their work with Wyler (himself the recipient of three Academy Awards, with eight additional nominations for best direction) and he helped those penurious studio heads carry home a few best picture Oscars for their mantels as well. But Wyler's meticulousness and imperious manner seem less significant than the question of whether his perfectionism drained the juice out of these paradigms of good taste, even while imbuing them with a patina of class and literacy. Was he, after all, merely (as David Thomson, among others, charges) a passionless technician who early on became "lost to respectability"?

Born in Mulhausen in Alsace-Lorraine, then part of Germany, Wyler was educated in Switzerland before moving to Paris at the age of twenty to study the violin. While there, he received a visit from distant cousin Carl Laemmle, the head of Universal, who invited him to America to work for the studio. Wyler began in Universal's New York–based publicity department in 1922, but was transferred to the Universal City lot a few months later, and by 1924 was working as an assistant director on two-reel Westerns and, more significantly, Fred Niblo's *Ben-Hur*. Between 1925 and 1928 Wyler directed a couple of dozen silent Westerns with titles like *Ridin' for Love, Lazy Lightning*, and *The Border Cavalier* before graduating finally to the (slightly) more prestigious genre of romantic comedy with *Anybody Here Seen Kelly?* (1928) starring Bessie Love.

*The Love Trap* and *The Shakedown* (both 1929) were Wyler's first partial talkies, the former with Laura La Plante as a chorus girl married to taxi driver Neil Hamilton, the latter with James Murray as a crooked boxer reformed by a young orphan. The all-talking *Hell's Heroes* (1930), shot on location near Death Valley, was another in a long line of screen versions of Peter Bernard Kyne's story "The Three Godfathers" and one of the most popular. *The Storm* (1930) was built around the competition between pals William Boyd and Paul Cavanagh for the affections of wildcat Lupe Velez while the three are stranded in a log cabin in the Canadian wilderness. The tastefully melodramatic *A House Divided* (1932) offered Walter Huston as a widowed fisherman who orders Helen Chandler from a matrimonial agency, only to lose her affections to his son (Kent Douglass).

*Tom Brown of Culver* (1932) starred, appropriately enough, Tom Brown as the chipper military understudy who has to come to terms with the fact that his father was a deserter in World War I. *Her First Mate* (1933) was a minor comedy with ZaSu Pitts and Slim Summerville, but *Counsellor-at-Law* (1933), from a play by Elmer Rice, was cut out of more distinguished cloth; John Barrymore plays a Jewish lawyer facing disbarment (a role made famous by Paul Muni on Broadway in the 1931 production), and Rice adapted the play for the screen with its then-bold examination of anti-Semitism virtually intact. But *Glamour* (1934) was tedious junk, with Constance Cummings as an erstwhile chorus girl who dumps husband Paul Lukas for young dance partner Philip Reed, who cuts her loose in turn.

A clever adaptation of a Ferenc Molnár play by Preston Sturges, *The Good Fairy* (1935) was a delightful comedy starring Margaret Sullavan—newly wed to Wyler—as the winsome Luisa Gingelbusher (a role performed on Broadway in 1931 by Helen Hayes) and Frank Morgan as the would-be sugar daddy who offers to make her rich. Successful though it was, *Fairy* would prove to be Wyler's last picture at Universal after eleven years there. He made *The Gay*

*Deception* (1935) at Fox, a forgettable romantic comedy with the underwhelming cast of Francis Lederer and Frances Dee, before signing with Samuel Goldwyn in 1936. It was a career move that would make his fame.

Wyler's first picture under his new arrangement was *These Three* (1936), Lillian Hellman's faithful translation of her controversial play *The Children's Hour*, with the lesbian theme supplanted by Code-sanctioned charges of heterosexual hanky panky among Joel McCrea and teachers Merle Oberon and Miriam Hopkins; Bonita Granville was Oscar-nominated for her performance as the student whose malicious charges ruin everyone's lives. This was Wyler's first collaboration with cinematographer Gregg Toland, a specialist in deep-focus composition, and the picture has a look superior to that of his previous work. (Wyler would be given the opportunity to film Hellman's original scenario some twenty-five years later under less stringent Code restrictions.)

*Dodsworth* (1936) was another classy transposition of a Broadway hit, with Sidney Howard adapting his play (itself based on the Sinclair Lewis novel). Walter Huston re-creates his acclaimed stage performance as a retired auto magnate whose sojourn to Europe opens his eyes to wife Ruth Chatterton's transparent status seeking while opening his heart to the attentions of sympathetic widow Mary Astor. Huston was nominated for an Academy Award as best actor (and did win the New York Film Critics Circle Award) while Wyler, Howard, Maria Ouspenskaya (as the Baroness), and the picture were also nominated. In the space of a year, Wyler had now established himself as one of the industry's premier talents.

He wrapped the last scenes of *Come and Get It* (1936) after Howard Hawks and Sam Goldwyn butted heads once too often (which explains why the final encounter between Joel McCrea and Frances Farmer resembles a moment from *These Three*), then took on Sidney Kingsley's socially conscious Broadway drama *Dead End* (1937). Adapted (and toned down) by Lillian Hellman, it was staged with Richard Day's highly stylized sets in place of the New York City locations Wyler wanted (and needed); the unfortunate effect was having Hell's Kitchen located two doors down from Sutton Place on the East Side. The dramaturgy was more than a little heavy-handed as well, with Humphrey Bogart's cad of a gangster, Baby Face Martin, and Joel McCrea's insufferably noble hero among the worst offenders. But Claire Trevor was memorable as Bogart's syphilitic ex-moll, as was Marjorie Main as his decrepit mother, and the Dead End Kids provided some raucous moments. The film, cinematographer Gregg Toland, Trevor, and art director Richard Day (who had won the year before for *Dodsworth*) were all nominated for Academy Awards.

*Jezebel* (1938) was a canny attempt by Warner Bros. to exploit the national publicity David O. Selznick had been fostering in anticipation of *Gone with the Wind*, and while this tale of the antebellum South was not mounted with the grandeur (or the Technicolor) of *GWTW*, it did have one asset: the great Bette Davis as a New Orleans belle who shatters the city's social conventions, losing the affections of stolid Henry Fonda in the process. The film was one of ten nominated that year for Academy Awards, and both Davis (who was having a brief but intense affair with the now-divorced Wyler) and Fay Bainter won acting Oscars.

*Wuthering Heights* (1939) is one of the enduring

screen romances of the day, and Laurence Olivier certainly makes a mesmerizing Heathcliff. Merle Oberon, on the other hand, is comparatively pallid as Cathy; Olivier had asked that Vivien Leigh be cast, but, alas, Goldwyn refused to change his mind about Oberon. Ben Hecht and Charles MacArthur were nominated for an Academy Award for their screenplay, and Wyler, the picture, Olivier, Geraldine Fitzgerald, and Alfred Newman's score also were nominated—but only Gregg Toland took home an Oscar, for his cinematography. (California's Conejo Hills, located about forty miles north of Los Angeles, should have been nominated as well for their impersonation of England's moors.)

From Broadway and the classics, Wyler now returned to the American West, but *The Westerner* (1940) bore little resemblance to the silent, low-budget oaters he had fashioned during his early days in Hollywood. Although it is not an epic in the usual sense, the film's brooding use of the landscape (brilliantly photographed by Gregg Toland) and Gary Cooper's iconic presence as laconic drifter Cole Hardin make it one of the handsomest Westerns ever filmed. Still, what really set it apart was Walter Brennan's caustic performance as Judge Roy Bean, a ripely evil turn that earned him his third Academy Award as best supporting actor in the span of five years. (Stuart Lake's original story was also nominated for an Oscar.)

*The Letter*, which had already been through several incarnations—a story by Somerset Maugham, a play starring Katharine Cornell, a 1929 film with Jeanne Eagels—became one of 1940's biggest hits. Bette Davis submitted one of her most formidable performances as the straying wife of rubber plantation owner Herbert Marshall, who goes broke (in more ways than one) trying to keep her out of prison for killing his longtime friend in what she claims was self-defense. (In actuality, the fellow was her lover and was shot in cold blood for wanting to end the affair.) Davis was nominated for an Oscar but somehow lost to Ginger Rogers; Wyler, the film, James Stephenson (who played her lawyer), and cinematographer Gaetano Gaudio were also nominated.

Wyler and Davis (whose affair had long since run its course, with Wyler remarrying) next collaborated on Lillian Hellman's Southern gothic *The Little Foxes* in 1941. But Davis failed to light a fire with her strident interpretation of the loathsome Regina Giddens (as Tallulah Bankhead had done more successfully on Broadway), a lack that kept the heavy melodrama (scripted by Hellman with Dorothy Parker and Alan Campbell) from igniting. And yet the film was a critical favorite and was nominated for an Academy

▲ *Wyler cavorts during a break in the filming of* The Best Years of Our Lives

Award (along with Davis, Wyler, supporting actresses Teresa Wright and Patricia Collinge, and the screenplay).

*Mrs. Miniver* (1942) is very much an artifact of its time, but Wyler should be (and was) given credit for transforming the rather maudlin, stiff-upper-lip heroics into something affecting—manipulative, to be sure, but affecting. Greer Garson, whose work has aged less well than almost any other major star's of her day, is almost unbearably courageous as the eponymous heroine, but Walter Pidgeon, Teresa Wright, Dame May Whitty, and Reginald Owen manage to advance the cause of Anglophilia. The picture was a smash for MGM, and Wyler won his first Oscar (as well as the New York Film Critics Circle Award) for best direction; Academy Awards were also disbursed to Garson, Wright, the screenplay, and Joseph Ruttenberg's cinematography.

Ironically, Wyler wasn't on hand to pick up his statuette, leaving that task to his wife, since he was beginning his term of service as a major in the U.S. Army Air Corps and was now stationed in England. He made three documentaries about the bomber groups to which he was attached: *The Memphis Belle* (1944), *The Fighting Lady* (1944), and *Thunderbolt* (1945; co-directed with John Sturges). Wyler lost the hearing in one ear as the result of a bombing run over Italy, won a medal for valor, and was discharged when the war ended with the rank of lieutenant colonel.

Unlike such returning compatriots as Frank Capra and George Stevens, Wyler selected a subject directly related to his recent experiences for his first postwar film. *The Best Years of Our Lives* (1946) was suggested by a 1944 *Life* magazine article about the difficulties in adjusting to civilian life faced by returning Marines. When the project was announced by producer Sam Goldwyn, many in the Hollywood community thought he must have been financing the picture as a *pro bono* work of patriotism. But under Wyler's acute eye it became something quite special, a dignified box-office smash that made more money than any other movie to that point in history save *GWTW*; ultimately it would rank as the eighth-biggest-grossing picture of the decade, despite a groundbreaking length (172 minutes) that limited its play dates.

Developed from MacKinlay Kantor's blank verse novelette "Glory for Me" (commissioned by Goldwyn) by screenwriter Robert E. Sherwood, *Best Years'* multiple story lines featured Fredric March and Myrna Loy as an upscale couple trying to get used to the idea of living together again; Dana Andrews and Virginia Mayo as a blue-collar couple whose relationship the war has permanently sundered; and real-life amputee Harold Russell as a gob whose loss of hands inhibits his relationship with fiancée Cathy O'Donnell. Russell, a nonprofessional, was awarded both the Academy Award as best supporting actor and a special Oscar, and *Best Years* also won for best picture, direction, actor (March), screenplay, and score. (Surprisingly, Gregg Toland's pristine cinematography was not cited.)

Wyler had been Oscar-nominated for each of his last four commercial releases, winning for the last two, which probably made him the industry's most bankable director. But after participating in the founding of the independent Liberty Films with Frank Capra and George Stevens, Wyler turned his attention to helping John Huston found the left-wing Committee for the First Amendment in 1947. When it became clear that Liberty was not going to succeed, the partners sold its assets to Paramount in 1948 in exchange for stock in the studio. One of those assets was Wyler, who was committed to produce and direct five pictures for the studio for a salary of up to $156,000 per picture, which over the next seven years he fulfilled.

His first Paramount release was *The Heiress* (1949), a literate adaptation of Henry James's novel *Washington Square* (and the more recent Broadway play based on it by Ruth and Augustus Goetz). Olivia de Havilland plays the repressed, mousy daughter of wealthy, coldhearted doctor Ralph Richardson, and Montgomery Clift is the handsome fortune-hunting suitor whose attentions are rejected, despite the happiness he might have brought. De Havilland won the best actress Academy Award for her wonderful performance, and Richardson, Wyler, and the film were all nominated. Wyler looked to Broadway and *Dead End* playwright Sidney Kingsley for *Detective Story* (1951), a busy, loud, stagy, but generally engaging pioneer entry in the now-clichéd genre of the police-precinct drama. Kirk Douglas starred as an overly violent cop with a secret or two spurring him on,

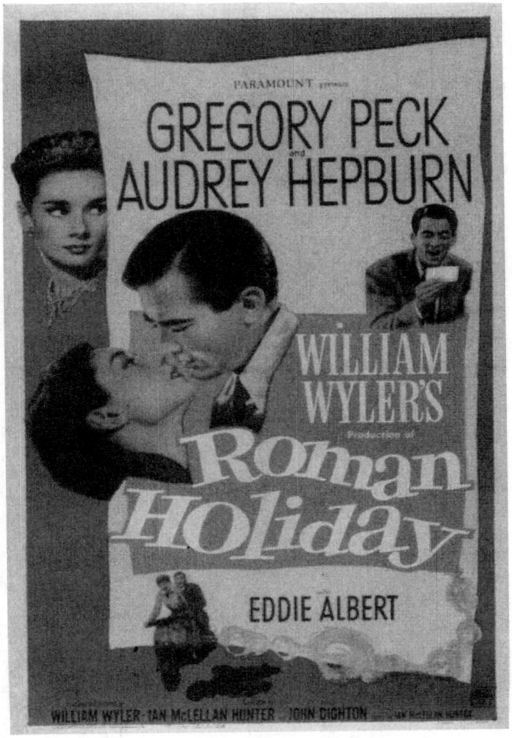


Eleanor Parker (in an Oscar-nominated turn) was his wife, and Joseph Wiseman and Lee Grant were among the colorful characters booked during the course of the action. Wyler was again nominated for an Academy Award for his direction (although this year he was not really a serious candidate).

*Carrie* (1952) was a well-intentioned (and well-adapted, by the Goetzes) version of Theodore Dreiser's great novel *Sister Carrie*. But even with Laurence Olivier at his most brilliant as the pathetic George Hurstwood, the downbeat story doesn't quite coalesce; perhaps Jennifer Jones's deficiencies as the title character are to blame. The charming *Roman Holiday* (1953) was more to the liking of ticket buyers, who flocked to see Audrey Hepburn in her star-making role as a European princess who goes AWOL in Rome and finds herself wooed (and won) by American reporter Gregory Peck. Wyler hadn't attempted a romantic comedy since 1935, but he looked like the second coming of George Cukor with this confection; it was nominated for ten Academy Awards, including best picture, best direction, and best actress—garnering Audrey Hepburn the only Oscar of her career.

*The Desperate Hours* (1955), Wyler's last picture under his agreement with Paramount, had been a

▲ *On location in Italy with Charlton Heston for* Ben-Hur

success as a novel and as a play (which had starred Paul Newman); now creator Joseph Hayes adapted it for Wyler. Humphrey Bogart stars as the leader of three escaped convicts who invade the home of Fredric March and Martha Scott, terrorizing them and their children while they wait for the delivery of money they had cached before going into prison. Although the schematic plot betrays its Broadway origins much as *Detective Story* and *Dead End* did, the film generates plenty of suspense, and the byplay between old pros Bogart and March is a delight.

*Friendly Persuasion* (1956), from stories by Jessamyn West, had been one of Capra's properties at Liberty Pictures, but ten years later it was Wyler who finally brought it to the screen. The tale of an Indiana Quaker family that faces dissension when the Civil War threatens, the film starred Gary Cooper and Dorothy McGuire as the peace-loving parents of young firebrand Anthony Perkins, whose insistence on joining his local militia to ward off a band of Confederate raiders forces Coop to lug his hunting rifle into the conflict. There was something of Coop's *Sergeant York* (1941) in the theme, which might account for its Academy Award nomination for best picture; Wyler, Perkins, and Michael Wilson's screenplay were also nominated. *The Big Country* (1958) was mighty big and mighty long—too close to three hours for comfort, and without the profound themes of *Best Years* to propel it. But the spectacle of Gregory Peck and Charlton Heston squaring off against each other like two petrified redwoods was perversely fascinating, and Burl Ives submitted a showy (and Oscar-winning) performance as a kind of Old West Big Daddy.

The deficiencies of *Country* were soon forgotten when Wyler's remake of *Ben-Hur* exploded onto screens in 1959. Where in the 1926 version Ramon Novarro and Francis X. Bushman had gamboled, Wyler had Charlton Heston as the Jewish prince and Stephen Boyd as his Roman friend Messala via novelist Lew Wallace's faux-biblical drama. *Ben-Hur* became a three and a half–hour spectacle on a scale never before attempted for the screen—it was even shot with experimental 65mm cameras. And yet the film seems more satisfying to ponder as an epic labor of moviemaking than to actually sit through.

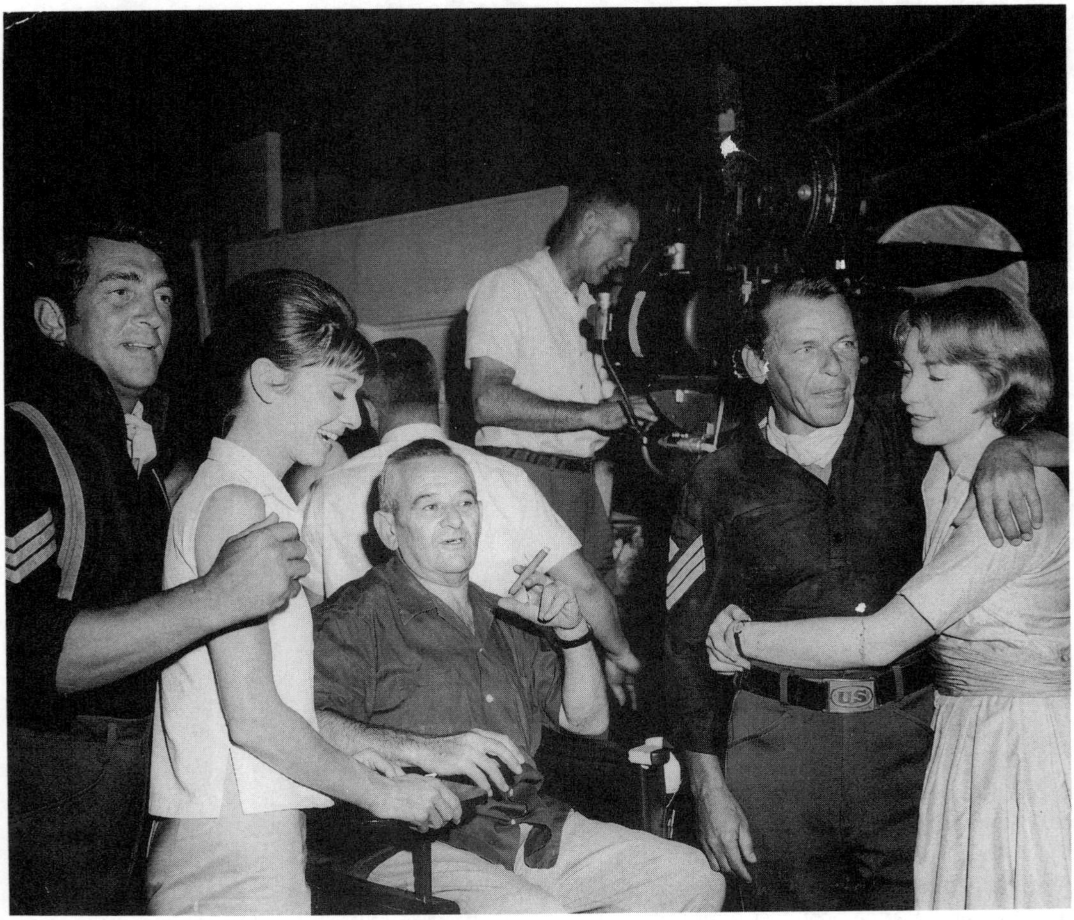

▲ *The Rat Pack invades the set of* The Children's Hour

The eye-popping statistics for its making include: 300 sets constructed; 200 statues sculpted; 8,000 extras employed; 40,000 tons of sand imported for the track in the famous chariot race, the arena which took 1,000 workers a year to erect; and a budget of more than $12 million (making it the most expensive production of all time—until *Cleopatra* erased the record a few years later). What this added up to was an enormous box-office gross of $37 million (still shy of what Cecil B. DeMille's *The Ten Commandments* had taken in in 1956) and twelve Academy Award nominations; it won eleven, including best picture, actor (Heston), supporting actor (Hugh Griffith), and direction—Wyler's third Oscar.

Wyler was now in a position to make any film he wanted, and what he wanted was another shot at Lillian Hellman's *The Children's Hour*. His 1962 remake, which restored the plot the Breen office had forced him to alter, starred Shirley MacLaine and Audrey Hepburn as the teachers accused by a student of having a lesbian affair, James Garner as the outraged fiancé, and Fay Bainter (whom Wyler had directed to an Oscar in *Jezebel*) as the ludicrously evil grandma. So the story, scripted again by Hellman, was intact—but it now lay on the screen inert. *The Collector* (1965) was more compelling; Terence Stamp plays a mild-mannered bank clerk whose collection of butterflies is expanded one day to include Samantha Eggar, whom he kidnaps and imprisons in his basement. Although not as chilling as John Fowles's source novel, the film is as perverse as the times would permit, and earned both Eggar and Wyler Oscar nominations (his eleventh and last).

*How to Steal a Million* (1966), with Audrey Hepburn and Peter O'Toole as amateur art thieves, gave Wyler the opportunity to make a romantic caper picture, a then-popular genre on the verge of flagging. The premise is clever enough, but *Million* never realizes the levels of charm and suspense of, say, Stanley Donen's *Charade* (but then, Wyler didn't have Cary Grant to draw on). He may just have been along for the ride for the big-budget adaptation of *Funny Girl* (1968), his first (and only) musical—the musical sequences were actually directed by Herbert Ross—but it was a smash nonetheless. Barbra Streisand, who had starred in the 1964 Broadway hit as vaudeville star Fanny Brice, here makes her film debut, and she carries this three-ring circus to the finish line. Streisand's a whirlwind, belting out the Bob Merrill–Jule Styne score (and original Brice hits like "My Man") and emoting all over the place with puppy-eyed Omar Sharif, who plays gambler Nicky Arnstein. It was enough for an Oscar, which she shared that year with Katharine Hepburn, while the film (a best picture nominee) went on to become the tenth-biggest moneymaker of the Sixties.

Wyler entered his sixth decade of filmmaking by making *The Liberation of L. B. Jones* (1970), a rather strident study of racism in the South that starred Lee J. Cobb, Anthony Zerbe, Roscoe Lee Browne, and Lola Falana. But the film failed to find an audience, convincing Wyler that perhaps he had, after all, stayed a bit too long at the fair. He could point to a career equaled by few of his peers—a body of work that, if it sometimes erred on the side of caution, nonetheless left a rich and enduring legacy.

## ● FRED ZINNEMANN (1907- )

With seven Academy Award nominations for best direction among just twenty-one feature film releases, two of them leading to best picture Oscars, Vienna-born Fred Zinnemann is one of the most honored of directors. Yet it took him over a dozen years after his 1929 arrival in Hollywood to be given the chance just to direct a "B" picture, and another six years after that before he made a film that was noticed. His movies are famed for their serious tastefulness and meticulous attention to detail—but those very qualities have often proven to be the bane of passion in his mature work, rendering it somewhat antiseptic and, at times, perilously close to being dull.

Trained as both a violinist and a lawyer, Zinnemann turned his back on both careers for the world of film. He worked with Robert Siodmak on the 1929 documentary *Menschen am Sonntag* (*People on Sunday*), then traveled to Hollywood, where he was put to work not behind the camera but before it, as an extra in Lewis Milestone's *All Quiet on the Western Front*. He assisted the likes of Robert Flaherty and Busby Berkeley in the early Thirties, then went to Mexico in 1934 to co-direct Paul Strand's documentary *Los Redes (The Wave)*. MGM signed him in 1937, but his initial assignments were the "Crime Does Not Pay" series and short subjects like *Weather Wizards*; one short, *That Mothers Might Live*, won an Oscar in 1938. MGM finally permitted him to direct a "B" in 1942 with *Kid Glove Killer*, an exciting mystery starring Van Heflin as a police chemist who solves a murder. The 1942 *Eyes in the Night* had Edward Arnold as Bayard Kendrick's blind detective Duncan McClain, while *The Seventh Cross* (1944) was a taut thriller, with Spencer Tracy as one of seven escapees from a concentration camp trying to outwit George Zucco and his Gestapo agents.

It was almost an insult—no, strike the "almost" —for MGM to next assign Zinnemann to *Little Mr. Jim* and *My Brother Talks to Horses* (both 1946), two inane vehicles for child star Butch Jenkins. But prestige was not lacking with *The Search* (1948), the first film shot in Germany after the war. It was a moving story about a GI (Montgomery Clift, in his second film) stationed in Berlin who tries to adopt a nine-year-old concentration-camp survivor and apparent orphan (Ivan Jandl), whose mother is even then scouring the war-torn city hoping to find him. Jandl—who never made another movie—was given a special Oscar, and Zinnemann and Clift also received nominations. *Act of Violence* (1949) was much darker, with crippled vet Robert Ryan seeking to avenge himself on former officer and POW Van Heflin, who betrayed his platoon while a prisoner.

*The Men* (1950) also dealt with crippled war veterans, but this time the emphasis was not on vengeance but rather on the long, laborious process of healing. Marlon Brando, in his film debut, gave a powerhouse performance as a paraplegic vet whose bitterness over his injury threatens to poison the entire ward and drive away his loyal fiancée (Teresa Wright). Written by Carl Foreman and produced by Stanley Kramer, *The Men* successfully trod the thin line between pathos and bathos. *Teresa* (1951) was the story of an Italian war bride who returns to the States with her GI husband to encounter prejudice in his hometown. It didn't add up to much, but the film is notable for introducing screen newcomers Pier Angeli (in the title role), Rod Steiger (as a psychiatrist), and Ralph Meeker.

Of far more import was *High Noon* (1952), another Stanley Kramer production. Aging Western icon Gary Cooper has one of his best roles as a marshal whose retirement and wedding day are interrupted by waiting for the imminent return of a gunman seeking revenge because the marshal sent him to prison. The eighty-five minutes the solitary Coop sweats out (literally—he had a bleeding ulcer

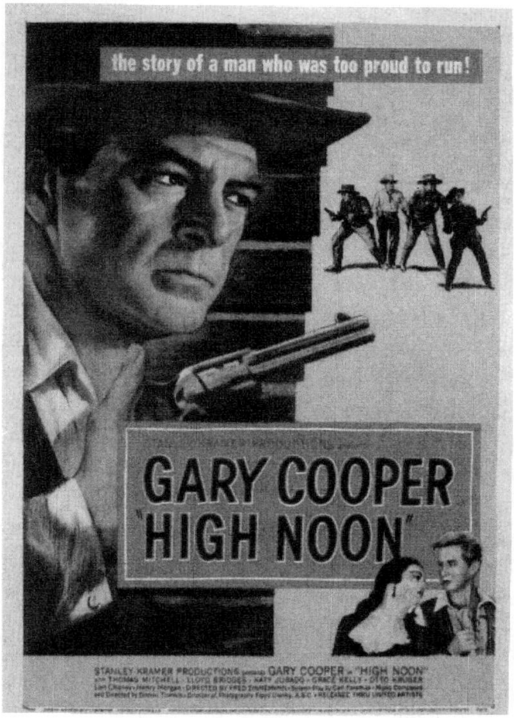


during filming and was in excruciating pain) correspond to the picture's running time, a device that Zinnemann (and Kramer, in postproduction) milk for every cent it was worth. Ultimately its worth proved to be Oscars for Cooper and Dimitri Tiomkin's theme song and score, and nominations for Zinnemann (who won the New York Film Critics Circle Award), the film, and Carl Foreman's screenplay. Zinnemann followed this triumph with *The Member of the Wedding* (1952), an adaptation of a lauded Broadway production (by way of Carson McCullers's coming-of-age novel) that used five members of the original cast, including twenty-five-year-old Julie Harris as the story's twelve-year-old protagonist, Ethel Waters, and Brandon de Wilde.

Then a real plum came Zinnemann's way. The screen version of James Jones's enormous and enormously successful bestseller, *From Here to Eternity* was easily the most anticipated movie of 1953. Zinnemann was handed a cast with plenty of star power, notably Montgomery Clift as rebel-with-a-cause Prewitt, Burt Lancaster as sympathetic Sergeant Warden, Deborah Kerr as Lancaster's surf-drenched mistress and wife of *his* CO, Donna Reed as Pru's "hostess" lover Alma, Frank Sinatra as the charming but luckless wise-guy Maggio, and Ernest Borgnine as the loathsome "Fatso." The film was a huge hit and won eight Academy Awards, including best picture, best direction, supporting actor (Sinatra), supporting actress (Reed), screenplay, and cinematography. (Clift, Lancaster, and Kerr were also nominated.) Like so many other multi-Oscar winners, its flaws have become more bothersome with time, particularly the softening of Reed's role (she was a very busy prostitute in the book) and the flavor of life in the barracks—but Zinnemann got as much of Jones's novel onto the screen as was thought possible in 1953, and then some. For his efforts he was also cited as best director by the New York Film Critics Circle.

*Oklahoma!* (1955) didn't present the censorship difficulties of *Eternity*, but adapting Rodgers and Hammerstein's Broadway smash to the screen carried its own set of problems, one of which was Zinnemann's decision to shoot on location in Arizona, an ordeal that took nearly eight months. The final, overlong film is more than adequate, but still less than the show, with Gordon MacRae and Shirley Jones complemented by Gloria Grahame as a surprisingly fine Ado Annie and Rod Steiger a predictably bombastic heavy. *A Hatful of Rain* (1957), from Michael Gazzo's play, was quite a change of pace, a low-budget, high-intensity drama starring Don Murray as a heroin addict whose pain is shared—willingly or not—by Eva Marie Saint, Tony Franciosa, and others in his life. Zinnemann then began what seemed a perfect project for a director of his sensibility—adapting Ernest Hemingway's *The Old Man and the Sea*. But in the midst of filming he withdrew, leaving the picture to be finished by John Sturges, who received the directing credit but failed to make it work.

*The Nun's Story* (1959) was a religious epic on an entirely different order from its contemporary *Ben-Hur*, which was as loud and splashy as this probing film (adaptated from Kathryn C. Hulme's autobiographical novel) is earnest and thoughtful. Audrey Hepburn gave an Oscar-nominated performance as the nun who braves the rigors of the Belgian Congo, the terrors of a mental hospital in Belgium, and the brutality of the Nazis before finally leaving her order to join the Resistance, while Peter Finch as a surgeon and Edith Evans as the Mother Superior also were memorable. Zinnemann and the film were both Oscar-nominated, and Zinnemann again won the

New York Film Critics Circle Award for best direction. *The Sundowners* (1960) was set in 1920s Australia and shot on location, with Deborah Kerr and Robert Mitchum as a husband and wife who set off with their teenage son and hiree Peter Ustinov to drive a thousand sheep a thousand miles; Kerr is eternally wishful that they might give up their migrant existence to farm, but Mitchum always presses on. It was a story like no other (from a novel by Jon Cleary), and Zinnemann captured its quiet heroism splendidly. Mitchum was compelling in an atypical role, and Kerr was deservedly Oscar-nominated, as were the film, the screenplay, supporting actress Glynis Johns, and Zinnemann.

*Behold a Pale Horse* (1964) was less successful on every level; Gregory Peck was hopelessly miscast as a Loyalist and Spanish Civil War hero twenty years on who is still waging his ideological battle with militia captain Anthony Quinn; preachy and dull, the film played to all of Zinnemann's worst tendencies. *A Man for All Seasons* (1966), from Robert Bolt's acclaimed play about the trials of Sir Thomas More, presented perils of its own, but Zinnemann navigated them masterfully. Adapted by Bolt himself, *Man* starred Paul Scofield (repeating his stage role) as the intractable More and Robert Shaw as the headstrong but charismatic King Henry VIII; Orson Welles and Wendy Hiller were also in the outstanding cast. The film was a runaway success at that year's Academy Awards, winning six Oscars, including ones for best picture, best actor, best screenplay; Zinnemann again won for best direction.

For some reason it took Zinnemann seven years to make his next film, the suspenseful but chilly political thriller *The Day of the Jackal* (1973), from Frederick Forsyth's bestseller about a plot to assassinate de Gaulle. The international cast and locations made for verisimilitude, but only Edward Fox as the brilliantly prepared assassin makes a lasting impression. *Julia* (1977) was easier to warm up to; Jane Fonda and Vanessa Redgrave provide genuine star power as, respectively, Lillian Hellman (admittedly, a stretch for Fonda) and her noble activist friend Julia (almost typecasting for Redgrave—but why not?), who enlists Hellman to aid in her efforts against the Nazis. Jason Robards makes an appealing Dashiell Hammett, and Meryl Streep has a small part in her film debut—but in the end, it's hard to comprehend how this exercise in perfectly tasteful, nigh-antispetic filmmaking warranted nine Academy Award nominations. (Robards and Redgrave won, as did Alvin Sargent's screenplay.)

Zinnemann took another five years to mount his final production, the regrettable *Five Days One Summer* (1982), with Sean Connery interminably climbing the Swiss Alps circa 1933 with a young woman who may or may not be his wife. It was lovely to look at but deficient in the storytelling department; still, if Zinnemann wanted to sign off with a mystical valentine, he had earned that right many times over.

► *Rehearsing* High Noon *with Grace Kelly and Katy Jurado*

# SHORT SUBJECTS:
# MORE PROFILES IN BRIEF

## LEWIS ALLEN (1905–1986)

Born in Shropshire, England, Lewis Allen acted and directed on stage in England before coming to the United States to work as an assistant director at Paramount. He made his first film in 1944 and never really topped it; in fact, *The Uninvited* may be the best ghost story to come out of Hollywood in the Forties, a marvelously atmospheric tale (from Dorothy Macardle's novel) enhanced by Gail Russell's naïve performance as the haunted girl and an evocative score that yielded the standard "Stella by Starlight." Russell was joined by Diana Lynn and Dorothy Gish in *Our Hearts Were Young and Gay* (1944), a dramatization of Cornelia Otis Skinner's memoir about her travels to Paris in the Twenties (oddly, Skinner herself had appeared in *The Uninvited*). Allen ventured again into the spectral world with *The Unseen* (1945), but its story about a governess (Russell again) whose predecessor was murdered petered out before the payoff.

*Those Endearing Young Charms* (1945) had Laraine Day trying to choose between evil suitor Robert Young and sincere Bill Williams during World War II, while *The Perfect Marriage* (1946) was a subpar marital comedy (via Broadway) in need of marital aids, with spoiled David Niven and spoiled Loretta Young feuding and making up. *The Imperfect Lady* (1947) was a dullish period drama with Parliament lord Ray Milland falling for music-hall dancer Teresa Wright in 1890s London, but *Desert Fury* (1947) was a fine crime yarn set out West; cop Burt Lancaster wrests rich Lizabeth Scott away from boyfriend (and compulsive gambler) John Hodiak at the behest of Scott's mom, gambling-hall owner Mary Astor. The suspenseful *So Evil My Love* (1948) sent Milland back to Victorian England once more, this time to seduce and betray Ann Todd and Geraldine Fitzgerald, until a well-placed dagger gives him his due.

Milland was in another kind of pickle in *Sealed Verdict* (1948), a courtroom melodrama in which he romances a Nazi's former mistress while preparing to prosecute her. *Chicago Deadline* (1949) featured Alan Ladd as an investigative reporter delving into the life and death of hooker Donna Reed, while *Appointment with Danger* (1951) was even more original: Ladd plays a two-fisted, airborne postal inspector who calls on nun Phyllis Calvert to help him infiltrate a mob of airmail crooks. (Now, *there's* a premise that hasn't been overused.)

Allen now left Paramount to freelance. His first stop was Columbia, where he made the dreadful *Valentino* (1951), one of the worst biopics of the era, and *At Sword's Point* (1952), a decent swashbuckler with Cornel Wilde and Maureen O'Hara. But *Suddenly* (1954) was a revelation, a gripping tale about a plot to kill the President in a backwater town, spearheaded by professional assassin Frank Sinatra —one of the best performances of his career.

*A Bullet for Joey* (1955) was a Cold War yarn that had old-timers George Raft and Edward G. Robinson struggling over the fate of an atomic scientist in Canada. *Illegal* (1955) used Robinson again, now as a criminal lawyer defending Nina Foch against a murder rap, while *Another Time, Another Place* (1958) had Lana Turner cracking up when lover Sean Connery is killed during World War II. Allen's last picture was *Whirlpool* (1959), a low-budget British production.

## JOHN G. AVILDSEN (1936– )

He parlayed one best direction Oscar and three or four hit movies into what is today considered a successful career, but John G. Avildsen's filmography on the whole is underwhelming. Born in Oak Park, Illinois, he began working in the Sixties as an assistant director on various films while holding a day job as a director of television commercials for an advertising agency.

Avildsen's first directing credits were on sexploitation movies, but he garnered attention with the garish *Joe* (1970); made for a pittance, it starred Peter Boyle as a virulent racist who finally goes over the edge. *Joe* captured the country's polarized mood and became a surprise hit, but neither the low-budget *Cry Uncle!* (1971), starring Allen Garfield as a private dick, nor *The Stoolie* (1972), with Jackie Mason in the title role, enjoyed the same result. Avildsen then got his shot at mainstream success with the male-weeper *Save the Tiger* (1973); written by Steve Shagan, whose screenplay was Oscar-nominated, it won an Academy Award for Jack Lemmon's performance as a businessman wallowing in a mid-life crisis. (For this orgy of self-pity, Lemmon beat out some of the best performances ever submitted by Brando, Nicholson, and Pacino.) The lively *W.W. and the Dixie Dancekings* (1975) found Burt Reynolds once again playing an amiable Southern con man.

Avildsen then caught lightning in a bottle with

*Rocky* (1976), the now legendary Sylvester Stallone project about an inarticulate but sensitive boxer who dreams of becoming champ. A huge box-office success, it became the *Marty* of the Seventies, winning the best picture Oscar and putting an Academy Award on Avildsen's shelf as well (Stallone had to settle for becoming the world's highest-paid star). But *Slow Dancing in the Big City* (1978), a laughable romantic drama starring Paul Sorvino, and *The Formula* (1980), a truly dull conspiracy "thriller" with Marlon Brando and George C. Scott, illustrated Avildsen's unique ability to squander opportunity after it had knocked down his door. His version of Thomas Berger's novel *Neighbors* (1981), starring John Belushi and Dan Aykroyd, was also a disaster.

But then came *The Karate Kid* (1984), the immensely popular, *Rocky*-ish tale of teenage wimp Ralph Macchio, whose life turns around after some tutelage in philosophy and the martial arts from unassuming Japanese janitor Pat Morita; Avildsen edited the picture himself and had the score composed by *Rocky* alumnus Bill Conti. "Manipulative," the critics complained, but it made $100 million. Not surprisingly, *The Karate Kid Part II* (1986) followed and did even better at the box office, although like most sequels it was just a diluted version of the original.

*Happy New Year* (1987) and *For Keeps* (1988) disappeared without a trace, but *Lean On Me* (1989), an inspirational biopic based on the exploits of New Jersey school principal "Crazy Joe" Clark (Morgan Freeman), was a hit. Of *The Karate Kid Part III* and *Rocky V* (1990) little need be said, and Avildsen also dropped the ball on *The Power of One* (1992), a sincere but mush-brained tale about a white South African lad (Stephen Dorff) who boxes black opponents to end apartheid. After making the little-seen *Eight Seconds* (1994), starring Luke Perry as a doomed rodeo star, Avildsen demonstrated his good sense by getting himself fired from the long-promised Howard Stern movie by the producers because of "creative differences."

## RICHARD BOLESLAWSKI (1889-1937)

Born in Warsaw as Ryszard Boleslawsky, he acted at the Moscow Arts Theatre, then went to New York, where he got work directing on Broadway and founded the avant-garde Laboratory Theater. Like so many other successful Broadway directors, he was invited to Hollywood with the advent of sound pictures. His first stop was at Columbia, where he made *The Last of the Lone Wolf* (1930). Then it was on to RKO for *The Gay Diplomat* and *The Woman Pursued*, both in 1931. He was put under contract at MGM specifically to direct *Rasputin and the Empress* (1932), in which John, Lionel, and Ethel Barrymore re-enact the palace intrigue that Boleslawski had grown up with. Next came the exotic *Storm at Daybreak* (1933), with Walter Huston betrayed by wife Kay Francis, and *Beauty for Sale* (1933), a good drama starring Madge Evans as a beauty-parlor worker

*Fugitive Lovers* (1934) was a farfetched romantic drama, with Robert Montgomery and Madge Evans drawn to each other while trying to escape their respective pursuers on a cross-country bus trip, and *Men in White* (1934) offered Clark Gable as an idealistic young doctor at loggerheads with Myrna Loy, his superficial society wife. *Operator 13* (1934) was Civil War hooey centered around Gary Cooper as a Confederate officer falling for Union spy Marion Davies, who disguises herself in blackface. *The Painted Veil* (1934) at least had dignity (as what Garbo vehicle does not?).

Moving to Fox for four pictures in 1935, Boleslawski hit his stride. *Clive of India* was a handsomely realized biopic: Ronald Colman played the cultivated imperialist who takes time off from his empire building to attend to Loretta Young. Better still was *Les Miserables* with Charles Laughton as the police inspector who hounds Fredric March, the man with a past; the film was one of twelve nominated for an Academy Award as best picture of 1935. *Metropolitan* was a showcase for opera star Lawrence Tibbett, while *O'Shaughnessy's Boy* reteamed Wallace Beery and Jackie Cooper without matching their earlier vehicles.

The sentimental Western *Three Godfathers* (1936) had an appealing (if low-wattage) cast that featured Chester Morris and Walter Brennan. But *Theodora Goes Wild* (1936) was a terrific romantic romp, with Irene Dunne (Oscar-nominated) and Melvyn Douglas both excellent as the author and artist fated to be in love. *Garden of Allah* (also 1936) was probably the year's most lavish picture, in Technicolor and with a Max Steiner score. But this Arabian lovefest forgot to give a decent script to appealing stars Charles Boyer and Marlene Dietrich (though Dietrich never looked better). Boleslawski's final film was *The Last of Mrs. Cheyney* (1937), a sophisticated romantic mystery about jewel thief William Powell and his affair with Joan Crawford. Only forty-eight years old, Boleslawski died halfway through the production, and the picture was completed by George Fitzmaurice.

## JAMES BRIDGES (1936–1993)

Former television actor and movie screenwriter James Bridges was born in Paris, Arkansas. He both scripted and directed *The Baby Maker* (1970), a low-budget drama about a childless couple who hire lovely hippie Barbara Hershey to serve as a surrogate mother, with unexpected results. More widely seen was *The Paper Chase* (1973), a vastly enjoyable drama about a Harvard Law School freshman (Timothy Bottoms) who struggles to survive the rigors of his course work with the demanding Professor Kingsfield (John Houseman, who won an Oscar) while courting the professor's free-spirited daughter (Lindsay Wagner); Bridge's adaptation of the source novel was also Oscar-nominated, and the picture was later spun off into a successful television series.

Bridges also wrote *9/30/55* (1978; aka *September 30, 1955*), an interesting dramatization of a fan's (Richard Thomas) struggle to come to grips with the death of idol James Dean in 1955. But it was the suspenseful *The China Syndrome* (1979) that became Bridges's first breakout hit. Jane Fonda plays a television reporter who stumbles onto a cover-up at a nuclear power plant that nearly suffered a meltdown, and Jack Lemmon is the engineer who blows the whistle on his criminally negligent superiors when he tumbles to their game; both actors were Oscar-nominated, as was Bridges for his share of the prescient original screenplay. The picture received an enormous boost when, a few weeks after it opened, the Three Mile Island nuclear disaster occurred.

Bridges also scored big with *Urban Cowboy* (1980), a formulaic but somehow irresistible story about young Texas construction worker John Travolta (never more endearing), who lets his marriage to spunky Debra Winger go to pot while he struggles to be accepted in the world of Gilley's, the famed Houston honky-tonk with its mechanical bull and competitive dance floors. Written by Bridges and Aaron Latham, from whose nonfiction magazine article the story was developed, *Cowboy* was a smash and spawned one of the bestselling sound tracks of all time. Bridges next wrote the existential murder mystery *Mike's Murder* for Winger, but his studio hated the cut he delivered in 1982 and kept it on the shelf until 1984, when a much-edited version was released to a deafening silence.

But it was *Perfect* (1985), one of the decade's definitive bombs, that ought to have stayed on the shelf. Developed from an Aaron Latham article about the new subculture of health clubs by Bridges and Latham, it starred John Travolta as a bright but unscrupulous, Lathamesque *Rolling Stone* reporter on the trail of a story and Jamie Lee Curtis as the club instructor he first exploits, then falls in love with. It took Travolta ten years to recover from this fiasco, and Bridges never did. His last film was *Bright Lights, Big City* (1988), an intelligent but curiously flat adaption (co-scripted by Bridges) of the Jay McInerney bestseller about the club-and-cocaine scene in 1980s New York City. Michael J. Fox was probably miscast as the overwhelmed protagonist, but Kiefer Sutherland was dead-on as his coked-up pal.

## DAVID BUTLER (1894–1979)

He made thirty-two movies for Fox between 1927 and 1938, another twenty-three for Warners between 1943 and 1956, and still had time for ten features at various other studios. The proficient Butler oversaw some of the best pictures made by Shirley Temple, Bob Hope, and Doris Day, never once intruding with any personal flourishes—who could ask for anything more? Born in San Francisco, Butler was practically raised in the theater by his stage-director dad, and by 1918 had become a silent-screen actor, appearing in pictures directed by D. W. Griffith, Tod Browning, King Vidor, Frank Borzage, and John Ford.

He began directing in 1927 at Fox, and made a number of silents before directing and scripting both the transitional sound musical *Sunny Side Up* (1929), featuring Janet Gaynor and Charles Farrel, and *Just Imagine* (1930), an ambitious futuristic musical starring comedian El Brendel as a sleeper who awakes after fifty years in 1980 and is amazed at the changes in society, fashion, and technology. Will Rogers starred for Butler in the first sound version of Mark Twain's *A Connecticut Yankee* (1931) alongside Maureen O'Sullivan, as well as in *Down to Earth* (1932), *Handy Andy* (1934), and *Doubting Thomas* (1935).

Butler directed new Fox discovery Shirley Temple for the first time in *Bright Eyes* (also 1934), for which he also co-wrote the story, then helped guide her to stardom in *The Little Colonel, The Littlest Rebel* (both 1935), and *Captain January* (1936). Butler's last Fox production, *Ali Baba Goes to Town* (1937), was a clever Eddie Cantor musical, and *Kentucky* (1938), starring Loretta Young and Richard Greene, helped Walter Brennan to a best supporting actor Oscar. *Kentucky Moonshine* (1938) was uninspired idiocy with the Ritz Brothers, but *East Side of Heaven* (1939) and *If I Had My Way* (1940) were acceptable Bing Crosby showcases. He handled the team of Bob Hope and Dorothy Lamour for the first time in *Caught in the Draft* (1941), and the results were so hiliarious that they joined forces again on *The Road to Morocco* (1942), one of the best in the series; *They Got Me Covered* (1943), a lesser espionage farce with Otto Preminger as one of the villains. *The Princess and the Pirate*, with Hope, found Lamour replaced by Virginia Mayo.

The biopic *Shine On, Harvest Moon* (1944) had Ann Sheridan as vaudeville star Nora Bayes and Jack Carson as Jack Norworth, while *San Antonio* (1945) was a solid Errol Flynn Western, co-starring Alexis Smith. Butler now entered his Dennis Morgan–Jack Carson phase, using them in *Two Guys from Milwaukee* (1946), the musical *The Time, the Place, and the Girl* (also 1946), *Two Guys from Texas* (1948), and the clever satire *It's a Great Feeling* (1949); in between it was Morgan alone in the biopic *My Wild Irish Rose* (1947). Butler was reunited with the adult Shirley Temple for *The Story of Seabiscuit* (1949) and handled the June Haver period musical, *The Daughter of Rosie O'Grady* (1950).

Butler was then entrusted with new Warners star Doris Day for the musicals *Tea for Two* (1950) and *Lullaby of Broadway* (1951). After making *Where's Charley?* (1952) with Ray Bolger, more hit Doris Day musicals unfurled: *April in Paris* (also 1952), *By the Light of the Silvery Moon* with Gordon MacRae, and *Calamity Jane* (both 1953) with Howard Keel and the Oscar-winning true "Secret Love." Inexplicably, Butler then began making action pictures like the Western *The Command*, the feeble *King Richard and the Crusaders* (both 1954), and the Indochina-based *Jump into Hell* (1955). He also directed the next generation of stars, Tab Hunter and Natalie Wood, in *The Girl He Left Behind* (1956). He came out of retirement for *C'mon, Let's Live a Little* (1967), a pop musical starring that immortal screen team Bobby Vee and Jackie De Shannon. After that one, Butler's retirement stuck.

## EDWARD (EDDIE) BUZZELL (1897–1985)

A onetime actor who performed in vaudeville and on Broadway, Brooklyn-born Eddie Buzzell directed many major stars during his long career, but rarely had them in a movie that transcended the run-of-the-mill, instead earning a reputation for speed and economy. After acting in a few silent comedies, in 1930 and 1931, Buzzell began directing a series of comedy shorts at Columbia, which he wrote and performed in.

He was promoted to director of featues in 1932, and during that first year directed *The Big Timer, Hollywood Speaks*, and *Virtue*, the last with Carole Lombard as a prostitute reformed by Pat O'Brien. *Child of Manhattan* with Nancy Carroll and *Ann Carver's Profession* (both 1933), with Fay Wray as a lawyer, were typical pre-Code melodramas, while *The Girl Friend* (1935) was a musical starring Ann Sothern and Jack Haley. Buzzell then spent three unproductive years at Universal, shooting a slate of "B" projects even more ephemeral than the Columbia work—*Transient Lady* (1935) and *As Good as Married* (1937).

Presumably he was relieved to move to MGM in 1938, where the "B" pictures were of a higher grade. Buzzell now worked with the likes of Robert Young and Eleanor Powell (*Honolulu*, 1939) and the Marx Brothers (*At the Circus*, 1939; *Go West*, 1940). *Ship Ahoy* (1942), in which Frank Sinatra croons with the Tommy Dorsey Orchestra to Eleanor Powell, was a bit better than it needed to be, while *Keep Your Powder Dry* (1945), starring Lana Turner, Laraine Day, and Susan Peters as feuding WACs, was less than it might have been. Buzzell remade the screwball classic *Libeled Lady* as *Easy to Wed* (1946), but how could Van Johnson, Lucille Ball, and Esther Williams ever replace William Powell, Jean Harlow, and Myrna Loy?

*Song of the Thin Man* (1947) *had* Loy and Powell, and was a good closing entry for the popular series, while *Neptune's Daughter* (1949)—Buzzell's final MGM picture—was a nice vehicle for Esther Williams, with "Baby, It's Cold Outside" almost making up for Red Skelton's presence. Buzzell's last pictures were light fare: the best, *Ain't Misbehavin'* (1955), was a happy mix of music, Piper Laurie, Mamie Van Doren, and Jack Carson.

## JAMES CRUZE (1894–1942)

A giant in the days of silent pictures, Utah native James Cruze becomes merely a footnote after the advent of sound pictures. Born to Mormon parents, Cruze gravitated to the stage at an early age, traveled with David Belasco's company, and appeared on Broadway. In 1908 he began his ten-year career as a screen actor, starring in serials, shorts, and features. He started directing in 1918 at Paramount, and over the next ten years made most of his forty-odd features there, including a number of Fatty Arbuckle comedies, the Western epic *The Covered Wagon* (1923), and *Merton of the Movies* (1924). But Cruze's bold decision to leave Paramount to form his own production company may have cost him the opportunity to make the transition to sound with the resources of a major studio, ultimately squandering the status he had earned through the Twenties.

Since so many of Cruze's silent films appear to be lost for all time, it's hard to evaluate how good a director he was in his prime, and his sound pictures offer little evidence of what his skills may once have been. *She Got What She Wanted* (1930) and *Salvation Nell* (1931) were made for the minor Tiffany studio, but in 1932 Cruze scored with *Washington Merry-Go-Round*, a crackling political drama starring Lee Tracy. He also directed one of the episodes in Paramount's all-star showcase *If I Had My Way. I Cover the Waterfront* (1933) was Cruze's most important pre-Code picture, starring Ben Lyon as an investigative reporter who uses Claudette Colbert to help crack a case involving smuggled Chinese immigrants.

At Fox he directed *Mr. Skitch* (1933) and *David Harum* (1934), pleasant diversions starring Will Rogers, and *Helldorado* (1935) with Richard Arlen and Madge Evans. *Two-Fisted* (1935) featured Lee Tracy as a prizefighter, while *Sutter's Gold* (1936) had Edward Arnold as explorer Johann Sutter. But Cruze's last four efforts—*The Wrong Road* (1937), *Prison Nurse*, *The Gangs of New York* (with a script by Sam Fuller), and *Come On, Leathernecks!* (all 1938)—were programmers made for lowly Republic, illustrating how far his once-lofty stature had slipped.

## ANDRÉ DE TOTH (1910– )

He was best-known for his no-nonsense action pictures, particularly Westerns made in the terse manner of Anthony Mann and Raoul Walsh, whose one-eyed visage the Hungarian-born André de Toth shared. In 1939 he fled his native country, in whose film industry he had worked since 1931, and settled in England, where he found work with Alexander Korda as a second-unit director on *The Thief of Bagdad* and *The Jungle Book*. In 1942 de Toth made his way to Hollywood, landing at Columbia, where he directed war-themed "B"s like *Passage to Suez* and *None Shall Escape* (both 1943). He then signed with United Artists, where he made the hard-boiled Western *Ramrod* (1947), featuring Joel McCrea and Veronia Lake (whom de Toth later married), and *The Pitfall* (1948), a good noir starring Dick Powell as a straying husband and slinky Lizabeth Scott as the treacherous woman who turns his life upside down.

*Slattery's Hurricane* (1949) put Richard Widmark to good use as a pilot who fears he might crash during a storm, but *Man in the Saddle*, *Carson City*, and *Springfield Rifle* (all 1952) were entirely conventional Westerns; the first two starred Randolph Scott, with whom de Toth would work many times. The best of de Toth's Fifties work includes *Last of the Comanches* (1952), a quasi-remake of Zoltan Korda's *Sahara*, with American Indians now standing in for the Nazi hordes of the original; *House of Wax* (1953), an excellent 3-D remake of the 1933 *Mystery of the Wax Museum*, with Vincent Price at his best as a deformed sculptor with murder on this mind; *The Indian Fighter* (1955), with Kirk Douglas and Walter Matthau; and, most interestingly, *Monkey on My Back* (1957), a biopic of drug-addicted boxer Barney Ross, starring Cameron Mitchell.

*Man on a String* (1960) was another good biopic, this time centering around the exploits of Soviet counterspy Boris Morros (well played by Ernest Borgnine). De Toth now began to work in Europe, filming action pictures like *Morgan the Pirate*, starring Steve Reeves, and *The Mongols* (both 1961), with Jack Palance as the son of Genghis Khan and Anita Ekberg as his spectacular mistress. Last came the taut World War II adventure *Play Dirty* (1968), in which Michael Caine, Nigel Green, Nigel Davenport, and several other fine British actors battle the Germans in North Africa.

## RAY ENRIGHT (1896–1965)

A former jack-of-all-trades for Mack Sennett, Hoosier Ray Enright began his directing career with the Rin-Tin-Tin adventure *Tracked by the Police* in 1927, then proceeded to make another fifty films for Warner Bros./First National between 1927 and 1942, most —but not all—low-budget genre entries. In fact, Enright made a career out of capable but wholly unexceptional "B" pictures.

His best-known Warners work includes the musicals *20 Million Sweethearts* and *Dames* (both 1934), both choreographed by Busby Berkeley and starring Dick Powell and Ruby Keeler; *The St. Louis Kid* with Jimmy Cagney; the Joe E. Brown vehicles *Alibi Ike* (1935) and *Earthworm Tractors* (1936); *Slim* (1937), with Henry Fonda and Pat O'Brien as high-wire linemen competing for the affections of Margaret Lindsay; *Angels Wash Their Faces* (1939), a juvenile-delinquent drama starring Ann Sheridan, Ronald Reagan, and the Dead End Kids; and the elaborate Vera Zorina showcase *On Your Toes* (1939), with Balanchine's "Slaughter on Tenth Avenue" and little else retained from the George Abbott Broadway hit. *The Wagons Roll at Night* (1941) had the dubious distinction of being Humphrey Bogart's only flop in the year that saw him rise to stardom in *High Sierra* and *The Maltese Falcon*.

Enright directed another eighteen pictures freelancing for Universal, Paramount, RKO, and Columbia between 1942 and 1953, the best of which were *The Spoilers* (1942), the finest rendering of Rex Beach's oft-filmed Yukon adventure, with the terrific cast of Marlene Dietrich, John Wayne, and Randolph Scott; *The Iron Major* (1943), a superior biopic starring Pat O'Brien as legendary Boston College football coach Frank Cavanaugh; and *Gung Ho!* (1943), a crackling war yarn with Randolph Scott that goes a bit off the deep end in equating partriotism with racism. After the war, Enright made Westerns primarily: *Return of the Bad Men* (1948), with Randolph Scott pitted against Billy the Kid, the Sundance Kid (Robert Ryan), and the Dalton Gang; *South of St. Louis* (1949), with Joel McCrea and Alexis Smith; and *Montana* (1950), starring Errol Flynn and Alexis Smith. Slightly more interesting was *Flaming Feather* (1952), in which Sterling Hayden helps save Barbara Rush from a band of renegade Indians. Enright retired a year later.

## NORMAN FOSTER (1900–1976)

Foster will always be associated with Orson Welles, with whom he worked closely on two projects in the Forties, but he produced little else of interest among the three dozen features he directed between 1936 and 1973. Born in Bloomington, Indiana, as Norman Hoeffer, he actually began his show-business career as a stage actor in the Twenties. By the dawn of talking pictures, Foster had made his way to Hollywood, appearing in films like *Play Girl*, *State Fair*, and *Smilin' Through*.

Foster decided to step behind the camera, and he went to work for Twentieth Century-Fox directing "B" mysteries. His first effort was *I Cover Chinatown* (1936), which was followed in short order by a number of entries in the popular Mr. Moto series with Peter Lorre (*Think Fast, Mr. Moto: Mysterious Mr. Moto; Mr. Moto Takes a Vacation*, 1937–39) and the Charlie Chan series, which now starred Sidney Toler (*Charlie Chan in Reno, Charlie Chan at Treasure Island, Charlie Chan in Panama*; all 1939–40).

Orson Welles had run into difficulty in 1942 with his documentary about South America, *It's All True*, and had fallen out of favor with RKO. Foster was hired to take over Welles's Mercury Production *Journey into Fear* (1943), an espionage yarn adapted from a complicated Eric Ambler novel, which was to star Welles and Mercury Players Joseph Cotten, Agnes Moorehead, and Everett Sloane. How much of the picture Welles actually directed without credit will always be a matter of dispute, but the film certainly doesn't resemble any of Foster's other pictures.

He spent the rest of the war years in Mexico shooting two Spanish-language films, then returned to Hollywood in 1948 with the charming Western romance *Rachel and the Stranger*, starring Loretta Young and Robert Mitchum, and the dank noir *Kiss the Blood Off My Hands* (aka *The Unafraid*), in which Burt Lancaster and Joan Fontaine run for their lives through London. *Tell It to the Judge* (1949) and *Father Is a Bachelor* (1950) were inane romantic comedies, but *Woman on the Run* (1950) was a proficient thriller starring Ann Sheridan and Dennis O'Keefe, and the low-budget, semi-documentary *Navajo* (1952) was an interesting project.

After a brief stop at MGM, Foster went to work for Walt Disney's Buena Vista, making live-action features for television, including *Davy Crockett, King of the Wild Frontier*—the one that started the national craze for the character in 1955—*The Nine Lives of Elfego Baca* (1959), and *The Sign of Zorro* (1960; co-directed with Lewis Foster). Although Foster made a handful of pictures over the next twelve years, like the coming-of-age saga *Indian Paint* (1964) with Johnny Crawford and Jay Silverheels, few received national theatrical release.

## SIDNEY FRANKLIN (1893–1972)

San Francisco–born Sidney Franklin got his start in films in 1913 as an actor and assistant cameraman. He worked primarily for First National and Warners from 1919 to 1925, and in 1926 moved to MGM, where he would remain for the next thirty-odd years. Franklin directed Norma Shearer in *The Actress*, and Greta Garbo in *Wild Orchids* (1929).

Now a favorite of Irving Thalberg, Franklin was entrusted with one of Shearer's first talkies, *The Last of Mrs. Cheyney* (1929), which he followed with *Devil May Care, The Lady of Scandal*, and *A Lady's Morals* (all 1930). *The Guardsman* (1931) was prime Lunt and Fontanne, their only appearance together on film, and *Private Lives* (1931) was an elegant adaptation of the Noël Coward play, in which Norma Shearer and Robert Montgomery merrily trade insults and barbs. *Smilin' Through* (1932) had Shearer again, now inheriting the tearjerking role Franklin had directed Norma Talmadge in back in 1922.

*Reunion in Vienna* (1933) was more upper-crust doings, enlivened by John Barrymore's sprightly performance. *The Barretts of Wimpole Street* (1934) was a lavishly mounted account of the love affair between Elizabeth Barrett and Robert Browning. Norma Shearer was Oscar-nominated for her performance. Less successful was *The Dark Angel* (1935), a remake of the 1925 Ronald Colman–Thelma Banky weeper. Merle Oberon was Oscar-nominated for her portrayal of the bereft woman.

Franklin's next production was the biggest of his career, and before it was completed, it would require the services of four other directors. But *The Good Earth* (1937) repaid the care lavished upon it by MGM. It became one of the year's top box-office draws and earned Academy Award nominations for best picture, direction, and actress (Luise Rainer). Thereafter Franklin worked only as a producer, with such classic weepers to his credit as *Waterloo Bridge, Mrs. Miniver*, and *Random Harvest*. He returned in 1957 to direct an inferior remake of *The Barretts of Wimpole Street* with Jennifer Jones.

## MICHAEL GORDON (1909– )

A minor figure in many ways, Michael Gordon nonetheless was attached to several films of merit during his three decades in Hollywood, although his career as a director was bisected by the nearly eight years he spent in exile after he was blacklisted. Born in Baltimore, Maryland, Gordon attended Johns Hopkins and then Yale Drama School. He acted on stage and also directed some productions before beginning in Hollywood as a film editor and dialogue coach at Columbia. His first directing credits were such "B" series entries as *Boston Blackie Goes Hollywood* and *Underground Agent* (both 1942), followed by *One Dangerous Night* (a "Lone Wolf" installment) and *Crime Doctor* (both 1943).

These programmers were capable if undistinguished, but when Gordon moved to Universal after the war he found a more respectable class of assignments awaiting him. The first was *The Web*, one of the many good noirs made during that banner year of 1947 (starring such genre icons as Edmond O'Brien, Vincent Price, Ella Raines, and William Bendix); Gordon handled its typically convoluted plot with facility. But instead of continuing in that vein, he was handed the tony *Another Part of the Forest* (1948), Lillian Hellman's prequel to *The Little Foxes*. The impressive cast (Fredric March, Edmond O'Brien, and *Foxes* veteran Dan Duryea) performed flawlessly, although Hellman's story wasn't quite as compelling as its 1941 companion piece.

*An Act of Murder* (1948), a drama about euthanasia, used March and O'Brien again to good effect, while *The Lady Gambles* (1949) was a great showcase for Barbara Stanwyck, who played a compulsive gambler. But *Woman in Hiding* (1950) was a giant step backward, with the usually reliable Ida Lupino and Howard Duff relentlessly chewing the scenery, the better to obfuscate the grade-C plot. *Cyrano de Bergerac* (1950) was made for Stanley Kramer's production company; it was a distinguished (if somewhat stagy) production that should have been Gordon's ticket to the top rank of directors—particularly after José Ferrer was awarded the Oscar for his performance. But after making two good films for Fox in 1951—the tangy garment industry drama *I Can Get It for You Wholesale* with Susan Hayward, and the Western suspenser *The Secret of Convict Lake* with Gene Tierney—Gordon was named as a former Party member in HUAC testimony, effectively ending his career for eight years. (He made one film in Australia in 1953.)

When Hollywood finally invited Gordon back, he was fortunate enough to be given the sprightly romantic comedy *Pillow Talk* (1959), probably the best of the enormously popular Rock Hudson–Doris Day films. The screenplay won an Oscar, and Day and Thelma Ritter were both nominated. *Portrait in Black* (1960) was a mediocre Lana Turner melodrama, while *Boys' Night Out* (1962) was a leering farce with a deft cast (James Garner, Kim Novak, Tony Randall) that probably delighted Hugh Hefner. *For Love or Money* (1963) tried to blend Kirk Douglas and bubbleheaded comedy—an oxymoron if ever there was one. *Move Over, Darling* (1963) was a decent remake of the 1940 screwball classic *My Favorite Wife* (intended to be *Something's Got to Give* before Marilyn Monroe's problems convinced Fox to shut down the production); James Garner does his damnedest to fill the Cary Grant role.

*Texas Across the River* (1966) was funny enough if one fancies Rat Packers Dean Martin and Joey Bishop out West, but the smarmy *The Impossible Years* (1968), from the Broadway play, placed David Niven in one of the decade's worst comedies. *How Do I Love Thee?* (1970), a hokey generation-gap drama starring Jackie Gleason and Maureen O'Hara, was nearly as bad. It brought down the curtain on Gordon's career, the two halves of which hardly match up as belonging to the same person. But looking at the films Gordon made just before and just after his blacklisting, one can easily speculate about the seven or eight good movies he might have made had those years not been stolen from him.

## ALFRED E. GREEN (1889-1960)

Green's glory days were with Warner Bros. in the early Thirties, but his career as a director spanned the Teens through the Fifties, with some tasty bonbons scattered among his seventy sound features. Born in Ferris, California, Green graduated from directing two-reel comedies to feature work in 1917. He was at Warners when sound came, and immediately made an impact with *Disraeli* (1929), *Old English* (1932), and *The Green Goddess* (1930), three upscale showcases for stage veteran George Arliss, who won a best actor Oscar for *Disraeli*. *Smart Money* (1931) was a tart crime yarn starring Edward G. Robinson, with James Cagney and Boris Karloff in support; Robinson was in fine form again in *Silver Dollar* (1932), a fact-based tale about the founding of Denver.

Green's pre-Code success continued with his 1933 slate: *Baby Face* with Barbara Stanwyck was the best of the group, although *The Narrow Corner* and *Parachute Jumper*, both with Doug Fairbanks, Jr., and *I Loved a Woman*, starring Edward G. Robinson and Kay Francis, also had vitality. Green shot seven features for Warners in 1934, including *Housewife*, in which advertising copywriter Bette Davis steals colleague George Brent from his wife (why bother?), and five more in 1935, the best of which were two Bette Davis melodramas: *Dangerous*, which won her her first Oscar (a consolation prize for being overlooked in the previous year's *Of Human Bondage*, wags murmured), and *The Girl from Tenth Avenue*.

*The Golden Arrow* (1936) was positively one of Davis's worst pictures, and it marked Green's exit from Warners. He did just fine freelancing, though: *More than a Secretary* (1936), a romantic comedy in which appealing Jean Arthur falls for boss George Brent (again: why bother?); *The League of Frightened Men* (1937), featuring Walter Connolly as a less-than-compelling Nero Wolfe; *Thoroughbreds Don't Cry* (1938), the first of many collaborations between Mickey Rooney and Judy Garland; and the goofy Philo Vance mystery *The Gracie Allen Murder Case* (1939).

Most of Green's work in the Forties was on "B"-level productions like the John Garfield dramas *Flowing Gold* and *East of the River* (both 1940); the wartime espionage thriller *Appointment in Berlin* (1943); and the biopic *The Jolson Story* (1946), a box-office smash that starred Larry Parks as the famed entertainer, with Jolson himself dubbing his songs. The dull *The Fabulous Dorseys* (1947) was one of the few biopics that had the stars—Jimmy and Tommy Dorsey—appearing as themselves, while *Copacabana* (also 1947) was strained Groucho Marx and Carmen Miranda. Of Green's last pictures, only *The Jackie Robinson Story* (1950) stands out; it was a low-budget but well-mounted biography of the legendary ballplayer, starring none other than the legendary ballplayer himself! *Invasion U.S.A.* (1952) had some value as Red-baiting camp shlock, while *The Eddie Cantor Story* (1953) was an insult to biopics everywhere. Green left Hollywood in 1954 and worked for several years in television before retiring.

## BYRON HASKIN (1899-1984)

He began working as a cinematographer in 1922, but Byron Haskin didn't become a full-time director until 1947, after which he made a handful of very nice genre entries, particularly in the film noir, science-fiction, and Western categories. Born in Portland, Oregon, Haskin worked as a newsreel cameraman before moving to Hollywood in 1919. There he found work first as an assistant cameraman, soon graduating to director of photography. He actually directed four silent features in 1927 and 1928, then moved to England, where he assisted director Herbert Wilcox for three years before returning to Hollywood and taking a slot in the special-effects department of Warner Bros., which he became head of in 1937.

*I Walk Alone* (1947) was his first feature in nearly twenty years; a respectable noir, it starred Burt Lancaster and Lizabeth Scott, with Kirk Douglas as the villain. *Too Late for Tears* (1949) was another hard-boiled yarn in which Lizabeth Scott tries to keep a bag of stolen loot out of the clutches of bad-guy Dan Duryea. Haskin's version of *Treasure Island* (1950), starring Robert Newton and Bobby Driscoll, was made under the Disney banner and was nearly the equal of Jack Conway's 1934 standard, and *Tarzan's Peril* (1951), with Lex Barker as the jungle king, was enhanced by Dorothy Dandridge in a supporting role.

Haskin's next three efforts were businesslike Westerns—*Warpath*, *Silver City* (both 1951), and *Denver and the Rio Grande* (1952)—all starring Edmond O'Brien. But *War of the Worlds* (1953) was an exceptional version of the H. G. Wells novel, with Oscar-winning special effects by George Pal (who also produced the film). *His Majesty O'Keefe* (1954) gave Burt Lancaster another opportunity to swash his buckles through the South Seas, while *The Naked Jungle* (also 1954), starring Charlton Heston and Eleanor Parker, was an excellent version of the classic adventure story "Leiningen vs. the Ants." After making an Australian version of *Treasure Island*, Haskin and Pal teamed again on *Conquest of Space* (1955), a rather dull account of man's first trip to Mars.

*The First Texan* cast Joel McCrea as Sam Houston, while *The Boss* (both 1956) gave John Payne a good role as the crime kingpin of St. Louis. Haskin's last pictures of interest were all science fiction. First came his slightly cheesy adaptation of Jules Verne's *From the Earth to the Moon* (1958), starring Joseph Cotten and George Sanders; then *Robinson Crusoe on Mars* (1964), a leisurely, almost contemplative updating of Defoe's tale that retains its charm after three decades; and finally, *The Power* (1968), a chilling tale about a killer with parapsychic powers that boasted a superb cast of character actors. On that up-note, Haskin retired.

## WILLIAM K. HOWARD (1899-1954)

Born in the small town of St. Mary's, Ohio, William K. Howard went on after his graduation from Ohio State to manage movie theaters and sell film stock. After serving in the First World War, Howard made his way to Hollywood, where he spent a year as an assistant director, and then began directing features. His first silents were primarily Westerns (*The Thundering Herd*, *Code of the West*), adventures (*Volcano*, *White Gold*, *The River Pirate*), and romantic melodramas (*Gigolo*, *Bachelor Brides*).

Howard's early Fox sound pictures remain obscure today: *The Valiant* (1929) with Paul Muni; *Scotland Yard* (1930); *Transatlantic* and *Don't Bet on Women* (both 1931)—the last three starring Edmund Lowe—but in 1932 he had modest hits with *First Year*, in which newlyweds Janet Gaynor and Charles Farrell struggle through some hard times, and *Sherlock Holmes*, starring dour Clive Brook as Holmes, pitting his wits against the diabolical Professor Moriarty (Ernest Torrence). Howard's most important picture was probably *The Power and the Glory* (1933), a searing account of the rise and fall of a powerful railroad tycoon (Spencer Tracy) who has committed suicide; written by Preston Sturges, the film employed a multiple-flashback structure that clearly had an effect on Orson Welles and Herman J. Mankiewicz when they scripted *Citizen Kane* in 1941.

Few of Howard's subsequent pictures were that ambitious. Moving to MGM, he made *Evelyn Prentice* (1934), a dullish melodrama starring William Powell and Myrna Loy, while *The Cat and the Fiddle* (1934) was a sprightly version of the Jerome Kern–Oscar Hammerstein operetta, starring Jeanette MacDonald and Ramon Novarro. *Vanessa, Her Love Story* was a maudlin romance between Helen Hayes and Robert Montgomery, although *Mary Burns—Fugitive* (both 1935) was a good gangster yarn in whch Melvyn Douglas tries to rescue Sylvia Sidney from thug Warner Baxter. *The Princess Comes Across* (1936) found the irresistible Carole Lombard posing as a princess while being romanced by Fred MacMurray on board an ocean liner.

Howard moved to England to make *Fire over England* (1937), a good historical romance set in the sixteenth century in which Laurence Olivier battles Raymond Massey for the love of Vivien Leigh. The hard-hitting Depression drama *Back Door to Heaven* (1939) featured Jimmy Lydon as a slum kid who has no choice but to become a thief. Howard's last films were modest crime "B"'s like *Money and the Woman* (1940) and *Bullets for O'Hara* (1941). The nearly forgotten James Cagney tale *Johnny Come Lately* (1943) was his penultimate project, and he retired in 1946.

## H. BRUCE (LUCKY) HUMBERSTONE (1903–1984)

A onetime assistant director to Allan Dwan, Edmund Goulding, and King Vidor, "Lucky" Humberstone was lucky enough to direct some of Fox's most enjoyable low-budget entries between 1935 and 1945. Born in Buffalo, he served his apprenticeship as an actor, a script clerk, and an assistant director before graduating to feature work at the humble Tiffany studio in 1932, directing something called *Strangers of the Evening*. He co-directed the cheesy Buster Crabbe Tarzan knockoff, *King of the Jungle* (1933), before going to Warners in 1934 to make *The Dragon Murder Case*, a good Philo Vance mystery starring Warren William.

He then signed with Fox, where he would spend the next fourteen years making a variety of mysteries, musicals, and action pictures. In 1936 he was assigned to the highly successful Charlie Chan series with Warner Oland, and turned out some of the best entries, including *Charlie Chan at the Race Trace*, *Charlie Chan at the Opera*, with Boris Karloff supplying the villainy (both 1936), and *Charlie Chan at the Olympics* (1937). *Time Out for Murder* and *While New York Sleeps* (both 1938) were snappy "B" mysteries, while *Pack Up Your Troubles* (1939) found the Ritz Brothers battling the Germans in World War I.

Humberstone stepped up a grade in 1941, getting such relatively prestigious assignments as *Sun Valley Serenade*, a top-notch Sonja Henie musical with John Payne and the Glenn Miller Orchestra, and *I Wake Up Screaming* (aka *Hot Spot*), a proto-film noir with the terrific cast of Victor Mature, Betty Grable, Carole Landis, and Laird Cregar. *To the Shores of Tripoli* (1942) was a Technicolor flag-waver featuring John Payne and Randolph Scott, and filmed with the cooperation of the Marines, while *Iceland* (also 1942) found Norwegian skating star Sonja Henie falling in love with visiting Marine John Payne (at least he didn't have to change uniforms).

*Hello Frisco, Hello* (1943), a period musical that starred Payne and Alice Faye, and *Pin Up Girl* (1944), a Betty Grable vehicle, were both hits, as was the prime Danny Kaye comedy *Wonder Man* (1945), in which Kaye plays twins. After the war, Humberstone's pictures rarely featured such stars and production values, particularly after he left Fox in 1948. But *Three Little Girls in Blue* (1946) was a nice Technicolor musical with June Haver, Vera-Ellen, and Vivian Blaine, and *She's Working Her Way Through College* (1952) provided Virginia Mayo with a good showcase as a burlesque star who goes back to school under the tutelage of Professor Ronald Reagan.



Late in the Fifties Humberstone worked in television, and also directed a trio of cheesy Tarzan pictures starring Gordon Scott that brought him full circle after a quarter century of moviemaking.

## GENE KELLY (1912– )

As an actor, dancer, and choreographer he was superstar; as a solo director, he was a mere mortal. Kelly and Stanley Donen joined forces in 1949 in *On the Town* and shared co-director status on both that and the classic *Singin' in the Rain* (1952) and *It's Always Fair Weather* (1955); one assumes Kelly's contributions to these began and ended with their deathless dance sequences. (And so, here he is, merely receiving credit for what he brought as "just" choreographer to such gems as the Minnelli-directed *The Pirate* and *An American in Paris*.)

Kelly began work on his ambitious "silent" musical *Invitation to the Dance* in 1952, but its three balletic segments were derivative of what he had created in his earlier screen work, and the gimmick of having neither dialogue nor songs succeeded only in making the picture seem far more pretentious than Kelly must have realized. But MGM realized it; they kept the film on the shelf for four years before releasing it in 1957 to a generally uninterested American public. *The Happy Road* (1957) was filmed on location in rural France, but otherwise it was a conventional tale of two single parents (Kelly and Barbara Laage) meeting cute when their children run away from school together.

*The Tunnel of Love* (1958), based on a Broadway play, was the first picture directed by Kelly in which he didn't also star; instead, the stars were Doris Day and Richard Widmark as a married couple who nearly drown in red tape when they try to adopt a child. Kelly returned to his favorite setting—Paris—for the heart-tugging *Gigot* (1962), an effective (if manipulative) story starring Jackie Gleason as a deaf-mute who takes waif Katherine Kath under his wing. He demonstrated a decent comic touch on the leering, guest-star-laden *A Guide for the Married Man* (1967), which finds Broadway star Robert Morse in top form as he instructs Walter Matthau on how to efficiently cheat on his gorgeous wife (Inger Stevens); presumably it was Hugh Hefner's favorite picture that year.



*Hello, Dolly!* (1969) was Kelly's garish, swollen adaptation of the Broadway brontosaurus . . . er, blockbuster. Barbra Streisand stars as the matchmaking Dolly Levi, and she overpowers everything in her path—including Walter Matthau and Louis Armstrong—just as she would a year later in Vincente Minnelli's *On a Clear Day . . .*; still, you can tell you're watching a star (just in case there was any doubt). The "naughty" Western comedy *The Cheyenne Social Club* (1970) made no apologies for its geriatric mindset, although stars Henry Fonda and James Stewart were still capable of holding down action roles at this stage of their careers. Kelly's final credit was as co-director (with Jack Haley, Jr.) of *That's Entertainment, Part 2* (1976), the predictable, and predictably self-congratulatory, follow-up to the 1974 original's compilation of highlights from MGM musicals. Here Kelly hosts with onetime co-star Fred Astaire—but the material isn't entirely culled from musicals and should have been.

## ROWLAND V. LEE (1891-1975)

Yet another erstwhile actor who converted to directing, Lee had a career that was split almost evenly between the thirty silent features he made between 1921 and 1929 and the twenty-eight sound pictures—most decent, few remarkable—that followed from 1929 to 1945. Born in Findlay, Ohio, to stage-veteran parents, he began performing himself at an early age. By 1915 he had broken into films as an actor, but after the First World War he returned to Hollywood intent on directing. As is typically the case, much of his early silent work has been lost for decades, but at Paramount in 1928 he made the silents *Doomsday* and *The First Kiss*, both featuring a young Gary Cooper, and *The Secret Hour*, *Loves of an Actress*, and *Three Sinners*, all with Pola Negri.

*The Mysterious Dr. Fu Manchu* (1929), with Warner Oland as Sax Rohmer's superhuman evil genius, remains one of the best talking pictures from that transitional year; it predictably spawned the 1930 sequel *The Return of Dr. Fu Manchu*, again with Oland and Jean Arthur. But otherwise Lee didn't contribute much of lasting value to the cinema's pre-Code years. Then came *The Count of Monte Cristo* (1934), an exemplary adaptation (co-scripted by Lee) of the classic adventure story, starring Robert Donat as a man unjustly imprisoned who gets the chance to savor his revenge. *Cardinal Richelieu* (1935) was a well-mounted bit of history Hollywood-style, starring George Arliss as the crafty Richelieu and Edward Arnold as the manipulatable Louis XIII.

Lee's version of *The Three Musketeers* (1935) suffered from a low-wattage cast (Walter Abel as D'Artagnan, in a year that saw Errol Flynn playing Captain Blood?), but the British-made *Love from a Stranger* (1937) gave Basil Rathbone a caddish role that he could chew for all it was worth, and *The Toast of New York* (also 1937) was a compelling (if fanciful) account of 1870s tycoon Jim Fisk; Edward Arnold, Cary Grant, and the ineffably lovely Frances Farmer starred. Next was the hopeless soaper *Mother Carey's Chickens* (1938), starring the luckless Anne Shirley and Ruby Keeler.

*The Son of Frankenstein* (1939) was the third entry in Universal's series, and the last to star Boris Karloff as the monster. Bela Lugosi was unforgettable as the demented Igor, Lionel Atwill was memorable as the one-armed Inspector Krogh, and Basil Rathbone was efficient as the eponymous Dr. Frankenstein, Jr. Less terrifying than James Whale's 1931 original and less sprightly than his 1935 *Bride of . . .* sequel, *Son of . . .* offers wonderful sets and a dignified approach that never again would be lavished on a Frankenstein picture; it's probably Lee's best film.

*Tower of London* (1939) wasn't up to that level, but Karloff and Rathbone were effective as, respectively, an implacable executioner and the cold-blooded Richard III. The historical adventure *The Sun Never Sets* (also 1939) teamed Rathbone and Atwill with Douglas Fairbanks, Jr., to good effect, and *The Son of Monte Cristo* (1940), with Louis Hayward avenging the wrongs his father left unsettled, was a solid swashbuckler. But *The Bridge of San Luis Rey* (1944) failed to capture the tragic scope of Thorton Wilder's novel, and *Captain Kidd* (1945) was a feeble pirate yarn, even with Charles Laughton as a florid Kidd.

## HENRY LEVIN (1909-1980)

Born in Trenton, New Jersey, Levin was an efficient contract director of "B"s and "B+"s after World War II, primarily for Columbia (1944–51), Fox (1952–59), and MGM (1960–64), ranging from film noir to historical adventure, from musicals to Westerns, from romantic comedy to horror and science fiction.

At Columbia, Levin's best pictures included *Cry of the Werewolf* (1944), an atmospheric chiller with Nina Foch and Osa Massen; *The Bandit of Sherwood Forest*, a Cornel Wilde swashbuckler, co-directed with George Sherman and one of seven features helmed by Levin in 1946; *The Guilt of Janet Ames* (1947), a taut melodrama starring Rosalind Russell and Melvyn Douglas; *Convicted* (1950), a prison drama with Glenn Ford and Broderick Crawford; *The Petty Girl* (1950), a silly romp with bland Bob Cummings cast as the famous pin-up artist, with his eye on coy Joan Caulfield; and *Two of a Kind* (1951), a good noir starring Edmond O'Brien and Lizabeth Scott as stone-hearted con artists.

Levin's work at Fox was generally innocuous, but *Belles on Their Toes* (1952), a sequel to *Cheaper by the Dozen*, was a big hit, as were *The Farmer Takes a Wife* (1953; a Betty Grable musical), and *April Love* (1957), a painless dose of Indiana corn with Pat Boone (whose title tune was a number-one hit) and Shirley Jones. *Journey to the Center of the Earth* (1959) also had Boone, but fortunately he was subordinate here to James Mason and the garden lizards standing in as dinosaurs. Levin's first picture for MGM was one of his biggest hits, and *Where the Boys Are* (1960), with its post-teen cast of Yvette Mimieux, George Hamilton, Jim Hutton, and Paula Prentiss on the prowl for romance and/or sex in Ft. Lauderdale, remains a classic of its kind.

Finally there was *Come Fly with Me* (1963), a leering romantic comedy starring Hugh O'Brien and Pamela Tiffin, and a pair of genuinely awful Dean Martin "Matt Helm" spy yarns, *Murderer's Row* (1966) and *The Ambushers* (1967). Levin's last effort was a television film, *Scout's Honor* (1980).

## ALBERT LEWIN (1894-1968)

Lewin spent the bulk of his Hollywood career as a screenwriter and producer, but he did direct six pictures between 1942 and 1957, several of which were quite interesting and most of which were more than a little pretentious; he also scripted all six. Born in Newark, New Jersey, Lewin was hired by MGM as a screenwriter in 1924, and by 1927 had become studio head Irving Thalberg's personal assistant and the head of MGM's story department. His producing credits during Thalberg's reign include *The Guardsman*, *Red-Headed Woman*, *Mutiny on the Bounty*, and *The Good Earth*.



The first picture Lewin directed was *The Moon and Sixpence* (1942), a classy adaptation of the Somerset Maugham story about an Englishman (George Sanders) who moves to Tahiti to paint; Herbert Marshall portrayed a Maugham-like writer. *The Picture of Dorian Gray* (1945), arguably Lewin's best movie, starred Hurd Hatfield as Oscar Wilde's ageless protagonist; the drop-dead decadent George Sanders and Angela Lansbury (who sings "Little Yellow Bird") are both wonderful in support, and Harry Stradling's cinematography won an Oscar. *The Private Affairs of Bel Ami* (1947), though nicely mounted, proved to be less popular; George Sanders and Angela Lansbury star again for Lewin, as Maupassant's roguish hero and the woman he foolishly forsakes.

*Pandora and the Flying Dutchman* (1947), shot in Spain, was a fascinating if longish (like most Lewin pictures, about two hours) romantic mystery; the exquisite Ava Gardner stars as an American playgirl whose love for supernatural drifter James Mason is literally doomed. Lewin had neither the luxury of top stars nor much of a story in *Saadia* (1954), but put Cornel Wilde, Mel Ferrer, and Rita Gam through their paces in this talky romance set in modern-day Morocco, while *The Living Idol* (1957) found archaeologists James Robertson Justice and Steve Forrest battling jaguars for the soul of Mayan reincarnee Liliane Montevecchi in the jungles of Mexico. Say this for Lewin, he never wasted his time (or ours) making a picture that moviegoers had seen before.

## JERRY LEWIS (1926- )

Either a certified genius or the most obnoxious actor/director on the face of the earth—or perhaps both—Newark-born Jerry Lewis (né Joseph Levitch) enjoyed an apotheosis of sorts as the spastic half of the Martin and Lewis team, which had started as a stage act in 1946 and then appeared in sixteen films for Paramount between 1949 and 1956. Their popularity reached such epic proportions that Lewis felt compelled to go solo. After a few years of enjoying the spotlight as a screen superstar who produced his own films, he decided—like Chaplin and Keaton before—to also direct himself, a function he probably had been assuming without portfolio for quite a while.



*The Bellboy* (1960) was his first effort behind the camera. Jerry played the eponymous hero, working at Miami Beach's Fountainbleau Hotel, to the dismay of guests Walter Winchell and Milton Berle; the film was fine, neither better nor worse than the bulk of the movies Lewis had made under the aegis of Frank Tashlin (who would continue to direct Lewis in alternating projects), Norman Taurog, Don McGuire, and various others. *The Ladies' Man* (1961) found Jerry working as a handyman at an all-girls school, under the unforgiving eye of Helen Traubel, while in *The Errand Boy* (1962), he goes beserk at a movie studio, driving old-timer Brian Donlevy to distraction. Better than any of these was *The Nutty Professor* (1963), which Lewis co-scripted from his own original story. Easily his best picture, it's a witty (and not entirely comical) takeoff on *Dr. Jekyll and Mr. Hyde*, with Jerry's hapless Professor Kelp transformed through the magic of chemistry into the smarmy, egocentric Buddy Love—a devastating parody of former partner Dean Martin—whose smug confidence helps attract the gorgeous Stella Stevens. (The 1995 remake with Eddie Murphy has its work cut out if it wants to top the original.)

The box-office success of *Professor* bode well for Lewis, but he never made another movie nearly as good. *The Patsy* (1964) was a lame farce about a bellhop who is trained to replace a recently deceased star, while *The Family Jewels* (1965) was a perverse *tour de force*; Jerry essays no fewer than seven roles—the sort of wretched excess that always had threatened to infect his career. His films grew progressively less funny, and ever more out of touch with the taste of American moviegoers: *Three on a Couch* (1966), with Jerry restricting himself to just five roles, as he tries to woo psychiatrist Janet Leigh; *The Big Mouth* (1967), with Jerry searching for treasure; the abysmal *One More Time* (1970), starring Peter Lawford and Sammy Davis, Jr. (and the only film Lewis directed without acting in it); and *Which Way to the Front?* (1970), a World War II comedy that was alarmingly unfunny.

As he established the garish spectacle of the Muscular Dystrophy Telethon in the seventies, a 24-hour, televised fund-raiser that is essentially beyond description, Lewis seemed to lose interest in filmmaking. His unreleased 1974 opus, *The Day the Clown Cried*, about a clown who helps lead concentration-camp children to the gas chambers, is the stuff of legend, while *Hardly Working* (1981) was hardly seen. *Smorgasbord* (1983; aka *Cracking Up*) was a barely released revue in which Jerry and pals Milton Berle and Sammy Davis, Jr., take turns appearing in "zany" sketches. He fared better as an actor in Martin Scorsese's *The King of Comedy*, willingly skewering his own reputation as a show-business mandarin of little warmth; in the television series *Wiseguy*, as a mobbed-up garment manufacturer; in Susan Seidelman's *Cookie*; and on stage in the 1995 revival of *Damn Yankees*. But it seems more and more likely that Jerry Lewis will never stand behind the camera again. Except for the French, whose love of his oeuvre is as genuine as it is inexplicable, few are likely to complain.

## GEORGE LUCAS (1944- )

It's increasingly difficult to recall that for most of the 1970s the names of Martin Scorsese, Francis Ford

Coppola, and Steven Spielberg were rarely uttered without that of George Lucas being invoked as well. But it's been nearly twenty years since he directed *Star Wars*, his third and (to date) last picture, and there is no indication that he intends to return to the ranks now that he's (arguably) the world's most successful producer.

Born in Modesto, California, during the Second World War, Lucas was a car-racing fanatic as a teenager until a near-fatal crash convinced him to give up the sport. He turned to moviemaking, graduating from U.C.L.A.'s film school in 1966 after a six-month internship at Warner Bros. and several highly acclaimed student films under his belt, including the futuristic parable *THX 1138: 4EB*, which took First Prize at the National Student Film Festival in 1965.

That was sufficient to win Lucas a scholarship that enabled him to assist Francis Ford Coppola on *Finian's Rainbow*. Lucas followed that experience by shooting "Making of . . ." documentaries about Coppola's *The Rain People* and the Carl Foreman–J. Lee Thompson adventure *Mackenna's Gold*. Lucas shot a portion of the Altamont documentary *Gimme Shelter* for the Maysles, then signed with Warners to direct a feature-length version of *THX 1138*, with Coppola executive-producing and Robert Duvall and Maggie McOmie starring as the illicit lovers. It was released in 1971 to respectful reviews, although its obvious debt to *1984* and overly deliberate pace kept it from being embraced too enthusiastically by either critics or audiences.

He found his next feature, *American Graffiti* (1973), much more warmly received. One of the year's biggest—and most unexpected—hits, it was co-scripted by Lucas and was redolent of his own days as a Modesto hot-rodding nerd back in '62, the year in which the film is set. Shot in less than a month for well under a million dollars, *Graffiti* became the sixteenth-biggest-grossing film of the decade—and with its modest cast of newcomers (including Richard Dreyfuss, Paul LeMat, Cindy Williams, and erstwhile child star Ron Howard) and unassuming L.A. locales may have been the most profitable. Executive producer Coppola had had to fight with Universal execs to ensure the film's release; $100 million later, Universal undoubtedly was glad they listened to him.

The success of *Graffiti* enabled Lucas to finance a project that had been dear to his heart for some time. Science fiction had traditionally been a poor box-office performer, with such rare exceptions as *Planet of the Apes* and *2001: A Space Odyssey* only proving the rule. But with *Star Wars* (1977), which he also wrote, Lucas eschewed high-tech dystopian allegory in favor of space opera synthesized with vintage Hollywood swashbucklers and frontier adventures. Lucas founded his Industrial Light and Magic state-of-the-art F/X company in Marin County specifically to serve the demands of *Star Wars*, which like *Graffiti* had an unprepossessing cast: Harrison Ford (*before* he was Harrison Ford), Mark Hamill, Carrie Fisher, the voice of James Earl Jones, and, in what amounted to a cameo, Alec Guinness.

Lucas came up with eye-popping (for the day) *F/X*, but his lively script—which included equal measures of suspense, humor, and drama—was just as responsible for the film's unprecedented success. It would be nominated for ten Oscars, and won six—but only in "minor" categories, a fate that had befallen Spielberg's *Jaws* two years earlier. But its box-office gross would grow to an astonishing $322 million by 1994, making it the third-biggest picture of all time, behind *E.T.* and *Jurassic Park*.

*Star Wars* also spawned two enormously popular sequels, *The Empire Strikes Back* (1980) and *Return of the Jedi* (1983), which collectively took in another $500 million—but Lucas did not direct them, instead handing over the reins to Irvin Kershner (*Empire*) and Richard Marquand (*Return*); their names may someday pop up in a Trivial Pursuit question. Through the '80s and '90s, Lucas has overseen (and sometimes written) such pictures as *Raiders of the Lost Ark*, *Indiana Jones and the Temple of Doom* (both directed by Spielberg), the mega-bomb *Howard the Duck*, Jim Henson's *Labyrinth*, the fine animated feature *The Land before Time*, Francis Ford Coppola's *Tucker: The Man and His Dreams*, Ron Howard's exciting sword-and-sorcery saga *Willow*, and *Indiana Jones and the Last Crusade* (Spielberg again).

His much-ballyhooed television series, *Young Indiana Jones*, failed to get the ratings that would have justified its enormous cost, and his production *The Radioland Murders* was so poor that it made barely a blip at the box office in 1994, despite a wave of national publicity by the suddenly accessible Lucas. In that publicity, he admitted that he had begun writing the screenplays for the *Star Wars* prequels, and that a fourth Indiana Jones film was on the drawing board. Whether he deigns to direct them or not, Lucas knows there's a billion dollars or two waiting to be spent by moviegoers the instant those pictures become reality—quite a testament to a man who's directed all of three films.

## DANIEL MANN (1912-1991)

As inexplicably happens with so many directors who come out of the theater, Daniel Mann's first few films proved to be his best—although he would make twenty-three in all, as well as some television films, one of which is among the best ever made. He also had the satisfaction of helping no fewer than three actresses to an Oscar. Born in Brooklyn as Daniel Chugerman, Mann was raised as something of a prodigy, attending New York's Professional Children's School and training as both a musician and an actor. After serving in World War II, he directed stage productions and worked on Broadway with Elia Kazan before moving briefly to television.

Mann's first film was an adaptation of the William Inge play *Come Back, Little Sheba* (1952). Shirley Booth repeated her stage role as a desperately unhappy, motor-mouthed wife whose ex-alcoholic husband (Burt Lancaster) cannot bear listening to her delusions; Booth won the best actress Oscar, and Terry Moore was also nominated for best supporting actress. The tearjerker *About Mrs. Leslie* (1954) found Booth in fine form again, now as the lover of tycoon Robert Ryan, while Tennessee Williams's lauded *The Rose Tattoo* (1955), which Mann had directed on stage in 1950, had Italian actress Anna Magnani as a repressed widow and Burt Lancaster as the hunky truck driver whose elemental passion gets her motor started again. The film was nominated for an Academy Award as best picture, and Magnani and cinematographer James Wong Howe won Oscars.

Mann's early success continued with *I'll Cry Tomorrow* (1955), an effective drama based on the autobiography of torch singer Lillian Roth; Susan Hayward was nominated for an Oscar for her performance as Roth, and Richard Conte was fine as her sadistic spouse. *Teahouse of the August Moon* (1957) was a first-rate adaptation of the Tony-award-winning Broadway play, which had starred David Wayne as the resourceful Okinawan Sakini; here the part is essayed by Marlon Brando, in a bold departure from his recent roles, while Glenn Ford plays straight man and Paul Ford re-creates his stage role.

To this point Mann had done nicely transferring Broadway hits to the screen, but as he moved away from that source, the quality of his work declined. *Hot Spell* (1958) was a turgid soap opera, with Shirley Booth, Shirley MacLaine, and Anthony Quinn, and *The Last Angry Man* (1959) was an only intermittently effective version of a Gerald Green novel, starring Paul Muni and David Wayne. *Butterfield 8* (1960) did win Elizabeth Taylor her first Academy Award, but it was a flavorless, bowdlerized version of the great John O'Hara novel, helped not at all by the casting of Liz's then-husband Eddie Fisher in a dramatic role beyond his pale. *Ada* (1961) managed to combine Susan Hayward and Dean Martin to good effect in this Washington, D.C., soaper, but Mann botched his adaptation of the play *Five Finger Exercise* (1962), while *Who's Got the Action?* (1962) and *Who's Been Sleeping in My Bed?* (1963) were a deadly pair of comic vehicles for Dean Martin.

*Our Man Flint* (1966) was a decent-enough parody of the James Bond pictures, starring James Coburn as the suavest of superspies and Gila Golan as his curvaceous romantic interest, but *For Love of Ivy* (1968) was an utterly embarrassing romantic comedy starring Sidney Poitier and Abbey Lincoln. Better was *A Dream of Kings* (1969), with Anthony Quinn and Irene Papas well cast as Greek immigrants trying to return to the old country, while *Willard* (1971) somehow translated an inane story of boy-rat love into an enormous box-office smash.

After a string of flops, Mann returned to television, where he scored a success with *How the West Was Won* (1977), an epic miniseries co-directed with Burt Kennedy, and *Playing for Time* (1980), a powerful drama based on the life of Fania Fenelon, a musician in a female orchestra at Auschwitz who survived the horrors of the camp because of her talent. Vanessa Redgrave won an Emmy for her nuanced performance as the indomitable Fenelon, as did Jane Alexander, scenarist Arthur Miller, and the production itself. Mann made two more television films, then retired in 1987.

## DELBERT MANN (1920- )

From television to the movies and back again, Delbert Mann reached the pinnacle of his career early on, then proceeded to labor in the near-anonymity of the made-for-television movie for more than twenty years. Born in Lawrence, Kansas, he attended the Yale School of Drama before serving in World War II as an Air Force bomber pilot. After the war he gravitated toward the stage, directing stock productions. In 1949 Mann joined NBC and soon was directing features for Philco Playhouse, one of the most prestigious live-television showcases for drama. He directed two of Paddy Chayevsky's best teleplays, *Marty* and *The Bachelor Party*, the success of which provided Mann with his entry to Hollywood.

*Marty* (1955) became his maiden big-screen effort, and its phenomenal popularity with critics and audiences propelled him to that rarest of achievements, an Academy Award for best direction on the first try. *Marty* won Oscars for best picture, actor (Ernest Borgnine), and screenplay (Chayevsky)—quite a sweep for a rather dull movie that basically re-creates the television version, although Rod Steiger is supplanted here by Borgnine. (Nearly forty years later, the film's immense popularity in 1955 remains something of a puzzle.) The caustic *The Bachelor Party* (1957), with Carolyn Jones, Don Murray, and E. G. Marshall holds up better, but *Desire under the Elms* (1958) was overcooked Eugene O'Neill; Sophia Loren and Anthony Perkins make one of the least convincing romantic tandems in movie history.

*Separate Tables* (1958), adapted from his play by Terence Rattigan, was a potent drama that covered adultery, divorce, spinsterhood, and most other forms of unhappiness. David Niven and Wendy Hiller won Oscars, and Rita Hayworth and Burt Lancaster were just as fine. But *Middle of the Night* (1959) was molasses onscreen, despite (or because of?) another Chayevsky screenplay. Mann's propensity for adapting stage vehicles continued with *The Dark at the Top of the Stairs* (1960), a tepid version of the William Inge play that at least offered a good turn by Angela Lansbury. *The Outsider* (1961), a biopic about the heroic American Indian Marine Ira Hamilton Hayes, who helped raise the flag at Iwo Jima, enabled Mann to finally break away from theatrical dramas; a strong performance by Tony Curtis as Hayes anchors the film.

With *Lover Come Back* (1961) and *That Touch of Mink* (1962) Mann demonstrated a deft comic touch; Doris Day and Rock Hudson in the former are just a tad more wonderful than Day and Cary Grant in *Mink*, although both films remain enjoyable examples of early Sixties romantic comedy. Hudson was also fine in the flyboy pic *A Gathering of Eagles* (1963), and Glenn Ford and Geraldine Page made the romantic agonies of *Dear Heart* (1964) more interesting than the title sounds. But *Quick Before It Melts* (also 1964), with researcher George Maharis trying to lure girls to an Antarctic compound, is a leading candidate for the decade's stupidest movie. *Mister Buddwing* (1966) had amnesia victim James Garner trying to learn about his past life from Suzanne Pleshette and Katharine Ross, but it was a pallid drama, and *Fitzwilly* (1967) was a poor comedy in which butler Dick Van Dyke tries to rob Gimbel's on Christmas Eve—for a good cause, of course.

This string of flops helped turn Mann's eye to directing films for television, which would comprise the bulk of his output over the next twenty-five years. Among the highlights: *Heidi* (1968), best remembered now for interrupting the classic New York Jets–Oakland Raiders football playoff game; *David Copperfield* (1970), with its impressive cast of Michael Redgrave, Edith Evans, Ralph Richardson, and Laurence Olivier; *Jane Eyre* (1971), starring George C. Scott and Susannah York; *Breaking Up* (1978), with Lee Remick as a mother of two deserted by her husband; and *All Quiet on the Western Front* (1979), with Patricia Neal, Ernest Borgnine, and Richard Thomas, which was nominated for several Emmy awards.

*Night Crossing* (1981) was a theatrically released Disney production based on the real-life escape by two families from East Germany via hot-air balloons, with John Hurt and Jane Alexander heading a good cast, while *Brontë* (1983) set Julie Harris's one-woman monologue about the life of Charlotte Brontë against stunning Irish locations. Mann then made the television films *A Death in California* (1985), a fact-based drama starring Sam Elliot and Cheryl Ladd as a rapist and victim who bond; *The Last Days of Patton* (1986), with George C. Scott returning to the scene of his earlier (and much more impressive) triumph; and *The Ted Kennedy, Jr., Story* (1986), a surprisingly good account of how the senator's son adjusted to losing his leg to cancer.

Mann's *Against Her Will: An Incident in Baltimore* (1992) was an excellent made-for-TV period drama, with Walter Matthau as a small-town attorney in the 1940s who takes on an unpopular case (as his character did in the 1991 predecessor, *The Incident*); *Incident in a Small Town* (1993) had Matthau reprising that rôle.

## RUDOLPH ("RUDY") MATÉ (1898–1964)

One of the greatest cinematographers of the 1930s and '40s, Rudy Maté was far less impressive as a director, although his name is attached to at least a few enduring genre classics. Born as Rudolf Matheh in Cracow, Poland, he began in films in 1919, after Alexander Korda hired him as an assistant cameraman. He spent years working in Berlin and Vienna before moving to France in the late Twenties, where he shot several of Carl Dreyer's most important pictures, including the 1932 *Vampyr*, and also photographed films directed by Fritz Lang and René Clair. In 1935, Maté followed Lang to Hollywood, where he soon established himself as one of the industry's most gifted directors of photography; his impressive credits in this capacity include *Dodsworth*, *Stella Dallas*, *Love Affair*, *Foreign Correspondent*, *That Hamilton Woman* (for which Maté was Oscar-nominated), *To Be or Not to Be*, *Sahara*, and *Gilda*.

Maté co-directed *It Had to Be You* with Don Hartman in 1947, then made his solo debut with *The Dark Past* (1949), a talky remake of the 1939 *Blind Alley*; here it's William Holden playing the disturbed killer and Lee J. Cobb the analyst being held hostage who uses the powers of psychoanalysis to outwit him. Far more impressive was *D.O.A.* (1950), a superior film noir that offered Edmond O'Brien at his tormented best as a businessman slowly dying of poison who has forty-eight hours to solve the mysteries of who wanted to kill him, why, and whether there's an antidote. Shot on location in Los Angeles and San Francisco, *D.O.A.* is a model of stylish suspense made on a low budget, with fine support from second-tier actors like Pamela Britton, Neville Brand, and Luther Adler.



Maté never made another picture that good, though not for want of trying. *Union Station* (1950) was a decent suspenser, with William Holden and Barry Fitzgerald as cops on the trail of kidnapper Lyle Bettger, but *Branded* (1951) was a formulaic Alan Ladd Western, and *The Prince Who Was a Thief* (also 1951), a silly (if colorful) costume adventure starring Tony Curtis and Piper Laurie. *When Worlds Collide* (1951) was a spectacular adaptation of a science-fiction novel by Edwin Balmer and Philip Wylie, but the best parts of the picture—George Pal's special effects—can hardly be credited to Maté.

Little of Maté's subsequent work rewards multiple viewing. There's *Paula* (1952), a soap opera starring Loretta Young, on whose television series Maté would work in years to come; *Second Chance* (1953), a passable noir originally released in 3-D and starring Robert Mitchum, Linda Darnell, and evil Jack Palance; the handsomely mounted but inane *The Black Shield of Falworth* (1954), with real-life newlyweds Tony Curtis and Janet Leigh seriously miscast as a medieval knight and his high-born lady; the forgettable Western *The Violent Men* (1955), starring Barbara Stanwyck and Glenn Ford; *The Far Horizons* (1955), with Fred MacMurray and Charlton Heston a rather unconvincing Lewis and Clark; and the tear-jerking *Miracle in the Rain* (1956), with Jane Wyman and Van Johnson adrift in New York City. Maté's last years were divided between action spectacles like the awful *The 300 Spartans* (1962) and various European productions. He died of a heart attack in 1964.

## WILLIAM CAMERON MENZIES (1896–1957)

His accomplishments as a director will always take a back seat to his reputation as an award-winning art director and set designer, most famously winning a special Oscar for "outstanding achievement in the use of color" in *Gone with the Wind*. And yet William Cameron Menzies did make a handful of films that will not soon be forgotten. Born in New Haven, he began his Hollywood career as the art director on *The Teeth of the Tiger* in 1919 and served the same function on such silent classics as the Douglas Fairbanks *The Thief of Bagdad*; *Cobra*, *The Eagle*, and *Son of the Sheik*, all with Valentino; and *Sadie Thompson*, before winning the first "interior direction" Academy Award ever given for the 1928 films *The Dove* and *The Tempest*.

He co-directed his first five pictures, low-budget affairs like the 1934 Bela Lugosi serial *Chandu the Magician*. Menzies's first solo directing credit was on Alexander Korda's spectacular $1.5 million British production *Things to Come* (1936), co-scripted by H. G. Wells himself; Raymond Massey starred in a dual role as the visionary Cabal, who survives the fall of one futuristic society and whose grandson (also Massey) helps rebuild the next. Talky, stilted, and long (although a half hour was chopped out of many U.S. releases), the film nonetheless possesses a singular visual beauty quite unlike any other film of its time, thanks both to Menzies and the day's *other* premier art director, Vincent Korda.

After directing one more picture in England, Menzies returned to the States to work on *Gone with the Wind*, on which he held the title of production designer. He followed that roaring success by designing such major productions as Hitchcock's *Foreign Correspondent* and Sam Woods's *For Whom the Bell Tolls* before directing the cautionary political fable *Address Unknown* (1944), starring Paul Lukas. He shot a few scenes in Selznick's *Duel in the Sun* after King Vidor was let go, but didn't direct again until 1951, when he made a pair of "B"s for RKO: *Drums in the Deep South*, a potboiler set during the Civil War, with Barbara Payton; and *The Whip Hand*, a quasi-science-fiction yarn about a Commie plot to conquer the United States by unleashing germ warfare from the Canadian border. Starring Raymond Burr as a Soviet thug, the film had an ideology that only rabid anti-Communists (including RKO studio head Howard Hughes) could love.

*Invaders from Mars* (1953) is probably Menzies's best-known and most-loved work. Made during the height of the science-fiction craze, it's a nightmarish, at times surrealistic, tale told from the perspective of little Jimmy Hunt, who sees a Martian saucer descend in a field but finds no adults willing to believe him until it's too late and most of the town has been turned into slaves—including parents Leif Erickson and Hillary Brooke. This gave an entire generation nightmares, and Menzies's art direction is still a model of low-budget resourcefulness. *The Maze* (1953), a horror yarn shot in 3-D and starring Richard Carlson, was less memorable, although Menzies bolstered the weak plot with his usual stylish art direction.

## ROY WILLIAM NEILL (1886–1946)

During a full thirty years of directing feature films, Roy William Neill (né Roland de Gostrie) rarely elevated a project above the level expected of it—generally the "B" end of a double bill. And yet his 1940s work for Universal, particularly on the Sherlock Holmes series, is still viewed with affection today, while so many bigger-budgeted contemporary productions have fallen by the wayside.

Born on a boat off the coast of Ireland, he went to work for Thomas Ince in 1915 and two years later found himself directing features. Few of his silents sound familiar, although the titles *Vive la France!*, *Radio-Mania*, and *The Kiss Barrier* intrigue. His early talkies seem just as obscure—*The Good Bad Girl*, *The Circus Queen Murder*, and *Fury of the Jungle* may be lost classics, or just lost. But we do know that *The Lone Wolf Returns* (1935), with Melvyn Douglas essaying the role of the suave jewel thief, was a fine genre entry. Neill then moved to England, where he made nine features between 1937 and 1939. The best of these is probably *Dr. Syn* (1937), starring George Arliss as a mild-mannered vicar who moonlights as a smuggler when the sun goes down.

In 1942 Neill returned to Hollywood, where he directed a string of modest but skillfully made "B"s for Universal. The best remembered are the Sherlock Holmes franchise with Basil Rathbone and Nigel Bruce, all just over an hour long: *Sherlock Holmes and the Secret Weapon* (1942); *Sherlock Holmes in Washington*, *Sherlock Holmes Faces Death* (both 1943); *Sherlock Holmes and the Spider Woman*, *The Scarlet Claw*, *The Pearl of Death* (all 1944); *The House of Fear*, *The Woman in Green*, *Pursuit to Algiers* (all 1945); and *Terror by Night* and *Dressed to Kill* (both 1946).

Also for Universal, Neill did an adequate job on the cult favorite *Frankenstein Meets the Wolfman* (1943) and the Maria Montez yarn *Gypsy Wildcat* (1944). The noir *Black Angel* (1946) was his last picture; a fine adaptation of the Cornell Woolrich thriller, it starred Dan Duryea, Peter Lorre, and the ineffable Ella Raines.



## RALPH NELSON (1916–1987)

Yet another of the many, many directors who began as actors before moving behind the camera, New York City–born Ralph Nelson began acting on stage as a teenager and appeared on Broadway in the late Thirties. He joined the Air Force in World War II and became a flight instructor, then returned to the stage. By 1948 he had broken into the nascent television industry, and began writing, directing, and occasionally acting in hundreds of live productions. Rod Serling's Playhouse 90 teleplay *Requiem for a Heavyweight* won a directing Emmy for Nelson in 1956; it starred Jack Palance as an over-the-hill boxer who turns to professional wrestling on the advice of his avaricious manager.

*Requiem* became Nelson's first theatrical film in 1962 when he directed it for the screen, with Anthony Quinn now in the title role and Jackie Gleason as his exploitive manager; Mickey Rooney and Julie Harris made an impact in supporting roles, and the young Cassius Clay had a cameo as a boxer who beats Quinn to a pulp. *Lilies of the Field* (1963) was even more successful, a well-observed, good-hearted drama about an antisocial, erstwhile G.I. (Sidney Poitier) whose travels around the United States are interrupted when he agrees to help a group of impoverished German nuns build a chapel; Nelson made his screen acting debut as a building contractor who donates his services. Poitier was awarded the best actor Oscar—the first black actor ever to receive one—and *Lilies* was also nominated as best picture.

*Soldier in the Rain* (1963), an eccentric but likable military yarn, starred Steve McQueen, Jackie Gleason, and Tuesday Weld, while *Fate Is the Hunter* (1964) was an adequate suspenser about a plane-crash investigation headed by Glenn Ford and Rod Taylor. The amiable *Father Goose* (1964) had Cary Grant cast against type as a South Seas beach bum, while *Duel at Diablo* (1966) was an excellent Western starring James Garner and Sidney Poitier. Nelson guided Cliff Robertson to the best-actor Oscar with *Charly* (1968), a popular expansion of Daniel Keyes's classic science-fiction story "Flowers for Algernon"; Cliff Robertson, repeating the role he had essayed on television in 1961, plays a retarded man temporarily transformed into a genius after scientists give him an experimental drug.

Nelson fared less well in the Seventies. The most infamous of his later pictures was *Soldier Blue* (1970), an ultra-violent "statement" about the U.S. Cavalry's Indian massacres that is clearly intended to parallel the government's policy in Vietnam. *The Wilby Conspiracy* (1975), with Sidney Poitier at his best as an African radical whose flight from the authorities takes unhappy companion Michael Caine along, has its moments. Nelson's last two films were made-for-television enterprises: *Christmas Lilies of the Field*, with Billy Dee Williams assuming the Poitier role, and *You Can't Go Home Again* (both 1979), a so-so version of Thomas Wolfe's famous novel, starring Chris Sarandon and Lee Grant.



## PAUL NEWMAN (1925- )

This Oscar-winning actor, who has moonlighted as an art-house director when not racing cars and developing new politically and nutritionally correct food products, might have become one of today's top directors had he committed all his energies to that profession. Newman was one of America's biggest box-office stars when he produced and directed *Rachel, Rachel* in 1968; it stars Joanne Woodward (Newman's wife since 1958) as a repressed spinster living with her widowed mother who tries to find love before it's too late. This subtle but powerful movie was nominated for a best picture Academy Award—an amazing honor for a first film to garner—and Woodward and screenwriter Stewart Stern also received Oscar nominations. Newman won the New York Film Critics Circle Award for best direction, and the same body gave Woodward the nod as best actress.

*Rachel* was a hard act to follow, and Newman's adaptation of Ken Kesey's sprawling novel about Oregon loggers, *Sometimes a Great Notion* (1971), fell short, even with a cast that includes himself, Henry Fonda, and Lee Remick. He next filmed the Pulitzer Prize–winning drama *The Effect of Gamma Rays on Man-in-the-Moon Marigolds* (1972), adapted by playwright Paul Zindel and starring Joanne Woodward as "Betty the Loon," a sarcastic mother whose daughters long to escape from her domineering presence. Made for television, the potent *The Shadow Box* (1980), about the interaction among three terminally ill patients and their visiting families, starred Woodward, Valerie Harper, and Christopher Plummer, and was adapted from his Tony Award–winning and Pulitzer Prize–winning play by Michael Cristofer.

The misconceived *Harry and Son* (1984) featured Newman and Robby Benson as a widowed father and his unsympathetic son, but its dynamics were less than convincing, despite Newman's having co-written the screenplay, while *The Glass Menagerie* (1987) was Newman's tasteful adaptation of Tennessee Williams's classic play; Joanne Woodward, John Malkovich, Karen Allen, and James Naughton starred, all of whom fared at least as well as their predecessors in Irving Rapper's 1950 version.

## ELLIOTT NUGENT (1899-1980)

His father, John Charles Nugent, was an actor and author of more than a hundred plays, and his mother a vaudeville performer, so it was perhaps inevitable that the pride of Dover, Ohio, was fated to become a part of show business. Elliott Nugent will always be thought of as a house director for Paramount—he did, after all, make eighteen of his thirty-one films there—but only a handful of them remain of interest today.

After performing in vaudeville with his parents as a child, Nugent began acting on Broadway in 1921, and thereafter alternated between treading the boards and playwriting. He broke into Hollywood as an actor in 1925, and went on to appear in a dozen movies. But by 1932 Nugent had made the decision to direct. His Thirties pictures alternated between screwball comedies and tearjerkers, none terribly memorable—*Whistling in the Dark*, about a radio sleuth; the breathless comedy *Three-Cornered Moon*, with Claudette Colbert and Mary Boland; the weepie *If I Were Free* (all 1933), with Irene Dunne and Clive Brook; the musical comedy *She Loves Me Not* (1934), starring that perpetual college sophomore, Bing Crosby; *Love in Bloom* (1935) with George Burns and Gracie Allen; and *Professor Beware* (1938), starring Harold Lloyd in his penultimate film as a hapless archaeologist.

In 1939 Nugent was assigned to mold radio comedian and budding screen draw Bob Hope into an "A" picture lead, and this he did impressively with *The Cat and the Canary*, a happy pairing of Hope with Paulette Goddard, and *Never Say Die* (also 1939), in which Hope is teamed with Martha Raye to good effect. Nugent then returned to Broadway and scored his biggest success there with *The Male Animal*, which he co-wrote with fellow Ohio State alumnus James Thurber; Nugent had the clout to also cast himself as the lead. After directing Hope and Goddard in the hilarious *Nothing but the Truth* (1941), Nugent adapted *The Male Animal* (1942) for the screen, although this time he was humble enough to let Henry Fonda play the lead role of a college professor who competes with Jack Carson for wife Olivia de Havilland's affections.

Nugent's subsequent pictures rarely reached that level. *The Crystal Ball* (1943) was a so-so romantic comedy starring Paulette Goddard and Ray Milland, while *Up in Arms* (1944) was a frenetic but not especially amusing Danny Kaye vehicle. The film noir spoof *My Favorite Brunette* (1947) certainly worked, with Bob Hope and Dorothy Lamour menaced by thugs Peter Lorre and Lon Chaney. But Nugent's sequel to *Sitting Pretty* with Clifton Webb, *Mr. Belvedere Goes to College* (1949), fell flat. So did *The Great Gatsby* (1949), Nugent's well-intentioned but dull version of the F. Scott Fitzgerald classic; Alan Ladd and Betty Field are hopelessly miscast as Jay and Daisy. After three more films, Nugent left Hollywood for good, directing and producing stage productions while battling mental illness. His autobiography, *Events Leading Up to the Comedy*, was published in 1965.

## GEORGE PAL (1908-1980)

A special-effects wizard—with five Academy Awards to prove it—George Pal always fared better with his mythical creatures, underground monsters, and colliding planets than with ordinary human actors. Yet each of his five feature films offers something special. Born in Cegled, Hungary, he studied architecture before becoming a set designer at Germany's UFA studio. Moving to Hollywood, where he signed a contract with Paramount, in 1940, Pal continued the screen experiments he had begun in Europe with stop-motion animated puppets by developing the Puppetoons series. There were eventually a total of forty-two, including "Hoola Boola," Dr. Seuss's "The 500 Hats of Bartholomew Cubbins," and "Jasper's Haunted House," and they earned Pal a special Oscar in 1943.

After the Puppetoons franchise was shuttered by Paramount in 1948 because of rising costs, Pal turned to feature-film work. His special effects for Irving Pichel's *Destination Moon* (1950), Rudy Maté's *When Worlds Collide* (1951), and Byron Haskin's *War of the Worlds* (1953) won him an entire mantelful of Oscars. Accepting a deal to produce and design films for MGM, Pal made his feature-directing debut with *tom thumb* (1958), a Disneyesque version of the famous children's story, featuring dancer Russ Tamblyn in the title role; Pal took the opportunity to toss in a Puppetoons sequence, and won another special-effects Academy Award for his trouble.

*The Time Machine* (1960), made in England, was even more spectacular. Rod Taylor starred as H. G. Wells's intrepid time traveler, and Yvette Mimieux was most appealing as Weena, the inarticulate Eloi girl he saves from the monstrous Morlocks, then falls in love with, 800,000 years into the future. The film was a major box-office success, and Pal won his fifth, and final, Oscar for special effects. *Atlantis, the Lost Continent* (1961) was Pal's only lemon—a no-name cast struggling through a so-what story until the island sinks, as we all knew it would in the first place. But *The Wonderful World of the Brothers Grimm*

(1962), a Cinerama production starring Laurence Harvey and Claire Bloom, delivered the goods. The film was co-directed with Henry Levin, but Pal's contributions are clear enough: lots and lots of exotic dragons and other creatures, and another terrific Puppetoons sequence.

Pal's last film, *7 Faces of Dr. Lao* (1964), based on Charles G. Finney's novel, was a fantasy set in the nineteenth-century American West. Tony Randall stars in the title role of a magician from the Orient whose exotic traveling circus is capable of teaching many lessons to those willing to listen. Randall was obliged to assume the aspects of Pan, Merlin, the Abominable Snowman, a dragon, and sundry other fantastic beings—fabulous stuff, and one can only imagine what wonders the pioneering Pal might have wrought had he lived into the modern-day era, with the technology now available. His Puppetoon shorts became available to a new generation with the release of the 1987 compilation *The Puppetoon Movie*.

## FRANK PERRY (1930– )

One of those rare directors whose very first feature was nominated for an Academy Award, Frank Perry failed to maintain that early promise, and his critical and commercial successes since then have been few and far between. Born in New York City, he worked as a stage manager and producer before moving into television and filmwork. He studied directing under Lee Strasberg and applied what he had learned impressively on the low-budget *David and Lisa* (1962), an independently made film (coproduced by Perry) about an emotionally ill young man (Keir Dullea) who is institutionalized by his parents; he learns to love fellow patient Janet Margolin under the care of a kindly psychiatrist (Howard Da Silva). Written by Perry's wife, Eleanor, who dramatized a case history from a book by Dr. Theodore Rubin, the film won an award for Perry at the Venice Film Festival and earned him an Academy Award nomination for best direction.

The fact-based *Ladybug, Ladybug* (1963), also written by Eleanor Perry, was a rather heavy-handed duck-'n'-cover drama about the effect of a civil defense miscue on a group of rural schoolchildren, while the existential allegory *The Swimmer* (1968) sent Burt Lancaster on an odyssey across the swimming pools of a wealthy Connecticut town; Eleanor Perry brilliantly adapted the disturbing John Cheever story. *Last Summer* (1969) was a provocative version of Evan Hunter's novel about four teenagers (Richard Thomas, Cathy Burns, Bruce Davison, and Barbara Hershey) whose sexual experimentation leads to tragedy.

The Perrys' greatest success may have been *Diary of a Mad Housewife* (1970), a chilling black comedy (adapted by Eleanor from the novel by Sue Kaufman) about the inexorable crack-up of an upscale suburban mother (the Oscar-nominated Carrie Snodgrass) whose monstrously self-centered husband (Richard Benjamin) and snotty kids have driven her into the arms of self-centered but passionate Frank Langella. It was all downhill from there for Frank Perry, whose marriage to Eleanor dissolved in 1970. *Doc* (1971), scripted by Pete Hamill, was a wise-guy debunking of the Wyatt Earp–Doc Holliday legend that starred Stacy Keach and Harris Yulin, while *Play It As It Lays* (1972) was a pretentious botch of the nihilistic Joan Didion novel, a waste of Tuesday Weld as the abused wife of movie director Anthony Perkins.

*Man on a Swing* (1974) was a muddled thriller, with Cliff Robertson as a cop who needs the help of clairvoyant Joel Grey. *Rancho Deluxe* (1975), scripted by Thomas McGuane, was an amiable contemporary Western about two hippie cattle rustlers (Jeff Bridges and Sam Waterston), while *Dummy* (1979), an excellent made-for-television drama, dealt with the true case of a deaf-and-dumb black boy (LeVar Burton) who is defended from a murder charge by a Chicago attorney (Paul Sorvino). But *Mommie Dearest* (1981) was a campy biopic of Joan Crawford, based on daughter Christina's bestselling memoir, starring a *way*-over-the-top Faye Dunaway. *Monsignor* (1982)—easily one of the decade's worst movies—starred the ludicrously miscast Christopher Reeve as a priest who rises to power at the Vatican while violating every tenet of Catholicism.

After these nuclear bombs, the modest deficiencies of the lightweight suburban murder mystery *Compromising Positions* (1985; from the bestseller by Susan Isaacs) and *Hello Again* (1987), a flat reincarnation comedy (again based on a book by Isaacs) seem practically irrelevant—although take the former, with Susan Sarandon and Judith Ivey, over the latter, with Shelley Long and Ivey, if push comes to shove. Perry's most recent work is the autobiographical documentary *On the Bridge* (1992).

## IRVING PICHEL (1891–1954)

There are a number of directors who performed in front of the camera before moving behind it, but not many who compiled impressive filmographies in both areas. The Pittsburgh-born Pichel acted on stage after finishing Harvard, then went to work for MGM as a writer in 1927. In 1930 he signed with Paramount as an actor, beginning a phase of his career that lasted intermittently throughout the decade. He was in *An American Tragedy*, *Madame Butterfly*, *Oliver Twist* (as Fagin), *Cleopatra*, *British Agent* (as Stalin!), *Dracula's Daughter*, *Jezebel*, and *Juárez*, among others.

But almost as soon as his screen-acting career commenced, Pichel also began to direct at RKO. His debut was the classic *The Most Dangerous Game* (1932), which he co-directed with Ernest B. Schoedsack. *Before Dawn* (1933) was next, followed by the imaginative *She* (1935), directed in collaboration with Lansing C. Holden. He spent the next few years at Republic working on "B" features like *Larceny of the Air* and *The Duke Comes Back* (both 1937) before moving to Fox, where more prestigious work awaited him. *Earthbound* and *The Man I Married* (both 1940) were his first two releases, the latter an effective Nazi-peril yarn with Joan Bennett, Francis Lederer, and Otto Kruger. *Hudson's Bay* (1941) was an elaborate historical adventure with Paul Muni and Gene Tierney, but *Dance Hall* (1941) was a Carole Landis musical more on the level of a Republic production.

*The Great Commandment* (1941) and *Secret Agent of Japan* (1942) were more low-budget stuff, but Academy Award nominee *The Pied Piper* (1942) was a top-notch thriller, with Monty Woolley (in an Oscar-nominated performance) and—as the Nazi commandant—Otto Preminger. *Life Begins at 8:30* (1942) had Monty Woolley again, this time as a drunk who ruins daughter Ida Lupino's life. *The Moon Is Down* (1943) was a good adaptation of John Steinbeck's novel about Norway's resistance to the Nazi invaders, while *The Happy Land* (1943) had Don Ameche in a sentimental yarn about a homefront tragedy. *And Now Tomorrow* (1944) was sentiment sans patriotism, leaving only Alan Ladd and Loretta Young to make goo-goo eyes while society keeps them apart.

*A Medal for Benny* (1945) returned to flag waving and did it very well indeed; it was a variation on Preston Sturges's *Hail the Conquering Hero*, without the frenzy and with Dorothy Lamour. *Colonel Effingham's Raid* (1945) wasn't quite as memorable, but Charles Coburn was fine per usual as a former soldier at loggerheads with the citizenry of a small town. Pichel continued his string of homefront dramas with *Tomorrow Is Forever* (1946), a three-handkerchief film in which Orson Welles plays a presumed-dead soldier returning home to find that wife Claudette Colbert has remarried. This plot had recently been played for laughs by Garson Kanin in *My Favorite Wife*, but Pichel wrings sufficient emotion from it, and showcases the young Natalie Wood for the third time.

*O.S.S.* was a better-than-average Alan Ladd espionage yarn, while *The Bride Wore Boots* (both 1946) was farce that had been left out too long in the sun, Barbara Stanwyck notwithstanding. The 1946 *Temptation* was pure soap, with Merle Oberon deciding whether to remain faithful to husband George Brent. But *They Won't Believe Me* (1947) was a superior RKO noir with the splendid cast of Susan Hayward, Jane Greer, and Robert Young and a wonderfully ironic ending; it made one wish that Pichel had worked in that genre more often. *Something in the Wind* (1947), with Deanna Durbin as a disc jockey, harmed absolutely no one, although the same cannot be said of *The Miracle of the Bells* (1948), a stupendously dumb picture with one of the most laughable casts ever assembled: Frank Sinatra, Fred MacMurray, Valli, and Lee J. Cobb. Pichel rebounded immediately from that disaster with the delightful *Mr. Peabody and the Mermaid* (1948): William Powell lands comely mermaid Ann Blyth while fishing, complicating his life most amusingly. (The 1984 *Splash* clearly is indebted to *Peabody*.)

*Without Honor* (1949), with Laraine Day and Dane Clark, was without merit, but *The Great Rupert* (1950) was another light fantasy; Jimmy Durante is surprisingly deft as a down-on-his-luck hoofer whose ship comes in when a trained squirrel drops a fortune into his hands. (Pichel himself appeared in a bit part, his first acting job in ten years.) *Quicksand* (1950) was a departure—a James Cainish story about auto mechanic Mickey Rooney's descent into hell after falling under the spell of bad girl Jeanne Cagney. The trailblazing *Destination Moon* (also 1950) was one of the first science-fiction movies, and though it was made on a small budget for tiny Eagle-Lion, with a no-name cast, Pichel and producer George Pal turned it into a creditable adventure with Oscar-winning special effects. *Sante Fe* (1951) was simply a bland Western with Randolph Scott that proved to be Pichel's last Hollywood film. He made two more movies with independent companies that saw only limited release, a rather anticlimactic conclusion to an interesting (if modest) career.

## SIDNEY POITIER (1924- )

It's his Oscar-winning performance in *Lilies of the Field* and his acting in films like *The Defiant Ones*, *In the Heat of the Night*, *A Patch of Blue*, and *To Sir with Love* that will always be his first claim to fame, but starting in 1972, Sidney Poitier also began directing, and some of his pictures became very big hits. He both starred in and directed *Buck and the Preacher* (1972), an amiable Western in which he played a con-man preacher; his co-stars were Harry Belafonte and Ruby Dee. *A Warm December* (1973), shot in England, was a tearjerker that found Poitier anguished at the impending death of Esther Anderson, but the silly *Uptown Saturday Night* (1974) was an enormous hit, thanks to the winning chemistry between Poitier and co-stars Bill Cosby and Harry Belafonte.

Poitier elected to do it again in *Let's Do It Again* (1975)—now he and Cosby hypnotize boxer Jimmy Walker to make their fortunes—while the overlong *A Piece of the Action* (1977) gave the formula a third run-through, sending Poitier and Cosby into the ghetto to help James Earl Jones in his battle to save underprivileged kids. Poitier didn't act in *Stir Crazy* (1980), but Gene Wilder and Richard Pryor did just fine without him as a pair of losers who mistakenly are sent to prison; the film was an enormous box-office smash, thanks in large part to Bruce Jay Friedman's deadpan script.

*Hanky Panky* (1982) *should* have reteamed Wilder and Pryor, but unfortunately settled for Wilder and his real-life wife, Gilda Radner, leaving the laughs in the lurch, while in *Fast Forward* (1985) Poitier eschewed slapstick comedy for a trite tale about a group of small-town Ohio kids who come to New York to make it big as—break dancers?!? His touch was no more sure on the saccharine *Ghost Dad* (1990), yet another in Bill Cosby's long string of big-screen flops; Poitier may have waited too long before asking his former co-star to resurrect the chemistry they had shared in the Seventies.

## H. C. ("HANK") POTTER (1904-1977)

Henry Codman Potter directed both motion pictures and stage productions, a talent he shared with many others and put to good use on several of his screen efforts. While he amassed a mere nineteen theatrical releases (along with one famous propaganda feature during the war), a high percentage of them have stayed popular through the years. Born in New York City, he attended Yale Drama School before entering films as a freelance director. His first feature was *Beloved Enemy* (1936), starring the beauteous Merle Oberon as an Englishwoman in love with Irish rebellion leader Brian Aherne. *Wings over Honolulu* (1937) was romantic nonsense betwixt Fred MacMurray, Ray Milland, and Wendy Barrie, while *Romance in the Dark* (1938) was another failed attempt to turn former opera star Gladys Swarthout into a bona fide movie star; John Barrymore and John Boles are just innocent bystanders.

*The Cowboy and the Lady* (1938) was a project with a better pedigree: Leo McCarey co-wrote the story, and stars Gary Cooper and Merle Oberon gave convincing portrayals of a rodeo cowboy and the high-born dame who falls for him. Even better was *The Shopworn Angel* (1938), an expert remake of the 1929 Gary Cooper–Nancy Carroll weeper; here it's Margaret Sullavan playing the hard-boiled Broadway actress who marries a shy young soldier (James Stewart) on the eve of the First World War and then waits helplessly to see if he'll survive combat. Sullavan's songs were dubbed by the young Mary Martin, and Walter Pidgeon was excellent in an against-type role as Sullavan's sugar daddy.

The handsomely mounted but perilously slow *The Story of Vernon and Irene Castle* (1939) was the last of RKO's enormously popular Fred Astaire–Ginger Rogers musicals; unlike the first eight, it was a period story, based on the lives of the world-famous dance team that thrilled audiences just before, and during, World War I. Potter next made a pair of "B"s for MGM—*Blackmail* (1939), with innocent Edward G. Robinson serving time in prison for Gene Lockhart's crime, and *Congo Maisie* (1940), the second entry in Ann Sothern's long-running series (and a pretty fair knockoff of the 1932 *Red Dust*). *Second Chorus*

(1940) reunited Potter and Astaire, but the notion of Fred as a trumpet-blowing bandleader (in reality, Artie Shaw's guys) competing with Burgess Meredith for the hand of tap dancer Paulette Goddard wasn't enough to make anyone forget *Top Hat*—even Astaire considered it a total dud.

Much better was *Hellzapoppin* (1941), a colorful restaging of the Broadway farce, with Shemp Howard, Olsen & Johnson, Hugh Herbert, and Martha Raye earning their share of yuks. After shooting the patriotic documentary *Victory Through Air Power*, Potter made *Mr. Lucky* (both 1943) with Cary Grant and Laraine Day; a low-key crime yarn with both romantic and patriotic spins, the film covered all the bases nicely and gave Grant the opportunity to show off some of his beloved cockney slang. *The Farmer's Daughter* (1947) was Potter's first release in four years, and it became his biggest hit. Loretta Young, in an Oscar-winning performance, stars as a Swedish housekeeper with so many pearls of wisdom that she decides to run for Congress against her employer, Joseph Cotten, even though she also happens to love him; Charles Bickford was also nominated for an Academy Award for his performance as a sympathetic butler.

*A Likely Story* (1947) was a strained romantic comedy that had the gimmick of real-life newlyweds Bill Williams and Barbara Hale as its stars. But *Mr. Blandings Builds His Dream House* (1948) was an utter delight: Cary Grant plays a New York City copywriter who, constrained by his family's tiny apartment, buys a dilapidated 200-year-old house in Connecticut; he then watches in growing horror as workmen of all stripes try to restore this money guzzler into something he and wife Myrna Loy might actually be able to live in. Grant has rarely been funnier, although the jokes and sight gags have seen greener pastures.

Potter's last pictures were less memorable. The stolid *The Time of Your Life* (1948) was a well-meaning adaptation of the William Saroyan play, starring James and Jeanne Cagney and William Bendix, while *The Miniver Story* (1950) was a predictable but not ineffective sequel to William Wyler's 1942 smash: Greer Garson and Walter Pidgeon are finally reunited in postwar England. After making *Top Secret Affair* (1957) with Kirk Douglas and Susan Hayward, Potter retired.

## RICHARD QUINE (1920–1989)

The son of an actor, Detroit-born Richard Quine found himself performing on the vaudeville stage before he was wearing long pants. He worked his way up from radio into films, taking his first screen role in Mervyn LeRoy's *The World Changes* in 1933. But he never graduated from supporting parts, and after fifteen years of acting decided to step behind the camera. Quine eventually became a reliable director for Columbia, where he spent his first twelve years specializing in comedy and often adapting Broadway plays for his source material.

In 1948 Quine co-directed the boxing yarn *Leather Gloves* with William Asher, but he then returned to acting and didn't take his first solo directing credit until 1951 with *Sunny Side of the Street*, a cheapie musical starring Terry Moore and singer Frankie Laine. *Sound Off* was a tepid Mickey Rooney service comedy, and *Rainbow 'Round My Shoulder* (both 1952) another Frankie Laine musical; Quine co-wrote both with Blake Edwards, who had acted in *Leather Gloves*. After *Siren of Bagdad* (1953) and a pair of Mickey Rooney potboilers, Quine extricated himself from this morass with *Pushover* (1954)—still a "B," but a decent little noir starring Fred MacMurray and new discovery Kim Novak, who soon would become Columbia's premier glamour girl.

Quine's assignments now improved markedly. *My Sister Eileen* (1955), starring Janet Leigh, Betty Garrett, and Jack Lemmon, was a crisp musical version of the former Broadway success and became Quine's first real hit. *The Solid Gold Cadillac* was a fine showcase for the comic genius of Judy Holliday, who also delivered as Richard Conte's very pregnant wife in *Full of Life* (both 1956). *Bell, Book, and Candle* (1958), adapted from a Broadway play, had Kim Novak literally bewitching James Stewart, to the amusement of pal Ernie Kovacs, who also lent a charge to the Doris Day–Jack Lemmon comedy *It Happened to Jane* (1959).

Quine examined the glamorous side of adultery in *Strangers When We Meet*, with the heavy breathing provided by Kirk Douglas and Kim Novak. The thrill of miscegenation informed *The World of Suzie Wong* (both 1960), which featured William Holden anguishing over prostitute Nancy Kwan. *The Notorious Landlady* (1962), which Quine wrote with Larry Gelbart, was a black comedy starring Kim Novak and

Jack Lemmon, but *Paris—When It Sizzles* (1964) was an appalling waste of Audrey Hepburn and William Holden. *Sex and the Single Girl* (1964), a leering romantic comedy starring Tony Curtis and Natalie Wood, had nothing whatever to do with Helen Gurley Brown's how-to guide, but *How to Murder Your Wife* was a deft black comedy in which Jack Lemmon inexplicably tries to knock off gorgeous Virna Lisi.

*Synanon* (also 1965) was a lugubrious drama about the famed drug-rehabilitation center, but *Oh, Dad, Poor Dad, Mama's Hung You in the Closet and I'm Feeling So Sad*, with Rosalind Russell and Robert Morse, was a tart adaptation of Arthur Kopit's dark Broadway comedy. The all-star shlockfest *Hotel* (both 1967), based on Arthur Hailey's bestseller, signaled the decline of Quine's work, although the maligned thriller *W* (1974) will always be savored for providing Twiggy with her most dramatic role.

## GREGORY RATOFF (1897-1960)

A man of parts who probably achieved more as an actor than he did as a director, Ratoff was born in St. Petersburg and trained in the Russian theater after surviving his term with the czar's army during the Revolution. Emigrating to the States, he joined the Yiddish Players in New York, both directing and acting in a number of productions. He graduated to Broadway later in the Twenties, acting, directing, and producing a number of plays. In 1931 he made his way to Hollywood, and within a year was performing in such films as Gregory La Cava's *Symphony of Six Million*, George Cukor's *What Price Hollywood?*, Frank Lloyd's *Under Two Flags*, and Howard Hawks's *The Road to Glory*. It was in 1936, a year in which he acted in three films, that he cut his teeth behind the camera, co-directing *Sins of Man* with Otto Brower for 20th Century-Fox.

*Lancer Spy* (1937) was his first solo flight and it was a good one, a thriller that offered the appealing cast of George Sanders, Peter Lorre, and Dolores Del Rio. In 1939 Ratoff helmed an impressive slate of six "A" features, five of them for Fox—but the one that he made on loan-out to Selznick, *Intermezzo: A Love Story*, was the best of the bunch. A glossy remake of the 1937 Swedish film of the same name that had starred Ingrid Bergman, who here makes her Hollywood debut, it also featured Leslie Howard (he reportedly helped Ratoff direct). Linda Darnell's film debut in the mediocre *Hotel for Women* was among the highlights of Ratoff's 1939 smorgasbord, while *Rose of Washington Square* with Alice Faye and Tyrone Power, *Wife, Husband and Friend* with Loretta Young and Warner Baxter, *Daytime Wife* with Darnell and Power, and *Barricade* with Faye and Warner Baxter completed his most prolific year.

Nineteen-forty was quieter. *I Was an Adventuress*, in which former jewel thief Vera Zorina is harassed by Eric Von Stroheim, and *Public Deb No. 1*—Brenda Joyce in hot water for supporting a Communist rally—were Ratoff's only credits. Departing Fox, Ratoff went to Columbia to make *Adam Had Four Sons*, starring Ingrid Bergman as a French governess who oversees defiant daughter Susan Hayward for widower Warner Baxter, and *The Men in Her Life* (1941), with Loretta Young as a ballerina who flashes back on her many past loves for our viewing pleasure. *The Corsican Brothers* (also 1941) was a top-notch swashbuckler via Alexandre Dumas, with Doug Fairbanks, Jr., as identical twins separated for most of their lives. *Two Yanks in Trinidad* (1942) was a lightweight Army yarn starring Pat O'Brien and Brian Donlevy, while *Footlight Serenade* (1942) was a nifty Betty Grable–Victor Mature–John Payne backstage musical; Phil Silvers provided some comic relief.

*Song of Russia* (1943) was MGM's laughably glossy pro-Soviet romantic drama, with concert pianist Robert Taylor wooing Russian peasant Susan Peters in Moscow as the bombs burst in the air—nutty stuff now, but it landed screenwriters Paul Jarrico and Richard Collins in hot water with HUAC a few years later. (Navy hero Taylor was, of course, beyond reproach.) But the appalling *The Heat's On* (1943) was Mae West's last film for twenty-seven years, and you can see why. *Something to Shout About* (1943), a backstage musical with Don Ameche and Janet Blair fronting for Hazel Scott and Teddy Wilson, wasn't much better, though *Irish Eyes Are Smiling* (1944) was a passable biopic about composer Ernest R. Ball, impersonated by Monty Woolley, with Dick Haymes and June Haver in support. *Where Do We Go from Here?* (1945) was a wild musical fantasy about a genie who whisks 4-F Fred MacMurray back through various conflicts in American history (songs by Ira Gershwin and Kurl Weill), while *Paris Underground* (1945) was a good drama in which POW internees Constance Bennett and Gracie Fields help to run a resistance movement.

*Do You Love Me?* (1946) had the unbearable Dick

Haymes wooing Maureen O'Hara, who made for a rather unlikely college dean, while *Carnival in Costa Rica* (1947) subjected Vera-Ellen to Haymes. (Why Ratoff kept getting assigned to musicals is a mystery, since few of them were much good.) *Moss Rose* (1947) was a flavorful murder mystery set in turn-of-the-century London; Peggy Cummins plays a chorus girl who suspects Victor Mature of killing several of her former co-workers. Ratoff's period drama about the eighteenth-century magician Cagliostro, *Black Magic* (1949), was even better—as well it might have been, with star Orson Welles co-directing it sans credit. Ratoff acted in *All About Eve* after directing the lumpy British dramas *If This Be Sin* (1949) and *Operation X* (1950), the latter with Peggy Cummins as tycoon Edward G. Robinson's daughter; then he made *Taxi* (1953), a bland comedy with Dan Dailey. He directed *Abdullah's Harem* (1956) and *Oscar Wilde* (1960) but his interest had shifted back to acting, and he appeared in *The Sun Also Rises* and *Exodus* before his death in 1960.

## CARL REINER (1922– )

One of television's all-time funniest writers, Carl Reiner's film career has been less impressive than son Rob's, except for four prime comedies he made between 1979 and 1984 with Steve Martin. Born in the Bronx, Reiner was a stage actor before hooking up with Sid Caesar from 1950 to 1954 on the classic television revue *Your Show of Shows*, on *Caesar's Hour* from 1954 to 1957, and on *The Sid Caesar Show* in 1958, serving as both an actor and a head writer and winning two Emmy Awards. In 1961 he created *The Dick Van Dyke Show*, which he originally intended to act in himself as protagonist Rob Petrie; CBS convinced him to settle for being a producer/writer/supporting actor. Six more Emmys followed over the next six years, while Reiner also acted in a variety of films and cut the comedy record *The 2,000-Year-Old-Man* with Mel Brooks.

Reiner's first screen-directing effort was *Enter Laughing* (1967), a rather flat adaptation of his quasi-autobiographical novel and play. With *The Comic* (1969), he attempted to elevate his TV superstar, Dick Van Dyke, to similar screen status, but this homage to the silent-screen comics came across only in fits and starts. *Where's Poppa?* (1970) was a daring, often hilarious black comedy starring George Segal as a frustrated lawyer and Ruth Gordon as his senile mom. Reiner then returned to television for several years, co-creating and producing *The New Dick Van Dyke Show* among other projects, before returning to Hollywood to make *Oh God!* (1977), a wholly unexpected blockbuster, in which John Denver plays a supermarket manager summoned to be the messenger of God (George Burns was entirely irresistible as the Supreme Being).

That surprise smash was followed by the mediocre *The One and Only* (1978), starring Henry Winkler as a reluctant wrestler. But then came *The Jerk*, one of the biggest hits of 1979 and the film that launched Steven Martin on the path to screen stardom; not since the heyday of Jerry Lewis had a comic made such a connection with moviegoers. The black-and-white film-noir parody *Dead Men Don't Wear Plaid* (1982) was a terrific idea for a thirty-minute sketch—private eye Martin finds himself interacting with characters from a number of Forties classics, including Barbara Stanwyck (in *Double Indemnity* blond wig), Humphrey Bogart, and Ava Gardner—but in spite of Michael Chapman's gorgeous cinematography and Rachel Ward's presence as Martin's curvaceous client, the script (by Reiner, Martin, and George Gipe) just isn't clever enough to fill an hour and a half.

*The Man with Two Brains* (1983) was a very funny yarn hatched by writers Martin, Reiner, and Gipe. Martin plays a neurosurgeon attending a convention in Vienna; his faithless wife (Kathleen Turner in her best comic performance) becomes insanely jealous when he falls in love with the disembodied brain of a murder victim (the voice of Sissy Spacek). About two out of every three gags work, a good ratio for such a precarious notion. *All of Me* (1984), probably Reiner's most sustained comic effort, has Martin as an attorney whose body becomes possessed by the soul of sour millionairess Lily Tomlin, much to his confused dismay; but all ends well, as Tomlin learns decency and Martin ends up in the arms of Victoria Tennant.

Reiner's subsequent films cannot claim that kind of quality: *Summer Rental* (1985) was amiable idiocy with John Candy and Richard Crenna, while *Summer School* (1987) had Mark Harmon as a high-school teacher with a roomful of hard-case kids. *Bert Rigby, You're a Fool* (1989), a musical comedy about a British coal miner (Robert Lindsay), seemed to exist in a time warp. *Sibling Rivalry* (1991) had the courage of its dark comic premise and little else, as leads Kirstie Alley and Bill Pullman failed to carry their weight. *Fatal Instinct* (1993) was a dead-on parody of the recent wave of ultra-violent, kinked-up thrillers like *Basic Instinct*; alas, it made its point in the first fifteen minutes and then had to hang on for dear life, although Sean Young was most amusing as the lethal temptress.

## STUART ROSENBERG (1928– )

One of the most anonymous of American directors despite more than thirty years of filmmaking, New Yorker Stuart Rosenberg came out of teaching at N.Y.U. into the golden age of television, directing episodes of *The Untouchables*, *Naked City*, and *The Defenders* by the score. His first feature film, *Murder, Inc.* (1960), was completed by Burt Balaban when an actors' strike interrupted filming for several months; a taut account of the notorious organization of killers for hire that flourished in the 1930s, it starred Peter Falk, Stuart Whitman, and May Britt. The low-budget West German production *Question 7* (1961) followed, and then Rosenberg was back in television, shooting the pilot films for *Fame Is the Name of the Game* (1966) and *Asylum for a Spy*.

He returned to moviemaking in impressive fashion with *Cool Hand Luke* (1967), an enormously popular updating of the rebel-within-a-prison formula. Paul Newman supplies one of his most charismatic performances as the irrepressible, indomitable convict who gives new hope to his chain-gang compatriots, and so does Strother Martin as the boss who tries but fails to break him. Newman, the screenplay, and the score all received Academy Award nominations, and George Kennedy won a best supporting actor Oscar for his work as the doomed Dragline. *The April Fools* (1969) was a flat, slightly askew romantic comedy that offered the unlikely pairing of Jack Lemmon and Catherine Deneuve as illicit lovers who intend to run away together; Charles Boyer and Myrna Loy as their sage advisors add some class to the affair.

*Move* (1970) was an irreverent black comedy starring Elliott Gould as a failed playwright who writes porno novels for a living; Gould was hot off his triumph in *M*A*S*H* at the time, but this awful film probably removed him from the "A" list pronto. Somewhat better was *WUSA* (1970), an adaptation of Robert Stone's novel *A Hall of Mirrors*, with Paul Newman as a disc jockey for a nefarious right-wing radio station in New Orleans who develops a conscience in the nick of time. Although didactic, the film had an exceptional cast that included Joanne Woodward, Anthony Perkins, Laurence Harvey, and Cloris Leachman. The slight comedy *Pocket Money* (1972) had Newman again, now as a modern-day cowboy who schemes (disastrously) with pal Lee Marvin to get out of hock by outconning professional crooks.

*The Laughing Policeman* (1973) was a middling adaptation of the fine "Martin Beck" police procedural by Maj Sjowall and Per Wahloo, with the action transposed from Sweden to San Francisco. Walter Matthau and Bruce Dern were acceptable as partners investigating a mass slaying on a bus, but the film is overlong and Rosenberg sustains neither the tension nor the sensibility of the novel. The same could be said of *The Drowning Pool* (1975), a plodding version of Ross MacDonald's 1950 novel about shamus Lew Archer, here played for the second time by Paul Newman (the 1965 *Harper* was the first), saving young Melanie Griffith. Nuance is all in an American private-eye yarn, and while Rosenberg dutifully lays out the plot, both the pace and tone of the picture are flat.

*Voyage of the Damned* (1976) was more ambitious, a Sir Lew Grade production that dramatizes the 1939 voyage of the S.S. *St. Louis*, which transported 937 German Jewish refugees who hoped to land in Havana; when permission to dock was denied there and everywhere else, the ship had to return to Germany. A kind of *Ship of Fools* without that film's ripe trashiness, *Damned* took its international cast of all-stars—including Max von Sydow, Faye Dunaway (in a monocle, yet!), James Mason, Oskar Werner (a veteran of *Ship*), Maria Schell, Ben Gazzara, and the indispensable Katharine Ross—and marched them through their doomed paces slowly, and at great length. *Love and Bullets* (1979) was just a typical Charles Bronson actionfest shot in Switzerland, with Jill Ireland as a potential FBI informant and Rod Steiger, Henry Silva, and Strother Martin the hoods Bronson implacably mows down to get to her.

Rosenberg hadn't had a real hit since *Luke*, but that was taken care of in spades with *The Amityville Horror* (1979). Based on the clichéd but wildly popular book by Jay Anson about a Long Island house possessed by demons, it starred James Brolin and

Margot Kidder as the unfortunate Lutzes and Rod Steiger as the priest who tries to exorcize the forces of darkness through the holy power of ham. It may not have been good, or even particularly scary, but *Amityville* was one of the year's top-ten grossers. Rosenberg then got the call to replace Bob Rafelson on the prison exposé *Brubaker* (1980), no doubt due to his success with *Cool Hand Luke*. Robert Redford plays the eponymous new warden who infiltrates his prison in the guise of a convict, experiencing the manifold horrors firsthand; he intends reform, but first he has to get out alive. A bit too unrelenting for its own good, this fact-based drama offers a terrific cast (Yaphet Kotto, Morgan Freeman, Tim McIntire) and an Oscar-nominated screenplay.

*The Pope of Greenwich Village* (1984) came by way of Vincent Patrick's tangy novel about hoods in Little Italy, and Rosenberg captures at least part of the book's quirky charm. Mickey Rourke gives one of his few good performances as a small-timer who aspires to greater things, and Eric Roberts is typically over-the-top as his hopelessly ill-fated cousin. The fine cast (Geraldine Page, Tony Musante, Kenneth McMillan) helps, and Burt Young and Daryl Hannah don't do any actual damage—but the feeling persists that this minor entertainment could have been much, much better.

*Let's Get Harry* (1986) was a little-seen, lame-brained actioner about drug dealers in South America; despite a cast that includes Robert Duvall, Ben Johnson, and Gary Busey, Rosenberg felt obliged to have his name removed from the credits (now "by Alan Smithee"), which tells us something. *My Heroes Have Always Been Cowboys* (1991) was at least a serviceable turn on the aging-rodeo-star tale, with Scott Glenn as the bone-weary (and -cracked) circuit veteran, Ben Johnson as his declining dad, and Tess Harper, Kate Capshaw, and Gary Busey doing what they can with soap-opera roles that fit like a very old boot.

## MARK RYDELL (1934- )

A talented actor who has directed just ten features over the course of twenty-six years, New York City–born Mark Rydell was trained at Juilliard and the Actors' Studio in the 1950s, developing the skills needed to appear on Broadway, to hold down a leading role on the popular television soap opera *As the World Turns*, and to act in Don Siegel's 1956 juvenile-delinquent saga *Crime in the Streets*. He then gravitated to television, where he directed episodes of *Gunsmoke* and *Ben Casey*, among other series.

Rydell made his film-directing debut with *The Fox* (1968), a brooding adaptation of a D. H. Lawrence novella, filmed in Canada and starring Sandy Dennis and Anne Heywood as housemates whose rural life—and lesbian relationship—is disrupted when handsome Keir Dullea moves in unexpectedly. *The Reivers* (1969) was a delightful version of William Faulkner's comic story, starring Steve McQueen as a high-spirited handyman who takes young Mitch Vogel and black friend Rupert Crosse in the family's new 1905 Winton Flyer on a ride to Memphis, where a wild time has been promised to all. Far less lively was *The Cowboys* (1972), Rydell's rather sour Western starring John Wayne as an old rancher who drags eleven youngsters along with him on an epic cattle drive.

Rydell made a great cameo appearance as a horrifying gangster in Robert Altman's *The Long Goodbye* in 1973, then adapted Darryl Ponisan's *Cinderella Liberty* (1973), a bittersweet romantic drama about a sailor (James Caan) who falls for a jaded hooker (Marsha Mason, nominated for an Oscar) who's raising her half-black son. *Harry and Walter Go to New York* (1976) was a strained comedy starring James Caan and Elliott Gould as a pair of unsuccessful Gay Nineties vaudeville performers who decided to make a career change and go into safecracking. But *The Rose* (1979) gave Bette Midler the role of her life as a Janis Joplinesque rock singer who self-destructively burns her candle at both ends. Frederic Forrest plays her hippie lover; both were nominated for Oscars, and the picture was a hit.



Rydell scored his biggest success—both critically and commercially—with the sentimental *On Golden Pond* (1981), Ernest Thompson's Oscar-winning adaptation of his play about the joys (not many) and pains (numerous) of growing old. Henry Fonda and Katharine Hepburn were obvious choices to play the long-married New Englanders, and Jane Fonda is their angry daughter. Hepburn and Henry Fonda won Oscars—he died less than a year later—and the film and Rydell were also nominated. On top of that, *Pond* took in $118 million at the box office, an incredible amount for a serious drama.

Since that triumph, Rydell has stumbled with *The River* (1984), a well-meaning drama in which Mel

Gibson and Sissy Spacek star as a farm couple struggling heroically to survive a flood; *For the Boys* (1991), a show-biz saga starring Bette Midler and James Caan as USO performers whose turbulent romance spans a half century; and the ludicrous *Intersection* (1994), in which Richard Gere portrays a man re-examining his love life (embodied by a deeroticized Sharon Stone and Lolita Davidovich) as he's experiencing a car crash.

## GEORGE SEATON (1911-1979)

Probably a better writer than he was a director, George Seaton (né Stenius) nevertheless contributed a handful of gems to the silver screen. Born in South Bend, Indiana, and raised in Detroit, he acted on stage and on radio (as the Lone Ranger!) before beginning his Hollywood career as a screenwriter at MGM in 1934. Among the hit films Seaton scripted are the Marx Brothers' *A Day at the Races*, *Charley's Aunt*, *The Song of Bernadette* (for which he was Oscar-nominated), and *Coney Island*. In 1945 he began a new phase at Fox as a writer-director, helming such productions as *Billy Rose's Diamond Horseshoe* (1945) and *The Shocking Miss Pilgrim* (1946), both with Betty Grable.



His breakthrough came in 1947 with the holiday classic *Miracle on 34th Street*, which won him an Oscar for his screenplay; "Santa" Edmund Gwenn and Valentine Davies's story also won Academy Awards. *Apartment for Peggy* (1948) was a light romance, with Jeanne Crain and William Holden as campus newlyweds, that is memorable only for Edmund Gwenn's performance, while *Chicken Every Sunday* (1949) was a harmless period piece with Dan Dailey and Celeste Holm. *The Big Lift* (1950) featured Montgomery Clift as a pilot during the Berlin airlift, with some tacked-on romantic subplots and good on-location photography, while *For Heaven's Sake* (1950) was a whimsical fantasy starring Clifton Webb and Edmund Gwenn as angels on a mission. Seaton now moved to Paramount, where he and longtime associate William Perlberg were given their own production unit. There Seaton wrote and directed *Anything Can Happen* (1952), a misconceived Cold War comedy with José Ferrer, and *Little Boy Lost* (1953)—unabashed hokum, with Bing Crosby searching a French orphanage for the son he has never seen.

Seaton's films hadn't made much of a splash since *Miracle*, but in 1954 he hit the jackpot with *The Country Girl*, an adaptation of Clifford Odets's play. It was Oscar-nominated for best picture, actor (Bing Crosby, cast against type as an alcholic singer), actress (Grace Kelly, ditto, as his dowdy wife), direction, and screenplay; the winners that emerged were Kelly and Seaton's screenplay adaptation. *The Proud and the Profane* (1956) had William Holden and Deborah Kerr in love during World War II, while *Teacher's Pet* (1958) was a delightful pairing of Clark Gable and Doris Day as, respectively, a newspaper editor and a journalism teacher who spar and (of course) finally fall in love; there is fine support from Gig Young and Mamie Van Doren. (This was the first Seaton-directed film that he didn't also write.)

*The Pleasure of His Company* (1961) was a deft comedy with Fred Astaire and Debbie Reynolds. The Seaton shifted gears with *The Counterfeit Traitor* (1962), an excellent espionage tale set during World War II, with fine performances by William Holden and Lilli Palmer, and *The Hook* (1963), a disturbing Korean War story starring Kirk Douglas. *36 Hours* (1966), a spy story set during World War II with James Garner, wasn't much better than, or different from, an episode of *Mission Impossible*, while *What's So Bad about Feeling Good?* (1968) was a good-natured attempt at whimsy, featuring George Peppard, Mary Tyler Moore, and a corny toucan.

Then came the smash hit *Airport*, one of 1970's most profitable releases and (rather incredibly) a best picture nominee. It earned Seaton his final Academy Award nomination for his screenplay adaptation of the Arthur Hailey bestseller, and ultimately spawned a number of inferior sequels (and even more parodies), none of which involved Seaton. His last film was *Showdown* (1973), an acceptable Western, with Rock Hudson and Dean Martin in fine fettle.

## WILLIAM A. SEITER (1892-1964)

He had a way with musicals and light romances, and for years seemed on the verge of moving into the front rank of directors—but somehow this onetime Keystone Kop never quite broke through the glass ceiling, despite working with the likes of Fred Astaire, Rita Hayworth, Shirley Temple, Barbara Stanwyck, Laurel and Hardy, Ava Gardner, the Marx Brothers, and Ginger Rogers, to name just a few of the major stars who appeared in his seventy sound features. Born in New York City, he graduated from the Hudson Military Academy with thoughts of becoming an artist, but ended up in Hollywood, acting for Mack Sennett and writing screenplays. Eventually he became an assistant director, and by 1919 was directing shorts.

Seiter began making features in 1921, and eventually directed several dozen silents, marrying silent star Laura La Plante in 1926. He was at Warners when sound arrived, and made such transitional talkies as *Why Be Good?*, *Synthetic Sin*, and *Smiling Irish Eyes* (all 1929), all starring Colleen Moore, while *Sunny* (1930) was an adaptation of the popular Broadway musical with original star Marilyn Miller. Moving to RKO in 1931, Seiter made the funny radio satire *Professional Sweetheart* with Ginger Rogers, in which future directors Gregory Ratoff and Norman Foster also had roles, and *Chance at Heaven* (both 1933), a weeper starring Rogers and Marian Nixon, whom Seiter would marry the following year.

*Sons of the Desert* (1933) is considered by many to be Laurel and Hardy's best feature film, while *Roberta* (1935) was a popular adaptation of the Jerome Kern–Otto Harbach musical (''Smoke Gets in Your Eyes,'' etc.); it nominally stars Irene Dunne, but only comes to life when Astaire and Rogers float by. Ginger Rogers had another good role in *In Person* (1935), an amusing satire of the movie industry. *The Moon's Our Home* (1936) was a painfully strained screwball farce starring Henry Fonda and Margaret Sullavan, but Seiter then engineered two of Shirley Temple's better vehicles, *Dimples* and *Stowaway* (both 1936). He made the effective period romantic adventure *This Is My Affair* (1937) with Barbara Stanwyck and Robert Taylor, and let the Marx Brothers run rampant through *Room Service* (1938), a successful transposition of the Broadway farce.

*Allegheny Uprising* (1939), with John Wayne and Claire Trevor, was good eighteenth-century Americana. Deanna Durbin was shepherded through *It's a Date* (1940) and *Nice Girl?* (1941) without mishap, but Seiter's best work of the Forties was represented by the fine Fred Astaire–Rita Hayworth musical *You Were Never Lovelier* (1942), with its great Kern-Mercer score. Thereafter his projects gradually decreased in importance and star power: *Destroyer* (1943), a solid World War II drama with Edward G. Robinson and Glenn Ford; the romantic comedy *The Lady Takes a Chance* (also 1943), starring the unlikely combo of John Wayne and Jean Arthur; and *Belle of the Yukon* (1944), a passable period adventure featuring Randolph Scott and Gypsy Rose Lee.

*Little Giant* was a bland Abbott and Costello outing, although *Lover Come Back* (both 1946) gave Lucille Ball a good comedy role. Deanna Durbin fared less well in *I'll Be Yours* (1947) and *Up in Central Park* (1948), and Seiter's version of *One Touch of Venus* (also 1948) didn't keep the comic edge of the Broadway hit, despite Ava Gardner as the lovely mannequin who comes to life for Robert Walker. *Borderline* (1950) was a modest noir, with Fred MacMurray and Claire Trevor. Seiter made his last three pictures at Republic, then retired in 1954.

# INDEX